# ENCYCLOPEDIA

## OF

## LATIN-AMERICAN

## HISTORY

# ENCYCLOPEDIA

## OF

# LATIN-AMERICAN

## HISTORY

MICHAEL RHETA MARTIN

GABRIEL H. LOVETT

*New York University*

Consulting Editor
FRITZ L. HOFFMANN
*University of Colorado*

Revised Edition by
L. ROBERT HUGHES
*Wright State University*

*THE BOBBS-MERRILL COMPANY, INC.*
A Subsidiary of Howard W. Sams & Co., Inc.
*Indianapolis* • *New York*

Copyright © 1968

*THE BOBBS-MERRILL COMPANY, INC.*

Printed in the United States of America
Library of Congress Catalog Card Number: 66-28231
Second Printing

# FOREWORD TO THE REVISED EDITION

The purpose of this book is to provide a convenient one-volume reference work on Latin-American history from the earliest times to the present. It includes comprehensive entries describing the major pre-Columbian civilizations, the founding and growth of European colonies in the region, and the political, social, and economic development of the Latin-American nations since their attainment of independence. The work gives attention to inter-American relations and Latin-American relations with other leading world powers. Other aspects of Latin-American culture such as religion, literature, and the creative arts are also treated. Additional entries cover the principal cities and geographic features, institutions of government, major wars and battles, agricultural, industrial, and labor development, as well as biographies of notable figures in political, military, and intellectual life. Definitions of Spanish and Portuguese words and phrases which have a special significance in Latin-American history are also given.

In order to make the fullest use of this book, the reader may find it useful to refer to several entries related to the same subject. For example, the history of a country during a particular administration is often described in greater detail in the biography of its president. This also applies to such obviously important items as the names of countries, large cities, major wars, religions, products, movements, etc. The use of SMALL CAPITALS—or, in some cases, of italics—for a name, word, or phrase indicates that it appears elsewhere as a separate entry.

The main effort in this revised edition of the *Encyclopedia of Latin-American History* has been to bring up to date the earlier version by incorporating events that have transpired in Latin America since 1956, when the previous volume was published. A few entries included in the earlier edition have been redone, but most necessary changes and corrections did not require that articles be completely rewritten.

Much has happened in Latin America during the past decade. All nations in the region have experienced political change, some of which has been peaceful and orderly and some violent and chaotic. Also, new persons have gained prominence in all fields. As in most works of this nature, a major problem has been the selection of material to be included. Space limitations have made it difficult to include every event and each person worthy of recognition. Further difficulties have arisen in determining exact dates; at times it has been impossible to fix doubtful or disputed dates with certainty. Another particularly vexatious problem has been the matter of names in the Portuguese and Spanish languages: the exact manner in which a name may be used depends to a great extent upon how the individual himself uses his name. Because there is no universally accepted manner of listing Brazilian names, it has been necessary to rely on common usage.

Every effort has been made to avoid blunders and to make this work as accurate as possible. Still it has been necessary to realize that one person, or many, could not record so much history with perfect reliability. Despite its shortcomings, however, this book should serve its purpose as a reference work for students of Latin-American history.

It is my good fortune to have received expert help and counsel in many ways from many sources during my work. I would like to express particular gratitude to Michael Rheta Martin, who deserves much of the credit for this revised edition, and to Dr. Fritz L. Hoffmann, whose long experience and expert judgement have contributed greatly to the merit of the book.

Dayton, Ohio         **L. Robert Hughes**
November 30, 1967

**Abad y Queipo, Manuel.** 1751–1825. Bishop, philosopher, and reformer. b. Asturias, Spain. Received degrees from Universities of Salamanca and Guadalajara, Mexico. Served for five years in Comayagua, Guatemala, as ecclesiastical attorney general and lawyer in the AUDIENCIA, and served as a bishop of Michoacán, Mexico. Denounced by his enemies to the INQUISITION, he was exonerated. He was deputy from Asturias to Spanish Cortes of 1820, and bishop of Tortosa, Spain. Imprisoned by FERDINAND VII in a convent near Toledo, where he died in 1825. A man of sound economic ideas, he tried to prevent Spain from losing her American colonies.

**Abascal y Souza, José Fernando.** 1743–ca. 1821. A native of Oviedo, Spain, Abascal pursued a military career until he became viceroy of Peru (1806–1816), where he successfully resisted the first movements for independence. In order to placate rebellious liberals he introduced many reforms, including the establishment of schools and the abolition of the INQUISITION in the viceroyalty. Efforts to maintain harmonious relations between Spaniards and Creoles earned for him the title of Marqués de la Concordia. FERDINAND VII replaced him with General Joaquín de la Pezuela (July 7, 1816).

**ABC Party of Cuba.** Organization formed to oppose the dictatorship of MACHADO Y MORALES in Cuba; largely responsible for the revolution of 1933. University students were especially active in the party.

**ABC Powers.** Argentina, Brazil, and Chile. The phrase came into use at the beginning of the 20th century to describe the ABC entente that continued to exist until WORLD WAR I.

**Abolition of Slavery.** Negro slavery was abolished first on the Caribbean island of HISPANIOLA (Haiti and Santo Domingo). The western half of the island, a French possession called Saint Domingue, was in the midst of a Negro revolt when a representative of the French revolutionary government, sent there to restore peace, proclaimed the abolition of slavery in 1793. In 1801, when the Negro leader TOUSSAINT L'OUVERTURE conquered the Spanish half of the island, he proclaimed the abolition of slavery there. On the other great Caribbean island, Cuba, the institution lasted much longer. Only in 1880 was gradual emancipation adopted, and in 1886 slavery was abolished. Mexico saw the end of slavery under President GUERRERO in 1829, and in Central America abolition was proclaimed by a Central-American Congress in 1824. As for South America, an Argentine assembly meeting at Buenos Aires in 1813 declared that henceforth all children born of slaves would be free. In Chile a constituent assembly abolished slavery in 1823. In Colombia it was done away with in 1851. In Brazil in 1888, while Emperor PEDRO II was away in Europe, his daughter ISABEL signed a law abolishing slavery without compensation to the owners; at that time, out of a population of 15,000,000 there were about 700,000 slaves.

**Academia dos Esquecidos** or **Academy of the Forgotten.** A society founded in Bahia, Brazil, in 1724, it was mainly concerned with the study of Brazilian history. The historian Rocha Pitta was one of its members.

1

**Acapulco.** The main Pacific port of the Republic of Mexico and a famous beach resort (approximately 600,000 tourists visit each year), 190 miles southwest of Mexico City; population, 49,000 (1960). It is built along a beautiful bay which is lined by high mountains. Ultramodern hotels and several fine beaches make it a popular vacation spot. It is connected by road and air with Mexico City and other centers in the country. The Acapulco area produces coffee, sugar cane, copra, nuts, and oil of limes. Industries in the town itself include the manufacturing of soap and muslin. Acapulco is the oldest port on the North American Pacific coast. It was from here that Spanish GALEONES, from 1565 to 1815, sailed to the Philippines and China. When the galleons, loaded with Oriental silk, muslins, spices, and aromatic oils, returned to Acapulco, fairs were held that became world-famous. There was much smuggling through Acapulco, and the Spanish Crown sought constantly to put an end to the contraband. In 1646 a customhouse was established in the port, but the illegal trade could not be stamped out. From Acapulco the East-Asian merchandise was transported on mule trains to Mexico City, over a winding distance of 325 miles, and, if necessary, from there to Veracruz, whence it was shipped to Europe. Some of the articles reaching Acapulco were shipped to Peru in spite of official prohibitions, and in return Acapulco was the destination point of much Peruvian silver. Acapulco was severely damaged by earthquakes in 1909.

**Acção Integralista Brasileira.** See INTE-GRALISTAS.

**Acción Democrática.** See DEMOCRATIC ACTION PARTY OF VENEZUELA.

**Acevedo Díaz, Eduardo.** 1851–1924. Uruguayan novelist, political leader, and diplomat. Author of a trilogy that he called "a hymn of blood," covering the period of the Uruguayan Wars for Independence: *Ismael*, 1888, *Nativa*, 1890, and *Grito De Gloria* (Cry of Glory), 1894. His most famous work is the Gaucho novel *Soledad*, 1894.

**Achá, José María de.** 1805–1868. President of Bolivia. Chosen in an election in 1861, he remained in office until 1865 when he was forced out by a revolt. He had given cabinet posts to all important political factions but could not stop unrest, uprisings, and intrigue. A constitution was passed in August 1861 which limited the term of the president to three years and established a unicameral legislature. During his administration in La Paz, 60 political prisoners, including a former president, were massacred on a false rumor.

**Acolhuas.** Also called **Texcocans.** Indians of the Nahua tribes, they lived near Lake Texcoco during the time of the Aztecs and formed a part of the Aztec confederacy. See AZTECS.

**Acordada.** A special tribunal set up in New Spain (Mexico) in 1710 to cope with the rapid growth of banditry. Throughout most of the 18th century it was empowered to hand out sentences from which there was no appeal, and to deal out severe punishments for crimes. In the last decade of the century and onward the viceroy and a special committee reviewed its sentences before execution.

**Acordada, Revolt of the.** Uprising in November 1828, of the troops quartered at the prison of the ACORDADA in Mexico City. Led by Zavala, the governor of the State of Mexico, they rose against the conservative Gómez Pedraza, who had been elected to succeed President Guadalupe VICTORIA by allegedly fraudulent methods. The revolt led to severe street fighting that lasted for days. Gómez Pedraza was defeated and went into exile, and in his place the liberal Vicente GUERRERO was declared president (April 1829).

**Acosta, José de.** *ca.* 1539–1600. Spanish JESUIT missionary. Spent 17 years, from 1570 to 1587, traveling through Peru and Mexico; author of the *Historia natural y moral de las Indias*, published in Seville in 1590. He wrote about the agriculture, political and social institutions, and the land systems of the Indians and is important for having transplanted European plants and animals to the New World, and for helping in the development of mining by the Spaniards in America. His studies of the religions of the Indians and the colonial people as seen through the eyes of a 16th century churchman are enlightening.

**Acosta, Vladimir.** 1900–    . Argentine architect. An outstanding example of his work is the Provincial Insane Asylum at San Lorenzo.

**Acosta García, Julio.** b. 1872. President of Costa Rica, 1920–1924. Served as minister of foreign affairs, 1915–1916, minister to Central America, and deputy in the national congress. He was a presidential candidate in 1933 and again in 1937.

**Acre Territory.** Territory of western Brazil bounded by the Brazilian state of Amazonas and by Peru and Bolivia, and crossed by the Acre (or Aquiry) River. A number of disputes arose between Bolivia and Brazil over control of the territory. The question was finally settled by the Treaty of Petrópolis, 1903, that awarded the area to Brazil for a payment of £2,000,000 to Bolivia.

**Acuerdo.** Spanish, meaning "agreement" or "resolution."

**Adelantado.** From the Spanish, *adelantar*, "to advance." The *adelantados* were officials vested with military, civil, and judicial powers, and were the promoters of colonization on the expanding frontiers of the Spanish empire. The office was transferred to the New World from Spain where the title had been used to designate the governors of frontier provinces in lands recaptured from the Moslems during the reconquest of the Spanish peninsula. The first to be so designated in the New World was probably Bartholomew Columbus, who was appointed to that position by his brother Christopher on his second voyage to the New World. In 1512 Juan PONCE DE LEÓN was the first to be promised that title by the Crown. The *adelantado* was in effect a governor, under the authority of the Crown. He was granted responsibility over an extensive territory and charged with the supervision of public order. He was also expected to keep the king informed of conditions that existed within his territory. The *adelantado* received a specified, tax-exempt income from the revenues of the province, held a large landed estate, and occasionally owned the fishing and trading rights of the area. He nominated municipal and ecclesiastical officials, distributed land and water rights, as well as *encomiendas* of Indians, among the soldiers and colonists. The *adelantados* were of importance only during the early period of Spanish settlement in the 16th century, after which they were replaced by viceroys. Few of them lived very long, since most were killed either in wars with the Indians or by assassination. There were four classes: the *adelantados mayores*, who were governors of provinces with judicial powers; *adelantados menores*, who were sometimes appointed by the former; the *adelantado de la corte o del rey*, who was a delegate of the king, and the *adelantado del mar*, who was entrusted with the command of a maritime expedition and was granted beforehand the governorship of the territories he might discover or conquer. The conquistadors were examples of the latter.

**Adelantado of the South Sea.** Title given to BALBOA by King Ferdinand of Spain in 1515.

**Aduana Seca.** Spanish, meaning "inland customhouse."

**Agiotista.** Spanish, meaning "profiteer," "bill broker," "usurer." Name given especially to Mexican businessmen who in the 19th century made huge profits by lending money to the government for short terms, and at high rates of interest, in exchange for mortgages on government property or on customs duties. When mortgages became payable, the *agiotistas* collected their profits, and as a result revenues diminished and the government usually was overthrown by revolution. Since they stood to benefit from government deficits, the *agiotistas* often took an active part in fomenting disorders in the country. They were especially powerful in the SANTA ANNA period, 1829–1855.

**Agrarianism** or **Agrarian Reform.** The revolutions that freed Latin America from Spain did not change the landholding system, called LATIFUNDISMO, that prevailed during the colonial era. Under that system a relatively small number of the population controlled most of the land. That minority, made up of wealthy CREOLES and members of the Church, formed a striking contrast with the masses of mestizos and Indians, who either

3

possessed small plots of less valuable land or were forced to work for negligible wages on the large estates. More often than not, they became indebted to rich landowners and fell into peonage, being forced to work the rest of their lives on the estates to repay their debts. The situation led to frequent demands for agrarian reform, and the organized demand for an equitable distribution of land became one of the most important social and political movements of a number of Latin-American countries. In the course of the 19th and 20th centuries, the governments have tried to give land to the destitute Indian peasants, and to free them from the system of peonage, but so far Mexico and Cuba are the only Latin-American nations to have effected a comprehensive program in land reform. In the former this was due mainly to the Mexican Revolution that derived much of its support from the peasantry, who had seen much of their land (private and communal) seized by powerful landholders under the DÍAZ dictatorship. Article 27 of the Mexican Constitution drafted in 1917 provided for the distribution of land to villages to be held as collective property and henceforth inalienable (see EJIDO). The distribution of land was gradually put into effect and by 1933 close to 19,000,000 acres had been granted to villages comprising some 750,000 heads of families. During the presidency of Lázaro CÁRDENAS (1934–1940) the program of land distribution was accelerated, and by 1940 it was estimated that from 60,000,000 to 70,000,000 acres had been allotted to nearly 2,000,000 heads of families since 1915. Cárdenas also sought to encourage co-operative farming and he established schools that taught Mexican peasants modern farming methods. Under ÁVILA CAMACHO, ALEMÁN VALDÉS, RUIZ CORTINES, and LÓPEZ MATEOS another 40,000,000 acres of land were added to the amount already distributed. Recent evaluations of the Mexican land reform program have deplored the disasters that have plagued that effort, particularly the weaknesses of the *ejido* system. The revolutionary program introduced by CASTRO in Cuba after January 1, 1959, included an agrarian reform program. Lands taken over from foreign interests, as well as Cuban-owned land, were

destined to be incorporated in the plan to give Cuba economic independence. Ownership of land was limited to 100 acres and collective farms were established. The Cuban Revolution has inspired agrarian reform efforts in Venezuela and in Brazil, where Francisco Julião has advocated seizure of privately-owned lands. Castro's program seems destined to have significant influence throughout Latin America.

**Aguascalientes, Convention of.** Convention that met in October 1914, at the Mexican town of Aguascalientes (state of Aguascalientes) to bring about a compromise between the two constitutionalist factions of CARRANZA and VILLA, then vying for power in revolution-torn Mexico. It named the idealistically-minded General Eulalio Gutiérrez, from San Luis Potosí, provisional president. Aguascalientes being filled with armed supporters of Villa, Gutiérrez was forced to appoint Villa as head of the army, after which civil war broke out between Villa and Carranza.

**Aguilar, Jerónimo de.** Spanish adventurer and interpreter. b. Ecija, Spain. Surviving a shipwreck, he landed at Cozumel Island, Yucatán, and spent eight years there. Having learned the Mayan language, he served as interpreter for CORTÉS, who landed there in March 1519.

**Aguirre, Lope de.** d. 1561. Spanish explorer in South America, notoriously cruel and hated by both the Spanish and Indians. He joined Ursúa's expedition in the search of EL DORADO, traveling from Peru eastward in 1560. A leader of the mutiny against URSÚA, he is believed to have killed him and to have taken control of the expedition himself. The expedition went down the Amazon and crossed over to the Orinoco, laying waste the villages it passed. He was executed by the Spanish official Barquisimeto after reaching the seacoast of Venezuela in 1561.

**Aguirre Cerda, Pedro.** 1879–1941. President of Chile. b. Los Andes, near Santiago, Chile. Lawyer; professor in the Pedagogical Institute, 1913; national deputy from Los Andes, 1915–1918; minister of justice and public instruction, 1918; national deputy from Santiago, 1918–1921; minister of the interior on three occasions, 1920–1924; national senator from Concepción, 1921–1927; president of the Radical Party and leader of the "popular front" comprised of the Radical Party, Socialists, and Communists. Aguirre was elected president in October 1938. As a result of a catastrophic earthquake a few months later, Aguirre instituted agencies for relief and reconstruction. The establishment of CORFO *Corporación de Fomento* (Development Corporation) in 1939 increased Chile's industrialization, aided the iron and steel industry, and led to the construction of hydroelectric plants. Aguirre and the Radical Party instituted a program of social legislation, including social security, old age pensions, and public housing. Internal friction within the party and the outbreak of the European war were problems confronting the president when he died on November 25, 1941.

**Aguirre y Salinas, Osmín.** Provisional president of El Salvador, October 21, 1944, until March 1, 1945, upon retirement of Andrés Ignacio Menéndez. He came into power as a result of the revolution that overthrew Maximiliano Hernández MARTÍNEZ. He promised to hold free elections in January 1945, but when the liberal Democratic Union put forward Arturo Romero as its candidate for the presidency, he opposed this choice and used police to break up the Union's meetings. The election was held in January 1945, and the only candidate, General Salvador CASTAÑEDA CASTRO, was elected. Aguirre staged a revolution in the summer of 1945, but it was suppressed.

**Agustín I.** See ITURBIDE.

**Alamán, Lucas.** 1792–1853. Mexican historian and statesman. b. Guanajuato, Mexico. Studied classics, physics, and chemistry; visited Spain, France, and other countries. He took an active part in the political activities of the period and worked for Mexican independence. In 1821, Alamán went to Paris and London, forming a company for the exploitation of Mexican mines. Secretary of the Interior and of State, 1823, he was the spokesman for Mexican conservatives favoring a monarchy, and a leading influence in the administration of BUSTAMANTE, 1830–1832. An opponent of the United States, he was largely responsible for the law of 1830, which prohibited further American immigration into Texas. He retired from political life after the fall of Bustamante, but helped SANTA ANNA become dictator of Mexico in 1853, still believing that he could be persuaded to carry out a serious political program. Alamán headed his cabinet and presented him with an elaborate program calling for economic improvements under the ministry of *fomento*, the building of roads and telegraphs, and the colonization of unoccupied lands. The army was increased, the government was centralized, censorship of newspapers was instituted. However, in June 1853, Alamán died. Considered the ablest conservative statesman of Mexico, he was also the author of several works including his *History of Mexico*, 1849.

**Alamo, Battle of the.** A battle famous in the annals of the history of Texas, drawing its name from the old mission building in San Antonio. In 1835, the Texans revolted against Mexico and defeated a Mexican army under General Cos. The Mexican general SANTA ANNA then hurried northward to crush the rebellion. When he reached San Antonio in February 1836 with 3,000 men, he found that the Texans, completely unprepared for resistance, had only 150 men under William Barrett Travis defending the mission of the Alamo. The Texans refused to surrender and held off the Mexican army for two weeks. On March 6, their trumpets sounding the *degüello*, the no quarter signal, the Mexicans then gathered for a final attack. The Alamo was stormed and its heroic defenders were killed to the last man. "Remember the Alamo" became the rallying cry for the Texan forces in the remaining weeks of the war, which finally saw the defeat of Santa Anna and the fulfillment of Texan independence at the Battle of SAN JACINTO, April 21, 1836, near Houston.

**Alarcón y Mendoza, Juan Ruiz de.** 1580–1639. Spanish playwright. A native of Tlacho, Mexico, Alarcón left his homeland at the age of twenty to study at Salamanca in Spain, returning only briefly to Mexico, and subsequently spent the greater part of his life

5

in Spain. A hunchback, he suffered constant ridicule because of his malformation. His twenty-three plays, among the best of the Spanish Golden Age, are outstanding examples of character study and perfection of language. His most famous play, *La verdad sospechosa* (The Suspicious Truth), was adapted by Corneille as *Le Menteur*. He died at Córdoba on August 4, 1639.

**Alberdi, Juan Bautista.** 1810–1884. Argentine publicist. b. Tucumán. Studied in Buenos Aires and received a law degree in Montevideo, 1840. After a voyage to Europe, he settled in Valparaíso, Chile. In 1844 he suggested the creation of a Hispanic American League which with the support of some European powers could settle boundary and other disputes. He supported Argentina's dictator ROSAS, but when he became aware of the latter's true character and aims, he became his bitter enemy. After the fall of Rosas in 1852, Alberdi held the posts of Argentine plenipotentiary in Paris, Madrid, the United States and London, drafting important agreements with these countries. A constitutional convention met at Santa Fe on May 1, 1853, and signed the constitution that incorporated many of Alberdi's views. He urged a strong federal government, with the greatest strength resting with the executive, having enough power to maintain order and national unity, but also granting autonomy to the provinces; he believed in free immigration and free navigation. This democratic constitution, which included a most liberal bill of rights in its introductory paragraphs, went into effect in all the provinces except Buenos Aires. Although Alberdi agreed to the help of Brazil in defeating Rosas and establishing URQUIZA as president in 1852, he cautioned that Brazil might continue on an imperialistic course and wrote *El imperio del Brasil ante la democracia de América* in 1869, which denounced Negro slavery, monarchy, and other aspects of Brazilian rule. He opposed the Paraguayan War. He also served as senator for Tucumán. A man of vast culture, he was one of Latin America's greatest political philosophers and the author of many works, one of the most important being his *Bases y puntos de partida para la organización política de la República Argentina*. He died in Paris.

**Alberto, João.** Brazilian statesman. b. Recife. Served as president of the National Council for Economic Defense and the Federal Council of Foreign Trade. He was one of the group of *tenentes*, or lieutenants, who staged the coup d'etat that helped Getulio VARGAS to power in 1930. He served as chief of police in Rio and as consular inspector abroad. Serving as minister to Canada, he was in charge of selling Great Britain Brazilian goods. He was made Co-ordinator of Economic Mobilization under Vargas in 1943, and had wide powers over mining, agriculture, industry, exports and imports, food supplies, rent control, etc. He controlled the coffee industry and was virtually economic dictator of the country.

**Alcabala.** Sales tax imposed in colonial Spanish America. It was introduced in New Spain in 1575, in Guatemala in 1576, and in Peru in 1591, where, when it was introduced in the province of Quito, it almost resulted in a revolution. The original rate was 2 per cent; by 1636 it was doubled; and later, although it went as high as 10 per cent, it became uniform at 6 per cent in most countries. The *alcabala* was levied on most saleable articles. On goods imported into Spanish-American ports, it was collected at the customhouse, whether the goods were sold or not. Indians, clergymen, churches, and monasteries were exempted, the latter three only in cases involving the sale of their own properties. In Mexico, the abuses connected with the collection of the *alcabala* became so great that customhouses had to be established within the country; sales taxes were abolished there in 1896.

**Alcalde.** Mayor, head of the town government. In Spanish-American colonies, an official acting both as mayor and judge. There were two main groups: *alcaldes ordinarios* were elected officials performing the duties of mayors and judges, there being two for each larger town; *alcaldes mayores* were officials appointed by the king or viceroy. The appointment was conferred for three years upon natives, for five upon Spaniards. The *alcaldes* *mayores* exercised civil and criminal jurisdiction and went from town to town. In New Spain the *alcalde mayor* governed, in the name of the king, a town that was not a provincial capital. Other *alcaldes* included: *alcaldes de la hermandad*, who were police magistrates for the rural districts and sometimes called *alcaldes de la mesta*; if the city was a large one, there were *alcaldes de barrio*, who had general supervision over several wards or parishes; an additional *alcalde provincial* was introduced into the *cabildos* of Peru in 1635 and most probably into New Spain at the same time; theoretically his duties were very much the same as those of the *alcalde de la hermandad*, but the crown ordered both to continue in operation.

**Alcaldía.** Office and jurisdiction of an *alcalde*.

**Alegría, Ciro.** 1909–1967. Peruvian novelist. Considered the outstanding writer of *novelas indianistas*, he is the author of the prize-winning *El mundo es ancho y ajeno* (Broad and Alien is the World), 1941, which tells of the destruction of an Indian village as the result of the greed of white men. The novel *La serpiente de oro* (The Golden Serpent), 1935, is a study of the Indians of the Marañón River. A member of the APRA party, Alegría was exiled from Peru.

**Alem, Leandro N.** 1842–1896. Argentine political leader. b. Buenos Aires. One of the leaders of the *Unión Cívica*, a political party formed prior to 1890, he led the revolt against the regime of President Juárez Celman, forcing him to resign. In 1891, after breaking with the conservative elements in the *Unión Cívica*, he formed the *Unión Cívica Radical*, which sought extensive political reforms. With YRIGOYEN he headed the unsuccessful revolt of 1893 against President Luis SÁENZ PEÑA. He committed suicide in 1896.

**Alemán Valdés, Miguel.** 1902– . President of Mexico. b. Sayula. Studied at the National University; practiced law in Mexico City; served as justice of superior court of Veracruz; senator and finally governor of that state, 1936–1940. He directed ÁVILA CAMACHO's campaign for the presidency in 1939, was named minister of the interior, 1940–

1945, and became president in 1946, the first popularly-elected president in 35 years who was not a general, but a civilian. The economic problems that faced Mexico during his administration were handled by businessmen, who entered his conservative cabinet; the influence of the labor unions declined. With a strong central government, Alemán was able to maintain a strong foreign policy and take an active part in the UN. His administration was marked by rapid economic progress, unfortunately accompanied by considerable corruption among government officials. He did little to carry forward the agrarian program of the revolution but embarked on large-scale irrigation enterprises modeled after the TVA. He supported the growth of industry, whose many problems made it necessary to attract foreign capital. A government corporation called the NACIONAL FINANCIERA aided in his economic program. He extended education and science, and in 1947 was the first Mexican president to visit the United States during his term of office. He was succeeded by Adolfo RUIZ CORTINES in 1952.

**Alessandri Palma, Arturo.** 1868–1950. President of Chile. b. Linares. Educated in Chile, he obtained his license as advocate, 1893. Associated with the liberal movement, he assisted in the candidacy of the younger ERRÁZURIZ, 1896; deputy from Curicó, 1897–1915; minister of industry and public works, 1908; minister of finance, 1913; elected senator, 1915; prime minister (with portfolio of minister of the interior) 1918; elected president, 1920. He attempted to institute much-needed reforms but was seriously handicapped by a split between the lower house and the senate, which were controlled by opposing parties. However, he received approval for some measures, with compromises, and the financial situation of the government was strengthened. Labor laws and laws to protect industry were also passed during his administration. He was called the "first president of the Chilean people." He resigned in September 1924, when trouble developed that he could not settle, but was recalled to the presidency, 1925, and exerted great influence on the constitution of 1925, which established a political democracy for Chile. He resigned the presidency, 1925, and after a period of exile returned to Chile and was re-elected president, 1932–1938. His second administration was considerably more conservative, and he was supported chiefly by rightists in his insistence on stronger government control of the nitrate industry. Succeeded by the radical leader AGUIRRE CERDA, he was subsequently senator from Tarapacá.

**Alexander VI (Rodrigo Borgia).** 1431–1503. Pope. b. Játiva, near Valencia, Spain. The most memorable of the corrupt and secular popes, he mediated in the dispute between Portugal and Spain over possessions in the New World during his pontificate (1492–1503). See DEMARCATION, LINE OF.

**Alfaro, Eloy.** 1842–1912. President of Ecuador. b. Montecristi. Fought President GARCÍA MORENO on side of the liberals, and after the failure of the revolt he was forced to emigrate to Panama, remaining there until García Moreno's death in 1875. He conspired against new governments and was forced to flee again. In 1895 the liberals and the anticlericals of Guayaquil "pronounced" in favor of the exiled Alfaro, and upon his return were able to overthrow the government. For the next 16 years, he controlled the country, occupying the presidency from 1895 to 1901 and again from 1906 to 1911. In 1897 a new constitution had been put into effect that changed the "clerical" conservative one, written 13 years before, and granted religious toleration; the government was centralized, and the president selected the provincial governors. In 1906 Alfaro returned to the presidency and instituted further changes. A new constitution was promulgated in that year, and his administration continued the degree of order that had been established. The construction of the 290-mile railroad between Guayaquil and the capital, Quito, was completed in 1909, marking the beginning of an expansion of modern transportation facilities. Alfaro continued his attack on the Church and attempted to curtail the power of the clergy. When the puppet whom Alfaro had named to succeed him died after a few months in office and anarchy again prevailed, Alfaro, in an abortive attempt to seize the presidency during the crisis, was arrested and imprisoned. In January 1912, the prison was stormed by an angry mob, and the former president was dragged out and brutally killed.

**Alfaro, Ricardo Joaquín.** b. 1882. Panamanian jurist and statesman. Studied in Colombia and Panama; official of ministry of foreign affairs; professor of history (1910); attaché, Panamanian Legation in Washington (1912); professor of law at the Escuela Nacional de Derecho, 1917–1923; premier, 1918–1922; minister plenipotentiary of Panama in Washington, 1933–1936. Alfaro has had a distinguished career as a jurist and historian, and also as a statesman. He is the author of a number of historical and juridical works.

**Alguacil Mayor.** The sheriff or chief constable attached to the colonial Spanish-American *cabildos* and *audiencias*. This post was highly lucrative and could be purchased.

**Alhóndiga.** Public granaries located in the main cities of colonial Spanish America, through which the colonial government tried to provide for the people a steady and adequate supply of bread at a reasonable price.

**Alliance for Progress.** A ten-year economic and social development program for Latin America proposed and supported by U.S. President John F. Kennedy. The long-term venture is based on the principle that the Latin-American countries will conduct extensive economic and social reforms in return for continued and expanded U.S. aid. The plan was first announced by Kennedy on March 13, 1961, shortly after his inauguration, and was enthusiastically approved by all the Latin-American nations, except Cuba, at a meeting (August 1961) of the Inter-American Economic and Social Council in Punta del Este, Uruguay. A charter to implement the plan was drawn up and signed (August 17) by all but the Cuban representatives. Goals of the ten-year plan included six years of schooling for all Latin-American children, literacy for 50,000,000 illiterate persons, eradication of malaria, large-scale public housing, and potable water for more than half the population. Any nation desiring to participate in the program was to submit a long-range development plan to a panel of nine advisers associated with the Inter-American Economic and Social Council. Agrarian reform measures and tax reforms were regarded as essential features of any plan to be submitted for approval. A minimum of $20,000,000,000 was pledged for the following decade, more than half of which would come from the United States in low-interest, long-term loans. It was expected that the balance of the funds would come from international agencies, western European sources, and private capital. Basic structural reforms and sweeping changes were pledged by the Latin-American nations in the fields of taxation, land reform, education, and housing. The magnitude of the Alliance program can be ascertained by a comparison of the anticipated expenditures in the period from 1961 to 1971 to the $4,000,000,000 of nonmilitary assistance given to Latin-American countries in the postwar period from 1945 through 1960. In the course of the first year of operation the United States committed more funds than were promised at the Punta del Este conference, thus enabling important projects to get underway, and Latin-American governments stepped up the tempo of reform efforts. At a conference of the Inter-American Economic and Social Council held in Mexico City in October 1962, a review of the first year's progress was undertaken. Five Latin-American countries had submitted ten-year development plans, four countries had passed agrarian reform laws (Mexico, Venezuela, Colombia, and Bolivia have had land reform programs underway for several years), and three countries had enacted tax-reform laws. Because the United States was concerned that the Alliance program had not been properly understood in the Latin-American countries, and that they viewed it as a charity rather than a cooperative venture, former presidents Juscelino Kubitshek of Brazil and Alberto LLERAS CAMARGO of Columbia were given the task of developing and propagating a convincing doctrine for the Alliance. During the first year the program had been frustrated by the resurgence of powerful conservative groups in Latin America who resisted reforms, and

also by the lack of capital resulting from the deterioration of trade and private investment. The declining prices of Latin-American exports and the rising costs of imports were tantamount to canceling out the aid received under the Alliance program. The Alliance was under attack in some areas because it was believed that the United States' attitude toward reforms was meddlesome and a danger to political stability. A second annual meeting to review Alliance progress was held in São Paulo, Brazil, on November 12, 1963. U.S. leadership and financing of the program was criticized because of the reckless administration of Alliance funds without regard for the potential productiveness of individual projects. The per capita national income had increased less than 1 per cent in 1962, far below the Alliance goal of 2.5 per cent. Population growth (7,000,000 annually) and unfavorable economic trends were outstripping the advantages derived from the aid received. The São Paulo conference delegates agreed to establish a permanent eight-man executive committee that would have collective responsibility for overseeing the operations of the Alliance. With the completion of the organizational phase of the program it was realized that greater performance, beyond the promises of the charter, would have to be achieved by the Latin-American countries. The resistance to economic and social reform by the entrenched elite of Latin America would have to be overcome to implement efficiently any program that would modernize traditional Latin-American society. The Alliance program, which has been regarded by many as heralding a new era in relations between the United States and Latin America, is accomplishing some of its goals, but it may very well take more than a decade to achieve the desired results.

**Almagro, Diego de.** 1475–1538. Spanish soldier and explorer. b. near Ciudad Real. Went to Panama in 1514; joined PIZARRO, 1522; and took part in the first voyage to the south, 1524–1525. He was Pizarro's partner in the conquest of Peru, 1533, and accompanied him on the march against Cuzco. He was the leader of an expedition of conquest into Chile, 1535–1536, and took issue with

Pizarro about ownership of Cuzco. He was defeated in war with the Pizarro brothers. Almagro was captured and executed. His son Diego (1520–1542) was born in Panama of an Indian mother, and accompanied his father on the expedition to Chile. He continued war with the Pizarros after the death of his father, his followers murdering Francisco Pizarro in 1541. He was defeated by royalist forces under VACA DE CASTRO at the Battle of Chupas and was executed.

**Almazán, Juan Andreu.** 1891–    . Mexican army officer. b. Guerrero. Served with MADERO, 1910, and commanded the army zone of Monterrey from 1924. He showed brilliant leadership in the suppression of the Escobar Rebellion, 1929. He became a candidate for the presidency, 1940, supported by the newly organized National Action Party (PAN), to oppose ÁVILA CAMACHO. His platform included a more lenient attitude toward the Church, complete freedom of speech and press, and a modification of the labor laws to control the right to strike. He won enthusiastic support from conservative elements opposed to the radical program of CÁRDENAS' administration. He lost the election and charged fraud, but Ávila Camacho became president of Mexico on December 1, 1940.

**Almojarifazgo.** Export-import tax or duty collected by the Spanish Crown during the colonial period on goods leaving Spain and bound for America and on goods arriving in the colonies, as well as on merchandise imported into Spain from America. An import duty of 7½ per cent in the Spanish-American colonies was levied until 1543, when it was cut to 5 per cent, with 2½ per cent collected on exports at Seville. American goods reaching Seville paid an *almojarifazgo* of 5 per cent and an *alcabala* of 10 per cent. In 1566 duties on European articles levied in American ports were raised to 5 and 10 per cent, with an additional export duty of 2½ per cent collected in the colonies on articles bound for Spain. From 1624 to 1660 *almojarifazgo* was levied on the basis of weight, but after a period during which duties were replaced altogether by an annual sum of 790,000 ducats paid by Spanish and Spanish-American traders, volume became a more common basis for assess-

ment. After 1720 *almojarifazgo* in American ports on trade with Spain was discontinued. By decrees in 1772 and later years, duties on many Spanish or American goods were reduced or abolished. The new rules of 1778 established an over-all payment in both Spanish and American ports on goods produced in Spain or originating in America, and the number of articles placed on the free list was increased. On foreign goods the *almojarifazgo* was still 7 per cent. There were some temporary increases during the wars following the French Revolution, but generally these rules prevailed until the beginning of the war for independence.

**Almonte, Juan Nepomuceno.** 1804–1869. Mexican general and conservative statesman, believed to be MORELOS' son. He was educated in the United States, served as lieutenant with SANTA ANNA in Texas, and was captured at SAN JACINTO, 1836. He was sent by Santa Anna as ambassador to Spain; minister to the United States, 1841–1845 and again in 1853; ambassador to France, 1857; supported French intervention, 1862, and headed the forces welcoming MAXIMILLIAN at Veracruz 1864.

**Alonso.** See LAUTARO.

**Alpaca.** Domesticated breed of South-American, camel-like, hoofed mammal, bred from the wild guanaco. Alpacas are kept in flocks on the level heights of the Andes in Bolivia, Chile, and Peru, at an elevation of 14,000 to 16,000 feet. The alpaca is the most important of the four kinds of indigenous fiber-bearing animals of South America; the others are the LLAMA, GUANACO, and VICUÑA. Alpacas are bred for their wool, and llamas as beasts of burden. The value of alpaca wool was recognized by the Peruvian Indians who wove it with great skill centuries before it was introduced into Europe. The first European importations of the wool, through Spain, resulted in its being condemned as an unworkable material. Although it was successfully spun into a yarn in 1808, it was not until 1836 that technological developments in the weaving industry facilitated the use of the wool for making cloth.

**Alsina, Valentín.** 1802–1869. Argentine political leader and journalist. A strong opponent of ROSAS' dictatorship, he carried on an unrelenting campaign from Montevideo. He led a revolutionary movement in 1852 against URQUIZA and served as governor of Buenos Aires for a short time in 1852; during a second term as governor, 1857–1859, the war between Buenos Aires and the Argentine Confederation broke out in 1859. He resigned his post after the defeat of the Buenos Aires forces, November 1859.

**Alvarado y Mesía, Pedro de.** *ca.* 1485–1541. Spanish explorer and adventurer. b. Badajoz, Spain. Served as second-in-command to CORTÉS in the conquest of Mexico, 1519–1521. In 1523 he was sent on an expedition into Guatemala and El Salvador, which he succeeded in conquering. In March 1534 with 500 Spaniards and 2,000 Indians he crossed the Andes and attempted to conquer Quito. He reached the Bay of Caráquez, met PIZARRO and ALMAGRO, and sold his expedition for 100,000 gold pesos. He was killed during the war with the Indians in Jalisco, Mexico.

**Alvares, Diego.** See CARAMURÚ.

**Álvarez, Juan.** 1780–1867. Mexican general and liberal leader. b. Atoyac, Guerrero, of Indian descent. Served with MORELOS in the war for Mexican independence; fought with SANTA ANNA against ITURBIDE, 1823; led a revolt against Anastasio BUSTAMANTE, 1830; served as general in the Mexican War with the United States, 1846–1848; first governor of Guerrero, 1849. With Colonel COMONFORT he started a Federalist revolt in the State of Guerrero under the PLAN OF AYUTLA early in 1854, and fighting continued for a year until Santa Anna went into exile, 1855. Álvarez acted as president of Mexico from October to December, 1855, and during his short term in office the LEY JUÁREZ and other liberal reforms were enacted. He resigned and was succeeded by Comonfort. Álvarez opposed the French invasion and MAXIMILIAN, 1862–1867.

**Alvear, Carlos María de.** 1789–1853. Argentine patriot. b. Santo Angel de la Guarda. Educated in Argentina and Spain, he served as an officer in the Spanish army and fought with SAN MARTÍN in the struggle for independence. He served in the constituent assembly of 1813 and was highly influential. In 1814 his uncle, Gervasio Antonio de Posadas, was elected "Supreme Director of the United Provinces of the River Plate." Alvear was named to succeed Posadas for a brief period in 1815 but was forced to flee to Brazil, 1820. He was appointed minister to the United States, 1824. When war broke out against Brazil in Uruguay, 1826, Alvear was placed in command of the Argentine forces and in January 1827 he invaded Brazilian territory with 8,000 men and won the Battle of ITUZAINGÓ. In 1832 he was again sent to the United States as a diplomatic representative. He continued to reside in the United States for many years and died at New York on November 2, 1853.

**Alvear, Marcelo Torcuato de.** 1868–1942. Argentine president and political leader. b. Buenos Aires. Leader of the radicals, he took part in the rebellions of 1890, 1893, and 1905, was national deputy from 1912–1917, and minister to France, 1917–1922. Elected to succeed IRIGOYEN as president of Argentina in 1922, he served until 1928. His administration was quiet and prosperous. He lived in exile, 1931–1932, and was an unsuccessful candidate of the Radical Party for the presidency in 1937. He was a strong supporter of the Allies in the first years of WORLD WAR II.

**Álzaga, Martín.** 1756–1812. Argentine merchant and royalist leader. He was head of the pro-Spanish forces in Buenos Aires, where he was a leading merchant, and probably the richest man in that area. He organized the defense of Buenos Aires in its fight against British attack in 1807. As chief *alcalde*, he dominated the *cabildo* during the important year 1808. He opposed LINIERS and at the end of June 1812 led a conspiracy to smother the revolution and to re-establish a monarchy headed by Princess CARLOTA JOAQUINA of Brazil, the elder sister of FERDINAND VII; but the plot was discovered and Álzaga was executed.

**Amador Guerrero, Manuel.** 1833–1909. President of Panama. Prominent physician; leader in struggle for independence; first president of Panama, 1904–1908. During his administration a constitution was adopted and a treaty was signed with the U.S. providing for the construction of a canal across a 10-mile-wide strip of Panamanian territory granted in perpetuity to the U.S.

**Amapala, Treaty of.** An agreement that temporarily united El Salvador, Honduras, and Nicaragua. The treaty, signed on June 20, 1895, created a loose confederation called the *República Mayor de Centro América*, later changed to *Los Estados Unidos de Centro América*. The existence of the union was seriously threatened three years later by a revolution begun in El Salvador. The dissolution of the treaty was officially announced on November 30, 1898.

**Amar y Borbón, Antonio.** Spanish viceroy. Sent to Bogotá as viceroy in 1803, he was the last of the Spanish viceroys of New Granada. He was deposed in 1810 by a patriotic junta, imprisoned, and then deported to Spain.

**Amat y Junient, Manuel de.** 1704–1790. Viceroy of Peru. Patron of the theater, largely responsible for the success of the actress "La Perricholi." Served as captain general of Chile, 1754–1761, and as viceroy of Peru, 1761–1776; on orders from the Crown, he expelled JESUITS from Peru. Believing in freedom of philosophic thought, he insisted that philosophy be taught at SAN MARCOS. In 1770 he established the excellent Convictorio of San Carlos, where emphasis was placed on the teaching of the Cartesian and Newtonian systems.

**Amazon Basin.** The huge Amazon region occupying almost two-thirds of colonial Brazil's total area was not included in the territory adjudicated to Portugal by the Treaty of TORDESILLAS. Consequently the Spaniards attempted to occupy it, but as they had to cross the forbidding chain of the Andes to reach it, they were at a considerable disadvantage; and in the 17th century their rivals, the Portuguese, ascending the river from its mouth at Pará (Belém), staked their claim to the whole area. In 1750 Spain recognized Portugal's rights to the territory. The Amazon Basin was exploited in the 18th century by the *Companhia Geral do Grão Pará e Maranhão* organized by Portugal's minister POMBAL

in 1755, and due solely to the activities of the company the cultivation of cotton and rice was fostered. The AMAZON RIVER was opened to navigation by merchant ships of all nations in 1867, and at the turn of the 20th century RUBBER became the main product of the Amazon valley and yielded tremendous profits. After 1912, however, when the Far-East plantations were producing rubber more inexpensively, the rubber boom came to an end. Under the VARGAS administration (1930–1945) increasing attention was paid to the development of the region. In 1940 Vargas suggested international development of the Amazon Basin jointly by Brazil and countries adjoining the area, and during WORLD WAR II the United States' need for Brazilian rubber considerably helped the Brazilian government in its Amazon development program. The close of the war marked the end of U.S. rubber purchases, and this fact, combined with a rising interest in the development of the São Francisco Valley, diverted public attention somewhat from the great Amazon Basin. However, during the presidency of Eurico Gaspar DUTRA (1946–1950), Brazil, in co-operation with Peru, Colombia, Venezuela, Bolivia, and Ecuador, and with the support of the UNESCO organization of the United Nations, established the Hylean Institute in 1947, designed to foster the development of Amazon resources by all these nations.

**Amazon River.** A river in South America, the largest in the world and third longest. It is 3,900 miles long and drains a basin 2,225,000 square miles in area. Its many tributaries, 17 of which are from 1,000 to 2,300 miles in length, include the great Ucayali, Madeira, and Xingu, and, together with the Amazon, constitute about 31,000 miles of navigable waterways. The Amazon has its source in the Peruvian Andes. It flows north and then east and is known as the Marañón, and from the junction of the Ucayali to the Brazilian border as the Amazonas. Flowing east through the immense Amazonian flood plain it is called the Solimões up to the river port of Manaus, where the Rio Negro joins it. From there to its 207-mile-wide mouth on the Atlantic Ocean near Pará (Belém) it is given the name of Amazonas. Its average width along much of its length is 5 miles, but along its lower reaches it is sometimes as much as 400 miles wide. The Amazon is navigable to ocean steamers as far as Iquitos, in Peru, a distance of 2,300 miles from the Atlantic Ocean. The chief cities along its course are Pará (Belém), near the mouth, Manaus, 1,000 miles from the Atlantic, and Iquitos, in Peru. The Amazon was discovered by the Spaniard Vicente Yáñez PINZÓN in 1500, and in 1541 another Spaniard, Francisco de ORELLANA, starting in Peru, descended the whole length of the river and came out into the Atlantic. He gave the river the name Amazonas, believing that its banks were inhabited by a nation of warlike women. In 1637 a Portuguese party led by Pedro Teixeira, setting out from Pará, reached Quito (capital of modern Ecuador) about a year later. A number of scientific expeditions, including that of the famous Alexander von HUMBOLDT (begun in 1799), explored the Amazon Basin in the 18th century, and were followed by more explorations in the 19th century (Wallace and Bates, Spruce, Agassiz, etc.). In the 20th century important expeditions have been the Roosevelt-Rondon Expedition (1914), the Rice Expeditions (1910–1924), the Ellsworth-Farabee-Fawcett Expedition (1923), and the Marshall Field Expedition of 1931.

**American Popular Revolutionary Alliance** *(Alianza Popular Revolucionaria Americana)*. Also known as **APRA, Aprista Movement.** Founded by Víctor Raúl HAYA DE LA TORRE of Peru in 1924, as a political movement opposed to foreign imperialism, both political and economic, dedicated to the integration of the Indians into the economic and political life of the Latin-American countries where they existed in large numbers. APRA supported nationalization of land and industry, opposition to "Yankee Imperialism," internationalization of the Panama Canal, close co-operation between the Latin-American republics, and opposition to Marxist Communism. Although Haya de la Torre was a candidate for the Peruvian presidency in 1931, the party was outlawed after 1933, and he was not allowed to run for election in 1936. In 1942, APRA was again barred from the elections, but in the free election of 1945 it was legally recognized and took the name of *Partido Popular* (Popular Party). With its support, BUSTAMANTE was elected to the presidency. APRA obtained a close majority in congress and three of its members were chosen for the cabinet. With the growth of the GOOD NEIGHBOR POLICY, APRA stopped attacking "Yankee Imperialism" and became pro-United States. Although the *apristas* wielded a good deal of influence from 1945 to 1947, they were faced with unrelenting opposition from the conservatives. In 1947 the *apristas* resigned from the cabinet, were accused of instigating the unsuccessful revolt of October 1948, and were declared illegal by Bustamante. Following the seizure of power by the conservatives under ODRÍA, Haya de la Torre was forced to seek asylum in the Colombian embassy in Lima, where he remained until given permission to leave the country in 1954. The *apristas* were again active in the election of 1956, forming a coalition with the *Movimiento Democrático Peruano* (M.D.P.) to successfully elect their old foe Manuel PRADO. The reactivation of the outlawed APRA was thereafter sponsored by Prado in 1957 and Haya de la Torre returned to Peru in July of that year. The aging APRA leader had become more an advocate of political serenity and political coexistence than he had in the past. Although the party was still considered to be left of center, the alliance with Prado had caused a serious loss of prestige among the Peruvian masses. Castro's revolution in Cuba brought about a split among the *apristas* when *APRA Rebelde*, a pro-Cuban dissident wing of the party, was formed in 1960; however, official policy remained anti-Communist and anti-Fidelista. Early in 1962 APRA announced that Haya de la Torre would be its candidate in the presidential election to be held in June of that year. Manuel Seoane and Alberto Arca Parró were candidates for first and second vice-presidents, respectively. In the bitterly-contested election none of the presidential candidates received the required number of votes for election and the selection of a president fell to the congress. Anticipating that the APRA candidate Haya de la Torre would be chosen, the conservative military intervened, deposing President Prado and annulling the election. Another election held in 1963 was more decisive; the APRA candidate was defeated by the Popular Action candidate Belaúnde Terry.

**American Revolution, Influence of.** Knowledge of the American Revolution and the ideals that inspired the North-American patriots had an unquestionable effect on discontented CREOLES of Latin America. Francisco de MIRANDA, Antonio NARIÑO, and other precursors of the independence movement in Latin America followed the events in the north with an avid interest and found inspiration in the success of their northern counterparts. Prior to the American Revolution direct contact between the British colonies and the Spanish and Portuguese colonies had been severely restricted by the policy of commercial exclusiveness of the mother countries. After the northern patriots achieved independence, Spain, in 1797, was forced to relax its commercial policy because of its involvement in a war with England. The emergency measure allowed the colonies to trade with neutral countries and brought about an economic liberation that established a strong commercial contact between the two Americas. American merchants and seamen disseminated their ideas of freedom and independence, distributed copies of the Constitution and the Declaration of Independence, sowed the seeds of sedition, and generally contributed to the political ferment that led to Latin-American independence. Aside from the growth in trade there was an increase in intellectual contact as well. Translations of U.S. books and pamphlets were read with increasing interest by creoles and a number of prominent statesmen of the United States became renowned in Latin America. Benjamin Franklin was especially well-known. Many of his works, translated into Spanish, were avidly commented upon in intellectual circles. A number of Latin Americans had traveled to the British colonies in North America before 1776, and others spent time in the United States after independence was achieved. Their reports of the achievements of the young republic did not fail to arouse strong interest among their countrymen, who dreamed of emulating their northern neighbors and throwing off the shackles of colonialism. Also, by allying itself with France against England in 1779, Spain helped the American colonials to free themselves of English domination. Spain's own colonials, admiring the freedom-loving British colonies, necessarily compared their own position with that of their northern counterparts; and devoting some thought to their status as second-rate citizens, they conceived the idea of independence in their own countries.

**Amézaga, Juan José.** b. 1881. Lawyer and president of Uruguay. A wealthy and successful lawyer chosen by BALDOMIR as his successor in 1942, he had served as an assemblyman and cabinet minister, and had been a representative to the League of Nations, but was not a prominent politician. He served as president from March 1, 1943 to March 1, 1947 and continued Uruguay's close co-operation with the U.S. during World War II. PERÓN put pressure on Uruguay by cutting off the normal supply of Argentine wheat causing a bread shortage in that nation. He finally offered to give the country wheat if it voted for the "right" man; however, this threat did not succeed, and Berreta, nominee of Amézaga's *Colorado Batllista* party, won the election of 1946.

**Amiguismo.** Spanish, meaning nepotism, or nomination to political office by reason of relationship or friendship.

**Amparo, Writ of.** The *amparo* is usually regarded as Mexico's unique and most important contribution to jurisprudence. The writ is issued only by federal courts and provides judicial protection against damage to individual interests or violation of constitutional guarantees, federal actions that infringe on the sovereignty of the states, and acts of the states that invade the federal sphere of action. The word *amparo* means "protection" and combines the characteristics of such English injunctions as *habeas corpus, mandamus,* and *certiorari.* Successful action on the part of the plaintiff whose right has been affected does not repeal the law in question, but merely prevents action from occurring in that particular instance. The writ had its origin in the state constitution of Yucatán in 1842 and its use has been specified in the national constitution of 1857 and in the present constitution.

**Amunátegui Aldunate, Miguel Luis.** 1828–1888. Chilean historian and reformer. He played an important part in the Liberal Convention. He was minister of the interior, 1868, the unsuccessful liberal candidate for the presidential nomination in 1875, and minister of public instruction under Aníbal PINTO GARMENDIA. He is important as a historian and is the author of *Vida de Andrés Bello, 1822, Crónica de 1810, Los precursores de la independencia de Chile.*

**Anáhuac.** Indian name for the valley of Mexico in the center of which Mexico City now stands. It means "place of waters." The valley formerly had several large lakes, now dried up.

**Anarcho-Syndicalism.** A movement aimed at the overthrow of the state by means of direct action on the part of workers organized in trade unions, with the ultimate purpose of establishing a cooperative society. Anarchosyndicalism, which has its roots mainly in the theories of the Russian Bakunin, the Frenchman Sorel, and the Spaniard Ferrer, has had great influence in Spain (Catalonia) and Italy. In some countries of Latin America it was fairly widespread among the working class from about 1890 to 1920, its rise being due partly to local social and economic conditions (poor wages, low standard of living), and partly because of the diffusion of syndicalist ideas by Italian and Spanish immigrants. It was especially active in Mexico under the leadership of Ricardo FLORES MAGÓN, in Argentina (chiefly in Buenos Aires) with Pedro Abad de Santillán, in Uruguay, and in Chile. As in Europe, Latin-American anarcho-syndicalism was violently opposed to Marxist socialism, mainly because of the latter's espousal of the doctrine of the "dictatorship of the proletariat." After 1920 its influence began to decrease and it lost ground to its rival and enemy, Marxism.

**Anchieta, José de.** *ca.* 1533–1597. Portuguese Jesuit missionary and educator. b. Canary Islands. Went to Brazil in 1553 when only 20 and founded on the plains near Piratininga a school called "College of São Paulo" for Portuguese children, for *mamelucos* (persons of mixed blood), and for Indians. In 1560, while an attack was made on the community by hostile Indians, Father Anchieta offered to go and talk to the opposing chiefs and was held as a hostage for five months. Author of an Indian grammar and many books on life in Brazil, he is often referred to as the "Apostle of Brazil."

**Ancón, Treaty of.** Treaty signed on October 20, 1883, between Peru and Chile, ending the WAR OF THE PACIFIC. By its terms, Peru gave up the territory of Tarapacá and Chile was empowered to occupy for the following ten years the provinces of Tacna and Arica. After that period the fate of the provinces was to be decided by a plebiscite.

**Andagoya, Pascual de.** 1495–1548. Spanish explorer. Andagoya arrived in the New World with Pedro ARIAS de ÁVILA in 1514, became a REGIDOR of Panama, and was appointed inspector general of the Indians. In 1522 he was sent on an expedition down the coast of what is now Colombia as far as the mouth of the San Juan River, where he obtained information later used by PIZARRO. Lack of sufficient equipment and illness prevented him from continuing south, and he was forced to return to Panama. He was appointed governor and *adelantado* of the San Juan River in 1539 by the Spanish crown. Because of charges brought against him by BENALCÁZAR he was imprisoned and later returned to Spain where he died. Since he was a highly intelligent and competent man it is often regretted that he did not become the conqueror of Peru. He wrote of his experiences in *Relación de sucesos de Pedrarias Dávila en las provincias de Tierra Firme.*

**Andes Mountains.** (From Quechua *Anti*, east, or *Antasuya*, metal region.) Also called *Cordillera*. The great South-American mountain system on the western side of the continent, running north-south, with a length of about 5,000 miles, from the Caribbean Sea to Tierra del Fuego. Its average width is 200 miles and its average altitude is 10,000 feet. It contains more than fifty peaks of over

20,000 feet, and the famous Mt. Aconcagua (22,835 feet) is the highest mountain in the Western Hemisphere. Gold and silver were once the coveted minerals of the Andes, but today tin, copper, lead, zinc, and other metals are just as important if not more so. The Indian population of the Andes is engaged in agriculture, raising maize, wheat, potatoes, and barley. In southern Peru and Bolivia a few Indians raise LLAMAS, ALPACAS, and sheep. Among the several rail lines that cross the Andes, the most famous is the Buenos Aires-Santiago de Chile line, 888 miles long, connecting Argentina and Chile at the Uspallata Pass, at an altitude of more than 10,500 feet. The Andes were the seat of the Incan civilization that ruled over the mountain area from northern Ecuador to central Chile, and of the Chibcha culture occupying the Cordillera Oriental of Colombia.

**Andrada e Silva, José Bonifácio de.** 1765–1838. Brazilian scientist and statesman. b. Santos, São Paulo. Educated at the University of Coimbra, Portugal, he spent ten years in Europe studying metallurgy and mineralogy and engaging in scientific research. He was responsible for the discovery of several new minerals and was one of the most brilliant men of his time. He fought at head of a group of students when French invaded Portugal, 1807; returned to Brazil, 1819, and became a political leader in São Paulo, where he led the almost bloodless revolution against Portugal that gained independence for Brazil. When Brazil was established as the only empire in the New World, besides Mexico, in 1822, he became prime minister to PEDRO I. His cabinet was accused of being tactless and arbitrary in the handling of political opponents. He attacked freedom of the press and set up a system of political espionage, and closed the masonic lodges, of which he had been a member. The emperor, jealous of Andrada's popularity, dismissed him in July 1823 and deported him to France along with his brothers, Martim Francisco and Antônio Carlos, both of whom had aided him. Andrada returned and was appointed guardian of five-year-old Pedro de Alcántara who on April 7, 1831 became Emperor PEDRO II. Andrada is credited with having said, long before Lincoln, that no country can exist that is half-slave and half-free.

**Andrade, Osvaldo de.** 1890–1954. Brazilian novelist. b. São Paulo. Considered by critics the *enfant terrible* of Brazilian letters, he is judged as an imitator of foreign styles and a sensation seeker. The books that have been considered "shocking" are *The Damned*, 1922, *The Star of Absinthe*, 1927, *The Vermillion Ladder*, 1934, and *Marco Zero*, 1943.

**Anglo–Latin American Relations.** From an early date England contested Spain's position in the New World. English contraband and piracy plagued Spanish-American possessions during the entire colonial period. In the 16th century the Englishmen John Hawkins, Francis Drake, and others made a number of attacks on the Caribbean coast and carried on much illegal trade throughout the whole Spanish Main. In the 17th century English privateers were particularly active in the Caribbean, and especially in the period from 1655 to 1670, when their frequent attacks on Spanish ships and on Spanish towns in the Caribbean region struck terror in the Spanish settlements of the area. At the same time, British forces were seizing important Caribbean bases, including Jamaica and other islands in the West Indies, and British buccaneers were establishing a foothold on the Central-American mainland by their log-cutting activities on the coast of present-day BRITISH HONDURAS. One of the most striking examples of British depredations during the colonial period was the destruction of Panama City carried out in 1671 by the buccaneer Henry Morgan. The British became interested from the beginning in the slave trade with Spanish America. Most of the time they smuggled Negro slaves into the Spanish colonies, but at the beginning of the 18th century, the British South Sea Company was granted by Spain the right to supply slaves to the colonies. However, as the Company took advantage of its privilege and carried out a considerable amount of illegal trade, Spain stepped in and tried to put an end to the contraband. England intervened on the side of the Company and the result was the "War of Jenkins' Ear" in 1739. The British were also active in smuggling with Brazil, and their privateers attacked and sacked Brazilian ports; the port of Santos was assailed and burned in 1591. Toward the end of the colonial period, in 1806 and 1807, England made two attempts to seize Buenos Aires, but was defeated twice. During the War for Independence, Britain maintained an attitude of official neutrality, but at the same time many Britons joined the South-American revolutionary movements and served as volunteers in the patriot armies. In 1823 Britain's foreign minister, George Canning, blocked the threat of French intervention on the side of Spain through the Polignac Memorandum, which was more important in preserving Latin-American liberties than the MONROE DOCTRINE. After the achievement of independence, Great Britain quickly recognized the Latin-American republics. Considerable British immigration occurred during the 19th century, especially into Argentina, although few British immigrants became assimilated. In the 19th century British interests largely dominated Latin-American economic development, while British diplomatic influence outweighed that of any other power. The frictions that occurred were caused by Great Britain's activities along the MOSQUITO COAST in Central America in the 1830's and 1840's; by a treaty violation on the part of the Argentine dictator ROSAS in 1845, resulting in a British and French blockade of Buenos Aires and a Franco-British landing at Montevideo to help anti-Rosas forces; and by controversies with Argentina (1833), Guatemala (1859), Mexico (1861), Nicaragua (1894), and Venezuela (1895 and 1902). In the 20th century the outstanding dispute between Great Britain and a Latin-American nation was the controversy with Mexico (1938), which was touched off by Mexico's expropriation of British oil concerns and led to a temporary breaking of diplomatic relations. Today Argentina still maintains claims on the Falkland Islands, which were annexed by Great Britain in 1833. Guatemala still claims British Honduras. By the first decade of the 20th century Great Britain had built up a considerable trade with Latin America, especially with Argentina, exporting manufactured goods and importing agricultural prod-

ucts. British investments in Latin America, especially in railroads and mining, were heavy and gave Great Britain a very important place in the commercial activities of that area of the world. British cultural activities in Latin America were maintained at a high level and today there are still many English clubs, newspapers, and schools in the big cities. Since WORLD WAR I, British influence has markedly decreased as a result of the growing strength of the United States, the rise of nationalistic sentiments and policies in Latin America, and the decline in Britain's world position.

**Angostura, Congress of.** On February 15, 1819, a congress met at the Venezuelan town of Angostura, confirming Simón BOLÍVAR as commander-in-chief of the patriot army and proclaiming him president of the republic of Venezuela. In December of the same year, the Congress of Angostura created the republic of Colombia, to be made up of Venezuela, New Granada, and the Presidency of Quito (Ecuador), after these territories had been liberated from Spanish rule. Simón Bolívar was elected president of the new republic, often referred to as *Gran Colombia* (Great Colombia).

**Antarctica.** Conflicting claims on Antarctic territories by Chile, Argentina, and Great Britain recently came to the fore. Argentina based her claims on voyages of discovery undertaken in the southern waters by the Argentine seaman Captain Luis Piedrabuena (1832–1883). Chile sent an expedition to Antarctic territories in 1947 and by 1950 had established a military base as well as radio and weather stations in the area also claimed by Argentina and Great Britain. All three countries maintain bases on Palmer Peninsula (Graham Land). A report on the Chilean expedition was written by Eugenio Orrego Vicuña, the distinguished Chilean historian (1948). Chilean president GONZÁLEZ VIDELA accompanied an expedition to Antarctica in 1948, where he raised the Chilean flag and renamed the area O'Higgins Land. In 1950 the Chilean government refused to recognize the British claim and rejected U.S. suggestions to internationalize the Antarctic.

17

**Antequera y Castro, José de.** 1690–1731. Creole leader of Paraguay (1721–1725). Sent by the *audiencia* of Chuquisaca as judge-investigator to inquire into charges that had been brought against the governor of Paraguay, Diego de los Reyes Balmaceda, Antequera promptly suspended Reyes and conspired to gain control of the government. He repeatedly defeated the forces sent by the viceroy of Peru to overthrow him and defied royal authority until 1725, when the governor of Buenos Aires, Bruno Mauricio de Zavala, occupied Asunción and caused Antequera to flee. He was later arrested in Chuquisaca and sent to Lima. While in prison Antequera inspired a fellow prisoner, Fernando Mompoz y Zayas, to carry on the intrigues he had begun. The rebellion in Paraguay was not completely suppressed until 1735. Antequera was executed in Lima on July 5, 1731.

**Anticlericalism.** It should be stated that anticlericalism connotes opposition to the political and economic power of the Church, and not to the Catholic religion. The Church had been inclined to support monarchy, and generally was opposed to the Spanish-American independence movements. Therefore it suffered somewhat during the wars of independence in Spanish America, but recovered quickly. The Church was still wealthy everywhere after the establishment of independence and retained most of its privileges or *fueros*. It also continued almost exclusive control over education. It was active in politics on the conservative side throughout the 19th century and was frequently under attack by liberal parties. The latter, advocating separation of Church and state, civil marriage and burial, lay education, and confiscation of Church estates by the state, brought their fire to bear on the Church, and usually took anticlerical measures when in power. In Mexico anticlericalism has been particularly strong in the last 130 years, especially during the JUÁREZ era, 1858–1872, and in the 1920's and early 1930's. Anticlericalism has been vigorous at different periods in Argentina, Colombia, Chile, Central America, Ecuador, and Venezuela. Today, anticlericalism has given way to a policy of compromise in almost all Spanish-American countries. The Church has become more liberal and has regained a good deal of its influence. In Brazil both the Church and the liberals have been much more tolerant of each other than in the other Latin-American republics and anticlericalism has been but a minor factor in the life of the country.

**Antigua.** City in Guatemala, situated in the south-central part of the country. In colonial times it was the capital of Guatemala with a population of more than 80,000 until 1773, when it was destroyed by an earthquake. The present population is approximately 14,000.

**Antilles, Netherlands.** See NETHERLANDS ANTILLES.

**Antilles, The.** Also called the **West Indies.** The island group stretches over an arc 1,940 miles long from Yucatán to the mouth of the ORINOCO RIVER (Venezuela). They are generally divided into two groups, the Greater Antilles (Cuba, Jamaica, Haiti, Dominican Republic, Puerto Rico) and the Lesser Antilles (the Leeward and Windward and other small islands). The name *Antilles* derives from the belief in the 14th century that there was a fabulous island called Antillia, situated between Europe and Asia.

**Antipersonalistas.** A group that seceded from the RADICAL CIVIC UNION PARTY OF ARGENTINA during the administration (1922–1928) of Marcelo T. de ALVEAR, in opposition to the party leader IRIGOYEN, who largely dominated party policies. The *antipersonalistas* backed Leopoldo Melo as their candidate in the presidential elections of 1928. After the overthrow of Irigoyen by a military coup d'état in 1930, the *antipersonalistas* joined forces with the conservatives in a coalition that dominated Argentina until 1943. *Antipersonalistas* were twice elected to the presidency: Agustín JUSTO, in 1931, and Roberto ORTIZ, in 1937.

**Antofagasta.** Chilean province, bounded on the west by the Pacific Ocean, on the north by the province of Tarapacá, on the east by Bolivia and Argentina, and on the south by Argentina and the province of Atacama. It has an area of 72,200 square miles and a population of 214,000. The capital is the important port of Antofagasta, with a population of 90,000, through which important minerals, including copper, are exported. The territory is rich in nitrates, which, by virtue of the treaties with Bolivia in 1866 and 1874, were exploited by Chile. When Bolivia revoked these treaties, the war of 1879 broke out. As a result of the war Bolivia recognized Chilean occupation of the province by a truce concluded in 1884, and finally ceded the area to Chile in the peace treaty signed in 1904.

**Antuñano, Esteban.** Mexican liberal, economist, writer. An industrialist who desired growth of Mexican industry through an increase in manufacturing, he was a leading economic liberal of the period 1834–1854, and his writings reflected his British education and his adherence to the principles of the Manchester Doctrine.

**Apatzingán Congress.** Mexican revolutionary convention called by the Mexican leader MORELOS Y PAVÓN, which met in 1814 at Apatzingán in the present-day state of Michoacán. The Congress adopted a republican constitution, providing for, among other things, equality before the law, and abolition of privileges and slavery. The constitution of Apatzingán was short-lived, for the revolutionaries who had promulgated it were soon crushed by superior royalist forces.

**Apodaca, Juan Ruiz de.** See RUIZ DE APODACA, JUAN.

**APRA.** See AMERICAN POPULAR REVOLUTIONARY ALLIANCE.

**Aprista Movement.** See AMERICAN POPULAR REVOLUTIONARY ALLIANCE.

**Aramayo, Carlos Victor.** 1889–    . Bolivian diplomat and financier. b. Paris. President of the Bolivian tin-producing organization, the Aramayo Mining Company; president of the Association of Mining Industries of Bolivia; director of the Central Bank of Bolivia; minister to the Court of St. James; national deputy; ambassador to Argentina, 1916; confidential agent to the United States; delegate to the League of Nations. Aramayo was one of the three tin barons whose mining

holdings were expropriated in 1952 by the PAZ ESTENSSORO administration.

**Aranha, Osvaldo.** 1894–1960. Brazilian lawyer, political leader, and diplomat. b. Alegrete, Rio Grande do Sul. Leader of the practically bloodless revolution of November 1930 that installed VARGAS as president and Aranha as minister of justice and internal affairs; in 1931, minister of finance; appointed ambassador to the United States, 1934–1938; minister of foreign affairs, 1938–1944, strongly pro-U.S. He broke with Vargas in 1944 and lived in retirement, supported Gomes, the National Democratic Union candidate in the election of 1950, was head of the Brazilian delegation to the United Nations, and was president of the UN General Assembly, 1947. He was appointed finance and agriculture minister by Vargas, 1953–1954, and left the government after Vargas' suicide.

**Araucanians.** A once warlike Indian people inhabiting the southern part of Chile and never subdued by the Spaniards in colonial times. At the time of the conquest Araucanian tribes, occupying the territory south of the Maule River, were a nation of hunters among whom the only forms of organized government were the confederacies they established in time of war. They had resisted the INCAS and had never been conquered by them. The Spaniards attempted to bring them under the sway of their empire in 1551, when Pedro de VALDIVIA began to push south from Concepción and founded the towns of Imperial and Valdivia. In 1553, the fierce Araucanians, led by the famous LAUTARO, rose against the invaders and ejected them from their land. In the course of the fighting Valdivia himself was captured and tortured to death. The Araucanians came close to taking Santiago, and the Spaniards were saved only by an epidemic of smallpox in the Indian ranks and by the death of Lautaro in battle. Another chieftain, called CAUPOLICÁN, who possessed qualities similar to those of Lautaro, continued the fight against the Spanish invaders. With skill and bravery he successfully led his troops in battle, but was finally betrayed and captured. The Spanish barbarously executed Caupolicán in 1558. Subsequently another campaign pushed the Araucanians back to the lands beyond the Bío Bío River, but in 1593 another revolt drove the Spaniards back and for the next 300 years the Araucanians were able to keep the whites north of the Bío Bío and to maintain their independence. After the WAR OF THE PACIFIC (1879–1883) the Chileans sent strong forces into Araucanian territory and the Araucanians were finally conquered. Today, remnants of the once-powerful tribes live on reservations. The great struggle of the conquistadors against the Araucanians is recounted in the famous epic *La Araucana* by Alonso de ERCILLA Y ZÚÑIGA.

**Arauco Domado.** Poem by the Chilean poet Pedro de OÑA (1570–*ca*. 1644) in which he deals with the rebellion of the ARAUCANIANS.

**Araujo de Azevedo, Antônio de.** Conde da Barca. 1754–1817. Portuguese statesman. b. Sa, near Ponte de Lima. Minister of foreign affairs, 1804, and prime minister, 1807–1808; went with the Portuguese court in March 1808 to Rio de Janeiro. He was the founder of schools of fine arts, medicine, and chemistry at Rio de Janeiro, and served as minister of the marine and as prime minister in 1817.

**Araujo Lima, Pedro de.** 1787–1870. Regent of Brazil who served from April 1838 until 1840. A conservative, he reduced the power of the provinces by subjecting their legislation to a veto of the national congress. In 1840 the congress requested the young 15-year-old Emperor PEDRO II to assume the throne, and Araujo Lima became Marques of Olinda.

**Arawaks.** The largest South-American linguistic group, originally occupying territories stretching from Florida to Argentina. Just before the discovery of the New World they were driven from the southern Antilles, the Guianas, and Venezuela by the fierce CARIB INDIANS. They cultivated corn, manioc, cotton, and tobacco, and were skilled weavers as well as accomplished craftsmen with stone, wood, and gold. Many tribes of this linguistic stock today occupy large regions of the Guianas, Venezuela, Colombia, Brazil, and Bolivia, and a tribe bearing the name Arawak still lives on the coast of Guyana and Dutch Guiana.

**Arbenz Guzmán, Jacobo.** 1914–      . President of Guatemala. Son of a Swiss pharmacist; lieutenant colonel in the Guatemalan army; joined a group of army officers and took part with them in the revolution against the dictator UBICO in 1944; member of the Revolutionary Junta; minister of war in the ARÉVALO BERMEJO government, 1949; elected president, November 1950, and inaugurated March 1951. Supported by the combination of left-wing political parties and the Guatemalan army, which brought him into power, Arbenz embarked on a program of far-reaching economic and social reform. Not a Communist but a nationalist bent on reducing the power and influence of foreign interests in his country, Arbenz received the full support of the small but active Guatemalan Communist Party. During his administration a considerable amount of land was distributed among landless Indians, and the power and influence of labor were increased. The Arbenz regime soon became involved in a bitter conflict with the American-owned UNITED FRUIT COMPANY, and in 1953 Arbenz signed a law expropriating much land held by the company without granting adequate compensation in return. The U.S. government became more and more alarmed at the left-wing character of the Arbenz government and at the increasingly important role the Communists were playing in Guatemala. The anti-Communist resolution sponsored by the U. S. at the CARACAS CONFERENCE in March 1954 was aimed directly at the Arbenz regime. In June 1954 Arbenz was overthrown by a revolution led by Colonel CASTILLO ARMAS. Having decided at first to fight it out, Arbenz later gave up the struggle after the Guatemalan army withdrew its support of him, and he sought refuge in the Mexican embassy in Guatemala City. He and his family were later given permission to leave Guatemala for Mexico. In recent years Arbenz has made his home in Cuba, and actively worked for the overthrow of the more conservative Guatemalan governments that have controlled the country.

**Arboleda, Julio.** 1817–1862. Colombian poet and patriot. Leader of the conservative revolt of 1856; became president of Colombia, 1860, and was later assassinated. Author of an unfinished modern epic, *Gonzalo de Oyón*, and other poems of merit; his work is of the romantic school and shows the influence of Byron.

**Arce, Manuel José.** 1783–1847. First president of the CENTRAL AMERICAN FEDERATION. b. San Salvador. A leader of the liberals, Arce served as president, 1825–1829. It was a stormy administration and Arce quarreled with his liberal supporters and had to seek the support of the conservatives. There was constant dissension between the federal and state authorities in Guatemala City. A revolt led by Father DELGADO, lasting two years, resulted in the final defeat of Arce and his government. He was replaced by MORAZÁN in 1830.

**Architecture.** The pre-Conquest Indians built many fine temples, palaces, and private dwellings in the central valley of Mexico, in Yucatán, and in the Andes. The Mayas in Yucatán were familiar with the corbeled arch and the beam and mortar roof. In Mexico many impressive pyramids and temples were constructed by the Toltecs, Aztecs, and other peoples. The Indians of the Andes were especially skillful in using enormous stones for their pyramids and fortresses, and they also used the corbeled arch, mainly in private houses. After the Conquest, architecture acquired an essentially European character, although a number of features of Indian architecture were kept. The true arch was used in all construction. Private buildings were devoid of ornamentation on the outside and were constructed around an inside court or patio. Aside from private dwellings, the emphasis was on churches and on public buildings. Church building went through three main stages: the simple, massive, classical-Renaissance style in the 16th century; the ornate baroque in the 17th century; and the heavily ornate churrigueresque in the 18th. In Brazil little building took place before the 18th century, when many impressive public buildings and churches were erected. In the 19th century, and at the beginning of the 20th century, more cosmopolitan architectural styles were employed, chiefly in the large cities. In more recent years an ultra-modern style in buildings with a view toward func-

tional motifs has been in use in many cities. In Rio de Janeiro there are many magnificent modern edifices, some of them designed by the famous French architect Le Corbusier. The new Brazilian capital Brasília, dedicated in 1960, is an outstanding example of brilliant modern architecture. The site for the new capital was chosen in 1956, and the entire city was constructed and readied for the transfer of the national capital by 1960. The plan for the city was boldly conceived by Bruno Giorgio Lúcio Costa, and Oscar Niemeyer designed most of the government buildings. Brasília is a modern example of town planning and an outstanding product of Brazil's imaginative architects. Many new and handsome modern buildings are being built in Caracas, Venezuela, as well as in all the larger cities of Latin America.

**Arévalo Bermejo, Juan José.** 1904– . President of Guatemala. Professor and well-known educator. In exile in Argentina during ten years of the UBICO administration, he enjoyed great prestige among democratic elements of Latin America and was supported by a new political group, the *Partido Acción Revolucionaria* (Revolutionary Action Party), composed mainly of professional classes, intellectuals, workers, and students. He was elected president and took office March 15, 1945. Succeeded in ousting Toriello, the finance minister, who attempted to control the government in 1946. He did not remove press censorship, and served his six-year term until 1951. In a general election (November 1950), his party supported Colonel Jacobo ARBENZ GUZMÁN, who was elected. With the advent of more conservative governments in Guatemala, and the revolution that ousted President Arbenz Guzmán in 1954, Arévalo was compelled to live in exile. He announced his intention to become a candidate in the 1963 election and to return to Guatemala in March of that year, precipitating the coup that upset the government of President Miguel YDÍGORAS FUENTES. See GUATEMALA.

**Arévalo Martínez, Rafael.** b. 1884. Guatemalan novelist and poet. Author of the psycho-zoological tale *El hombre que parecía un caballo* (The Man Who Resembled a Horse).

**Argentina.** Eighth largest country in the world, fourth in the Western Hemisphere, second in South America, with an area of 1,072,070 square miles (not including claims in Antarctica and South Atlantic Islands) and a population of 23,408,000 (est. 1967) of which 95 per cent are of European origin, mainly Spanish and Italian, and 5 per cent are Indians or of mixed descent. Argentina has the highest percentage of pure whites in Latin America. Spanish is the official language but Italian is widely used. The peso, 1967 exchange rate, 20¢ to the U. S. dollar, is the monetary unit. Argentina's chief cities and populations (1960) are Buenos Aires, the capital and principal port, 3,845,000; its industrial suburb Avellaneda, 355,000; Rosario, 566,000; Córdoba, 471,000; and La Plata, 258,000. The country is 2,291 miles long and its maximum width is 884 miles. The terrain includes the Andes and their foothills, running from northwest to southwest, the huge plains, comprising the GRAN CHACO (forests and savannas with a semitropical climate), the fertile pampas that are ideal for agriculture and cattle raising, and the arid steppes of Patagonia. The main rivers are the Paraguay (1,250 miles), the Paraná (2,800 miles), and the Uruguay (940 miles), the last two flowing into the huge Río de la Plata estuary (maximum width 70 miles). Most of Argentina is situated in the south temperate zone, and its mean temperature in the summer is 77 degrees and in the winter 54 degrees. The country comprises 23 provinces and the federal district, which is Buenos Aires. The president is elected by direct vote for six years. There is a senate, a chamber of deputies, and a judiciary branch. Senators and deputies hold office for six years. Voting is compulsory for all citizens over 18. Roman Catholicism is the official religion and is supported by the state, although a schism between the two occurred in 1955 (see below). Today Argentina is still a predominantly agricultural and pastoral country. It is one of the world's largest exporters of corn and wheat and is the third largest exporter of mutton and lamb after Australia and New Zealand. Argentina provides an extraordinarily favorable environment for sheep and cattle raising. In recent years the annual number of cattle in the country has been about 44,000,000, and sheep have totaled 45,000,000. Argentine grain is grown mostly in the pampas, while cotton, rice, sugar, tobacco, and *yerba maté* are cultivated in the north and northeast. The Chaco is a great producer of quebracho wood, yielding valuable tannin extract; and the mountain valleys of the west and northwest, as well as the Río de la Plata delta, are producers of fruits. Although there are deposits of iron, copper, manganese, and oil, Argentina lacks iron and coal, and approximately 75 per cent of manufactured products have to be imported. However, there is a steady industrial development in processing raw materials; and more plants, especially textile mills, are constantly being built. In 1960 steelworks, located at San Nicolás, began operation and an eventual annual output of 4,000,000 metric tons is anticipated. Argentina's rail network is the largest in Latin America, with 27,000 miles of state-owned railroads. Argentina's airlines, nationalized under the name *Aerolíneas Argentinas*, service many parts of the world, including New York and San Francisco. Argentine exports in 1966 totaled $1,492,500,000 and imports were valued at $1,198,600,000. The chief customers are the United Kingdom, the Netherlands, Italy, West Germany, and the United States. The chief suppliers are the United States, West Germany, Italy, and the United Kingdom. Argentina has the highest rate of education in Latin America. Literacy is estimated at 87 per cent, the highest rate in Latin America; over 90 per cent of children of elementary-school age attend school. However the number of students enrolled in high schools and in institutions of higher learning is relatively low.

It is probable that the Río de la Plata was first visited by Europeans in 1501–1502, when Amerigo VESPUCCI may have visited there during an early voyage. Juan DÍAZ DE SOLÍS was definitely there in 1516, and the first settlement on its shore was Nuestra Señora de Santa María del Buen Ayre, founded in 1536 by Pedro de MENDOZA. It was abandoned and later refounded in 1580. The colonists engaged in the raising of horses and cattle, and soon large herds were roaming the pampas around the settlement. At the same time the northwest and the west of the country were occupied by settlers from Peru and Chile, and agriculture developed rapidly in those regions. Córdoba was founded in 1573, Salta in 1582, and Jujuy in 1593. Until 1776, the Río de la Plata region, including the provinces of Paraguay, Tucumán, Buenos Aires, and Cuyo, each with its own governor, was nominally under the authority of the viceroy of Peru. In 1776 it became the viceroyalty of La Plata (Upper Peru, Paraguay, Argentina, and Uruguay). Until the last third of the 18th century, trade in the Río de la Plata area was hampered by Spanish mercantilist restrictions, but with the liberalization of the Spanish trade policy, Buenos Aires, now able to trade directly with the other Spanish-American colonies and with Spain, soon prospered as a great salted meat, hide, and tallow exporter. As a result Buenos Aires grew from a population of 2,200 in 1726 to 45,000 in 1800. Throughout the 18th century the nomadic Indians of the plains around Buenos Aires gave considerable trouble to the colonists, and frequently Indian cavalry was able to cut off Buenos Aires from Córdoba and other settlements. The CREOLES of Buenos Aires realized that they could rely upon themselves in an emergency when they repulsed two British invasion attempts in 1806 and 1807; and in 1810, after the armies of NAPOLEON had overrun Spain in 1808, they deposed the Spanish viceroy and set up a provisional junta representing the provinces of the Río de la Plata in the name of the Spanish king FERDINAND VII. Independence of the United Provinces of La Plata was formally declared by the Congress of Tucumán in 1816. Efforts of the junta to extend its authority over Upper Peru (Bolivia) and Paraguay had failed and the *Banda Oriental* (Uruguay), which had seceded from the federation, later became an independent state in 1828. José de SAN MARTÍN led the Argentine fight against Spanish royalists from 1814 on, and in the course of a brilliant campaign liberated Chile and Peru (1817–1822). Serious dissensions between Buenos Aires unitarians and provincial federalists prevented the new nation from acquiring a stable form of government and the country was in a state of anarchy, from 1816 to 1829, until the dictatorship (1829–1852) of Juan Manuel de ROSAS brought about some form of unity. Under his regime Argentina became involved in disputes with Great Britain and France over Uruguay. Rosas was finally overthrown (1852) by Justo José de URQUIZA, who became president of an Argentine Confederation that was shunned by the province of Buenos Aires (1853). A federal constitution, promulgated in 1853, provided for a bicameral congress, a president elected for a six-year term with no re-election, and a judiciary branch. After a period of discord between the Confederation and Buenos Aires, unification was finally achieved (1862) when Bartolomé MITRE became president of the unified Argentine Buenos Aires was made the capital. There was strong advance under Mitre, but Argentina became involved in the war with Paraguay (1865–1870). Material progress continued, immigration increased, and incursions into Indian territory were made by Domingo SARMIENTO (1874–1880) and Julio ROCA (1880–1886). In 1880 Buenos Aires became a federal district as the capital of Argentina. After a period of speculation and corruption under Juárez Celman (1886–1890) Argentina weathered an economic crisis and by 1914 was a thriving nation with a population of 8,000,000, exporting great quantities of wheat and cattle products. In 1916 the Radical Party, helped by the electoral reforms instituted under Roque SÁENZ PEÑA (1910–1913) and providing for the secret ballot, and universal suffrage, defeated the conservatives and elected its leader Hipólito YRIGOYEN president. Serving from 1916 to 1922, he introduced social reforms and maintained Argentina's neutrality during World War I. He was elected again in 1928, but the world-wide depression and his administration's inefficiency caused his ouster by General José URIBURU (1930), supported by the conservatives, who was followed by Agustín JUSTO (1932–1938). During the latter's administration there was strong internal tension between leftist and rightist groups, but a remarkable economic recovery took place. Argentina developed an active foreign policy, re-entered the League of Nations, which it had left in 1921, and took part in the negotiations dealing with the Chaco war. Roberto ORTIZ, elected president in 1937, pursued a fairly liberal policy, but illness forced him to relinquish his powers to Vice-president Ramón CASTILLO, a conservative, who maintained Argentine neutrality in the first years of World War II. Castillo was overthrown by a military group (1943), which pursued somewhat pro-Fascist policies, although Argentina finally declared war on the Axis (March 1945), in order to secure admission to the United Nations. In 1946 Vice-president Juan Domingo PERÓN was elected president and moved to institute a semitotalitarian regime in Argentina known today as *peronismo* or *justicialismo*. Perón developed his regime along lines of economic and political nationalism. Social reforms were instituted that had as their objective the redistribution of wealth in favor of the masses. The support of the working people, the *descamisados* (shirtless ones), was important in the rise of Perón. He won their backing by means of wage increases and demagogic appeals, and organized their support by means of the *Confederación General de Trabajo*. Perón's policy of rapid industrialization was promoted at the expense of the nation's agriculture and dangerously crippled the entire economy. Through the Argentine Trade Promotion Institute (*Instituto Argentino de Promoción del Intercambio,* known as I.A.P.I.) the Argentine government acquired the power to purchase major crops at their source and resell them in international markets. Perón's use of those powers resulted in ruinously low prices being given the nation's farmers in an attempt to promote the government's industrialization program. The Argentine constitution of 1853 was abrogated in 1949 and a new constitution was voted that included an amendment allowing a president to be re-elected. Perón, re-elected in 1951, continued his program of economic reorganization and social legislation. The loss of his wife (Eva Duarte or Evita) in 1952 proved to be a great loss to Perón as she had been a favorite among his followers and an astute politician. Perón's policies were altered in the years of his second term in office and gave offense to many of his followers. Fewer favors were given to the *descamisados*, the government increas-ingly curried the support of Argentine businessmen, foreign capital investments were encouraged, and the president launched an attack against the Catholic Church in Argentina. In May 1955, the Peronist congress enacted legislation designed to carry out the separation of Church and state in Argentina. The following June, Argentine military elements revolted against the Perón regime. Although the revolt was successfully contained by government forces, it was followed by another revolt in September that quickly crushed Perón's support. While Perón sought refuge in neighboring Paraguay, the rebel leader, General Eduardo Lonardi, was proclaimed provisional president. In November, General Pedro E. Aramburu replaced Lonardi. The overthrow of the Perón regime left Argentina in serious difficulties. The short-sighted economic policies of Perón bequeathed the nation serious economic troubles. Politically the country was divided between loosely organized anti-Perón elements and a strong Peronist following. Despite difficulties the Aramburu government effected the return to constitutional government by 1958. The constitution of 1853 was re-established in 1957, and in 1958 national elections were held. Arturo Frondizi, candidate of the Intransigent Radical party, was elected president and his party won a majority of the seats in both houses of congress. Constitutional democracy did not bring peace to Argentina, however, and political unrest continued to plague the country. The immediate cause for dissatisfaction was the austerity plan instituted to bring about economic recovery. In March 1960, President Frondizi's party suffered an overwhelming defeat in the congressional elections. Frondizi had been elected by a substantial majority in 1958, but by 1960 he had lost the support of his country. The elections held in March 1962, showed considerable strength for the Peronist party that had been allowed to have candidates on the ballot for the first time since 1955. The strongly anti-Peronist military organization reacted violently and swiftly. The elections won by Peronists were annulled and a coup, led by General Raúl A. Poggi, removed the president from office in March 1962. Senate President José María

Guido was installed as president on March 30, congress was recessed in May, and later dissolved. A struggle for power between discordant military elements kept the country upset throughout the remainder of 1962 and into 1963. Military leaders were opposed on the question of whether to take a strict or liberal attitude toward the Peronist movement. Elections held in July 1963 chose Dr. Arturo U. Illia president for a six-year term. The new government moved to appease nationalist sentiment by annulling government petroleum contracts with foreign companies. In June, 1966, another military coup, led by General Juan Carlos Onganía, ousted President Illia and installed a military dictatorship with General Onganía as head of state.

**Argüedas, Alcides.** See LITERATURE.

**Arias, Harmodio.** 1886–1962. President of Panama. b. Penonomé. Educated in England and received his doctorate of law at the University of London; successful lawyer; member, commission on codification; member advisory commission, ministry of foreign affairs; delegate to the League of Nations; minister to Argentina and the United States. He was the leader of the uprising in Panama City, January 2, 1931, that led to the overthrow of Florencio Harmodio Arosemena by the *Acción Comunal*, a group of independents and conservatives, and as leader of the Doctrinal Liberal Party he was elected president on June 5, 1932. He visited with President F. D. Roosevelt in July of 1933. A revision of the Treaty of 1903, in relation to the PANAMA CANAL, was concluded during his administration, which ended in 1936. He was the author of many books.

**Arias de Ávila, Pedro.** Usually called **Pedrarias Dávila** 1442–1531. Spanish soldier and colonial administrator. b. near Segovia. Sent to the New World to govern Darién from 1514 to 1526, he was responsible for the trial and execution of BALBOA in 1517. He founded Panama City in 1519. He sent CÓRDOBA to Nicaragua in 1522 and, when the latter attempted to revolt, was able to surprise and kill him in 1526. He was transferred to Nicaragua in 1526.

**Arica.** See TACNA-ARICA QUESTION.

**Arista, Mariano.** 1802–1855. Mexican general, leader, and president. During the War for Independence he served with ITURBIDE; exiled, 1833–1836; defeated by the Americans in May 1846 at Matamoros, Palo Alto, and Resaca de la Palma. He served as minister of war under HERRERA, 1848, and was elected to succeed him in 1851 as president. An honest administrator, he reduced the army appropriation. Attempts at establishing a stable economy met with difficulties, and he was overthrown in January 1853, the conservatives resuming power and SANTA ANNA becoming dictator.

**Arosemena, Alcibíades.** 1883–1958. President of Panama. b. Los Santos. Succeeded Arnulfo Arias Madrid when he was overthrown in the revolt of May 1951 and completed Arias' term of office to October 1, 1952. He was succeeded by José Antonio REMÓN CANTERA, and appointed ambassador to France.

**Arosemena, Juan Demóstenes.** 1879–1939. President of Panama. Winner of a bitter presidential election campaign held in 1936, he represented the National Revolutionary Party and took office on October 1. In February 1938, the right of the Japanese to fish in territorial waters was terminated. Arosemena died of a heart attack on December 15, 1939.

**Arroyo del Río, Carlos Alberto.** b. 1894. President of Ecuador. b. Guayaquil. Distinguished educator, lawyer, and public administrator, he temporarily assumed executive power on the death of President Narváez, 1939, and was elected president for the 1940–1944 term. A few months after his taking office a boundary dispute with Peru developed into an undeclared war. It was several months before the United States, Brazil, and Argentina, acting as mediators, could establish a neutral zone that put an end to the fighting. At the Rio de Janeiro conference early in 1942 a boundary line was agreed upon and Ecuador had to give up her claim to a large area in the upper Amazon basin; this agreement weakened Arroyo del Río, who had had to put down revolts and plots many times during his administration. He continued in office, however, and was able to aid the United

States during World War II by supplying important bases in the Galápagos Islands. Ecuador was given in return lend-lease and loans through the EXPORT-IMPORT BANK OF WASHINGTON; roads and public buildings were constructed; exports of important strategic material, however, caused inflation. In May 1944, a general strike in Quito and a revolt in Guayaquil led to the resignation of Arroyo del Río and to the formation of a junta composed of representatives of all opposition parties, which took charge of the government and placed VELASCO IBARRA in power.

**Art.** The pre-Columbian civilizations (Maya, Aztec, Inca) are renowned above all for their architectural achievements. Their temples and palaces were greatly admired by the *conquistadores*, and the ruins that remain today are still impressive. The Indians were also skilled in stone carving, in pottery, and in working with gold and jade. The architecture of the Indians had not produced buildings suitable for everyday life, and it fell to the Europeans to bring to the New World the dwelling provided with sufficient light and space. The standard private house of the colonial period was, therefore, the home made of stone or adobe, erected around an inner court, the patio, with most of the decoration in the interior of the house. Many churches and public buildings were erected throughout the colonial period in Hispanic America. The famous Cathedral of Mexico, standing on the site of the Aztec temple of HUITZILOPOCHTLI, was begun in the last third of the 16th century and completed in the first half of the 19th. In Brazil, due mainly to a lack of funds, there was little public building until the 18th century, when many edifices, especially churches, were built. The construction of churches in Latin America went through three periods: first, the Renaissance style with its classical symmetry and simplicity; then, the baroque style of the 17th century, which emphasized ornamentation; and finally, the ornate churrigueresque evolved in the 18th century. Some of the most beautiful churches of colonial Brazil were built by Francisco Lisboa Antônio, who followed the baroque style. Sculpture and painting in colonial times, to a great extent of a

religious nature, flourished mainly in Mexico. There the Spaniard Manuel de TOLSA became famous for his statue of Charles IV and as the founder of a school of sculpture at the end of the 18th century. The Indian Manuel Chile of Quito was renowned for his sculpture *Assumption of the Virgin*. In the field of colonial painting the Mexican Nicolás Rodríguez Juárez deserves special mention, because he was the founder of the 18th century school of Mexican painting. Miguel Cabrera and José María Ibarra achieved fame in the same period. Miguel de Santiago, of Quito, was the founder of a school of religious painting. Throughout the colonial period in a number of regions the Indians continued to carve stone, metals, and wood, mainly for religious purposes. In their work they were encouraged, but closely supervised, by the Church, which also controlled the work of sculptors and painters of religious subjects. More individualism might have been achieved in the colonial arts if the artists had not been controlled by guilds which employed inspectors to regulate the output. The post-independence artistic achievements of the Latin-American republics are many. In Mexico painting was given great impetus in the 20th century by the remarkable work of three outstanding painters, David A. SIQUEIROS, José C. OROZCO, and Diego RIVERA. The Mexican Revolution and the Mexican Indian are the main themes running through their paintings and frescoes. Sculptors of note are Gabriel Guerra and Manuel de Arzave. In Venezuela the post-independence painters were Martín Tovar y Tovar (1828–1902), known for his historical works, and Otero, Golding, and Monasterios, the modern painters. In Colombia Gustave Arcila Uribe (b. 1895) and Rozo Paña (b. 1899) are sculptors of note. In Ecuador Antonio Salas and his sons Ramón and Rafael are outstanding 19th century painters. Peru's leading painters are Francisco Laso (1823–69) and José Sabogal (b. 1888). Bolivia has produced Cecilio Guzmán de Rojas (b. 1900) and Arturo Reque Meruvia (b. 1906), painters of merit. Chile has given to the world Miguel Antonio Caro (1843–1908), Rameri Subercasseaux (1854–1937), and Matta (Roberto Sebastián Matta Echaurren, b. 1912), outstanding painters;

and Rebecca Matte de Iñíguez (1875–1929) and Nicanor Plaza (1844–1918), first-rate sculptors. In Argentina Jorge Bermúdez (1883–1926), Pablo Tosto (b. 1899), and Eduardo Sívori (1847–1918) are painters of note, while Francisco Cafferata (1861–90), Troiano Troiani, and Gyula Kosice (b. 1924) produced fine works of sculpture. Uruguay is represented by the well-known painters Juan and Nicanor Blanes. Brazil has produced many fine painters including Victor Meirelles de Lima, Almeida Reis, Pedro Américo de Figueiredo (1843–1905), Henrique Cavaleiro, Cândido Portinari (b. 1903), and Mary Vieira (b. 1927); J. Figuerar and Leão H. Velloso are well-known sculptors. At the present time there are noteworthy contemporary Indian crafts. Modern painters and sculptors have been influenced by European art but have retained a definite native quality in their work; and modern architecture, although some of it is designed by architects of other countries, has produced some of the most magnificent buildings in the world today. See ARCHITECTURE.

**Artigas, José Gervasio.** 1764–1850. Uruguayan patriot. b. Montevideo. BANDA ORIENTAL gaucho leader who led the attack against the Spanish forces at Montevideo in 1811 but was forced to retreat. He besieged Montevideo again in 1812. A constituent assembly was convened the following year and Artigas as the CAUDILLO of the Banda Oriental sent delegates to Buenos Aires with instructions to vote for a federal republic and autonomy for all provinces; the delegates were refused seats or recognition. Once again Artigas withdrew with his forces to the countryside, and was branded a traitor. He succeeded in 1815 in driving the PORTEÑOS from the whole Banda Oriental, declaring the area independent. The Portuguese invaded in 1816 and finally routed Artigas at Tacuarembó in 1820 and he was forced to flee in exile to Paraguay where he lived out his days a virtual prisoner of the Paraguayan dictator FRANCIA. He is regarded as the original leader and inspiration of Uruguayan national feeling and desire for unity.

**Aruba.** An island of the Dutch Antilles situated 20 miles north of the Paraguaná Penin-sula, Venezuela, and 45 miles west of Curaçao Island. Aruba has an area of 67 square miles and a population of approximately 59,000. The oil industry was introduced in 1925; since then the island has become important as a transshipment and refining center for Venezuelan petroleum and is the site of one of the largest oil refineries in the world.

**Asiento.** In full, *Asiento de negros*. Name given to the slave-trade monopoly that was granted by the Spanish government to a private individual or to a nation. The *asentista* (slave trader) committed himself to pay a determined sum for this privilege and he imported a determined number of slaves of both sexes. The first *asiento*, which was granted to a Genoese company in 1517, contracted for 1,000 Negro slaves to be delivered to the colonies within eight years. In 1528 two Germans received the *asiento* and exclusive right to furnish Negroes to the colonies overseas. They were to send 4,000 to America, to be sold at not more than 45 ducats each. They paid the royal treasury 20,000 ducats for exclusive rights to such trade for a period of four years. Subsequent *asientos* were granted in 1552, 1595, 1609, 1615, 1696, 1701, and in 1713 (English South Sea Company). This last *asiento*, for which a stipulation was provided in the Treaty of Utrecht, is perhaps the best-known of these contracts. The English received the right to furnish Negroes at the rate of 4,800 a year for 30 years. Between 1600 and 1750, *asiento* contracts permitted the introduction of about 3,000 Negro slaves annually into the Spanish colonies.

**Assembly of Notables.** A group of Mexican conservatives who, in 1863, gathering in French-occupied Mexico City, offered a Mexican imperial crown to Archduke MAXIMILIAN, brother of Franz Joseph, emperor of Austria.

**Assis, Joaquim Maria Machado de.** See MACHADO DE ASSIS.

**Astronomy, Indian** and **Colonial.** The Mayas, the Aztecs, and the Incas had a knowledge of astronomy. This is borne out by their remarkable calendars. The Mayas established an astonishingly accurate solar calendar (365 days, with 366 every fourth year) that was supplemented by two more calendars, one of them based on the planet Venus and the other on a 260-day-year for religious purposes. The Aztecs seem to have borrowed their calendar from the Mayas. They also knew the reasons for eclipses and had some understanding of astronomy, although their conclusions were mostly of an astrological nature. The Incas devised a lunar calendar. In the colonial period, astronomy received the attention of the famous Mexican mathematician and philosopher Carlos de SIGÜENZA Y GÓNGORA (1645–1700) in his work *Libro astronómico*. The Mexican astronomer Antonio de Alzate observed the transit of Venus (1769). In New Granada (Colombia) the famous scientist Celestino MUTIS lectured on the Copernican system at Bogotá in 1773 and, therefore, incurred the wrath of the Inquisition.

**Asunción.** Capital of Paraguay, situated on the east bank of the Paraguay River about 935 rail miles north of Buenos Aires. Asunción is the chief port of the country and is connected with Buenos Aires by rail and river steamer facilities. A road from Asunción to Iguassú, on the Brazilian frontier, has been completed, and another to Bolivia, the *Ruta Trans-Chaco*, is nearing completion. Air services are furnished by seven airlines, one of which uses seaplanes, following the river between Asunción and Buenos Aires. The city, including suburbs, has a population of over 300,000 and is the major commercial, industrial, and cultural center of Paraguay. It completely dominates all phases of life in the country, having over 16 per cent of the country's population, and handling nearly all of its imports and exports. Processing plants for agricultural and forest products are located in the city in addition to cotton, wool, and rayon mills, shipbuilding yards, railroad shops, and lesser manufacturing industries. Among the outstanding buildings are the *Palacio Gobierno, Palacio Legislativo, Panteón Nacional de los Héroes, La Catedral Iglesia Metropolitana*, and the church of Recoleta. Asunción is laid out in rectangular fashion and has retained little of its colonial aspect, although a few examples of colonial architecture do remain. Bullet-spattered walls

and buildings evidence the internal troubles Paraguay has experienced. The city was founded on the feast of the Assumption, August 15, 1537, by the Spaniard Juan de Salazar de Espinosa. At that time a stockade, or *casa fuerte*, was erected and named *Nuestra Señora de la Asunción*. The settlement flourished under Domingo Martínez de IRALA and became the most important town in the RÍO DE LA PLATA region. Its prominence was destroyed by the rise of Buenos Aires in the 17th century. During the dictatorship of FRANCIA the city was rebuilt to satisfy the tyrant. The city has enjoyed a steady growth in recent years.

**Atacama, Desert of.** Desert in Chile that stretches from the Peruvian-Chilean frontier to the latitude of 30 degrees south. In some sections it is so arid that no rainfall has ever been recorded, while in others, the total annual rainfall equals that of one good summer thunderstorm. It is crowned by many high mountains and much of its territory is at altitudes of 3,000 to 5,000 feet. The region is rich in minerals, especially nitrates. Part of the Atacama Desert, the province of ANTOFAGASTA, formerly belonged to Bolivia, but after the WAR OF THE PACIFIC, 1879–1883, the area was ceded to Chile.

**Atahualpa.** 1500–1533. Ruler of Peru, son of the Inca emperor HUAYNA CAPAC and of the daughter of the sovereign of Quito. After the death of Huayna Capac, Atahualpa and his half-brother HUÁSCAR fought a bitter civil war, each wanting to be undisputed ruler of the Incan empire. In 1532, the year the Spaniards under Francisco PIZARRO disembarked in northern Peru, Atahualpa defeated Huáscar decisively and took him prisoner. He then met Pizarro at Cajamarca, where the latter, taking advantage of the fact that Atahualpa had gone into the town with only a small part of his army of 50,000 men, fell upon him with his soldiers and seized him. Atahualpa thought that his brother had instigated the ambush, and although a prisoner, he managed to give the order to have Huáscar killed. Pizarro promised Atahualpa to release him if he would fill the room where he was held with gold. Atahualpa complied and soon the room, which was 22 feet long, 17 feet wide, and 9 feet high, was filled with coins and objects of gold. Pizarro staged a mock trial, as a result of which Atahualpa was put to death August 29, 1533.

**Atlantic Charter.** Originally a joint declaration of peace aims signed in August 1941, by the United States and Great Britain, it has been signed by other nations, including the Latin-American countries, until today all members of the United Nations are signatories. It provides that the member nations will not seek territory or other aggrandizement; no territorial changes not in accord with the wishes of the inhabitants concerned will be recognized; the right of the self-determination of all peoples will be provided for; the restoration of self-government to those who had lost it will be granted; the nations will attempt to improve labor standards; social security and better economic conditions will be sought; a peace providing security and freedom from fear and want would follow the defeat of the enemy; freedom of the seas will be established; and the disarmament of potential aggressors established.

**Atlantic Ocean.** The great body of water with an area of 31,830,800 square miles and an average depth of 12,880 feet (greatest known depth off Puerto Rico, 30,246 feet) fired the imagination of sailors for centuries before COLUMBUS' epic voyage. As early as A.D. 1,000 the Norseman Leif Ericson discovered the American coast, and after him America was visited by other Norse sailors. Throughout the Middle Ages stories of islands lying far out in the Ocean were told by sailors. Some of these, e.g., Antillia and Brazil, were even marked on maps. There exists a legend of seven Portuguese bishops who had sailed west after the conquest of their country by the Moors, and who had founded seven cities. During the reign of Affonso IV of Portugal (1325–1357) Portuguese explorations were undertaken in the Atlantic and these were followed by Italian, Spanish, and Portuguese explorations in the 14th century. The Canary Islands were occupied by the Spaniards at the beginning of the 15th century, while the Portuguese occupied the Azores in 1427–1432, and the Cape Verde Islands in 1457. In colonial times, Spanish and Portuguese fleets were crossing the Atlantic carrying goods to and from the colonies and were frequently set upon by freebooters and pirates of all nations. After Latin-American independence was achieved, passenger service was established between Europe and Latin America, and steamships of many nations bore multitudes of immigrants to the shores of Latin-American countries. During both World Wars German submarines roamed the South Atlantic, sinking Allied and neutral ships, and in both conflicts Brazil, at war with Germany, collaborated with the Allies in patrolling Atlantic waters. In WORLD WAR I, a German fleet was all but destroyed by a British squadron in the Battle of the Falkland Islands (December 1914), and in WORLD WAR II, the German pocket battleship "Graf Spee" was driven into Montevideo harbor by three lighter British units and was subsequently scuttled by its crew.

**Ato Adicional of 1834.** An amendment to the Brazilian Constitution of 1824, issued in 1834, providing for the right of the Brazilian provinces to elect their own lawmaking assemblies, for the abolishing of the entailing of estates, and the suppression of the Council of States, a bulwark of reaction under Dom PEDRO I. The number of regents was reduced from three to one, and the provincial governments were given control of primary and secondary education. The adoption of the *ato adicional* was the result of agitation on the part of the provinces for more self-government and introduced a form of federalism in an attempt to preserve the threatened unity of Brazil.

**Audiencia.** The *audiencia* was the highest royal court of appeal within a given district of colonial Spanish America, and it served as a consultative council to the viceroy or captain general; it had some legislative powers as well. It was strong because, while ultimate decisions lay in most cases with the viceroy, a hostile *audiencia* could cause considerable difficulty, and, if it so desired, effectively clog the wheels of the royal government. It could hear the complaints of individuals against viceroys and captains general and often took measures to restrain these officials. In Mexico City the *audiencia* originally consisted of four judges or *oidores* and a president. By the 18th century the number of *oidores* had increased to ten. The lesser *audiencias* had, by law, three to five judges. As a court of justice it tried civil and criminal cases. Unusually important cases could be appealed from the *audiencia* to the Council of the Indies. An important function of the *audiencia* was to protect the interests of the Indians and usually two days a week were set aside for suits between Indians, or Indians and Spaniards. The viceroy or captain general was president of this tribunal, but had no voice or vote in judicial decisions unless he was a lawyer. Next to the viceroy the *audiencia* was the most important institution in the government of the Spanish Indies. It served as the principal curb upon the colonial governors. The first *audiencia* was established in Santo Domingo in 1511 with jurisdiction over the Carribbean area. Next came the *audiencia* of Mexico (1527), with power over a large portion of Mexico and over the Gulf Coast and Florida. The *audiencia* of Lima was set up in 1542 and that of Guatemala in 1543. By the middle of the 16th century there were seven *audiencias* in Spanish America, and by the end of the 18th century there were thirteen, forming important territorial subdivisions of the viceroyalties.

**Augustinians.** Members of the Augustinian order, active with other orders (FRANCISCAN, DOMINICAN, JESUIT, etc.) in the propagation of the Christian faith throughout colonial Latin America. The Augustinians together with the Franciscans were active in establishing hospitals. They also possessed great wealth, especially in Mexico.

**Avellaneda, Nicolás.** 1837–1885. President of Argentina. b. Tucumán. Well-known journalist; minister of justice and public instruction for SARMIENTO and largely responsible for educational progress and enlightened policies that won prestige for the federal government. He defeated MITRE for the presidency in the election of 1874, effected many economic reforms, and suppressed a Mitre revolt. On September 21, 1880, Buenos Aires as the national capital was formed into a federal district, separated from the province of Buenos Aires. During Avellaneda's administration

which lasted until 1880, minister of war ROCA was able to subdue the hostile Indians of the southern pampas and the entire region was divided into sections to be administered by the central government.

**Ávila, Pedro Arias de.** See ARIAS DE ÁVILA, PEDRO.

**Ávila Camacho, Manuel.** 1897–1955. President of Mexico. b. Teziutlán, state of Puebla. In military service during and after Revolution, rising to the rank of general; minister of war and marine under President Abelardo RODRÍGUEZ, 1932–1934; secretary of national defense in CÁRDENAS administration, 1939; president, 1940–1946. Although he owed his election to support of Cárdenas and of the Party of the Mexican Revolution (PRM), he followed much more conservative policies, checking land reform, curbing powers of organized labor, and stimulating business expansion. A practicing Catholic, he worked for better relations between Church and State and revised the public education system in accordance with clerical views. He worked for close relations with the United States, settled the oil dispute, 1942, and adopted a program of close economic co-operation. He broke relations with the Axis after Pearl Harbor and declared war, June 1, 1942. Mexican economy was largely devoted to war production to meet the needs of the United States, which resulted in rapid expansion of industrial production in Mexico but also in sharp inflation that caused severe hardships for the mass of the people.

**Axis Influence.** The prestige and influence of the Rome-Berlin Axis were strong in a number of South American countries in the years preceding WORLD WAR II and continued to be so until it became obvious that Hitler and Mussolini were doomed to defeat. Playing upon South-American fears of Communism and on the traditional suspicion with which U.S. policy was looked upon, Germany exerted particularly strong influence in South America, especially in Brazil, Argentina, and Chile. In Brazil, Nazi propaganda enjoyed great success among the approximately 1,000,000 persons of German origin living in the southern states of Rio Grande do Sul,

Santa Catarina, and Paraná, emphasizing the retention of their native language and national consciousness. A serious menace to the Brazilian government was revealed when the German legation in Rio de Janeiro was implicated in the INTEGRALISTA revolt against the VARGAS regime in May 1938. The Brazilian government subsequently spared no efforts to eradicate any loyalty to Nazi Germany among its German minority, one of the measures taken being the closing of schools maintained by foreign minorities. In Argentina there were in 1938 more than 230,000 Germans, including German-born and persons of German descent. There were more than 200 German schools, 22 of them in Buenos Aires. There were 1,800 German families living in the Chaco Territory, and German settlements studded the Misiones Territory. Since approximately one-third of the Argentine population was made up of Italians or persons of Italian descent, Fascist propaganda found fertile ground, although the percentage of pro-fascists among the Italian minority was much smaller than that of pro-Nazis among the German minority. In Chile, Hitler propagandized the large German minority in southern Chile. Germany and Italy did not limit their efforts to their national minorities in South America. They tried to gain the good will of South Americans by various means including trade, cultural propaganda, tourism, etc. The net of efficient German-operated airlines covering South America before the war was a trump card of German influence. So was the fact that many South-American military men, especially Argentines, had received their training at German military colleges. Italy gained much sympathy when she initiated a program of distributing free telegraphic news service to many South-American (especially Argentine) newspapers. The dispatch to South America of a squadron of Italian stunt fliers in 1937 was another clever move on the part of the Fascist regime, because the fliers were received with great enthusiasm in Peru, Chile, Argentina, and Brazil. During World War II, the intensive propaganda that the Axis had conducted throughout South America paid off mainly in Argentina. For several years the Argentine government, though officially neutral, favored the Axis nations and their Japanese allies in many ways, and only in March 1945 did it declare war on Germany. Axis activities were also in evidence in Uruguay, Bolivia, and Paraguay. In Uruguay a German plot to seize control was crushed in May 1940, and in Bolivia a pro-Axis party under Colonel VILLARROEL overthrew the Peñaranda government with the complicity of Argentine officials and German agents in Buenos Aires in December 1943. President MORÍNIGO of Paraguay ostensibly followed a pro-Allied course to ensure receiving lend-lease army equipment but hypocritically allowed Paraguay to become a refuge for Axis spies and encouraged the distribution of Axis propaganda among Germans living within the country. On the whole, however, Latin America cooperated with the United States in its war against Japan and the Axis. Aside from the Latin-American nations who declared war on the Axis powers after Pearl Harbor, all Latin American countries except Argentina and Chile broke off diplomatic relations with Germany, Italy, and Japan during and after the Rio de Janeiro Conference of January 1942, and Chile did so in January 1943. Axis agents and saboteurs were rounded up and German airlines in the various countries were nationalized. In Argentina, Nazi influence survived the German collapse, but in 1947 the Argentine government took measures against Nazi firms and individuals.

**Ayacucho, Battle of.** The last important battle of the Spanish-American wars for independence. It was fought on December 9, 1824, near the city of Ayacucho, in central Peru, between the Spanish forces under Viceroy La Serna, and the South-American army under General SUCRE. La Serna's 9,000 soldiers were faced by only 5,000 South Americans, but in spite of their numerical superiority, the royalist forces were decisively defeated. Viceroy La Serna, taken prisoner, signed the capitulation of his army, recognizing at the same time the independence of Peru.

**Ayala, Eligio.** 1879–1931. Lawyer and president of Paraguay. Served as president on two occasions, from April 11, 1923, to March 17, 1924 (provisional), and from August 15,

1925, to August 15, 1928. The country had its first four years of internal peace since 1899. He began preparing the country for the CHACO WAR. He served in the cabinet of his successor, GUGGIARI, as minister of finance until his death.

**Ayala, Eusebio.** 1875–1942. President of Paraguay. b. Barrero Grande. Educator, lawyer, and banker, Ayala was president of the chamber of deputies, 1910; three times senator from Asunción; held portfolios of the treasury, public instruction, and foreign affairs; provisional president of Paraguay, 1921–1923; minister plenipotentiary to the United States, 1925; ambassador to Peru; elected president of Paraguay, 1932–1936. The CHACO WAR with Bolivia was declared on May 10, 1933, and economic depression aggravated by war losses and political discontent brought about his overthrow on February 17, 1936, by the revolt of army leaders. He was exiled to Buenos Aires and the government fell to Colonel Rafael Franco and the FEBRERISTA PARTY. Ayala died in Buenos Aires on June 4, 1942.

**Ayllu.** A village community and unit of government in the vast Incan empire of Peru. The people and the land they tilled were included in the *ayllu*. The term has persisted to the present day, being used to designate an Indian community.

**Aymarás.** Indians inhabiting Peru and Bolivia, who in pre-Columbian times developed an advanced civilization. The impressive ruins of TIAHUANACO are thought most probably to have been built by their ancestors. The Aymarás, once concentrated in the region just south of Lake TITICACA, were for the most part farmers and shepherds. They were divided into *ayllus* or clans, which were the basic units of the tribe. They became part of the Incan empire at the time of the fifth Inca Capac Iupanqui in the 15th century, but retained a certain number of privileges. During the colonial era, they suffered greatly from work in Spanish-owned mines, and in 1780 participated in the TUPAC AMARU II rebellion, but were defeated. In the 19th century many *ayllus* lost their lands through fraud and violence. Today, although they are still indispensable in the mines of Bolivia, where they are often the only people who can stand the high altitudes, they are largely engaged in agriculture, growing potatoes and quinoa, and in raising sheep, LLAMAS, and ALPACAS. The *ayllu*, with its communal landholding custom, still is the basis of their social organization. They have also preserved their language, which is guttural and of energetic pronunciation. It is widely spoken in Peru, Bolivia, and northern Argentina. They are Roman Catholics, but have retained many pagan rituals.

**Ayora, Isidro.** b. 1879. President of Ecuador and physician. He was made provisional president in 1926; and in order to stabilize the currency, on the advice of Professor KEMMERER of Princeton University, a central bank was established that had the sole right to issue notes. He was elected president by a constituent assembly and assumed office on April 17, 1929, under a constitution that had been promulgated on March 25th. Due to the depression and political unrest, he was forced to resign in 1931 and retired to medical practice.

**Ayuntamiento.** Municipal government, or town council, in Spanish American colonies. See CABILDO.

**Ayutla, Plan of.** Name given to the proclamation issued in March 1854, in the state of Guerrero, Mexico, by the liberal opponents of dictator SANTA ANNA. The plan, which called for the election of a convention to draft a new constitution, received more and more support in the country and led to Santa Anna's defeat and exile in 1855.

**Aztecs.** Members of an Indian tribe inhabiting the central valley of Mexico at the time of the Spanish conquest. One of the NAHUA-speaking tribes that invaded central Mexico in the 12th century, the Aztecs settled in the lake region of the central valley, where in the early 14th century, probably in 1325, they built their capital, TENOCHTITLÁN, on an island near the western shore of Lake Texcoco, in the area of present-day Mexico City. Forming a powerful confederation with two neighboring city states, Texcoco and Tlacopán, they soon controlled vast territories of Mexico and extended their sway as far south as the Isthmus of Tehuantepec. They were governed by a chieftain who was leader of the army and chief justice, and by a tribal council representing 20 clans into which the city was divided. The chieftain, later called emperor by the Spaniards, was elected by the tribal council from among the members of one ruling family, and he lived in great luxury. Land was owned in common by each one of the different clans and privately by hereditary nobles who had a great number of serfs cultivating their property. The nobles were exempt from taxation but owed military service to the ruler. At the bottom of the social scale were the slaves, who were criminals, prisoners of war, and children sold by their parents. Religion was of the greatest importance and consequently the priests occupied a privileged position together with the aristocracy. Every year many hundreds of persons were sacrificed to the Aztec gods and one of the aims of the many wars of conquest fought by the Aztec Confederacy with its neighbors was to acquire an ever-growing number of prisoners of war to be sacrificed. A thorough system of tax-collecting was in force throughout the territory of the Confederation and that of subject tribes. The Aztecs were skilled in architecture, gold and silver work, in weaving, and in pottery making. They had a pictorial system of writing, an intricate calendar, and musical instruments. Because of their many acts of aggression against their neighbors, they had bitter enemies and this was the main cause of their inability to offer successful resistance to the Spaniards, who used thousands of Indian allies in the conquest of Tenochtitlán (1521), in which the Aztecs were almost exterminated.

**Azuela, Mariano.** 1873–1952. Mexican novelist. By profession, he was a doctor in Mexico City. In 1916 he wrote *Los de abajo* (The Underdogs), a realistic story of the Mexican Revolution, which was one of the earliest and most famous novels of this type. He also wrote *Mala yerba* (translated into English as Marcela and published in New York in 1932), and numerous other books.

# B

**Báez, Buenaventura.** 1810–1884. President of the Dominican Republic. First chosen president in 1849, but before he could serve his full term, he was driven from power by SANTANA, who became a president-dictator. Báez again became president in 1856 and was again ousted by Santana in 1858. He returned to become chief executive for a short time in 1866, and after a period of exile he became president again, for the fourth time, serving from 1868 to 1873. Fearing attack from Haiti, Báez favored annexing the Dominican Republic to the United States, and although President Grant favored the idea, it was opposed by the U. S. Congress (1870). In 1878, Báez was again elected to the presidency, but was ousted by a fresh revolt.

**Bagé, Capture of.** An important incident in the war between Brazil and Argentina (1825–1828). The town of Bagé, situated in the Brazilian province of Rio Grande do Sul, was a key center of communications for the towns of Rio Grande, Rio Pardo, and Pôrto Alegre, and was also the source of vital supplies for the Brazilian army. The capture of the town by the Uruguayan General LAVALLEJA on January 26, 1827, was a severe blow to the Brazilian army.

**Bahia** or **Baía.** Federal state in Brazil bordering on the Atlantic Ocean, between the state of Minas Gerais to the south and the states of Maranhão, Piauí, and Pernambuco to the north, with an area of 217,688 square miles. The population is 5,990,605 (1960), with a high percentage of Negroes and mulattoes. The state is mostly mountainous and is cut by many rivers. The climate is warm and humid along the coast and temperate in the interior. The bay that gave its name to the state was discovered in 1501, and in 1503 an expedition led by Amerigo VESPUCCI penetrated into the interior of that region. In 1534 Francisco Pereira Coutinho founded a settlement on the site of present-day SALVADOR (Bahia), the capital of the state, but it was soon destroyed by hostile Indians. In 1549 Thomé de SOUZA built a strong, permanent settlement on the same site and named it São Salvador da Bahia de Todos os Santos. The city was to be Brazil's capital until 1763. The province prospered during the colonial period because of the sugar industry, which developed rapidly. Bahia became the center of the great sugar plantations worked by Negro slaves and owned by Portuguese aristocrats who ruled over their properties like feudal lords. The removal of the capital to Rio in 1763 did not affect in the main the prosperity of the province, nor did Brazilian independence in 1822. Only the rise of São Paulo and the growth of coffee in the second half of the century, combined with the ABOLITION OF SLAVERY in 1888, reduced the importance of Bahia in the economy of the country. Today the main agricultural products of the state are cacao, coffee, cotton, sugar, and tobacco. Stock raising is also important. The state is rich in natural resources; diamonds and oil have been discovered. There still are plantations, but there has been a growth of small independent holdings. Manufactured products include cigars, cigarettes, sugar, textiles, and beverages. The influence of the Negro on the culture has been strong and is evident in local music and folklore.

**Bahía Blanca.** An important port in Argentina on the Atlantic Ocean, 397 miles southwest of Buenos Aires, with a population of approximately 140,000 (1960). It is a naval base and is furnished with large shipyards and drydocks. Bahía Blanca ranks second to Buenos Aires in commercial importance. Grain is the chief product exported through it, and petroleum products, agricultural machinery, and lumber are the main imports. Rail, highway, and air connections link the port with Buenos Aires and other cities in South America. Bahía Blanca was founded in 1828 during the war between Argentina and Brazil, when a fort was built there to protect the coast from a possible invasion by Brazilian forces. The fort subsequently served as a base for campaigns against the Indians. Many Italian immigrants settled in the area, giving great impetus to agriculture. After the completion in 1884 of a railroad from Buenos Aires, the city's importance increased rapidly.

**Balboa, Vasco Núñez de.** 1475–1517. Spanish conquistador. b. Jerez de los Caballeros (Badajoz). Accompanied Rodrigo de BASTIDAS on his explorations in 1500 and settled on Hispaniola Island, dedicating himself to agriculture. Unsuccessful in this undertaking, he embarked as a stowaway on a caravel captained by Fernández de ENCISO in 1510. He founded a colony on the banks of the Darién River, on the Isthmus of Panama, naming it Santa María la Antigua de Darién, and when the governor of the territory, Nicuesa, appeared on the scene, Balboa and Enciso had him imprisoned in a brigantine together with 18 men, and sent the ship out in the open ocean in March 1511. Nicuesa was never heard from again. After confiscating Enciso's property and forcing him to leave the colony, Balboa became sole governor of the region in 1512. He gained the good will of a number of Indian chieftains and in the course of one of his expeditions discovered the Pacific Ocean on September 25, 1513. His enemies were hard at work to bring him into the king's disfavor, and finally a new governor of the Darién territory was sent to replace Balboa. The new governor, Pedro ARIAS DE ÁVILA ordered Balboa to pay for all damages caused by him during his stay in power, thus ruining him. Balboa, however, received from the king the title of Adelantado of the South Sea and governor of the provinces of Coiba and Panama under the supreme command of Pedrarias. Subsequently, Balboa set out on an expedition across the Isthmus, helping his men to carry wood earmarked for the construction of four brigantines. After accomplishing the difficult feat, he was about to set out with his vessels and 300 men, when Pedrarias had him turn back, claiming that he had acted without his permission. He was taken into custody by Francisco PIZARRO and beheaded on orders from Pedrarias at the newly-founded port of Acla, together with several of his friends, in 1517.

**Baldomir, Alfredo.** 1884–1948. Uruguayan president. b. Montevideo. Soldier and architect; minister of national defense with rank of general, 1935; president, 1938–1943. He increased trade, proposed to pay all national debts, established a barter treaty with Germany, and a "most-favored-nation" trade agreement with Brazil, 1939. On December 13, 1939, the "Graf Spee" was driven into the port of Montevideo by British warships; this proved embarrassing to Uruguay, and the crew put out to sea and scuttled the ship. Negotiations for a trade agreement with the United States collapsed. Uruguay discovered a Nazi plot in 1940 involving Germans from Argentina and Brazil, and the United States sent along two cruisers; this action led ultimately to co-operation between the two nations; protests in Uruguay were silenced by a loan from the EXPORT-IMPORT BANK of Washington for $7,500,000. At the time of Pearl Harbor, Uruguay denounced the action and froze Axis funds, and in January 1942 broke off diplomatic relations. Because of unrelenting opposition from the Nationalist Party, Baldomir dissolved the congress in February 1942, and he and an appointed council of state governed for the next twelve months.

**Ballivián, José.** 1804–1852. Bolivian general and politician. b. La Paz. President of Bolivia. Ballivián seized leadership of the government (1841) and defeated a Peruvian invasion led by GAMARRA (1841); Ballivián's administration imposed order and adopted a new constitution (1843), and internal quiet was promoted when SANTA CRUZ, his chief opponent, was given a pension and sent to Europe. Ballivián attempted to build roads and improve education. The first real newspaper was published. He resigned his office (1847) in the midst of a revolution fomented by President CASTILLA of Peru.

**Balmaceda Fernández, José Manuel.** 1840–1891. President of Chile. b. Santiago. Leader of the Liberal Party; deputy in congress, from 1870; minister to Argentina, 1878–1881; minister of foreign affairs and minister of the interior, 1881–1886; succeeded SANTA MARÍA GONZÁLEZ as President of Chile, 1886–1891. His administration was for the most part successful, due in large measure to the country's prosperity at that time. He launched a great program of public works including railways, roads, and bridges; extended telegraphic and postal services; had government buildings erected; and fostered education by building many schools. There were prison reforms and new penal institutions built. A council for health was created and more than 20 hospitals and clinics set up. Although considered anticlerical, he compromised with the conservatives and the Church, with the appointment of a new archbishop. Balmaceda favored his minister of public works, SANFUENTES, as the next presidential candidate, but this met with opposition, so he appointed Sanfuentes minister of the interior and Sanfuentes withdrew his candidacy. There was dissension within the Liberal Party, and congress, whose power had steadily increased since 1871, was forcing its wishes on the president by suspending action on the tax laws and the budget. Balmaceda had to give way further and appoint a neutral cabinet, and then, although the tax laws were passed, the budget was not approved. The new ministers resigned and the budget was again held up. Balmaceda, with no other way to get government funds, announced that the budget from the previous year would remain in force. This caused the worst civil war in Chile's history (1891). The navy sided with congress, but the army remained loyal to the president. The insurgents seized the nitrate

provinces where they could not be reached by attack on land; the government forces were defeated in two battles near Valparaíso, in August 1891; and Balmaceda turned the government over to General Baquedano. Balmaceda sought asylum in the Argentine legation and three weeks later committed suicide. The war cost thousands of lives and millions of dollars, and led to the looting of Santiago and Valparaíso by mobs before order was restored.

**Balta, José.** 1816–1872. President of Peru. b. Lima. Colonel in the army; served in PRADO's cabinet, 1865–1867; leader of revolution that overthrew Pedro Díaz Canseco in 1868; president of Peru, 1868–1872. During his administration Henry MEIGGS built several railroads, agricultural production was expanded, and labor problems caused the import of Chinese coolies. When the army revolted, Balta was murdered.

**Baltimore Affair.** A serious incident involving the United States and Chile, coming on the heels of the Chilean civil war of 1891. The supporters of the Chilean congress, which had led the revolt against President BALMACEDA, were enraged by the ITATA AFFAIR and what they considered U.S. partiality to the Balmaceda forces. Their fury reached its highest pitch when, after the defeat of Balmaceda, several members of his party were given asylum by the American minister. On October 16, 1891, a group of U.S. sailors from the cruiser U.S.S. "Baltimore," on shore leave at Valparaíso, were set upon by a mob. Two of the sailors were killed and seventeen were seriously wounded. The United States took a strong line and threatened war if Chile failed to pay reparations. Chile, while putting the blame on the American sailors, paid an indemnity of $75,000; for a long time after the incident relations between the two countries were strained.

**Banana Industry.** The banana is grown in the tropical lowlands of Latin America, especially in the Caribbean area. There the leading growers are Honduras and Costa Rica. Other important centers of production are Colombia, Ecuador, Guatemala, and Mexico. In recent years Ecuador has stepped up its production considerably and is today the world's leading exporter. Extensive banana planting was begun in Costa Rica in 1872, by a North American, Minor C. KEITH, who subsequently built plantations in Panama and Colombia and at the end of the century contributed to the formation of the UNITED FRUIT COMPANY. In the first decade of the 20th century, the United Fruit as well as other North-American companies established plantations in the Atlantic coast areas of Guatemala and Honduras. Railroads were built to bring the bananas to the ports, and fleets of steamers were formed to ship the fruit and to transport passengers as well. At first the Caribbean lowlands were chosen for the growing of bananas, but later the Pacific coast also became the site of the plantations. The banana industry contributed strongly to the economic development of the countries in which the product was grown, since large jungle areas were cultivated and many workers were employed on the plantations. In Central America bananas became the second-ranking export product after coffee. Before WORLD WAR I, the leading producer was Costa Rica, but subsequently Honduras took command, exporting 31,000,000 stems in 1932. Before the outbreak of WORLD WAR II the *sigatoka* disease threatened for a while to wipe out all the Caribbean plantations and to ruin the industry. A chemical spray discovered by the United Fruit Company saved the banana, however, but the necessity of operating spray systems has changed banana growing in a number of ways since World War II. The company built a special fleet of ships earmarked for the transportation of bananas to the United States, and in Honduras these shipments represented, before World War II, about 75 per cent of the country's exports. Although the United Fruit Company has in most cases endeavored to establish decent working conditions for its employees in Central America and is providing medical care for them, there have been instances of exploitation and of interference in the countries' internal affairs, which have created bitter memories in the isthmus republics.

**Banda Oriental.** The name given the territory east of the Uruguay River in the 17th century, as distinguished from the land lying to the west of the river. The region was known as *Banda Oriental,* or Eastern Bank, until 1828, when it became an independent nation bearing the name República Oriental del Uruguay, or Eastern Republic of the Uruguay (River). Present-day Uruguayans still prefer to be known as *orientales.*

**Bandeirante.** Member of a *bandeira;* also the chief of the expedition. Among the most famous *bandeirantes* were Antônio Raposo Tavares, Fernão Dias Pais Leme, Bartolomeu Bueno de Siqueira, and Pedro Teixeira. The last of these navigated up the Amazon River in 1637 and reached Quito. See BANDEIRAS.

**Bandeiras.** Name given to expeditions organized in the 17th century by the Portuguese in Brazil, with the aims of exploring the interior of the country, discovering precious mines, founding new centers of colonization, and taking native slaves. The principal points of departure for these expeditions were São Paulo and Taubaté. The *bandeiras* were organized by well-to-do individuals who became the undisputed lords and masters of the exploring groups. They usually included priests, judges, and writers. The first real *bandeira* was the one formed in 1628 by Antônio Raposo Tavares. The most famous was that of Fernão Dias Pais Leme. The *bandeiras* contributed immensely to the development of the colony. There has as yet been no entirely satisfactory explanation for the origin of the word, the most plausible being that it is due to the fact that a *bandeira* (standard or banner) was usually carried at the head of the expedition.

**Banking.** Until the last years of the colonial period there was little organized banking in Latin America because of a lack of surplus liquid capital. Many of the activities that are usually performed by banks were carried out by monasteries, since they were the only institutions having a surplus to invest. By 1716 there were only two banks in Mexico. Toward the middle of the century a number of private banks in Mexico City extended loans to miners. When the *Cuerpo de minería* was established in 1777 to promote the mining industry, a mining bank, the *banco de avíos,* was created at the same time. It was decided that the bank would raise a capital of 2,000,000 pesos from which loans were to be made for the purpose of mining development. For many reasons, including mismanagement, the bank eventually went bankrupt to the extent of 4,000,000 pesos. In 1783–1784, the Bank of San Carlos was established. Mexican state banks flourished in the 19th century until the establishment of the Bank of Mexico in the 1880's introduced bank centralism. The secretary of finance under Porfirio DÍAZ, José Ives LIMANTOUR, after taking office in 1893, strengthened centralized banking and almost eliminated state banking. The rhythm of bank centralization was accelerated under ÁVILA CAMACHO, 1940–1946, and today banking, both public and private, is concentrated in Mexico City. The Banco de México, established in 1925, has its own branches and has established what amounts to a monopoly over Mexican banking. In addition to banking institutions, modern Mexico has many other auxiliary institutions that make up its highly complex financial community, resembling in this respect the system in use in the United States. Mortgage institutions, investment banks, clearing houses, credit unions, and saving and loan associations are representative of these latter institutions. In Argentina the Banco de Buenos Aires, a private and provincial bank with the exclusive privilege of discount and note issue, was established in 1822. In 1826 it was replaced by the Banco Nacional, which had branches in the provinces. The establishment of central banking aroused opposition in the provinces, where local banks were doing business, and in 1836 the Banco Nacional was dissolved. A new Banco Nacional was established in 1872, but due to unsettled economic conditions it made limited progress. In 1887 a system of 20 National Guaranty Banks, modeled after the national banking system of the United States, was founded, but the disastrous corruption and mismanagement of the Celman administration (1886–1890) brought about a loss of public confidence in the banks. As a result, the financial crisis of 1890 wiped out the system. The Banco de la Nación was created in 1891, restoring public faith in government credit. After the depression of the

early 1930's, the Banco Central was established in 1934, which greatly strengthened the whole banking system. The Banco Central, controlled by member banks of the federal system, was to be a bank of issue and was expected to control credit operations through the discounting of the paper of the private banks. When war broke out in 1939, the initial panic was curbed by virtue of the Banco Central's buying of all government securities offered for sale on the stock exchange. It bought 33,000,000 pesos' worth of such securities. Under the PERÓN regime the Banco Central was taken over by the government in 1946. In Brazil, the Bank of Brazil with a 20-year charter was established in 1808, its main activities consisting of the discount of letters of exchange and the issuance of drafts. It also acted as a bank of deposit for the Crown's diamonds, gold, and silver, and was backed mainly by the Crown and wealthy Portuguese. It was liquidated in 1829, and Brazil assumed the obligation for its notes of issue. In 1851 a second Bank of Brazil was founded that merged with the Commercial Bank of Brazil in 1854, and became the Bank of the Republic of Brazil in 1892. A fourth bank of Brazil was established in 1905, which took over the resources and privileges of the Bank of the Republic. Under President Affonso PENNA, 1906–1909, a *caixa de conversão*, or conversion office, was established that fixed the value of the milreis and guaranteed the redemption of Brazil's depreciated paper currency by notes backed up by gold. Today Brazil has no central bank, but many functions of central banking are carried out by the Bank of Brazil. The bank not only manages all exchange and exercises important control over export and import transactions, but it also acts as a financial agent for national, state, and municipal governments, and holds large deposits for retirement and pension institutions. The bank also serves as a depository for the superintendency of money and credit. The Brazilian government, by law, holds more than 50 per cent of the bank's total capital. Brazil is also served by 750 commercial banks that vary in size from large institutions with branch systems to small local banks serving limited trade areas. The Bank of Brazil, however, transacts about one-third of the country's banking business. In Chile the banking system dates from 1860. A Central Bank system was established in 1925, with control of currency issue and a currency based on the gold standard. The Central Bank assumed other functions, such as managements of exchange rates and the administration of exchange controls. In Uruguay the Banco de la República was founded in 1896 and is entirely state-owned. In 1950 a law increased the capital of the bank to 70,000,000 pesos. One of the principal purposes of the bank is to extend cheap rural credit. There are ten private banks in Uruguay.

**Baptista, Mariano.** 1832–1907. President of Bolivia. Conservative political leader, newspaper editor, and well-known orator, he became president of Bolivia and served from 1892–1896. There were Indian revolts, and General Camacho tried to overthrow the government, but Baptista was able to suppress all uprisings.

**Baquerizo Moreno, Alfredo.** 1859–1950. President of Ecuador. Served as president from 1916–1920; was made provisional president in 1931 but was ousted during election disturbances in 1932. During his first administration yellow fever and other tropical diseases slowed up traffic in the port of Guayaquil, but with the help of the Rockefeller Foundation a successful sanitation program was carried out.

**Barbosa, Ruy.** 1848–1923. Brazilian jurist and statesman. b. São Salvador. Gained his reputation as an important jurist and was an ardent abolitionist and supporter of republican government under the monarchy. He drafted a decree separating Church and state, which was issued in January 1890; aided in the drafting of the first republican constitution of Brazil, which was finally adopted in 1891; responsible for a criminal code, and reforms in the organization of the courts. He was minister of finance in the provisional government of Manoel Deodoro da FONSECA, but his unsound financial policies weakened the country considerably. Barbosa energetically opposed the army's influence in governmental affairs. He was the Brazilian representative at the Second Hague Conference, 1907, and the presidential candidate of Civilista party in the first popular political campaign, 1910. He served on the Permanent Court of International Justice.

**Barra, Francisco León de la.** 1863–1939. Mexican statesman and Catholic leader. Minister for foreign affairs under DÍAZ, 1911; served as ambassador to the United States; provisional president after the Díaz abdication, May to November 1911; cabinet member under HUERTA, 1913; professor of international law at the Sorbonne; arbitral commissioner of World Court at The Hague from 1914.

**Barranquilla.** The chief seaport of Colombia as well as an important airport. A city of 452,140 inhabitants (1961), it is situated on the west bank of the Magdalena River seven miles from the Caribbean coast. The sand bars that in former times prevented large ships from entering the harbor were cleared away, 1928–1935, and today Barranquilla is reached by ocean liners, for which modern docks have been built. The climate, although hot, is tempered by trade winds from November to March. The founding of the city dates back to 1629, when cowboys on the trail of lost cattle found a good watering place on the site where the city stands today. Barranquilla was sacked in 1815 by royalist forces during the War of Independence. Its main industries include textiles, sawmills, flour mills, cement works, steel plants, foundries, and shipyards. The cathedral is a most attractive structure, and before it on the Central Plaza there is a statue of BOLÍVAR.

**Barreda, Gabino.** 1820–1881. Mexican educator. Studied at the University of Paris with scientist and sociologist Auguste Comte. He believed in the doctrines of POSITIVISM and worked with JUÁREZ in advancing science as opposed to theology. His influence for progressive, scientific, and liberal education was felt for generations. He was head of the then newly-created National Preparatory School, 1868.

**Barreda Laos, Felipe.** 1888–    . Peruvian lawyer and statesman. b. Lima. Professor of history at the University of San Marcos, 1912–1919; deputy in the national congress,

1916–1919; editor of *La República*, Lima, 1926–1930; delegate to the seventh Pan-American conference in Montevideo, 1933; ambassador to Argentina and to Uruguay, 1930–1938; delegate to Permanent Court of International Justice (World Court).

**Barrios, Eduardo.** 1884–  . Chilean novelist, noted for his gift for psychological analysis, impeccable prose, and his mastery of emotional writing. He is the author of *El niño que enloqueció de amor* (Sentimental Madness), 1915; *Un Perdido* (A Lost Soul), 1917; *El hermano asno* (Brother Ass), 1922; and others.

**Barrios, Justo Rufino.** 1835–1885. President of Guatemala. b. San Lorenzo. Commander-in-chief of the army, 1871–1873; president of Guatemala, 1873–1885. A belligerent liberal, intent on limiting the power of the Church, he had the religious orders exiled, and the archbishop and bishops expelled. Tithes were abolished, Church properties were put under the control of the state, and the clergy was forbidden to teach. He enlarged the functions of the provincial officials, the *jefes políticos*, under his control, in an attempt to strengthen local administration. He improved education throughout the country. He sought to extend the railroads; the highway to El Salvador was begun and all other roads improved. He encouraged progress in the coffee, rubber, cotton, and rice industries, and the nation improved during his term as virtual dictator. He was anxious to unite the countries of Central America under his leadership, but in this he failed. However he constantly interfered in the internal governments of Honduras and El Salvador, attempting to have liberal rather than conservative governments in power. In 1885 when he went into El Salvador to force his leadership, he was killed in the Battle of CHALCHUAPA.

**Barros Arana, Diego.** 1830–1907. Chilean historian. b. Santiago. Student of law, literature and history; professor of history of literature at the University of Chile, Santiago; exiled during the administration of Manuel MONTT TORRES; twice rector of the University of Chile; rector of the National Institute,

1863. He is best-known for his *Historia general de Chile* (16 vols., 1884–1902), which covers Chile's past from primitive times to 1833, and is considered outstanding among Chilean national historians.

**Barros Borgoño, Luis.** 1858–1943. Chilean author and statesman, and son of the well-known Chilean historian Diego BARROS ARANA. b. Santiago. Professor of history, University of Chile, Santiago; served as minister of war and marine, 1889, 1902; minister of war, 1892; minister of foreign affairs, 1894, 1918–1919; candidate for the presidency, 1920; vice-president of Chile and acting president, 1925; ambassador to Argentina, 1925–1938. He was the author of several books.

**Barros Jarpa, Ernesto.** 1894–  . Chilean lawyer and statesman. b. Chillán. Graduate, University of Chile, Santiago; minister of foreign affairs, 1921, 1941; minister of finance and interior, 1932; professor of international public law, University of Chile; author of many books on international law.

**Barroso, Gustavo.** 1888–1959. Brazilian jurist and journalist. b. Fortaleza, Ceará. Studied for the bar at Fortaleza, 1907–1909, and at Rio de Janeiro, 1910–1911; prominent as editor, *Jornal do Ceará*, 1908–1909, and *Jornal do Comércio*, 1911–1913; secretary of the Brazilian delegation at Versailles peace conference, 1919; director of National Historical Museum from 1922. The leader of the INTEGRALISTA movement, 1932, which imitated Italian fascism, Barroso, as a historian, attempted to invite intellectuals into his movement, and tried to foster anti-Argentine feeling. His book on integralism, *O que o integralismo deve saber*, was published in 1935.

**Bases, Naval and Air.** In the 20th century the United States, aware of the strategic importance of the Caribbean area, lost no opportunity in acquiring bases there. In 1903 Cuba gave the United States the right to establish coaling and naval bases at Guantánamo Bay and Bahía Honda. No base was built at Bahía Honda, however, and this project was eventually abandoned, but, by the treaty of 1934, the base constructed at Guantánamo Bay was maintained. The defense of the Panama Canal made it more and more imperative for the United States to make the Caribbean an "American lake." In March 1941, Panama granted the United States the right to extend its defenses outside the Canal Zone. At the same time naval bases at Guantánamo, Cuba; San Juan, Puerto Rico; and St. Thomas, Virgin Islands; were speedily modernized. By the famous "destroyer-for-bases" exchange of September 1940, the United States received from Great Britain important naval and air bases in the Bahamas, Jamaica, St. Lucia, Trinidad, Antigua, and the British Guianas, among others, on 99-year leases in exchange for 50 World War I destroyers. In conformity with agreements reached at various Pan-American conferences, the Latin-American nations were given the use of these bases. During WORLD WAR II the use by U.S. planes of Brazilian airfields proved of great help to Allied operations in Africa and the Mediterranean. In September 1942, Ecuador granted the United States naval bases in the Galápagos Islands and the Santa Elena peninsula.

**Bases Orgánicas of 1843.** Conservative, centralist Mexican constitution promulgated on June 13 of that year, with the title "Bases of the Political Organization of the Mexican Republic." This constitution replaced the Seven Constitutional Laws, which had been in use since 1836, and permitted the election of SANTA ANNA on January 2, 1844. It lasted only until 1846, when the federalist constitution of 1824 was re-established.

**Bassols, Narciso.** b. 1898. Mexican political leader and diplomat. b. Tenango del Valle. Educated at law school, Universidad Nacional de México; secretary of interior, state of Mexico, 1924; professor of constitutional law, and director, faculty of law and social science, Universidad Nacional de México, 1929; secretary of education during the RODRÍGUEZ administration. In 1933 he instituted a general reform of the school system, raising wages, extending federal control over the state schools, and applying the ideals of the rural school system to the urban schools; the following year he attempted to install a socialist-type education in Mexico. He was secretary of finance under CÁRDENAS, 1935–1936; minister to Great Britain, 1936; delegate to the League of Nations, 1937; minister to France, 1938; and ambassador to Russia, 1945. He is the author of *La Ley agraria, Garantías y amparo*, and other works.

**Bastidas, Rodrigo de.** 1460–1526. Spanish explorer and conquistador. b. Seville. Explored coastal region of Colombia, 1501, accompanied by Juan de la Cosa and Vasco Núñez de BALBOA; gave name to Santa Marta. A year later he was shipwrecked on the coast of Santo Domingo, his gold was confiscated, and he was imprisoned by order of the governor of the island, Francisco de BOBADILLA, who had him sent to Spain as a prisoner. In Spain, he obtained his freedom and recovered part of his fortune. Assigned a lifelong pension by the king, he founded a colony in Colombia near the bay of Santa Marta 1525. Friction quickly developed between him and the other colonists because of his generous attitude toward the Indians, which manifested itself in his refusal to let his countrymen use them as slaves. He was stabbed by a rebel as a result of this ill feeling and died shortly afterwards in Cuba.

**Batista y Zaldívar, Fulgencio.** 1901– . President of Cuba. b. Banes. Educated at a Quaker missionary school and at public schools; worked at various trades before he began his army career as a recruit in 1921; promoted to sergeant. He became a member of the ABC PARTY, which actively opposed the dictatorship of MACHADO. After the revolt that ousted Machado in August 1933, he led a coup that deposed the provisional president CÉSPEDES in September 1933 and named GRAU SAN MARTÍN the new provisional president. He was promoted to colonel and made chief of staff of the army, and from 1933 to 1940 he effectively controlled the country through presidents who were dependent on his support to remain in office. He was elected president, 1940–1944, elected senator, 1948, and carried out a second successful coup, 1952. He became provisional president in 1952 and for the second time was elected to the office of president in 1954 for a four-year term beginning February 24, 1955. He resigned the presidency January 1, 1959, because of opposition led by Fidel CASTRO, and fled to the United States. See CUBA.

**Batlle, Lorenzo.** 1812–1872. President of Uruguay. b. Montevideo. General in the army and political leader. He served as president from 1868 to 1872.

**Batlle Berres, Luis Conrado.** 1897–1964. President of Uruguay. b. Montevideo. Nephew of José BATLLE Y ORDÓÑEZ. Successful political leader for 25 years before running for vice-presidency; owner of Montevideo's principal radio stations, which he used for political purposes, including anti-PERÓN speeches by refugee liberals from Argentina; national deputy, 1923–1933, 1942–1947; political exile, 1933–1937; president of the chamber of deputies, 1943–1945; elected vice-president with BERRETA on November 24, 1946. When Berreta died in August of the following year, he became president. Under his administration, 1947–1951, Uruguay enjoyed general prosperity; meat and wool exports were at a high level, and industries, mainly textile, were developed with the help of the government's protectionist policies. After an interval of several years during which he was out of power, he was elected in December 1954, as the head of the liberal wing of the Colorado party, to the presidency of the National Council of Government, which by virtue of a constitutional amendment adopted in 1951 served as the country's executive branch, and he was inaugurated as president of the newly-elected council on March 1, 1955.

**Batlle y Ordóñez, José.** 1856–1929. President of Uruguay. b. Montevideo. Son of Lorenzo BATLLE. Educated in Uruguay and Europe. He devoted himself to politics and journalism during his early career, founded the newspaper *El Día*, 1886, and attempted to rebuild a stronger and more democratic Colorado Party. He was elected senator, 1898, served as member of council of state, was president of the senate under Cuestas, and was elected to the presidency as a candidate of the Colorado Party, 1903. The first years of his administration were plagued by a civil war that lasted nearly two years. The remainder of his time in office (to 1907) he devoted to the reorganization and reconstruction of the country, and the introduction of a system of modified European socialism. His second administration (1911–1915) brought further reform and an expansion of the system of public ownership; Uruguay became one of the most completely socialized countries in the world. Batlle y Ordóñez proposed a number of labor and social laws including a comprehensive workman's compensation scheme, a law providing an obligatory day of rest each week, the "law of the chair" (stipulating that women workers must have available chairs upon which to sit while working), and a law requiring leave with pay for women workers for a month before and after giving birth. He also established research organizations to promote new industries and a government insurance company that operated in many fields and had a monopoly in workman's compensation insurance. Although Batlle used authoritarian methods to promote his liberal program, he saw the danger of a strong executive, and during his second administration he strenuously advocated the adoption of a plural or collegiate form for the executive office. He was successful in bringing about a constitutional convention, 1917, which adopted a modified form of his proposals. The National Council of Administration was created, the members being elected by a system of proportional representation that gave both *blancos* and *colorados* a voice in the national government; presidential powers were divided between the president and the council, with some cabinet members reporting to the president and others to the council; and control of foreign affairs, finances, and defense remained in the hands of the president. Batlle served twice as the head of the National Council and did much to discredit *caudillismo* and *personalismo*, leading the way to political stability in Uruguay. He contributed greatly to the establishment of a pattern of democratic government, and all but a few of his successors have followed his example.

**Belaúnde Terry, Fernando.** 1912–   · Peruvian architect and politician; elected president of Peru in 1963.

**Belgrano, Manuel.** 1770–1820. Argentine general and patriot. Considered intellectual leader of the Creoles; studied in Spain; secretary of the Buenos Aires *Consulado*,

1794. He proposed the adoption of measures designed to promote agriculture, manufacturing, trade, education, sciences, and the arts. He took part in the revolution of 1810, and led forces of the Buenos Aires junta against Paraguay, 1811. Although untrained as a military man he became general of the patriot army. He defeated Peruvian royalists in the Battle of Tucumán, 1812, and won the Battle of Salta, 1813. He was defeated at Vilcapugio and Ayohuma, 1813, and was replaced as commander of the army by SAN MARTÍN, 1814. He was sent on diplomatic mission to Europe with RIVADAVIA, 1815, to secure recognition of the independence of the United Provinces by Spain and England, and to search for an acceptable monarch for a proposed constitutional monarchy. He urged an Inca monarchy for Argentina at the CONGRESS OF TUCUMÁN, 1816. He designed the Argentine flag.

**Belize** or **Belice.** See BRITISH HONDURAS.

**Bello López, Andrés.** 1781–1865. Venezuelan poet, lawyer, educator, grammarian, publicist, journalist, and statesman. b. Caracas, Venezuela. While a student he was influenced by HUMBOLDT, who visited Caracas. He accompanied BOLÍVAR on his mission to Great Britain in 1810 in an effort to obtain recognition of Venezuelan independence, hoping also to recruit some legionnaires for the service, but the mission was not successful. He served as representative in London for the revolutionary government until 1829. He then went to Chile where he spent the remainder of his life. He worked for the Chilean government and formulated a new civil code and served as Chilean representative in cases of international arbitration. He was head of the University of Chile from 1843. One of Chile's greatest educators, and one of its great literary figures, he wrote what is still considered the best grammar of the Spanish language. He was an outstanding Latin and Greek scholar, and wrote many works of poetry.

**Belo Horizonte.** Capital of the state of Minas Gerais in southeastern Brazil, about 200 miles north of Rio de Janeiro, altitude 2,500 feet, population 583,019 (est. 1960). The second largest of Brazil's inland cities (after São Paulo), Belo Horizonte was founded in 1898 because of its beautiful surroundings and healthful climate. Today it is an important mining, industrial, and diamond-cutting center. Its main products are gold, iron, manganese, and cattle, and its industrial strength is based on its cotton mills. The city is connected by rail with Rio de Janeiro.

**Belzú, Manuel Isidoro.** 1808–1866. President of Bolivia. b. La Paz. Professional soldier who rose to rank of general. Uneducated, he assumed power in a military coup in 1848 and gained popularity by appealing to class hatred and encouraging mobs to ruin and sack the properties of the upper class. He was the idol of the people, but his rule was constantly troubled by conspiracies and revolts, and even his ruthless killing of his opponents did not stop them; at one time the president of the congress met his death as a conspirator. A new constitution was drawn in 1851 that limited his term to five years, but continued his dictatorial powers. He gave up the "anarchy" and "ungovernable Bolivians" in 1855 in favor of his illegitimate son Jorge CÓRDOBA. He seized the presidency again in 1865 but was deposed and assassinated in 1866.

**Benalcázar,** or **Belalcázar, Sebastián de.** Real name, **Sebastián Moyano.** 1495–1550. Spanish conquistador. b. Estremadura. Sailed with PEDRARIAS in 1514 and arrived at Darién with a party of men later to become famous; conquered Nicaragua, 1524; served with ALMAGRO and PIZARRO, 1532. While Pizarro went south, Benalcázar stayed in Ecuador, and after disposing of ALVARADO Y MESÍA, defeated the Inca chief, Ruminahui, and conquered Quito, 1533. Leaving there, he joined in the search for EL DORADO in 1536, and in 1538 met JIMÉNEZ DE QUESADA and FEDERMANN in Santa Fe de Bogotá. The three conquistadors asked the Crown to divide the spoils, and Benalcázar became governor of the lush lands of Popayán from 1538.

**Benavides, Oscar Raimundo.** 1876–1945. President of Peru. b. Lima. Chief of general staff, 1913. During the revolution of 1914 he was chief of the governing junta that worked with the *civilistas* to overthrow the govern-

43

ment. Provisional president in 1915; appointed minister to Italy and served 1917–1920; minister to Spain, 1931; minister to England, 1932–1933; chief of national defense, 1933; conservative president of Peru, 1933–1939; ambassador to Spain, 1940–1945.

**Berbeo, Juan Francisco de.** See COMUNERO REVOLT.

**Bermejo.** See CHRIST OF THE ANDES.

**Berreta, Tomás.** 1871–1947. President of Uruguay. Born of a poor family on a small farm, he was largely self-educated and worked as a laborer and policeman. He joined the *batllista* wing of the Colorado Party and was elected to the National Council of Administration in 1929. Forced into exile by TERRA in 1933, when he returned he was elected senator. He served as minister of public works in AMÉZAGA's cabinet. Nominated for the presidency, he was elected in November 1946. He visited the United States in February 1947. He died in August of that year and was succeeded by BATLLE BERRES.

**Bertrand, Francisco.** President of Honduras. Served as provisional president in 1912 and as vice-president under Bonilla. He became president in 1913 when his predecessor died. His popularity was strong and his administration so successful that he was re-elected in 1915 to serve until 1920.

**Betancourt, Rómulo.** 1908– . President of Venezuela. b. Guatire, Miranda. Educated at the Liceo Caracas and the law school of the Central University of Venezuela. He actively opposed President Juan Vicente GÓMEZ and was exiled in 1928. A member of the Communist Party in Costa Rica in 1930, he later quit the party, and returning to Venezuela, founded the newspaper *Orve* in 1936. He was again exiled in 1940. He was founder and secretary general of *Acción Democrática* in 1941, and co-founder of the newspaper *El País* in 1943. He joined the revolutionary forces that brought about the fall of President MEDINA ANGARITA in 1945. He was president of the seven-man ruling junta, 1945–1948, and headed the Venezuelan delegation to the CONFERENCE OF BOGOTÁ (Ninth Pan-American Conference) in 1948. He was exiled

after the 1948 coup. Following the overthrow of Pérez Jiménez in 1958, Betancourt returned to Venezuela to reorganize his party, the *Acción Democrática,* and was the successful candidate for president in 1958. He initiated an ambitious economic development program that included industrial expansion, agricultural education, and the improvement of communications. See VENEZUELA.

**Bidlack Treaty.** (Also called **New Granada Treaty.**) Treaty concluded between the United States and New Granada (Colombia) on December 12, 1846, giving the United States right of transit across the Isthmus of Panama by any means of transport. In exchange the United States guaranteed the neutrality of the isthmus and the sovereignty of New Granada over it. The U. S. Senate was suspicious of possible entanglements and did not approve the pact until June 3, 1848. After the California gold rush, the United States took advantage of the treaty terms and an American company built a railroad across the isthmus, 1855. In conformity with the provisions of the treaty, the Colombian government in later years often appealed to the United States to intervene in order to keep the isthmus route open in time of civil war. American influence in that area was thus considerably increased.

**Big Stick Policy.** Term applied to the U. S. policy in the early years of the 20th century, based on President Theodore ROOSEVELT'S phrase "speak softly and carry a big stick," and involving American intervention in the affairs of Latin-American countries. The policy was the outgrowth of financial exploitation (DOLLAR DIPLOMACY) and threatened the Latin-American nations with force unless they faithfully observed their financial obligations to U. S. investors. The Big Stick Policy created considerable animosity toward the United States in Latin America. See ROOSEVELT COROLLARY.

**Billinghurst, Guillermo Enrique.** 1851–1915. President of Peru. b. Arica. His father was English and his mother a native Peruvian. A successful businessman and leader of the radical group, he was elected president in September 1912, as the candidate of the *pierolistas* (see Nicolás de PIÉROLA). Forced to resign by a military coup d'etat in February 1914, he was exiled to Panama. One of the reasons for his overthrow was his stopping of the exploitation of Indians in the Putumayo rubber district. He had the good of his people in mind but quarreled with his congress and made an unfortunate attempt to compromise with Chile on the TACNA-ARICA QUESTION.

**Bimini.** A mythical island where a miraculous fountain of youth was thought to be located. PONCE DE LEÓN was searching for the island of Indian legend when he discovered the mainland in 1513. He renamed the newly-discovered land "Florida."

**Black Legend** or **La Leyenda Negra.** A term used to deprecate the Spaniards and their extremely cruel treatment of the natives of Latin America. LAS CASAS wrote of the brutality inflicted upon the Indians, and his work was used as propaganda by the enemies of Spain, particularly by the Dutch and the British. Although there was some truth in what he had to say, it was exaggerated to such an extent as to make the people of the Iberian peninsula seem inhuman. Only in the 20th century have these exaggerations been recognized as such.

**Blaine, James Gillespie.** 1830–1893. Secretary of State of the United States, 1881 and from 1889 to 1892, during the administrations of Garfield and Harrison. He argued for the abrogation of the CLAYTON-BULWER TREATY to give the United States exclusive rights in the building of an Isthmian canal, 1881. He had a deep admiration for Latin America as a whole but managed to alienate several Latin-American republics as a result of his policies. He attempted to influence the settlement of the WAR OF THE PACIFIC by opposing the ceding of Peruvian and Bolivian land to Chile and was Secretary of State during the unfortunate ITATA and BALTIMORE AFFAIRS, which further estranged Chile. Blaine presided over the first PAN-AMERICAN CONFERENCE, 1889, which created the Pan-American Union. He was the chief exponent of reciprocal trade agreements with Latin-American nations and advocated closer commercial and cultural ties with Latin America. Despite his lack of immediate achievements, Blaine laid the foundations for better relations with Latin America upon which others have built.

**Blanco Encalada, Manuel.** 1790–1876. Argentine and Chilean patriot, admiral, and naval hero. b. Buenos Aires. Educated in Spain, he served in the Spanish navy and was sent to America after the outbreak of revolt there. He joined the revolutionary forces in Chile, 1813, and organized the Chilean navy, serving under COCHRANE. He was president *ad interim* of Chile, 1826. He commanded the Chilean army in the war with Bolivia, 1837. He was Chilean diplomatic agent in Paris and directed naval operations against the Spanish fleet, 1865.

**Blanco Fombona, Rufino.** 1874–1944. Venezuelan writer and publisher. b. Caracas. As a result of his opposition to the rule of Juan Vicente GÓMEZ in 1910, he was sent into exile. He lived in Madrid from 1914 and founded a publishing house in 1915. He returned to Venezuela in 1935. He was the author of *Cantos de la Prisión y del Destierro*, poems written in prison, 1911, *Cuentos de Poeta*, 1900, *El Hombre de Hierro* (The Man of Iron), 1907, *El Secreto de la Felicidad* (The Secret of Happiness), 1932, and many other works. In 1920 he wrote *El Hombre de Oro* (The Man of Gold), which was a strong satire on political life in Caracas. He was a strong opponent of "Yankee Imperialism."

**Blancos.** From Spanish *blanco*, meaning white. Name given in the 19th century to the Uruguayan conservatives. In the 1830's the rural population and the clergy, rallying around Manuel ORIBE, adopted the white flag as their emblem and fought against the liberals (*colorados*, or reds) of RIVERA. In this civil war the *blancos* had the support of the Argentine dictator ROSAS. Throughout the 19th century and the beginning of the 20th, the history of Uruguay was marked by the struggle between *blancos* and *colorados*.

**Blest Gana, Alberto.** 1830–1920. Chilean novelist. He was influenced by the French Realists of the 19th century. A prolific writer, he was the author of *Martín Rivas, Durante la*

*Reconquista, Los Trasplantados* (The Transplanted), and numerous other works.

**Blue Book on Argentina.** A document issued by the U. S. State Department twelve days before the Argentine presidential elections of February 1946. Using captured German papers as evidence against the official candidate, Juan PERÓN, it accused him of having collaborated, together with other Argentines, with the Axis powers during WORLD WAR II. In spite of the Blue Book, Perón won the election and it is believed that many Argentines, although disagreeing with him, voted in his favor because of what they considered an American attempt to interfere in the affairs of Argentina. See BRADEN.

**Bobadilla, Francisco de.** d. 1502. Spanish colonial governor of the Indies, succeeding COLUMBUS, 1499. Knight Commander of the Order of Calatrava and officer in the royal household, he was sent to the Indies in 1500 to investigate the activities of Columbus. He imprisoned Columbus on the latter's arrival at Santo Domingo in 1500 and sent him back to Spain in chains. He functioned as governor until 1502, ruling ruthlessly, and the Indians were treated harshly while he was in control. He was recalled to Spain and placed under arrest.

**Bogotá.** The capital of the republic of Colombia, situated on a high plateau of the Andes mountains at an altitude of 8,600 feet above sea level. Its population is 1,256,640 (est. 1961). A great number of public buildings, monuments, and churches, many centuries old, give the city an impressive historic atmosphere. There are about twenty theaters and a million-dollar bull ring. Points of interest include the Plaza Bolívar, with the statue of Simón BOLÍVAR, the residence of the president, the Congress, the Cathedral, the University, and the National Library. The area around the city grows coffee, cacao, tobacco, and cotton, and raises cattle. Manufactured products turned out by Bogotá's plants include textiles, leather goods, cigarettes, glassware, soap, and matches. The city is best reached by plane, the trip from Barranquilla to Bogotá taking about two hours. The only other connection with the Caribbean coast is the 1,000-mile long Río Magdalena and a railroad leading from the river to the city. This voyage, however, takes about seven days. Bogotá was founded in August 1538, by the Spanish conquistador, Gonzalo JIMÉNEZ DE QUESADA, after an epic two-year trek from the Caribbean coast. Jiménez de Quesada, with fewer than two hundred companions surviving out of an original group of 800, built a church and twelve huts, each bearing the name of an Apostle, and called the settlement Santa Fe de Bogotá. The name Bogotá itself was that of a CHIBCHA Indian chieftain, who resisted the Spaniards but was finally killed. During the colonial period the city was a center of learning. In 1563 the DOMINICANS established a chair of arts, and in 1573 they founded the University of Santo Tomás, the ancestor of today's National University. The Jesuit University, founded in 1622, was revived in the 20th century (1931). The University City, located in the suburbs, today includes the professional schools of the National University. At the time of the Ninth Inter-American Conference in April 1948, the city was swept by destructive riots on the heels of the assassination of the liberal leader, Jorge Eliécer GAITÁN, April 9th.

**Bogotá Conference.** The Ninth Pan-American Conference that met in the capital of Colombia in March 1948. Latin-American delegates were disappointed by U. S. Secretary of State Marshall's announcement that the U. S. Congress had been asked by President Truman to earmark half a billion dollars for loans to Latin-American nations by the EXPORT-IMPORT BANK; they had hoped for a much larger sum. During the conference, there occurred violent popular riots, attributed to Communist influence and provoked by the murder of liberal leader GAITÁN, nearly destroying the city. In spite of disappointments and mishaps, the conference was able to adopt the Charter of the ORGANIZATION OF AMERICAN STATES and the American Treaty on Pacific Settlement, which outlaws war in the Western Hemisphere.

**Bolas.** See BOLEADORAS.

**Boleadoras.** A lasso made from two or three united thongs with weights at the end of each. Boleadoras were used originally by the Indians of the Argentine PAMPAS for hunting, and later were adopted by the GAUCHOS.

**Bolívar, Simón.** 1783–1830. World-renowned as the Liberator of large parts of Spanish South America, and often called the "George Washington of South America." b. Caracas, Venezuela. Heir to a large fortune; tutored by Simón Rodríguez (1771–1854), who taught him democratic ideas of government; studied in Madrid and entered court life there. Married at 20, his wife died a year later. Inspired by the French Revolution and Napoleon, he traveled through Europe, and while in Rome, in 1805, decided to free his native land from Spanish rule. He returned to Venezuela by way of the United States in 1807; member of the Caracas junta which in 1810 forced the Spanish captain general of Venezuela to abdicate. He was requested by the junta in 1810 to go to England on behalf of his country in the hope that he would obtain recognition of independence. His mission was not a success, since all he was able to obtain was moral support for his country; he returned to Venezuela; with Francisco de MIRANDA fought against the Spanish. After the defeat of the revolutionary forces in 1812, he fled to Curaçao and later to Cartagena (Colombia). Returning to Venezuela at the head of a small force, he seized Caracas in 1813 but was defeated and forced to flee again to New Granada (Colombia), 1814; after Spanish victory there forced into exile in Jamaica, 1815; sailed to Haiti; landed in Venezuela and led a successful revolt there, 1816–1818; entered New Granada and with a small army defeated the Spanish at the battle of BOYACÁ, 1819. As president of the new republic of Gran Colombia, 1819, that included the modern states of Colombia, Venezuela, and Ecuador, he had unlimited power. He won the Battle of CARABOBO in 1821, which was the last struggle for Venezuela. He captured Quito, 1822, and met with SAN MARTÍN on July 26th and 27th, 1822, at Guayaquil; while nothing is known of what was said or agreed, San Martín resigned his command and left Peru in September. Bolívar succeeded in finally freeing Peru from Spain, 1824–1826, and was given dicta-

torial powers. He planned a Pan-American federation, but failed to get support for it at the Panama Conference of 1826. Returning to Colombia in 1826, his plans for a strong central government met with large opposition, and in 1828 he was forced to suspend the constitution of 1821 and assume dictatorial powers in an effort to curb the unrest in the provinces. He was almost assassinated in 1828; greatly upset by the murder of SUCRE. He was unable to prevent the breaking up of the republic of Gran Colombia; Colombia, Venezuela, and Ecuador became independent republics in 1830. He resigned as president of Gran Colombia, 1830, and planned to sail for Europe, but became ill and died on December 17, 1830. Bolívar was great both as a military leader and as a political thinker, but his career was marred by personal ambition and his desire for glory. He will, unquestionably, live on in the memories of all Latin Americans as a great inspiration for freedom.

**Bolivia.** The fifth largest country in South America, with an area of 424,163 square miles. One of the two landlocked countries in Latin America, Bolivia is surrounded by Chile and Peru to the west and the northwest, Brazil to the north and east, Paraguay and Argentina to the south. Of a population of 4,188,000 (est. 1965), approximately 63 per cent are pure Indians, both AYMARÁS and QUECHUAS, the remainder of the population is composed of whites and *cholos* (mixed). The official language is Spanish, but Aymará, Quechua, and GUARANÍ are still widely spoken among the Indians. In 1963 a new currency, the peso boliviano, was distributed; the rate of exchange was twelve to the U. S. dollar. Under the provisions of the constitution of 1961 Bolivia is a republic, whose president is elected every four years by popular vote. The members of the senate are elected for six years, and those of the chamber of deputies for four. It is a predominantly Roman Catholic country. Bolivia's chief cities and their populations (est. 1962) are LA PAZ, the seat of the government, 352,912, Sucre, the legal capital, 54,270, Cochabamba, a business center, 92,008, and the mining towns Oruro, 86,985, and Potosí, 55,233. The eastern part, constituting two-thirds of the country and formed by low plains and jungles, is sparsely populated. Most of the population is concentrated in the highlands and on the *altiplano* (high plateau), situated between the western ranges of the Andes, about 450 miles long and 8 miles wide, at an average altitude of 12,000 feet. With Tibet, this high plateau is the highest inhabited area in the world. The *altiplano* is the main center of the economic life of the country and contains La Paz, the highest capital in the world, as well as LAKE TITICACA, the largest lake in South America and the highest steam-navigated lake in the world (altitude 12,500 feet). The climate of the *altiplano* is cool, 50.4 degrees on the average in La Paz, and that of the lowlands is hot, with an average temperature of about 77 degrees.

The section around Lake Titicaca was the seat of a well-developed culture that found its zenith about A.D. 900. The INCAS, who founded their empire in the same general area in the twelfth century and then extended their hold northward as far as Ecuador, were conquered by the Spaniards under PIZARRO, 1532–1535. The conquest of Peru opened the door to the high plateau of present-day Bolivia. In 1538 the town of La Plata (later known as Charcas, Chuquisaca, and Sucre) was founded, and in 1545 the fabulous silver mountain, Cerro Rico de Potosí, was discovered and the town of Potosí at its foot became world-famous. The Aymará and Quechua Indians were forced to work in the mines and many of them died from hardship and disease. During the colonial era the country, known as Upper Peru, was a part of the viceroyalty of Peru until 1776, although it functioned under the jurisdiction of the separate *audiencia* of Charcas. In 1776 it became a part of the viceroyalty of La Plata. In the course of the colonial period there were a number of Indian and mestizo uprisings, one of the most serious being the one led by TUPAC AMARÚ II in 1780–1781. Upper Peru revolted against Spain in 1809, and for many years there was bitter fighting in the territory between patriots and royalists. The country finally gained its independence in 1825, due chiefly to the victories of the armies of BOLÍVAR and SUCRE. After liberation it adopted the name of Bolivia, in honor of the great

liberator, who was given the title of "Father of the Republic." Bolívar framed the country's first constitution, which was ratified in 1826, and Antonio José Sucre was elected president. The name of the capital of the new nation was changed from Chuquisaca to Sucre. A revolt overthrew the president in 1828, and in 1829, Andrés SANTA CRUZ, who had been a general in Bolívar's army, assumed power. He introduced many reforms and succeeded in forming a confederation of Peru and Bolivia that lasted from 1836 to 1839, when Santa Cruz was overthrown by a combined army of Chileans and Peruvians. The balance of the 19th century proved a chaotic period for Bolivia. There was extreme political instability, and the country lost considerable territory as well as its outlet on the Pacific Ocean after the disastrous war with Chile (1879–1883). Under the administration of the liberal presidents, José Manuel PANDO (1899–1904) and Ismael MONTES (1904–1909, 1913–1917), some reforms were initiated. Boundary agreements negotiated with Chile and Brazil led to the building of railroads which provided badly needed outlets to the Pacific and the Amazon. The production of copper, lead, and tin made great strides, and during this period, also, La Paz became the seat of government. In the 20th century Bolivia has generally continued on the road of political instability. Moreover the country was plunged into the disastrous Chaco War with Paraguay (1932–1935), as a result of which it lost about three-quarters of the Chaco in exchange for getting an outlet to the Río Paraguay. During WORLD WAR II Bolivian tin became vital to the Allied war effort after Japanese seizure of Malaya. Bolivia declared war on the Axis powers in April 1943. In December of the same year, however, the pro-Ally Peñaranda government was overthrown by a pro-Axis group that remained in power until July 1946, when its leader, President Gualberto VILLARROEL was killed by a mob in La Paz. The moderate Enrique Herzog, who became president in 1947, had to contend with labor unrest and with the political opposition of the M.N.R. (*Movimiento Nacional Revolucionario*). Because of ill health Herzog was forced to resign in October 1949. His successor, Mamerto Urriolagoitia, was defeated in the 1951 elections by the M.N.R leader Víctor PAZ ESTENSSORO, who had to oust a military junta to assume office in April 1952. Paz Estenssoro embarked on a program of economic and social reforms, including the nationalization of the country's three largest tin companies and the distribution of land to farmworkers. Paz Estenssoro was the first president to complete his term of office since SAAVEDRA in 1925. The elections held in May 1956 elevated Hernán Siles Zuazo to the presidency. Siles Zuazo had served as vice-president under Paz Estenssoro and was the candidate of the M.N.R. The period from 1956 to 1960 was one of economic depression and political unrest. Inflation continued, exports declined, and despite substantial international aid the Bolivian economic position failed to improve. In June 1960 former president Paz Estenssoro replaced Siles Zuazo after a bitter campaign that split the M.N.R. Continuing economic difficulties provoked serious disturbances and strikes in 1961, and Bolivian supporters of Fidel CASTRO, backed by Communists and leftist labor elements, attacked the government. Paz Estenssoro announced a ten-year economic development program in 1962 that was designed to raise the standard of living of the people and generally bolster the entire economy. Despite strong opposition from the Popular Bolivian Alliance, a coalition of parties opposed to the M.N.R., President Paz Estenssoro was re-elected in May 1964 but was ousted by the military in November. A junta, headed by General René Barrientos Ortuño suppressed a leftist oriented uprising by the tin miners in 1965. In 1966 elections were held and General Barrientos was elected president.

Bolivia's economy today is still based upon its mineral resources. The country is the world's second largest producer of tin, which constitutes approximately 68.5 per cent of Bolivia's exports. Tin mining is carried out mostly in the Potosí and Oruro districts at altitudes of from 13,000 to 15,000 feet. The labor supply is made up of Andean Indians, who alone can stand the work at such tremendous heights. Other metals produced are lead, copper, tungsten, zinc, gold, and silver. Although Bolivia has rich oil deposits, production is still low. The great majority of the people continue to be engaged in agriculture. There are a great number of large estates, but they are being broken up to give acreage to landless peasants and farm workers. In many places, aside from the big estates, the land is still cultivated by the Indians on a communal basis. In the lowlands of the east, coffee, cacao, brazil nuts, and mahogany, are grown, and rubber, cinchona, and quebracho are extracted. The Indians of the high plateaus raise LLAMAS, ALPACAS, and VICUÑAS, and breed chinchillas; in the highlands as well as on the plains of the east, cattle are raised. Many foodstuffs still have to be imported, and because of the peculiar geographical features of the country, imports as well as exports face problems of transportation. Three rail lines connect the *altiplano* region to the Pacific outlets of Mollendo (Peru), Arica, and Antofagasta (Chile), but the costs of running these lines is high. There still is no rail connection between the *altiplano* and the food-producing areas of the east, and Bolivia has to depend a great deal for its transportation on the national airlines. In January 1955 the vital Corumbá-Santa Cruz rail line linking the railway systems of Brazil and Bolivia was dedicated by the presidents of both countries. Thus Bolivia finally gained a direct outlet to the Atlantic Ocean. The new railroad also provides an important link between Bolivia's new oil industry near Santa Cruz and the Brazilian city of São Paulo. Bolivian manufacturing is limited and what industry exists is carried out in La Paz.

Bolivia today is struggling with many problems. The Indians, who are in the majority, take practically no part in the political life of the country. Education is at a low level and illiteracy is estimated to be as high as 70 per cent. Wages in the nationalized tin companies have been raised, but continuing inflation is disastrous to the workers, and although land is being distributed among farm workers, food production has actually dropped. Bolivia is suffering a lack of foreign exchange and the purchase of foodstuffs abroad faces increasing obstacles. The drop in world tin prices is adding to the country's economic woes, for it threatens the country's main source of wealth. The government is participating in the ALLIANCE FOR PROGRESS and plans to invest $1,300,000,000 in the ten-year plan for the coming decade. In 1961, tin, antimony, tungsten, and sulfur production were increased over the previous year but other minerals and petroleum production suffered decreased yields. Bolivia became involved in a dispute with Chile in 1962 over Chile's construction and operation of a hydro-electric dam that diverted the waters of the Lauca River for irrigation purposes. The river has its source in Chile but flows through Bolivia. Efforts to settle the dispute continued into 1963, but no settlement was reached.

**Bonampak.** Site in southern Mexico of remarkable Mayan ruins famous for their extraordinary murals. The Indian name means "painted walls."

**Borges, Jorge Luis.** 1899–    . Argentine short story writer, poet, and essayist. b. Buenos Aires. One of the foremost contemporary Spanish-American writers. Author of essay collections: *Inquisiciones* (1925) and *Otras inquisiciones* (1960) as well as collections of short stories, among them *Ficciones* (1944) and *El Aleph* (1949).

**Borno, Louis Eustache Antoine François Joseph.** 1865–1942. President of Haiti. b. Port-au-Prince. Lawyer and public official. Foreign minister in the government of General Nord Alexis; member of the World Court (Permanent Court of International Justice) at the Hague, 1919–1922. He served two terms as president of Haiti, 1922–1930. He was the author of several works on jurisprudence.

**Boundary Disputes and Settlements.** The earliest question of boundaries, the problem of delimitation of Spanish and Portuguese possessions in the New World, arose with COLUMBUS' discovery in 1492. It was settled by Pope ALEXANDER VI's drawing of the LINE OF DEMARCATION, 1493, and by the TREATY OF TORDESILLAS, 1494, that moved the Line further to the west. Throughout the colonial period, Portugal and Spain were in conflict over the area that is Uruguay today. Armed clashes over the disputed region were frequent and, after both Spain and Portugal had lost their South-American possessions, the

struggle was continued by Argentina and Brazil, the question being resolved only in 1828 when Uruguay became an independent nation. Portuguese claims to vast territories in the Amazon and Paraná basins were recognized by Spain in the Treaty of San Ildefonso, 1777. In the 19th and 20th centuries, at the time of the achievement of independence by the colonies, boundaries between them were not well-defined, and there were numerous geographical disputes; many settlements had to be worked out, a number of them by neutral arbitrators. The more important boundary disputes were: the controversy between Peru and Colombia, 1828; the TACNA-ARICA QUESTION involving Peru and Chile, which was a result of the War of the Pacific, 1879–1883, and which was settled only in 1929; the dispute between Paraguay and Argentina, 1878, arbitrated by President Hayes of the United States, who decided the issue in favor of Paraguay; the controversy between Nicaragua and Costa Rica concerning the Nicoya district and the status of the San Juan River as a boundary river, which was submitted to the arbitration of U. S. President Cleveland and decided by him in 1888 in favor of Costa Rica; the quarrel between Brazil and Argentina over the boundary in the Misiones area, arbitrated by President Cleveland in 1895 in favor of Brazil; the controversy between Brazil and Bolivia over the Acre Territory, concluded by the ceding of the territory by Bolivia to Brazil in 1903; the boundary controversies between Argentina and Chile, which were settled by mutual agreement in the Patagonian area in 1881, and by submitting further disputes to arbitration by the queen of England (accepted in 1902) and the United States minister in Buenos Aires (accepted in 1903), after which the CHRIST OF THE ANDES was erected in commemoration of the settlements; the conflict over the Amazon port of LETICIA involving Peru and Colombia, settled by Peru's relinquishing all claims to Leticia, 1935; the boundary disagreement between Bolivia and Paraguay over the Gran Chaco, perhaps the most serious of them all, which had international repercussions. The latter controversy began in the late 1870's and led eventually to full-fledged warfare between the two countries, 1932–1935. The issue was not settled until 1938. The war between Peru and Ecuador over the Oriente region, 1941, was settled at the Foreign Ministers' Conference at Rio de Janeiro in January 1942, with Ecuador relinquishing claims to territory east of the Andes, but keeping the eastern slope, supposed to be rich in oil, and receiving an outlet to the Atlantic through the tributaries of the Amazon and through the Amazon itself. In late 1960 the interesting Honduras-Nicaragua boundary dispute reached a final settlement. Under an earlier treaty (1894) the two countries had agreed to submit their dispute to the arbitration of the king of Spain, who handed down his decision in 1906 only to have it refused by Nicaragua. The ORGANIZATION OF AMERICAN STATES brought about a new agreement in 1957 whereby the disputants agreed to submit the case to the World Court (International Court of Justice). The court ruled in 1960 that Nicaragua was obliged to recognize and carry out the Alfonso XIII decision. Both nations agreed to abide by the court's decision. An attempt to submit boundary disputes among Spanish-American States to a Hispanic-American Convention was made at the Panama Conference of 1826, but the attempt failed. Provisions for settling boundary conflicts by peaceful means have been adopted in the 20th century at several PAN-AMERICAN CONFERENCES, such as the Fifth Conference at Santiago, Chile, in 1923, the Sixth Conference at Havana, Cuba, in 1928, and the Ninth Conference at Bogotá, Colombia, in 1948.

**Bourbons.** An old French family that produced the three dynasties that ruled over France (1589–1792, 1814–1848), Spain (1700–1931), and Naples (1735–1806, 1815–1860). The Bourbons replaced the Hapsburgs in Spain in 1700, when Philip of Anjou, the grandson of Louis XIV, ascended the Spanish throne. The rule of the Spanish Bourbons in the 18th century (PHILIP V, 1700–1746; Ferdinand VI, 1746–1759; CHARLES III, 1759–1788; and CHARLES IV, 1788–1808) was marked by a series of measures intended to pull the Spanish-American colonies out of the political and economic stagnation in which they found themselves at the beginning

of the 18th century. The Bourbon kings, advised by French experts, realized that reforms were in order if the overseas empire was to be strengthened and if the economic yield of the colonies was to be increased. Important administrative changes included the creation of the viceroyalty of New Granada, 1718 (abolished in 1723, but re-established in 1740), comprising what is now Colombia, Panama, Ecuador, and Venezuela; the formation of captaincies general in Venezuela (1731), Cuba (1777), and Chile (1778); the establishment of the viceroyalty of La Plata, 1776; and the subdivision, in the second half of the century, of viceroyalties into INTENDENCIES with intendents wielding administrative, financial, and military powers in place of *alcaldes mayores* and *corregidores*. The expulsion of the Jesuits from Spanish dominions was carried out under Charles III in 1767. The removal of many restrictions on trade between Spain and Spanish America resulted in a stimulation of economic life in the colonies. Particularly beneficial was the opening to trade of more ports in Spain and in America, after 1765, and the relaxation of many restrictions on intercolonial trade. The FLEET SYSTEM went out of existence in 1748 and the *Casa de Contratación* was abolished in 1790. In order to stem the rising wave of smuggling and develop the trade of certain colonial provinces, trading companies with special privileges were formed. The most famous of these was the Caracas or Guipúzcoa Company organized in 1728. Under Charles III the *repartimiento* was abolished, the *corregidores de indios* were removed. The *encomienda* system gradually went out of existence throughout the 18th century. The condition of the Indians was thus eased somewhat. New mints were established and internal trade was correspondingly stimulated. Education, science, and the arts were encouraged, and printing increased considerably. The French occupation of Spain and the struggle for independence that followed brought an end to the constructive efforts of the Bourbon rulers in Spanish America.

**Boves, José Tomás.** Real surname, Rodríguez. *ca.* 1770–1814. Spanish soldier. b. Asturias. Boves, condemned to a lengthy imprisonment at Puerto Cabello, Venezuela, adopted the name of Boves in gratitude to a benefactor who obtained his pardon. During the War of Independence Boves recruited an army of LLANEROS to fight on behalf of Spain, defeated the force of patriots under Bolívar and Mariño at La Puerta on June 15, 1814, and entered Caracas in triumph on July 10th. He was known for his ruthless brutality toward the patriots. The *llaneros* were eventually persuaded to fight for the patriot cause by José Antonio PÁEZ and became a significant factor in turning the tide of battle against the Spaniards.

**Boyacá, Battle of.** An important engagement of the Spanish-American War for Independence. At the end of May 1819, in the rainy season, Simón BOLÍVAR, at the head of an army of 2,000 men including several hundred British volunteers, started out from San Miguel del Montecal in Venezuela with the intention of marching into the upper Orinoco valley and then crossing the eastern range of the Andes into New Granada (Colombia). His purpose was to surprise the Spanish forces stationed there, crush them, and thus liberate that province. After crossing the plains inundated by the swollen tributaries of the Orinoco, Bolívar and his men joined an army of about 1,200 men under the Colombian patriot, General SANTANDER, and the combined force undertook in the first week of July the forbidding task of crossing the Andes. The patriot troops accomplished the feat but suffered severely from the merciless cold and wind of the mountains. Hundreds died on the epic trek and the army arrived on the high plateau north of Bogotá in a lamentable state. Nevertheless Bolívar instilled sufficient spirit into it to fall on the surprised Spanish forces under General Barreiro and defeat them in the engagements of Gameza, July 12, and Vargas Swamp, July 25. On August 5 Tunja fell, and two days later the patriot forces, now numbering 3,000 men because of forced levies, faced General Barreiro's army of about equal strength close to the Boyacá River. Bolívar ordered the attack, and while forces under Santander isolated the Spanish vanguard near the bridge over the Boyacá, Bolívar's main force under Anzoátegui charged the main

body of the royalists half a mile away. In spite of fierce resistance, the advancing army crushed the enemy. The patriots took 1,800 prisoners, among them the Spanish commander, General Barreiro. On August 10 the capital of New Granada, Bogotá, fell and New Granada was thus made secure for the patriot cause.

**Boyer, Jean Pierre.** 1776–1850. President of Haiti. b. Port-au-Prince. A free mulatto, he was educated in France, joined the Haitian revolutionary forces under RIGAUD, 1792, and distinguished himself in battle. Forced by the intrigues of TOUSSAINT L'OUVERTURE to flee to France, he returned with LECLERC's expedition but deserted to aid the revolutionary forces. After independence was achieved in 1804, Boyer joined PÉTION, helped to establish the republic of Haiti in the south, supported Pétion in his resistance to CHRISTOPHE, and succeeded Pétion as president of the republic, 1818. Upon the death of Christophe, 1820, Boyer brought the whole of the western portion of the island under his control, and in 1822 he conquered the eastern portion of the island. During his presidency Haiti secured recognition of its independence by France, 1825. Boyer instituted a general policy of compulsory labor to build roads and was forced to sign a treaty of indebtedness with France that caused much dissatisfaction. In 1843 a revolution inspired by liberals brought about his overthrow, and Boyer fled to France where he remained until his death.

**Braden, Spruille.** 1894–    . American diplomat. b. Montana. Member of the American delegation to the Seventh Pan-American Conference at Montevideo, 1933; U. S. minister to Colombia, 1939–1942; minister to Chile, 1942; ambassador to Argentina, May–October, 1945; Assistant Secretary of State of Affairs of American Republics (Latin-American Affairs); resigned in 1947. As ambassador to Argentina and Assistant Secretary of State, he became known as a militant champion of democracy and opponent of PERÓN. His unsuccessful efforts to bring about the defeat of the latter in the Argentine election of 1946 were denounced by Argentine nationalists. See BLUE BOOK ON ARGENTINA.

**Brado do Ypiranga.** See GRITO DO YPIRANGA.

**Brasília.** The new federal capital of Brazil, located on the great central plateau in the central state of Goiás. Population 185,000 (est. 1962). The federal district covers 2,245 square miles and is 550 miles north of Saõ Paulo and 580 miles northwest of Rio de Janeiro, the old capital. The idea of relocating the Brazilian capital on an inland site is not new to Brazilian history. In 1789, when the Inconfidentes Mineiros began their abortive independence movement to free Brazil from Portuguese domination, it was planned to relocate the federal capital, and a search was begun for a likely site. In 1822 José Bonifácio de ANDRADA E SILVA, prime minister under PEDRO I, also proposed the transfer of the capital to the interior. After the downfall of the monarchy in 1889, the government of the new republic announced its intention to move the capital to the central plateau by incorporating the proposal in the new constitution. Commissions formed in 1894 and 1948 made no progress toward the selection of a site, and it was not until 1956 that the present site was finally chosen by a commission headed by Marechal José Pessoa. A joint Brazilian-United States team made the selection after considering topography, climate, drainage, water supply, power sources, recreation, availability of building materials, and many other factors. After the site was chosen the government appointed a committee to take charge of finances and construction and conduct the actual transfer of the capital to the new city. The plan for the new capital city was designed by the sculptor, Bruno Giorgio Lúcio Costa, and the public buildings were designed by the eminent architect, Oscar Niemeyer. On June 30, 1958, President Kubitschek and other officials were present for a dedication of the new capital in a religious ceremony at the *Palácio da Alvorada* (Palace of the Dawn). The transfer of the seat of the federal government was accomplished in April 1960. Highways connecting the capital with different parts of the country are partially completed and the plan to build an ocean port on the peninsula of Maraú in the state of Bahia will provide a natural sea approach to the capital.

**Bravo, Nicolás.** 1787?–1854. Mexican general and political leader. b. Chilpancingo of a CREOLE landowning family. Fought under MORELOS Y PAVÓN during the War of Independence; one of the leaders of the group that succeeded in overthrowing ITURBIDE in 1823; served as vice-president of Mexico, 1824–1827. He led a rebellion against President VICTORIA in 1827, was defeated, and exiled, 1828. He held various posts under SANTA ANNA and served as acting president in 1839 and again, 1842–1843. He was president for only a few days in 1846. Starting his career as a liberal and a rebel, he became a conservative and pawn of the reactionary elements of his country.

**Braz Pereira Gomes, Wenceslau.** b. 1868 in Brasópolis, Minas Gerais. President of Brazil. President of Minas Gerais, 1909–1910; vice-president of Brazil, 1910–1914; president 1914–1918. During his administration the nation made great strides as an economic power among the nations of the world. At the time of his election, the nation was suffering financial difficulties, but he was able to secure a large loan from the Rothschilds to meet needs. A number of Brazilian ships were sunk by German submarines, and Brazil declared war on Germany in 1917, thus becoming the only South-American republic to join the Allies as a belligerent.

**Brazil.** The largest country in South America, third in the Western Hemisphere, fifth in the world, with an area of 3,287,204 square miles. Its population of 82,696,000 (est. 1965) is the greatest in Latin America and accounts for nearly half of the population of South America. Approximately 61 per cent of the population are white, 11 per cent are Negro, 26 per cent are of mixed ancestry, and the remainder are Asians, Indians, and others. The language is Portuguese, but Italian and German are spoken in the southern states. The monetary unit for this country is the cruzeiro. The prevailing religion is Roman Catholicism, but there is complete freedom of worship. Brazil is a federal republic consisting of twenty-two states, four territories, and one federal district. The president of the republic is elected every five years by popular vote and cannot succeed himself. There is a congress formed by a senate and a chamber of deputies. Senators are elected for an eight-year term and members of the chamber of deputies serve four years. Voting is open to all literate citizens upon reaching the age of 18. The chief cities and their populations (1960) are: Rio de Janeiro, 3,307,163, the old capital and main port; São Paulo, 3,825,321, the great coffee center and fastest growing city in Latin America; Recife (Pernambuco), 797,234, an important seaport; Salvador (Bahia), 655,735, a seaport and old capital; Pôrto Alegre, 641,173; Belo Horizonte, 693,328, the mining center; and Belém (Pará), 402,000, the Atlantic port of the Amazon River. Brasília, the new capital, has a population of 185,000 (est. 1962). Brazil can be divided into three main geographical regions: the tropical and sparsely populated Amazon Basin, the largest drainage area in the world, that extends over more than one-third of Brazil's total area and is covered with a limitless equatorial forest filled with reptiles, birds, and small animals; the Brazilian plateau, 1,000 to 3,000 feet high, that includes the very little explored Mato Grosso, with a semi-tropical climate, its southern portion drained by the Paraguay River, and populated even more sparsely than the Amazon Basin; and finally, the Atlantic coastal region, composed of a low-lying plain and mountain ranges running parallel to the Atlantic coast. Most of the population is concentrated in this rich section, comprising the northeastern sugar-producing area, the rich mining district around Belo Horizonte, the coffee-producing state of São Paulo, Rio de Janeiro, and the southern rolling plains. The important river is the 1,800-mile-long São Francisco, navigable for about 1,000 miles and forming, near the Atlantic Ocean, the 260-foot Paulo Affonso Falls. The climate is generally warm on the coast and temperate toward the mountainous interior. Brazil is still mainly an agricultural country, with 60 per cent of the population engaged in that pursuit and related employments, but only approximately 4 per cent of its land surface is cultivated. More than half the producing land lies in the states of São Paulo, Minas Gerais, and Rio Grande do Sul. The most important crops are coffee, constituting 53

per cent of Brazil's total exports in 1962, and almost half the world's supply, rice, cotton, sugar, wheat, cacao, of which Brazil is the world's third largest grower, tobacco (in Bahia and Rio Grande do Sul), corn, and rubber (Manaus and Pará). Cattle are raised in all sections, but Rio Grande do Sul, the chief exporting center for Brazilian beef, supplies about 25 per cent of the total. After Argentina, Brazil ranks second in South America in the production and export of hides and skins. Among the country's mineral riches are coal and iron ore (Minas Gerais), manganese, diamonds, and oil. Industry is expanding rapidly, and Brazil is the most highly industrialized country in South America. Most of the manufactured products, however, are consumer goods, and Brazil has to import fuel, machines, chemicals, vehicles, and a few foodstuffs. The most important industries are the processing of foods and the production of textiles. The steel plant at Volta Redonda (State of Rio de Janeiro), 90 miles from São Paulo, is the largest producer of steel in the country. A valuable factor in Brazilian industrial development is the presence of unlimited water power. However it has not yet been harnessed to a sufficient degree to meet Brazilian needs. The one chief obstacle to the development of the country is the problem of transportation. The peculiar geographical features of Brazil make the construction of railroads difficult, and today the building of roads and motor transport are emphasized. About 75 per cent of the total railroad mileage (23,823) branches out from São Paulo and Rio de Janeiro. Approximately 50 per cent of the railroads, and 80 per cent of the mileage are owned by the federal government. About twenty-six Brazilian airlines serve many areas of the country, and even the most remote parts of the interior can be reached by air. Brazilian exports in 1962 totaled $1,214,000,000, and imports $1,475,000,000. The United States took 44.36 per cent of the exports and provided 30.30 per cent of the imports. According to the law, education in Brazil is compulsory and free, yet less than 49 per cent of the population is literate. There are ten universities, including one that is federalized, the University of Brazil in Rio de Janeiro, and six state universities.

Under the Treaty of TORDESILLAS (1494), which moved the demarcation line between Spanish and Portuguese possessions 270 leagues further to the west, Portugal acquired a large part of what is today Brazil. In 1500 the Brazilian coast was explored by Vicente Yáñez PINZÓN, who discovered the mouth of the Amazon. In May of the same year, the Portuguese commander Pedro Álvares CABRAL landed near present-day Bahia and in the name of the Portuguese Crown took possession of the territory, which he believed to be an island and to which he gave the name of Santa Cruz. The name Brazil came into being because redwood similar to Oriental brazilwood was found in great quantity on the newly-found coast. In 1532 the Portuguese Martim Affonso de SOUZA founded São Vicente on the coast southwest of present-day Santos, bringing in European grains, fruits, and cattle. Between 1534 and 1549 colonization was carried out under a *capitania* system that provided for twelve feudal captaincies along the Atlantic Ocean for a length of 150 miles and extending inland to the demarcation line, under the almost absolute authority of *donatários* (noble grantees), who were to administer the territory and promote colonization of their respective captaincies. The experiment proved generally unsuccessful, and in 1549 the post of governor general was created. The first governor general was Thomé de SOUZA, who founded the capital of the colony, São Salvador (Bahia) in 1549, fostered colonization, and created general prosperity in the colony. The cultivation of sugar cane, begun about 1520, developed rapidly, and the areas of Bahia and Pernambuco saw the establishment of many large plantations that used slave labor, Indian at first, Negro later. Under the third governor, Mem de SÁ (1558–1572), Rio de Janeiro was founded, colonization was furthered, and a French colony on the bay of Rio de Janeiro was destroyed. From 1580 to 1640, as a result of PHILIP II of Spain's acquisition in 1580 of the Portuguese throne, Brazil was a Spanish colony, and the Portuguese colonists had to fight against British attacks on coastal towns toward the end of the 16th century and later against the Dutch occupation of the northeast territory between the province of Maran-

hão and the São Francisco River, 1630–1654. In the south, the city of São Paulo was founded on the Piratininga plains after the middle of the 16th century, and the inhabitants of the region, the PAULISTAS, of mixed Indian and white blood, after having hunted Indian slaves in the coastal areas, began to organize expeditions into the interior in the early 17th century. These well-equipped parties, called *bandeiras*, explored the hinterland and brought back Indian slaves. They came into constant conflict with the Spanish JESUITS, who gathered the Indians into missions or *reducciones*. In 1629, after the destruction of these missions by the *paulistas* the Jesuits were forced to remove the Indians further south. After the middle of the 16th century the Portuguese government tried to eliminate Indian slavery, and increasing numbers of Negroes were imported from Africa to take the place of Indian slaves. However it was not until the middle of the 18th century that Indian slavery was legally prohibited. The 18th century was marked by: the development of the captaincy of Minas Gerais, where gold in great quantities had been discovered toward the end of the 17th century, and diamonds were found in 1727; the frequent conflicts between the Portuguese and the Spaniards over possession of the Banda Oriental (Uruguay); the recognition by Spain of Portuguese claims to large areas in the Amazon and Paraná basins (Treaties of Madrid, 1750, and San Ildefonso, 1777); the vigorous colonial administration of the Portuguese minister Pombal, who fostered commerce between Brazil and Portugal, easing many restrictions and organizing trading companies; the expulsion of the Jesuits in 1759; and an unsuccessful revolt against Portugal in Minas Gerais by Joaquim José da Silva Xavier (TIRADENTES) in 1789. In 1808, as a result of NAPOLEON's invasion of the Iberian Peninsula, the Portuguese Royal family, led by the regent Dom João, fled to Rio de Janeiro, where the regent became João VI on the death of his mentally-ill mother in 1816. Under Dom João, the economic life of Brazil was greatly stimulated and measures were taken to modernize the colony. The Banda Oriental (Uruguay) was conquered and attached to Brazil as the *Província Cis-*

*platina* (Cisplatine Province). In 1821, after a liberal upheaval in Portugal and because of growing demands in the mother country for João's return, he embarked for Lisbon, leaving his son PEDRO behind as regent. A year later Brazil revolted against the Portuguese government's attempts to restore the old colonial status, and Pedro, ordered to return to Portugal, refused and proclaimed Brazilian independence. He became Brazil's first emperor as Pedro I. Because of irregularities in his private life, his preference for Portuguese ministers over native Brazilians, his interest in Portuguese affairs, and his loss of the Cisplatine Province after a losing war with Argentina (1828), Pedro I was forced to abdicate (1831) in favor of his son PEDRO II (1825–1891). During the regency (1831–1840) there was much unrest and a number of federalist revolts took place in the provinces. After 1840, when Pedro was declared of age and ascended the throne as Pedro II, the revolts were brought under control and the country was able to develop peacefully except for a victorious but costly war with Paraguay (1864–1870). Agriculture, industry, and commerce developed and railroads were built. After 1850 coffee grown in São Paulo displaced sugar as Brazil's first crop, and after 1880 rubber became an important product of the Amazon Basin. There was much European immigration, especially to the southern states, and after slavery was abolished in 1888, the rate of immigration increased, most of the immigrants coming from Italy, Portugal, and Spain. Although Pedro II was an enlightened monarch, he was unpopular with a number of groups in the country because of various policies of his administration. Republicanism grew, and the army and landowners stopped giving the Empire their support, the former because of the spreading of republican propaganda in its ranks and the latter because of the suppression of slavery. A republic was proclaimed when a revolution forced the emperor to abdicate in 1889. The constitution of 1891 established a federal republic, the United States of Brazil, with a president elected for four years and two chambers. After some initial unrest Brazil enjoyed a period of stability under a succession of civilian presidents (1894–1910). After 1910 Brazil

had to weather a financial crisis because of the decline in rubber production due to foreign competition, and a drop in the production of coffee. During WORLD WAR I Brazil declared war on Germany in 1917, and the Brazilian navy cooperated with the Allies. Postwar Brazil was rocked by an antigovernmental revolt in 1924 and social unrest during the presidency of Washington Luis Pereira de SOUZA (1926–1930). In 1930 a revolt led by Getulio VARGAS, governor of Rio Grande do Sul, overthrew the government, and in 1934 Vargas, the provisional president, was elected president under a new constitution that provided for greater centralization, the election of the president by congress, and his nonreelection. The depression of the early thirties that had forced the government to destroy great quantities of coffee, in the hope of preserving a favorable price in the world market, was brought under control, but Vargas had to face unrest from the Communists on the left and the Fascist-minded INTEGRALISTAS on the right. In 1937 he proclaimed a new constitution, giving him dictatorial powers, setting up a corporate state, and making the president eligible to succeed himself. During WORLD WAR II Brazil declared war on the Axis in 1942 and sent an expeditionary force to Italy. In October 1945 Vargas was overthrown in a bloodless revolution, and in December of the same year General Eurico Gaspar DUTRA was elected president. A new constitution, adopted in 1946, made it impossible for a president to succeed himself. The Communist Party was outlawed in 1948. Under Dutra the economic development of the country was given a new impetus. Agriculture, industry, and commerce expanded rapidly, the state and city of São Paulo being the fastest-developing in the country. In the 1950 elections Getulio Vargas showed that his name still had great appeal among Brazilian voters. After having run on the ticket of the Brazilian Labor Party and advocating civil liberty, he was elected president. In the early 1950's Brazil was plagued by droughts and labor disturbances. Industrial expansion however, continued at an accelerated pace. In June 1954 a move to impeach President Vargas was initiated in the Brazilian congress because of Vargas' alleged intrigues with

PERÓN. After an air force major was killed by Vargas supporters on August 5, 1954 (the victim of shots actually directed at a newspaper editor who was an avowed enemy of the Vargas regime), the army insisted on the resignation of Vargas. On August 24th Vargas committed suicide. His successor was the vice-president, João Café Filho, a leader of the conservatives. The presidential election held in October 1955 chose the former Minas Gerais state governor, Juscelino Kubitschek de Oliveira; he took office in January 1956, after a brief military intervention. In 1956 Brasília was chosen as the new federal district to replace the old capital of Rio de Janeiro, and a federal commission was designated to finance, construct, and move the capital by 1960; in April of that year, the official transfer of the national capital was accomplished. In the elections of 1960 Jânio da Silva Quadros was elected to replace Kubitschek. The new president remained in office only seven months and then resigned. After an attempt by the military to prevent him from taking office, the vice-president, João Belchior Marques Goulart, became president for the balance of the term ending January 31, 1966. Because of a lack of confidence in Goulart the Brazilian congress, at the behest of the military, approved an amendment that established a parliamentary system giving the president of the council of ministers, or premier, increased responsibilities and a share of the executive power. Rising inflation and the government's inability to agree on economic and social reforms led to almost constant strikes, demonstrations, riots, and military action to preserve order. President Goulart persisted in maintaining friendly relations with Cuba despite pressure from the United States and from conservative elements within Brazil. Early in 1963 Brazilians voted to restore the presidential form of government and to abolish the parliamentary system that had taken away power from the president and made his office ineffectual. The leftist trend of the Goulart government and a desire to maintain a more conservative middle-ground position in the political spectrum led to a revolt against President Goulart, beginning on March 31, 1964. The president retired to his native state of Rio Grande do Sul. When it became evident that he had few supporters and could not maintain his position, he left Brazil on April 4 for Uruguay, where he had been granted asylum. Pascoal Ranieri Mazzili, president of the chamber of deputies, became acting president on April 2, in accordance with the constitution, and was replaced a short time later by General Humberto Castelo Branco, one of the military officers who engineered the revolt that overthrew the Goulart government. The administration of President Castelo Branco was able to improve the Brazilian economy, but the increasingly undemocratic nature of the new government alienated broad sectors of the population. Breaking with Brazils' recent practice of direct, popular elections, the Castelo Branco regime had Congress elect Arthur da Costa e Silva president in October 1966. He was inaugurated on March 15, 1967.

**Brazil, National Democratic Union of.** See NATIONAL DEMOCRATIC UNION OF BRAZIL.

**British Guiana or Guyana.** Former British crown colony on the Caribbean shore of South America, bounded on the northwest by Venezuela, on the west and south by Brazil, and on the east by Surinam, or Dutch Guiana. It has an area of 83,000 square miles and a population of about 683,000 (est. 1965), of which 44.5 per cent are East Indians, 38.2 per cent Negroes, 10 per cent mestizos, 2.9 per cent whites, and 4.3 per cent South American Indians. The capital is Georgetown with a population of 148,451 (1960). The country's economy is based on agriculture and mining. The main crops are sugar cane, rice, and coconuts. There are valuable bauxite deposits in the interior that are being increasingly exploited; bauxite made up about 24 per cent of the income realized from exports in 1962. The territory, originally consisting of three colonies, was captured by the British from the Dutch in 1796 and was formally acquired during 1814 and 1815. In 1831 the three colonies (Berbice, Demerara, and Essequibo) were consolidated into British Guiana. The abolition of slavery in 1834 and the Sugar Act of 1846, putting an end to the preference given to colonial sugar in the British market, proved disastrous for the sugar-based economy of Guiana, which suffered a severe crisis in 1847.

The shortage of labor was remedied by the arrival of Portuguese and Chinese laborers and especially by the importation of East Indians. Another crisis struck the economy at the end of the 19th century and another during the depression of the early 1930's. In the 19th century Great Britain and Venezuela became involved in a boundary dispute covering 42,000 square miles. In 1895, with the situation exceedingly tense, the United States urged both parties to submit their dispute to arbitration. This was done, and an international commission, meeting in Paris in 1899, handed down its decision, by which the greater part of the area in dispute was awarded to Great Britain. A boundary controversy with Brazil was settled in 1904 by the arbitration of the king of Italy, who awarded most of the disputed territory to Great Britain. Toward the end of 1953 British Guiana suddenly sprang into world news when Great Britain, worried over the possibility that the newly-elected government, dominated by the People's Progressive Party and Dr. Cheddi Jagan, would lead to Communism, sent warships and troops to the colony. The new constitution that had been inaugurated on April 1, 1953, was suspended on October 9 of the same year, and an interim legislative council governed the colony until 1957. In the elections of 1957 the left-wing People's Progressive Party won the majority of seats in the legislative assembly, and Cheddi Jagan was recognized as the chief minister. Internal autonomy was achieved with a new constitution that came into force after the 1961 elections and affirmed the dominant position of the People's Progressive Party. Independence within the British Commonwealth of Nations was accepted in principle in 1960 and obtained in May, 1966.

**British Honduras.** Known as **Belize** or **Belice** by the Guatemalans. A British crown colony in Central America, bounded by the Caribbean Sea on the east, Mexico on the north, and Guatemala on the west and south. It has an area of 8,867 square miles and a population of approximately 98,000 (est. 1962), of which 38.3 per cent are Negroes, 23.9 per cent Indians, 31 per cent mixed (mainly Negro and white parentage), 4 per cent whites, and 2.4 per cent Asian. The capital is Belize, with an approximate population of 32,864 (1960). The chief products of the colony are sugar, citrus fruits, mahogany, chicle, logwood, and cedar. Sugar, citrus fruits, and lumber constitute the chief exports, the greater part of these supplies going to Great Britain and other Commonwealth countries. English settlers established themselves in the Belize area about 1638, and the region soon became a logwood industry center. The British seized the territory at the end of the 18th century and it remained under their rule, although the surrounding areas were fighting for their independence from Spain. Guatemala claimed the territory in vain, and in 1859 finally ceded the disputed area to Great Britain, with a number of conditions attached to the agreement. The United States ignored this apparent violation of the MONROE DOCTRINE. In 1862 a lieutenant governor, acting under the governor of Jamaica, was in control of the government. A governor took over the administration in 1884. In 1948 a long-standing dispute between Great Britain and Guatemala over possession of British Honduras came to a head, and at one point Guatemala closed the border and Great Britain sent three warships to the vicinity. Guatemala claimed that since the road that was to have been built into northern Guatemala according to the treaty of 1859 had indeed never been constructed, it was under no obligation to abide any longer by the treaty in which British possession was recognized. In spite of the tension created, the dispute eventually subsided. In 1960 a new constitution was announced that permitted the people to choose their own prime minister, and the country remained a crown colony. On January 1, 1964, another new constitution took effect that gave the colony internal autonomy. The latter constitution provided for a cabinet headed by a premier, and a bicameral national assembly. The British governor of the colony retained his jurisdiction over defense and foreign affairs. The Guatemalan government severed relations with Great Britain on July 24, 1963, in a renewal of the dispute over the colony. The granting of internal self-government by Great Britain was interpreted as a violation of Guatemalan rights.

**British West Indian Colonies.** A number of islands belonging to the British Crown, situated in, or adjacent to, the Caribbean Sea. The islands include the Bahamas, Barbados, Bermuda, the Cayman Islands, and the Turks and Caicos Islands, the Leeward Islands composed of Antigua (with its dependencies Barbuda and Redonda), the component entity of St. Christopher (commonly called St. Kitts), Nevis, Anguilla, and Montserrat; the Windward Islands composed of Dominica, Grenada (with its dependencies in the Grenadines), St. Lucia, and St. Vincent ( with its dependencies in the Grenadines) ; and the British Virgin Islands. The combined area of the British insular possessions is 6,106 square miles, the total population is 883,000 (est. 1960). The population of the islands is largely Negro and mulatto. In August 1962 the former colonies of Jamaica (4,411 square miles, 1960 population 1,614,000) and Trinidad-Tobago (1,980 square miles, 1960 population 828,000) became independent members of the British Commonwealth of Nations. The economy of the islands is based on agriculture, the most important products being sugar, bananas, cotton, and cocoa. Rum is an important by-product. British occupation of the West Indies dates from the first half of the 17th century, when English settlers established themselves in the Lesser Antilles (St. Kitts, Nevis, Antigua, Montserrat, etc.). In 1655 an English expedition captured Jamaica from Spain, and notwithstanding frequent conflicts with the Dutch, the French, and the Spaniards, Great Britain was able to consolidate its position in the Caribbean, In the 18th century the intermittent conflict with Spain was marked by Admiral Vernon's capture of Porto Bello in the War of Jenkins' Ear (1739) and the British capture of Havana in the Seven Years' War (1762). During the War of American Independence, Great Britain was opposed by France, Spain, and the Netherlands and lost almost all its possessions in the West Indies. In the end, by the Treaty of Versailles of 1783, it was able to hold on to all except Tobago. During WORLD WAR II, the United States leased naval and air bases in the British West Indies for a period of ninety-nine years in exchange for fifty U.S. WORLD WAR I destroyers. From

1958 to 1962 Barbados, Jamaica, the Leeward Islands, Trinidad-Tobago, and the Windward Islands were incorporated into the Federation of the West Indies. The federation was dissolved in the latter year following Jamaica's decision to secede and become an independent state. Trinidad-Tobago, administered through a central government, became an independent nation immediately after Jamaica. Barbados gained its independence in 1966, and discussions have been held concerning the possibility of creating a new federation out of the colonies of the Windward and Leeward Islands.

**Brown, William** or **Guillermo.** 1777–1857. Irish-American naval fighter who aided the patriots in Buenos Aires. In the employ of Argentina as an admiral, he was placed in command of the newly-formed armada and ordered to block Montevideo and destroy the royalist fleet; he was successful, 1814. In 1826 he blockaded Colonia in Argentina's fight against Brazil, and was successful in breaking the Brazilian blockade of Buenos Aires and in defeating the Brazilian fleet at Juncal and Pozos, 1827. Under orders from Rosas to blockade Montevideo in 1845, Brown was obliged to surrender his squadron to an Anglo-French fleet.

**Brum, Baltasar.** 1883–1933. President of Uruguay. Journalist and political leader; served as foreign minister under President VIERA; president of Uruguay, 1919–1923. Considered one of the most enlightened and progressive leaders ever serving any Latin-American nation, he proposed in 1922 to abolish the office of the presidency in favor of a commission of nine men to run the country. On April 21, 1920, he delivered a speech at the University of Montevideo entitled "American Solidarity," in which he suggested that all American nations "formulate a declaration, similar to that of Monroe," thereby transforming the MONROE DOCTRINE to benefit all the countries of the Western Hemisphere. He is best-known for the "Brum Doctrine," which called for the establishment of an American league of nations.

**Bryan-Chamorro Treaty.** A treaty between Nicaragua and the United States, 1916, providing a payment to Nicaragua of $3,000,000 in return for the exclusive right of the United States to build a canal across the country. By virtue of the treaty, the United States was also granted a 99-year lease of the Great and Little Corn Islands and the right to a naval base in the Gulf of Fonseca. The treaty aroused protests from neighboring Costa Rica and El Salvador, who claimed the agreement violated their territorial rights, and they appealed to the Central American Court of Justice. The court handed down decisions condemning Nicaragua for signing the treaty and declaring that Nicaragua had infringed upon these neighbors' rights, but did not invalidate the treaty. The fact that neither Nicaragua nor the United States recognized the court's decision brought about that court's dissolution in 1918. To date no naval base has been built and the United States has not enforced its lease on the Corn Islands. The canal has not been constructed, and it does not seem that the project will be carried out in the foreseeable future.

**Bucareli y Ursúa, Antonio María.** 1717–1779. Spanish general and colonial administrator. Governor of Cuba, 1760–1771; viceroy of New Spain, 1771–1779. He was considered exceedingly able.

**Buccaneers** or **Freebooters.** The term buccaneer is no doubt derived from the French word *boucan,* a spit upon which meat is roasted or barbecued. A person using the *boucan* is a *boucanier.* Originally the term was used to designate the French freebooters who settled on the island of Tortuga, off Hispaniola. They made their living by selling the meat and hides from the animals they killed. Their chief sustenance was beef, which they roasted on *boucans.* In time the French term was corrupted and applied to European adventurers of the West Indies who preyed on Spanish shipping and colonists. Similarly, the term freebooter is a corruption of the Dutch word *vrijbuiter* (*vrij,* free, and *buit,* booty). In the 16th century buccaneers settled in the Antilles, especially in the occidental portion of Hispaniola (Santo Domingo), and hunted and sold hides in the neighboring posts. Later, with the consent of their governments, these French, English, and Dutch buccaneers

operated against the Spanish colonies in the Antilles. In 1640 they called themselves the "Brethren of the Coast" and were organized under the leadership of an admiral. Their main base of operations was the island of Tortuga, from which they set forth to attack and terrorize the Spanish Main and the Spanish Antilles. The Peace of Ryswick (1697) practically outlawed buccaneering. Those freebooters who continued their predatory activities instead of turning to lawful occupations were considered pirates and treated as such by the powers. They were vigorously pursued by French and Spanish naval forces and finally lost the island of Tortuga. Most famous and picturesque leaders of the buccaneers were Pierre le Grand, Henry Morgan, Jacques Cassard, Edward Teach (Blackbeard), and Captain Kidd.

**Buena Vista, Battle of.** An important engagement of the war between Mexico and the United States (1846–1848), called by the Mexicans the battle of La Angostura. At the beginning of 1847 an American army about 5,000 strong under General Zachary Taylor was encamped in open country 18 miles north of Saltillo (Coahuila). The Mexican general SANTA ANNA, who had returned from exile in September 1846 and had been appointed acting president of Mexico, set out from San Luis Potosí at the head of an army of about 25,000 to overwhelm the American army to the north. On February 21, Taylor learned of the approach of Santa Anna and hastily burned his stores and then retreated a dozen miles to La Angostura, near the hacienda of Buena Vista, where two high mountain ranges enclosed a road running through a broad pass. On February 23 Santa Anna attacked, and the Mexican army, flinging itself into a gap between the American army and the mountains on the eastern side of the pass, which had been left undefended by Taylor, succeeded in pushing back the left flank of the Americans. The latter were in a precarious position for a while, but finally their devastating artillery fire proved too much for the Indian conscripts of the Mexican army, and by nightfall the gap had been closed. Santa Anna, having suffered heavy losses, was in no mood to resume the battle and withdrew from the field during the night, leaving fires burning to conceal his retreat. The Mexicans had captured two American standards, but their losses exceeded 3,000, while those of the Americans amounted to little over 700.

**Buenos Aires** (province). The largest and most important province of the republic of Argentina with an area of 118,752 square miles and a population of 6,734,548 (est. 1960). It is separated from Uruguay by the Río de la Plata and is bounded on the east and south by the Atlantic Ocean. The rich, humid pampa constitutes most of its area and agriculture has prospered, the province growing the largest crops of corn, wheat, and linseed in the country. Cattle raising, however, carried on on large cattle ranches *(estancias)*, is still an important occupation of the area. Buenos Aires province is also the most important industrial region of Argentina and contains about one-third of the nation's railroad mileage. In cities like Avellaneda and Bahía Blanca there are meat-packing establishments *(frigoríficos)*, flour mills, shipyards, textile mills, and other industries. The principal ports are La Plata and Bahía Blanca, and there is a famous seashore resort at Mar del Plata. The capital of the province, La Plata, founded in 1880, has a population of 258,000 (1960). The largest city in the province is Avellaneda with a population of 355,000 (1960).

**Buenos Aires** (city). The federal capital of the republic of Argentina and the largest city in South America. It ranks very high as one of the largest cities in the world and has a population of more than 3,845,000 (1960). It is situated on the west bank of the Río de la Plata, about 170 miles from the Atlantic, and is endowed with an excellent port. The city is located in the southern temperate zone, the high temperature (about 92 degrees) being registered in January and the low (about 30 degrees) in July. The rainfall is abundant (annual average 33 inches). Buenos Aires is a cosmopolitan city, with a European appearance, which does not prevent it, however, from keeping its own original character. The streets of the city are mainly laid out in square blocks, and there are many wide avenues shaded by trees. The principal artery is the famous Avenida de Mayo, one mile long and 120 feet wide. At one of its ends is the Plaza de Mayo where the residence of the president, the CASA ROSADA (Pink House), is located. At the other extremity of the Avenida de Mayo is the national Capitol, the Palacio del Congreso. Other important buildings are the Cabildo, now a museum; the old Congress Hall; the Banco de la Nación; the important railroad station. El Retiro; the Stock Exchange; the opera house, Teatro Colón, which can seat 3,750 people; the Mitre Museum and Library; and the National Library. Northeast of the city is the beautiful Park of Buenos Aires, the Parque 3 de Febrero, occupying an area of five square miles, near which are found the popular Zoological and Botanical Gardens. The city is also the seat of the University of Buenos Aires and of a number of scientific institutions. Means of transportation are ample and include five subway systems. The port of Buenos Aires, which ranks among the largest in the world and is surpassed only by that of New York in the Western Hemisphere, is provided with the latest loading devices and accommodates ships from all parts of the world. Since Argentina's railroads branch out from Buenos Aires, the city is the focal transportation point in the country. Buenos Aires' airport, opened in 1949 and one of the largest in the world, links the city with the rest of the world by air. Branches of the Pan-American Highway connect it with Chile and Bolivia. Together with its suburbs, especially that of Avellaneda, Buenos Aires is the industrial center of the nation and is competing with São Paulo for first place in South America. Most of the industries are concentrated in Avellaneda and include meat packing (still the most important industry), flour milling, textiles, shipbuilding, and the production of chemicals. For history, see ARGENTINA.

**Buenos Aires, Conference of.** An Inter-American Conference for the Maintenance of Peace that met in December 1936. Its chief achievements were: the Declaration of Inter-American Solidarity and Co-operation, by which all the American states pledged themselves to the peaceful settlement of all disputes; the Convention for the Maintenance,

Preservation and Re-establishment of Peace, providing for consultation between the American states in the event of any threat to the peace of the hemisphere; and the Special Protocol Relative to Nonintervention, by which the American states declared inadmissible "the intervention of any one of them, directly or indirectly, and for whatever reason, in the internal or external affairs of any other." The United States accepted the Nonintervention Protocol without any reservations, thus definitely repudiating the BIG STICK policies pursued in the Caribbean area during the early years of the 20th century.

**Bula de Cruzada.** Spanish, meaning bull of crusade. An indulgence originally issued by the pope to Spanish kings granting privileges similar to those conferred upon the crusaders. In the 15th century, the kings of Spain and Portugal were allowed to sell these bulls to raise money for wars against the Moors. They were valid in the colonies, where their sale was administered by local Church authorities. It was, for all practical purposes, a tax, since the people were placed under great pressure to buy them. The institution lasted until the end of the colonial period.

**Bulnes, Francisco.** 1847–1924. Mexican critic, educator, engineer, and publicist. Associated with the *científicos* of the DÍAZ era, he aroused considerable antagonism by attempting to derogate JUÁREZ and other national heroes. Bulnes' best-known work is *El porvenir de las naciones hispano-americanas ante las conquistas de Europa y los Estados Unidos* (The Future of the Hispanic-American Nations in the Face of the Recent Conquests of Europe and the United States). He was also the author of *Las grandes mentiras de nuestra Historia* (The Great Lies of Our History), *El Verdadero Juárez* (The Real Juárez), *El Verdadero Díaz* (The Real Díaz), *La Verdad completa sobre México* (The Full Truth about Mexico), and others.

**Bulnes Prieto, Manuel.** 1799–1866. President of Chile. b. Concepción. Espoused the revolutionary cause and fought under SAN MARTÍN; commander-in-chief of the Chilean army at Yungay in 1839, where he destroyed SANTA CRUZ' forces and put an end to the

Peruvian-Bolivian Confederation. He served as president of Chile for two terms, 1841–1851, and was leader of the Conservative Party. During his administration there was peace and prosperity, and he instituted educational and economic reforms. A Chilean expedition built a fort in 1843 on the north coast of the Strait of Magellan, which it called Bulnes (today Punta Arenas). He appointed the capable Manuel MONTT TORRES minister of education, founded 300 new schools, and in 1842 had the University of Chile chartered. He also opened a school of agriculture, one for training in arts and crafts, and conservatories of music and art.

**Bunau-Varilla, Philippe Jean.** 1860–1940. French engineer. Endeavored to get the French government to construct a Panama canal and worked on the attempts made in 1884–1889 and again in 1894. Representing the New Panama Canal Company, successor to the defunct de Lesseps organization, he worked to persuade the U. S. government to adopt the Panama route in preference to Nicaragua, and after Colombian failure to ratify the HAY-HERRÁN TREATY, helped to bring about the movement for the independence of Panama. He was minister from the new Republic of Panama to the United States in 1903; he negotiated and was largely responsible for the HAY-BUNAU-VARILLA TREATY that gained control of the Panama Canal Zone for the United States.

**Burgos, Laws of.** The first Spanish code of laws dealing with the government and the instruction of the American Indians. The controversy over the status of the Indians, precipitated in 1511 by the DOMINICAN friar Antonio de Montesinos' denunciation of the enslavement of the natives, led King FERDINAND V of Castile to promulgate a body of thirty-two laws at Burgos, Spain, on December 27, 1512. Under the laws Indian labor was regulated and maximum working hours were established. The natives were assured of adequate food and shelter, and royal officials were to insure the good treatment of the Indians. However the laws stipulated that a third of all Indians were to work in the mines and that during at least nine months of the year they were to work for the Spaniards. The laws were intended to eliminate the many abuses perpetrated against the natives, but they were never properly enforced and the Indians continued to be exploited and mistreated.

**Busch, Germán.** 1904–1939. President of Bolivia. As a lieutenant colonel and acting chief of the army general staff, he directed a bloodless coup to oust President TEJADA SÓRZANO and install David TORO (1936). He became provisional president after a coup d'etat in July 1937, which ousted Toro. The government abandoned state socialism and returned to a democratic-republican form of government. When Busch was formally elected president and inaugurated in May 1938, there were many economic problems that his administration attempted to solve: an agreement was signed with Brazil (1938) that established railroad communication between the two countries; oil was to be exploited. In October 1938 he promulgated a new constitution, and a treaty of peace and a boundary settlement with Paraguay were signed (1938). Early in 1939 the economic and political conditions of the country were so bad that Busch was forced to dismiss congress and set up a dictatorship; the lower courts were abolished and he ruled by decree. On May 10, 1939, the government, with the approval of the supreme court, expropriated the oil properties of the Standard Oil Company. A barter agreement was signed with Germany, exchanging oil, minerals, and other products for German manufactured goods worth four million marks. He had other economic plans, which were never carried out because of his death, probably by suicide, in August 1939.

**Bustamante, Anastasio.** 1780–1853. General and conservative president of Mexico. b. Jiquilpan, Michoacán. Fought with the Spanish against the independence movement headed by HIDALGO and MORELOS; supported ITURBIDE and the PLAN OF IGUALA in 1821; served as vice-president under Gómez Pedraza in 1828, and held the same position under Gómez Pedraza's successor, GUERRERO, from 1829 to 1830. He joined the conservatives in revolt against Guerrero, became president of Mexico, and served from January 1830 to August 1832, when he was driven out by liberals led by SANTA ANNA. Forced into exile, he was recalled from England to become president during the period of conservative rule and served from 1837 to 1841. Considered an honest, well-intentioned man who was often led by stronger men, he was overthrown in 1841 by a military coup d'etat headed by Santa Anna and PAREDES Y ARRILLAGA.

**Bustamante, Carlos María de.** 1774–1848. Mexican historian, publisher, soldier, and liberal statesman. b. Oaxaca. He was editor of the first daily newspaper, *El Diario de Méjico*, from about 1805 until 1812, when he served as an army officer in Mexico's first war for independence. He accompanied ITURBIDE as his secretary on his march to the capital in 1821. He founded the weekly newspaper *La Avispa de Chilpancingo*. He was considered an outstanding 19th-century historian of the revolutionary period in Mexico, and was the author of *Cuadro histórico de la Revolución de América, Galería de antiguos príncipes Mejicanos, Apuntes para la historia del gobierno del general Santa Ana,* and other works.

**Bustamante y Rivero, José Luis.** 1894– . President of Peru. Distinguished jurist and diplomat. He served as minister of justice, minister to Uruguay, and ambassador to Bolivia, 1945. Nominated by the liberals on the acceptance of his Memorandum of La Paz, which placed the country above the special interest of the party, he was backed by HAYA DE LA TORRE and elected president in July 1945, largely through the vote of the *apristas*. The conflict between the conservatives and the liberal elements in his cabinet caused the president's position to be a difficult one, and in January 1947 *apristas* in his cabinet resigned and the conservatives refused to cooperate, causing the government to come to a virtual standstill. In October 1948 his government was overthrown by the conservatives in a military coup d'etat and he departed for Argentina.

# C

**Caamaño, José María Plácido.** 1838–1901. President of Ecuador. b. Guayaquil. Leader of a conspiracy against the anti-clerical dictator VEINTEMILLA and exiled in 1882, he led the successful conservative revolt ousting him in 1883. Caamaño served first as provisional president in 1883 and then, after the adoption of the new constitution, served as president from 1884 to 1888. He served as minister to Washington, 1889–1890. He retired to Spain in 1895.

**Caatinga.** Semiarid area of northeastern Brazil; also a thornbush native to the region.

**Caballerías.** Small land grants awarded by the Spanish Crown to *caballeros* (mounted soldiers) during the period of the reconquest of Spanish soil from the Moors, and during the conquest of the New World. In 1513 a law encouraging settlement in the New World was passed stipulating that two general types of land grants, the *peonía* and *caballería*, would be allotted. The *peonía*, the smaller of the two grants, contained approximately 100 acres and was awarded to pensioned-off soldiers or as spoils; the *caballería* contained from 500 to 1,000 acres and was granted to *caballeros*. Title to the land was granted on the condition that the recipient occupied the land, and only after improvements were carried out. The *caballería* is also a varying unit of land measure in several of the Latin-American countries.

**Caballero, Bernardino.** 1831–*ca.* 1892. President of Paraguay and founder of the Colorado Party. b. in Brazil. Served as general in the PARAGUAYAN WAR (1865–1870);

taken prisoner in 1870. He also served as minister of war and marine during Rivarola's administration (1870), minister of the interior under Jovellanos (1871–1874), minister of justice and education under Gill Aquinaga (1874–1877) and minister of the interior under Barreiro (1878–1880). Acting president, 1880–1882, and president for the four-year term, 1882–1886, he continued to wield political influence through the Colorado Party until his death.

**Cabello y Mesa, Francisco Antonio.** d. 1812. Spanish colonel and journalist. Publisher of the first newspaper in colonial Argentina, entitled *Telégrafo Mercantil, Rural, Político, Económico e Historiógrafo del Río de la Plata*, first printed in 1801. He had had, at one time, some editorial connection with the *Mercurio Peruano*, which was published at Lima, Peru, from 1791 to 1795. Cabello succeeded through his paper in stimulating CREOLE intellectual activity and a national feeling. However, it had difficulties and financial troubles and lasted only one year. He founded the *Sociedad Patriótica Literaria y Económica* (Patriotic Literary and Economic Society). He died in Spain, fighting French invasion forces.

**Cabeza de Vaca, Álvar Núñez.** 1490–1560. Spanish explorer and colonial administrator. b. Jerez de la Frontera. Served as a soldier in several European campaigns; treasurer of NARVÁEZ expedition of 1527–1528. Imprisoned by Indians after being wrecked off the Texas coast in 1528, he was able to escape and reached Mexico City by traveling across the northern part of the country from 1530 to

1536. His report of the Narváez expedition led to those of Niza, 1539, and CORONADO Y VALDÉS. He returned to Spain in 1537 and was made *adelantado* and governor of the La Plata territory. He set out from Spain in 1540 and led the expedition to the coast of Brazil. From there he proceeded overland to Asunción, arriving on March 11, 1542, but failed in an attempt to reach Peru by overland route in 1543. He was imprisoned in Asunción by his enemies, who elected IRALA in his place in 1544, and was sent back to Spain where he was tried and convicted in 1551 of charges brought against him. He was banished to Africa for a period of five years after which he was recalled and appointed to a judgeship in Seville.

**Cabildo.** The town government of Spanish America. It consisted of from four to twelve *regidores* (town councilmen), who in the 16th century were elected annually, and in the 17th century could purchase their offices; two *alcaldes ordinarios* (judges) chosen by the council; an *alférez* (ensign); an *alguacil* (constable), and other officials. The many duties of the *cabildo* included the supervision of public works, sanitation and health, enforcement of police regulations, administration of property, regulation of prices and wages, and numerous other functions. The authority exercised by the *cabildo* varied. It had more autonomy in outlying provinces than in the large cities. Particularly powerful were the *cabildos* of Buenos Aires and Asunción (Paraguay). Although the *cabildo* lost much power in the late colonial period, it still retained sufficient vigor to permit the colonists to gain experience in self-government.

**Cabildo Abierto.** An extension of the *cabildo.* When matters of grave importance were to be discussed, the governor, on his own initiative or at the request of the *cabildo,* called an open *(abierto)* meeting of all the principal citizens of the town. Although all members of the *cabildo abierto* were entitled to speak and to vote, they functioned more as an advisory body. The *cabildo abierto* played an important role in the defense of Buenos Aires against the British in 1807. In 1810 *cabildos abiertos* in a number of different cities put forward demands for self-government as long as the French were in occupation of Spain. This was the beginning of the struggle for independence.

**Caboclo.** Brazilian term first applied to Indian farmers. Later *caboclo* was used to designate a crossbreed of white and Indian stock, and now is generally used to mean any lower-class rural person.

**Cabot, Sebastián.** *ca.* 1476–1557. Explorer. Son of John Cabot. b. Venice. Commander of the expedition that explored the La Plata area from 1526 to 1530. Authorized by Charles V, in April 1526, Cabot, a pilot major of Spain in the employ of Seville merchants, started on an expedition to the Moluccas and Cathay. He arrived instead in La Plata in 1527, decided to explore that territory, and found and rescued survivors of previous expeditions. He explored the Paraná River. He built a fort at Sancti-Spiritus, which was the first settlement in the Plata region, lasting until 1532. He explored the Paraguay River, returning to Spain in 1530 with samples of gold and silver.

**Cabral, Pedro Álvares.** *ca.* 1460–1526. Portuguese navigator and explorer. Sent by King Manoel I of Portugal in 1500 to establish trade with East Indies, after Vasco da Gama's return announcing his discovery of a new route to India. He was in command of a fleet of 13 vessels, which traveled west, landed on the coast of Brazil on April 22, 1500, and took possession of the territory in the name of Portugal. It is uncertain whether Cabral reached Brazil by accident because of a storm, or whether he was obeying secret orders from the Portuguese government. Cabral believed Brazil to be an island, calling it SANTA CRUZ, and sent a ship and messenger back to inform the king of his new land. His expedition strengthened Portugal's claim to Brazil, already established by the TREATY OF TORDESILLAS. He then traveled east, losing four ships in a storm off the Cape of Good Hope, but finally succeeded in reaching Calicut, India, where he was able to establish a trading post.

**Cabrillo, Juan Rodríguez de.** d. 1543. Portuguese explorer. b. Portugal. Went to Mexico with NARVÁEZ in 1520, and served with CORTÉS at the capture of Mexico City in 1521. Sent by Antonio de MENDOZA, the viceroy of New Spain, to search for the elusive "Strait of Anian" that was supposed to cross Mexico, he set sail in 1542 and discovered San Diego Bay. He then sailed northward beyond the Golden Gate, passing, but without seeing, San Francisco Bay. He turned back and died on the small island of San Miguel in the Santa Barbara Channel, January 3, 1543. Bartolomé Ferrelo, his pilot and successor, turned northward the following year and reached the Oregon coast.

**Cacao.** The cacao tree is native to the New World and was widely cultivated in America at the time of the conquest. In the colonial period it was, for a long time, one of the principal crops of the Caribbean area, the main producer being the territory around Caracas, Venezuela. It also became the staple crop of the *audiencia* of Quito (Ecuador). The success of cacao was due to its tremendous popularity in Europe, its high nutritive value, and the fact that relatively few slaves were needed for its production. On the other hand there were certain drawbacks in the cultivation of the product, such as, the difficulty of keeping it in damp climates, and the prolonged period of eight to ten years required for maturity of the tree. Venezuela began to export cacao in the first decades of the 17th century and profited greatly from smuggling carried out by the Dutch after they captured the island of Curaçao in 1634. Venezuela's annual production for the period 1800–1806 amounted to 21,230,000 pounds and by 1814 it was supplying two-thirds of Europe's total consumption. During the 19th century Ecuador considerably increased its output and for a time was the first producer of cacao in the world, until it was overtaken by Brazil around 1910. Beginning in 1924 Ecuador's production was severely reduced by the witch broom disease attacking its cacao trees, but today the country still remains one of the world's largest producers. Brazil, where cacao is grown mostly in the south of the state of Bahia, produces about 175,000 metric tons of beans annually, of which the greater part is exported to the United States. In the Caribbean area the Dominican Republic is at present the leading producer of cacao, with Venezuela second. While cacao is still an important crop in Latin America, its former predominance in world markets has been lost; African countries supply about 63 per cent of the world's annual production, with Ghana and Nigeria the major producers.

**Cáceres, Andrés Avelino.** *ca.* 1833–1923. President of Peru. b. Ayacucho. Military attaché at Peruvian legation in Paris, 1857–1860; fought as general in WAR OF THE PACIFIC, 1879–1883; head of provisional government of Lima, after its capture by Chileans, 1883. He led the revolt, 1885–1886, against President IGLESIAS, who had been supported by Chileans; president of Peru (military dictator), 1886–1890. Under Cáceres the government was organized on a more modest and economical scale and a new revenue system was introduced that included various excises and heavy taxes on exports and imports. He was minister to France and Great Britain, 1890–1894, and served again as president in 1894–1895. He was defeated by PIÉROLA, leader of the Democratic Party, and lived outside Peru from 1895 to 1903. He was again active in political affairs in Peru and served as minister to Italy, 1905–1911.

**Cacique.** Word of Indian origin meaning chief, first heard by Spanish conquistadores in Cuba. The *cacique* was an Indian prince, the head of a tribe, or the governor of a region. Throughout the Spanish-speaking countries the word has been extensively applied to those individuals who exert too great an influence on local politics. It is the equivalent of the English "boss."

**Caciquismo.** The equivalent of the English "boss rule," a system under which the CACIQUE or local boss rules local politics. Throughout Latin American history *caciquismo* has been a distinctive trait.

**Cacos.** Haitian peasants used as political armies by succeeding presidents and men of power. In 1918, during the period of intervention by the United States, there was an order for compulsory labor on the roads. The *Cacos* in the north and west revolted, and for two years fought against the government.

In the course of the insurrection almost 2,000 people lost their lives. The struggle was finally suppressed by the U.S. Marines. The term *Cacos* was also used to designate one of the two chief political factions that came into being in Central America during the period immediately preceding independence. The *Cacos*, led by prominent CREOLES, among them José Matías DELGADO and Dr. Pedro Molina, favored independence and professed liberal political tenets. Opposed to the *Cacos* were the *Gazistas*, led by José Cecilio de Valle, who took a more conservative view of the political future of Central America. Although Valle was interested in liberty and the political rights of Central Americans, he had a deep interest in the protection of property and a belief in evolutionary change. The conflict between the two factions was more a struggle for political power than a clear-cut issue over the question of independence.

**Cafuso** or **cafús.** In Brazil, a term used to describe a person of Indian and Negro descent.

**Caldas, Francisco José de.** 1770–1816. Colombian scholar, teacher, and patriot. b. Popayán. Considered a brilliant scientist, he was the author of books on geography and natural history. He studied under MUTIS, directed (1808–1811) the *Semanario del nuevo reyno de Granada*, one of the first periodicals published in colonial Latin America and noted for its scientific contributions. He worked with HUMBOLDT and Bonpland. He was shot during Morillo's "Reign of Terror."

**Caldera Rodríguez, Rafael.** 1916– . Venezuelan political leader. Head of C.O.P.E.I. (Committee Organized for Independent Elections), he was sympathetic to the 1945 revolution by *Acción Democrática*, but opposed the new government's socialist policies, preferring closer cooperation with the Church and opposing educational reforms as anticlerical. A lawyer, he served as attorney general under a junta. Nominated by C.O.P.E.I. and the Democratic Republican Union as presidential candidate in election of 1947, he was defeated by GALLEGOS. After the overthrow of the Pérez Jiménez government (1952–1958) Caldera was a candidate for the

presidency, 1958. Candidate of the Social Christian Party for President, 1963, he ran second in the field of seven candidates.

**Calderón Guardia, Rafael Ángel.** 1900– . President of Costa Rica. Educated at the Colegio Seminario de Costa Rica; received his M.D. at the University of Louvain; chief surgeon, San Juan de Dios Hospital; deputy, national congress, 1934–1942, serving as vice-president, 1935–1937, and president, 1938–1939; leader of the National Republican party; president of Costa Rica, 1940–1944; toured United States, Guatemala, and Cuba. The U.S. EXPORT-IMPORT BANK loaned Costa Rica $4,600,000 for the completion of the Pan-American Highway through the country. He established a National University in which were to be incorporated all existing professional schools. A candidate of the Liberal Party in the presidential elections of 1948, he was forced into exile in Nicaragua after the FIGUERES FERRER revolt. Supported by Nicaraguan *calderonista* elements, he attempted unsuccessful invasions of Costa Rica in December 1948, and again in January 1955. Elected to the national congress in February 1958, he returned from exile for the first time, June 1958, and was enthusiastically received. He was the unsuccessful presidential candidate of the National Republican Party in 1962.

**Callao.** The chief port of the republic of Peru, 18 miles southwest of Lima, with a population of 161,000 (est. 1964). It has excellent shipping facilities, including a 570-foot-long drydock. It is also important as an industrial center, its manufacturing establishments including foundries, flour mills, and lumber mills. The city was founded in 1537. In the colonial period it was the richest port on the Pacific, where goods from Europe were landed, and Peruvian silver and gold were loaded for shipment to Spain. Callao's prosperity aroused the greed of such pirates as Drake and Cavendish, who attacked it in 1578 and 1587 respectively. In 1746 it was destroyed by a tidal wave coming on the heels of a severe earthquake; it was rebuilt at a distance of less than one mile from the first port. During the War for Independence, Callao changed hands several times and was the last Spanish-held position in South America. It finally surrendered in 1826 to the South-American patriots. In 1866 it was shelled by Spanish naval forces during the war between Spain and Chile and Peru. In 1881 Callao surrendered to the Chilean Army during the WAR OF THE PACIFIC, and was returned to Peru after the signing of the Treaty of ANCÓN, 1883. In May 1940 an earthquake caused considerable damage.

**Calleja Del Rey, Félix María.** Conde de Calderón. 1750–1820. Spanish general and viceroy of New Spain. b. Medina del Campo. Sent to Mexico about 1789, he succeeded in defeating HIDALGO and MORELOS in 1811 and 1814 respectively. He was called "the butcher" because of his vicious treatment of prisoners, but was one of Spain's ablest generals. He served as viceroy of New Spain, 1813–1816.

**Calles, Plutarco Elías.** 1877–1945. President of Mexico. b. Guaymas. Schoolteacher and farmer; military service under OBREGÓN in conflicts with HUERTA and VILLA during the Revolution; governor of Sonora, 1917; secretary of *gobernación* in Obregón administration, 1920–1924; president, 1924–1928. He carried forward the program of the Revolution, pushing agrarian reform, supporting organized labor, building rural schools, and launching measures for public health. His attempt to enforce the constitutional provision calling for the registration of priests by state caused a serious conflict with the Church, 1926. The order that oil companies should exchange ownership of fields for fifty-year leases led to diplomatic conflict with the United States in 1926, which was settled by compromise in 1927 through the efforts of U.S. representative Dwight MORROW. After retiring from the presidency in 1928, Calles continued to be the real ruler of Mexico during the administrations of PORTES GIL, ORTIZ RUBIO, and Abelardo RODRÍGUEZ, 1928–1934, and was known as *jefe máximo*. During this period he swung over to more conservative policies, opposing further land and labor reform, but continued to attack the Church. He rapidly lost power after the election of CÁRDENAS in 1934, and was expelled from Mexico in 1936 on the charge of plotting rebellion. He lived in the United States but was allowed to return in 1941 and resume his post in the army.

**Calvo, Carlos.** 1824–1906. Argentine diplomat and historian. b. Montevideo. Best known as an authority on international law, he is responsible for the CALVO DOCTRINE. He served as Paraguayan envoy to London and played an important part in the settlement of the Alabama Claims. His outstanding work was the *International Law of Europe and America in Theory and Practice*, published in two volumes in 1868, with an additional six volumes, 1887–1896.

**Calvo Doctrine.** Proposed by the Argentine diplomat Carlos CALVO in a treatise on international law published in 1868, it maintained that all countries should have equal rights over aliens and that the collection of indemnity should be equal for all, giving no advantage to stronger states. It attempted to force foreign property owners to seek judicial review in their claims against Latin-American countries within each country itself, rather than to rely on diplomatic intervention. Calvo also claimed in his book on international law that no country had the right to resort to armed intervention in the collection of a debt. A Calvo clause in an official document of any Latin-American country provides that an alien receiving a concession contract must renounce any right to prefer diplomatic claims in regard to that contract.

**Cámara de Indias.** See CONSEJO DE CÁMARA DE LAS INDIAS.

**Campero, Narciso.** 1815–1896. President of Bolivia. Served as minister of war in 1872; president, 1880–1884. He was commander of the Peruvian and Bolivian armies in the war with Chile at Tacna and was defeated, 1880. It was a difficult time for Bolivia because Chile succeeded in closing off its access to the sea.

**Campisteguy, Juan.** 1859–1937. President of Uruguay. b. Montevideo of Basque descent. Teacher and journalist. He took an active part in the overthrow of the Santos government in 1886. A *colorado* member, he served as secretary of the treasury in 1897 and again in 1899, and as president, 1927–1931.

**Campomanes, Pedro Rodríguez, Count of.** 1723–1803. Spanish economist and statesman. b. Asturias. President of the Council of Castile, 1762; director, Royal Academy of History. He studied the causes of Spain's financial difficulties and advocated important reforms, which were adopted by the Crown and resulted in changes in the monopolistic trade practices with the colonies and brought about an increase in trade. He was the author of *Tratado de la regalía de la amortización*, 1765, *Discurso sobre la educación popular de los artesanos y su fomento*, 1774–1776, and other works.

**Campos, Francisco da Silva.** 1891–   . Brazilian political leader. b. Dôres do Indaya, Minas Gerais. Close aide to VARGAS; sponsored the University Reform movement of 1931; writer of the constitution of 1937, which had fascistic overtones; minister of justice and minister of the interior in the cabinet of Vargas, 1937–1943. He wrote the book entitled *O Estado nacional*, published in 1939, which described the "New State." In 1942, when Brazil entered World War II and joined the Pan-American front, Campos was forced out of the government.

**Campos Salles, Manoel Ferraz de.** 1846–1913. President of Brazil. b. Campinas, São Paulo state. Served as deputy from 1884–1889; minister of justice; governor of São Paulo, 1896–1898. President of Brazil from 1898 to 1902, his was an able and constructive administration that enacted many reforms and settled boundary disputes, including one with Bolivia over the Acre territory, and one with French Guiana. He was able to put the economic and financial conditions of the country in good order for the first time in many years. Campos went to Europe and from the Rothschild banking house secured a funding loan of $10,000,000, which permitted a three-year suspension of service on debt and arranged for the issuing of bonds bearing interest at five per cent. The Rothschild loan was to be guaranteed by the customs revenue from Rio de Janeiro and other Brazilian ports, and the Brazilian government pledged itself to incur no other debt without the consent of the bankers, and to arrange for the retirement of paper money to the amount of the loan; payment on foreign debt was resumed in 1901. During his administration Brazil was able to maintain friendly relations with her neighbors.

**Capitania.** Old territorial division used in the Portuguese colonies, particularly in Brazil. In 1532, in order to develop the recently acquired colony of Brazil and to counteract the danger from French operations against Portugal in that part of the world, the Portuguese king, João III, divided it into twelve *capitanias*, giving each to a Portuguese noble, known as the *donatário*, who was to colonize and develop his grant. The results were not satisfactory except in São Vicente and in Pernambuco. In 1549 João III appointed Thomé de SOUZA as governor general of Brazil and made Bahia the capital of the colony, thus sharply reducing the powers of the *donatários*, who, however, remained in possession of their grants. Officials called captains or governors took over the functions of the *donatários* and the *capitanias* gradually went out of existence, the last reverting to the Crown in 1754.

**Capitão-do-mato.** Portuguese, meaning captain of the forest. It was the name given the official in colonial Brazil who was charged with the responsibility of recapturing fugitive slaves.

**Capitão-mor.** In colonial Brazil, the commander-in-chief of the military forces of a province.

**Capitulación of 1492.** A contract entered into by Queen ISABELLA of Castile and Christopher COLUMBUS in April 1492, stipulating that Columbus was to be viceroy and governor for the Crown of Castile of all lands to be discovered, and therefore was to be entitled to one-tenth of all revenues from the discovered territories, and that he should have the right of presenting three candidates for any post of profit under him, from whom the Crown was to select one; that he would also bear the title of admiral and as such would have the final word in matters pertaining to the trade of the new-found regions; that he would be entitled to one-eighth of the profits accruing from the Indies if he contributed one-eighth of the cost of the expedition; and that he was accorded the title of captain general. Eventually the Spanish sovereigns regretted the granting of such vast powers to Columbus, and upon the latter's failure in the colonization of Hispaniola (Santo Domingo), his former authority was rescinded in 1500.

**Captain General.** In colonial Spanish America, a captain general was an official who had practically the same responsibilities as the viceroy, but in less important areas, particularly in regions where the danger from Indian depredations and foreign aggression presented problems of defense. Generally a captain general was dependent on the viceroy and needed his permission on important decisions. However, in some cases, as in Chile, they were given considerable autonomy and were directly responsible to the COUNCIL OF THE INDIES. Primarily, the title of captain general denoted military rank and was not only bestowed on high military officials but also on other high officials, such as a viceroy or a president of an *audiencia*, who were given military jurisdiction. After the middle of the sixteenth century the title was used to designate a royal governor who was independent of viceregal authority and subject directly to the king and council. Captain general was also the title by which the governor of colonial Brazil was known in the 16th and 17th centuries.

**Capuchins.** Religious order active in the colonization of Latin America. They settled in the 16th century in Brazil, first in Bahia and later in Rio de Janeiro. By the middle of the 18th century they controlled 15 Indian villages in northern Brazil. The Capuchins were also instrumental in bringing under control the lower Orinoco valley in Venezuela. Their first mission in the area dates from 1724 and by 1766 there were 18 villages with more than 5,000 Indians under their control.

**Carabobo, Battle of.** Famous battle of June 24, 1821, which assured the independence of Venezuela from Spain. Marching north toward the town of Valencia with an army of 6,500 men, including English, Scotch, and Irish volunteers, BOLÍVAR, ably seconded by PÁEZ, attacked the Spanish forces, numbering about 5,000 men, on the plains of Carabobo. There the Spanish general, LA TORRE, had drawn up his army to block the road to Valencia. Patriot columns under Páez assaulted the Spanish right wing and after fierce fighting, in which the British Legion distinguished itself, succeeded in forcing the enemy to retreat. At the same time, South-American cavalry smashed the Spanish forces in the center. Soon the whole Spanish army dissolved under the blows of the South Americans. About 3,500 of its men were dead or prisoners. The rest managed to escape through Valencia to Puerto Cabello. The battle that had begun at eleven o'clock in the morning, lasted only an hour. Bolívar's losses were not heavy, but a number of first-rate officers had been killed. A month later Bolívar entered Caracas, and all Venezuela, with the exception of Puerto Cabello and Cumaná, was free of Spanish troops.

**Caracas.** The capital of the republic of Venezuela, situated 3,100 feet above sea level on the slopes of the Venezuelan coastal range, about 6½ miles from its port La Guaira, with a population of about 739,255 (metropolitan area, 1,265,001, 1961). Because of its altitude the city has a relatively healthy climate, with annual temperatures varying little (average maximum 72 degrees, average minimum 68 degrees). Regularly laid out, Caracas has broad avenues and many parks and plazas. It has an Old-World aspect, but in many respects is a modern city. The new Avenida Bolívar, running through the heart of the town, has three levels: The top level is reserved for local traffic, the second for parking, and the bottom level is a through avenue. The main square is the Plaza Bolívar, with a statue of the Liberator. Close by are the Capitol, the Government Palace, the Bolívar Museum, the National Pantheon containing the remains of Bolívar, the Central University, and the Casa Bolívar, birthplace of the Liberator, now a national shrine. Because it is surrounded by mountains, Caracas is difficult to reach and until recently the journey from its nearby port of La Guaira took two hours by rail and one hour by car, as the railroad and the highway had to wind their way around the steep slopes of the Andes while making the ascent. In 1953 a new highway was completed, cutting through the mountains and reducing travel time to twenty minutes. A railroad 99 miles long, using 86 tunnels and 217 bridges, connects Caracas with Valencia. The city is also served by air transportation. Industries in Caracas include textiles, clothing, shoes, paper, glassware, perfumes, an auto-assembly plant, sugar refineries, meat-packing plants, furniture making, brewing, and the making of cigarettes and matches. As cacao, coffee, and tobacco are all grown in the Caracas area, the city is an export center for these products. Caracas was founded in 1567 by Diego de Losada, who, having in mind the Indian Caracas tribe of the region, called it Santiago de León de Caracas. In colonial times Caracas was a prosperous town, deriving its wealth mainly from the nearby cacao and tobacco plantations. In 1595 it was sacked by the English and in 1766 it was raided by the French. Caracas is the birthplace of Simón BOLÍVAR (1783) and of the famous patriot Francisco de MIRANDA (ca. 1750). In 1811 Venezuelan independence was proclaimed in Caracas and the long War of Independence began. The following year the city suffered greatly from an earthquake, which contributed to a comeback of the royalist forces, as they convinced the population that the earthquake was a manifestation of the wrath of God aroused by the revolutionist activities of the patriots. In 1829, after Venezuela had been part of Great Colombia for a few years, Caracas became the capital of the independent nation of Venezuela. In 1954 Caracas was the site of the Tenth Inter-American Conference (CARACAS CONFERENCE).

**Caracas Conference.** The Tenth Inter-American Conference that met at Caracas, Venezuela in March 1954, and was attended by all American republics except Costa Rica, the latter refusing to take part in the meeting because the host nation, Venezuela, was ruled by a dictatorship. Among the 97 resolutions voted by the delegates, the anti-Communist declaration, sponsored by the United States

and approved by 17 votes to 1, with Mexico and Argentina abstaining and Guatemala dissenting, attracted the most attention. The resolution, brought before the Conference by the United States because of Communist influence in the ARBENZ government in Guatemala, was officially called the "declaration of solidarity for the preservation of the political integrity of the American states against international Communist intervention." Another important resolution demanded complete elimination of European colonies in the Americas. The vote was 19 to 0 in favor of the resolution, with the United States abstaining. Latin-American hopes that the United States would come to the Conference with a Marshall Plan for its Latin neighbors were not fulfilled and there was considerable disappointment among Latin-American delegates at the failure of the United States to offer more economic aid. The Conference decided, however, that a special economic conference of the American Republics would be held later.

**Caramurú.** Real name **Diogo Álvares.** Shipwrecked Portuguese who lived among the Tupí Indians in Bahia, Brazil. Supposedly he saved his own life by awing the natives with a display of musketry (hence the name Caramurú, meaning the fire maker). He returned to Europe with his favorite wife, Catarina Paraguassú, on a French vessel, and then made his way back to Brazil where he remained. When Thomé de SOUZA landed in Bahia in 1549, he was greeted by Caramurú who aided in the establishment of the new city of Bahia. His adventures were commemorated in *O Caramurú*, an epic poem on the discovery of Brazil written by José de Santa Rita DURÃO in 1781.

**Caravellas, Manuel Alves Branco, Viscount of.** 1797–*ca.* 1855. Brazilian statesman. b. Bahia. Studied law and mathematics at Coimbra, Portugal; elected deputy to the assembly; charged with writing the penal code. It was due largely to his efforts that religious freedom was proclaimed in Brazil. He was head of the government under Emperor PEDRO II from 1847 to 1849. As a reward for his services he was named Viscount of Caravellas by the emperor.

**Cárdenas, Lázaro.** 1895–    . President of Mexico. Born at Jiquilpan de Juárez, Michoacán, of mixed white and Tarascan Indian ancestry. Joined revolutionary forces, 1913; made brigadier general, 1924; provisional governor of Michoacán, 1920; governor, 1928–1932; minister of the interior, 1931; minister of war and marine, 1933; elected president, 1934–1940. Successfully asserting his independence of ex-President CALLES, who had dominated Mexican politics throughout the previous decade, he pushed forward the revolutionary program authorized by the constitution of 1917 with unprecedented speed. During his term some 40,000,000 acres were expropriated from large landowners and organized into *ejidos* for the use of village communities. The labor movement, organized into the *Confederación de Trabajadores de México*, 1936, was supported in struggles with both native and foreign capital; and a number of enterprises, especially the railroads, were turned over to the workers to operate. The building of rural schools was promoted. The most spectacular episode of the administration was the expropriation of the foreign oil companies, both British and American, 1938, as a result of their refusal to obey government orders to grant higher wages and other benefits to their employees. Although there was much criticism of the economic wisdom of Cárdenas' policies, his integrity was generally recognized, as well as his belief in democracy, which was displayed in the freedom of speech and press enjoyed by opposition elements. He was placed in command of Mexican forces on the Pacific coast, 1942, and the following year named minister of national defense. After the war Cárdenas retired to private life at Pátzcuaro but remained interested in national politics. Since 1960 he has evidenced a pro-Castro attitude and sympathy for the Cuban reform movement and has also spoken out against U. S. aid to Cuban refugees who have attempted to invade the island. In May 1961 the ex-president withdrew from the INSTITUTIONAL REVOLUTIONARY PARTY (*Partido Revolucionario Institucional* or P.R.I.) and in a public statement asked the peasants to support greater social reform. He is an outspoken advocate of more "revolution" for Mexico.

**Carías Andino, Tiburcio.** b. 1876. President of Honduras. General; leader of the conservatives; unsuccessful presidential candidate in 1924. Although Carías received a plurality of the votes he failed to gain an absolute majority and the election was referred to the congress where U. S.-sponsored negotiations resulted in the naming of Miguel Paz Baraona, Carías' vice-presidential running mate, as president. Again defeated as candidate of the National party in 1928, he was elected president in 1933 and ruled as a virtual dictator until 1949. He was able to put down continual liberal uprisings in his country against his regime and succeeded in placing Juan Manuel Gálvez, his minister of war, in the presidency in 1949.

**Caribbean Sea.** A body of water between the West Indies and Central and South America, with a total area of about 750,000 square miles, connected with the Gulf of Mexico by the Yucatán Channel, 120 miles wide. A shallow area that extends from Honduras to Jamaica divides the sea into two basins, both of which are over 10,000 feet deep and contain depths to about 25,000 feet. Most of the year the Caribbean is a calm body of water, but it is also known for its devastating hurricanes which usually occur in September. The Caribbean was discovered and explored by COLUMBUS and was named after the fierce CARIB INDIANS, who inhabited some of the West Indies and parts of Venezuela at the time of the discovery. In the colonial era it was the highway for the Spanish fleets bringing European products to the Spanish-American colonies and taking back to the Old World the gold and silver of the Spanish colonial empire. Many battles were fought between Spanish convoys and foreign privateers and pirates, and also between ships of other European powers who wanted to establish themselves in the area. With the opening of the Panama Canal in 1914, the Caribbean took on new importance as a route of trade and acquired new strategic importance for the United States. The defense of the canal requires strategic control of the sea by the United States, whose naval and air bases in the West Indies, leased from Great Britain in 1940, insure this control.

**Carib Indians.** An important South-American linguistic stock. At the time of their discovery, the Caribs inhabited the Lesser Antilles and a large portion of Venezuela and the Guianas. When COLUMBUS met them, they had, a relatively short time before, driven out the Arawakan Indians. The CARIBBEAN SEA was named after the Caribs, who were known for their fierceness and cannibalism, yet were also skilled in canoe making and in using sails for navigation.

**Carioca.** A citizen of Rio de Janeiro.

**Carlota Joaquina.** In full, **Joaquina Carlota de Borbón.** 1775–1830. Queen of Portugal. Daughter of CHARLES IV of Spain; married Prince John of Portugal in 1790. At the time of the Napoleonic invasion of Portugal fled with her husband and royal court to Brazil, 1807. The ambitious and unprincipled sister of the imprisoned FERDINAND VII of Spain, she considered herself heir to his realms in America and aspired to establish control over the Plata basin. She constantly plotted to obtain a throne for herself in the Spanish-American colonies and carried on intrigue with Creole leaders in the River Plate and Chile for some years. People were executed in Buenos Aires when a plot in her favor was discovered in 1812. She was notoriously unfaithful to her husband, and encouraged her son Dom Miguel in a revolt against Dom Pedro (PEDRO I) and Maria, 1828–1830 in their struggle to obtain the Portuguese throne.

**Carmelites.** One of the four mendicant orders of the Roman Catholic Church. A reform movement within the Carmelite order beginning in 1562 resulted in the establishment of a new order, the Descalced (or Barefoot) Carmelites, in 1593. This latter order was active in the establishment of missions and in missionary work in both Portuguese and Spanish colonial America. Although the order was not as effective as some of the other Catholic orders in the New World, it became increasingly influential as its members increased during the 17th century.

**Caro, Miguel Antonio.** 1843–1909. President of Colombia. b. Bogotá. Related to Rafael NÚÑEZ, whom he succeeded to the presidency; editor of conservative journal; helped in the writing of the constitution of 1886; vice-president, 1892–1894; president, 1894–1898. He is known for his writings on philosophy, politics, and history, but is best-known in the literary field as poet and author of a collection of poems, *Horas de Amor* (Hours of Love).

**Carranza, Venustiano.** 1859–1920. President of Mexico. b. Cuatro Ciénegas, Coahuila. Well-to-do landowner; served as a senator under the DÍAZ regime, 1901–1910; supported MADERO in revolution of 1910 and was elected governor of Coahuila, 1911; headed constitutionalist revolution against HUERTA after the latter's seizure of power and murder of Madero, 1913; assumed title of "first chief." After the overthrow of Huerta in 1914, his claims to the presidency were disputed by VILLA and ZAPATA, resulting in another period of civil war during which Carranza was supported by the U. S. Government and made a bid for popular support by promising extensive land and labor reforms. He was recognized as *de facto* president, 1915, and after the election continued to serve as legal president, 1917–1920. He opposed U. S. attempts to secure protection for its citizens in Mexico, but had to allow the PERSHING expedition against Villa, 1916, and remained strictly neutral during World War I. He accepted the revolutionary constitution of 1917, drafted by the convention at Querétaro, but did little to enforce any of its provisions. As his term ended, he indicated that he would turn over the presidency to a little-known supporter named Bonillas. This precipitated a rebellion headed by OBREGÓN, which was immediately successful. Carranza fled from Mexico City and was murdered in the remote Indian village of Tlaxcalantongo in the state of Puebla, where he had taken refuge, May 21, 1920.

**Carrera, José Miguel de.** 1785–1821. Chilean dictator and revolutionist. b. Santiago. Served in the Spanish army in Europe; joined his brothers in the revolutionary army in Chile in 1810; overthrew the conservative junta in 1811; ruled as military dictator, 1811–1813. As a consequence of the rivalry that existed between Carrera and O'HIGGINS, Carrera failed to support O'Higgins in the crucial Battle of Rancagua, and Chile was lost to the royalist forces in October 1814. Both leaders and 3,000 men fled across the Andes to Mendoza. Carrera went to Buenos Aires, then the United States, returned to Argentina in 1816, and plotted to overthrow O'Higgins, who had supported SAN MARTÍN in the final attack against the royalists in Chile. Carrera remained a powerful opponent of the government in power in Chile, until he himself was put to death in Argentina in 1821.

**Carrera, Rafael.** 1814–1865. President of Guatemala. b. Guatemala City. He was of mixed Indian, white, and Negro parentage. The leader of the conservative insurgents who finally destroyed the CENTRAL AMERICAN FEDERATION, 1839, he completely dominated the political life of Guatemala as a dictator from 1840 to 1865, and was able to extend his influence over other Central-American states as well. He was president of Guatemala from 1844 to 1848 and from 1854 to 1865. In 1854 he was made president for life. He led the war against El Salvador from 1850 to 1853, and in 1863. He was conservative and illiterate and strongly supported the Church.

**Carrillo, Braulio.** 1800–1845. President of Costa Rica from 1835 to 1837 and again from 1838 to 1842. b. Cartago. An able administrator, and, though he ruled virtually as a dictator and would have liked to make himself president for life, he was able to accomplish many things for his country. He promoted the growth of coffee and made it the country's chief export. He strengthened the position of the peasant by taking common lands away from the towns and subdividing them among the people. He was overthrown by a revolution under the leadership of MORAZÁN in 1842.

**Cartagena.** Important Colombian port on the Caribbean Sea. Capital of Bolívar department with a population of about 179,250 (est. 1961), it is one of the most interesting cities in the New World. Its fortifications, built against pirate raids, have undergone almost no change. Coffee is exported through Cartagena, and it is also an important center for imports. An oil pipeline from the Barrancabermeja oil fields terminates at nearby Mamonal and makes the area a principal outlet for petroleum. Founded in 1533 by Pedro de Heredia, the city sustained a number of attacks and sieges. It was sacked by the French in 1544 and by the British under Drake in 1585. It repelled a well-organized landing attempt by British forces under Admiral Vernon in 1741. Cartagena was one of the first cities in Colombia to proclaim its independence from Spain (November 11, 1811), but in 1815, following a siege of almost four months, it surrendered to Spanish forces after the greater part of its inhabitants had died. The Spaniards finally lost the port on October 15, 1821. For the heroism it showed during the War of Independence, Cartagena received from BOLÍVAR the title of *Ciudad Heróica* (Heroic City).

**Casa de Contratación.** House of Trade. Earliest institution created specifically for the governance of the Spanish-American empire, it was founded by royal decree on January 20, 1503, by FERDINAND and ISABELLA of Spain and organized by Bishop Juan Rodríguez de FONSECA at Seville. Its main purpose was the organization and regulation of Spanish trade with the West Indies. All Spanish ships carrying goods to the colonies had to pass through Seville and through the customs service of the *Casa*. It was a government bureau that licensed and supervised all ships and merchants, passengers and goods, crews and equipment, passing to and from the Indies, and enforced the laws and ordinances relating to such matters. The *Casa* received all revenues in gold, silver, and precious stones remitted to the Crown by the colonies, and collected the *avería* or convoy tax, customs, and other duties. It was also a court of law in charge of cases involving trade. In 1718, the *Casa* was transferred to Cádiz. It was abolished in 1790.

**Casado, Carlos.** 1833–1893. Argentine empire builder. From 1850 he engaged in profitable economic activities up and down the Paraná River, and with his activities and holdings in Santa Fe, he became the owner of a vast empire that included railroads, shipping, plantations, and forests. He worked through banks in Buenos Aires and laid the foundation for a family fortune that has lasted through his descendants to this day.

**Casa Grande.** Spanish and Portuguese meaning a large or great house. In Brazil it refers to a manor house. In colonial Brazil the *casa grande*, residence of the *fazendeiro*, (plantation owner), who was the undisputed lord of his domain, came to symbolize the power of the landed aristocracy.

**Casa Mata, Plan of.** The pronouncement that hastened the overthrow of ITURBIDE, emperor of Mexico. The plan was published in February 1823, by General Echávarri, supporting SANTA ANNA, and although declaring that Agustín I (Iturbide) should keep his throne, it called for the election of a new congress that was to be allowed to meet freely. The position of Iturbide soon became untenable and he lost support in all quarters. In March he was forced to abdicate and to go into exile.

**Casa Rosada.** Until recently the *Casa Rosada* (Pink House) was the official home of the president of Argentina. It is now used for presidential and other offices and the president has an official home elsewhere. It is a magnificent pink building that fronts on the Plaza de Mayo in the heart of Buenos Aires.

**Casas, Bartolomé de las.** 1474–1566. Spanish DOMINICAN missionary, bishop, and historian. b. Seville. Famous as the "Apostle of the Indies." First priest to be ordained and preach his first Mass in the New World, 1510, in Hispaniola. He had been an *encomendero* until the suffering of the natives resolved him to devote his life to helping them. He went to Spain in 1515 to intercede in their behalf with FERDINAND V and was sent by the Crown and Cardinal Jiménez to Santo Domingo as Protector of the Indians. However he was constantly opposed by the colonists. He attempted a model Indian village in Venezuela, 1520–1521, but it failed. He was partly responsible for the NEW LAWS passed in 1542 for the protection of the Indians. He was bishop of Chiapas from 1544 until 1547, when he retired to Spain. He wrote important historical works including *Breuissima relación de la destruycion de las Indias*, printed in 1552, which exaggerated the cruelty of the Spanish to the Indians and was used by the British and the other enemies of Spain as a basis for

the BLACK LEGEND. His *Historia de las Indias* was published in several volumes.

**Caseros, Battle of.** Battle fought on February 3, 1852, at the town of Monte Caseros in the province of Buenos Aires between the Argentine, Brazilian, and Uruguayan troops of the Argentine general URQUIZA and those of the dictator ROSAS. The victory of Urquiza put an end to Rosas' tyranny.

**Castañeda Castro, Salvador.** *ca.* 1888–1965. President of El Salvador and army officer. b. Cojutepeque. Entered army, 1905; promoted to brigadier general in 1929; minister of the interior, 1931–1934; candidate of *Partido Unificación* in 1944–1945 and elected president in January 1945. He was expected to take orders from AGUIRRE Y SALINAS, but he had a mind of his own. He introduced a number of reforms primarily in the field of education and labor. He advocated Central American union and promoted the political merger of Guatemala and El Salvador, 1945. He insisted on referring to the constitution of 1886, which was a fairly liberal document, but was forced to arrest opponents and suppress the opposition press. However he gave the country the closest thing to a democracy that it had known in years. After promising an honest election in 1948, he was removed from office by a revolution of army officers.

**Castellanos, Aarón.** 1800–1880. Argentine land promoter, interested in acquiring river navigation and railroad contracts. He was able to persuade the Sante Fe provisional government in 1853 to authorize a contract permitting the immigration and settlement of 1,000 Swiss families at Esperanza, which was farm land a few miles outside the city of Santa Fe. He established pioneer tenant farms and was aided by URQUIZA in his attempt to free Santa Fe from both the strong influence of the cattlemen and the PORTEÑO monopoly.

**Castilla, Ramón.** *ca.* 1797–1867. President of Peru. b. Tarapacá. Fought with the royalist army in Chile during the Wars for Independence, but later joined the patriots and fought under SUCRE at AYACUCHO, 1824; took part in civil wars in Peru, 1841–1845; served in various political positions and was minister of war in 1837; served as president of Peru,

1845–1851. Economic prosperity enabled Castilla to improve the country which had fallen into a state of decay. Guano and fertilizers were exported. WHEELWRIGHT's steamship line, which started service about 1840 and carried goods to Europe and the United States, helped a great deal. This contact with the outside world created a civilian liberal party within the country, and joined by liberals, Castilla led a revolution that resulted in the overthrow of President José ECHENIQUE and became president for the second time, serving from 1855 to 1862. He abolished slavery in Peru, 1856, and announced the adoption of a new constitution, 1860.

**Castillo, Ramón S.** 1871–1944. President of Argentina. b. Catamarca. Educated in Catamarca and at the University of Buenos Aires; received law degree, 1894; secretary of the commercial court; criminal judge of Buenos Aires province, 1895; commercial judge of Buenos Aires, 1905; justice of the criminal court, 1910; dean of the faculty of law of the University of La Plata, 1923–1928; dean of the faculty of law and social sciences at the University of Buenos Aires; member of the constituent convention, 1931; federal senator from Catamarca, 1932–1935; named minister of justice and public instruction, 1936; leader of the conservatives; served as minister of the interior, 1936–1937; vice-president of Argentina, 1938–1940; and when President Roberto ORTIZ became incapacitated and unable to resume his duties, Castillo became acting president, 1940–1942. Immediately he showed his sympathies to be with the wealthier classes of the country. He insisted on a neutral position during World War II. Becoming president upon the death of Ortiz in 1942, Castillo's partiality toward the Axis powers rendered his government unpopular with the majority of the people. At the Rio de Janeiro Conference in January 1942, Argentina's attitude prevented the passage of a resolution calling for severance of relations with Germany and Japan by all American republics. Castillo was ousted on June 4, 1943, by a military group that placed General Rawson in the presidency.

**Castillo Armas, Carlos.** 1914–1957. President of Guatemala. b. near Escuintla. Educated at the military school of Guatemala; studied military tactics and strategy in the United States, 1945–1946. He participated in the unsuccessful revolt against the government of Juan José ARÉVALO BERMEJO, was captured and given a sentence of death, but escaped from prison and fled into exile. He led a successful revolt against the pro-Communist government of ARBENZ GUZMÁN in June 1954, and assumed control of the military junta that ruled the country, becoming constitutional president after a national election in October 1954. He was assassinated by a member of the presidential guard on July 26, 1957, and was succeeded by the vice-president, Luis Arturo González López.

**Castizo.** Spanish, meaning "of good origin"; also designates pure Castilian language without foreign words or idioms. In Spanish America, it also has the special meaning "the son of a mestizo (half breed) and a Spanish woman."

**Castro, Cipriano.** *ca.* 1858–1924. President of Venezuela. b. near San Antonio, Tachira state. An illiterate but courageous cowboy, he came down from the Andes to lead a successful insurrection against President Ignacio Andrade and took control of the government in October 1899. He was provisional president, although a "supreme military leader" from 1899 to 1902 and was elected president in 1902. He ruled as a dictator and was troubled by many revolts, and his administration reached a new high in Latin America for corruption and graft. In 1902 he involved Venezuela in blockades of the ports by Germany, Italy, and England, who were creditor nations. The United States offered to arbitrate, and the claims were finally submitted to the Hague Tribunal, which declared that Venezuela must reserve 30 per cent of customs receipts to pay the creditors. In 1908 his health failed and he was obliged to go to Europe for treatment, leaving the government in the hands of his vice-president, Juan Vicente GÓMEZ, who became dictator and ruled for 27 years.

**Castro, Juan José.** b. 1895. Argentine composer and conductor. b. Buenos Aires. Studied with Vincent d'Indy in Paris;

founded the Renacimiento Orchestra in Buenos Aires in 1929; conducted modern ballet at the Colón Theater. His compositions are fairly modern in feeling and are based on native melodies. His ballets *Mêkhâno* and *Sinfonía Argentina* were presented in Buenos Aires in 1937.

**Castro Alves, Antônio de.** 1847–1871. Brazilian poet, best-known for his writings on the theme of slavery and social justice. His poems include *O Poema dos Escavos* (The Poem of the Slaves).

**Castro Madriz, José María.** 1818–1893. President of Costa Rica. b. San José. Served as president, 1847–1849, 1866–1868. He broke the last bond that united Costa Rica to the CENTRAL AMERICAN FEDERATION by declaring the country an independent republic in 1848 and is, therefore, referred to as the "Founder of the Republic."

**Castro Ruz, Fidel.** 1927–     . Cuban premier, political leader, and lawyer. b. Mayarí. Educated at the Colegio Dolores in Santiago and the Colegio Belén, Havana; received the doctor of law degree from the University of Havana, 1950; associated with political and revolutionary movements from an early age. He advocated the overthrow of the BATISTA government, and on July 26, 1953, led an unsuccessful attack on the Moncada army barracks in Santiago. Captured and sentenced to prison for fifteen years, Castro was released in 1955 under a general amnesty. He visited the United States and Mexico, where he gathered together Cuban exiles and trained them in guerrilla tactics, and returned to invade Cuba in December 1956, with about eighty followers. After initial defeats, his 26th of July movement, named for the date of the earlier attack on the Moncada barracks, gathered support and succeeded in carrying on a highly successful guerrilla warfare. He occupied Havana and began his control of the country when Batista's government collapsed on January 1, 1959. He had Manuel URRUTIA LLEO named provisional president and himself designated premier in February 1959. He resigned the premiership in July 1959, but resumed those duties after Osvaldo DORTICÓS TORRADO was appointed president

during the same month. Since Castro's rise to power in 1959, the nationalization of industry, the agrarian and educational reforms, and Castro's attacks on religion have followed the Communist pattern. Cuban-U. S. relations deteriorated rapidly, while Castro brought Cuba closer to the Sino-Soviet orbit. In December 1961 he publicly referred to himself as a Marxist-Leninist. Castro suffered a loss of prestige as a result of economic difficulties and the Soviet withdrawal of offensive ballistic missiles from Cuba in the last months of 1962. See CUBA.

**Caudillismo.** System by which the reins of government are held by different *caudillos* (leaders) wielding dictatorial powers and generally suppressing all manifestations of political democracy. *Caudillismo* has been one of the salient features of Latin-American history, it being a direct result of the social and political instability that has frequently plagued the Latin-American republics. It began during the Wars of Independence, and BOLÍVAR was the first great *caudillo*. The period immediately following independence is often called the "age of the *caudillos*." More advanced countries, such as Argentina and Chile, achieved constitutional government during the 19th century. Some countries are still governed by *caudillos* today. Although *caudillismo* has persisted to the present day in many Latin-American countries, it has tended to become less violent and has more of the characteristics of political bossism in the United States. Some of the more famous *caudillos* or dictators of the 19th and 20th century were Juan Manuel de ROSAS of Argentina, Francisco Solano LÓPEZ of Paraguay, and Juan Vicente GÓMEZ of Venezuela.

**Caudillo.** Spanish meaning "chief" or "leader," and by extension, "dictator." The *caudillo* has been a recurring figure in Latin-American politics. See CAUDILLISMO.

**Caupolicán.** d. 1558. Araucanian Indian hero. b. near Palmaiquén, Chile. Fought with the famous Araucanian chieftain LAUTARO in resisting the conquest of Chile by the Spanish conquistadors VALDIVIA and Villagrán. Following Lautaro's death, he assumed command of the Araucanians, who were probably the fiercest fighters Spain faced in the New World. Disastrously routed by García HURTADO DE MENDOZA and Alonso de Reinoso, he was barbarously executed by the latter in the city of Cañete (1558). He is immortalized in a statue by the distinguished Chilean sculptor Nicanor Plaza and in the poem *La Araucana* by Alonzo de ERCILLA Y ZÚÑIGA.

**Caxias, Luiz Alves de Lima e Silva, Duke of.** 1803–1880. Brazilian general and statesman. b. Rio de Janeiro. Brazil's most famous military figure; suppressed revolt in Maranhão in 1841 and was given the title of Baron of Caxias for that service; commanded military forces that defeated the liberal revolt in the provinces of Minas Gerais and São Paulo, 1842; crushed revolution in Rio Grande do Sul, 1842–1845; appointed minister of war, introduced needed reforms in the army; given title of Marquis. The Brazilian commander during the PARAGUAYAN WAR, he became commander-in-chief of the allied forces in January 1868 upon the retirement of General MITRE and held this commission until March 1869. He was honored with the title of duke for his military service in Paraguay, the only commoner to hold that title in the entire history of the Brazilian empire. He served as president of the council of state, or prime minister, 1850, 1856–1857, 1861–1862, 1875–1878.

**Cedillo, Saturnino,** d. 1939. Mexican general and political figure. Developed from a peasant leader during the revolution into a wealthy landowner and conservative politician. He was governor of the state of San Luis Potosí and secretary of agriculture, 1934–1937. He opposed the liberal CÁRDENAS administration and revolted in May 1938, using his own private army. The movement was crushed in two or three weeks and Cedillo was killed in January 1939.

**Celaya, Battle of.** Battle between the constitutionalist forces under OBREGÓN, supporting CARRANZA, and those of VILLA at Celaya, Mexico, 1915. Obregón dug trenches and threw up barbed-wire entanglements and posted machine guns. For three days Villa, on three different occasions, flung his cavalry against Obregón's fortifications and saw them shot down by machine guns. Ultimately, after the greatest series of battles ever fought on Mexican soil, Villa was forced northward in retreat, and the control of Mexico by Carranza was assured. Obregón lost an arm in the battle.

**Censorship.** In Spain strict censorship of books was established by FERDINAND and ISABELLA in 1502. All publications printed, imported, or placed on sale were subject to examination and required to have a license from the Royal Council. The censorship was vigorously enforced by the Crown and the INQUISITION, especially after Lutheran ideas had found their way into Spain. Books that incurred the wrath of the Church were listed in an index, the *Index Librorum Prohibitorum*, and severe penalties, including death, were meted out to individuals found in possession of heretical works. Only a few persons were granted from time to time a special license to read and possess prohibited works. The same system was in force in the Spanish-American colonies throughout the colonial period. Books going to the colonies were first approved by Spanish secular and ecclesiastical authorities, then had to be licensed again by the COUNCIL OF THE INDIES, passed on by authorities at the time of embarkation at Seville or Cádiz, and again upon arrival in the New World. Penalties for infraction against the censorship law in the colonies were as severe as in Spain, and also included the death sentence. In spite of all the measures taken by the Spanish Crown and the Church, prohibited books did reach the colonies, but their number was relatively small. The seizure of banned books illustrated the Inquisition's uncompromising stand. On order of the Inquisitor General of Spain, the archbishop of Mexico seized all the books listed by the *Index Prohibitorius* of 1559. Other book removals took place at the same time throughout the Spanish-American empire. Often the Inquisition seized books that were not even listed on the *Index*. Some of the works prohibited during the colonial period were Milton's *Paradise Lost,* Voltaire's books, the *Encyclopédie,* Marmontel's *Les Incas,* works of Montesquieu and Condorcet, and the *Social Contract* of Rousseau. Censorship was not limited to written works. Speech was just as much controlled and it was extremely dangerous to utter ideas that might run counter to the *Weltanschauung* of the Crown and the Church. In colonial Brazil censorship, although it existed, was never as strictly enforced, partly because there were no Inquisition tribunals, inquisitorial powers being held chiefly by bishops. In more modern times censorship in Latin America has accompanied many dictatorial regimes, such as that of ROSAS in Argentina (1829–1850), Juan GÓMEZ in Venezuela (1908–1935), and PERÓN in Argentina. An odd revival of ecclesiastical censorship took place under GARCÍA MORENO, the president of Ecuador (1861–1875). García Moreno was a fervent Catholic, and restored to the Church all the privileges it had enjoyed in colonial times, including censorship over all printed matter.

**Central America.** In geographical terms, the isthmus connecting North and South America, stretching between the isthmus of Tehuantepec to the north and that of Panama to the south. As a political designation Central America includes Guatemala, Honduras, El Salvador, Nicaragua, Costa Rica, Panama, the Panama Canal Zone, and British Honduras. While the inclusion of Panama as a Central-American country is now common, tradition dictates that the five northern republics constitute Central America, and that Panama should be included with South America. This tradition is largely based on the boundaries assigned to the old Spanish colonial administrative areas of the captaincy general of Guatemala and the viceroyalty of Nueva Granada. Panama was part of the latter area and never politically associated with its northern neighbors. Since 1903, when Panama achieved independence from Colombia, it has become common usage to group all of the isthmian republics as being Central-American. With an area of approximately 210,000 square miles and a population of approximately 12,-250,000 (est. 1961), the isthmus is constituted to a great extent by a chain of highlands and is studded with volcano areas. The climate varies between the low and hot *tierra caliente* (hot country), with an annual temperature average of more than 75 degrees; the *tierra*

*templada* (temperate zone), with an average of 65 to 75 degrees; and the *tierra fría* (cold country), with an average of 55 to 65 degrees. The crop grown in the widest area is maize, and the main exports are cotton, coffee, and bananas. The population is concentrated on the western side of the isthmus where the highlands offer a more temperate climate than that in the lowlands of the eastern or Caribbean side. In Guatemala the population is predominantly pure Indian, in Costa Rica pure white, and in Honduras, El Salvador, Nicaragua, and Panama, MESTIZO. Central America was first explored and settled in present-day Panama by Ojeda, Nicuesa, and BALBOA in the first two decades of the 16th century. Subsequently it was explored and conquered by Pedro de ALVARADO Y MESÍA (1523–1524), who pushed down from Mexico as far south as present-day El Salvador; by Cristóbal de Olid and Hernán CORTÉS (1524–1525), who conquered Honduras; and by Spanish expeditions pushing north from Panama. In the colonial period, Central America, including the present Mexican state of Chiapas and the present republics of Guatemala, Nicaragua, Honduras, El Salvador, and Costa Rica, formed part of the viceroyalty of New Spain and the captaincy general of Guatemala. In the 17th century English log-cutting buccaneers settled on the Belize River (now in British Honduras) and along the so-called Mosquito Coast, today part of Honduras and Nicaragua. In the 19th century the history of Central America is marked by: the achievement of independence from Spain in 1821; a short interlude as part of ITURBIDE's Mexican empire (1822–1823); the CENTRAL AMERICAN FEDERATION (1823–1838); general internal instability in the various Central-American nations, of which the curious episode of the American filibusters in Nicaragua led by William WALKER (1855–1857) is an example; the emergence of coffee as the leading crop of the area; and British and American rivalry over influence in the region. This conflict of interests was settled by the CLAYTON-BULWER TREATY of 1850, by which both parties pledged themselves not to acquire sovereignty over any part of the isthmus or to exercise exclusive control over any waterway that might be built across it. The Clayton-Bulwer Treaty was followed by the British ceding the Bay Islands to Honduras in 1859 and the relinquishing of the Mosquito protectorate in 1860. In 1903 Panama seceded from Colombia, and the United States acquired the concession to build the PANAMA CANAL. The construction of the canal, the ever-growing banana industry, developed by the UNITED FRUIT COMPANY and other firms, and the adoption of the ROOSEVELT COROLLARY to the MONROE DOCTRINE, focused American attention on Central America. In 1907, when it seemed that a general war was imminent in Central America because of Nicaragua's interference in El Salvador's internal affairs, the United States called a conference of all Central-American republics (except Panama) in order to reduce tension in the area. The conference met in Washington and its most important achievement was the creation of the Central American Court of Justice, at which each nation would be represented by one judge and to which all future disputes in Central America should be submitted. The Court functioned until 1918, accomplishing relatively little. It finally ceased to exist because of its inability to settle the quarrel that had arisen over the BRYAN-CHAMORRO TREATY of 1916. U. S. interference in Central-American affairs became more pronounced under the Taft administration (1909–1913), when the American government, fearing that European nations might take action in the Caribbean area to protect their investments, tried to forestall this intervention by establishing a control over the revenues of the Central-American states and by the refunding of their foreign debts. The United States kept armed forces in Nicaragua from 1912 to 1925 and from 1926 to 1933. This BIG STICK POLICY was discontinued with the initiation in the early thirties of the GOOD NEIGHBOR POLICY. During WORLD WAR II all Central-American governments declared war on the Axis and cooperated in the defense of the Panama Canal. Since that war there has been much internal unrest and increased Communist influence in the Central-American countries. There have been numerous successful and unsuccessful attempts at revolution in all of the Central-American states. Guatemala experienced a revolution in 1954 that ousted the leftist administration of Jacobo ARBENZ GUZMÁN, a presidential assassination in 1957, and a successful military coup in 1963. The government of El Salvador was forcibly replaced in 1960 by a military junta that was deposed a few months later by another junta. Honduras had election difficulties in 1954 and its government was twice overthrown by coups in 1956 and 1963. The Somoza dynasty in Nicaragua has successfully held the reins of government since 1937, but has been continually plagued by revolutionary activity. In 1956 President Anastasio SOMOZA was assassinated and was succeeded by his son Luis Somoza Debayle. Costa Rica has had constitutional democratic governments since the 1880's except for the dictatorial regime of Federico Tinoco, 1917–1919, and a brief period of civil war in 1948. Anti-FIGUERES Costa Ricans made attempts to invade the country from Nicaraguan soil in 1948 and 1955, but the intervention of the ORGANIZATION OF AMERICAN STATES settled that threat to Central-American peace. In Panama domestic tranquility has always been an elusive goal. The assassination of President REMÓN CANTERRA in 1955 was followed by a confused interval of government and the eventual election of Ernesto de la Guardia, the first president to complete a four-year term for a quarter of a century. Beginning in 1951, an attempt to create a regional organization known as the ORGANIZATION OF CENTRAL AMERICAN STATES (ODECA) has achieved limited success. The goal of the organization has been economic integration through a common market and the coordination of cultural and educational activities in the several countries. Panama has evidenced increasing interest in cooperating with her northern neighbors in the endeavor. See COSTA RICA, EL SALVADOR, GUATEMALA, HONDURAS, NICARAGUA, and PANAMA.

**Central American Federation.** A union of the states of Guatemala, El Salvador, Honduras, Nicaragua, and Costa Rica. From the 1520's, when that region became a part of the Spanish empire in the New World, to 1821 they, together with the present Mexican state of Chiapas, formed the captaincy general of Guatemala, a part of the viceroyalty of New Spain. In the latter year they achieved their independence from Spain and in the following year became a part of the Mexican empire under the rule of Agustín de ITURBIDE. With the overthrow of the Mexican emperor in 1823, Central American ties with Mexico were broken. In June 1823 deputies from the several provinces met in a constituent assembly in Guatemala City declaring themselves independent of any power and formally creating "The United Provinces of Central America." The federation adopted a constitution and established its capital at Guatemala City. Manuel José ARCE became the first president of Central America in 1825. Dissensions over a variety of questions and a growing antagonism between liberals and conservatives led to civil war. The liberals were victorious, and their leader, Francisco MORAZÁN, became dictator in 1829 and president in 1830. His administration put through a liberal program that included control of the Church, religious freedom, and the promotion of industry and commerce. The seat of government was moved to San Salvador, in 1835. Morazán's government aroused the opposition of the conservatives, and in 1837 the smoldering resentment broke out in civil war. The leader of the conservative forces was the Guatemalan MESTIZO Rafael CARRERA. Morazán was defeated and the Central American Federation collapsed in 1838. The states thereafter resumed the status of independent nations. Since that time about twenty-five attempts have been made to unite the countries of Central America again, but all have failed. Recently exponents of union have enjoyed limited success in restoring the unity of the Central American countries. In October 1951 the ORGANIZATION OF CENTRAL AMERICAN STATES was formally created to promote regional cooperation among its members. This latest effort is directed at economic integration through a customs union and a common market, and at coordinating cultural and educational facilities in the Central American countries. See CENTRAL AMERICA.

**Centralism.** The principle of strong central government. During the first half-century of Latin-American independence there were fre-

quent conflicts between the advocates of centralism and those of federalism, especially Mexico, Colombia, Venezuela, Chile, and Argentina. Federalism was generally supported by liberal elements while centralism proved more attractive to the conservatives, who in some instances became advocates of constitutional monarchy. A number of countries, however, found by practical experience that federalism was likely to result in virtually anarchical conditions, and most Latin-American political leaders, liberal as well as conservative, finally became convinced of the need for some form of centralism. The particularly bitter struggle between these two factions in Argentina ended in the adoption of a moderate form of federalism that recognized the necessity of consolidated authority.

**Cepeda, Battles of.** The name given to two engagements that took place at the town of Cepeda, in the province of Buenos Aires, during the long period of organization of the Argentina republic. The first Battle of Cepeda was fought on February 1, 1820, between the forces of General José Rondeau, Supreme Director of the United Provinces and leader of the Buenos Aires unitarians, and the federalist forces of the provinces. The defeat of the Buenos Aires forces led to the dissolution of the Buenos Aires Congress and the termination of the Directory. The second battle was fought on October 23, 1859, between the Buenos Aires forces under MITRE and those of the Argentine Confederation. Mitre was defeated and as a result Buenos Aires was incorporated into the Confederation.

**Cerro Gordo, Battle of.** The battle that opened the road to Puebla and Mexico City for U. S. forces under Winfield Scott during the Mexican War, 1846–1848. SANTA ANNA, after losing the important Battle of BUENA VISTA in February 1847, turned eastward to meet an American army led by General Scott, which had landed on March 7 at Veracruz. Santa Anna entrenched himself in a strongly fortified position at Cerro Gordo, 50 miles northwest of Veracruz, where the road wound upward into the mountains, and thus hoped to bar the way to the Mexican capital to the enemy. However, the American engineers, in a maneuver as spectacular as it was daring, dragged their guns through deep ravines and thick woods around the northern flank of the Mexican army. The latter soon found itself facing an attack on its front and on its left and was quickly routed, April 17th and 18th. As a result of his victory Scott could proceed unmolested to Puebla.

**Cervantes, Vicente.** Mexican botanist of the late 18th and 19th century, who, as head of the Botanical Gardens in Mexico, introduced new horticultural methods into New Spain.

**Céspedes, Carlos Manuel de, the Elder.** 1819–1874. Cuban revolutionist. b. Bayamo. Studied in Spain; participated in Prim y Prat's revolution in 1843. He led an armed revolt on his return to Cuba in 1868 that began the Ten Years' War. Elected president of the revolutionists in 1869, he was deposed in 1873, and killed in 1874 by Spanish soldiers.

**Céspedes y Quesada, Carlos Manuel de.** 1871–1939. Son of Carlos Manuel de CÉS-PEDES, the Elder. Cuban lawyer and diplomat, Served as ambassador to Washington, 1913–1922; was provisional president of Cuba from August 12 to September 5, 1933, after the overthrow of MACHADO. The country had financial difficulties, and he was overthrown by BATISTA and GRAU SAN MARTÍN. In 1936 Céspedes was the unsuccessful presidential candidate of the Centralist Party.

**Chacabuco, Battle of.** An important engagement of the South-American War for Independence. José de SAN MARTÍN, realizing that the most effective way of crushing Spanish power in Peru was by a march over the formidable Andes into Chile and from there to Peru, obtained the governorship of the western Argentine province of Cuyo (1814). In the provincial capital, Mendoza, he spent more than two years in organizing an army capable of crossing the great mountain range. In January 1817, in the middle of the southern summer, the only time of the year when the mountains were passable, San Martín divided his forces, slightly more than 5,000 men strong, into two main columns, with smaller units on the flanks, and the army crossed the Andes, the main groups going through the passes of Uspallata and Los Patos, each

12,000 feet above sea level. The "Army of the Andes" counted in its ranks many Chilean patriots, including the famous O'HIGGINS, who was put in charge of one division. The passage, one of the great feats of history, considering the forbidding terrain and the tremendous altitudes, was made possible by the extensive preparations that had provided the army with all the equipment and supplies necessary for such an undertaking. The royalist army in Chile, cleverly kept in the dark by San Martín's spies and emissaries as to the actual route to be taken by the main Argentine-Chilean forces, was trying to defend as many points of the country as it could, but its widely scattered groups could not unite in time to stem the patriot army. Nevertheless the royalist General Maroto, gathering what troops he could, awaited San Martín with 1,500 men on the hill of Chacabuco, at the northern entrance to the valley of the capital, Santiago. San Martín had been able to unite most of his forces and on February 12, 1817, faced Maroto's troops with 3,000 men. The initial phase of the battle was imprudently executed with the result that O'Higgins' forces had to retire in disorder before the Spanish infantry. A charge of grenadiers led by San Martín beat back the Spanish cavalry that had rushed in to destroy the retreating battalions, thus giving O'Higgins time to regroup his division. Soler, whose flanking movement had been delayed because of difficult terrain, then joined the battle, completely surprising the Spaniards and turning the engagement into a royalist disaster. Two days later San Martín and O'Higgins entered Santiago.

**Chaco, Gran.** An extensive lowland plain today divided among Paraguay, Bolivia, and Argentina. The region is bounded on the north by tropical woodlands, on the south by the Salado River, on the east by the Paraguay River, and on the west by the Andean piedmont. The region is divided into three parts by the Bermejo and Pilcomayo rivers: That part north of the Pilcomayo is the Chaco Boreal (100,000 square-miles); the Chaco Central (50,000 square miles) is located between the two rivers; and the Chaco Austral (100,000 square miles) is south of the Bermejo, extending south to the Salado River. It is largely an area of open savannahs and scrub forest dotted with carandai palms and occasionally broken by islands of dense jungle. The heavy soil, almost impermeable, is covered with water from the torrential rains that occur during the rainy season. The Chaco Boreal belongs almost entirely to Paraguay, with only the extreme western and northern portions lying within the boundaries of Bolivia. The boundary dispute between the two countries, involving the ownership of the Chaco Boreal, precipitated the sanguinary CHACO WAR, 1932–1935, which resulted in the present boundaries. The Chaco Central corresponds to the northern Argentine province of Formosa and the northeast part of the province of Salta. The Chaco Austral corresponds to the Argentine province of Chaco and parts of Santa Fe, Santiago del Estero, and Salta provinces. The region is very sparsely populated, the Paraguayan Chaco having approximately 70,000 inhabitants. Indians, once fierce and hostile to missionary and colonization efforts, still lead a nomadic, but more peaceful, existence in the Chaco. An attempt to establish settlements in the Paraguayan Chaco was begun in 1926 by Russo-German Mennonites from Canada. This project now comprises about 36 villages, the largest being Filadelfia. The region is rich in quebracho wood and there is an abundance of lumber and cattle. In the west oil deposits have been located.

**Chaco War.** A conflict that was fought intermittently from 1928 to 1935 between Bolivia and Paraguay over possession of the Chaco Boreal. The question of the ownership of the Chaco region first received attention in 1852 and from that time efforts were made by both countries to mark the Paraguayan-Bolivian boundary in the region. All attempts at a settlement failed, and meanwhile, both Bolivia and Paraguay pushed a line of fortified posts into the territory. The inevitable armed clash took place in 1928, when the Paraguayans attacked and captured a Bolivian fort. The LEAGUE OF NATIONS and the Pan-American Conference on Arbitration, then in session, offered to arbitrate, but although both parties

accepted the offer of the latter group, no satisfactory solution was found, and fighting in the Chaco continued until April 1930, when a temporary truce was negotiated. Full-fledged warfare broke out again in 1932 and war was formally declared in the following year. Although Bolivia's army was larger and better-equipped, it had to fight far from the country's settled areas and its soldiers, accustomed to the climate of the cold highlands, suffered considerably from the heat. By 1935 the Paraguayan army had managed to overrun most of the Chaco and to invade eastern Bolivia, but counterattacks forced it back from the latter area. Both sides were now thoroughly exhausted, and in June of the same year the United States and a number of South-American governments were able to arrange a truce. On July 21, 1938, as a result of the work of the Chaco Peace Conference which included the United States, Argentina, Brazil, Chile, Peru, and Uruguay, a peace treaty was signed at Buenos Aires. It provided that Paraguay was to receive 70,000 square miles of the disputed territory and Bolivia 30,000 square miles. Bolivia was granted an outlet to the Atlantic Ocean by way of the Paraguay River, as well as the use of the Paraguayan Chaco port of Puerto Casado as a free port. The war, which cost Bolivia about 52,000 lives and Paraguay about 36,000, drained them economically and led to political upheavals in the postwar period.

**Chacón, Lázaro.** 1873–1931. President of Guatemala. b. Teculután. Soldier and politician, president, 1926–1930. Chosen to serve for the presidential term ending in 1932, he was incapacitated by illness and forced to relinquish his position on December 12, 1930. He settled a boundary dispute with Honduras.

**Chalchuapa, Battle of.** A battle fought on April 2, 1885, at Chalchuapa, El Salvador, between the Guatemalan army under President Justo Rufino BARRIOS and the forces of El Salvador. The engagement resulted in the defeat and the death of Barrios, thus ending his dream of uniting Central America under his own leadership.

**Chamorro Vargas, Emiliano.** 1871–1966. President of Nicaragua, 1917–1920. General and political leader. b. Acoyapa. Graduated from the University of Pennsylvania; minister plenipotentiary to the United States, 1913–1916, 1921–1923. He signed the BRYAN-CHAMORRO TREATY of 1914 (ratified by the United States in 1916) by which the United States purchased the right to build a canal across Nicaragua. He seized power by a coup d'etat from Carlos Solórzano, the legally elected president, shortly after the termination of U. S. intervention in 1925. He held the presidency for a short time in 1926, but when the United States refused to recognize his administration and sent armed forces back to Nicaragua to enforce constitutional order, he resigned and left the country. He was senator (from 1928) and head of the Conservative Party from 1933.

**Chapetón.** In the Spanish colonies of South America, the name given to a native-born Spaniard.

**Chapultepec.** In the Nahuan language, "the hill of the grasshopper." An isolated rocky hill, nearly 200 feet high, located about three miles southwest of the center of Mexico City. The scene of a battle in the pre-Conquest era, it became a place of worship and a resort for the Aztec emperors. After conquering the valley, the Spaniards erected a chapel, dedicated to San Javier, on its heights in 1554. In the 18th century the hill became the site of a castle that served as a summerhouse and place of recreation for the Spanish viceroys. In 1841 a military school was established on the hill. As the last Mexican stronghold in the Mexican War, the position fell to the American forces on September 13, 1847, after a heroic resistance by the defenders. The castle was rebuilt by MAXIMILIAN and became the official residence of the emperor and the presidents that succeeded him. In 1940 the castle became a national museum. Chapultepec was the meeting place of the Inter-American Conference on Problems of War and Peace (1945), which resulted in the signing of the ACT OF CHAPULTEPEC, advocating reciprocal assistance and hemispheric solidarity.

**Chapultepec, Act of.** Measure adopted at the Inter-American Conference on Problems of War and Peace held at Mexico City in February and March 1945. It stipulated that an act of aggression upon an American state, whether from within the American states or from without, would be considered an act of aggression against all, and called for collective action by the American republics. An inter-American defense treaty was recommended. Such a treaty was signed at the inter-American conference at Rio de Janeiro in 1947. See RIO CONFERENCE OF 1947.

**Chapultepec, Battle of.** The battle that sealed the fate of Mexico City in the Mexican War, 1846–1848, fought on September 12–13, 1847. When the American army under General Winfield Scott approached Mexico City, it did so from the southwest, and found that before it could enter the city proper, it had to capture Chapultepec, a hill 200 feet high, in the southwestern outskirts of the Mexican capital. The hill itself was an excellently fortified position defended by more than 7,000 men, including cadets from the nearby military college. After an intense artillery preparation American troops, about 7,000 strong, attacked from three directions. The force attacking from the west, using scaling ladders, managed after a desperate hand-to-hand struggle to fight its way to the top of the hill. The most heroic resistance was offered by the Mexican cadets, who suffered heavily while defending the position. At 9:30 A.M., September 13, the hill was surrendered by the Mexican commander. Losses on the Mexican side were placed at 1,800, those on the American side at 450.

**Chapultepec Conference of 1945.** Name given to the Inter-American Conference on Problems of War and Peace that met at the Chapultepec Castle in Mexico City in February and March 1945. The Conference, attended by all American states except Argentina, discussed hemispheric security and adopted measures to achieve this aim. There was also discussion of the forthcoming United Nations Conference at San Francisco. Among the more important decisions were the adoption of an Economic Charter of the Americas and the ACT OF CHAPULTEPEC, the latter dealing with steps to be taken in case of aggression against any American state.

**Charles I.** Also, **Charles V** of the Holy Roman Empire. Spanish, **Carlos.** 1500–1558. King of Spain, 1516–1556. Son of Philip of Burgundy and Joanna, who was the daughter and third child of FERDINAND and ISABELLA, and grandson of Emperor Maximilian I; inherited Burgundy and the Netherlands in 1506, was crowned emperor in 1520, and married Isabella of Portugal in 1525. The unnatural aggregate of distinct territories and races within the lands he ruled made Charles' reign extremely complex and difficult. His reign in America was the age of conquest and organization, and the holdings of the Spanish Crown on the mainland were insignificant upon his accession, but by 1556 the Conquest was practically complete and Spanish rule was firmly established. He resigned his Spanish kingdoms in favor of his son PHILIP II in 1556.

**Charles II.** Spanish, **Carlos.** 1661–1700. King of Spain from 1665 to 1700. Son of Philip IV. Joined Grand Alliance in war against Louis XIV, which ended with the Treaty of Ryswick, 1697. Feeble in both mind and body, he was the last of the Spanish Hapsburgs and during his reign the Spanish Empire grew weaker and more corrupt. He had no children and immediately before his death he signed a new will making Philip of Anjou, the grandson of Louis XIV, his heir. The question of Charles' successor came to a climax upon his death and was the signal for the beginning of the War of the Spanish Succession.

**Charles III.** Spanish, **Carlos.** 1716–1788. Son of PHILIP V and Elizabeth Farnese of Parma. An enlightened despot, he was the ablest of the Spanish Bourbon kings, under whose reign the administration of the colonies was highly efficient. In 1732 he was sent to rule as duke of Parma; conquered Naples and Sicily and became king as Charles IV, first of the Neapolitan Bourbons, 1734–1759. He became king of Spain, as Charles III, on the death of his half-brother Ferdinand VI, and reigned, 1759–1788. He reformed finances, aided commerce and agriculture, and encouraged education, particularly military schools. In 1761 he signed the Family Compact with France against England. He participated in the last year of the Seven Years' War, 1762–1763, and joined France against England during the North American Revolution. He expelled the JESUITS in 1767 and was responsible for many reforms in colonial administration designed to stimulate economic and cultural progress, and to improve efficiency and honesty.

**Charles IV.** Spanish, **Carlos.** 1748–1819. King of Spain from 1788 to 1808. Second son of Charles III. b. Naples. He was dominated by his wife, María Luisa of Parma. Manuel de Godoy, the Queen's favorite, was made prime minister in 1792. Wars with France, England, and Portugal were waged during his reign, and Louisiana was ceded to France in 1800. Spain was invaded by French armies in 1807–1808. Economic conditions and relations with the colonies became increasingly worse. Forced to abdicate in 1808, he died in Rome.

**Charles V.** See CHARLES I.

**Charro.** Name given to the colorful, lavishly dressed Mexican horseman.

**Chartered Companies in Latin America.** To put an end to illicit trade between the Spanish-American colonies and foreign merchants, and to promote trade with underdeveloped areas of its overseas empire, the Spanish government in the 18th century formed monopoly companies with wide powers to eliminate smuggling and to protect their interests. The majority of these privileged organizations were formed with capital from northern Spain and Catalonia. In exchange for the exclusive privilege to trade with specified territories they were often under obligation to build ships for the Spanish navy, to arm vessels in order to stamp out smuggling, and to render other services without charge to the Crown. The earliest of these was the Honduras Company (1714), followed by the Guipúzcoa (Caracas) Company (1728), the most important of the monopoly organizations, operating in Venezuela. The Guipúzcoa Company had its own troops and in the War of Jenkins' Ear (1739–1748) helped to fight off British attacks on Venezuela. It was successful in eliminating Dutch contraband in cacao off the Venezuelan coast, and it introduced other crops besides cacao, such as cotton, indigo, and tobacco, thus contributing greatly to the prosperity of the area. At times the Guipúzcoa Company abused its privileges, and in 1749 a revolt against it broke out. It was put down three years later. The company ceased operating in the 1780's. Other monopoly groups included the Galicia Company (1734), which was permitted to send two ships a year to Campeche, Mexico, the Havana Company (1740), and the Barcelona Company (1755), which was given the privilege of trading with Hispaniola, Puerto Rico, and Margarita. All of these organizations were financial failures except the Guipúzcoa Company. Monopoly companies were also set up by Portugal for trade with Brazil. The first of these was the Companhia do Brasil, established in 1649, which in return for a monopoly over a number of products, including wine, oil, and brazilwood, took upon itself certain obligations including the convoying of merchant vessels. It was also granted an exclusive concession to manufacture distilled liquors from sugar. Investors included Jews in difficulties with the Inquisition, who were given the choice of placing their capital in the company as an alternative to confiscation by the Holy Office. In the course of the 17th century the company underwent a number of reforms and was abolished in 1720–1721. The Companhia do Brasil was followed by the Companhia do Maranhão (1678), which was at first granted an *asiento* to deliver Negro slaves to the provinces of Maranhão and Pará, and later obtained a twenty-year monopoly over the trade between Portugal and those provinces. It was abolished in 1684. In the 18th century, due to the initiative of the Portuguese minister Pombal, another organization, the Companhia Geral do Grão Pará e Maranhão, was established in 1755. Granted a monopoly of the wholesale trade in the Amazon Valley, it stimulated the economic development of northern Brazil, fostering among other things the growing of such important crops as rice and cotton, and bringing labor into the area. It came to an end in 1778–1779. The Companhia de Pernambuco e Paraíba, formed in 1759 with a large capital, functioned until 1779. The Portuguese monopoly companies succeeded to a certain

extent in replacing British merchants in the trade with Brazil, and contributed to the development of the northern provinces of the colony.

**Chibchas.** A number of Indian tribes inhabiting the high plateau of present-day Colombia, who, at the time of the discovery, had attained a relatively advanced stage of culture. There were five nations, each ruled by a priest-king. The Chibcha religion included worship of the sun and the moon, and human sacrifices. They were skilled in the manufacture of pottery and cotton, and worked with gold and emeralds. They carried on an extensive trade with the surrounding tribes and had developed a currency. Unlike the Incas they did not have pack animals, and unlike the stone-made Inca buildings the houses of their towns were made of wood and cane. The custom of one of the Chibcha tribes that consisted in the king's being covered with gold and immersing himself in water probably gave rise to the legend of El Dorado, the gilded man. The Chibchas were conquered by JIMÉNEZ DE QUESADA (1537–1538).

**Chichén Itzá or Chichén.** An ancient Mayan city, now in ruins, in the south-central part of the state of Yucatán, Mexico. The city derived its name from wells around which it was built, *Chi*, meaning "mouths," *chen*, "wells," and *Itzá*, the name of the tribe that first settled there. The entire name means the "Mouths of Wells of the Itzá." The city was founded not later than A.D. 530 but abandoned in the middle of the 7th century. This early period is usually referred to as the Old, or First, Empire. The following period, two to three centuries, has been described as the "Dark Ages" of Mayan history. In 964 the Itzás returned to the city and initiated an era of renaissance in Mayan culture. An alliance of the three greater Mayan cities was formed about 1000 and lasted for 200 years before it was disrupted by wars between the member cities. Elements of Toltec-Aztec culture were introduced into Chichén when these people were allied with the enemies of the Itzás and conquered them. In spite of its loss of dominance, the Itzá city continued to flourish until the middle of the

15th century when it was rather suddenly and finally abandoned.

**Chichimecs** or **Chichimecas.** A group of Nahua-speaking Indian tribes, including the Aztecs, who, toward the end of the 12th century, invaded the central Mexican valley from the north and displaced the Toltecs as rulers of the area. The Aztecs eventually became the dominant Chichimec tribe and formed their powerful empire with the support of the Tlacopán and the Texcoco city states.

**Chicle Industry.** Chicle, the main ingredient of chewing gum, is extracted from the sapote tree (*Achras Sapote*) which is found in large, forested regions of Mexico (Campeche, Yucatán, Quintana Roo), British Honduras, and Guatemala (Petén). The chicle industry began in the 19th century, and has always had a transportation problem. The plantations are at a great distance from the coast and the gum has to be carried on muleback or by airplane to the ports of shipment. The United States is the biggest customer in the world market, but the high cost of the raw material, the fact that the trees have been grown successfully in Florida, and the possibility that a substitute product may be used in the making of chewing gum, all combine to threaten the future of the chicle industry.

**Chile.** Sometimes referred to as the Shoestring Republic, it is about 2,650 miles long and an average of 110 miles wide, situated on the west coast of South America between the Andes and the South Pacific. Its area is 286,397 square miles and its population about 8,950,000 (est. 1966), of which the overwhelming majority is white, with only 2 per cent of the population Indian. The monetary unit is the escudo, and 4.29 escudos equal the U. S. dollar (1966). The language is Spanish and the predominant religion is Roman Catholicism, although religious freedom is guaranteed. The chief cities and their populations (est. 1961) are Santiago, the capital, 2,001,000 (includes environs and suburbia), the important port of Valparaíso, 280,000, Concepción, 174,000, Viña del Mar, 110,000, and Antofagasta, 90,000. The powers of government are in the hands of a president elected for six years, a chamber of deputies,

and a senate. Voting is open to all literate citizens over twenty-one years of age. The country may be divided into three general regions: the northern desert, containing mineral deposits; the central valley, where agriculture flourishes; and the southern mountains covered by forests. Mining is the mainstay of the economy, with iron ore leading the field in 1962 with more than 8,150,000 metric tons; other minerals include coal, nitrates, copper, gold, silver, lead, and petroleum. Oil production, begun in 1945 in the far south, reached approximately 1,208,-000 metric tons in 1961. Chile is the second largest copper-producing country in the world, and produces 95 per cent of the world's natural nitrates and 70 per cent of the world's supply of iodine, a by-product of nitrates. The chief agricultural product is wheat, and other important crops include rice, beet sugar, potatoes, oats, barley, corn, and grapes, Chile being a high-ranking wine producer. There are about 3,000,000 cattle and 500,000 horses, and sheep raising is an important occupation. Manufacturing has developed considerably since 1939, and the Huachipato steel plant near Concepción is the second largest in Latin America. The textile industry utilizes the wool from the country's sheep and manufactures 85 per cent of the silk and rayon fabrics used in Chile. The chief exports are copper and nitrates, and the principal imports are machinery, petroleum, and vehicles, the principal customers, as well as the chief suppliers, being the United States, West Germany, the United Kingdom, and Argentina. The government controls two-thirds of the 6,000 miles of railroads, and there are more than 28,900 miles of roads. The airport at Santiago is served by 12 international airlines. Education is compulsory and free between ages of 7 and 15. There are a number of outstanding universities and a national library. The literacy rate is more than 80 per cent, ranking Chile the third highest Latin-American country in education.

The first Spanish leader to make his way into Chile from Peru was Diego de ALMAGRO, PIZARRO's colleague, in 1536, when he attempted to establish a colony in the new country, but failed. A fort was built in 1541 by Pedro de VALDIVIA on the site of what is now Santiago. The Spaniards encountered fierce opposition from the ARAUCANIAN INDIANS, Valdivia being killed in 1555, but after 1557 the Spaniards were able to gain control of central Chile as far as the Bío-Bío River. The Araucanian Indians refused to give up and were still fighting long after the War for Independence from Spain. During the colonial period, when Chile was under the control of governors and captains general, who were called presidents, it was an economically impoverished area.

The Chilean fight for independence started in 1810. The Chilean O'HIGGINS and the Argentinian SAN MARTÍN were the heroes in the struggle for national sovereignty, and defeated the Spaniards at CHACABUCO in 1817, and at MAIPÚ in 1818. These two battles insured the independence of Chile. O'Higgins served for several years as dictator, finally being forced into exile in 1823. From 1831 to 1861 the country was ruled by a series of conservative presidents functioning chiefly in the interests of the landowning oligarchy. For another 30 years a more benevolent and more liberal administration guided the fortunes of Chile, even though the Constitution of 1833 had established a strong centralized government. During these 60 years there was expansion to the south under BULNES PRIETO in 1843, and to the north by the WAR OF THE PACIFIC, 1879–1883, a conflict between Chile and a coalition of Peru and Bolivia, arising out of a bitter dispute over valuable nitrate lands. The Chileans marched into Lima, the capital of Peru, victorious. They gained possession of the Bolivian littoral, including the port of Antofagasta (thus depriving Bolivia of its outlet to the sea) and the Peruvian province of Tarapacá, and also took possession of the Peruvian provinces of Tacna and Arica on the understanding (never fulfilled) that a plebiscite, ten years later, would determine ownership. In 1923 the United States entered as arbitrator and in 1929 the dispute was settled (see TACNA-ARICA). Following a civil war between the supporters of President BALMACEDA FERNÁNDEZ and those of the Chilean congress in 1891, there was a period of unstable government. The forces of congress had won out, but the number of political parties fighting for control lessened

the efficiency of the lawmaking body. The ever-increasing rate of nitrate exports as well as the opening in 1911 and 1915 of the important copper mines brought much income to the government and the upper classes, but the working class did not generally benefit from the economic prosperity. Moreover, most people had little to say in the operation of the government since they were excluded from suffrage largely by literacy qualifications. The middle and laboring classes were finally able to express their dissatisfaction with the ruling group when they elected Arturo ALESSANDRI PALMA to the presidency in 1920. He was prevented by the conservatives from carrying out his program of reform in the legislative branch of government. The economic depression caused by the decrease in Chile's exports resulted in difficulties for the administration, but the newly-elected congress of 1924 was favorable to the policies of the administration. However the army was dissatisfied with the new economic program and forced Alessandri's resignation. The military junta was unable to solve the situation and Alessandri was recalled. In 1925 a new constitution was promulgated, which returned to the executive the powers held in the 19th century, provided for universal male suffrage, separation of Church and state, election of the president by direct vote, and judicial reform. The government was generally modeled after that of the United States. Under Carlos IBÁÑEZ DEL CAMPO, who became president in 1927 and ruled as a virtual dictator until 1931, the Tacna-Arica question was settled, labor laws were enacted, a modest agrarian program got under way and educational facilities were improved. With the depression of the 1930's, Ibáñez's administration collapsed. After Chile attempted to create a short and unsuccessful socialist government, in 1932, Alessandri was called back to the presidency. He succeeded in supporting and having some laws passed that aided the laborers and *inquilinos* (tenant farmers). The condition of the country was much improved as industry expanded and the national finances were put on a sound basis. There was strong opposition to the decidedly conservative leanings of the Alessandri administration. With the backing of all the parties of the left and center, grouped into the "popular front," Pedro AGUIRRE CERDA won the election for the presidency in 1938. A vast earthquake in the Concepción-Chillán area killed more than 25,000 people in January 1939, destroyed considerable property, and drained the resources of the country. Juan Antonio RÍOS MORALES, also supported by the Popular Front organizations, was elected to succeed Aguirre Cerda in 1941. Chile, although she followed Argentina's lead and remained neutral after the Japanese attack on Pearl Harbor, finally broke diplomatic relations with Germany and Japan in 1943 and declared war on Japan in 1945. In 1946 GONZÁLEZ VIDELA was elected to the presidency. He was backed by the Communists in the election and was forced to give them three cabinet posts but, after a few months, he broke with them and the Communist members resigned. In September 1948 the Communist Party was outlawed. A disciple of Aguirre Cerda, he expanded the industrialization of Chile. In 1952 former president Carlos Ibáñez del Campo was elected to the presidency. His term in office was marked by economic troubles, including a considerable drop in Chile's exports of copper to the United States, severe inflation, and strikes. The troublesome labor situation prompted the president to declare a state of siege in September 1954. However, in December of the same year, the congress lifted the state of siege. Late in 1954 the Chilean government announced that foreign and domestic capital had been invited to take part in the exploration and exploitation of oil. In 1958 Ibáñez del Campo was succeeded by Jorge Alessandri Rodríguez, the son of the former president, Arturo Alessandri Palma. The new administration enjoyed immediate success in achieving a balanced budget and checking inflation but was later beset by economic difficulties. An austerity program and mild social and economic reforms were instituted to promote recovery, but labor-management trouble and industrial strikes added to the administration's economic problems. As the situation worsened, confidence ebbed in the fiscal policies of the government. Multiple earthquakes struck in Chile's south central region in May 1960, killing approximately 5,000 persons and leaving 350,000 homeless.

Accompanying floods, landslides, and tidal waves increased the damage. International aid was rushed to the stricken area and helped the Chilean government to alleviate suffering. Relations with Bolivia reached a crisis in 1962 when that country objected to Chile's diversion of water from the Lauca River for irrigation purposes. The river rises in Chilean territory but flows through Bolivian lands. Later, in 1963, the dispute was broadened by Bolivia into a demand for revision of the 1904 peace treaty and a revival of Bolivia's desire to have an access to the Pacific Ocean. Chile signed the LATIN-AMERICAN FREE TRADE ASSOCIATION agreement in 1960 and became a member of the organization in 1961 when the treaty was approved by the congress. In November 1964, Christian Democrat Eduardo Frei Montalva was elected president, defeating the candidate of a left-wing coalition. His victory in the 1965 congressional election should enable Frei to push through much needed social and economic reforms, which offer Latin-Americans an alternative to the type of violent upheaval propounded by Fidel CASTRO.

**Chimu Indians.** A nation of Indians who began their culture in the late years B.C. along the northern reaches of the Peruvian coast in river valleys. Their powerful nation, with its capital at Chan-Chan (near modern Trujillo), was conquered by the Incas in the 15th century. The remains found in their territory show an advanced culture; they lived in large, well-organized communities and produced beautiful portrait vases and other magnificent pottery.

**China Poblana.** A red and green costume traditionally worn by Mexican women while performing certain national dances. According to a popular legend, the costume originated with a Chinese princess of the 17th century who was captured by pirates, sold into slavery in Mexico, and lived in the city of Puebla. She was converted to Christianity and became renowned for her sanctity.

**Chincha Islands.** A group of small islands in the Pacific Ocean about 12 miles off the coast of Peru, to which country they belong. The largest island, Isla del Norte, is less than one mile in length, and only one-third of a mile wide. They are of granitic formation and reach a maximum elevation of 113 feet. Formerly the islands were known for their vast deposits of guano, which were exported by the Peruvian government as early as 1840. The supply was exhausted by 1875. At a time when relations between Peru and Spain were severely strained, and when Peru refused to grant satisfaction to a Spanish royal commissioner over a minor dispute, the islands were seized by the Spanish fleet in April 1864. They were returned on payment of an indemnity to Spain. The act of surrender to Spain so infuriated the people of Peru that General Pezet was overthrown by General PRADO. With the support of Chile, war was declared against Spain and fought, 1865–1866. A peace treaty was not signed until 1879.

**Chinese.** Chinese labor was imported in the 19th century into British Guiana and Peru in order to remedy the labor shortage in those countries. In 1849 a law was enacted in Peru that granted subsidies to contractors bringing immigrants to the country. As a result, about 4,000 foreign laborers, most of them Chinese, were imported under contracts that forced them to work for low pay over a period of many years. The 1849 law was abrogated in 1853, and in 1856 Chinese immigration was made illegal, but the new law was reversed in 1861. In the next 14 years almost 85,000 Chinese were imported. During the earlier period the Chinese coolies were brought in mainly to work the guano deposits in the islands off the Peruvian coast, where they lived and worked under unbelievably bad conditions. Later arrivals were employed in the railroad building program of the 1860's and 1870's. In 1875 Peru signed a treaty with China, according to which only voluntary migration was henceforth to be allowed. Today Chinese comprise an important element in the retail trade business of Peru. Chinese immigration into Mexico was significant after 1910, but tapered off due to government restrictions and an agreement made with the Chinese government. The Chinese in Mexico suffered many indignities during the first years of the Revolution. The Chinese colony in Havana, Cuba, where they are engaged in retail business and truck gardening is perhaps the largest in all Latin America.

**Chocano, José Santos.** 1875–1934. Peruvian poet. An admirer of the United States, he wrote two poems reflecting this attitude, called *Istmo de Panamá* and *El Canto del Porvenir* ("Song of the Future"). However, he was an ardent revolutionist and complained about "Yankee Imperialism." He also wrote *Alma América* ("Soul of America"), 1906, *¿Quién Sabe?*, 1913, and *Oro de Indias*, 1934. He is considered an important modern poet.

**Cholos.** Term used to designate MESTIZOS, or the mixture of Indian and white, in the central-Andean countries. It is also used to refer to Indians or servants.

**Christ of the Andes.** Pass in the chain of the Andes, also called Bermejo, between Chile and Argentina. The monument, Christ of the Andes, was dedicated in March 1904. This statue, cast from melted cannon and situated at an altitude of 13,000 feet, represents a heroic figure of Christ holding a colossal cross in his hand. At the base the emblematic figures of Chile and Argentina are clasping hands, symbolizing the harmony reached between the two countries over the question of boundaries.

**Christophe, Henri.** 1767–1820. Negro king of Haiti. b. a slave in Grenada in the Windward Islands. Served as lieutenant under TOUSSAINT L'OUVERTURE in revolution of 1791 against the French; fought against LECLERC in 1802; joined in the uprising of DESSALINES, 1803–1804. When Dessalines was killed in a fight against the rebels in 1806, Christophe became his successor in the north as King Henry I. He was proclaimed king of all Haiti in 1811 and crowned in 1812. Though uneducated, he was intelligent and an able administrator. He could speak English as well as French and he made an effort to establish schools. He grew despotic toward the end of his reign, suffered a paralytic stroke in 1820, and his followers, who had been afraid of him, deserted him. Rather than fall helpless into the hands of his enemies, he committed suicide by shooting himself with a silver bullet.

**Church.** Throughout the colonial period the Catholic Church was one of the main pillars of Spain's power in the New World, and its influence upon the development of the colonies was incalculable. From the very beginning, the Spanish Crown exercised tight control over the ecclesiastical realm in the colonies. This control, granted to the king of Spain by a series of bulls by the popes ALEXANDER VI (1493, 1501) and Julius II (1508), was called the *real patronato de Indias* (royal patronage of the Indies). The Spanish Crown was entitled to control the emigration of ecclesiastics to the New World through the granting of licenses, to make clerical appointments, to collect the tithes, and to settle disputes between ecclesiastics. In spite of the right of patronage, however, clashes between civil and religious authorities were frequent and the rivalry between Church and State constantly marred the smooth functioning of colonial government. One important factor in this friction was the existence of special Church tribunals with jurisdiction over all religious affairs, but whose authority as opposed to that of civil courts was not always easy to delimit. Friction not only occurred between the civil and religious authorities, but also within the ranks of the clergy itself. The more important religious offices were in the hands of Spaniards, whereas the parish priests were in most cases Creoles. The latter were usually poor, for they had to rely on contributions in the rural areas for their maintenance, while higher Church officials, such as bishops, enjoyed a comfortable income. This disparity often caused tension between the two groups. Other conflicts existed among the various religious orders. The friars and the secular clergy also quarreled, because the former, who carried out most of the missionary work, tried to remain in the Indian villages as parish priests, while the latter, who arrived later, tried to dislodge them. The Church was instrumental in converting the Indians to Christianity and in extending the influence of the Crown. It played a major role in education, since it maintained almost all the schools and colleges

in the colonies. It also provided the hospitals and directed all charity. All phases of colonial life were permeated with its influence. Through the INQUISITION, established in Lima and Mexico in 1569, it exercised strong supervision over religious and political thought. Much wealth was amassed by the Church during the colonial period, most of it derived from the tithes along with gifts and bequests. Often this wealth took the form of large real-estate properties and by the end of the colonial period much of the land in Spanish America was in its hands. While there were many virtuous churchmen, there were many cases in which clerics merely used their position to enrich themselves and to engage in many types of reprehensible activities. Idleness, concubinage, and exploitation of the Indians by unscrupulous members of the clergy were fairly common. On the other hand there were many instances when churchmen had the welfare of the natives at heart, and did their best to defend them from abuse on the part of settlers and civil authorities. The Church was fully organized very soon after the Conquest. In 1511 the first American bishoprics were founded in Hispaniola (Santo Domingo) and Puerto Rico, followed in 1522 by that of Cuba. The diocese of Mexico was set up in 1527, and that of Santa Marta in Colombia in 1529. Peru received its first bishopric in 1534 and Venezuela in 1532. At the end of the 16th century Spanish America had five archbishoprics and twenty-seven bishoprics, and by the end of the colonial period there were seven archbishoprics and about thirty-five dioceses. In Brazil, too, the Church was under the authority of the Crown, which, as in the Spanish colonies, exercised patronage. The Church, however, had less influence than in Spanish America. It was relatively poor in comparison to the Spanish-American Church, and its control over religious thought could not be compared with that of its sister in the Spanish colonies. Some non-Catholic foreigners were allowed to reside in Brazil and no tribunal of the Inquisition was established there, although inquisitorial activities were carried out and there were cases of heretics burned at the stake or sent to Portugal for trial. The Jesuits were the most important group in the Brazilian Church. They were in the forefront of missionary activities, and contributed greatly to the conversion of the Indians. During the Spanish-American War for Independence, most of the higher officials in the Catholic hierarchy remained loyal to Spain, and thus the clergy was deprived of its leadership. As a result the number of priests decreased considerably. After independence the papacy refused for a number of years to recognize the new governments and opposed the contention of the new republics that they were automatically entitled to the right of patronage. In spite of the conflict, it was not long before the number of clergymen grew again, and for a long time the Church retained its influence in all phases of life. The Catholic religion was at first the only denomination tolerated, and the Church still maintained its special privileges, including the right to special ecclesiastical courts, exemption from taxation, and control of education. The dispute over patronage, however, marred relations with the civil authorities for a considerable period. The Church soon took sides in the early struggles between liberals and conservatives, for it saw in the liberals irreconcilable enemies of its prerogatives, threatening to end its privileges, and establish State control over education, marriage, and burial, as well as to confiscate its great wealth. In the conservatives the Church saw the supporters of the traditional order of things, and hence of the power and influence of the Church. The history of the Spanish-American republics revolves to a large extent around the struggle between the Church and the civil authorities. When the liberals were in power they almost invariably pushed through programs of lay control over education, marriage, and burial, of expropriation of Church property, etc. The conservatives usually saw to it that the Church preserved its ascendancy in the life of the nation. Among the regimes which were favorably inclined toward the Church were those of Rafael CARRERA in Guatemala (1844–1865), NÚÑEZ in Colombia (1880–1882, 1884–1894), and especially GARCÍA MORENO in Ecuador (1861–1865, 1869–1875), who went so far as to have his country consecrated to the "Sacred Heart of Jesus." Liberal regimes antagonistic toward the Church included those of MORAZÁN in Central

America (1830–1940), JUÁREZ in Mexico (1861–1872), and GUZMÁN BLANCO in Venezuela (1870–1888). In Mexico the struggle between Church and State was particularly bitter during the War of the Reform (1858–1860). Under the leadership of Juárez, all properties of the Church were nationalized and the monastic orders were suppressed. Under Porfirio DÍAZ (1877–1911), the Church was able to recoup many of its losses, but it was hit sharply by the revolution of 1910. In the 1920's and 1930's, the Church suffered much from succeeding anticlerical administrations, especially under that of CALLES (1924–1928). In recent years, however, peace has gradually come to Mexico in the religious field and it seems, for the time being, that relations between Church and State will continue on an even keel. In Venezuela, during the first years of Guzmán Blanco's presidency, the Church saw itself on the verge of losing all its influence. All Church properties were confiscated, parish schools were abolished, and an attempt at nationalizing the Church was made. Relations between Church and State have developed along much friendlier lines in Chile, where the separation of Church and State was decreed by law in 1925, and the Church owns properties and controls its own schools, and in Uruguay, where the separation has not been the result of bitterness and strife. In Argentina until recently the Church enjoyed a special status. It received an annual subsidy from the government, but the latter did not use its right of patronage to any great extent. In 1954–1955 Argentina witnessed a souring of Church and State relations. The PERÓN regime accused ecclesiastics of interfering in the political affairs of the country, and of carrying out anti-Peronist propaganda, and in some instances the regime took drastic measures, such as arresting a number of clerics, to underline the government's determination not to brook interference with its program. Congress passed legislation aimed at separating Church and State, religious education in State-supported schools was discontinued, and Perón was excommunicated by the pope. After the June 1955 revolt, however, Perón seemed ready to normalize Church and State relations. In Colombia the Church was disestablished by the constitution of 1936, but it still exercises a powerful influence in the nation. In 1957 the Church co-operated with liberal democratic groups in the overthrow of the Colombian military chief Rojas Pinilla. Similarly, in Venezuela the Church co-operated with the forces that brought about the fall of the dictator Pérez Jiménez. The Venezuelan government gives financial support to the Church, and Catholic instruction in public schools is compulsory. In Ecuador the Church has lost its former influence, whereas in Peru it enjoys a strong position, owning large properties and exercising considerable influence in the field of education. In Brazil the history of State and Church relations during the 19th and 20th centuries is devoid of the bitterness often found in Spanish America in the same period. Church and State were separated in 1890. The Church in Latin America has done much in the last twenty-five years to strengthen its position, and by the 1960's there was no major anti-Church movement anywhere in Latin America, with the exception of Cuba. As of 1960, the Church was subsidized by the State in nine of the Latin-American countries and was a legal participant in politics in Chile, Costa Rica, the Dominican Republic, Panama, Peru, and Uruguay. Its educational program has been given a great deal of attention; it operates at least 10 universities and 8,000 elementary and secondary schools with a total enrollment of approximately 2,000,000. The Church has taken an active part in social work and has tried to improve its public services. It has performed yeoman service in Latin America through the *Acción Católica* (lay groups) that keeps up an intense propaganda among the people. The importance of the Catholic Church in Latin America was underlined in 1946, when the offices of six new cardinals were created; three more were added in 1953.

**Churrigueresque.** A style of Spanish architecture, baroque in feeling, named after José Churriguera, (1650–1723). The term is applied especially to the extremely ornate style used in churches in Mexico during the first half of the 18th century.

**Churubusco, Battle of.** On August 20, 1847, the forces of the United States defeated the Mexicans in the battle of Churubusco, a suburb of Mexico City, in a swift, fierce assault. This was an important part of the battle for Mexico City itself.

**Cíbola.** See SEVEN CITIES OF CÍBOLA.

**Científicos.** Name given to a group of officials of the regime of the Mexican president Porfirio DÍAZ, because of their belief that all national problems must be handled with positivist, scientific methods, putting aside considerations of a spiritual, idealistic character. This group took shape in the 1890's, and largely dominated the government during the last twelve years of the Díaz regime. Originally organized by Rosenda Pineda, leadership fell to Romero RUBIO until his death in 1895 when José Yves LIMANTOUR became the leading figure. Cooperation with foreign capital, and their own wealth and power, made them unpopular with the mass of Mexican people. They lost more of their influence with the fall of Díaz in 1911. See POSITIVISM.

**Cieza de León, Pedro de.** 1518–1560. Spanish soldier and historian. b. Llerena. He came to America in about 1532 and remained until 1552, serving with the Spanish armies. He was the author of *Crónica del Perú* (in 4 parts), *Historia de la Nueva España*, and many other works.

**Cifuentes, Rodrigo de.** b. 1493. Spanish painter. A student of Bartolomé de Meza, he was the first European artist to paint in Mexico, where he arrived in 1523. He was known for his portraits of CORTÉS, Doña MARINA, Martín de Valencia, Nuño de GUZMÁN, and Viceroy Antonio de MENDOZA.

**Cimarrón.** Spanish term for a runaway Negro slave. Cimarrón has other meanings as well: shy, bitter (YERBA MATE), wild, and lazy.

**Ciudad Bolívar.** City in eastern Venezuela, the capital of the state of Bolívar, on the southern bank of the Orinoco River, about 200 miles from the east coast, with a population of 64,133 (1961). Ciudad Bolívar is an important commercial center, where tonka beans, gold, diamonds, balata, chicle, and other products are brought from the surrounding area for export. The town was founded in

1764 and was given the name of San Tomás de la Nueva Guayana, which was later changed to Angostura (The Narrows), for it was set on a narrow section of the Orinoco. Angostura played an important part in the Spanish-American War for Independence. It was here that BOLÍVAR reorganized his forces after suffering defeat. In 1819 a revolutionary congress met in Angostura and proclaimed Bolívar President of the Republic of Venezuela and in December of the same year president of the new state of Colombia. Angostura became Ciudad Bolívar in 1849.

**Ciudad Trujillo.** See SANTO DOMINGO.

**Civilistas.** The civilian party of Peru, as opposed to military groups. The *partido civil* was organized in opposition to the administration of BALTA. In 1872 it succeeded in electing Manuel PARDO to the presidency and, in fact, it was the first time an official candidate had lost an election since 1833. The *civilistas* placed General PARDO in office in 1876. The War of the Pacific found Peru unprepared, for the civilian government had reduced the army strength, and in 1879 PIÉROLA seized control of the government. The *civilistas* supported MORALES BERMÚDEZ in the election of 1890, but the government was overthrown by the *Pierolistas*, the supporters of Piérola. The *civilista* candidate Eduardo de Romaña succeeded Piérola in 1899 and continued in power for twelve years. However, the *civilistas*' power decreased as they remained conservative in changing times.

**Clark Memorandum.** On December 17, 1928, Undersecretary of State for the United States, J. Reuben Clark, Jr., submitted his celebrated work, *Memorandum on the Monroe Doctrine*, to Secretary of State Kellogg. Clark's basic conclusion was "it is not believed that this corollary (ROOSEVELT COROLLARY) is justified by the terms of the MONROE DOCTRINE, however much it may be justified by the application of the doctrine of self-preservation." The Clark Memorandum repudiated the policing of the hemisphere and considered that his nation was no longer responsible for the internal conditions of Latin-American countries, or for the protection of foreigners within those countries. In

1931 Secretary Stimson said "The Monroe Doctrine was a declaration of the United States versus Europe . . . not of the United States versus Latin America." The Clark Memorandum was an important step toward the GOOD NEIGHBOR POLICY of the 1930's.

**Clay, Henry.** 1777–1852. American lawyer and statesman. b. Virginia. U. S. Senator and member of the House of Representatives. When Speaker of the House in 1817, he was sponsor of recognition of Latin-American republics and his speeches did much to influence public sentiment, thus helping to bring about the MONROE DOCTRINE. He served as U. S. Secretary of State in the John Quincy Adams administration from 1825 to 1829, and was the unsuccessful candidate for the presidency 1824, 1832, and 1844. He was the first influential exponent of ideals of Pan-Americanism.

**Clayton-Bulwer Treaty.** Treaty between the United States and Great Britain signed in 1850 by the American Secretary of State, John Clayton and the English ambassador, Sir Henry Lytton Bulwer. It guaranteed the strict neutrality of any interoceanic canal opened across Central America. The countries agreed that neither would seek to control any canal that might be built, nor to occupy or plant colonies in or exercise dominion over any part of Central America. It was abrogated by the HAY-PAUNCEFOTE TREATY in 1901.

**Coal Industry.** Argentina, Brazil, Chile, Colombia, Mexico, and Peru are the Latin-American countries in which coal mining has acquired importance. Deposits of low-grade coal have been found in various parts of Argentina, the best quality being located in the province of Mendoza. Argentina produced 217,000 metric tons in 1960. It is estimated that Brazil has coal reserves amounting to 5 billion metric tons. Annual production reached 2,400,000 metric tons in 1960. Chile's important coal fields are found to the south of the city of Concepción and are provided with good transportation facilities, both by rail and by sea. Chilean coal reserves are estimated at more than 2 billion metric tons. Coal production in 1958 was 1,741,000 metric tons. Colombia produces about 2,500,000 metric tons annually in the mines òf the Cauca basin. In Mexico the great coal deposits are in the state of Coahuila. The most important source is the Nueva Rosita mine at Sabinas. Mexican production exceeded 1,750,-000 metric tons in 1958. Almost all of Peru's bituminous coal is extracted at the Goyllarisquisga mine, belonging to the Cerro de Pasco company. Peru is the only country in Latin America with known anthracite fields. The main hard-coal area is located between Trujillo and Huánuco and another large deposit is found in the Río Santa Valley. Peruvian mines produced 172,000 metric tons in 1958.

**Cochrane, Thomas Alexander.** 10th Earl of Dundonald. 1775–1860. b. Anesfield, Lanarkshire, Scotland. British naval commander. He was dismissed by the British admiralty, took command of Chile's navy in war for independence, 1818, directed naval operations against Spanish along Peruvian coast, 1819, and captured Valdivia, 1820. He set sail from Valparaíso on August 20, 1820, with eight warships and sixteen transports carrying more than 4,000 Argentine and Chilean soldiers. He dropped the men at Pisco, south of Callao, kept the Spaniards in the harbor town in fear, and successfully neutralized the Spanish squadron. He was in command of the Brazilian navy and helped secure Brazilian independence, 1823. He commanded the Greek navy and was reinstated in the British navy as a vice-admiral, 1842, and was made an admiral, 1852.

**Cocoa.** See CACAO.

**Coffee.** Coffee planting in the New World began in the latter part of the 18th century in the Caribbean area. It was introduced first in Haiti where it soon became an important crop. After the native uprising in 1791 many Haitian coffee planters fled to Cuba where the product soon prospered. At the same time coffee reached the shores of Caribbean South America, and by 1812 Venezuela was an important producer. In that year the leading coffee-growing countries were Haiti, Jamaica, Cuba, and Venezuela, and the total American export amounted to 100,000,000 pounds. Toward the end of the 18th century coffee began to be produced in Brazil, the first

plantings taking place in the Paraíba valley, where the *terra roxa* (red soil) is present on the São Paulo plateau, and subsequently São Paulo became the great center of Brazilian coffee production. After 1850 coffee became Brazil's leading export product, and by the end of the 19th century the country was providing 75 per cent of the world supply. Brazilian coffee was grown chiefly on great plantations or *fazendas*. In Colombia planting began between 1840 and 1850 on the plateau of Cundinamarca around Bogotá, and soon spread to the Antioquia and Cauca valleys. The industry there was carried out on relatively small farms and gave rise to a strong class of peasant proprietors. In Central America Costa Rica began to plant coffee in the first half of the 19th century, and the product soon became the country's leading export. By the end of the 19th century it was the chief crop of Costa Rica, Guatemala, and El Salvador. In Guatemala the rise of coffee benefited the upper class, but also led to an extensive loss of land by the Indians, who constituted the bulk of the population. Greedy planters, frequently by illegal methods, appropriated Indian holdings and the original Indian owners were often forced into debt slavery. Brazil and Colombia have been the two leading Latin-American coffee producers in the 20th century. In Brazil, as a result of a decline in the price of coffee in the first decade of the century, the government introduced a measure known as valorization, in order to keep prices at profitable levels. With financial support from abroad, Brazil purchased a substantial amount of coffee and withheld it from the world market until prices increased. The operation was successful and valorization became a feature of the nation's economy. After 1929, however, valorization collapsed when the tight money market barred Brazil's credit abroad. At the same time there was a vast oversupply. As a result the price of coffee dropped from 25 cents a pound in 1929 to 7 cents in 1931, and many planters were ruined. The Vargas government took drastic measures. Surplus coffee was burned, dumped in the ocean, or used as fuel for locomotives. By 1934 the number of bags burned totaled more than 26,000,000. Prices dropped again in 1935 in spite of the wholesale destruction. However in subsequent years prices improved as world demand rose. In 1962–1963 Brazilian production amounted to more than 27,000,000 bags of 132 pounds each. At that time, heavy frost and fires caused damage to important coffee producing areas. Nevertheless, Brazil's recent annual production averages approximately 4,597,-000,000 pounds. Ranking next to Brazil as the leading coffee producer in the world is Colombia. Its 1962–1963 production was more than 7,700,000 bags of 132 pounds each, most of which were bought by the United States. As for other areas in Latin America, coffee is the leading export of Costa Rica, El Salvador, Guatemala, Nicaragua, and Haiti. During World War II Latin-American coffee producers suffered greatly from the closing of European markets. To remedy the situation the Inter-American Coffee Marketing Agreement was signed in November 1940, fixing a quota for imports into the United States for each coffee-producing country in Latin America. Competition was thus restricted and the quantity purchased was assured a fairly good price. More recently the United Nations Coffee Conference has also attempted to accomplish the same goal. In 1958 the International Coffee Organization was established by Portugal and fourteen Latin-American coffee-producing countries. The aim of the organization is to promote the consumption of coffee throughout the world, and to conduct research on ways to reduce production costs and improve the quality of coffee. Brazil has recently initiated a program to control overproduction by cutting down 2,000,000 coffee trees and replacing them with fewer small trees of higher quality.

**Colombia.** The fourth largest republic in South America and the only country in South America bounded by both the Pacific Ocean and the Caribbean Sea. It has an area of 439,513 square miles and a population of 18,566,000 (est. 1966) of which 74 per cent are MESTIZO, 20 per cent white, 4 per cent Negro, and 2 per cent Indian. The language is Spanish and the monetary unit is the peso, which is worth approximately 6 cents. The population is predominantly Roman Catholic. The government consists of a president,

elected by direct vote for four years, and a bicameral congress of a senate and house of representatives. A temporary provision in the constitution provides that from 1957 to 1974 the presidency will alternate between candidates of the Conservative and Liberal parties and that the administrative and legislative posts will be shared equally. All Colombians 21 years of age and over are permitted to vote, women having been given the right to vote in 1954. The main cities and populations (est. 1962) are Bogotá, the capital, 1,329,230; Medellín, 690,710; Barranquilla, the chief port, 474,000; Cali, 693,120; and Cartagena, 185,160. Colombia is bounded on the north by the Caribbean Sea, on the northwest and west by Panama and the Pacific Ocean, on the southwest and south by Ecuador and Peru, and on the southeast and east by Brazil and Venezuela. It is crossed by three great mountain chains of the Andes, running from southwest to northeast, with peaks rising to almost 20,000 feet above sea level. In the northeast of the country there is another lofty range, containing the peak of Sierra Nevada de Santa Marta (19,309 feet above sea level). The southern part of the country consists of low plains or *llanos*, some of which are covered with thick forests. Colombia has a fertile soil, but the country's agriculture has not reached its maximum capacity. The chief crop and one that constitutes about 72 per cent of all exports is mild coffee. Cotton, tobacco, and sugar cane are also grown. There are abundant mineral deposits, including emeralds, salt, gold, silver, copper, and petroleum. There was little manufacturing carried on in the first years of the present century, but there has been an increasing activity in industry recently and the country has met all requirements for domestic consumption for textiles, footwear, foodstuffs, tobacco, beverages, industrial chemicals, cement, and other building materials. Two auto assembly plants were in operation in 1963. Chief imports are textiles, food, machinery, and chemicals. Transportation in Colombia faces formidable obstacles in the topography of the country. The 1,000-mile-long Magdalena River flowing north into the Caribbean is still much used for inland shipping, but there has been a steady development in railroad and road building and the communication problem has been considerably eased by an efficient air service linking Colombia's cities. The benefits of elementary education are not yet enjoyed by the whole population, but real progress has been made in this field in recent years. More schools are continually being built, and the number of illiterates is decreasing. The literacy rate is about 62 per cent. There are more than 60 colleges and universities, the oldest of these being the National University at Bogotá, founded in 1572.

The Caribbean coast of Colombia was first discovered by Rodrigo de Bastidas in 1500. The conquest of the region began in 1525 when Bastidas founded the town of Santa Marta on the northern coast. Pedro Fernández de Lugo became governor of Santa Marta and Cartagena in 1535, and the next year Gonzalo JIMÉNEZ DE QUESADA set out from Santa Marta at the head of an expedition and after much hardship was able to make his way to the plateau of Bogotá, where he defeated the CHIBCHA INDIANS. Shortly after this exploit he discovered an abundant treasure of gold and emeralds at Tunja and declared himself master of the entire central plateau, founding the city of Bogotá in 1538. Most of the territory of present-day Colombia was soon conquered by the Spaniards and a number of settlements were established. As Quesada's home was in Granada, Spain, the newly-conquered region was given the name of New Granada. It was later incorporated as a presidency into the viceroyalty of Peru (1564) and in the 18th century it became the viceroyalty of New Granada, including present-day Colombia, Venezuela, Ecuador, and Panama. During the colonial period the territory was the main source of gold in the Spanish colonial empire, but it also occupied an important place in agriculture, and trade with Spain. For a long time, throughout the 17th century, the port of Cartagena enjoyed great prosperity, as it was a port of call for the Spanish trade fleets and a host to commercial fairs. In the latter part of the 18th century the colony was shaken by the uprising of the *comuneros,* a revolt against high taxes (1780–1781), and in that period the ideas of the French philosophers of the 18th century as well as some ideas of the French

Revolution began to find their way into New Granada. The independence movement, begun in 1810 at Bogotá, was finally successful in August 1819, after BOLÍVAR's victory at Boyacá. Bolívar set up the Republic of Colombia, which by 1822 included Venezuela, Colombia, Panama, and Ecuador; but internal dissensions soon undid Bolívar's work, and in 1830 Venezuela and Ecuador broke away and declared themselves independent republics. New Granada, given the name of the United States of Colombia in 1863, suffered a long period of internal instability marked by a struggle between liberals and conservatives. In 1886 the conservative president Rafael NÚÑEZ had a strongly centralist constitution adopted, thus doing away with the federalism favored by the liberals, which had kept the country in a state of anarchy for a long time. Under this constitution the country was renamed the Republic of Colombia. A bloody civil war between liberals and conservatives, 1899–1902, ravaged the country. In addition, the following year, Panama seceded from Colombia after the congress refused to ratify the HAY HERRÁN TREATY with the United States, giving the latter the right to build a canal through the isthmus of Panama. The conservatives ruled until 1930 and the liberals from 1930 until 1946, when the conservatives returned to power. During World War II Colombia granted naval and air bases to the United States and in 1942 it broke off diplomatic relations with the Axis, proclaiming a state of belligerency against Germany in 1943. The postwar period has been marked by considerable political instability and even strife. At the time of the Ninth Conference of American States at Bogotá in April 1948, there were serious riots in the capital after the assassination of the leftwing leader Jorge Eliécer GAITÁN, and for a number of years the country was torn by intermittent civil war between liberals and conservatives. In November 1949 the conservative Laureano GÓMEZ was elected to the presidency and took office in August 1950. In 1953 he was ousted by a military coup headed by General Gustavo Rojas Pinilla, who took charge as provisional president and succeeded in restoring order throughout the country. A constitutional assembly met in 1953, approved Rojas as provisional president, and then elected him president for the 1954–1958 term. The administration of Rojas proved to be a dictatorship not unlike the one he helped to overthrow. In an attempt to restore civil constitutional government, the Liberal and Conservative parties reconciled their differences and organized the National Front (*Frente Nacional*). This coalition was based on an agreement to split government offices between them and to alternate the presidency. The agreement was given an expiration date of 1974. In 1957 the arrest of the presidential candidate of the National Front precipitated demonstrations and a national strike that brought about the resignation of President Rojas on May 10. A military junta was appointed to preserve peace and conduct the transition to a constitutionally elected government. The agreement concerning the National Front was made a part of the constitution in December 1957. In 1958 the Liberal party leader Alberto LLERAS CAMARGO took office as president after the first free elections in nine years. Violence, banditry, and terrorism occurred throughout the country during the administration, making it necessary to impose a state of siege on several occasions, and the high cost of living contributed to the general discontent. Political difficulties arose when political factions opposing the National Front made gains in the 1960 congressional elections. In an effort to hold the bipartisan government together the president reorganized his cabinet to include members of opposing factions. Despite vigorous opposition the National Front won a clear-cut victory in the congressional elections in March 1962, and in the presidential elections that followed in May, Dr. Guillermo León Valencia, the successful Conservative Party and National Front candidate, was inaugurated in August 1962. The new president announced a desire to stop the chronic violence in the hinterland. The banditry and terrorism that began with the civil war in 1948 has continued to the present day and in 1962 alone accounted for the loss of 4,360 lives. The president also announced programs to promote education and increase agricultural production. In the 1966 elections, the National Front Candidate Carlos Lieras Restrepo was elected and took office in Au-

gust. Although many social and economic as well as political problems remain unsolved, the country has made solid gains in recent years. Colombia became a member of the LATIN AMERICAN FREE TRADE ASSOCIATION in 1961 and is co-operating in the ALLIANCE FOR PROGRESS program sponsored by the U.S. government. New oil fields have been located in the north and near the Venezuelan border that will augment the increasing production of wells already in operation.

**Colorados.** See BLANCOS.

**Columbus, Christopher.** 1451–1506. Known as the discoverer of America. b. Genoa, Italy. Spent his early years as a weaver and at sea; moved to Lisbon, Portugal, 1477. Influenced by Portuguese navigators and his brother, Bartolomé, who was a chart maker, he believed that the earth was round and wanted to sail west in order to find a new route to Asia. He had no success in setting up an expedition until he went to Spain in about 1485 and was able to convince Queen ISABELLA that she should support his plans. He signed an agreement with her making him governor of the territories to be discovered, April 17, 1492. He sailed from Spain on August 3, 1492, with three small ships, the *Santa María*, the *Niña*, and the *Pinta*. He sighted land on October 12, 1492, and landed at San Salvador of the Bahama Islands. He sailed along the north coast of Cuba and Haiti, then returned home, and was accorded a royal reception. On his second voyage, he landed at the Leeward Islands, St. Christopher, Puerto Rico, and Jamaica. His third voyage landed him at Trinidad, and at the mouth of the Orinoco River, August 1, 1498, which was his first discovery of the mainland of South America. He was not a good administrator, and because he did not find the treasure expected of him, he was replaced by BOBADILLA, who had him sent back to Spain in chains. He was released, but lost his honors and the lands that had been given him. On his fourth voyage, he discovered Honduras and Panama, 1502. He died in poverty and neglect, still believing he had discovered the coast of Asia. His explorations changed the course of world history.

**Communism in Latin America.** Communism developed in Latin America after World War I, its growth being facilitated by the stepped-up pace of industrialization. Communist ideas found a fertile ground among the underprivileged factory workers, miners, and port workers of many areas, and Communists successfully infiltrated a number of trade unions. In Argentina the Communist movement grew under such leaders as Victorio Codovilla and Rodolfo Ghioldi; in Chile a Communist party was set up in the early twenties by Luis Recabarren, but it was outlawed under the IBÁÑEZ DEL CAMPO dictatorship (1927–1931); and in Peru, in the late twenties, the Communist intellectual José Carlos Mariátegui wielded considerable influence among Peruvian radicals through the literary journal and review *Amauta*. During the depression of the thirties, Communism gained rapidly, especially in Brazil and Chile. In Brazil, under the leadership of Luiz Carlos Prestes, the Brazilian Communist Party became one of the largest in Latin America. In 1935 Brazilian Communists combined with trade unions, Socialists, and Liberals to form the *Aliança Nacional Libertadora* (National Liberation Alliance) to oppose the totalitarian regime of VARGAS and the Brazilian Integralists (Fascists). The *Aliança* was declared illegal by the government and was dissolved; the Communist party was outlawed (November 1935) and Prestes and other leaders were arrested. However, in spite of its being driven underground, Communism continued to be an important factor in Brazilian politics. In Chile, following the tactics of Communist parties in France, Spain, and Brazil, the Chilean Communist Party entered into a Popular Front composed of leftist parties, including the moderate Radicals, to oppose the conservative government of ALESSANDRI PALMA (1936). At about the same time in Colombia, the Colombian Communist Party (organized 1930) reached its zenith under Gilberto Vieira, who co-operated with trade unions and other left-wing parties in support of the administration of Alfonso LÓPEZ PUMAREJO. In Mexico, there never was a strong Communist party, but through the widespread influence of Vicente LOMBARDO TOLEDANO, leader (1936–1946) of the *Conferación de Trabajadores de México* and head

of the *Confederación de Trabajadores de América Latina* (organized 1938), and known for his pro-Soviet sympathies, Communist ideas succeeded in infiltrating not only the Mexican labor movement but also the ranks of labor in other Latin-American countries. After the start of World War II, Latin-American Communists, adopting the then prevalent world-wide Communist technique, co-operated with the Axis; but when Germany invaded the Soviet Union in 1941, they changed their attitude and co-operated with democratic forces in prosecuting the war against Germany, Italy, and Japan. After the war, however, they reverted to a militant, anti-imperialist, anti-U. S. policy and have shared the basic objectives of all Communist parties throughout the world: to support the policies of the Soviet Union and to establish the hegemony of their own party within their particular countries. For a short time Latin-American Communism surged ahead and it seemed it would continue its ascent. A reaction set in, however, and Communism lost considerable ground during the following decade because of the close association of Communists with the Soviet Union. When the cold war began, the majority of Latin Americans chose the anti-Soviet side, and the popularity acquired during World War II was lost. During the late 1950's and early 1960's, Communists have regained some of the ground that had been lost. The postwar surge of Communism was especially strong in Brazil, where Prestes was released in 1945, and by 1947 the Communist party there became the largest in the New World. But in the same year the party was outlawed and Brazil broke diplomatic relations with the Soviet Union. In 1948, Prestes as well as fifteen deputies were expelled from the Brazilian congress. The estimate stands today at 35,000 Brazilian Communist Party members. Although officially outlawed, the Brazilian Communist Party is still a fairly potent factor in the political life of the country and openly engages in political activities. Approximately the same pattern was followed in Chile. The government of Juan RÍOS MORALES (1942–1946) rejected the support of Chilean Communists, but under his successor, GONZÁLEZ VIDELA, three Communists entered the first cabinet of the president. In April 1947, however, González Videla formed a new cabinet without them. Later in the same year the Communists were accused of having instigated the costly coal strike near Concepción, and Chile broke diplomatic relations with the Soviet Union. The government arrested hundreds of Communist leaders and the party was outlawed in 1948. The party continued its operations in a clandestine manner until 1958, when it was again declared legal and allowed to participate in political activity. The membership of the party is now estimated to be about 25,000. In Colombia the Communists, an estimated 5,000, were blamed for the Bogotá riots in 1948 and a number of Communist leaders were arrested, while diplomatic relations with the Soviet Union were severed. In spite of setbacks, the Colombian Communist Party has had a certain degree of success and has managed to increase its membership. The membership is now estimated to be about 10,000. In Mexico, Communist influence has been on the decline since 1946, when Lombardo Toledano lost his position as head of the *Confederación de Trabadjadores de México*. In Guatemala, where surprisingly enough there are only an estimated 1,100 Communists, they attained a dominant position in recent years. These Communists, led by Fortuny and Pellecar, co-operated with former President Jacobo ARBENZ GUZMÁN who, though not a Communist himself, put through far-reaching labor and agrarian reforms. In return for their support, they were allowed to become the main force in the labor unions of the country. The growing Communist influence in Guatemala was clearly in the mind of the U. S. Secretary of State John Foster Dulles when he pressed for the adoption of the anti-Communist resolution by the Tenth Inter-American Conference at Caracas in March 1954. The Arbenz regime was subsequently ousted by a revolt headed by Colonel Castillo Armas, and the Communist Party was proscribed. Since then, the Communists have again developed considerable influence and have increased their membership. It is estimated that today there are approximately 50,000 Communists in Argentina, 60,000 in Cuba, 30,000 in Venezuela, 5,000 in Uruguay, and 10,000 in Peru. Today

Communist parties are legal only in Mexico, Colombia, Ecuador, Bolivia, Chile, Cuba, Peru, and Uruguay. The revolution in Cuba has given the Communists a splendid opportunity to capitalize on anti-U. S. feeling and to promote Communist goals. The Communist movement in Latin America is presently enjoying a modest success in increasing its membership and in influencing certain governments. It has been active in combating the ALLIANCE FOR PROGRESS program, U. S. economic holdings and political influence, and U. S. actions against Cuba. The tensions created by the Sino-Soviet quarrel have profoundly affected the entire movement in Latin America. Most of the Communist parties have officially supported Moscow against Peking, but others have developed serious splits within their party organizations.

**Comonfort, Ignacio.** 1812–1863. Mexican liberal political leader. b. Puebla. Creole; customs collector at port of Acapulco. Dismissed by SANTA ANNA, he visited the United States and returned with a supply of munitions after being joined by other exiles in New Orleans. He led a revolution for the PLAN OF AYUTLA that overthrew Santa Anna in 1855. Minister of war under Juan ÁLVAREZ in 1855; made provisional president and served from 1855–1857. He was elected president under the new constitution in December 1857, but was forced to flee to the United States in 1858 after having been ousted by ZULOAGA. An honest moderate, his virtues were his downfall. In the hope of conciliation he agreed to the LEY LERDO of June 1856, the purpose of which was to increase the revenues of the government and stimulate economic progress. Trapped in a fight between Church and State, and hoping to satisfy both conservatives and liberals, he was left without supporters. He returned from exile to fight French invaders, 1861–1863, and was killed in ambush.

**Composiciones.** In colonial Spanish America, the procedure to legalize the title to lands through agreement with the government.

**Comunero Revolt.** A revolt that broke out in New Granada (Colombia) in 1781 as a result of an increase in taxes. The rebels were at first successful, finding support in sixty towns. However, the Spanish viceroy took drastic measures and the movement was crushed. Its leaders, Juan Francisco de Berbeo and José Antonio Galán, were executed in 1782 and 1783, respectively. This revolt fanned the latent antagonism between Colombian patriots and Spaniards, which was to break out with renewed intensity in the War of Independence thirty years later.

**Concepción.** The third largest city in the republic of Chile, the most important in the south of the country, located on the Bío-Bío River about 360 miles southwest of Santiago by rail. Concepción is the capital of the province of the same name and has a population of 174,000 (1961). It is situated less than 10 miles from its Pacific port, Talcahuano. Points of interest include: Caracol hill, from which there is a magnificent view; the Cerro Amarillo or Yellow Hill in the center of the city; the Plaza Independencia; the new cathedral; and the university. Concepción has good rail connections with Santiago and southern Chile, and is connected by air with many important Latin-American cities. It is located in a coal-producing region. The modern Huachipato steel plant near Talcahuano has contributed to the industrial expansion of the area. In Concepción itself there are flour mills, textile mills, and clothing plants The city was founded in 1550 by Pedro de VALDIVIA on the Pacific Ocean, on the site where present-day Penco is situated. The independence of Chile was proclaimed at Concepción on January 1, 1818. In colonial times it was sacked several times by the ARAUCANIAN INDIANS and was often wrecked by earthquakes. In March 1751, an earthquake destroyed it completely, and in 1755 it was rebuilt at its present location. It was again destroyed by an earthquake in 1835, and it suffered heavily from another in 1939. Traces of the latter can still be seen in the city. The most recent earthquakes took place on May 20, 1960, and March 28, 1965, when the city suffered extensive damage.

**Concepción.** City in the republic of Paraguay on the east bank of the Paraguay River, about 130 miles north of Asunción, with a population of 29,354 (est. 1961). It is the trade center of northern Paraguay and is connected by steamship service with Asunción and Corumbá, Brazil. Yerba maté, lumber, and cattle are produced in this area.

**Concordancia.** The name given to the coalition of Argentine right-wing radicals and conservatives that was in power from 1932 to 1940.

**Congrega** or **Congregación.** During the colonial period, any Indian town. The Spanish Crown realized early that it was necessary to concentrate the Indians in villages or towns if they were to be converted rapidly to Christianity and if labor was to be exacted from them. From about the middle of the 16th century on, the Spaniards pursued the policy of concentrating Indians in *congregas*. Often the Indians reacted unfavorably toward the system, and there were many revolts against it.

**Conquistadores.** English, conquistadors. Name given to the Spaniards who conquered the New World.

**Consejo de Cámara de las Indias.** A tribunal founded in 1600, composed of ministers from the CONSEJO DE INDIAS (Council of the Indies), with the attributes of a private council of the Spanish king in matters relating to the colonies. It was abolished in 1609, reestablished in 1644, and permanently abolished in 1834.

**Consejo de Indias** or **Real y Supremo Consejo de las Indias.** Council of the Indies, founded in Spain by CHARLES V on August 1, 1524, exercising supreme governing and judicial powers in the Spanish-American colonies. The composition of the council varied and the number of councilors started at six but was increased to nine or ten. After 1569 the men traveled to the Indies and attempted to understand the problems involved in colonial administration. All laws and decrees relating to the administration, taxation, and police of the American dominions were prepared and dispatched by the council, with the approval of the king and in his name. No important local scheme of government or colonial expenditure was put into operation by American officials without the approval of the council. It sat as a court of last resort in important civil suits appealed from the colonial *audiencias*. It had power of censorship of the press in regard to material published about or for the Indies. The code of law governing the Indies was called *Recopilación de leyes de las Indias* and was not issued until 1681, with approximately 6,400 laws in nine books. CHARLES III asked for revision of the code in 1765. Acting only as an advisor to the king in 1790, the council lost a great deal of its power. It was abolished by decree in 1812, re-established by FERDINAND VII in 1814, and again abolished by law in 1834. In 1851, it reappeared under the name of *Consejo de Ultramar* (Transmarine Council), but it went out of existence in 1854.

**Conselheiro, Antônio.** Real name, Antônio Vicente Mendes Maciel. 1828–1897. Brazilian religious fanatic who in 1897 led a rebellion in Bahia against the Brazilian government. After suffering heavy losses, the Brazilian army was finally able to crush the uprising, and Conselheiro was killed in battle. This episode is the theme of Euclydes da CUNHA's great novel, *Os sertões*.

**Conselho da India.** The Portuguese equivalent of the Spanish CONSEJO DE INDIAS, created in 1604 by PHILIP III of Spain, at the time when Portugal formed part of the Spanish Crown.

**Conselho do Ultamar.** Portuguese for Overseas Council. The body which replaced the CONSELHO DA INDIA (Council of the Indies) in Portugal in 1642 after the Portuguese regained their independence from Spain in 1640. It controlled the civil, religious, and military affairs of the colonies.

**Consolidación, Law of.** A royal Spanish decree enforced in Mexico between 1805 and 1809 that provided for the conversion of the landholdings of religious foundations into cash, and for the transfer of this capital to the Spanish treasury. The measure was a hard blow to the religious foundations in Mexico, for they held much real estate and owned many mortgages, and also to the rich conservatives, who were deeply involved in loans and debts on realty. The *consolidación*, in essence a financial operation aimed at the nationalization of the land held by the religious communities in Mexico, netted approximately 10,600,000 pesos during the period of its enforcement.

**Constant de Magalhães, Benjamin.** Also, **Botelho de Magalhães, Benjamin Constant.** 1838–1891. Brazilian statesman, Best-known for his liberal and republican teaching when professor at the military academy. He was the leader in the revolution that caused the overthrow of PEDRO II and established the republic in 1889.

**Constitución vitalicia.** From Spanish *vitalicia*, meaning "lasting for life." The name given to the constitution framed by BOLÍVAR in 1826 for Bolivia which he felt should be adopted in Peru and Colombia. It provided for a life-long presidency and the right of the president to name his own successor. It provided also that the vice-president was the responsible head of the administration, subject to impeachment by congress and the supreme court. The judiciary was entirely independent. There was no provision for real local self-government, although there was a complicated procedure advanced for the appointment of local officials. The congress was divided into three chambers: the tribunes who served four years; the senators who served eight; and the censors who were elected for life. There was to be freedom of worship for non-Catholics, and the exercise of the right of ecclesiastical patronage by the government was provided for. It was adopted in Bolivia. In Peru a similar system was adopted, but later put aside. Colombia never accepted it.

**Consulado.** A guild of merchants in the Spanish colonies. Representing the European residents and traders, it wielded considerable influence as a kind of chamber of commerce, and as a tribunal handling matters of contracts, freights, bankruptcy, and similar questions.

**Continuísmo.** Term used throughout Latin America to describe the act of continuing the president in power beyond his legal tenure.

**Contraband.** See SMUGGLING.

**Copán.** An ancient center of Mayan civilization situated in western Honduras, a few miles from the Guatemalan border, and the site of impressive ruins. The artifacts include temples, pyramids, stelae, an acropolis, and a stairway covered with hieroglyphics. The ruins were first described in a letter to the king of Spain by Diego Garcia de Palacios in 1576. The first archaeological expedition to Copán was undertaken in 1834 by the Irish adventurer John Gallagher. An important exploration was that of the Englishman, Alfred P. Maudsley, in 1881. In 1936, at the urging of Doctor Sylvanus G. Morley, the leading authority on the ruins, the Honduran Government and the Carnegie Institution of Washington embarked on the joint project of restoring the ruins. The work was completed in 1950.

**C.O.P.E.I.** In full, **Comité Organizador Pro Elección Independiente,** or **Committee Organized for Independent Elections.** A political party in Venezuela formed in 1945 in opposition to the policies of the government. COPEI, led by Rafael CALDERA, favored a more sympathetic attitude toward the church, and although revolutionary, it did not like the socialist policies of the BETANCOURT government. It gained nineteen seats in the constitutional assembly election of 1946. The party's name was later changed to the Social Christian Party (*Partido Social Cristiano*), but it is still known as COPEI. Although political parties were banned during the dictatorship of Pérez Jiménez (1952–1958)), the party was reorganized in 1958 and was represented in the presidential election by its candidate Rafael Caldera. Caldera was the party's presidential candidate again in 1963, at which time he polled the second highest number of votes.

**Copper.** Before the Spanish Conquest, copper, as well as tin and bronze, was known and worked by the Indians of Mexico and the Andes. Since iron was unknown, copper and stone served to make tools. However, when the Spaniards introduced iron, it gradually replaced copper until the electrical age again put copper in demand. After the Conquest, copper continued to be mined in Cuba, Haiti, Mexico, Venezuela, and Chile. Because the metal was difficult to smelt and because of the long journey to Europe, it could not compete with European copper and

therefore little was exported. It was used for the making of cannon, bells, and similar objects. It is estimated that during the colonial period Chile produced 83,000 metric tons, which is a small quantity compared with today's needs, but substantial if it is remembered that this was before the industrial age. Today copper is one of Latin America's leading metals. The major share of all Latin-American copper is produced in Chile, whose most important mines are located at Chuquicamata in the northern province of Antofagasta. Chilean production in 1964 amounted to 611,000 metric tons, making it the world's third copper producer. In Peru the Cerro de Pasco Copper Corporation and the Southern Peru Copper Corporation are important producers. The latter company is working the recently developed deposits at Toquepala, a mountain in southern Peru that contains an estimated 400,000,000 tons of copper ore. The open-pit operation was begun in 1956 and actual production of copper ore began in 1959. Today Toquepala is yielding more than 12,000 metric tons of 99 per cent pure copper every month. In Bolivia there is some copper mining in the Corocoro area. In Mexico copper is mined chiefly in the north in the states of Baja California, Sonora, and Coahuila. In Cuba the metal is exploited in the west, at Matahambre, and to a lesser extent in the eastern province of Oriente.

**Cordillera.** See ANDES MOUNTAINS.

**Córdoba.** A large central province of Argentina endowed with great agricultural wealth, having an area of 64,894 square miles and a population of 1,957,500 (est. 1960). A highly-developed agriculture and a growing industrial economy have made the province one of the most prosperous regions in the country. Among the most important crops of the province are wheat, corn, flax, rye, and oats. The famous Dique San Roque Reservoir, near the capital, Córdoba, holds about 825,000 cubic feet of water and irrigates a large part of the province's farmlands.

**Córdoba.** The third largest city of the republic of Argentina, capital of the province of the same name, situated at an altitude of about 1,400 feet, in the valley of the Río Primero, 430 miles northwest of Buenos Aires, with a population of 471,000 (1960). The city has retained to a great extent its colonial character, but it contains at the same time modern buildings, fine parks, and broad thoroughfares. Points of interest are the Plaza San Martín in the old section, the viceroy's house, the government house, the cathedral, and the university. Córdoba is a popular summer and winter resort, its attraction being the beautiful mountains surrounding it. It is connected by rail and air with other large South-American cities. Economically the city is important because of the agricultural wealth of the area around it. Wheat, corn, linseed, barley, and cattle are some of the regional products. Local industries include furniture, soap, leather and leather goods, textiles, cement, ceramics, and aircraft factories. The city was founded in 1573 by the governor of Tucumán province, Jerónimo Luis de Cabrera, who called it *Córdoba la Ilana*. The famous University of Córdoba, the oldest in Argentina and one of the oldest in the New World, was established in 1613 and contributed largely to the city's becoming a leading intellectual center in colonial South America. The city took an active part in the tumultuous political history of Argentina in the first half of the 19th century. After the achievement of independence, Córdoba opposed the Buenos Aires unitarians and was ruled by Juan Antonio Bustos from 1820 until his defeat by General PAZ in 1829. Córdoba suffered greatly under the tyranny of ROSAS (1835–1852), who imposed his will on the province through his local representative, Colonel Manuel López. The railroad to Córdoba, built in 1869, was the decisive factor in the city's rapid development in the late 19th century. Córdoba has been called the "American Seville" and the "American Rome."

**Córdoba, Francisco Hernández de.** *ca.* 1475–1518. Spanish soldier and explorer. He accompanied Pedro ARIAS DE ÁVILA to Panama in 1514, and went to Cuba with VELÁSQUEZ, who agreed to his leading an expedition westward to find slaves in 1517. He explored Yucatán, discovering the remnants of the great Mayan civilization. He suffered losses in a clash with the natives and returned home. On the way back to Cuba, he touched on the coast of Florida. Seriously wounded in battle, he died shortly afterward. His had been the first Spanish expedition to discover Mexico, leading to the expeditions of GRIJALVA in 1518 and CORTÉS in 1519.

**Córdoba, Jorge.** 1822–1861. President of Bolivia. b. La Paz. A son-in-law of Manuel BELZÚ, his presidency was imposed on the country by the retiring Belzú in 1855. He occupied the position for less than three years, and was then deposed and driven into exile by LINARES. Córdoba's administration was characterized by the continuation of the policies of his predecessor, which encouraged the CHOLO class in their opposition to the propertied class of Bolivia.

**Córdoba, Treaty of.** Treaty signed in the Mexican town of Córdoba, on August 24, 1821, by the Spanish viceroy O'DONOJÚ and the Mexican leader ITURBIDE. It followed substantially the PLAN OF IGUALA and provided for the withdrawal of Spanish forces from Mexico.

**Córdoba League.** Name given to an Argentine provincial political group formed by politicians of the Argentine provinces in opposition to the *porteños* of Buenos Aires. It controlled the country's political scene during the administrations of SARMIENTO (1868–1874), although Sarmiento himself attempted to remain neutral; of AVELLANEDA (1874–1880), who defeated the PORTEÑO candidate, MITRE; of ROCA (1880–1886), under whom the municipality of Buenos Aires separated from the province and became a federal district, with La Plata the new capital of the province; and of Juárez Celman (1886–1890). Its domination ended in 1890, when Juárez Celman was forced to resign because of the corruption and inefficiency of his administration.

**Corfo.** In full, **Corporación de Fomento** or **Development Corporation.** Established in Chile in 1939 during the administration of AGUIRRE CERDA, its purpose was the development of national industries. The government desired to stimulate production and plan the economic future of the country. Free from strict government control and given a wide latitude of operation, it accomplished great strides, and is one of the most successful examples of national planning carried out with international cooperation. The EXPORT-IMPORT BANK has advanced loans of over $70,000,000 to aid in the projects of the organization. A good deal of its work has been in the field of hydroelectric development, but it also works in the petroleum industry, agriculture, transport, steel, copper, cement, and irrigation fields. In 1961 CORFO presented a ten-year development program that was approved and put into operation by the government of Alessandri Rodríguez. The plan calls for increases in agricultural production, mining, manufacturing, and electrical power output and will be coordinated with the ALLIANCE FOR PROGRESS program. The overall capital investment will total more than ten billion escudos and will be supported by international monetary aid.

**Corn Islands.** Islands off the Caribbean coast of Nicaragua that, under the BRYAN-CHAMORRO TREATY of 1914, were to be the sites of U. S. naval bases. The bases, however, were never built.

**Coronado y Valdés, Francisco Vásquez de.** 1510–1554. Spanish explorer in America. b. Salamanca, Spain. Sailed for Mexico, 1535; in 1539 went as commander of the large exploring expedition sent by Viceroy MENDOZA northward to search for legendary QUIVIRA and CÍBOLA, lands of riches. He probed the Colorado River and discovered the Grand Canyon. He followed the Río Grande, went into Arizona, New Mexico, Texas, Oklahoma, and central Kansas, 1540–1542. He returned to Mexico in 1542, disappointed at his failure to find any rich Indian civilization.

**Corral, Ramón.** 1854–1912. Vice-president under DÍAZ of Mexico in 1904. Although an able administrator as governor of Sonora and responsible for having built a few schools, he was one of the most hated men in Mexico because he was said to have made his fortune by selling the Yaqui Indians into servitude. Allied with the CIENTÍFICOS, he was again vice-president in 1910, when DÍAZ had Bernardo REYES, the popular choice, exiled to Europe. Corral lost power when MADERO defeated Díaz and, unnoticed, he went into exile. Díaz' insistence on making the unpopular Corral his official successor in case of his death in office was a leading cause of the Madero revolution of 1910.

**Corregidor.** Local official, both of Spain and Spanish America, with administrative and judicial powers. In Spanish America there were two types of *corregidores;* the *corregidor de españoles* (of Spaniards) and the *corregidor de indios* (of Indians). The former was appointed by the Crown and lived in the Spanish settlements. The latter was appointed by the AUDIENCIA and lived in Indian villages. Each presided over his respective *cabildo* or municipal council. The duties of the *corregidor* were to foster economic development of his district, to make at least one tour of his district during his term of office, and to resolve administrative and judicial problems. Special duties of the *corregidor de indios* were the collection of tribute from the Indians, the supervision of forced labor that was demanded of the Indians, and the protection of the natives from the Spaniards. The tyranny and corruption of the *corregidores,* especially in their relations with the Indians, were often extreme. CHARLES III, in his reforms, gradually replaced the *corregidores* by *intendentes,* and by 1790 the new system was in operation throughout Spanish America.

**Correo.** Spanish, meaning mail, or post office.

**Cortés, Hernán.** 1485–1547. Spanish conqueror of Mexico. b. Medellín. Went to Hispaniola (Santo Domingo) in 1504 when 19 years old; officer on expedition led by Diego VELÁSQUEZ to Cuba, 1511; commanded expedition that set out to explore the mainland, February 1519, along the coast of Yucatán and Mexico; aided by Jerónimo de AGUILAR, who had been shipwrecked about eight years earlier and had learned the Mayan language; slaughtered the Indians at Tabasco; met MARINA, an Indian girl, who became his mistress and acted as interpreter and guide; founded Veracruz; destroyed his fleet so that there would be no turning back; defeated and made alliance with Tlaxcalans;

entered the Aztec capital Tenochtitlán (Mexico City) on November 8, 1519; held Aztec chief MOCTEZUMA as a hostage; captured NARVÁEZ, who had been sent to arrest and replace him; fought Aztec revolt in 1520; forced to lead Spaniards out of the city in June 1520; retreated to Tlaxcala; made another assault on Tenochtitlán and captured it in August 1521; in 1523–1524 Cortés sent two expeditions into Central America, one of which, led by Pedro de ALVARADO Y MESÍA, overcame the Mayan tribes in Guatemala; journeyed to Honduras, 1524–1526; deprived of governorship in 1526 and returned to Spain in 1528; given honors and married to daughter of Count of Aguilar; returned to Mexico in 1530 not as governor, but only as captain general; on an expedition he discovered lower California in 1536; returned to Spain in 1540 and died there, his body being afterward shipped to Mexico for burial; as governor of New Spain he did much to protect the Indians, promote economic growth, and spread Christianity; probably the greatest of the conquistadors.

**Cortés Castro, León.** 1882–1946. President of Costa Rica, 1936–1940. During his term of office a board of agricultural cooperation was organized and improvements were made in the agriculture of the country. The government expropriated the holdings of the Electric Bond and Share Company of New York, but paid the company an indemnity. Cortés Castro also launched an anti-Communist program.

**COSACH.** In full, **Compañía Salitrera de Chile** or **Nitrate Company of Chile.** A Chilean state monopoly organized under President Carlos IBÁÑEZ DEL CAMPO in 1930. One half of the shares of its capital (3,000,000 pesos) was owned by the national treasury, and the other half by private nitrate companies. Its function was to control foreign sales and exports of nitrate, and it was granted many concessions, including the removal of export taxes on nitrates and the transfer to it of government-owned nitrate reserve lands. In spite of the fact that COSACH reduced production in order to profit by the ensuing scarcity on the world market, it suffered heavy losses during the depression years; and although it possessed control over the industry, it soon came under attack from many sides. It was accused of corruption and of being an instrument of foreign bankers. It was also charged with granting to foreign companies larger production quotas than to Chilean concerns. COSACH was dissolved in 1934 under the ALESSANDRI PALMA administration.

**Costa, Cláudio Manuel da.** ca. 1729–1790. Brazilian poet. b. Marianna, Minas Gerais. Studied law at the University of Coimbra, Portugal, but is primarily known for his poetry. His most popular work, the epic *Villarica*, written in 1773 and published in 1841, is considered a classic.

**Costa, Hipólito da.** 1774–1823. Brazilian journalist. b. Colonia (now part of Uruguay) ; edited the *Correio Brasiliense* which was printed in London from 1808 to 1822. A liberal who believed in reform but not revolution, he was a Freemason, and wrote editorials denouncing abuses in Brazil, which provoked the Pernambucan movement in 1817. Actually a monarchist, he did not believe democracy was possible in Brazil; nevertheless he fought for independence and the abolition of slavery.

**Costa Rica.** Spanish, meaning rich coast. Costa Rica is the second smallest republic in Central America. Almost cut off from its neighbors by water, it is washed on its low eastern coast by the Caribbean Sea, and on the west by the Pacific Ocean. It is bounded on the north by Nicaragua and on the south by Panama. It has an area of 19,575 square miles, extending 200 miles at its greatest length and 150 miles at its widest point. The Caribbean coast line is 180 miles long, and the Pacific coast line extends 360 miles. The most important mountain ranges are the Sierra de Tilarán and the Talamanca Mountains. The crater atop Poas Volcano is the largest in the world. The mountains, which are volcanic and the cause of common earthquakes, rise more than 12,000 feet in southern Costa Rica. The volcanic dust and ashes, however, make for a rich soil in the central plain area. The important rivers are the Río Grande, Revantazón, and the Diquis. Orosi

Falls is the chief waterfall of the country. The rivers are not navigable because the steep slopes of the mountains cause swift currents, but the water provides power and irrigation. The climate is moderate and pleasant, and the rainfall is average. Costa Rica has rich natural resources, but they have not been developed to capacity. Gold and silver are mined in the Pacific Coast area along with copper, quartz, alabaster, sulphur, and mercury. Some granite and oil are found in the hills, while in the forests fine hardwoods such as rosewood, cedar, mahogany, and ebony are plentiful. The population is 1,507,000 (est. 1966), of which more than 97 per cent are white and MESTIZO, 2 per cent Negro, and less than 1 per cent Indian. Most of the people live on the central highland and lower mountain slopes. Roman Catholicism is the state religion, but there is complete freedom of worship. The official language is Spanish. The monetary unit is the colón, worth approximately 15.10 cents. The Costa Ricans take pride in the fact that there are more teachers than soldiers in their country and that school attendance on the elementary level is free and compulsory. Less than 21 per cent of those ten years of age and over are illiterate. The University of Costa Rica, first founded in 1843 and re-established in 1941, along with the National School of Agriculture, are both in San José, the capital of the country, which has a population of 119,482 (1962). Alojuela, population 20,642 (1962), and Puntarenas, population 20,170 (1962), are also important cities. Agriculture is the leading occupation. The chief products are coffee, bananas, rubber, cacao, rice, tobacco, corn, and sugar. Abacá and hemp are fibers produced and used in the manufacture of rope. The distillation of spirits is a government monopoly. The United States is Costa Rica's chief trading partner, supplying almost one-half of the country's imports and taking more than one-half of its exports. The nation is divided into seven provinces, each with a governor, appointed by the president and responsible to the minister of government in the cabinet; however the people choose their own mayors in the municipalities. A bill of rights guarantees individual liberty. Voting is compulsory for all men; by a direct vote of the people the president is elected for a period of four years, and he may not be immediately re-elected. There is no vicepresident, but a cabinet of eight members; the congress (chamber of deputies) is a unicameral body with 57 deputies serving for four years; the supreme court has 17 members chosen by the congress; there is no jury system.

Costa Rica was discovered by Christopher COLUMBUS in 1502. Cartago in upper Costa Rica was settled by the Spanish in 1564. Until 1821 it was part of the captaincy general of Guatemala, when it joined other Central-American countries in becoming a part of Mexico. In 1823 the CENTRAL AMERICAN FEDERATION was formed. Costa Rica became an independent government in 1838. From 1838 to 1870 the country was torn apart by rivalries between two groups of landowning families. Tomás GUARDIA, an army officer, overthrew the government in 1870 and dominated the affairs of the nation until his death in 1882. The era of modern democratic government in Costa Rica started in 1902 with the election of Ascensión Esquivel, who administered an efficient and honest government. With the assistance of the United States, the important boundary dispute between Costa Rica and Panama was settled in 1921. In 1941 the country declared war on the Axis powers and took part in the defense of the Western Hemisphere in World War II.

Constitutional democratic government has been preserved during the 20th century, except for the seizure of power by Federico Tinoco in 1917, who held power until 1919, and except for the civil war of 1948. After the 1948 election, the defeated candidate, CALDERÓN GUARDIA, charging fraud, had the congress annul the election, whereupon Colonel José FIGUERES FERRER, protesting illegal electoral procedures, led a successful rebellion and installed a junta under his leadership. A national assembly called to draw up a new constitution validated the election of ULATE BLANCO, the victorious candidate in the 1948 election. Provisional President Figueres turned over the government to Ulate in November 1949. Figueres became a candidate for the presidency in 1953 and was elected to succeed Ulate in

November of that year. On two occasions, December 1948 and January 1955, supporters of ex-President Calderón Guardia invaded Costa Rica from Nicaragua with the support of SOMOZA, dictator of that country. These conflicts were settled by the intervention of the ORGANIZATION OF AMERICAN STATES. Costa Rica refused to attend the Inter-American Conference of 1954 in Venezuela, chiefly because the host country was under the control of a dictator. In 1958 Mario Echandi Jiménez was chosen to succeed Figueres in an election that was observed by a three-man team sent by the Secretary General of the United Nations upon the invitation of the Costa Rican government. Echandi was succeeded in 1962 by Francisco José Orlich Bolmarich, who had been backed by Figueres. José Joaquín trejos Fernández was inaugurated as president in May 1966. Since 1950 Costa Rica has made basic changes in its economic production. Although the country has continued to rely on agricultural exports, it has increasingly taken on the aspects of an industrial state. From 1952 to 1956 the number of commercial and industrial establishments were doubled, and the first national industrial fair was held at San José from December 28, 1954, to January 6, 1955. In addition to the program of economic diversification, President Orlich sponsored regional cooperation in the Central-American Common Market. In March 1963, U. S. President Kennedy met with the presidents of the five Central-American countries and Panama in San José. The seven presidents pledged their support to the containment of Communism emanating from Cuba, the principles of the ALLIANCE FOR PROGRESS, and the economic integration of Central America. See CENTRAL AMERICA and ORGANIZATION OF CENTRAL AMERICAN STATES.

**Cotton.** A native American crop, cotton was widely grown by the Indians of pre-Conquest America and was an all-important product for clothing. During the colonial period cotton textiles were manufactured in many parts of Latin America. By the end of the 18th century this commodity ranked among the leading agricultural products of Mexico, Brazil, the Caribbean area, and the northern coast of South America. Today the leading Latin-American producers are Mexico and Central America, Brazil, and Argentina. In Mexico and Central America there has been a radical increase in cotton production in recent years, the 1962–1963 crop for this area amounting to about 3,293,000 bales as compared with 2,118,326 bales for the 1954-1955 crop. In Mexico a record 2,380,000 bales were produced in 1962–1963 compared with 1,800,000 bales in 1961–1962. In Central America, Guatemala, El Salvador, and Nicaragua are the largest producers.

**Council of the Indies.** See CONSEJO DE INDIAS.

**Courts.** Aside from the regular courts of first instance in towns and supreme courts or *audiencias,* the Spanish colonial administration included a great number of special courts, among them the tribunals of the *gremios* or guilds, the ecclesiastical courts, military courts, the *consulados* or courts for commerce, the *tribunal de minería* or court for mining, the Indian courts, and others. The smooth functioning of the judicial system was constantly hampered by ceaseless conflicts between civil and ecclesiastical groups, and this antagonism erupted at times into armed clashes. In colonial Brazil the judicial system was far less developed than in the Spanish colonies. The municipalities had courts of first instance. A high court, the *Relação da Bahia,* was established in 1608, abolished in 1626 and re-established in 1652. Special courts included the *Casa de Supplicação,* the *Desembargo do Paço,* and ecclesiastical courts. By the close of the 18th century there were two superior judicial districts, with high courts at Bahia and Rio. Appeals from these courts were received directly by Lisbon. In modern Latin-American history the power of the courts is in large measure determined by the power of the executive. In a liberal, democratic government, the judiciary has independence; in a dictatorship or a government with a strong executive, the judiciary has only secondary power. See AUDIENCIA.

**Creelman Interview.** In 1908 DÍAZ of Mexico gave an interview to the American journalist James Creelman, published in the

March issue of *Pearson's Magazine*, stating that Mexico was ready for a democratic form of government and that he, the dictator Díaz, would welcome an opposition party and would be willing to turn over his power to any candidate who was legally elected president. Re-elected in 1910, Díaz did not carry out these promises, but they helped to stimulate opposition and eventually led to the MADERO revolution.

**Creoles.** Spanish, *criollos*, Portuguese, *crioulos*. The Latin-American whites born in America. Although there was no law debarring them from public offices, they were usually excluded from high administrative positions in both Church and State in the Spanish colonies; this fact contributed much to the antagonism between them and the Spaniards. In Brazil, according to a royal order of the late 17th century, creoles were to be given preferential treatment in the matter of appointments to vital positions. In practice, however, the important posts were usually filled by the more influential Portuguese. It was in the town governments, the *cabildo* in the Spanish colonies and the *senado da cámara* in Brazil, that the creoles were represented and had considerable influence. The growing hostility of the creoles toward the peninsular Spaniards was the most important cause of the discontent in the Spanish colonies on the eve of the War for Independence, and did its share in fanning the flame of revolt. In Brazil, too, the hostility of Brazilians toward peninsular Portuguese played an important role in the movement for the country's independence, 1822, and in the ouster of PEDRO I, 1831.

**Crespo, Joaquín.** 1845-1898. President of Venezuela. b. San Francisco, Cuba. As a general, he supported GUZMÁN BLANCO and agreed to serve as figurehead president under Blanco's guidance, 1884-1886. He led the revolution that succeeded in deposing President Andueza Palacio in 1892 and set up a dictatorship, 1892-1894; a new constitution issued under the Crespo administration, 1893; elected president and served, 1894-1898. This professional soldier from the *llanos* gave the country comparative peace from 1894 to 1898. His administration was chiefly notable for the sensational controversy over the boundary between Venezuela and British Guiana, when gold was discovered in the disputed territory. This led to U. S. diplomatic intervention, 1895-1897. In an unsuccessful attempt to defend his successor, Ignacio Andrade, he was killed.

**Cristeros of Mexico.** Name given to the militant Catholics who often resorted to armed violence in combatting the anticlerical policy of the Mexican government in the late 1920's. Their slogan was *Cristo Rey* (Christ the King). Their revolt lasted from 1927 to 1930 and functioned chiefly in Jalisco and other west-central states.

**C.R.O.M.** In full, **Confederación Regional Obrera Mexicana.** A Mexican federation of labor unions formed as the result of the convention of Mexican labor leaders at Saltillo in the state of Coahuila in May 1918. Under the leadership of its secretary general, Luis MORONES, it was organized on a craft-union basis and modeled closely after the American Federation of Labor. Through the *Grupo Acción*, an inner circle of eighteen men who controlled the C.R.O.M.'s activities, the latter was able to organize a Mexican Labor Party, the purpose of which was to sponsor OBREGÓN's candidacy to the presidency. During Obregón's term of office, 1920-1924, the chieftains of the C.R.O.M. were rewarded with political patronage and with support against rival trade-union organizations. The *Grupo Acción* entered on a program of smashing the independent unions, and this practice continued throughout the CALLES administration, 1924-1928. Meanwhile the leaders of the C.R.O.M. were becoming rich and corrupt. Little of this wealth came directly from the workers. At the height of its power, the C.R.O.M. claimed a membership of a million and a half, but only thirteen thousand of them paid any union dues. Much of it was acquired, by processes that resembled blackmail, from employers. After the ascension to the presidency of PORTES GIL at the end of 1928, the C.R.O.M. was smashed by the government with the help of revolutionary unions that had retained their independence. In the textile districts of Veracruz, C.R.O.M. unions maintained themselves for years, but in the country as a whole, the federation rapidly disintegrated. Its successor was the C.G.O.C. *(Confederación General de Obreros y Campesinos)*, organized in 1932 by LOMBARDO TOLEDANO, long a member of the old C.R.O.M.

**Crowder, Enoch Herbert.** 1859–1932. American army officer and ambassador. b. Missouri. Graduated U.S.M.A., West Point, 1881. During the provisional government established by Secretary Taft in Cuba in 1906, an advisory commission headed by Colonel Crowder drafted laws covering elections, civil service, the judiciary, municipal and provincial government, and other matters that should have been drafted by the Cuban congress. He was head of the board that supervised elections in Cuba in 1908, and he set up new electoral laws in Cuba in 1919. Sent as personal representative of the president of the United States in 1921, he attempted to straighten out Cuba's economic problems, and arranged for a loan of $50,000,000 in 1922. He served as U. S. ambassador to Cuba from 1923 to 1927.

**Cruz, Oswaldo.** 1872–1917. Brazilian physician and hygienist, who was responsible for freeing Rio de Janeiro from yellow fever, 1903–1909, rendering it one of the most healthful tropical cities in the world; aided by the research work of the scientist, Adolpho Lutz.

**Cruz, Sor Juana Inés de la.** Called **The Tenth Muse.** Real name, **Juana María Inés de Asbaje y Ramírez de Cantillana.** 1651–1695. Mexican poetess, the greatest Spanish-American poet of the colonial period. She spent some time at the court of the viceroy, where her beauty and intelligence gained her the admiration of all. At the age of 18 she entered a convent, where she died at the age of 44. She wrote secular and religious poetry, the exquisite quality of her love poems gaining her wide fame. Her best-known works are *Sonetos* (Sonnets), *Liras, Romancero de la ausencia,* and *Sueño.*

**Cruzada.** See BULA DE CRUZADA.

**C.T.M.** In full, **Confederación de Trabajadores de México.** A Mexican federation of labor unions organized in the spring of 1936, under the leadership of the radical Vicente LOMBARDO TOLEDANO, who became its secretary. The C.T.M., organized on a basis of industrial unionism, was a powerful factor in Mexico's economic life during the administration of President CÁRDENAS and was incorporated into the labor sector of the official party when it was reorganized by President Cárdenas into the P.R.M. By 1940, according to Lombardo Toledano, C.T.M. unions were operating a number of sugar mills and textile factories, the railroads, all of the Mexican ships trading in the Gulf of Mexico, trolleys, buses, etc. The more conservative administrations of ÁVILA CAMACHO, ALEMÁN VALDÉS, RUIZ CORTINES, and LÓPEZ MATEOS have cut back the militant activities of C.T.M. The P.R.I has purged the organization of Communism and imposed discipline to help develop a sense of responsibility to the Mexican economy. In recent years the C.T.M. has become less occupied with politics and more concerned with social and economic questions. There are no recent figures of the C.T.M. membership, but the confederation without doubt dominates and overshadows its smaller rivals. Estimates of its membership in 1962 ranged from 500,000 to 1,300,000, including unions in the fields of railways, mining, communications, electric power, petroleum, and nearly all the branches of industrial economy. Its membership includes twenty national unions, thirty-one state federations, and more than one hundred local and regional federations. The C.T.M. has continued to be the official representative of organized labor within the P.R.I.

**Cuartelazo.** From Spanish *cuartel,* meaning barracks. Literally, a blow from the barracks. In Spanish America, *cuartelazo* is the name given to any military uprising against the established authority.

**Cuatequil.** Name given in New Spain, during the colonial period, to the forced wage *(repartimiento)* system.

**Cuauhtémoc.** Sometimes called **Guatemotzin.** *ca.* 1495–1525. Last AZTEC emperor of Mexico; nephew and son-in-law of MOCTEZUMA II (Montezuma). Leader of the Aztec forces that opposed CORTÉS after the death of

Moctezuma's successor, CUITLAHUAC, he attempted to defend Mexico City against Cortés in 1521. He was captured and tortured, but would not reveal the hiding place of the Aztec treasures, and his stoical courage while under torture has become legendary. He was taken as hostage, marched to Honduras and executed on charges of treachery. The alleged discovery of his bones in Mexico recently has caused considerable interest.

**Cuba.** Called the **Pearl of the Antilles.** The largest island of the West Indies, lying among the Greater Antilles. To the north lie the Gulf of Mexico and the Strait of Florida; the Atlantic Ocean is to the northeast; to the south is the Caribbean Sea; to the east, separated by the Windward Passage (50 miles wide) is Haiti, and Jamaica is 85 miles to the south. Key West in Florida is about 90 miles away, and Yucatán is 130 miles to the west. The area of Cuba is 44,218 square miles. It is 730 miles long and its width averages 50 miles, although it expands to a width of 160 miles. Including the larger Keys, the coast line is 2,500 miles long. Cuba has a population of 7,750,000 (est. 1966), 73 per cent white, 15 per cent mulatto, and 12 per cent Negro. Its outstanding harbor at Havana is one of the finest and safest in the world. Havana is also the capital of the country, and has a population of 1,305,000 (1960). Guantánamo and Bahía Honda are other important harbors. The second city is Holguín, population 226,779 (1960), followed by Camagüey, population 191,379 (1960). The mountains, reaching a general elevation of 3,000 feet are in Pinar del Río Province in the west, and in Oriente in the east. The highest point, at Pico Turquino, reaches an altitude of 8,230 feet. The soil is fertile and rich in vegetation; there are about 3,500,000 acres of dense forest. Cuba is the largest cane sugar producer in the world, with about 2,285,000 acres devoted to this crop. In the past sugar produced about two-thirds of the national income and was the most important crop. Mismanagement of production by the government caused a decline from 6,767,000 tons in 1961 to 3,800,000 tons in 1963. By 1966 sugar production had risen to 4,500,000 tons. Sugar imports from Cuba were embargoed by the United States in 1960.

The second most important industry is tobacco. Grown chiefly in the renowned Vuelta Abajo area, it is used in the manufacture of world-famous Havana cigars and cigarettes. Bananas, coffee, molasses, pineapples, citrus fruits, coconuts, dyewoods, fibers, mahogany, cedar woods, oils, and resins are also important commercially. There are 11,250 miles of railroad track and 5,000 miles of good all-weather roads distributed throughout the island. The entire transportation system steadily deteriorated after 1958 but in 1963 purchases of buses from England and locomotives from France were made in an attempt to improve services. In June 1951 the U. S. dollar was no longer legal tender in Cuba, and the sole monetary unit, the peso, was established at a par with the dollar. The language is Spanish, but English is widely understood. The prevailing religion is Roman Catholicism, but all faiths are tolerated. Education has made rapid advances according to claims made by the Castro regime. The number of students enrolled in primary and secondary schools doubled after 1959, and adult education schools have virtually eliminated illiteracy. The important University of Havana was founded in 1728.

Cuba was discovered by COLUMBUS on his first voyage on October 28, 1492. Its conquest was undertaken by Diego de VELÁSQUEZ in 1511, and a number of communities were quickly established. The Indians were soon wiped out as a result of mistreatment and disease, and the importation of Negro slaves was begun in 1512. In 1519 Havana was established on its present site and developed rapidly, soon becoming the most important base in the Caribbean. During the colonial period Cuba was a great producer of sugar, and in the 18th century it also increased its production of tobacco and coffee. Foreign pirates frequently attacked the island, and in 1762 the British were able to capture Havana and occupy it for a year. From the beginning of the 19th century there were frequent rebellions against the authoritarian rule of the Spanish, and these movements culminated in the Ten Year War, 1868–1878. Despite reforms undertaken by the Spanish government after this conflict, Cuba remained determined to gain her freedom. Another revolt broke out in 1895 under the leadership of the famous patriots José MARTÍ and Máximo GÓMEZ. Martí was killed shortly after the hostilities began, but the revolutionaries carried on the fight, which was waged with great ferocity on both sides. In 1898 the United States intervened, and after the short SPANISH-AMERICAN WAR, Cuba gained her independence as established by the Treaty of Paris, signed December 10, 1898. The United States withdrew in 1902 and Cuba became a republic. The PLATT AMENDMENT, written into a treaty of 1903, gave the United States the power to intervene in Cuban affairs, but this right was revoked in 1934. The first two decades of the 20th century were periods of political instability causing the United States to intervene in the internal affairs of Cuba, 1906–1909, 1912, and 1917–1922. The administration of General Gerardo MACHADO Y MORALES (1925–1933) was a virtual dictatorship, punctuated by constant rebellions. Machado was finally forced to leave the country when the army turned against him. His successor, Carlos Manuel de CÉSPEDES Y QUESADA, was forced out in turn by a coup led by Colonel Fulgencio BATISTA Y ZALDÍVAR, who appointed GRAU SAN MARTÍN as provisional president. While the country was in the throes of a severe economic depression, Batista was able to force Grau's resignation, 1934. Cuba entered into a period of *de facto* governments, one election of Batista succeeding the other. Batista was officially elected president, 1940–1944; then, after a free election, he was succeeded by Grau, who held office until 1948. PRÍO SOCARRÁS was elected by a large majority in 1948 and served until 1952 when a coup d'etat led by Batista forced him to leave the country; Batista again became head of Cuba. Batista suspended the 1940 constitution and called himself *Jefe del Estado* (Head of State). Batista was elected president in November 1954, his opponent, Grau San Martín, having withdrawn from the race a short time before the election. Strong opposition developed against Batista, denying the validity of the election and organizing a campaign of harassment and sabotage in the provinces. The opposition, led by Fidel CASTRO, carried on guerrilla warfare that rapidly brought a state of virtual

civil war. The Batista government collapsed on January 1, 1959; the president resigned and fled the country. Manuel URRUTIA LLEO was designated president of the new provisional government immediately, and Fidel Castro took the position of premier in the following month. Castro resigned his position as premier on July 17 but resumed that office after Urrutia resigned as president in the same month. Osvaldo DORTICÓS TORRADO was named to replace Urrutia. The new Cuban government soon began a propaganda campaign blaming the ills of Cuba on the United States and expressing warm friendship for the Communist countries. Relations with the United States rapidly deteriorated while economic ties between the two countries were all but severed. By the end of 1960 the Cuban government had seized U. S. investments in that country amounting to $1,500,000,000. On January 3, 1961, the U. S. government broke off diplomatic relations with the Castro government because of a campaign of vilification that included the charge that the U. S. government was planning an invasion of Cuba and a demand that the staff of the U. S. embassy in Havana be drastically cut. In April 1961 armed forces attempted an invasion of Cuba. The invaders were defeated and forced to surrender. The participation of the U. S. government in the organizational phase of the invasion caused serious repercussions throughout Latin America and the entire world. The meeting of the foreign ministers of the ORGANIZATION OF AMERICAN STATES in January 1962, at Punta del Este, Uruguay, excluded Cuba from participation in the inter-American system, because of the Cuban government's adherence to Communism. Late in 1962 evidence that the Communist nations were sending military weapons and armed forces to Cuba led to an international crisis. On October 22, 1962, the U. S. government demanded that offensive weapons capable of constituting a threat to the Western Hemisphere be removed from Cuba. A quarantine of the island was maintained by the U. S. Navy, which searched all ships thought to be carrying offensive ballistic missiles to Cuba. The Soviet Union agreed to the U. S. demand and ordered the dismantling of the missile bases on October 28.

In October 1963 the island suffered extreme damage in a hurricane that hovered over Cuba for five days and was the worst of the century in the Caribbean area. From October 4th to the 8th the shattering hurricane destroyed crops and took the lives of more than 1,000 Cubans. Recent developments include the dropping from public view of former war minister Che Guevara; a steady worsening of economic conditions; Castro's consent to an airlift from Cuba to Florida of 300,000 Cuban emigrés, excluding men of conscription age and essential workers; and a severing of relations between Cuba and Communist China, a by-product of the Sino-Soviet split.

**Cúcuta, Congress of.** The constituent assembly that met in Cúcuta, New Granada (Colombia), in 1821. It drew up a federal constitution for the recently-created nation of Colombia (Great Colombia), and confirmed BOLÍVAR in his office as president, and Francisco de Paula SANTANDER as vice-president. The constitution of Cúcuta was abrogated by BOLÍVAR in 1828, who then assumed dictatorial powers in order to hold the new state together.

**Cuerpo de Minería.** See REAL CUERPO DE MINERÍA.

**Cuervo, Rufino José.** 1844–1911. Colombian philologist and grammarian. Author of *Apuntaciones críticas al lenguaje bogotano*, *Notas a la gramática de Bello*, and *Diccionario de construcción y régimen de la lengua castellana*.

**Cuestas, Juan Lindolfo.** 1837–1905. President of Uruguay from 1897 to 1903. b. Paysandú. On February 10, 1898, he dissolved congress and declared himself dictator, and in March 1899 he was legally elected president. In 1902 he was able to avert an attempted plot on his life, which was the result of his anti-Catholic reform measures.

**Cuevas, Mariano.** b. 1879. Jesuit historian, author of *Historia de la Iglesia, en México*, an important five-volume ecclesiastical history of Mexico.

**Cuitlahuac.** Aztec leader, succeeded MOCTEZUMA in June 1520. He fought bravely against CORTÉS and the Spaniards and sent ambassadors to the other Indian tribes, endeavoring to form a federation against the Spaniards, but the TLAXCALANS, for example, remembered the long years of Aztec domination and refused. He died of smallpox, 1520, and was succeeded by CUAUHTÉMOC.

**Cumaná.** Venezuelan port and capital of the state of Sucre, situated on the northeastern coast of Venezuela, 185 miles east of Caracas. Population approximates 71,000. The principal products of the surrounding area are coffee, tobacco, cocoa, sugar, and hides. Important local industries are the manufacturing of cotton goods, and fishing. The town is connected with other centers by ship and air. Founded by Diego Castellón in 1523, Cumaná was at first known as Nuevo Toledo. It is the oldest existing European-built settlement on the South-American mainland. In colonial times it was an important Spanish-American center of trade with Spain. Severe earthquakes wrecked the town in 1766, 1797, and 1929.

**Cunha, Euclydes da.** 1866–1909. Brazilian novelist. He was a military engineer by profession, a journalist by trade, and a sociologist by avocation. He is most famous for his work *Os sertões*, 1902 (translated as Rebellion in the Backlands, 1944) which is the powerful story of the rural mystic, Antonio CONSELHEIRO, who gathers a fanatic group and settles down with them in the *sertão*, a vast area in the interior of northeast Brazil. The community is rebellious, and the government is forced to send military expeditions to subdue it. This is finally accomplished after three unsuccessful attempts are made. The book is beautifully written, although somber in mood. *Os sertões* is considered by some critics to be one of the best books ever to have emerged from Brazil.

**Curaçao.** See NETHERLANDS ANTILLES.

**Cuzco.** City in the south of Peru, 365 miles southeast of Lima, standing at an elevation of 11,440 feet, with a population of about 70,000 (est. 1960), mostly Quechua-speaking Indians. The climate of the city is cool. Once the capital of the Incan empire, Cuzco has been for centuries a center of interest for archaeologists. Everywhere in the city there are vestiges of Incan architecture. The walls of perfect stonework lining many streets; the remains of the temple of the Sun; the ruins of the temples of the Moon, the Stars, Thunder and Lightning, and the Rainbow; the many Inca palaces, later embellished by the Spaniards; and the ruins of Sacsahuaman Fortress near the city are points of interest. Recent excavations have uncovered more ruins, and in 1946 the remains of PIZZARRO's half-brother Gonzalo and of the two ALMAGROS were discovered. Cuzco, apart from being the site of Inca ruins, is also a Spanish colonial city with many religious buildings. The most notable of these is the cathedral, a structure of Renaissance style completed in 1564, and reconstructed after the earthquake of 1650. The building is made entirely from granite taken from Incan structures. Other important edifices are the prefecture, formerly the palace of Francisco Pizarro, the university (founded in 1598), and the museum of Peruvian antiquities. Many buildings were damaged extensively by an earthquake in 1950. A railroad connects Cuzco with the port of Mollendo, 400 miles to the south. Industries include cotton mills, distilleries, tanneries, and chocolate and sugar refineries. The city was founded in the 11th century by the first Inca ruler, MANCO CAPAC, and became the capital of the vast Incan empire. It was protected by heavy walls and by the fortress of Sacsahuaman, and within the city the Incas held court, the splendor of which had no equal in South America. Pizarro took formal possession of the city in 1534, granting it the title of *La Muy Noble y Gran Ciudad del Cuzco* (Very Great and Noble City of Cuzco). The conquerors made many Incan buildings into private dwellings and others were converted into churches and convents. In early colonial times, the city suffered from the civil wars among the conquerors and from Incan uprisings. The native population was rapidly reduced from 200,000 to 20,000, and the city consequently declined soon after the establishment of the viceroyalty.

# D

**Danish West Indies.** In 1671 King Christian V of Denmark was persuaded by a group of Dutch traders to found a Danish West India Company and to occupy the island of St. Thomas. The action of the Dutch was prompted by the fact that Holland was at war with France and had difficulties in carrying on trade in Dutch ships. St. Thomas developed into an important center for the slave trade and prospered during the 18th century. The islands of St. Croix, St. Thomas, and St. John, which were taken over by Denmark, are known today as the Virgin Islands and are U. S. territory with a population of 32,000. The United States purchased them from Denmark in 1917 for $25,000,000. The majority of the population is Negro, and supports itself by farming, cattle raising, and fishing, and by the tourist trade. The capital, Charlotte Amalie, is on St. Thomas. The inhabitants of the territory are U. S. citizens, ruled by a governor who is appointed by the president.

**Darío, Rubén.** 1867–1916. Nicaraguan poet and writer. b. Metapa. One of the greatest poets of the Spanish language; considered the chief representative of the Modernist movement in Latin America. It is easy to tell whether a Spanish poem was written before or after Darío, so strong was the originality of his style. His works are characterized not only by great pioneering of style, but by the uniqueness of the subject matter and the exquisite quality of his verse. He not only revived old Spanish meters but introduced a number of bold metrical innovations; his work was replete with colorful imagery, literary allusion, and boundless variety, showing much flexibility and rhythmical skill. His efforts are often considered lacking in great warmth or philosophical depth, but his *Songs of Life and Hope* (1905) and *Poem of Autumn* reach the abyss of despair. He was the author of the collections *Azul, Rimas, Prosas profanas,* and others. He lived in South America and Europe as consul for Nicaragua. See LITERATURE.

**Dartiguenave, Philippe Sudré.** b. 1863. President of Haiti. Named chief executive under American supervision and served 1915–1922. The United States established political and economic control for a period of ten years, and a new constitution was introduced in 1918. He helped to suppress a revolt directed against the United States, 1918–1919.

**Dávila, Miguel R.** d. 1927. President of Honduras. General; leader in Liberal Party; minister in Policarpo Bonilla's government, 1895–1898; provisional president of Honduras, 1907–1908; placed in power by ZELAYA of Nicaragua. He was elected president, serving 1908–1911. Overthrown by former president Manuel Bonilla, he resigned in 1911.

**Dávila Espinoza, Carlos Guillermo.** 1885–1955. Chilean political leader and diplomat. b. Los Angeles, Chile. Studied law at the University of Santiago but abandoned a legal career for journalism; newspaper editor; founder of the newspaper *La Nación* at Santiago, 1917; served as ambassador to the United States, 1927–1932; participated in the successful arbitration of the TACNA-ARICA boundary dispute between Chile and Peru, 1929; founder of the Chilean news magazine *Hoy,*

1932. He took part in the overthrow of President MONTERO RODRÍGUEZ in 1932, and served as acting president from July to September of that year. He believed in state socialism but was unable to carry out the social reforms that he issued by executive order while in office. After 1932 he lived mainly in the United States as journalist and lecturer. He was made Secretary-General of the ORGANIZATION OF AMERICAN STATES in July 1954.

**Dávila y Padilla, Agustín.** Called *"Chronicler of the Indies."* 1562–1604. Mexican historian. b. Mexico City. Entered the Dominican order, 1579; bishop of Santo Domingo, 1599–1604. His chief work, commissioned by the government, was the *Historia de la fundación de la provincia de Santiago de Méjico de la Orden de Predicadores*, 1596; republished, 1624.

**Dawson Agreement.** An accord (November 1910) among the leaders of the Nicaraguan Revolution of 1910, arranged by the U.S. representative Thomas C. Dawson, which made General Juan J. Estrada president, and Adolfo DÍAZ vice-president of Nicaragua for a two-year term, and also provided for the creation of a commission including U.S. representatives to take up the problem of foreign claims.

**Daza, Hilarión Grosolé.** See GROSOLÉ DAZA, HILARIÓN.

**Degollado, Santos.** d. 1861. Mexican leader, known as the "Hero of Defeats." Professor of law at Morelia. He was devoted to limiting ecclesiastical power and to the scientific improvement of agriculture. In the fight against SANTA ANNA, he organized guerrilla bands in Jalisco. Appointed general of the armies of the west by JUÁREZ before the latter's move to Veracruz in 1858, he was defeated in April 1859 by Leonardo MÁRQUEZ at Tacubaya, and again in November, near Celaya. Alarmed by seizure of British property and afraid of intervention, he suggested mediation by foreign governments, for which he was relieved of his command by Juárez in 1860 and was succeeded by GONZÁLEZ ORTEGA. The tide turned in favor of the liberals, and he was given credit for his efforts. He was killed by Márquez in 1861.

**Delgado, José Matías.** 1768–1833. Salvadoran priest and political leader. He led the uprising against the colonial regime in 1811; led resistance to the incorporation of El Salvador into the Mexican Empire, 1822–1823. He was president of the congress that drew up a constitution for the CENTRAL AMERICAN FEDERATION, 1823. Delgado was the leader of the revolt that overthrew the first president of the federation, Manuel José ARCE, 1829.

**Demarcation, Line of.** The decision of Pope ALEXANDER VI in 1493 to divide the non-Christian or New World possessions of Castile and Portugal by drawing a north-south line on the map of the Atlantic Ocean, which ran 100 leagues west of the Cape Verde Islands. It did not satisfy the Portuguese, for they wanted more room in the Atlantic to seek a passage to India by sailing around the Cape of Good Hope, or by navigating westward to the south of the territories discovered by Columbus. This led to the TREATY OF TORDESILLAS of 1494.

**Democratic Action Party of Venezuela,** (*Acción Democrática*, or *A.D.*). A radical party formed in Venezuela in 1936 to oppose the regime of LÓPEZ CONTRERAS. By 1940 this party, relying chiefly on labor and the intellectuals of the country, supported author Rómulo GALLEGOS for the presidency. He was defeated when congress met in joint session and voted almost unanimously for López Contreras' selection, MEDINA ANGARITA. The Democratic Action Party achieved temporary success in 1945, when the leader of the party, Rómulo BETANCOURT, took over the government by revolution. The party's candidate, Rómulo Gallegos, was elected president in December 1947 and took office on February 15, 1948, only to be overthrown by revolution on November 24. In addition to economic reforms, the main interest of the party was in securing a democratic constitution that would call for the direct election of the president for a limited period. In 1947 it succeeded in having a democratic constitution adopted. During the dictatorship of Pérez Jiménez (1952–1958), political parties were banned, but once the dictator was overthrown, the party was reorganized and has been successful in maintaining itself in power. Betancourt represented the party in the 1958 presidential election and served, 1959–1964. In recent years the party has suffered from internal dissensions. In 1960 and again in 1962 dissatisfied members formed separate factions. In December 1963 Dr. Raúl Leoni was the successful presidential candidate.

**Democratic Alliance of Ecuador.** Members of all parties from the extreme right to the extreme left formed a coalition in Ecuador in 1944, called the Democratic Alliance, for the purpose of overthrowing ARROYO DEL RÍO. Former president VELASCO IBARRA, in exile, was to be their candidate in the election of 1944. Many persons were imprisoned or exiled by the government, which was determined to prevent Ibarra's return. Revolution was the only solution and was successful. However, once in control, the discordant elements in the Democratic Alliance were incapable of successfully running the government, and the various parties split away.

**Democratic Socialist Coalition of Cuba.** A group of parties formed to support Carlos Saladrigas, a well-known lawyer, in the election of 1944. This coalition, backing BATISTA'S candidate, included the old-time Liberal Party, the A.B.C. PARTY, the Democratic Party, and the Communists (Popular Socialist Party). They were opposed by the Republican Authentic Alliance. These *auténticos* had been in existence since the end of MACHADO's regime, when they had succeeded in making their leader, GRAU SAN MARTÍN, president in 1933. He was again their candidate in this campaign and was victorious.

**Democratic Union of Argentina** or (**Unión Democrática**). A coalition of Argentine parties formed to oppose the candidacy of Juan PERÓN in 1946. This group included the Radicals, Progressive Democrats, Socialists, and the Communists. Their candidate was José TAMBORINI, leader of the Radicals. They were unsuccessful.

**Descamisados.** Refers to "the shirtless ones," so named by Juan PERÓN of Argentina. *Descamisados* were the poverty-stricken, poorer elements of the population, that formed the bulk of his support.

**De Soto, Hernando.** See SOTO, HERNANDO DE.

**Dessalines, Jean Jacques.** 1758–1806. Negro emperor of Haiti. b. a slave, at Grande Rivière, and took the name of his French master. He joined the revolutionary independents in 1791 and fought with TOUSSAINT L'OUVERTURE in 1797. By 1800 Toussaint had put down mulatto uprisings in the north, and also had control of the south. Dessalines followed the victory with the murder of 10,000 persons of mixed blood. He was finally forced to submit to the French under LECLERC in 1802, but, helped by the British, he succeeded in driving out the French in 1803. On January 1, 1804, as leader of the rebel army, he proclaimed the independence of Haiti, the first free nation in Latin America. Dessalines took the title of governor general, but in September 1804, in imitation of NAPOLEON, he had himself proclaimed emperor and ruled as Jacques I from 1804 to 1806. As a former slave entirely without education, his qualifications were courage and ferocity. His administration was a military despotism. The French were murdered, but the British were allowed to continue trade. Depriving many mulatto planters of their lands caused a revolt, and in October 1806, marching against the rebels, he was killed in ambush in the outskirts of Port-au-Prince. Today Dessalines is the national hero of Haiti and is remembered as the Father of Haitian Independence.

**Diamonds.** Diamonds are found in South America in Brazil, Guyana, and Venezuela. Diamonds were discovered in the province of Minas Gerais, Brazil, in 1728. Mining was developed by 1740, and from then until the discovery of the deposits in South Africa in 1867, Brazil was the world's largest producer of diamonds. During the first hundred years after the discovery, the total production was approximately 3,000,000 carats. When Brazilian diamonds threatened to cause a disastrous drop in world prices, the Portuguese government in 1771 took diamond production into its own hands. The most important deposits are in Minas Gerais, Bahia, and Mato Grosso, but diamonds are also found in the states of Goiás, São Paulo, Paraná, Piauí, Maranhão, and Amazonas. In recent years the annual production in South American countries has been about 300,000 carats in Brazil, 100,000 carats in British Guiana, and 90,000 carats in Venezuela.

**Díaz, Adolfo.** 1874–1964. President of Nicaragua. Served as vice-president under Estrada: took office as provisional president in May 1911. A conservative, he was friendly to the United States. Able to suppress President-elect Luis Mena's revolt; he was elected president and served, 1913–1917. Again chosen president by the congress in November 1926, he served with the support of the United States until 1928.

**Díaz, Félix.** Nephew of Porfirio DÍAZ. Mexican chief of police. He led a rebellion in October 1912, which was crushed by MADERO and led to Díaz' imprisonment. He was released in February 1913. He arranged with HUERTA that he would succeed him as president, but instead he was sent to Japan on a military mission.

**Díaz, José de la Cruz Porfirio.** 1830–1915. Mexican general and president. b. Oaxaca. A MESTIZO, he started to study for the priesthood but changed to law and studied under JUÁREZ at the Institute of Oaxaca. He fought with liberals against SANTA ANNA and served in the War of the Reform. He was the leading Mexican general in the war against the French, 1863–1867, and captured Mexico City in 1867. The unsuccessful candidate for the presidency several times, he finally overthrew LERDO DE TEJADA and was made provisional president of Mexico, 1876–1877. He was elected president and served, 1877–1880, and then served for seven terms, 1884–1911. His dictatorial administration did very little for the great mass of the people but was marked by peace and prosperity for the country and brought to the masses a new respect for law and order. Graft and corruption were reduced in his administration; investment of foreign capital was encouraged; exports, particularly of petroleum, were increased; and railroads and roads were built. It has been said that during the Díaz administration Mexico was "mother of the foreigner and step-mother of the Mexican." The land went into the hands of the upper classes and the foreigner, and

the power of the church was increased. He was forced to abdicate by the revolution led by MADERO in May 1911. Exiled to Paris, he died there on July 2, 1915.

**Díaz del Castillo, Bernal.** 1492–1584. Spanish soldier and historian. Went to Darién in 1514 under PEDRARIAS, to Yucatán with CÓRDOBA in 1517, and was with CORTÉS during the conquest of Mexico, 1519–1521. He is famous for his eyewitness account of the conquest of Mexico in his *Verdadera Historia de la Conquista de la Nueva España* (True History of the Conquest of New Spain), written about 1568. He had read the *Historia de las Indias y Conquista de México* by Francisco de Gómara in 1552–1553 and determined to write a reply to the errors he found therein. His book remained in manuscript form until it was published in three volumes in 1632 by the Mercedarian Friars in Madrid; it appeared, however, in a changed form pleasing to the Friars. In 1904–1905, the Mexican historian Genaro García issued an authentic edition based on the photographic copy of the original manuscript that is in the Guatemala National Library. In 1908–1916, the Hakluyt Society of London published Alfred Maudslay's translation in five volumes. Archibald MacLeish, the American poet, based his epic poem *Conquistador* on Díaz' work. Although not a literary work of the highest quality, it does reflect the Spanish mind of the 16th century and is an important contribution to scholarship. Díaz settled in Guatemala and died there.

**Díaz de Solís, Juan.** 1470–1516. Spanish navigator and explorer. With PINZÓN he made two voyages along the Atlantic coast of South America, 1497–1498, and 1508–1509. He was made chief pilot by King FERDINAND and made a voyage to South America in 1515, entering the great estuary of the RÍO DE LA PLATA. Near the mouth of the Paraná he was ambushed and killed, possibly by the Charrúa Indians, in 1516.

**Díaz Rodríguez, Manuel.** 1868–1927. Venezuelan author. He was a master stylist and his work, *Sensaciones de Viaje* (Impressions of Travel), 1896, made him famous. He wrote realistic descriptions of the outward aspects of the life of his characters, but made them self-centered and individualistic, so that there is a lack of oneness between the individual lives and that of the environment in which they lived. His other works include *Cuentos de color*, 1898, *Idolos rotos* (Broken Idols), 1907, and *Sangre patricia* (Noble Blood).

**Didapp, Juan Pedro.** Mexican liberal. Supporter of suffrage and representative government. Enemy of the *científicos* and Porfirio DÍAZ, he wrote articles in 1901 and 1904 demanding government by political parties and not one-man rule. Although not quite successful in having an immediate effect upon his readers, he did convince many that suffrage and representative government had to come first, and that social and economic progress would slowly but surely develop.

**Diezmo.** In Brazil, *dizimo*, church tithe, meaning one-tenth. This ecclesiastical tax was collected in the American colonies by the Spanish (Portuguese) government for the purpose of defraying the cost of maintenance and construction of churches and other religious buildings.

**Direeu.** See GONZAGA, THOMAZ (OR THOMÉ) ANTÔNIO.

**Dollar Diplomacy.** A phrase used by hostile critics to describe certain aspects of U.S. policy toward Latin America during the early years of the 20th century, especially during the administration of President Taft (1909–1913). It was alleged that one of the primary motives of U.S. diplomacy was to promote the interests of business corporations by securing commercial and investment opportunities in foreign countries, and when necessary, by resorting to force to protect their properties. U.S. interventions in the Dominican Republic, Nicaragua, and other Caribbean countries under the ROOSEVELT COROLLARY to the MONROE DOCTRINE were regarded as manifestations of Dollar Diplomacy. President Wilson, in 1913, lashed out at his predecessor's policies in Latin America by announcing that he did not intend to support any "special group or interest," but found that his idealistic opposition to Dollar Diplomacy was not in keeping with the realities of international relations. While the U.S. Government, both before World War I and during the 1920's, continued to be interested in promoting and protecting the investment of capital abroad, it is probable that its Caribbean policy was motivated by considerations of national security more strongly than by economic interest. It wished to increase American investments in the Caribbean in order to promote American influence and minimize the influence of European powers in that region. Accusations of Dollar Diplomacy, nevertheless, did much to stimulate antagonism in all Latin-American countries. One of the primary purposes of the GOOD NEIGHBOR POLICY of the administration of Franklin ROOSEVELT was to put an end to this resentment by demonstrating that the United States had wholly abandoned this alleged policy.

**Dolphin, Incident of the.** See VERACRUZ INCIDENT.

**Dominican Republic.** This nation, occupying the eastern two-thirds of the island of Hispaniola, is the second largest of the Antillean republics and is situated between Cuba on the west and Puerto Rico on the east. The boundary line that separates the Dominican Republic from Haiti, its western neighbor, is 193 miles long. The area comprises 18,816 square miles, with a coast line 1,017 miles long. The climate is subtropical. The capital of the country is Santo Domingo, (called Ciudad Trujillo, 1936–1961), with a population of about 367,000 (1960). The population of approximately 3,783,000 (est. 1966) includes whites (28.1 per cent), MESTIZOS and mulattoes (60.4 per cent), and Negroes (11.5 per cent). There is no state religion, and although all faiths are tolerated, the majority of the people are Roman Catholic. Education is free and compulsory between the ages of seven and fourteen, but more than 55 per cent of the population are illiterate. The University of Santo Domingo, one of the three oldest universities in the New World, was founded in 1538 by the Dominican friars. The language of the country is Spanish, although English is widely spoken. Recent constitutions (the country has had more than twenty) have called for a separation of powers between the legislative and executive branches; the

119

preponderance of power, however, has resided in the executive. There are 1,680,000 acres of arable land and land under tree crops, making agriculture and stock raising the principal industries. Sugar, the outstanding crop, is exported primarily to Great Britain. Cacao, coffee, rice, corn, molasses, and tobacco are the other chief products. Chief industrial products are cement, cigars and cigarettes, lumber, shoes, textiles, and rum. There are deposits of silver, platinum, copper, iron, salt, bauxite, and petroleum, and an attempt has been undertaken to establish a larger mining industry. In 1954 an effort was made to expand the fish industry. The peso is the monetary unit, being on a par with the U.S. dollar. Dominican exports totaled $180,000,000 in 1965 and imports amounted to $220,000,000. The United States is the nation's principal trading partner, taking almost 90 per cent of the country's exports and supplying about 57 per cent of the imports.

The island was discovered in December 1492 by COLUMBUS, who named it ESPAÑOLA. The city of Santo Domingo, established by Columbus' brother Bartolomé, was the first permanent European settlement in the Western Hemisphere. The colony prospered, but the Indians were cruelly exploited, and as a result of mistreatments and disease they soon died out. To compensate for the loss of a labor supply, Negro slaves were imported into the island in increasing numbers. After the discovery of Mexico and Peru, many settlers left the island, and by 1564 the city of Santo Domingo was inhabited by only 500 persons. By the beginning of the 17th century the colony had lost its former importance and at the end of that century the western part of the island, for a long time the site of settlements by French colonists and buccaneers, was ceded to France. In the 18th century the Spanish colonists in the east were relatively prosperous. Sugar and tobacco were the main crops, and active trade was carried on with the French section of the island. By the last third of the century the population of the colony of Santo Domingo was approximately 125,000, including 15,000 Negro slaves. In 1795 France also acquired Santo Domingo. However, in 1801 TOUSSAINT L'OUVERTURE, who at that time controlled Haiti, the western

section, invaded Santo Domingo and freed the slaves, causing many Spanish colonists to flee. The French defeated Toussaint in 1802 and remained in the Spanish section until 1808, when the Spanish colonials, with the help of the British, expelled them and regained control. In 1821 the colonists declared their independence from Spain and joined BOLÍVAR's Great Colombia, but were immediately conquered by the Haitians under BOYER in 1822, and remained under Haitian rule until 1844, when they revolted and achieved independence, proclaiming the Dominican Republic. The first president of the new nation was General Pedro SANTANA, who ruled until 1848, when Manuel Jiménez, minister of war, succeeded him. After the war with Haiti, 1849, Colonel Buenaventura BÁEZ became the chief executive. In 1853 Santana returned to power, took steps against the clergy, and exiled Báez. After a constant change of leadership the Dominican Republic was annexed to Spain in 1861, at the suggestion of Santana. Partly because of pressure from the United States, Spain withdrew, and independence was again declared in 1865. During the administration of President Grant in the United States, there was considerable sentiment in favor of annexing the Dominican Republic, but opposition in the U.S. Senate prevented ratification of the plan. Pedro Pimentel became dictator but was overthrown and again a succession of leaders followed. General Ulises HEUREAUX was president from 1882 until his assassination in 1899. Heureaux's regime was cruel and despotic but gave the country its first long period of peace. As a result of Dominican inability to maintain payments on its foreign debt, the United States assumed control of the finances of the country in 1905, with the consent of the Dominican government. There followed several revolutions and new presidents until 1914, when Juan Isidro Jiménez was established as president under the protection of the United States. He was overthrown in 1916, after which the country was governed by U.S. officials until 1922, when Burgos became provisional president. The United States withdrew its occupation forces in 1924 and ended its financial supervision in 1941. In 1927 a new constitution was adopted. In

1930 VÁSQUEZ was overthrown and Rafael TRUJILLO was elected president. Trujillo continued to rule the country, sometimes serving as president himself and sometimes governing through a friend or relative, until his assassination in 1961. Although the dictatorial character of the government caused it to be severely criticized, the nation enjoyed some progress and there were no important internal disturbances for almost thirty years (rarely possible under dictatorship). In 1937 the massacre of many thousands of Haitians living in the Dominican Republican brought the two countries to the brink of war. A conflict was narrowly averted by the interposition of friendly powers. When President Trujillo was assassinated on May 30, 1961, the executive power was nominally in the hands of President Joaquín Balaguer, a figurehead installed by Trujillo in 1960. Although Balaguer weathered the chaotic period immediately following the assassination, he was replaced by the vice-president, Dr. Rafael Bonnelly, as the result of an air-force coup carried out in January 1962. On December 20, 1962, the first free elections in thirty-eight years were held and Juan Bosch was elected president. The hopes that a free election might provide a stable government were disappointed in the following September, when a military coup brought about the downfall of the Bosch administration. A three-man civilian junta dissolved the constitution and the national legislature. In April 1965 a revolt, launched by civilian and army elements, overthrew the regime of Donald Reid Cabral, who had remained in command of the country after the resignation in May 1964 of the other two members of the junta. This revolt precipitated a civil war between conservatives (mostly military personnel, including the Air Force) and liberals, led by Colonel Francisco Caamaño Deno, who included in their ranks left-wing elements of all shades of political opinion. U. S. President Lyndon B. Johnson, claiming that the lives of United States citizens were in danger, and fearing a Castro-type take over of the country, ordered a force of marines to Santo Domingo. In a short time there were more than 20,000 U. S. Marines and paratroopers in the area. Other hemispheric forces, especially Brazilian units, joined the U. S. troops after the ORGANIZATION OF AMERICAN STATES had agreed to establish an inter-American military force in the strife-torn Dominican Republic. In spite of continuing unrest, the OAS intervention succeeded in setting up a provisional government under García-Godoy, which prepared for general elections. In these elections, held in June 1966, the moderate Joaquín Balaguer defeated former president Juan Bosch, the liberal candidate, who had returned from exile in Puerto Rico. It is estimated that about 3,000 Dominicans were killed in the civil war. On July 1, Balaguer was sworn in as president, and on September 19, the last elements of the American Peace Force were withdrawn from the country. The intervention of U. S. troops before concerted OAS action had been decided upon did considerable harm to U. S. prestige in Latin America.

**Dominicans.** A Roman Catholic religious order that was among the first to spread the gospel in the New World. They arrived in Hispaniola in 1510, and almost at once protested against the exploitation of the natives. They were well known for their work as educators. An outstanding Dominican was Bartolomé de LAS CASAS.

**Donatário.** See CAPITANIA.

**Dorrego, Manuel.** 1787–1828. Argentine statesman. b. Buenos Aires. Served in the military during separatist movements in Chile, Bolivia, Uruguay, and Argentina; came to the United States as an exile. He returned in 1820 and acted as provisional governor of Buenos Aires, played a leading role in the constituent assembly of 1826, and was elected governor of Buenos Aires in 1827. As governor, he resumed peace negotiations with Brazil in 1828, and through intervention of the British government was able to apply pressure upon PEDRO I of Brazil; a treaty was negotiated that created the independent republic of Uruguay. He served as provisional president, and during an attempt to put down a revolt, was captured and killed by the rebels.

**Dorticós Torrado, Osvaldo.** 1919–
President of Cuba. b. Cienfuegos. Educated in Roman Catholic primary schools; attended

the Colegio Champagnat and the Instituto de Segundo Enseñanza in Cienfuegos; studied philosophy and law at the University of Havana, where he received a doctorate of civil law, 1941; began revolutionary activities as a student leader, 1939. He practiced law until he joined CASTRO's revolutionary movement against the BATISTA government. Leader of the revolutionary underground in Cienfuegos, 1957–1958, he was arrested and imprisoned, 1958. He escaped to Mexico and returned to Cuba soon after Castro's victory. He was appointed minister of laws in the new cabinet and made president upon the resignation of Manuel URRUTIA. As president, Dorticós generally echoed Castro's policies and those of the Soviet Union.

**Drago, Luis María.** 1859–1921. Argentine jurist. Served as minister of foreign affairs, 1902–1903; member of Hague Tribunal. He formulated the DRAGO DOCTRINE which maintains that, since imprisonment for debt in private relations has been universally negated, the use of armed forces to collect public debts among nations should be abolished.

**Drago Doctrine.** During the controversy in 1902 between Venezuela on the one hand and Great Britain, Italy, and Germany on the other, over the collection of Venezuela's debts by the other countries, Dr. Luis DRAGO, minister of foreign relations of Argentina, protested to the U. S. government against the use of force for the purpose of collecting the debts. He maintained that foreign debts could not be used as an excuse by a European power for intervention in any American nation, nor could they be collected by force. A similar idea had been proposed twenty years earlier by Carlos CALVO of Argentina. A modified form of the doctrine proposed by Drago was approved by the United States at the Hague Convention (Second Peace Conference) in 1907 (the Porter Resolution).

**Duarte, Juan Pablo.** 1813–1876. General and political leader of the Dominican Republic. Educated abroad, he formed a secret society, "La Trinitaria," in 1838 upon his return to Santo Domingo. This group joined the Haitian liberals against BOYER and made the revolt a success. He was sent into exile by the Haitian government, but his friends seized forts at Santo Domingo on February 27, 1844, and declared the independence of the Dominican Republic. Duarte returned from Curaçao, where he had been in exile, and became a member of the *Junta Central* that controlled the government. Pedro SANTANA, commander of the army, became president against Duarte's wishes.

**Duhalde Vázquez, Alfredo.** Chilean political leader. Served as minister of the interior under RÍOS MORALES, and upon the latter's illness became acting president in January 1946. He was a moderate Radical and supporter of Ríos, although more conservative in his views. A labor crisis caused widespread strikes, and Radical members of the cabinet resigned. Duhalde Vázquez replaced them with Socialists and was expelled from the Radical Party. He campaigned for the presidency but was defeated.

**Durão, José de Santa Rita.** 1721–1784. Brazilian poet. b. Minas Gerais. Educated in Portugal; received Doctor of Theology degree from University of Coimbra; member of the Order of St. Augustine. He is noted for his poem *O Caramurú* (1781) that holds a high place in Portuguese epic poetry and has been called the *"Lusiads* of Brazil." See CARAMURÚ.

**Dutch-Latin American Relations.** In the second half of the 16th century the Dutch, who at the time were waging a relentless war for independence against the Spaniards in their homeland, began to engage in raiding the Spanish and Portuguese possessions in the New World, and at the same time established a profitable although illegal trade with the Spanish colonies in the Caribbean area. They soon built up a monopoly over the cocoa and tobacco trade with the north coast of South America and were also active in bringing Negro slaves to the Spanish colonies, receiving in return gold, silver, salt, coffee, and sugar. Dutch trade with America was put on an even more solid foundation with the formation in 1621 of the DUTCH WEST INDIA COMPANY, which was able to fit out large fleets of merchant vessels and warships. In 1628 a Dutch fleet captured a huge Spanish fleet loaded with treasure. As a result, the Dutch West India Company was in a position to pay a 50 per cent dividend. In 1634 the Dutch gained possession of the important Caribbean island of Curaçao, which became a base for their raiding operations and for their trade with the Spanish Main. It was in Brazil that the Dutch achieved some of their most resounding successes during the 17th century. In 1630, after a series of raids on the Brazilian mainland, an expedition organized by the West India Company was able to occupy Olinda and Recife in the province of Pernambuco, and subsequently extended its foothold, until it was in possession of most of the northeastern part of the country. Under the capable leadership of Jan MAURITZ (1637–1644) the Dutch colony prospered but faced increasing resistance from the Portuguese colonists after 1641. The Dutch maintained themselves in Brazil until 1654, when Portugal was able to defeat them at Recife to end the era of Dutch occupation. In the Caribbean, however, Holland continued to remain a powerful and feared force until the end of the 18th century.

**Dutch West India Company.** A monopoly company established in Holland in 1621 with a view to breaking the power of the Spanish-Portuguese trade in the New World. Among its stockholders there were many Portuguese Jews residing in Holland, whose trade with Brazil had suffered severely from Spain's annexation of Portugal in 1580. The company seized and held for a number of years the richest part of Brazil, Pernambuco (1630–1654). In the Caribbean it captured Curaçao from the Spaniards in 1634, and carried on contraband trade on a large scale with the Spanish Main. Its fleets were a constant threat to Spanish convoys. In the second half of the 17th century, the power of the company declined after the Portuguese recovered their Brazilian and African possessions.

**Dutra, Eurico Gaspar.** 1885–    . President of Brazil. b. Cuiabá, Mato Grosso. Brigadier general in the army; minister of war; supporter of VARGAS; conservative and at one time a supporter of Germany, climbing onto the Allied bandwagon at a late date. He was supported in the campaign of 1945 by the Social Democratic Party which did not seek the support of Vargas, but rather that of the upper classes, the Church, and the army. Gomes, supported by the National Democratic Union, was expected to win, but on December 2, when the first election in fifteen years was held, Dutra won with a margin of over 1,000,000 over Gomes and was inaugurated on January 31, 1946. To the surprise of local as well as international observers, he was not a Vargas puppet and had definite and determined ideas. His new constitution was of a liberal character. There were economic problems, some being offset by a large loan from the EXPORT-IMPORT BANK of the United States, and the Communist party was outlawed. He was succeeded by Vargas in 1951.

# E

**Earthquakes.** During the colonial period, earthquakes often devastated vast regions of Latin America. A large part of Chile was affected by a disastrous upheaval, 1647, and a gigantic quake obliterated part of the city of Lima, Peru, 1746. The city of Antigua, Guatemala, was completely destroyed, 1773, while in modern times the most famous quakes have been the one in Chile (January 1939) that devastated about 50,000 square miles and killed about 30,000 persons, and the one in Ecuador (August 1949) that destroyed 50 towns and killed about 6,000. During the past few years there have been severe earthquakes in Mexico and South America. The Mexican earthquake occurred in the region around Mexico City and Guerrero State on July 28, 1957, killing 56 persons, injuring 500 others, and causing extensive damage to buildings in the capital. A disaster occurred in Chile's south-central region in late May 1960. The death toll was about 5,000, and some 300,000 persons were left homeless. Total damage in Chile was estimated at more than $550,000,000. Peru suffered damage in January 1958, when 128 people were killed by a landslide and earthquake in the region around Arequipa in the southern part of the country. In December 1961, an earthquake struck in Colombia in the departments of Caldas, Antioquia, Tolima, and Cundinamarca killing 18 persons and injuring more than 100.

**Echave, Baltasar de.** 1548–1630. Painted in the churches of Mexico at the end of the 16th and the beginning of the 17th century, working in the meticulous style of the old masters. He was known as *El Viejo* to distinguish him from his son who was also a painter.

**Echenique, José Rufino.** 1808–1879. President of Peru. General of the army who served as president from 1851 until his overthrow by CASTILLA, his predecessor, in January 1855. During his administration a new civil code was put into effect in 1852, but the national prosperity declined.

**Echeverría, Esteban.** 1805–1851. Argentine socialist, political leader, and poet. Mainly known for his opposition to the dictator ROSAS and for his doctrines of social democracy, Echeverría was also a poet and writer of considerable distinction who introduced European romanticism into the literature of Argentina. He went to Europe in 1825 where he was greatly influenced by French intellectuals, returned to Argentina in 1829, and began his literary career. Exiled to Uruguay by Rosas, he wrote violent attacks on the dictator that were smuggled into Argentina. Author of *Profecía del Plata*, 1831, *Elvira o la novia de la Plata*, 1832, *Los Consuelos*, 1834, *Rimas*, 1837, *El Matadero*, (translated as The Slaughter House), 1837, *Dogma socialista*, 1839, and other works. See SOCIALISM, POSITIVISM, and LITERATURE.

**Economic Nationalism.** In Latin America during the 19th century commerce and business were almost exclusively controlled by foreigners. Railroads, mines, banks, etc., were in the hands of foreign investors, and the natives had almost no say in their management. In the 20th century there has been an increasing tendency to shake off the control of outsiders in the economic field. This movement has expressed itself mainly in sustained efforts to build up national industries, to restrict the privileges of foreign companies, to promote greater participation by nationals in foreign enterprises, and also in seizures of foreign property. The growth of local industries was fostered especially during the depression years of the thirties, when Latin-American countries had difficulties selling their goods in the world market, and the resulting scarcity of foreign exchange was a serious obstacle to obtaining goods from abroad. There have been several outstanding examples of expropriation of foreign holdings by Latin-American governments in recent years. In 1938 the Mexican government seized American and British oil properties and set up a national agency to control the acquired reserves. The expropriation of holdings of the UNITED FRUIT COMPANY by the ARBENZ GUZMÁN government of Guatemala in 1953 further exemplified the feeling of violent economic nationalism. The most recent example of such seizures has been in Cuba, where the CASTRO government has confiscated American property valued at more than $1,000,000,000.

**Ecuador.** The republic of Ecuador lies on the Pacific coast of South America and extends from approximately 100 miles north of the equator to 400 miles south of it. It is bounded on the north by Colombia, and on the east and south by Peru. The area of the country is approximately 105,000 square miles (indefinite because the Ecuador-Peru border has not yet been delimited), and the population 5,243,000 (1966), of which 39 per cent are Indian, 41 per cent MESTIZO, 10 per cent white and 5 per cent Negro. The monetary unit is the sucre, valued at 18.18 to the U.S. dollar. The language is Spanish, but Quechua is widely spoken among the Indian population. The dominant religion is Roman Catholicism, but there is complete religious freedom. The constitution of 1946 provides for a president elected every four years by direct popular vote, and for a bicameral congress. The congress is composed of a lower house having seventy-three deputies elected every two years and a senate with forty-seven elected for four years. Twelve

senators are elected to represent the armed forces, education, labor, business, and journalism. The country is naturally divided into three sections: a tropical coastal area, where the main seaport, Guayaquil (population est. 1962, 680,000), is located, and where the chief crops, bananas and cacao, are raised; a temperate mountainous section formed by two cordilleras of the Andes where 60 per cent of the population live, and where the capital, Quito (population est. 1962, 420,000), is located; and a trans-Andean region covered with forests and sparsely populated. The Galápagos Islands 650 miles off the coast of Ecuador, with 2,869 square miles and a population of 1,900 (1960), form a part of the country. Important agricultural products are bananas, cacao, potatoes, rice, corn, sugar, barley, wheat, and coffee, the chief export in 1962 being bananas. The country is rich in minerals, but these are not fully exploited. They include silver, gold, petroleum, copper, iron, and lead. Ecuador is still the world's leading supplier of balsa wood, widely used in aircraft and marine construction. The principal industrial products are crude petroleum, cement, textiles, edible oils, sugar, and chemicals. Panama hats are a well-known product of Ecuador. Largest customers are the United States and Germany, and the United States is the main source of the country's imports, which include cotton goods, metals, foodstuffs, drugs, chemicals, and textiles. The 700 miles of railroads include the famous Guayaquil-Quito line, one of the great engineering accomplishments in the Western Hemisphere, climbing to an altitude of almost 12,000 feet. Education is compulsory and free, but about 45 per cent of the people are illiterate.

Ruled by the Incas in pre-Conquest times, the territory of Ecuador was occupied by the Spaniards during the period of Francisco PIZARRO's conquest of the Incas of Peru. Quito was conquered in 1533 by Sebastián de BENALCÁZAR, who was the first governor of the territory. In colonial times the area was first organized as the *audiencia* of Quito and was a part of the viceroyalty of Peru. With the formation in the 18th century of the viceroyalty of New Granada, it was included under this jurisdiction. Colonial Ecuador raised sugar cane, cacao, and livestock, and up to the 18th century was an important center of textile manufacture. The Ecuadorian independence movement began in 1809, and freedom from Spain was finally achieved in 1822, after the victory of Pichincha, won by General SUCRE, a lieutenant of BOLÍVAR. For a few years Ecuador was part of Greater Colombia but declared itself an independent republic in 1830. In the next thirty years the history of the country was marked by great political instability and a general lack of economic progress. From 1860 to 1875 it was ruled by President GARCÍA MORENO, who suppressed all opposition with great ferocity. He granted extensive privileges to the Church, placing in its hands the importation and publication of books and the control over education. After his assassination in 1875, there was a period of struggle between conservatives and liberals, and the latter finally gained power in 1895, when Eloy ALFARO became president after a short civil war. The liberals pushed through a number of anticlerical measures, and in 1906 a new constitution, which took control of education away from the Church, was adopted. Under Alfaro the important rail link between the Pacific port of Guayaquil and the capital of Quito was completed. The first half of the 20th century was a period of general political instability, few presidents being able to remain in office for the full four-year term. During World War II Ecuador broke off relations with Germany, and granted the United States a naval base on the Galápagos Islands. President Galo PLAZA LASSO, elected in 1948, served four years, and was succeeded by José María VELASCO IBARRA, who had twice before been elected to the presidency. Velasco Ibarra's third term as president was characterized by an anti-U.S. attitude and the revival of the boundary dispute with Peru. In the course of its history, Ecuador has had a number of boundary disputes with its neighbors, the most important one being with Peru. The disagreement resulted in an undeclared war in 1941, which was settled through the mediation of the United States, Chile, and Argentina, with Ecuador having to relinquish its claims to much territory in the Amazon Basin. The fixing of the new boundary in unexplored areas proved difficult and has continued to be

a source of ill feeling between the two countries. The Velasco government, realizing the great need for more transportation, announced in 1954 plans for a road-building program to extend over a four-year period, with an estimated cost of $40,000,000. Velasco Ibarra, succeeded in 1956 by Camilio Ponce Enríquez, candidate of the Conservative party, was elected president for a fourth term in 1960 but was overthrown by an air-force coup in November 1961. The new government, headed by Carlos Julio Arosemena Monroy, vice-president under Velasco Ibarra, was plagued by strikes and demonstrations. Dissatisfaction with Arosemena caused impeachment proceedings to be initiated in the congress, and in July 1963, he was ousted and replaced by a four-member junta. A reform program begun by the new government promised a new constitution, initiated agrarian reform, and made an effort to have Communists ousted from positions in educational institutions. In March 1966, the military junta was deposed by the armed forces, and in October a constituent assembly elected Otto Arosemena Gómez provisional president.

**Egaña Fabres, Mariano.** 1793–1846. Chilean publicist. Brilliant conservative who followed in the footsteps of his illustrious father, Juan EGAÑA RIESCO. In the constitutions that they wrote together, they attempted to create an independent country with progressive views, yet maintaining Spanish colonial traditions. He had worked in the FREIRE SERRANO ministry for educational reform for the National Institute. He was sent on a mission to Peru in 1836 with several ships of the Chilean navy, but his demands were rejected and war was declared in November 1836. He served for five years as a diplomat in Europe.

**Egaña Riesco, Juan.** 1769–1836. Chilean writer, jurist, and statesman. b. Lima, Peru. Creole. He went to Santiago, Chile, to practice law and became one of the leaders of the Chilean revolution in 1810; imprisoned with other Chilean revolutionists on Juan Fernández Island and freed by O'HIGGINS. In 1811 he drew up a declaration of rights in which he proposed that a congress of independent American states be called with the idea of federation. He collaborated with HENRÍQUEZ

GONZÁLEZ in the publication of the first newspaper in Chile, *La aurora de Chile*, in 1812. He served as president of the constituent congress of Chile in 1823 and was a planner of the Chilean constitution in 1823. He was an intellectual conservative who wanted to shape laws and political power to the already existing practices and customs and strive for slow reform, mainly through education. He believed that mining was as important to Chile as agriculture and secured the exclusive right to mining lands in southern Chile. A strong foe of religious freedom, he was the spokesman of the ecclesiastical oligarchy. He was the author of ten volumes of collected essays, textbooks, poems, and other works.

**Ejido.** Spanish, meaning literally, "the way out." Derived from the Latin word *exitus*. In Spain this meant the common lands attached to a town or village, used by the inhabitants for pasturing their cattle and gathering firewood. In Spanish America it was applied to the common lands held by the Indian communities and used for agriculture. In accordance with Indian tradition, the lands were usually divided into individual family plots, but ownership remained with the community. During the colonial period, the Spanish government endeavored to protect the Indian *ejidos* from encroachment by white settlers. The Indians, nevertheless, were gradually deprived of much of their land, largely because they generally lacked legal titles of ownership. This process continued during the 19th century, especially in Mexico where the LEY LERDO of 1856 ordered all *ejidos* to be divided into private properties. As enforced during the administration of Porfirio DÍAZ, the *Ley Lerdo* caused the Indians to lose most of their lands, being either induced to sell them on easy terms or deprived of them by legalized robbery. The grievances of the expropriated peasants were one of the main causes of the Mexican Revolution of 1910–1917, and the restoration of the *ejido* system of land ownership became one of its chief objectives. The constitution of 1917 declared in Article 27 that all alienations of *ejidos* since the *Ley Lerdo* should be annulled, and that if this was not sufficient to supply the needs of the villages, additional lands might be expropriated from neighboring properties. The *ejidos* were henceforth to be inalienable and to remain as the communal property of the villages, although it was anticipated that they would be divided into plots for the individual use of the peasants. The redistribution of land began during the revolution and by 1934 about 17,000,000 acres had been granted to peasants. During the administration of President Lázaro CÁRDENAS (1934–1940) the total was more than doubled, to about 41,000,000 acres. Presidents ÁVILA CAMACHO, ALEMÁN VALDÉS, and RUIZ CORTINES made impressive contributions to the redistribution program, but on a lesser scale than Cárdenas. During the first nine months of his administration, LÓPEZ MATEOS distributed about 4,500,000 acres, and by September 1963, had granted nearly 30,000,000 acres to peasants. Since 1915 approximately 125,000,000 acres have been parceled out to about 2,700,000 families, and 2,500 *ejidos* have been established. One of the problems of the *ejido* program has been that too many peasants have flocked to the best land, dividing it into very small units, creating a problem aptly termed *minifundia*, even more serious than *latifundia*. The Agrarian Code of December 30, 1949, set the minimum *ejido* grant at 10 hectares (24.7 acres) of irrigated land or 20 hectares of seasonal land. Most of the *ejidos* are divided into family plots; on the other hand, about 500 are operated as units on a co-operative profit-sharing basis.

**El Dorado or The Legend of the Gilded Man.** According to rumors that the Indians insisted were true, in the interior of present-day Colombia was a king who each morning had resin spread over his naked body and was then dusted with gold from head to foot; each evening he bathed. It was true that once a year an Indian CACIQUE who lived far in the interior of Colombia was thus dusted with gold, and as an offering to the gods, he bathed in Lake Guatavita and washed the precious metal into the water. The white explorers expected that there was a limitless amount of gold available for such rituals. Tales of this kind, of course, sent many men in search of these kingdoms with limitless gold and precious stones. It attracted such explorers as

Gonzalo PIZARRO (1541), who also searched for the "Land of Cinnamon," Gonzalo JIMÉNEZ DE QUESADA and Felipe de Hutten (1545), and Pedro de Silva (1569). The German settlers of Venezuela Hohemut and FEDERMANN (1535) also searched the interior, proving that the Spaniards were not the only gullible folk of the time. Even Sir Walter Raleigh, the British adventurer, explored the area in 1617 for El Dorado.

**Elhuyar, Fausto de.** 1755–1833. Spanish scientist who went to Mexico and taught at the School of Mines. He conducted scientific experiments and is considered a father of science in Mexico. His brother, Juan José de Elhuyar, went to New Granada as director of mines, the purpose being to stimulate and increase silver output by recommending new scientific methods and techniques.

**Elío, Francisco Javier de.** 1767–1822. Spanish colonial administrator and general. Went to the Río de la Plata estuary in 1805 in command of forces that were opposing the British. He recaptured Montevideo in 1807, served as an ultraroyalist governor, and organized a junta in 1808 to oppose Viceroy LINIERS, but it failed. He was viceroy of Buenos Aires in 1810. He returned to Spain to command the Catalonian and Valencian army in 1812 and served as governor of Murcia and Valencia from 1813 until he was deposed by liberal insurgents in 1822 and executed.

**El Salvador.** The smallest of the Central-American republics, bounded on the north and east by Honduras, on the northwest and west by Guatemala, and on the south by the Pacific Ocean, has an area of 8,260 square miles and a population of about 2,908,000 (1965), of which 75 per cent are MESTIZO, 20 per cent Indian, and 5 per cent white. The monetary unit is the colón ($.40). The language is Spanish, and Roman Catholicism is the predominant religion, although all other faiths are tolerated. The chief cities are San Salvador, the capital, population 263,275 (1961), Santa Ana, population 146,048 (1961), and San Miguel, population 80,263 (1961). The powers of government are in the hands of a president elected for a five-year term, who may not succeed himself, and a one-house congress. The country is divided into fourteen departments for administrative purposes, each with a governor appointed by the president. It is a country of mountains and high plateaus, with a number of volcanoes, including the famous Mount Izalco. Coffee is the chief product and constitutes about 70 per cent of the country's exports. Other important crops are cotton and sugar. El Salvador is rich in minerals, particularly gold and silver. The United States is one of the country's chief customers and its principal supplier. Education is compulsory and free, but the illiteracy rate runs to more than 50 per cent.

El Salvador was conquered by Pedro de ALVARADO Y MESÍA, who arrived in the area in 1524. During the colonial period the territory was a part of the captaincy general of Guatemala. The town of San Salvador, founded in 1525, was the first in Central America to proclaim independence from Spain (November 5, 1811), in a movement led by the priest José Matías DELGADO. The territory was not liberated, however, until 1821. El Salvador refused to become a part of the Mexican empire of ITURBIDE, and decided to ask the United States for admission as a state in the North American Union, but before the United States was advised of the request, the province was occupied by Iturbide's troops, who faced strong resistance by Salvadoran patriots. After Iturbide's downfall in 1823, El Salvador joined the CENTRAL AMERICAN FEDERATION, and San Salvador became the capital of that state in 1834. After the disintegration of the federation in 1838, El Salvador went through a long period of internal instability and conflicts with neighboring states. From 1931 to 1944 it was ruled by General Maximiliano Hernández MARTÍNEZ who was ousted by a fierce revolt that inaugurated another period of unrest. In 1950 a new constitution was adopted and Oscar Osorio took the office of president and remained for a full term of office. During Osorio's presidency the Lempa River hydroelectric power plant began operations in 1954, and the 191-mile stretch of PAN-AMERICAN HIGHWAY running through the country was completed. Lieutenant Colonel José María Lemus became president in 1956 and served until October

1960, when his government was overthrown. The military junta that succeeded Lemus was deposed a few months later in January 1961, and another junta took its place. The following year a new constitution was announced in January and Julio Adalberto Rivera was elected president. During Rivera's administration the government's fiscal position improved steadily, and business confidence in Rivera led to increased manufacturing activity and a general economic upturn. The country's first labor code was passed by the national legislature in January 1963, and went into effect the following month. Since 1951 El Salvador has been active in the ORGANIZATION OF CENTRAL AMERICAN STATES, which has as its aim the eventual economic and political union of the five Central-American states. See CENTRAL AMERICA.

**El Supremo.** Name given the Paraguayan dictator José Gaspar Rodríguez de FRANCIA (1766–1840). The appellation was no doubt derived from his official title *Dictador Supremo de la República*.

**Emancipation.** See ABOLITION OF SLAVERY.

**Emboabas, War of the.** After the PAULISTAS had discovered gold in Minas Gerais province, Brazil, at the end of the 17th century, many people began to settle in the region. Tensions soon developed between the Paulistas and the outsiders, who were called *emboabas* and were for the most part immigrants from Europe. Civil war over possession of the mines finally broke out in 1709. The Paulistas were successful at first, but they were outnumbered and in the end the *emboabas*, who were supported by the government, defeated them in 1711. As a result of the civil war the Paulistas went farther west and discovered other gold mines in MATO GROSSO and in Goyaz.

**Emphyteusis.** Grant of land for a long time or for perpetuity with the conditions that it be kept cultivated and that a fixed annual rent be paid the true owner. It was used in Argentina by RIVADAVIA in the 1820's with a view to encouraging immigration as well as cultivation of the land. ROSAS continued this plan for the distribution of public lands but later abandoned the program.

**Encilhamento.** In the first years of the Brazilian republic, *encilhamento* was the name given to the great movement of financial speculation.

**Encina, Francisco A.** b. 1874. Chilean historian and critic who became famous as a social thinker with the publication in 1912 of his *Nuestra inferioridad económica, sus causas, sus consecuencias*. It attributed a great deal of the lag in progress in Chile to the lack of education. Encina had great influence upon the thinking of his period and his country.

**Enciso, Martín Fernández de.** *ca.* 1470–1528. Spanish writer and colonizer. b. Seville. Went to America in 1500, settled as a lawyer in Santo Domingo, and founded Santa María la Antigua, Darién, 1510. He was the author of the first account in Spanish of discoveries in the New World, *Suma de Geografía*, 1519.

**Encomienda.** Institution originally used by Spanish kings in the conquest of Moorish territories in Spain, it was brought to the New World by the Spaniards and established there with some modifications. In the early stages of the Spanish conquest in the West Indies, the *encomienda* was the grant to Spanish colonists of a number of Indians concentrated in villages near the European settlements. Each colonist was put in charge of a village and was given the task of teaching the natives Christianity and protecting them. In return he could demand the payment of tribute as well as work, provided he compensated the Indians for their labor. The *encomenderos* usually did not fulfill their obligations and treated the Indians with utmost cruelty, and as a result of the heavy work, the bad treatment, and disease, the native population on the islands was soon wiped out. After the conquest of the mainland, the system was extended to the newly-acquired territories. There the *encomienda* took on a hereditary character, the grant being allowed in some cases to extend through several generations. Theoretically the Indians did not owe any labor, but merely the payment of tribute to the *encomendero*. In practice it usually happened that the Indians not only had to pay tribute but also were forced to work on the estates of their masters. Although no grant of land was included in the *encomienda,* in a number of cases, particularly in Mexico, the *encomendero* eventually appropriated the land of the Indians by various means. The abuses connected with this system gave rise to many protests, and as a result of the indignation of a number of conscientious Spaniards like Bartolomé de las CASAS, the Spanish Crown promulgated in 1542 the NEW LAWS, designed to bring about the gradual elimination of the *encomienda.* But the New Laws could not be enforced because of the violent opposition of the colonists. A royal order proclaimed the abolition of the system in 1720, but it was only by a gradual process, continuing throughout the 18th century, that the *encomienda* was done away with in the Spanish colonies in America.

**Enríquez Gallo, Alberto.** Army general who served as president of Ecuador for ten months, starting on October 22, 1937. His cabinet was composed entirely of army officers. He was the candidate of the Liberal-Radical Party in the presidential campaign of 1948, but was defeated.

**Entrada.** Literally, "entrance," or "arrival at a place." It is the term applied to the conversion of the Indians to Christianity as the result of military coercion; also known as *conquista de almas* ("conquest of souls"). However the missionaries most often relied on gentle methods of persuasion.

**Ercilla y Zúñiga, Alonso de.** 1533–1594. Spanish poet. b. Madrid. Went to Chile in 1554 to aid in suppressing the rebellion of the ARAUCANIANS. Their heroic fight inspired him to write the epic poem *La Araucana,* composed of thirty-seven cantos and considered the first major literary work produced in the Americas. Much of it was written on the field of battle and is vigorous in feeling; its heroes are Araucanian Indian chieftains. The first part of the poem was published in 1569, the second in 1578, and the third in 1589.

**Errázuriz, Eulogio Sánchez.** See SÁNCHEZ ERRÁZURIZ, EULOGIO.

**Errázuriz Echaurren, Federico.** 1850–1901. Called the younger. President of Chile,

serving from 1896 to 1901, and supported by the conservatives. His chief problems were domestic economic and financial affairs.

**Errázuriz Valdivieso, Crescente.** 1839–1931. Chilean archbishop and historian. b. Santiago. Ordained presbyter, 1863; became professor in the seminary of Santiago and held chair of canonical law at the University of Chile; founded *El estandarte católico,* 1874; entered Dominican Order, 1884. Made Archbishop of Santiago, 1919, he is best-known for helping to bring about the peaceful separation of Church and State in Chile. The disestablishment of the Church was accomplished under the new constitution of 1925 with the sincere co-operation of governmental and Church officials, and in such an exemplary manner that it has added greatly to the prestige of the Church, Chile being one of the few Latin-American countries that have solved this delicate problem without bloodshed. Errázuriz made notable contributions in the field of historical writing with his *Los orígenes de la iglesia chilena, 1540–1603* (1873), and his investigations into the early history of the country.

**Errázuriz Zañartu, Federico.** 1825–1877. President of Chile. Took part in the insurrection of 1851; served in PÉREZ MOSCAYANO's government. During Errázuriz's administration (1871–1876) a constitutional amendment was adopted that prohibited the president from accepting two successive terms and further increased the power of congress over that of the executive. He was the first president to serve under the amended constitution as a liberal. The press was given more freedom, the power of the church was diminished, and a criminal code was passed that gave the civil courts jurisdiction over the clergy.

**Escoceses.** Spanish meaning, "Scotchmen." Name given to the members of the Mexican Masonic lodges of the Scottish rite, founded around 1806. They played an important role in the overthrow of ITURBIDE. As their views were on the conservative side, they were actively opposed by the federalist-minded Masons of the York rite or YORKINO lodges. They took a prominent part in the conservative revolt of 1827 led by Nicolás BRAVO, who was the vice-president of the republic and grand master of the Scottish rite lodge. When the revolt proved a failure, the power of the *escoceses* was broken and a number of their leaders were forced into exile.

**Esmeralda Affair.** In 1895 the government of Ecuador, under the presidency of Luis Cordero, permitted the government of Chile to transfer the Chilean warship *Esmeralda* nominally to Ecuador before selling it to Japan. In this manner Chile tried to maintain a front of neutrality in the war between China and Japan. When this deal became known in Ecuador, popular indignation was great, and the liberals used the affair as a pretext to revolt against the government. The success of their revolt carried the liberal Eloy ALFARO into power.

**Española.** Name given by Christopher CO-LUMBUS to the island of Haiti when he discovered it on December 6, 1492. The choice of the name was due to the resemblance that Columbus saw in the landscape of the island with that of southern Spain. The name was later Latinized as Hispaniola. The entire island is now referred to as either Haiti or Santo Domingo.

**Espejo, Francisco Javier Eugenio.** 1747–1796. b. Quito. A doctor of medicine who organized many cultural societies in New Granada (Colombia). He was a contributor to *Papel Periódico de la Ciudad de Santafé de Bogotá*, a weekly that was the first real newspaper in New Granada. He was often censored by the viceroy and was imprisoned.

**Estado Novo.** Portuguese. Literally, "New State." Name given to the dictatorial regime established by the Brazilian president Getulio VARGAS, which lasted from 1937 to 1945.

**Estancias.** The term used in the region of the Río de la Plata to designate the large rural estates, usually cattle ranches, which still occupy much of the region's arable soil. Formerly (and in many cases today) the *estancia* was a huge, almost self-sufficient community, with the all-powerful *estanciero* (owner) supervising his servants and tenant farmers. His power could be compared with that of the feudal lord of the Middle Ages. On his *estancia* he was judge and lawmaker. This system often led to abuses, if the *estan-ciero* was not animated by paternal feelings toward his dependents, or if he left the management to a cruel overseer. Often he would lead the life of a wealthy absentee landlord, and reside in the big cities of the region or in Europe, surrounded by luxury. Until recently the *estanciero* wielded considerable influence in the political life of the country. In Argentina, however, the PERÓN regime, with its emphasis on the lower middle class and the workers, somewhat diminished the power and influence of the landed aristocrat. The *estanciero* has his counterpart in the Brazilian *fazendeiro* and the Mexican *hacendado*.

**Estigarribia, José Félix.** 1888–1940. President of Paraguay. b. Caraguatay. General of the army who was serving as inspector general when the CHACO WAR broke out in 1932. He served as commander-in-chief and led the army to many victories, 1932–1935; exiled, 1936–1937. He served as minister to the United States, 1938–1939, and helped to arrange the peace settlement between Bolivia and Paraguay in 1938. He served as Liberal president of Paraguay, 1939–1940, proclaimed himself dictator of the country, 1940, and initiated action to draw up the new constitution of 1940. He was killed in an airplane crash on September 7, 1940.

**Estimé, Dumarsais.** 1900–1953. President of Haiti, 1946–1950. Moderate politically, he had worked as a farmer and rural school teacher. He instituted many reforms and internal improvements including the elimination of the nation's caste system, and the economic and social privileges of the mulattoes. He had new roads constructed, organized collective farms, and had model villages built. Payment of the balance of the external loan of 1922 made it possible to offset foreign control of the country's financial administration, and all of his program was financed by the first income tax in the country's history. He had slight trouble with TRUJILLO in 1949, but it was amicably settled by the ORGANIZA-TION OF AMERICAN STATES. He tried to amend the constitution to allow his continuing as president, but was superseded by a military junta and forced to resign.

**Estrada Cabrera, Manuel.** 1857–1924. President of Guatemala. Of obscure origin, he served as vice-president until February 8, 1898, when President Justo BARRIOS was assassinated, and he assumed the office, serving from 1898 to 1920 and being "re-elected" in 1904, 1910, and 1916. He was a corrupt dictator, intoxicated with power, who favored the wealthy classes and did nothing for the poor Indians of Guatemala. He was able to attract foreign capital which, invested in the development of the sugar and banana industries, gave the country products for export. He was finally ousted by a revolution led by Carlos Herrera y Luna in 1920.

**Estrada Palma, Tomás.** 1835–1908. First president of Cuba. Patriot who served in Cuban Ten Years' War, 1868–1878; president of provisional government of Cuba; captured and imprisoned, 1877–1878; went into exile in Honduras and the United States until 1902; served as minister to the United States while the revolution was in progress, 1898; elected first president of Cuba in 1901 and served 1902–1906; re-elected; an honest man and greatly respected, but not a forceful leader, he had strong opposition from the liberals; Estrada Palma asked the United States to intervene in Cuba in 1906 which it did; he resigned.

**Expropriation Law of 1938.** The decree by which the British and U. S. oil companies were expropriated by the Mexican government in March 1938. The conflict between the Mexican workers employed by the foreign oil companies and the latter came to a head in May 1937, when the workers struck for higher wages and a voice in the management of the oil industry. The dispute was submitted to an arbitration board, which in December of the same year handed down a decision considered unacceptable by the companies. On March 18, 1938, President Lázaro CÁRDENAS ordered the expropriation of all the more important foreign companies. This action put a severe strain on Mexico's relations with Great Britain and the United States, and on the country's own economy. Mexico's oil could be exported only with the greatest difficulty, for most of the world's tankers were under the control of the expropriated companies. Furthermore the official organization

that now operated the oil fields had to face a decrease in production and an increase in costs. In spite of these economic difficulties, however, the Mexican public gave its wholehearted support to the expropriation policy of the Cárdenas government. The dispute with the United States was settled in 1942, Mexico agreeing to pay $23,995,991 in compensation, plus $8,500,000 previously paid to Sinclair interests.

**Export-Import Bank of Washington** or **Eximbank.** A U.S. government bank chartered by Congress in 1934. It is empowered to extend loans or to guarantee private loans when there is a scarcity of private credit resources. These loans are generally intended to finance commerce between the United States and other nations. In 1938 the bank was given the authorization to extend loans to foreign governments, corporations, or individuals, and the amount of money in loans it was permitted to have outstanding at any one time was allowed to go as high as $700,000,-000. By 1941 most of the Latin-American republics benefited from the aid given by the Export-Import Bank. Loans were made especially for the purpose of improving transportation in order to facilitate the delivery to the United States of strategic materials. One of the projects that was financed by the bank was the furthering of work on the PAN-AMERICAN HIGHWAY between Mexico City and the Canal Zone. The authorized capital of the bank has been augmented from time to time, most recently in 1963 when the U.S. Congress increased the lending authority of the bank to $9,000,000,000. At that time the life of the bank was also extended for another five years, to June 30, 1968. Loans to the Latin-American countries have increased greatly over the years. Loans to those countries from 1952 to 1956 totaled $1,100,000,000, and during the fiscal year ending June 30, 1961 they received $773,200,000. Among the projects that gained greatly from the loans were: the Brazilian steel industry, hospitals, and public works; road building in Bolivia; electric-power development in Chile; irrigation, road building, and other public works in Cuba; and the development of a rubber industry and agriculture in Haiti.

# F

**Facundo.** An important book by the Argentine statesman and author Domingo Faustino SARMIENTO, published in 1845. The complete title is *Facundo, o la civilización y la barbarie* (Facundo, or Civilization and Barbarism). The book tells of the life of the terrible *caudillo* Facundo Quiroga, a local tyrant who achieved power after the establishment of Argentine independence. It also gives a fine picture of the Argentine countryside of that period and is an indictment of ROSAS and the whole *caudillo* system, which Sarmiento predicted would collapse. The book is considered an outstanding example of the Argentine romantic school of writing.

**Falcón, Juan Crisóstomo.** 1820–1870. President of Venezuela. General of the army, member of the federalists. The leader of the liberals who overthrew PÁEZ in 1863, he was made provisional president upon the withdrawal of Páez. A new constitution was framed in 1864 establishing the principles of federalism, the name of the country was changed to the United States of Venezuela, and in the same year Falcón was elected to serve as president for a term of four years. He was constantly forced to put down revolts and was finally overthrown toward the end of his term of office by José Tadeo MONAGAS and the *Azules* (Blues), 1868, and went into exile.

**Falkland Islands.** See ANGLO-LATIN AMERICAN RELATIONS.

**Farrapos.** See GUERRA DOS FARRAPOS.

**Farrell, Edelmiro J.** b. 1887. President of Argentina. A general, he served as minister of war under Pedro RAMÍREZ in 1943, whom he succeeded in March 1944. He was part of the Fascistic military group and many countries, including the United States, withheld recognition because of his pro-Axis policies. He allowed the suppression of the press and created a large army that called for heavy government expenditures. In response to the CHAPULTEPEC CONFERENCE he declared war on Germany and Japan in March 1945, and was accorded U.S. recognition. He was succeeded by PERÓN, who won the election of February 1946.

**Fascism.** Latin-American Fascist movements emulating the pre-World War II type of German and Italian Fascism were especially active in Brazil, Chile, and Mexico. Argentine *peronismo* has often been compared to the European Fascist systems. It should, however, be considered in the light of purely Argentine history and politics, and not as a movement endeavoring to emulate foreign systems. In Brazil a Fascistlike organization arose during the 1930's, called the Integralist movement. Its leader, Plinio Salgado, modeled it on the Italian and German movements, having his followers wear green shirts, give the Fascist salute, and train with military precision. At first the Brazilian dictator VARGAS was sympathetic toward the INTEGRALISTAS, but in 1938 he dissolved their party, and when they staged an armed uprising, he crushed it mercilessly and put an end to Integralism. In Chile a similar movement developed under the leadership of Jorge González von Marées. Members of this organization called themselves *nacistas* or Nazis. They claimed that they were Chileans first and that their movement was a purely national product. However their slogans and tactics were closely patterned after those of Hitler and Mussolini. They staged an uprising in September 1938 that was easily put down, for the *nacistas* were not numerous and were not supported by public opinion. In Mexico SINARQUISMO, with its strong emphasis on religion, nationalism, and order, and its use of uniforms and Fascist-type salute, was another such group. The Mexican government took effective measures against it during World War II. See also AXIS INFLUENCE.

**Faustin I.** See SOULOUQUE, FAUSTIN ÉLIE.

**Fazenda.** Any large estate in Brazil. Formerly, it was a self-sufficient community with the owner or *fazendeiro* being not only the acknowledged lord and master of his family, the freemen, and the Negro slaves working on his land, but also a powerful local chieftain. Very often the *fazendeiro* spent much time in neighboring towns or cities, leaving the care of the plantation in the hands of an overseer. Today, the term still applies generally to large plantations. See also ESTANCIAS and HACIENDA.

**Febrerista Party of Paraguay.** Also, **Partido Revolucionario Febrerista.** A political party originally composed of the followers of former President Rafael Franco. The name of the party was derived from the fact that the revolution that had elevated Franco to the presidency had broken out in February 1936. The party opposed the dictatorship of Higinio MORÍNIGO and attempted to overthrow his government in 1941. Party members participated in the coalition government under Morínigo in 1946 but resigned from the cabinet early in 1947. The Febrerista Party led a rebellion that almost succeeded in overthrowing the same government in 1947. It purged itself of Communist elements that had infiltrated its ranks in 1954 and is now a member of the *Federación de Partidos Revolucionarios Latinoamericanos*, with APRA of Peru, ACCIÓN DEMOCRÁTICA of Venezuela, and MNR of Bolivia. The party is still active but has refrained from participating in recent national elections because of the dictatorial

nature of the present regime in power in Paraguay.

**Federalism.** The federal principle of national organization had many supporters in Latin America during the period immediately following the winning of independence, largely because of the example of the United States. In most countries the liberals were federalists, while the conservatives advocated strong central authority. In practice, however, any consistent application of federalism usually resulted in anarchy, and its supporters often paid only lip service to its principles when they achieved power. In Argentina two decades of conflict between federalists and unitarians ended in 1835 when ROSAS, who was officially a federalist, established an absolute dictatorship. Federalism had the upper hand in Chile during the 1820's, but came to an end in 1830 with the defeat of the liberals on the battlefields. In Colombia federalism was dominant from about 1853 to the early 1880's, when Rafael NÚÑEZ greatly strengthened the central government. Venezuela adopted a federal constitution in 1864, but it did not prevent GUZMÁN BLANCO from ruling as dictator from 1870 to 1888. Finally, in Mexico, a federalist constitution was adopted in 1824. Replaced by a conservative system in 1836, it was reestablished in 1846, and extensively revised in 1857. Today a number of Latin-American countries, including Argentina, Brazil, and Mexico, have constitutions based in some degree on the federal principle, but the central governments exercise more power over the local authorities, both legally and actually, than has been the case in the United States, and federalism remains a theory rather than a concrete reality.

**Federmann, Nicolás** or **Nikolaus.** *ca.* 1501–1543. German explorer and adventurer in South America. Member of the German colony in Venezuela, he led an expedition that reached the highlands near Santa Fe de Bogotá by way of the upper tributaries of the Orinoco River. As agent of the German bankers, the House of WELSER, he made trips into the interior looking for cities of gold and slaves.

**Feijó, Diogo Antônio.** 1784–1843. Regent of Brazil. b. São Paulo. Ordained a Roman Catholic priest in 1807; made Brazilian deputy to the Cortes at Lisbon in 1822; resigned on the announcement of Brazilian independence in 1822; deputy to the Brazilian Cortes, serving 1823–1833; senator; minister of justice; regent of Brazil, 1835–1837, during the infancy of PEDRO II. One of the worst local civil wars, the GUERRA DOS FARRAPOS, took place in Rio Grande do Sul. Feijó had an inflexible disposition and his fairly radical ideas alienated the liberals as well as conservatives, and continued revolts caused him to resign.

**Feitoria.** Trading post on the coast of Brazil in the early days of Portuguese colonization, through which goods passed to and from Portugal and other countries.

**Ferdinand V of Castile** or **Ferdinand II of Aragón.** Called The Catholic. 1452–1516. Son of John II of Aragón. b. Sos, Aragón. Married ISABEL I OF CASTILE and became sole ruler of the Spanish Empire upon her death in 1504.

**Ferdinand VII.** 1784–1833. Son of Charles IV of Spain. b. San Ildefonso. Became king after forced abdication of CHARLES IV in 1808. Invited to a conference at Bayonne by NAPOLEON, he was taken prisoner. Regaining the throne after the expulsion of the French in 1814, he was a cruel and despotic ruler. The constitutionalists curbed his power from 1820 to 1823, but the Holy Alliance, using French troops, restored absolutism in 1823. His reign saw the loss of all colonies in North and South America, except Cuba and Puerto Rico, and Spain was thereafter a secondary power in Europe.

**Fernandes Pinheiro, José Feliciano. Visconde de São Leopoldo.** 1774–1847. Brazilian statesman and writer. b. Santos. Organized the first German colony, Saõ Leopoldo. He served as the first president of Rio Grande do Sul, 1823–1825; minister of justice, 1825–1827; and senator, 1827 until his death.

**Fernández, Juan.** *ca.* 1536–1602. Spanish navigator and explorer. He explored the southern Pacific between Panama and the settlements in Peru and Chile from about 1550 to 1590 and discovered the islands named for him, 1563.

**Fernández, Juan Manuel Félix.** See VICTORIA, GUADALUPE.

**Fernández de Córdoba, Diego. Marqués de Guadalcázar** and **Conde de Posadas.** Viceroy of Mexico, 1612–1621. He founded Lerma, 1613, Córdoba, 1618, and Guadalcázar, 1620. Served as viceroy of Peru, 1622–1629.

**Fernández de Enciso, Martín.** See ENCISO, MARTÍN FERNÁNDEZ DE.

**Fernández de Lizardi, José Joaquín.** 1776–1827. Mexican writer. His novel *El Periquillo Sarniento*, written in 1816 and published in four volumes in 1830, was the first novel written by a native of Latin America and printed in the Western Hemisphere; translated into English and published in 1941 as The Itching Parrot. Called *El Pensador Mexicano* (The Mexican Thinker), he was a famous pamphleteer who battled against monarchy in support of democracy, fought for benefits to the poor in social and economic reforms, and for a written constitution and forceful laws.

**Fernández de Oviedo.** See OVIEDO Y VALDÉS, GONZALO FERNÁNDEZ DE.

**Fernández Madrid, José.** 1789–1830. Colombian physician, writer, and statesman. b. Cartagena, Colombia. Educated in Bogotá; active in the fight for independence in 1810. He was elected president of Colombia in 1816 but was captured by the Spanish and interned at Havana, Cuba, 1816–1825. He served from 1825 as minister to England. He wrote many scientific works and two poetic tragedies, *Atala* (1822) and *Guatimozín* (1827).

**Ferreira da Veiga, Evaristo.** 1799–1837. Brazilian liberal and newspaper publisher. b. Rio de Janeiro. Published *Aurora Fluminense*, an opposition and liberal paper, founded in 1827. He became the chief figure in the liberal movement of that period and for a time led a group known as *moderados*, who wanted a constitutional monarchy. He succeeded in having PEDRO I enact some changes in the latter's administration.

135

**Ferrera** or **Ferrer, Francisco.** President of Honduras. While president, 1841–1844, he defeated several attempts to overthrow the government and pacified the country. He became minister of war and commander-in-chief of the military forces after his term of office expired and was the real ruler of Honduras until 1848. During his presidency Honduras was united in a confederation with Nicaragua and El Salvador, 1842–1845.

**Fidalgo.** Portuguese term applied to a person who inherited a title of nobility or was granted it by the king.

**Figueres Ferrer, José** or **"Pepe."** 1906– . President of Costa Rica. b. San Ramón. Studied at M.I.T. and University of Mexico; coffee planter in Costa Rica; exiled for his opposition to President CALDERÓN GUARDIA, 1942; colonel in the army. In March 1948, at the head of the socialist National Liberation movement, he led the military revolt in support of the opposition candidate in the February elections, ULATE BLANCO, whose victory had been annulled by the Costa Rican congress. After about six weeks of bitter fighting, he overcame the resistance of a coalition of government forces and Communists, both supporting the defeated candidate, Calderón Guardia. He entered the capital, San José, April 28, set up a junta, over which he presided, abolished the army, and outlawed the Communist Party. He called a constitutional assembly that, in January 1949, confirmed Ulate Blanco's election and drafted a new constitution, and Figueres turned over the government to Ulate Blanco in 1949. Figueres was elected president of Costa Rica, July 1953, and served until 1958, when he was succeeded by Mario Echandi Jiménez. Figueres attracted world-wide attention with his firm stand against the Nicaraguan-supported invasion of Costa Rica, January 1955, by supporters of ex-President MICHALSKY PICADO, and is known for his opposition to authoritarian government in Latin America.

**Figueroa Larraín, Emiliano.** 1866–1931. President of Chile. Lawyer; conservative; served in congress, in the cabinet, and in the diplomatic service; acting president, September–December, 1910; instrumental in the formation of the entente between the ABC POWERS. He was supported by all parties in the election of 1925 and served until 1927. During his administration, many much-needed economic reforms were put into effect. An honest man, but not a strong enough leader for the times, he was forced to resign by pressure exerted by IBÁÑEZ DEL CAMPO, a military officer who had been serving first as minister of the interior and then as vice-president.

**Financial Administration in the Spanish-American Colonies.** The Spanish Crown derived a considerable revenue from its American possessions in colonial times. From about 165,000 ducats annually in the first half of the 16th century, it rose to between 2 and 3 million in the reign of PHILIP II (1556–1598); it then fell off somewhat in the 17th century, but soared to from 5 to 6 million before 1800. The Crown's revenues were derived mostly from the mines, which paid one-fifth (*quinto*) of the returns to the king; from duties (*almojarifazgo*) on goods exported from Spain to the colonies; from the tribute paid by the natives to the Crown; from taxes, such as the *cruzada*, which originally had been collected in Spain for the purpose of fighting the Moors; from the *alcabala* or sales tax; from the sale of public offices; from the *mesada* and the *media anata*, or payments to the Crown from the income of newly appointed secular and ecclesiastical officials; and from monopolies (quicksilver, salt, gunpowder, playing cards, etc.). The collection of revenues in each colony was in the hands of *oficiales reales* (royal officials), who were four in number: a treasurer, a *contador* or comptroller, a *factor* or business manager, and a *veedor* or inspector. However, from the middle of the 16th century on, the offices of *veedor* and *factor* were substantially discarded. Taxes were often collected by private individuals as well as by Crown officials. Financial questions were discussed in each province by a *junta superior de real hacienda* (higher board of royal treasury), meeting once a week and including the viceroy or governor, the *oficiales reales*, the senior judge, and the *fiscal* or prosecutor of the *audiencia*. Up to 1605, the CONSEJO DE INDIAS

(Council of the Indies) acted as supreme court of audit, but from that date on, three tribunals of accounts with the power of auditing all public accounts were established in the Spanish colonies, one in Santa Fe de Bogotá, one in Mexico City, and one in Lima. A special accountant for the West Indies resided at Havana, and another one for Venezuela was located at Caracas. The first royal mint was founded in Mexico in 1535, and in Lima in 1568; private individuals or companies called *compañías de fabricantes de moneda* were granted the operation of colonial mints under a fixed tax. In the 18th century, under PHILIP V (1700–1746), mints were operated directly by the Crown. The Spanish Bourbons, worried by the inefficiency and the waste prevalent in the financial management of the colonies, introduced in the second half of the 18th century the system of the *intendentes* or intendants, who were officials with wide powers of reorganization and revenue collection. As a result of this reform, the financial situation was greatly improved, and revenues increased.

**Finca.** Spanish for farm, country land, or coffee plantation.

**Finlay, Carlos (Charles) Juan.** 1833–1915. Cuban physician and biologist. b. Camagüey, Cuba of Scottish-French parentage. Known for his investigation into the cause of yellow fever. He wrote a paper in 1881 saying that the disease was carried by a mosquito and his later belief that it was carried by the mosquito *stegomyia* was proved to be correct by Dr. Walter REED in 1900. Finlay was made chairman of a commission on infectious diseases in Havana, 1899–1902, and chief sanitary officer of Cuba, 1902–1909.

**Fleet** or **Flota System.** From the beginning of the colonial period the Spanish government was concerned with the safe transportation of the gold and silver from the American mines to Spain. From the very start pirates attacked Spanish ships carrying the precious metals to the motherland as well as those carrying European goods to the colonies. It became necessary to have merchant ships escorted by war vessels. Thus the fleet system came into existence. After the middle of the 16th century and until the latter half of the 18th century, trade was carried on by well-protected fleets. Each year two fleets left Spain for the American colonies. The number of ships in each was usually from thirty to ninety in the 16th century, but afterward the quantity decreased. One fleet, the *galeones* (galleons), sailed for Cartagena in New Granada, where goods for this colony were unloaded. From there the fleet proceeded to Porto Bello on the Isthmus of Panama, where traders and officials remained more than a month until the exchange of European goods for South-American gold, silver, and other products, had been completed. European goods were carried overland to Panama City (always a difficult journey) and thence shipped to the ports of the South-American west coast. The second fleet, called *flota*, sailed for Veracruz in Mexico, detaching a few ships after its arrival in Caribbean waters to supply the West Indies. In the spring of the following year the two fleets met at Havana and started on the homeward journey together. The counterpart of the Porto Bello fair in Mexico took place at Jalapa, a much healthier place than the Panamanian town where many traders died of various diseases. From Veracruz goods were transported to Mexico City, a journey far less expensive than that from Porto Bello to Lima. As a result, trade with New Spain superseded that with Peru in later colonial times. Toward the middle of the 18th century the Panama fleet was discontinued and trade with South America was carried on with individual ships, some of which were now permitted to sail around Cape Horn. The Mexican fleets were discontinued in 1789.

**Flores, Juan José.** 1800–1864. President of Ecuador. b. Puerto Cabello, Venezuela. Started as a common soldier, and although of obscure origin and with no schooling, he married into one of the best families in Quito and was highly regarded. He served under BOLÍVAR in the War of Independence, won the victory of Tarqui, 1829, became the first president of Ecuador after declaring it independent of Gran Colombia in 1830, and served until 1835. When ROCAFUERTE led a revolt against the government and was captured, Flores, instead of having him shot, promised he would be president in 1835, which occurred. Flores was again president from 1839 to 1845 and ruled without a congress. His administration was rather corrupt and arbitrary, and he was overthrown by a revolution and sent into exile. He was recalled to defend Ecuador against New Granada in 1863.

**Flores, Venancio.** 1809–1868. President of Uruguay. b. Paysandú. Colonel in the army; leader of the *colorados,* following the civil war of 1842–1851, in a revolt against the government. Elected president in 1854, he was overthrown in a civil war with the *blancos* and exiled to Argentina. With the aid of Brazil and Argentina he returned with an army in 1863 and by 1865 had captured Montevideo and taken over. He joined Brazil and Argentina in war against Paraguay, 1865, and returned in 1867 to govern his country. That year the first rail line was laid in Uruguay and a civil code of laws was promulgated in January of the next year. In 1868 he decided that he would run for election to the presidency, for he had only been provisional head of the country, but on February 15th of that year he was assassinated.

**Flores Magón, Ricardo.** 1873–1922. Mexican revolutionist. b. Teotitlán del Camino. Began opposition to DÍAZ; published and edited the journal *La Regeneración,* the organ of the junta of his so-called Mexican Liberal Party. Imprisoned for his opposition to the Díaz government, he escaped to the United States where he, his brother, Jesús, and other comrades surreptitiously published their newspaper. He was an anarchist and syndicalist who opposed communist philosophy based on a dictatorship of the proletariat. Captured by the U.S. authorities in Texas after an abortive attempt to organize a revolution, Flores Magón escaped only to be recaptured and imprisoned in Leavenworth prison where he died. By 1918 his ideas were being replaced by the views held by MORONES and the CROM.

**Fomento.** Spanish for development, promotion, fomentation.

**Fonseca, Hermes da.** 1865–1923. President of Brazil. Marshal of the army. He became president in 1910 and served as dictator until 1914. The candidate of the conservative republicans, he was militaristic and reactionary in the extreme. His term was upset by a heavy financial depression caused by a drop in coffee and rubber prices.

**Fonseca, Juan Rodríguez de.** 1451–1524. Spanish prelate. As Archdeacon of Seville, he served ISABEL and FERDINAND as chaplain; made bishop of Badajoz, and then archbishop of Burgos. He was head of colonial affairs from 1493 until his death. Responsible for the early colonial policy of Spain, he was suspicious of the conquistadors, and anxious to help the Indians. He sent BOBADILLA to the New World to investigate COLUMBUS and also opposed CORTÉS. In 1503 he established the *Casa de Contratación* at Seville to assist him with his many duties. After his death the Council of the Indies was established. The Gulf of Fonseca was named in his honor by its discoverer, Gil González de Ávila.

**Fonseca, Manael Deodoro da.** 1827–1892. Brazilian president and general. b. Alagoas. Took an active part in the war with Paraguay, 1864–1870; governor of Rio Grande do Sul, 1887–1889; headed the movement in opposition to PEDRO II; made head of the provisional government and served 1889–1891. He was president of Brazil from February 25 to November 23, 1891, when he was forced to resign because he had dissolved congress and declared himself dictator. During his time in office a complete reorganization of the national and local administrations was instituted. The right of suffrage was extended; separation of Church and State was decreed on January 7, 1890. The new constitution which went into effect on February 24, 1891, was modeled after that of the United States, and was generally liberal. Fonseca, an honest, popular man, and a good soldier, was not a good executive.

**Foral.** In colonial Brazil, the charter that formulated the relationship between the proprietor of a captaincy or *donatário* on the one hand, and the Portuguese Crown and the Portuguese colonists on the other.

**Foreign Trade.** In colonial times the Spanish Crown, and to some extent the Portuguese Crown, tried to maintain a tight monopoly over trade between the Latin-American colonies and Europe. Other nations, seeing themselves shut out from profitable trade with the Spanish-American colonies and Brazil, resorted to contraband and to piracy. The ebbing of Spanish world power in the 18th century, and the more enlightened attitude of the Spanish Bourbons, led to the liberalizing of trade policies. Montevideo, for instance, was permitted to trade directly with the firm of Brentano, Vobara, and Urbieta of Hamburg, the company of Joaquín Fernández da Silva of Oporto, Portugal, and other neutrals in Spain's wars. At the end of the War of the Spanish Succession (1701–1713) the British were granted the *asiento,* or contract, permitting them to import slaves into the Spanish-American colonies. During the same war, since France and Spain were allies, the French were permitted to trade directly. After the colonies achieved independence, their trade with European nations increased greatly. Great Britain soon took the lead in this movement and maintained this position in Latin-American trade during the 19th century. In the 20th century the United States has superseded Great Britain in Latin-American trade. The great economic expansion of the United States, the proximity of the United States to the southern republics, the opening of the Panama Canal, and World War II have been strong factors contributing to this change. Great Britain, however, still is an important customer of the Latin-American nations. Germany and Italy competed successfully with other nations for Latin-American markets before World War II, and, after the war Germany again emerged as an important supplier of the Latin-American republics. In recent years Latin-American countries have been endeavoring to achieve a higher degree of economic independence. They have been trying to change the age-old pattern of bartering Latin-American raw materials for foreign manufactured products. Increased industrialization is leading to a reorientation of the pattern of Latin-American trade. At the same time Latin-American governments are trying to bolster the drive for economic independence by intervening in the direction of the countries' foreign commerce. The levying of special surtaxes on imports, prohibitions affecting specific types of imported goods, the creation of quotas, and other regulations reflect this tendency on the part of these governments toward self-sufficiency. This growing economic nationalism has put many obstacles in the way of trade with Latin America. More consumer goods are being produced as a result of increased industrialization, but on the other hand, the greater need on the part of Latin-American nations for industrial machinery points the way to increased business in this field. After World War II there was a considerable increase in commerce among the Latin-American republics, and in the late 1950's the Central-American republics and the South-American nations created common markets in the hope of increasing intra-Latin American trade and strengthening its world bargaining position. The nine-member LATIN AMERICAN FREE TRADE ASSOCIATION (LAFTA), organized in 1960, includes Mexico and all the South-American countries except Bolivia and Venezuela. Trade between the LAFTA countries increased from $12,000,000 to $23,000,000 in its first two years and reached $40,000,000 in 1963. The CENTRAL AMERICAN COMMON MARKET (CACM), consisting of all the Central-American countries except Panama, has stimulated a 30 per cent growth in internal trade. The CACM nations established a common tariff on 98 per cent of all products from outside the area by the end of 1965.

**Foros.** In colonial Brazil, privileges including exemptions from certain taxes.

**Francia, José Gaspar Rodríguez de.** 1766–1840. Paraguayan dictator. A lawyer and political figure before independence, Francia became a leader in the rebellion against Spanish authority. He was a member of revolutionary juntas, 1811, shared consulate executive with Fulgencio Yegros, 1813, was given absolute power for three years, 1814, and became dictator for life, 1816. During his long rule he relied for support on the Indian masses of the country, who constituted the bulk of the population. Toward the CREOLES and the clergy, he assumed an uncompromising attitude and instituted a reign of terror designed to eliminate the influence of the upper classes and the Church. He isolated the country from the outside, barring all foreigners, and in attempting to render Paraguay self-sufficient, he fostered the raising of cotton and indispensable food crops, and established a fairly large army, created from among his Indian subjects. In his old age, Francia became more and more despotic and resorted to frequent liquidations of people whom he suspected of plotting against him.

**Franciscans.** Religious order that took an active part in the colonization of the Spanish and Portuguese territories in America. During the conquest of Mexico, Franciscan missionaries were the first to set foot in that country and to preach and convert the Indians to Christianity. They accompanied the conquistadors on their expeditions and succeeded in converting large numbers of natives. They founded many missions in northern Mexico and later in California and Texas. Soon after the conquest of Mexico, Franciscan friars established schools there. The important early schools were that of Pedro de Gante, founded for Indians in 1522 and that of Santa Cruz de Tlaltelulco, also for Indians, founded in 1536 with the assistance of viceroy Antonio de MENDOZA. In the course of time the Franciscans became powerful. They were granted extensive privileges by the pope and the crown, and considered themselves practically independent of state jurisdiction. They were also active in South America. At an early date they went among the Chanaes Indians along the Uruguay River and founded the missions of Santo Domingo de Soriano (1624), Víboras, and Espinillo. In Brazil they were active in the 17th century in establishing missions among the Indians of the Amazon Valley.

**Free Trade Act.** Full title, **Reglamento y aranceles reales para el comercio libre de España e Indias.** A decree promulgated in 1778 allowing all colonial provinces except New Spain and Venezuela to carry on trade with the more important Spanish ports instead of only with Cádiz, as had formerly been the rule. Foreigners were excluded from this trade, and it was further stipulated that goods were to be transported exclusively in ships of Spanish construction and the property of Spaniards. As a result of the act the ports of Santiago, Montevideo, and Buenos Aires prospered greatly. The act was extended to include New Spain and Venezuela in 1789.

**Freire Serrano, Ramón,** 1787–1851. Dictator of Chile, b. Santiago. Served in the war for independence of Chile from 1811 to 1820; made leader of the liberal party. He led the revolt of the army at Concepción in 1822; joined by military forces in other parts of the country, and when a *cabildo abierto* demanded and obtained the resignation of O'HIGGINS in January 1823, Freire became dictator of the country. He was a better soldier than politician. He was forced to suspend the constitution of 1823 that restricted the power of the executive and gave it to congress, because it was unworkable. The principal achievement of his administration, with all its troubles, was the conquest of the island of Chiloé, 1826, which until then had remained under Spanish control. He resigned in 1826, was reelected in 1827, but was forced to resign by the conservatives. He led an army revolt against the government, was defeated by PRIETO VIAL, and sent into exile in Peru in 1830. He returned to Chile in 1842.

**French-Latin American Relations.** From the beginning the French tried to obtain a hold over Latin-American trade. Throughout the 16th century they backed this policy with organized piracy, and French corsairs constantly attacked Spanish ships and settlements in the West Indies and on the Spanish Main. In the same century they established posts along the coast of Brazil, from which they shipped large quantities of dyewood. In 1555 they founded a colony in Rio de Janeiro Bay, and although they were expelled in 1560 they later captured the port of Recife. In the course of the 17th century France acquired the western end of the island of Hispaniola (Santo Domingo), and the French-held island of Tortuga became a famous base for buccaneers and pirates. In the early years of the

18th century, when Spain and France were allies in the War of the Spanish Succession, French ships were granted the privilege of taking on provisions in Spanish-American ports. They took advantage of this concession by trading in those ports, and many French products entered Spanish America. Until the end of the colonial period French smugglers carried on a profitable illicit trade with the Spanish colonies. During the War for Independence, France, under a monarchy sympathetic to the Holy Alliance, would have welcomed the restoration of Spanish royal authority, but did not intervene, partly because she looked forward to profitable trade with the new republics, and partly because of British opposition expressed by Foreign Secretary Canning in 1823. In 1838, and again in 1845, France became involved in a conflict with the Argentine dictator ROSAS, and twice blockaded Buenos Aires, the second time in conjunction with Great Britain. Also, in 1838, a French fleet was sent to the Mexican port of Veracruz to back up French financial claims against the Mexican government. In this so-called PASTRY WAR, the French occupied Veracruz and blockaded other Mexican ports. In 1862 French troops intervened in Mexico, installing MAXIMILIAN as emperor in 1864, but left in 1867. In the Caribbean area France had lost Haiti in 1802–1804, but recognized the independence of the new republic in 1825 in exchange for the payment of an indemnity. The economic development of Haiti greatly interested French bankers who, by the first decade of the 20th century, had extended most of the loans saddling the Haitian government. Although the French political role in Latin America has been negligible in the last eighty years, French cultural influence has been considerable. Most educated Latin Americans consider France to be their intellectual home. The French language is still the second language, and French books are widely read. Many Latin Americans have spent much time in France, absorbing French culture, and studying the arts and the sciences. At present French cultural influence is somewhat diminishing, mainly because of the ever-increasing nationalism, economic and cultural, of the Latin-American republics.

**Freyre, Gilberto de Mello.** 1900–      . Brazilian sociologist and anthropologist. b. Recife. Educated in Recife and in the United States; secretary to governor of Pernambuco, four years; professor of sociology, 1928–1930. He took part in Brazilian politics under VARGAS and was imprisoned because of opposition to the latter's policies, 1934. He was professor of sociology at the law school of Recife, 1935, technical adviser to the National Department for the Care of Historical Documents, 1937, and went on a lecture tour in the United States, visiting universities, 1939. Among his many works are *Apologia pro generatione sua*, 1924; *Casa grande e senzala*, 1933, which was translated as The Masters and the Slaves, 1946; and *Sombrados e mucambos*, 1936, translated as The Mansions and the Shanties, 1963. *Casa grande e senzala* is probably his best-known work and is a remarkable study of Brazilian life in the slave-holding era.

**Fruit Industry.** Among fruits native to the Western Hemisphere are the pineapple, the papaya, and the avocado. Bananas, mangoes, oranges, and grapes were some of the fruits introduced into America by the Spanish and Portuguese colonizers. Vineyards developed especially well in the valleys of Peru and Chile. In colonial times there was such an abundance of fruit in Chile that its value in terms of money was extremely low. They were sold only in Santiago and Valparaíso. Fruits were also produced in great abundance in the Río de la Plata region. Today the fruit industry has become an important factor in the Brazilian economy. Before the decline in recent years of the Brazilian orange industry, due to a root disease and lessened demand abroad, Brazil's industry was the second-ranking in the world. Brazil exports bananas to the countries of the Río de la Plata region and grows, aside from a large number of native fruits, papayas, guavas, mangoes, peaches, melons, grapes, pineapples, and grapefruit. Argentina, too, has an important fruit industry. Grapes have been grown since early colonial times in the Mendoza and San Juan regions, where today the production of wine grapes in a normal year reaches 1,-000,000 tons. In the provinces of the north and in the Paraná delta many citrus fruits are produced. Apples, pears, and peaches are grown in the southwest districts of Río Negro and Neuquén. About 40,000 tons of fresh and dried fruits are exported each year. Central America today is still a great banana-producing area, with Honduras holding first rank. See BANANA INDUSTRY.

**Fueros.** Special privileges granted in colonial Spanish America to members of the clergy, the military, and to civil officials, according to which members of these classes had the right to be tried by their own courts in both civil and criminal cases. This system caused frequent conflicts over jurisdictional problems and led to much confusion and even violence. Abolition of *fueros* during the 19th century also led to much conflict, especially in Mexico. *Fuero* is also the name given to a body of laws, particularly the municipal laws of the Spanish colonial towns. See LEY JUÁREZ.

**Fundo.** In Chile, a *fundo* is a rural estate.

**Funes, Gregorio.** 1749–1830. Argentine historian. b. Córdoba. Ordained priest; rector of the University of Córdoba; dean, cathedral of Córdoba. A liberal, secular churchman who preached regionalism, he was deputy for Córdoba in the Buenos Aires junta, 1810. His notion of federalism resembled the final arrangements of the Spanish colonial system, and after 1813 he lost power to the GAUCHO and *caudillo*. He was editor of *El Argos de Buenos Aires*. His best-known work is *Ensayo de la historia civil del Paraguay, Buenos Aires, y Tucumán*, published in three volumes, 1816.

# G

**Gachupín.** Mexican term, meaning "person of Spanish birth." During the colonial period, it was applied to royal officials and to immigrants and is still used today, often derogatorily. Its derivation is uncertain, but it is probably from an Aztec word meaning "man who wears spurs."

**Gadsden Purchase.** The acquisition in 1853 by the United States of a 45,535-square-mile strip of land belonging to Mexico and located in southern Arizona and New Mexico. The purchase, which cost the United States the sum of $10,000,000, was negotiated by James Gadsden, the U.S. minister to Mexico, and was prompted by U. S. desire to build a railroad to the West Coast through the southern Rocky Mountains.

**Gainza Gabino.** Acting captain general of Guatemala in 1821. When it declared its independence from Spain, Gainza remained as head of the new government and called a *cabildo abierto* to find out what the people wanted from their government. He was forced to share his power with a *junta consultiva* of important people, both liberal and conservative. There was dissension, and the Spanish governors of Honduras and Nicaragua, who adhered to Iturbide's PLAN OF IGUALA, deposed him.

**Gaitán, Jorge Eliécer.** 1903–1948. Colombian political leader. Head of the more radical faction of liberals, he was known for his defense of the workers in their strike against the United Fruit Company in 1928. He gained a large following from 1942 to 1946 and was a presidential candidate in the election of 1946. However, the liberals were split, and although their combined total vote was greater than that of the conservative OSPINA PÉREZ, they were defeated. Gaitán was assassinated on the streets of Bogotá on April 9, 1948. His murder was followed by rioting, attributed to the Communists, while the Ninth PAN AMERICAN CONFERENCE was meeting.

**Galán, José Antonio.** See COMUNERO REVOLT.

**Galápagos Islands.** Group of islands about 700 miles off the coast of Ecuador, belonging to that republic. The islands have attracted naturalists and travelers because of their interesting geographic characteristics, but the Ecuadorian government has done little to exploit them. During World War II the United States was granted bases on the islands.

**Galeones.** English, **galleons.** Sailing vessels similar to galleys and dating from the end of the Middle Ages. The term also was used for a fleet carrying European goods to the Spanish-American colonies and treasures from the Spanish-American colonies to Spain. The ships (between thirty and ninety in a fleet during the 16th century, less later) would leave Seville and go to Cartagena (Colombia) and from there to Porto Bello on the Isthmus of Panama. The *galeones* were the coveted prize of the corsairs and pirates of various nations and many sea battles were fought between Spanish and British, French, and Dutch ships over silver and other treasures. The *galeones* were no longer used after 1740.

**Galindo, Carlos Blanco.** Bolivian general who headed a revolutionary military junta that took charge of the government from June 29, 1930, until the newly-elected SALAMANCA took office on March 5, 1931. Galindo instituted many political and economic reforms.

**Gallegos, Rómulo.** b. 1844. President of Venezuela and distinguished novelist. Elected by the DEMOCRATIC ACTION PARTY in the first genuinely free election, he served as president from February until November 1948, when he was overthrown by a military junta. He is the author of *Doña Barbara*, 1929, *Chanticler*, 1934, and many other well-known works.

**Gallo Goyenechea, Pedro León.** 1830–1877. b. Copiapó. Wealthy Chilean miner who organized and financed the Chilean Radical Party in 1859, which is still in existence today. He led the revolutionary movement of 1859 and was exiled, 1859–1863. He was a liberal from the northern nitrate-copper region who was anxious to reform Chilean politics, seeking a constitution change and a more equal system of representation. He also wanted more and better public education.

**Gálvez, José de, Marqués de la Sonora.** 1729–1786. Spanish administrator and statesman. b. Vélez Málaga. *Visitador general* or inspector general sent by King CHARLES III to New Spain, he was the last and greatest of the *visitadores*. When he landed in New Spain in July 1765, he insisted on the recall of the viceroy, who was replaced, and the government moved ahead with an efficiency previously unheard of in America. He sent an expedition to Upper California to establish garrisons and missions at San Diego and Monterey, and created the first settlements there in 1769. In his General Report of 1771, he recommended many reforms including a new mining code and the organization of a miners' guild. He took the collection of taxes out of private hands and placed it under the direct administration of the Crown. He was president of the COUNCIL OF THE INDIES, 1774.

**Gálvez, Manuel.** 1882–1962. Argentine writer. b. Paraná. Author of realistic novels including *La maestra normal* (The Grade Teacher), *Nacha Regules*, 1919, *La sombra del convento* (The Shadow of the Convent), and *Hombres en soledad* (Men in Solitude), 1948. He has also written many historical novels and biographies.

**Gama, José Basílio da.** 1740–1795. Brazilian poet known for his epic work, *O Uruguay*, 1769. It was an anti-Jesuit account of the Portuguese-Spanish campaign against the GUARANÍ INDIANS.

**Gamarra, Agustín.** 1785–1841. Peruvian general and political leader. One of a group of officers called the "marshals of Ayachucho"; mestizo *caudillo*. He revolted against MAR in 1829 and became president of Peru, serving from 1829 to 1833. He commanded the Chilean reserve division in the war between Chile and the Peru-Bolivian confederation in 1839, and after the Chilean victory at YUNGAY, he was made president of Peru for a second time in 1839. He set himself up as dictator and was unpopular, increasing the taxes and exiling citizens without trial. He was forced to place the country under martial law and a new constitution was put into effect in November 1839. In the war against Bolivia in 1841, he was killed at the Battle of Ingaví.

**Gamboa, Federico.** 1864–1939. Mexican novelist. His work is realistic, with some traces of Modernism. Author of *Suprema ley* (Supreme Law), *La llaga* (The Wound), *Santa*, and numerous others.

**Gamio, Manuel.** 1883–1960. Mexican Indianist, scholar, and archaeologist. b. Mexico City. Considered one of the outstanding Indian archaeologists and ethnologists in the world; he was the author of *Investigaciones arqueológicas en México*; *Teotihuacán*; *El templo de Quetzalcoatl*, and other scholarly writings.

**Gamonal.** In Peru, Bolivia, and Ecuador, a term used in referring to a large landowner.

**Gamonalismo.** Term similar to "bossism"; applied in Peru, and also in Bolivia and Ecuador, to the exploitation practiced on the Indian natives of those countries, chiefly by landowners.

**Garay, Juan de.** 1541–1584. Spanish colonial administrator. Basque of noble blood, he went to Paraguay in about 1565, founded the city of Santa Fe, 1573, and served as governor of Paraguay in 1576. He was lieutenant governor and captain general of Río de la Plata and founded Buenos Aires on the site of the abandoned settlement of Pedro de MENDOZA on June 11, 1580. He was killed by Indians.

**García, Calixto.** 1832–1898. Cuban lawyer, soldier, and revolutionist. b. Holguín, Santiago. Served as a leader in the Ten Years' War against Spain, 1868-1878. He arrived from the United States in 1896 with munitions and 180 men to aid the insurgents against the Spanish. In the Spanish-American War he led a force at El Caney, 1898. In negotiations with the United States, involving Cuban independence, he was appointed to represent Cuba, 1898, and became famous in the United States as the result of Elbert Hubbard's essay, *A Message to García*.

**García, Diego.** *ca.* 1471–*ca.* 1535. Portuguese navigator who served the Spanish. b. Lisbon. In 1526 he commanded an expedition to South America and explored Uruguay and the Paraná River. He joined forces with Sebastián CABOT who had arrived in the Río de la Plata region shortly before. García returned to Spain in 1530.

**García, Genaro.** 1867-1920. Mexican historian. A vigorous critic of Spanish conquest and heritage, he fought for the rights of women in Mexico. He was the author of *Carácter de la conquista española en América y en México;* among his other works is a biography of Leona Vicario, the patriot-wife of QUINTANA ROO.

**García Calderón, Francisco.** 1834–1905. Peruvian statesman. b. Arequipa. Member of congress, 1867; minister of the treasury, 1868. He became provisional president, 1881, after the flight of PIÉROLA during the WAR OF THE PACIFIC and asked the help of the United States in establishing a new government. Refusing to surrender Tacna and Arica to Chile, he was taken prisoner by Chileans and sent to Valparaíso. He returned to Peru in 1886, became president of the senate, and served as rector of the University of San Marcos.

**García Calderón, Francisco.** 1883–1953. Peruvian diplomat. Son of President Francisco GARCÍA CALDERÓN. Delegate to the Peace Conference in Paris held in 1919; served as minister to Belgium from 1918 to 1921; ambassador to France, 1930. He was the author of histories and political essays, such as *Hombres e ideas de nuestro tiempo, Démocraties latines de l'Amérique, Profesores de idealismo*.

**García Moreno, Gabriel.** 1821–1875. President of Ecuador. b. Guayaquil. Journalist, political leader, and lawyer. While a political exile he studied in France and, during the civil war in 1859, attempted unsuccessfully to make Ecuador a protectorate of France. He was first a "nationalist" against Juan José FLORES, then an extreme conservative against URBINA and Robles. He came into power with Flores' support but was not influenced by him. He was president of Ecuador from 1861 to 1865 and again from 1869 until he was assassinated on August 5, 1875. He was a dictator who completely dominated Ecuadorian political life for fifteen years, although he allowed others to serve as president. A concordat promulgated in 1863 gave the Church authorities control over the publication and importation of books, and supervision of all education. He was essentially honest and hard-working, but an extremely dogmatic individual. He attempted to beautify the cities and increase the number of schools, and most important, he had a cart road built from Quito to Guayaquil that allowed transportation from the coast to the interior.

**Garcilaso de la Vega,** Called **El Inca.** *ca.* 1539–1616. Peruvian historian. b. Cuzco. Descended from the Incas through his mother, he is best known for his works *La Florida del Inca: Historia del Adelantado Hernando de Soto*, 1605, and *Comentarios Reales* (Royal Commentaries), a history of the Incas in two volumes, published 1609, 1616, translated into English, 1869–1871. He was the son of Sebastián Garcilaso de la Vega y Vargas, *ca.* 1500–1559, who served with CORTÉS in Mexico, went with ALVARADO Y MESÍA to Peru, 1534, and became governor of Cuzco.

**Garibaldi, Giuseppe.** 1807–1882. Italian

patriot who fought for Italian freedom along with Mazzini. He was forced to flee Italy, 1834, and lived in exile in Uruguay, 1836–1848, where he fought with José Fructuoso RIVERA and the *colorados* against the *blancos*. He returned to Italy, where he attempted to free and unify his country (1854–1867).

**Gasca, Pedro de la.** 1485–1567. Spanish bishop and colonial administrator. b. near Ávila. President of the *audiencia* of Peru, 1547–1550. An exceedingly capable administrator and talented lawyer, he was sent to America by the Spanish king with the title President of the Royal *Audienca* of Lima to re-establish royal authority in Peru and put an end to the civil wars there. He was granted many extraordinary powers including the right to revoke laws. He left Spain for Peru in 1546 and spent some time in Panama. He defeated Gonzalo PIZARRO and Carvajal in the Battle of Xaquizaguana on April 5, 1548, when they attempted a rebellion, and arrived at Cuzco, Peru, in April 1548, after having captured and executed the rebellious Gonzalo Pizarro. He left Peru in January 1550 and returned to Spain. He was Bishop of Palencia, 1550–1561, and of Sigüenza, 1561–1567.

**Gaucho.** The true gaucho rode the plains of Argentina and Uruguay. He was Indian, European, Negro, or any combination of the three. A nomadic and fearless rider who wore *bombachas*, the long, full riding pantaloons that fell in accordion pleats to fit tightly at the ankle, and covered the tops of the boots. He was the hero of the armies of liberation in the colonial wars of independence against Spain. The gauchos supported ROSAS and were the backbone of his private armies. But since the pampas have been fenced in, and although they helped build up the vast cattle empire of today, they are no longer the picturesque gauchos of folklore and music. The name gaúcho is a popular designation for the inhabitants of the Brazilian State of Rio Grande do Sul.

**Gazistas.** See CACOS.

**Geffrard, Nicholas Fabre.** 1806–1879. Haitian general and political leader. A mulatto, he was head of the general staff serving under SOULOUQUE. When he learned he had fallen under suspicion for disloyalty, he decided to act and became leader of the insurrection that overthrew Soulouque, 1858–1859. Haiti was declared a republic, and Geffrard became president, serving from 1859 to 1867. During his administration he concluded a concordat with the Holy See in 1860, the United States recognized the government of Haiti, 1862, and public schools were started. He was forced to resign following a revolt by the liberals and went into exile in Jamaica.

**German-Latin American Relations.** The relations between Germany and the Latin-American republics acquired importance relatively late. At about the turn of the 20th century Germany became involved in the Caribbean area, when in 1896 it sent two men-of-war to Port-au-Prince in Haiti to exact the payment of an indemnity to a German national, and when it participated in the international blockade of Venezuela during the presidency of Cipriano CASTRO (1902). In the years preceding World War I, Germany began to occupy an important place in the trade of Latin America and became a strong competitor of the United States and Great Britain. Germany's economic influence was sharply curtailed during World War I and did not become prominent again until the Nazi government made a determined effort in the 1930's to regain lost ground. The Germans resorted to such devices as barter deals and government subsidies to strengthen their position. They were especially successful in Brazil. World War II again all but wiped out Germany's economic gains in Latin America. Before and during the war, relying on German nationals living in various parts of Latin America, and on native fascist parties, the Nazi government tried to whip up sentiment for Nazi Germany, but its plans ultimately failed. In postwar years Germany has been successful in her efforts to regain her standing in the economic sphere. German cultural influence in Latin America has been negligible. Military circles, however, have adopted German methods, and German missions have had an important role in the training of Latin-American armies. See AXIS INFLUENCE.

**Girón, Francisco Hernández.** *ca.* 1505–

1554. Spanish soldier and adventurer. b. Cáceres, Estremadura. He went to South America in 1535, aided in the conquest of New Granada, and served with the royalist army against Gonzalo PIZARRO in Peru, 1545–48. He led a revolt against the government at Cuzco on November 12, 1553, seized power, and controlled the surrounding territory. He was captured on December 6, 1554, and beheaded.

**Gobernador.** Spanish, meaning governor.

**Godo.** Spanish, meaning Goth. During the colonial period, *godos* was the name given to Spaniards from the mother country. The term is synonymous with *peninsulares*. European-born whites were also called *chapetones* in South America and *gachupines* in New Spain.

**Goethals, George Washington.** 1858–1928. U. S. army officer and engineer. b. Brooklyn, N.Y. Graduated from West Point, 1880. He was appointed chief engineer on the Panama Canal Commission, 1907, by President Theodore ROOSEVELT and carried the canal project through to completion in 1914. He was made a major general, 1915, and served as governor of the Canal Zone until 1916.

**Golpe de estado.** Spanish, meaning coup d'etat. In Latin America most political maneuvers aimed at unseating the existing government through the use of force are, properly speaking, *golpes de estado* and not revolutions. The *golpe de estado* characteristically brings about a shift of power from one group to another without the fundamental change in philosophy and political organization usually connected with a revolution.

**Gomes, Carlos.** 1836–1896. Brazilian composer. b. Campinas, São Paulo. Considered the greatest musician of the 19th century in Brazil, he is best known for his opera *Il Guarany*, which had its world premiere at La Scala, Milan, March 19, 1870. This opera gained him recognition in Europe and the United States. His other operas include *Maria Tudor*, 1879, and *Lo Schiavo*, 1889.

**Gómez, José Miguel.** 1858–1921. President of Cuba. General; served as liberal president, 1909–1913. Popular, astute, and scheming, he used the government's treasury to pay his followers and maintain his power. This was popular because of the wealth of the island at the time, but there were many riots during his administration, including the race war of 1912. He revolted against MENOCAL in 1917, but was defeated.

**Gómez, Juan Vicente.** *ca.* 1857–1935. President of Venezuela. Soldier and political leader; supporter of Cipriano CASTRO in 1899; served as vice-president and commander of the army, 1902–1908. He seized the government when Castro was absent and was dictator from 1908 to 1935, although he was first provisional president and then was duly elected a number of times. He was commander in chief of the army from 1915 to 1935 and dominated the provisional presidents who served in intervening terms. A shrewd man, with little or no education, he ruled with an iron hand and often treated his enemies with brutality. The foreign debt was paid and the petroleum industry thrived. Although never married, he had an enormous family. He died in office.

**Gómez, Laureano.** 1889–1965. President of Colombia. Ultraconservative; publisher of *El Siglo*, a pro-Franco journal. He served as a senator and had considerable influence on the conservatives. He opposed the reforms and liberalism of the LÓPEZ PUMAREJO administration of 1936, and opposed the United States and the United Nations. After the assassination of GAITÁN, 1948, the mob set fire to the building that housed his newspaper and he was forced to resign his post as minister of the interior; elected president, 1950. An extremely wealthy landed aristocrat, he was also religious, and opposed to any separation of Church and State. Due to poor health he was inactive from October 1951, to June 1953, and was ousted by a coup d'etat led by Rojas Pinilla on the day he resumed control of the presidency. He remained politically active, leading the Laureanista Conservatives in opposition to the government, until his death.

**Gómez Farías, Valentín.** 1781–1858. Leader of the *puros* or liberal party of Mexico. b. Zacatecas. Physician. He served as vice-president under SANTA ANNA in 1833 and inspired the new congress to institute a number of reforms, including the abolition of compulsory tithes, the building of schools, and a reduction in the size of the army. He was removed from office by Santa Anna in 1834 and driven into exile to New Orleans. He returned in 1840 to lead a liberal uprising in Mexico City but was forced back into exile. During the Mexican war with the United States, the *puros* returned to power and Gómez Farías became acting president from December 1846 to March 1847, when Santa Anna was called back to lead the troops in the war. Gómez Farías' attempt to reduce the power of the clergy was again thwarted and he was once more driven into exile. He returned in 1857, and when the constitution, for which he had fought for thirty years, was completed, this patriarch of the liberal party was carried into the hall in a litter and was the first to pledge allegiance to it.

**Gondra Treaty.** At the Fifth PAN-AMERICAN CONFERENCE held in 1923 at Santiago, Chile, Manuel Gondra of Paraguay suggested a treaty that provided for the submission of all inter-American controversies that could not be settled by diplomatic negotiations, to a commission of inquiry for investigation and report. No hostile move was to be made until six months after the commission's report had been rendered. Two such commissions, one to be established at Washington and one at Montevideo, were to consist of five men each, and were to report within one year from the date of first meeting; these reports, though not final, would be afforded serious consideration. The commissions were to act as conciliatory bodies and would work until the parties to the dispute would themselves set up a commission of conciliation. The treaty failed to be ratified in many of the participating states.

**Gonzaga, Thomaz** (or **Thomé**) **Antônio.** Known as **Dirceu.** 1744–1807. Portuguese poet who lived in Brazil after 1768. b. Oporto. Served as a judge in Minas Gerais and was nominated to be a member of the supreme court of Bahia. When he was found guilty of participation in the alleged TIRADENTES conspiracy of 1789, he was exiled to Mozambique in 1792 and died insane. He was known for his collection of love poems titled *A Marília de Dirceu.*

**González, Manuel.** 1833–1893. President of Mexico. General; served with DÍAZ against the French, and in the revolution of Tuxtépec in October 1876; defeated the *lerdista* general Alatorre at Tecoac; succeeded Díaz, 1880. His administration was marked by rapid economic progress, but also by increased corruption. Authorities disagree as to whether González was indeed guilty, or whether his unsavory reputation was due to Díaz, who gained power again and succeeded González in 1884.

**González Flores, Alfredo.** b. 1877. Served as president of Costa Rica, 1914–1917. When no candidate had a majority of the votes, he was made president by the congress. He advocated heavy taxation on wealth and was overthrown by a coup d'etat in 1917.

**González Ortega, Jesús.** 1824–1881. Mexican general and liberal leader in the Three Years War, 1858–1860. Defeated MIRAMÓN in August, 1860, and was given the privilege of finishing the war by JUÁREZ. In October of that year he took Guadalajara, in November he crushed Leonardo MÁRQUEZ at Calderón, and marched on the Valley of Mexico. By December 22nd at San Miguel Calpulalpan, the liberals had defeated the last of the conservatives and on January 1, at the head of 25,000 men, he rode into Mexico City. He served as chief justice of the supreme court under Juárez. He was forced to surrender Puebla to the French after a gallant defense of the city on March 16, 1863, and fled in exile to New York City. He was unsuccessful in his attempt to return to Mexico to claim the presidency.

**González Prada, Manuel.** Called "the grand old man." 1848–1918. Peruvian socialist, journalist, poet, and critic. The influence of his teachings on the youth of Peru, on HAYA DE LA TORRE and many others, led to the formation of APRA.

**González Videla, Gabriel.** 1899–    . President of Chile. b. La Serena, northern Chile. Headed the popular front that had succeeded in electing AGUIRRE CERDÁ to the presidency in

1938. After the election of 1946, when there was no majority, it was up to congress to choose a president. González Videla was chosen. Having had the support of the Communists in congress, he appointed three to his cabinet, but broke with the Communists who were outlawed in 1948. He was interested in extending Chilean resources to the south, and supported the first Antarctic polar expedition that took place in 1947. He had many economic and social problems and was forced to suppress several revolts against the government. Woman suffrage went into effect in 1949. A railway was constructed from Salta in Argentina across the Andes to Antofagasta, which connected northwest Argentina with the Chilean Pacific Coast. One of the important achievements of his administration occurred on November 25, 1950, when the Huachipato Steel Plant, near Concepción, was opened, and steel was supplied to Chile, Argentina, Bolivia, and Ecuador from this large installation. He was succeeded by Carlos IBÁÑEZ DEL CAMPO, September 1952.

**Good Neighbor Policy.** Spanish, *Política del buen vecino.* A policy initiated by the Franklin D. ROOSEVELT administration, directed at establishing friendly relations, and economic as well as cultural co-operation between the United States and the Latin-American countries. Although it had become clear as early as 1929–1930 that the United States was willing to abandon its policy of intervention in the affairs of Latin-American countries, the really constructive measure in this direction was taken in 1933. In December of that year, at the Seventh Inter-American Conference at Montevideo, the American delegation headed by Cordell HULL signed a Convention of Rights and Duties of States, Article 8 of which declared that "No state has the right to intervene in the external or internal affairs of another." The following year the PLATT AMENDMENT was abrogated, and American troops were withdrawn from Haiti. In 1936, by a new treaty signed with Panama, the United States gave up several rights in the Canal Zone and in the Republic of Panama, which it had been granted in the treaty of 1903. The same year at the BUENOS AIRES CONFERENCE it was decided that the American

republics should consult with one another if a threat to the peace of the American nations developed. The expropriation of foreign oil properties by the Mexican government brought a test of the Good Neighbor Policy in 1938. The Roosevelt administration continued to observe its policy of nonintervention and the crisis passed when the CÁRDENAS government announced its intentions to pay all proper claims. Inter-American collaboration became even more manifest at the LIMA CONFERENCE of 1938, the Panama meeting of Foreign Ministers in September 1939, and the HAVANA CONFERENCE of 1940.

During World War II the great majority of the Latin-American republics co-operated with the United States. Pan-American solidarity was welded even further by the Inter-American Treaty of Reciprocal Assistance signed at the RIO CONFERENCE OF 1947, and by the formation of the ORGANIZATION OF AMERICAN STATES, decided upon at the BOGOTÁ CONFERENCE of 1948. Co-operation extends into the economic and cultural fields as well. Through the EXPORT-IMPORT BANK, the U.S. government has extended important financial aid to the Latin-American republics. Through the Division of Cultural Relations established in Washington in 1938, the Office of the Coordinator of Inter-American Affairs was created in 1940. More recently, the Institute of Inter-American Affairs, the exchange of students, and other means of intellectual and cultural communication such as art, music, and literature have been fostered.

**G.O.U.** Full name, *Grupo de Oficiales Unidos.* The ultranationalist Argentine army group that seized power in the country in 1943, and whose leader by 1945 was Juan Domingo PERÓN. The G.O.U. was composed of extreme nationalists, including some Axis sympathizers. Its motto was "Government, Order, Unity" and it looked to the establishment of a totalitarian regime. Other members of the group were Generals Pedro RAMÍREZ and Edelmiro FARRELL, each of whom was president for a short time, Ramírez in 1943 and Farrell from 1944 to 1946.

**Graça Aranha, José Pereira da.** 1868–1931. Important Brazilian novelist and essayist, author of the novel *Canaan,* 1902, in which the question of European racial superiority over native culture is discussed amid tropical settings.

**Gran Chaco.** See CHACO, GRAN.

**Gran Colombia.** The name given by historians to the state comprising New Granada (Colombia proper), Venezuela, and the Presidency of Quito (Ecuador), whose existence was proclaimed by the revolutionary Congress of Angostura (Venezuela) during the South American War for Independence in December 1819. Quito actually joined the new republic only in 1822, when it was definitely freed from Spain. Gran Colombia was soon torn by dissensions and separatist movements, and only the authority of BOLÍVAR, its president, managed to hold it together. It finally broke up in 1830, when Venezuela and Ecuador seceded and became independent republics.

**Grau, Miguel.** 1838–1879. Peruvian naval officer who succeeded in holding off the Chilean navy in 1879. He commanded the ironclad "Huáscar," which defied the entire Chilean navy for several months until the ship was finally captured on October 8 in the Battle of Angamos. Grau was killed in the battle.

**Grau San Martín, Ramón.** b. 1889. President of Cuba. b. Pinar del Río. Physician; head of the provisional junta and provisional president of Cuba from September 10, 1933 to January 15, 1934, following the revolution that overthrew the MACHADO regime. He had been dean of the medical school at the University of Havana. He was a popular president, but with little administrative and political experience. The economic problems were due largely to the failure of sugar crops and the cutback in the export market. BATISTA, who was the most powerful man in the country, became dissatisfied with Grau's administration and forced him to resign, 1934. He was defeated by Batista in the election of 1940. As candidate of the Republican Authentic Alliance, 1944, he was elected by a large majority and served until 1948. There were minor political problems and strikes, but generally speaking, the economic and political conditions of the country were good. He was

essentially an honest man, but his administration was corrupt.

**Great Britain.** See ANGLO-LATIN AMERICAN RELATIONS.

**Grijalva, Juan de.** ca. 1489–1527. Spanish explorer. b. Cuéllar, Segovia. Nephew of Diego VELÁSQUEZ; sent on an expedition to Yucatán in 1518, to continue where CÓRDOBA left off. He sailed along the east coast of Mexico from Yucatán to Veracruz and discovered the island of Cozumel. He told of the rich Aztec region in the interior of Mexico. He was the first to call the new territory New Spain, and his explorations led to the famous CORTÉS expedition of 1519.

**Grito de Dolores.** Spanish, meaning Cry of Dolores. Name given to the revolutionary act of Miguel HIDALGO Y COSTILLA, who on September 16, 1810, proclaimed the revolt against Spanish authorities in Mexico at the village of Dolores, near Querétaro. September 16 is now celebrated as Mexico's Independence Day.

**Grito do Ypiranga.** Portuguese, meaning Cry of Ypiranga. Name given to the action of Portuguese Regent Pedro, later PEDRO I, who when summoned on September 7, 1822, to return to Portugal from Brazil, drew his sword on the banks of the Ypiranga river, Province of São Paulo, and proclaimed the independence of Brazil.

**Grosolé Daza, Hilarión.** 1840–1894. President of Bolivia. b. Sucre. General; president, 1876–1879; notoriously unscrupulous dictator of Bolivia. He induced congress to pass a law placing a tax of ten centavos upon each hundredweight of nitrates sent out by the Chilean Nitrate Company of Antofagasta and when the company refused to pay, the Bolivian government (which was Daza) seized the property of the company. He joined Peruvian forces at Tacna in war against Chile, 1879, the troops mutinied, and he was forced into exile. He returned in 1894 only to be killed by a mob.

**Guadalajara.** The capital of the Mexican state of Jalisco, and the second city of Mexico, at an altitude of 5,000 feet, 290 miles northwest of Mexico City. Population is approximately 734,000 (1960). Its cleanliness and its architecture, similar to that of southern Spain, as well as its many gardens and squares, combine to make it one of the most attractive cities in Mexico. Among the outstanding buildings are the cathedral, finished in 1618, the government palace, the state museum, and the state university. Guadalajara is connected with Mexico City by air, by rail, and by road. The city is situated in an agricultural and mining region. Among the products mined in the area are silver, copper, lead, and zinc. Sugar, coffee, and bananas are grown. The city is well-known for its pottery and also produces glassware, textiles, soap, and flour. The city was founded in 1530 or 1531 by order of Nuño de GUZMÁN. It was first called Espíritu Santo, and in 1542 it was given its present name. In the colonial period it was from here that Spanish influence extended northward along the west coast. The Mexican martyr HIDALGO Y COSTILLA stayed here briefly during his uprising against Spain, 1810–1811, and the liberal leader Benito JUÁREZ was almost killed by mutinous troops when he stopped in the city on his flight from the Mexican conservative forces in 1858.

**Guadalupe, Basilica of.** Famous Mexican shrine near Mexico City. According to tradition, in 1531 on the site where the Indians had been worshipping Tonantzin, the mother goddess, the Virgin appeared and asked Juan Diego, a poor peasant, to inform the Bishop of Mexico that she wished a church built on that spot. She also gave him evidence of the authenticity of the vision by causing a picture of herself to be impressed on his blanket. This picture, in which the Virgin Mary is given the appearance of an Indian woman, is still preserved in the church at Guadalupe, and even today it is the most revered object in Mexico. During the wars of independence, the Virgin of Guadalupe became the adopted symbol of the insurgents.

**Guadalupe-Hidalgo, Treaty of.** Treaty signed on February 2, 1848, between the United States and Mexico, putting an end to the war between the two countries. Under the stipulations of the treaty, Mexico ceded to the United States the territory that includes the present-day states of New Mexico, California, Arizona, Nevada, Utah, part of Colorado, and confirmed the title to Texas as far as the Rio Grande, in return for the payment of $15,000,000. The United States also assumed the claims of U.S. citizens against the Mexican government to the value of $3,250,000.

**Guanaco.** One of the two wild members of the South American camel family. The two domesticated forms of the species, the LLAMA and the ALPACA, are related to the guanaco. Guanacos inhabit the Andes mountain chain from Peru to Cape Horn but are found in the greatest numbers in Patagonia. They live in herds ranging in number from five to thirty. The flesh of the animal is palatable and its skin furnishes the chief clothing material for the Indians of Patagonia.

**Guano.** The deposits of seabird fertilizer found in abundant quantities on the islands off the Peruvian coast. Guano was used as fertilizer by the Indians in pre-Colombian times. The great value of the product was not recognized until the 19th century, when the demand for guano from abroad made many Peruvians rich. The peak of the guano era was reached in the late 1860's. The prosperity led to large expenditures that in time could only be met by borrowing against shipments of guano that were expected in the future. When the price dropped on the world market, Peru was beset by financial troubles. Eventually the deposits were threatened with depletion and practically all exports had to be forbidden by the Peruvian government in order to save it for local agriculture.

**Guaraní Indians.** The Guaraní tribes, at first known as Carijó or Cario, belong to the Tupí-Guaraní family of South American Indians. During the 16th and 17th centuries the primitive Guaraní occupied an area of the Atlantic coast from the southern part of the modern state of São Paulo in Brazil to present-day Uruguay, and from there extended their control westward to the Uruguay, Paraná, and Paraguay rivers. To the south the tribe was found along both shores of the Río de la Plata estuary and extended north along the principal rivers. North of the confluence of the Paraná and Paraguay rivers these Indians were found only on the eastern side of the latter river. Those members of the Guaraní who have preserved their cultural identity are today found in isolated groups in Paraguay and southern Brazil. The Guaraní of the upper Paraná and Uruguay river basins were converted to Christianity by the JESUITS, who from the beginning of the 17th century to the latter part of the 18th century maintained a large number of missions forming what amounted to an independent state within that part of the Spanish empire in the New World. The Guaraní language is still spoken in Paraguay and in the northern Argentine states of Corrientes and Misiones. As the result of the diligence of Jesuit and FRANCISCAN priests, who found the language indispensable for their Christianizing efforts, the Guaraní language was given a written form and a grammar. There exists a considerable body of Guaraní literature and poetry at the present time. Today the rural population of modern Paraguay is often called "Guaraní."

**Guardia, Ricardo Adolfo de la.** 1899–    ·
President of Panama. Became president, October 1941, when President Arnulfo Arias was overthrown in a coup d'etat. The United States was involved in rumors that claimed it had aided the change of presidents, since de la Guardia was friendly to the United States, but Secretary HULL denied any U.S. participation in the affairs of Panama. He retired as president, 1945, to his work as a newspaper publisher.

**Guardia, Tomás.** 1832–1882. Dictator of Costa Rica, 1876–1882, after having served as the duly elected president from 1870 to 1876. He had been an army officer, and when he seized power he had the leaders of the opposing political parties exiled. The constitution adopted on December 7, 1871, still stands with but few changes. He encouraged the KEITH brothers, who began the first railroad line in Costa Rica in 1871, and he introduced banana cultivation.

**Guatemala.** The third largest republic in Central America, bounded on the north and west by Mexico, on the southwest by the Pacific Ocean, on the south and east by El Salvador and Honduras, and on the east by British Honduras, with an area of 42,042 square miles, and a population of 4,540,000 (est. 1966), of whom 60 per cent are Indian, 35 per cent MESTIZO, and 5 per cent white. The language is Spanish but many Indian dialects are used. The monetary unit is the quetzal (linked to the dollar at 1 to 1). The predominant religion is Roman Catholicism with tolerance for other creeds. The constitution of 1956 stipulates that a president shall be elected for six years by direct vote of the people and cannot be immediately re-elected, and that a one-chamber, 66-member congress shall carry out legislative duties. The chief cities are Guatemala City, the capital and largest city in Central America, population 407,401 (1961), Quezaltenango, and the Caribbean port of Puerto Barrios. The greater part of the country is mountainous and there are many volcanoes, the only flatlands being the hot and humid coastal plains and the equally hot plain of Petén in the north. Most of the population is concentrated on the fertile, well-watered, and temperate western slope near the Pacific Ocean. The longest waterway is the Motagua River, which flows 250 miles east into the Caribbean. Agriculture forms the basis of the economy, providing about 35 per cent of the total gross domestic product and 95 per cent of the earnings through foreign exchange. Coffee is the main crop of the country and other important agricultural products include cotton, bananas, sugar, and beans. Guatemala's forests produce chicle gum, cinchona bark, a number of woods, and some rubber. There are deposits of gold, copper, tin, lead, and other minerals, but mining has not developed to a great extent. Guatemala exports mostly coffee, cotton, and bananas, and imports are chiefly textiles, petroleum, drugs, and automobiles. The United States is the largest customer and supplier. The most important rail line links the capital with the Caribbean port of Puerto Barrios and there are about 5,000 miles of highways. Education is compulsory and free, but more than 70 per cent of the people are illiterate. The famed University of San Carlos is in Guatemala City.

In pre-Conquest times, Guatemala was inhabited by the Maya Indians, whose settlements are also found in present-day Chiapas (Mexico), in the Yucatán peninsula and in Honduras, and whose civilization probably had its greatest period from the fourth until the ninth century A.D. The territory was conquered by the Spanish conquistador Pedro de ALVARADO Y MESÍA in 1524. The AUDIENCIA of Guatemala was established in 1542, and during the colonial period the area was a captaincy general and included all of Central America. In 1821 Guatemala declared itself independent from Spain, then for a short time joined the Mexican empire of ITURBIDE, but broke away in 1823 and the same year became a part of the CENTRAL AMERICAN FEDERATION. In 1839 Guatemala again set itself up as an independent state, and for the next twenty-six years it was controlled by the ultraconservative Rafael CARRERA, who, after being the real power in the country for several years, became president in 1843. He was again elected to the presidency in 1851, and in 1854 was proclaimed president for life. During his rule, Carrera made war on Honduras and El Salvador, and in 1859 he signed a treaty with Great Britain by which he recognized the latter's claim to the territory of Belize (British Honduras). From 1873 to 1885 power was in the hands of the liberal Justo Rufino BARRIOS, who ruled as a dictator but introduced a number of economic and social reforms. Another long dictatorship was that of Manuel ESTRADA CABRERA (1898–1920). During his administration there were many revolts, one of which in 1906 caused international complications in Central America and led to the Central American Peace Conference in Washington in 1907. Estrada Cabrera encouraged the development of the coffee and banana industries by American and German concerns but kept the Indians in a state of poverty and semi-servitude. General Jorge UBICO, dictator from 1931 to 1944, brought about some social reforms, settled boundary disputes with El Salvador and Honduras, and co-operated with the United States in World War II. After Ubico was overthrown by a popular revolt, General Federico Ponce was elected president in July 1944, but he in turn was ousted by a combination of army officers and liberals. In November of that year Juan José ARÉVALO BERMEJO,

a schoolteacher, was elected on a left-wing ticket, and proceeded to push through advanced social legislation with the aim of bettering the lot of the Guatemalan Indian. The left-wing trend in the political life of the country was accentuated after the election of Jacobo ARBENZ GUZMÁN, who assumed the presidency in March 1951. Far-reaching land reforms were initiated in 1952, and about 30 per cent of Guatemala's cultivated land was seized from big landowners and redistributed to landless Indian peasants. There was constant friction with the UNITED FRUIT COMPANY, which operates great banana plantations in the country, and in 1953 the government seized 233,973 acres of the United Fruit Company's banana reserve lands at Tiquisate. Toward the end of the same year the International Railways of Central America, in which the United Fruit Company owns 42.68 per cent of the stock, was taken over by the government after a strike of rail workers. All these measures received the wholehearted support of the small but vocal Guatemalan Communist Party. The latter had infiltrated into government agencies and non-Communist parties of the Democratic Electoral Front (the government coalition) and had established control over the Confederation of Labor. The United States became increasingly alarmed at the left-wing policies of the Arbenz regime and the role Communists were playing in Guatemala. It was because of the Guatemalan situation that the United States brought before the Tenth Inter-American Conference at Caracas in March 1954, the anti-Communist resolution, which was then voted by the delegates. Meanwhile in Honduras, a group of revolutionaries led by Colonel Carlos CASTILLO ARMAS was preparing an uprising against the Arbenz government. Castillo Armas struck from across the Honduran border in June 1954, and after some fighting, in the course of which a few planes of Castillo Armas's tiny air force strafed the capital, the revolutionaries were victorious. Arbenz was forced to seek refuge in the Mexican embassy, and a military junta headed by Castillo Armas was formed. The United States was not long in recognizing the new regime. After overcoming an army revolt directed against him, Castillo Armas dissolved the governing junta and assumed the presidency in September. He formally took office in November 1954. The new government attempted to moderate the extreme social reforms inaugurated by Arbenz and to restore the confidence of foreign investors. This work was cut short by the assassination of President Castillo Armas on July 26, 1957. Two short-lived governments held power from then to March 1958, when Miguel YDÍGORAS FUENTES took office. Harassed by both right- and left-wing extremists, the Ydígoras government managed to stay in power until March 31, 1963, when military elements ousted the president. The coup was led by the minister of defense Colonel Enrique Peralta Azurdia who cited irresponsibility and corruption in the government as reasons for the take-over. A more important reason for the revolt centered around the return of former President Juan José Arévalo Bermejo to Guatemala. His announced intention to become a candidate in the November election awakened in conservative elements the fear of an extremist victory. Although Ydígoras had publicly warned Arévalo that he was not welcome in his homeland, army leaders suspected Ydígoras' secret approval of the candidacy of Arévalo in November. Once in power, Peralta canceled the November elections, dissolved the legislature, suspended the constitution, and began to govern through decrees. The return to constitutional government was promised as soon as an election could be held. The United States government recognized the new government of Guatemala on April 17, 1963. In March 1966 Julio César Méndez Montenegro, a moderate reformist, was elected president. Left-wing guerrilla activities, patterned after the CASTRO formula, which have been plaguing the country for several years, are continuing in spite of the efforts of the new government to restore national peace and harmony. See CENTRAL AMERICA, and ORGANIZATION OF CENTRAL AMERICAN STATES.

**Guatemala City.** The capital of Guatemala, situated 75 miles from the Pacific port of San José, on a plateau 4,880 feet above sea level. Population is 382,000 (est. 1960). The city, built in a valley and surrounded by hills and volcanoes, has many modern buildings including the University, the Chamber of Deputies, the National Palace, and the Post Office. Guatemala City is connected by rail and by road with the port of Puerto Barrios on the Atlantic, the ports of Champerico and San José on the Pacific, and with Mexico and El Salvador. There are air connections with North and South America as well as with other Central-American countries. It is the commercial center of the country and has industrial establishments for producing cement, furniture, leather goods, soap, beverages, and textiles. The city was built in 1776, 25 miles northeast of the old capital of Antigua, which was destroyed by an earthquake in 1773. It was severely battered by another in 1874 and was again nearly destroyed in 1917–1918. But it has been rebuilt since then and today not much of the old capital remains.

**Guatemotzin.** See CUAUHTÉMOC.

**Guayaquil.** Official name, **Santiago de Guayaquil.** The chief seaport and the largest city of Ecuador, situated on the west bank of the Guayas River, 35 miles from the Pacific Ocean, having a population of 450,000 (est. 1960). The climate is hot, but during the dry season from May to December the nights are cool. The city's aspect has changed greatly in recent years, and today it has many modern buildings, theaters, and clubs. Parks and gardens are found in a great number of places. Along the famous waterfront promenade, the Malecón Simón Bolívar, stand the beautiful Palacio Municipal and the Government Palace. Other important buildings are the University of Guayaquil, the National Conservatory of Music, and the Academy of Painting. The harbor, which is 2.5 miles long, is visited by large ocean liners. Industrial establishments include steam sawmills, foundries, machine shops, and breweries. Guayaquil is connected by air and rail with Quito and by air with other South-American centers. The city was founded by the Spanish conquistador Sebastián de BENALCÁZAR in 1531. After having been destroyed by an Indian uprising, it was rebuilt by Francisco de ORELLANA in 1537. Another Indian revolt was put down in 1541. In the colonial period

Guayaquil, ridden with deadly diseases such as yellow fever, malaria, and bubonic plague, was one of the unhealthiest places in the New World. In 1587 a smallpox epidemic killed more than 12,000 persons. In 1687 and 1709 it was attacked by British pirates. In 1822 Guayaquil was the scene of the well-known GUAYAQUIL CONFERENCE between Simón BOLÍVAR and José de SAN MARTÍN, as a result of which Bolívar became the sole leader of the South-American movement of liberation and San Martín went back to private life. A campaign to eradicate yellow fever, malaria, and bubonic plague was launched in the second decade of the 20th century by the Rockefeller Foundation. The task was successfully accomplished and by 1920 Guayaquil had been freed of the deadly diseases that had hampered its development.

**Guayaquil Conference.** The conference that took place on July 26 and 27, 1822, at Guayaquil, Ecuador, between BOLÍVAR and SAN MARTÍN. It is not known what passed between the two liberators at this meeting, which was held to map out future military operations against Spanish forces in Peru, as well as to plan the future political configuration of the country. It is surmised that Bolívar refused to carry out the liberation of Peru in partnership with San Martín and that he opposed San Martín's plan to have a European prince rule Peru under a constitutional monarchy. As a result of the conference San Martín decided to leave Peru. In September of the same year he gave up his title of Protector and left for Chile.

**Güemes, Martín.** 1785–1821. Argentine patriot. With his army of GAUCHOS, he aided the patriot cause with his heroic resistance against Spanish royalist forces at the frontier in the northern part of Argentina in 1815.

**Guerra dos Farrapos.** Literally, **War of the Ragged Ones.** A federalist revolt in the Brazilian province of Rio Grande do Sul, initiated in 1835 by Bento Gonçalves da Silva, which resulted in proclamation of the Republic of Piratiní in 1836. The revolutionaries were eventually defeated by troops under General CAXIAS and the insurrection came to an end in 1845. All those who had taken part in the revolt were granted an amnesty.

**Guerrero, Vicente.** 1782–1831. Mexican soldier and political leader. Served with MORELOS Y PAVÓN in war for independence, 1810; leader of guerrilla forces; accepted ITURBIDE's PLAN OF IGUALA, 1821. He was chosen president by the congress in March 1829, but was overthrown by revolution in December of that year. As president he instituted a number of reforms, including abolition of slavery, which took effect as of September 16, 1829, and the expulsion of native Spaniards from Mexico. He was a generous man who made the mistake of pardoning his enemies and trusting those who did not deserve to be trusted. SANTA ANNA turned against him, BUSTAMANTE led a revolt; Guerrero was forced to resign, and was shot on orders of Bustamante.

**Guggiari, José Patricio.** 1884–1957. President of Paraguay. b. Asunción. Lawyer and political leader, he was president of Paraguay from 1928 to 1931, when he was forced from office in October. In 1929 there was border friction with Bolivia, and the administration was criticized for the handling of the incident. Guggiari found it necessary to declare martial law for many months. He served again as president from January to August 1932.

**Guipúzcoa Company.** See CHARTERED COMPANIES IN LATIN AMERICA.

**Güiraldes, Ricardo.** 1882–1927. Argentine poet and novelist, author of *Don Segundo Sombra*, 1926 (translated as Shadows on the Pampas, 1935), a novel based on life on the Argentine PAMPAS, in which he portrays the ideal GAUCHO. He is considered an important modern Argentine writer. His other works include *Xaimaca* and *Cuentos de amor y de muerte* (Tales of Love and Death).

**Guirior, Manuel.** Enlightened Spanish viceroy of New Granada who served from 1773 to 1776. He attempted to improve education, trade, and the economic condition of the colony. He recommended to Madrid that it establish a university for the youth of the colony, but he met with opposition from the DOMINICANS. He later served as viceroy of Peru.

**Gutiérrez González, Gregorio.** 1826–1872.

Colombian poet. b. Antioquia. His greatest poem is an agricultural epic called *Sobre el cultivo del maíz en Antioquia,* 1866. He also wrote *¿Por qué no canto?* and other works.

**Gutiérrez Guerra, José.** 1869–1929. President of Bolivia. Served 1917–1920, after which he was overthrown by a bloodless revolution. A liberal, he was interested in establishing friendly relations with Chile, but the project proved unpopular.

**Gutiérrez Nájera, Manuel.** 1859–1895. Mexican poet. A Romantic, he was nevertheless a forerunner of the Modernist movement. He was a poet of sorrow and resignation and some of his works are among the best ever written in Spanish America. *Serenata de Schubert, Pax Animae, Non omnis moriar,* and *Almas y Aves* are among his best known works.

**Guzmán, Antonio Leocadio.** 1801–1884. Venezuelan political leader and journalist. Father of GUZMÁN BLANCO. Founded *El Venezolano,* which attacked the conservative government of Venezuela, and in 1840 Guzmán, who had been one of the chief advisers of the regime during the MONAGAS monopoly, organized the liberal party. He was badly defeated in the elections of 1842.

**Guyana.** See BRITISH GUIANA.

**Guzmán, Gonzalo Nuño de.** d. 1539. Spanish colonial administrator and conquistador. Governor of Pánuco, on the Gulf of Mexico; appointed president of the *audiencia* of New Spain (Mexico) in May 1527, and arrived in New Spain late in 1528. He confiscated *encomiendas* that CORTÉS had given to his followers, in order to redistribute them among his own friends, sold Indians into slavery, exacted heavy tributes from the *caciques,* kidnaped attractive women, and kept watch over the seaports to prevent any news of his activities from being carried to Spain. He was excommunicated together with the *audiencia* by Bishop ZUMÁRRAGA, 1529, and in the same year he set out on an expedition to Michoacán with an army of 10,000 men, where he treated the TARASCAN Indians with great cruelty. He continued northward into Jalisco, where he goaded the Indians into rebellion in order

that the Spaniards might have a pretext for enslaving them. He went as far as Sinaloa, thinking he was on the way to the country of the Amazons, but then retreated and established himself in Jalisco, where he built the towns of Compostela and Guadalajara, and organized *encomiendas.* He gave the grandiose name of Greater Spain to his conquests and ruled as governor at Compostela. The authorities finally realized the extent of his crimes and ordered him to return to Mexico City. Jalisco and the adjacent territories were rechristened Nueva Galicia, and the governorship was transferred in 1536 to Pérez de la Torre. Guzmán spent two years in the common prison in Mexico City, and was then shipped to Spain, where he soon died in obscurity.

**Guzmán, Martín Luis.** 1890–    . Mexican novelist and journalist. b. Chihuahua. Author of *El águila y la serpiente* (translated as The Eagle and the Serpent, 1930), a fascinating account of episodes of the Mexican Revolution, *La sombra del caudillo, Memorias de Pancho Villa* (1928), and others.

**Guzmán Blanco, Antonio.** 1829–1899. President of Venezuela. b. Caracas. His father was a journalist and had been the liberal candidate for the presidency in the 1840's. During the MONAGAS regime Guzmán Blanco served as consul in Philadelphia and New York, and as secretary of the Venezuelan embassy in Washington; served as vice-president to FALCÓN, 1863–1868, when he succeeded in floating loans to his country in Europe. He became leader of the liberal party, the *Amarillos* (Yellows), in 1870, which captured the capital during a revolt. He dominated Venezuelan politics for the next 18 years and was one of Latin America's most colorful *caudillos.* He was vain and loved pomp and ceremony, but he was a very able executive and in the course of his administration, during which he ruled with an iron hand, roads were built and ports were improved, railroads were constructed, the large cities were modernized, public education became compulsory and free, the national debt was refunded, national credit restored, the economic condition grew to be sound, and the penal system was modernized. He was unfriendly toward the Church. During his administration there were two new constitutions, one in 1874 and the other in 1881. The presidential office was limited to a two-year term, but it was provided that a federal council composed of senators and deputies could elect him. Thus he continued to rule the country either as constitutional president or through puppet executives whom he controlled. He spent many years abroad, especially in Paris, became exceedingly wealthy at his country's expense, and his popularity waned. In 1888 he named Dr. Juan Paúl as president, thinking him to be a willing puppet, but he was wrong and Paúl broke with the dictator in 1889. Guzmán Blanco remained in Europe where he spent the rest of his life.

# H

**Hacienda.** The great landed estate that for centuries constituted the main form of landholding in large portions of Latin America and is still an important factor today. The *hacienda* emerged soon after the Conquest, existing side by side with the *encomienda*. Although the *hacendado* (owner of the estate) could not legally treat the Indians living on the estate as serfs, he wielded considerable powers over them. They could not easily move away from the estate, and the debts they incurred kept them solidly bound to the *hacienda*. The *hacendado*, moreover, frequently controlled the local government and was for all practical purposes the local chieftain. While some *haciendas* produced crops for the market, many functioned as self-sufficient economic units, the result being a lack of incentive for efficient use of the land. In many parts of Latin America the *hacienda* is still the prevailing type of landed property. In Argentina the equivalent of the *hacienda* is the *estancia*, and in Brazil the *fazenda*. The Spanish word *hacienda* also has other meanings. It may be defined as treasury, as in *Ministerio de Hacienda* (Ministry of the Treasury), and in some parts of Latin America the word is used to refer to cattle in general.

**Haiti.** The smallest of the Antillean republics, and the only Negro republic in the Western Hemisphere, situated on the island of Hispaniola (Santo Domingo), of which it occupies the western third. To the east it borders on the Dominican Republic, and the Windward Passage separates it from Cuba to the west. The area is 10,714 square miles,

and the population 4,820,000 (est. 1966), of which 95 per cent are Negro and 5 per cent mulatto, rendering it the most densely populated republic in the Americas. The monetary unit is the gourde (20 cents). The language is French and the predominant religion is Roman Catholicism, although there is complete freedom of religion. The chief cities are Port-au-Prince, the capital and principal port, population 250,000 (est. 1961), the ports of Cap Haitien, Gonáives, and Les Cayes. Haiti was a democratic republic whose president was until recently elected for a six-year term by a majority of voters in a secret ballot. A new constitution promulgated in 1957 provided for a single-chamber legislature, composed of 67 members elected for six years, to replace the bicameral legislature in 1963. The country is divided into a number of isolated valleys by three mountain ranges that run from east to west. The coastal plains are hot, whereas the climate in the mountains is temperate. The main occupation of the population is agriculture, with coffee the chief crop and the principal export product. Other important agricultural products are sisal, cotton, sugar cane, bananas, and cacao. Railroad mileage totals about 220 miles, and there are about 2,000 miles of roads that are, for the most part, not suitable for motor transportation. Because of the lack of adequate transportation, there is much coastwise trade. The illiteracy rate is still high (90 per cent).

The island of Hispaniola (Santo Domingo) was discovered by COLUMBUS in December 1492 and became a Spanish colony. African slaves were soon brought to Hispaniola, and the importation of slaves continued at a rapid rate. In the 17th century, French buccaneers, operating mostly from the nearby island of Tortuga, settled in the western part of the island and in the second half of the century, France took over that portion of Hispaniola, with Spain recognizing French sovereignty in 1697. The colony, known as Saint Domingue, prospered during the 18th century, and became France's richest overseas possession. It produced a large part of the world's sugar and the greater part of the world's coffee. By the end of the 18th century, out of a total population of 520,000, about 450,000 were slaves, 28,000 were freed slaves owning about one-tenth of the land, and the rest were white. A revolt by the freed slaves, fired by news of the French Revolution, was brutally suppressed by white planters in 1790, but the next year a massive uprising by slaves in the north resulted in widespread massacres of white landowners. Commissioners sent to Saint Domingue by the French National Assembly in 1791 were unable to stop the revolt, and another commission, sent in 1792, was no more successful. In the following years the leadership of the rebel Negroes was taken over by the highly talented TOUSSAINT L'OUVERTURE, who helped repel a Spanish invasion of the northern part of the island in 1794, and then induced the former slaves to go back to the plantations and work as free men. While outwardly respecting the authority of France, he was in fact in command of the northern part of Saint Domingue. He was able to occupy Port-au-Prince in 1798, by virtue of an agreement with the British, who had occupied the town in 1793 and were now ready to evacuate it. Toussaint then wiped out the mulattoes who were holding the southern part of the colony, and in 1800 he attacked the Spanish part of Hispaniola, completing his conquest of the area in 1801. A French expeditionary corps sent by NAPOLEON I in 1802 defeated the Haitians and forced the capitulation of Toussaint L'Ouverture who was treacherously seized and sent as a prisoner to France. The French forces began to suffer heavily from yellow fever, and the Haitians took up arms again. A British blockade made the position of the French forces, already decimated by yellow fever and the war against the Haitians, untenable.

Toward the end of 1803, the remaining French evacuated the island. On January 1, 1804, Jean-Jacques DESSALINES, the head of the revolting Negroes, proclaimed the independence of the western portion of Hispaniola, calling it the Republic of Haiti, a word of Indian origin meaning "mountainous." Haiti thus became the first Latin-American country to achieve freedom. Dessalines had himself declared emperor in the same year and ruled as a despot. After his assassination in 1806, the country was split into two states, the northern "State of Haiti" under Henri CHRISTOPHE, who had himself proclaimed king and built the famous fortress of Laferrière, and the southern "Republic of Haiti," dominated by mulattoes and ruled by Alexandre PÉTION until 1818. In 1820, after Christophe committed suicide, Pétion's successor, Jean Pierre BOYER, occupied the north and ruled over a unified Haiti. In 1822 he occupied the Spanish portion to the east, after the colonists there had freed themselves from Spanish rule. The Haitians ruled over the entire island until 1844, when the Spanish section rose against Haitian rule and achieved freedom as the Dominican Republic. The rest of the 19th century and the beginning of the 20th were marked by considerable turbulence and civil strife. Unrest was especially great from 1911 to 1915, and in 1915 the United States, landing marines at Port-au-Prince, intervened to restore order. American occupation continued until 1934 and a financial expert supervising customs remained until 1941. The American occupation aroused considerable opposition in Haiti during the first years and was never too popular in the country, but it was able to restore sound finances, political tranquillity, and to make improvements in transportation, sanitation, and health. In 1946 a revolution ousted President Élie LESCOT, and the next president, Dumarsais ESTIMÉ, was overthrown in 1950. Colonel Paul E. Magloire became the first president to be elected by the direct vote of the people in 1950. Magloire sought to remain in office at the end of his term in defiance of the constitution of 1950, which provided that no president could seek immediate re-election. The opposition to Magloire, reinforced by army elements, forced the president to resign his office in 1956. After several provisional governments tried their hand at governing the country, the Haitians elected François Duvalier for a six-year term in 1957. After four years in office President Duvalier dissolved the bicameral legislature and called for the election of new representatives to a single-chamber legislature. Duvalier presented a list of candidates of his own choosing and included his own name on the ballots. The election was proclaimed a unanimous victory for the regime and Duvalier was declared re-elected for a new six-year term in spite of the fact that a presidential election had not been announced and he still had two years to serve of his first term. Foes of the Duvalier government demanded the president's resignation on the grounds that his actions had violated the constitution. Opposition to the repressive regime continued to mount and broke out in open revolt in 1963. Exiled rebels invaded Haiti in August 1963 but failed to inspire a general revolt among the Haitian people. Terrorist tactics used by the Duvalier government succeeded in suppressing further revolts against the government. Long-standing difficulties between Haiti and the Dominican Republic erupted into violence early in 1963. Because of a Haitian violation of the extraterritorial rights of the Dominican embassy in Port-au-Prince, the Dominican President Juan Bosch suspended diplomatic relations with Haiti and threatened to use armed force to obtain satisfaction. The good offices of the ORGANIZATION OF AMERICAN STATES were accepted by both countries to bring the explosive situation under control. In October 1963 a hurricane struck the island killing more than 2,500 persons, leaving 100,000 persons homeless, and causing extensive crop damage. In April 1964 Duvalier proclaimed himself president for life. A new constitution was enacted which ratified Duvalier's decision and changed the colors of Haiti's flag from red and blue to red and black.

**Hapsburgs.** The Spanish sovereigns belonging to the Austrian dynasty of the Hapsburgs, include the Emperor Charles V (CHARLES I of Spain) (1516–1556), PHILIP II (1556–1598), PHILIP III (1598–1621), PHILIP IV (1621–1665), and CHARLES II (1665–1700).

**Havana.** Spanish, *La Habana.* The capital of Cuba and its main port, on the northwest coast of the island, about 90 miles southwest of Key West, Florida. Population 1,305,000 (1960). The city is built on a peninsula and has a beautiful and well-protected harbor two miles long, one mile wide, the entrance to which is protected by the La Punta fortress and the famous Morro Castle. Havana offers a fascinating mixture of the modern and the old. Together with many modern buildings, avenues and parks, there are colonial buildings, churches, fortresses, and picturesque, narrow streets. Havana has a number of residential suburbs, the best known of which is El Vedado. The famous Malecón, a wide and well-paved boulevard facing the sea and the harbor, extends around the city and permits sightseers to enjoy a most interesting drive. The main avenue is the Paseo de Martí, or Prado, a wide and well-shaded thoroughfare that extends from the Parque de Colón to the Malecón on the north shore. Important and outstanding edifices include the Capitol building, opened in 1929; the City Hall, completed in 1792; the University, opened in 1728; the Presidential Palace, finished in 1922; the Castillo de la Real Fuerza, built in 1538; and Morro Castle, erected in 1588–1597. Before the advent of the present regime under Fidel CASTRO, the city was noted as a tourist attraction. In recent years some 250,000 tourists visited the island and its capital city, annually spending more than $50,000,000. Havana is connected by rail and highways with all parts of the island, and by air with Mexico, Spain, and the Soviet Union. Havana is the main trading center in the West Indies. Through its important port, sugar, tobacco, cigars, rum, and other products are exported. The city has many tobacco plants as well as leather, soap, clothing, and perfume manufacturing establishments. Havana was established on its present site in 1519 after a town called San Cristóbal de la Habana, situated on the south coast and founded in 1514 by Diego de VELÁZQUEZ, had later been moved north to what today is called La Chorrera. The original place was considered unhealthful, and then moved again, for the second site seemed too exposed to assaults by pirates. Havana developed rapidly and soon became the most important settlement in the Caribbean. In 1592 it was made the capital of the island, and in 1634 a royal decree proclaimed it the "Key to the New World and the Bulwark of the West Indies." The English, French, and Dutch, and foreign pirates constantly attacked, sacked, and burned the city; and to defend the port against these depredations, the La Punta and Morro Castles were erected and completed in 1597. In 1762 the British under Lord Albemarle captured Havana after a siege of two and a half months. The conquerors kept the city for a year, cleaned it up, and made it an important center of world commerce, especially in the slave trade. The city continued to grow in area, population, and wealth, and in 1834 its development was given further impetus by Miguel Tacón, who became governor that year. He eliminated crime and constructed many new public buildings. In 1898 the United States warship "Maine" blew up in the harbor of Havana, and this incident led to the war between the United States and Spain. American occupation (1898–1902) proved of great importance to Havana, because contagious diseases, such as yellow fever, were eliminated, the streets were paved, and the entire city was modernized. Profound and drastic changes in the life of the city have been brought about since the fall of the BATISTA government on January 1, 1959. The luxury hotels, gambling casinos, and other entertainment sites have suffered from the decline in tourism. Many of the fashionable clubs and hotels have been expropriated by the government for use as public facilities.

**Havana, Act of.** Name given to the Declaration of Reciprocal Assistance and Co-operation for the Defense of the Nations of the Americas, adopted at the HAVANA CONFERENCE OF 1940, a meeting of foreign ministers of the American republics held at Havana, July 21–30, 1940. According to this act the Latin-American nations declared their right to defend European possessions in the Western Hemisphere against foreign aggression if the situation should warrant such action. Such possessions might be occupied and held in trusteeship until the end of the war. The act was designed to prevent British, French, and Dutch possessions in the New World from falling into the hands of Nazi Germany. It thus gave Pan-American sanction to the traditional NO-TRANSFER DOCTRINE of the United States. In accordance with the Act of Havana, the United States intervened in Dutch Guiana in November 1941.

**Havana Conference of 1928.** The Sixth Pan-American Conference, meeting in Havana in 1928, saw much Latin-American ill-will displayed toward the United States because of the latter's policy in the Caribbean. The American delegation was able, only with great difficulties, to prevent the passing of a resolution condemning the intervention on the part of one state in the affairs of another. If passed, the resolution would have been a condemnation of U. S. intervention in Haiti and Nicaragua.

**Havana Conference of 1940.** A conference of the foreign ministers of the American republics in July 1940 held in order to meet the threat to the Western Hemisphere caused by German occupation of the Netherlands and France, and the possibility of German victory over Britain. It adopted the ACT OF HAVANA, the purpose of which was to prevent any change in sovereignty for European possessions in America, thus giving Pan-American sanction to the NO-TRANSFER DOCTRINE. If there was danger of such a change, the American nations, or any one of them, might intervene and set up a provisional administration. The conference also passed resolutions providing for action against propaganda and espionage by agents of the Axis powers and for economic co-operation to meet the dislocations caused by the European war. Its most important achievement, however, was a declaration stating that "any attempt on the part of a non-American state against the integrity or inviolability of the territory, the sovereignty, or the political independence of an American State shall be considered as an act of aggression against the States which sign this declaration."

**Haya de la Torre, Víctor Raúl.** 1895–    . Peruvian political leader. b. Trujillo. Studied at the University of Trujillo, the University of San Marcos in Lima, and the University of Cuzco. Attempting to raise the standard of living of Peru, he took a leading part in establishing workers' colleges. He led a mass demonstration to protest the dedication of Peru to the Sacred Heart of Jesus. Jailed and exiled in 1923, he studied in Mexico, 1923–1924. While in Mexico, he founded the AMERICAN POPULAR REVOLUTIONARY ALLI-ANCE (*Alianza Popular Revolucionaria Americana*), popularly known as APRA, or the Aprista movement, 1924. He was secretary to the Mexican minister of education, José VAS-CONCELOS, traveled in England, where he pursued postgraduate studies at Oxford, toured Europe, the United States, and all of Latin America, 1924–1927, and lived in Germany, 1927–1930. He opposed Marxist Communism, returned to Peru after the overthrow of the dictator LEGUÍA, and became the Aprista candidate for president, 1931. Despite his overwhelming popularity and success at the polls, SÁNCHEZ CERRO was declared the winner and inaugurated as president. Haya de la Torre was imprisoned without a trial for one and one-half years, 1932–1933, and went into hiding in Peru, 1934–1945. He was denied the chance to be a candidate in the election of 1936, because APRA was considered an international rather than a Peruvian political party. He reorganized the Aprista Party, which took the name Popular Party (*Partido Popular*), backed BUSTAMANTE for president, 1945; after APRA's victory in the elections, he wielded considerable influence under the new government. The Aprista Party was again declared illegal, 1948, because of a revolt for which the party was held responsible. When the Bustamante government was overthrown by conservatives under ODRÍA, Haya de la Torre was forced to seek refuge in the Colombian embassy in Lima, where he remained until 1954, when he was given permission to leave the country. He went into exile in Mexico and from there to Europe. In the presidential election of 1956, the Apristas formed a coalition with the *Movimiento Democrático Peruano* to elect PRADO Y UGAR-TECHE president. He returned to Peru in July 1957 and became less a militant revolutionary and more inclined to advocate peaceful and constructive revolution. He then spent considerable time in Europe, and made a study

of the agrarian reforms in Japan, Formosa, and India, 1957–1962. He was the candidate of the Aprista party in the 1962 election and because no candidate polled the necessary one-third of the vote (Haya de la Torre had 32.97 per cent of the vote), the congress had the task of selecting a president from among the three leading candidates. Before a president could be chosen a military coup deposed President Prado y Ugarteche and annulled the election. Haya de la Torre was again a candidate for the presidency in the 1963 elections but was narrowly defeated by the Popular Action party candidate, Fernando BELAÚNDE TERRY.

**Hay-Bunau-Varilla Treaty.** The treaty of November 18, 1903, negotiated by the U. S. Secretary of State John Hay and Philippe BUNAU-VARILLA, a French engineer connected with the New Panama Canal Company, who was appointed minister to Washington by the new Republic of Panama. It provided for the construction by the United States of a canal across the Isthmus of Panama. The United States was given the perpetual "use, occupation, and control" of a zone ten miles wide, and the right to take such additional lands as might be needed for the construction, maintenance, sanitation, operation, and protection of the canal. Panama was to receive $10,000,-000 along with $250,000 annually beginning nine years from the day the treaty went into effect. On August 15, 1914, the first steamer passed through the canal.

**Hay-Herrán Treaty.** Treaty signed in January 1903, by the U. S. Secretary of State John Hay and the Colombian chargé in Washington, Tomás Herrán, providing for the building by the United States of a canal across the Isthmus of Panama. The United States was to be granted the right to operate the canal for one hundred years as well as the option of extending this time for an indefinite period. The United States was also to be given a lease of a strip of land three miles wide on each side of the canal. In exchange Colombia was to receive $10,000,000 at once and an annuity of $250,000 was to begin nine years after the treaty was ratified. The treaty was not ratified by the Colombian Senate, because it hoped to get better terms. As a result, Panama seceded from Colombia.

**Hay-Pauncefote Treaty.** Treaty signed between the United States and Great Britain in November 1901, which abrogated the CLAYTON-BULWER TREATY. The latter prevented the United States from achieving control over any canal built across the Central-American Isthmus. The Hay-Pauncefote Treaty paved the way for American construction, operation, and fortification of such a canal.

**Health, Departments of.** Latin-American public health services have made considerable advances in the 20th century; they have been helped by U. S. organizations such as the International Health Board of the Rockefeller Foundation, which has done outstanding work in combating malaria and yellow fever. Among the health departments of Latin America the Brazilian *Saúde Pública* (Bureau of Public Health) is a very efficient organization. It has eliminated malaria and yellow fever in the cities of Rio de Janeiro and Santos; its Rural Sanitary Service (*Prophylaxia Rural*) fights disease in the interior of the country. There are many efficiently-run general hospitals in Latin America. Outstanding examples are the national hospitals of Uruguay, functioning in Montevideo. The low mortality rate of Uruguay makes it one of the healthiest countries in the world. Other progressive Latin-American hospitals are those of Buenos Aires, the Calixto García Hospital in Havana, and those of the Mexican *Beneficencia Pública*, which include a hospital for prostitutes. In spite of the activity of Latin-American Public Health departments, the rate of disease is still high. Rural areas generally suffer from a variety of diseases, among which malaria, yellow fever, and hookworm are prevalent. One of the most serious problems is the impurity of the water supply in most cities. Through its specialized agencies the ORGANIZATION OF AMERICAN STATES gives appreciable help to the individual governments and provides invaluable aid to Latin America's fight against disease. It cooperates with the World Health Organization (WHO), a specialized agency of the United Nations, established in 1948, which operates in Latin America mainly through the Pan-American Sanitary Bureau, the WHO's regional office since 1949.

**Henríquez González, Camilo.** Pen name, **Quirino Lemachez.** 1769–1825. Chilean patriot, writer, priest. b. Valdivia. Educated in Lima where he was subjected to trial by the INQUISITION for the possession of prohibited works. Sent to Quito to found a convent, he was suspected of taking part in an uprising (1809) agitating for Chilean independence. Under his pen name of Quirino Lemachez, he wrote fiery articles for independence and self-government. He preached a sermon of optimism on the opening of the first Chilean congress, July 4, 1811. Constantly pushing the democratic ideals as established by the United States and France, he had a great deal to do with making Chile the first Latin-American country to abolish slavery. He became editor of *La aurora de Chile* (The Dawn of Chile), the first newspaper in the country, February 13, 1812, and nine other newspapers in Santiago and Buenos Aires, where he fled after the defeat of Rancagua. He was recalled to Santiago by Bernardo O'HIGGINS, 1822, became a member of congress, 1824, and was the leader of the liberals until his death.

**Heredia, José María de.** 1803–1839. Cuban poet. b. Santiago. He was banished from Cuba, 1823, as an insurrectionist, traveled through the United States, 1823–1825, and settled in Mexico. He is considered one of Cuba's greatest writers and his best-known poem is *Al Niágara*. He also translated Voltaire and other French writers and is the author of *Lecciones de Historia Universal*, 1830–1831.

**Heredia, Pedro de.** *ca.* 1500–1554. Spanish colonizer. Founded the town of Cartagena, Colombia, on January 20, 1533.

**Hernández, José.** 1834–1886. Important Argentine poet. He wrote *Martín Fierro*, 1872, an outstanding example of GAUCHO epic poetry.

**Herrán, Pedro Alcántara.** 1800–1872. Colombian statesman. b. Bogotá. Served under SUCRE in the republican army in Ecuador, Peru, and Bolivia, 1824–1826; hero at BATTLE

OF AYACUCHO, 1824; general; elected president of New Granada (Colombia) in 1841. The constitution of 1843 gave power to the central government at the expense of individual and local freedoms, and restricted freedom of the press. JESUITS who had been in exile were permitted to return in 1844, and there was closer co-operation with the Church. He served until 1845.

**Herrera, José Joaquín.** 1792–1854. President of Mexico. General and political leader. He supported ITURBIDE in the revolution of 1821 but opposed him later when he became too powerful. Serving as acting president of Mexico, 1844–1845, he was anxious to negotiate the matter of boundaries and Texan independence with President Polk of the United States but was overthrown by the more nationalistic PAREDES Y ARRILLAGA. Although opposed to the war, he was second in command to SANTA ANNA, 1846–1847. He was president from 1848 to 1851 and was generally unsuccessful in his attempts to introduce liberal reforms into the government. A race war in Yucatán caused serious damage and he was forced to put down several minor revolts. He was a mild and honest man whose administration was one of the most conscientious Mexico had seen.

**Heureaux, Ulises.** 1844–1899. President of the Dominican Republic. b. Cap-Haïtien. He dominated the life of his country for 17 years, although he was president only from 1882 to 1883 and 1887 to 1899. A Negro, the illegitimate son of a Haitian and a woman from one of the West Indian islands, with little education but native intelligence, he distinguished himself in the war against Spain. At first his administration was comparatively liberal, but it turned into one of cruel greed. The country was prosperous, but Heureaux' financial transactions (heavy foreign debts were incurred) led the Dominican Republic into economic difficulties. He was assassinated on July 26, 1899.

**Hidalgo y Costilla, Miguel.** Called **The Father of Mexican Independence.** 1753–1811. Mexican patriot. Priest in small village of Dolores near Querétaro; former dean of the College of San Nicolás at Valladolid (now Morelia); in trouble with the INQUISITION and Spanish authorities for his advanced ideas; started war of independence with his GRITO DE DOLORES ("Cry of Dolores"), September 16, 1810; led army of revolt against the Spanish government; joined by others and with an army of 80,000, marched on Mexico City, October 10, 1810, but failed to capture it. He was defeated in 1811 near Guadalajara, and while fleeing north, was captured and imprisoned, and is said to have written a document retracting his actions and saying that Mexico was not ready for independence. He was executed and his head, with those of others, was hung on the walls of the Alhóndiga, Guanajuato, until 1821. September 16th, the day of revolt, is celebrated as independence day in Mexico.

**Hides Industry.** From an early date, hides constituted a valuable export from the colonies to Spain. In the first decades of the Conquest, the Caribbean islands provided an important source of hides taken from such animals as horses, mules, and goats, which had been imported from Spain. These animals were also taken to the mainland where they rapidly multiplied and provided abundant sources of the material. Articles such as sheepskins, sole leather, and cordovans were made from them. Chile and the Río de la Plata were the most important areas in Spanish America for this industry. Northern Mexico and eastern Venezuela also produced hides in the colonial period. In the Río de la Plata the industry developed particularly in the 18th century, especially after the Plata ports were allowed to trade directly with Europe. On one occasion, in 1781, a convoy of ships sailed with 432,000 cowhides. It has been estimated that in 1782, about 1,500,000 hides were awaiting shipment. In 1783, 1,400,000 hides were shipped from Buenos Aires. In Brazil the hide industry made great strides in the 18th century, the exports of hides in 1806 being four times more valuable than those of tobacco. Today the export of this product is an important factor in the foreign trade of a number of Latin-American countries, especially Argentina, Chile, Colombia, Uruguay, and Venezuela.

**Hispaniola.** Latinized form of ESPAÑOLA, the name given by COLUMBUS to the island of Haiti.

**Hochschild, Mauricio.** Argentine tin magnate of German ancestry who until recently owned large tin mines in Bolivia. His company, with headquarters in Buenos Aires, dominated about 20 per cent of all of the nation's tin production.

**Honduras.** The second largest Central-American republic, bounded on the north by the Caribbean Sea, on the west and south by Guatemala, El Salvador, and the Pacific Ocean, and on the south and southeast by Nicaragua, with an area of 43,277 square miles and a population of 2,298,000 (est. 1966), of which 90 per cent are MESTIZO, 7 per cent Indian, 2 per cent Negro, and 1 per cent white. The monetary unit is the lempira (50 cents). The language is Spanish and most of the population is Roman Catholic, but all other religions are tolerated. The country elects a president (who in theory cannot succeed himself) for a six-year term, and legislative functions are carried on by a one-chamber congress. Chief among the large cities are Tegucigalpa, the capital, population 132,778 (est. 1963), San Pedro Sula, population 78,925 (est. 1963), and La Ceiba, population 47,870 (est. 1963), the banana port on the Caribbean. Most of the country is mountainous, but there are a number of plains, including the coastal area along the Caribbean, where bananas are grown, and the fertile 40-mile-long and 5-to-15-mile-wide Comayagua plain near Tegucigalpa. The basis of the Honduran economy is the banana crop grown on large American-owned plantations along the Caribbean coast, and exported through the port of La Ceiba. Bananas constitute about one-half of the exports, the greater part of which are taken by the United States. Other products are coffee, tobacco, and lumber, as well as sarsaparilla. Transportation by road or rail is underdeveloped, but this lack is compensated in part today by an efficient air network. Education is compulsory and free, but the illiteracy rate is still more than 60 per cent.

The coasts of Honduras were discovered by Christopher COLUMBUS in 1502. The Spaniards Francisco de las Casas and Cristóbal de OLID founded the towns of Trujillo, 1523, and Triunfo de la Cruz, 1524, respectively. During the colonial period Honduras was part of the capitancy general of Guatemala, but in 1821 it gained freedom from Spain. Until 1823 it formed part of the Mexican empire and, from then until 1839, part of the CENTRAL AMERICAN FEDERATION. The rest of the 19th century and the first three decades of the 20th century were periods of constant internal upheavals and wars with neighboring countries. General CARÍAS ANDINO, who was to rule for sixteen years as a dictator, took office in 1933. During his administration, Honduras almost went to war with Nicaragua over a boundary dispute, and the country declared war against the Axis powers in 1941. In 1948 Carías withdrew from the presidency and was succeeded by Juan Manuel Gálvez. The most important events of Gálvez' administration were the general strike of the workers of the Tela Railroad Company, a UNITED FRUIT COMPANY subsidiary, which lasted from May 3 to July 9, 1954, and the launching of the invasion of Guatemala by CASTILLO ARMAS' revolutionaries from Honduran bases. Presidential elections in October 1954 failed to select a president from among the three candidates and as a result of a constitutional impasse in congress Acting President Julio Lozano Díaz proclaimed himself chief of state. Díaz was unseated by a bloodless coup in October 1956 and a three-man junta took control of the country. During 1957 there was a border dispute with Nicaragua over territorial claims to an area north of the Segovia river; the ORGANIZATION OF AMERICAN STATES prevented hostilities through prompt and effective action of its agencies. The International Court of Justice later awarded the area to Honduras in a decision handed down in 1960. A constituent assembly was elected in September 1957 and met in October to draft a new constitution and choose a president. Ramón Villeda Morales was elected for a six-year term and took office in December 1957. Shortly before the scheduled elections in October 1963 a military coup led by Colonel Osvaldo López Arellano deposed President Villeda Morales. Colonel Arellano justified his seizure of the government on the grounds that the government had tolerated pro-Castro and Communist infiltration into all levels of the government. A month after the election of February 1965, in which his National Party was victorious, López Arellano was elected president by the new constituent assembly. See CENTRAL AMERICA and ORGANIZATION OF CENTRAL AMERICAN STATES.

**Houssay, Bernardo Alberto.** b. 1887. Argentine scientist and physiologist. b. Buenos Aires. He has done important work in the field of endocrinology, pharmacology, hypertension, diabetes, and other fields. He won the Nobel Prize for medicine, 1947.

**Houston, Samuel.** 1793–1863. Frontier hero and political leader of the United States. b. Virginia. Lived with the Cherokee Indians as a boy and served in the Creek campaign with Andrew Jackson; studied law and was admitted to the bar. He was a member of the House of Representatives, 1823–1827, governor of Tennessee, 1827–1829, and moved to Texas in 1833. He was commander in chief of forces in the war with Mexico, and defeated SANTA ANNA at SAN JACINTO in 1836. He was the first president of the Republic of Texas, 1836–1838 and was re-elected 1841–1844. When Texas was admitted to the Union he became one of the first U. S. senators from that state and served from 1846 to 1859. He was again governor, 1859–1861, refused to join the Confederacy and retired.

**Huancavélica.** From Inca, *huanca villca*, meaning "great temple." Capital of the Peruvian department and province of the same name. Famous during the colonial period for its deposits of mercury, a metal essential in the extraction of silver from the native ore.

**Huáscar.** *ca.* 1495–1533. Inca prince. Son of HUAYNA CAPAC. Defeated in battle in 1532, he was imprisoned and put to death on orders of his half brother ATAHUALPA, who had shared equally in the empire of his father.

**Huayna Capac.** *ca.* 1450–1525. Eleventh Inca ruler of Peru. He controlled an empire about 3,000 miles long and 400 miles wide from 1487 to 1525. The capital was at Cuzco. When he died, his empire was equally divided

between his two sons, HUÁSCAR and ATAHUALPA. This appears to have been the first time that such an arrangement had occurred in Inca history.

**Huerta, Adolfo de la.** 1881–1955. Mexican political leader. b. Guaymas. Played a part in the revolution of 1920 against the government. Governor of Sonora State when CARRANZA died, Huerta was made provisional president from May to November 1920. He served as minister of finance under OBREGÓN, 1920–1923, and played an important part in the oil property discussion of 1921. He led a revolt against Obregón and CALLES, 1923–1924, and was defeated. He was forced to live in exile in the United States from 1924 to 1935; became inspector general of Mexican consulates, 1936.

**Huerta, Victoriano.** 1854–1916. Mexican general and political leader. b. Colotán, Jalisco. Took an active part in the revolution that brought DÍAZ to power; rose to rank of brigadier general in 1902. During the MADERO administration he led the troops against OROZCO and succeeded in crushing the rebellion but would not account for the million pesos of war department funds that had been entrusted to him; retired; recalled by Madero and given command during a military revolt headed by Félix DÍAZ. He led a revolt against Madero in February 1913, and arrested and deposed him; is said to have been responsible for Madero's death. He was provisional president of Mexico from 1913 to 1914 and his policies while in power were reactionary and dictatorial. He tried to continue DÍAZ' system. He was not recognized by the United States, and was defeated by the revolutionary forces of CARRANZA, VILLA, and ZAPATA. He resigned on July 15, 1914, and went into exile in Europe and the United States, 1914–1916. Arrested on the Mexican border of the United States for a revolutionary conspiracy, he died while in the custody of the U. S. government.

**Huitzilopochtli.** From Aztec *huitzizilin*, meaning "humming bird," and *opochtli*, meaning "sinister." An important deity of the Aztec Indians of Mexico. His cult was characterized by human sacrifices, which included the slaying of slaves and prisoners of war. The victim was strapped on a stone and held down by five priests while a sixth tore out his heart, held it up to the sun and threw it at the feet of an image of Huitzilopochtli. Because of the many wars that the Aztecs fought, the number of prisoners immolated reached incredible proportions.

**Hull, Cordell.** 1871–1955. United States Secretary of State. b. Tennessee. Lawyer; judge; member, House of Representatives; U. S. Senator, 1931–1933; author of federal income tax law. He was appointed by Franklin D. ROOSEVELT as U. S. Secretary of State, 1933–1944. A leader in the GOOD NEIGHBOR POLICY, he worked for the lowering of tariff barriers. He was awarded the Nobel Peace Prize, 1945.

**Humaitá, Siege of.** The Paraguayan fortress of Humaitá, situated at a strategic point on the Paraguay River a few miles north of its confluence with the Paraná, is famous for the heroic resistance it offered the combined naval and land forces of Brazil, Argentina, and Uruguay during the Paraguayan War (1864–1870). Ideally located for defense of the river and protection of the communications with Asunción, the fortress was the key to the entire defense system of the Paraguayans. In February 1868, Brazilian ironclads ran the gauntlet of the fortress' river batteries and shortly thereafter the position became untenable. After the garrison had made a final courageous stand against the numerically superior allied forces, the fortress was surrendered on July 25, 1868.

**Humboldt, Alexander von.** 1769–1859. German naturalist, traveler and author. b. Berlin. Educated at the universities of Frankfort, Berlin, Gottingen, and the mining school in Freiberg. He accompanied the French botanist Aimé Bonpland on his scientific journey to Cuba, Mexico, and South America from 1799 to 1804 and with him wrote *Voyage aux régions équinoxiales du Nouveau Continent* (30 volumes. Paris, 1807–1834.) He introduced Peruvian GUANO into Europe. The Humboldt Current, which carries a steady flow of cold water northward from the Antarctic regions to the Peruvian coast, is named

after him. He believed in the Phoenician theory of the origin of early man in America and was the author of many important works, including *Kosmos*, a study of the physical universe, published 1845–1862.

**Hundred Days Government.** The regime that ousted the MONTERO administration in Chile in June 1932, and remained in power until September of that year when it was toppled by the Chilean army. Its proponents were the diplomat and newspaper editor, Carlos DÁVILA ESPINOZA, and the Socialist leader, Colonel Marmaduque Grove. As soon as they came into power, they announced sweeping reforms such as the nationalization of industry and of the Central Bank, higher taxation on large fortunes, unemployment relief, and other measures that gave the government the name of "Socialist Republic" and gained it the good will of labor but the hostility of the conservatives. Soon Dávila broke with Grove and remained alone in power as president. He set about establishing a form of state socialism and established a number of state corporations, including a state agricultural corporation and a state mining corporation. But Dávila did not have time to carry out his program for he was turned out of office by a military revolt on September 13, 1932.

**Hurtado de Mendoza, Andrés.** Title, **Marqués de Cañete.** ca. 1490–1560. Viceroy of Peru. Arrived in Peru on June 29, 1556, as viceroy; forbade immigration from Spain or travel out of Peru. He instituted reforms including the sending of certain undesirable colonists to explore and settle other areas, and grouped families in communities along the frontier, which became the bases for future cities. He encouraged agriculture, introducing grape and olive plantations.

**Hurtado de Mendoza, García.** 1535–1609. Governor of Chile and Viceroy of Peru. b. Cuenca, Spain. Son of Andrés HURTADO DE MENDOZA. Appointed governor of Chile after the death of Pedro de VALDIVIA, 1554, he arrived in the colony in April 1557 and led successful campaigns against the ARAUCANIAN Indians. He arranged for exploration of the colony and the establishment of new settlements. He retired from the governorship, 1562, was appointed Viceroy of Peru, 1588, and returned to Spain, 1596. He is mentioned in the works of the poets Pedro de OÑA and Alonso de ERCILLA Y ZÚÑIGA.

**Hyppolite, Louis Modestin Florville.** 1827–1896. President of Haiti, 1889–1896. Under his regime Haiti enjoyed a period of peace and comparative prosperity, and took part in the 1893 Chicago World's Fair.

# I

**IAPI** or **Argentine Trade Promotion Institute.** The official agency for trade promotion in Argentina. It was founded before the accession of PERÓN to the presidency in 1946 but became infamous through the manner in which it was used by Perón. An important activity of the IAPI was to buy meat and grain at low prices from Argentine producers and to sell these products to foreign consumers at high prices. The government was thus able to accumulate handsome profits.

**Ibáñez del Campo, Carlos.** 1877–1960. Chilean president. b. Chillán. Colonel, minister of war under ALESSANDRI PALMA, BARROS BORGOÑO, and FIGUEROA LARRAÍN. He became vice-president upon the resignation of Figueroa, April 1927, and served as president from 1927 to 1931. He suppressed political opposition and controlled the press. The most important event in his administration was the settlement of the TACNA-ARICA question, Chile keeping Arica and Peru getting Tacna. Ibáñez tried to improve the labor laws and introduce a modest agrarian program. With loans from the United States and Europe, an extensive program of public works was introduced, wages were raised, and the standard of living improved. When prosperity ended with world depression, the Ibáñez regime collapsed. He was in exile, 1931–1937. He was the unsuccessful candidate for the presidency in 1938 and 1942, but was elected in 1952 with the support of a coalition of right-wing parties. Problems of inflation and labor trouble caused him to declare a state of siege in September 1954. Deterioration of the national economy as the result of a serious decline in copper prices prevented Ibáñez from fully implementing his program. He was succeeded in 1958 by Jorge Alessandri Rodríguez. See CHILE.

**Ibarbourou, Juana de.** 1895– . Uruguayan poetess. b. Melo. Nature and love are the main themes of her poetic works, including the collections *Las lenguas de diamante* (The Diamond Tongues), *Raíz salvaje* (Wild Root), and *La rosa de los vientos* (The Rose of the Winds).

**Ibarra, Francisco de.** 1539–1575. Spanish explorer and colonizer. In 1554 he began to prospect north of Zacatecas, Mexico, and by 1562 he had successfully opened at least six mines. He was governor and captain general of the new province of Nueva Vizcaya. He founded Nombre de Dios and Durango in 1564 and San Sebastián in 1565. He explored for three more years, returning to Mexico City, where he retired and died in 1575.

**Icaza, Jorge.** 1906– . Ecuadorian novelist and playwright. Best known for his *Huasipungo*, 1934, which depicts the burning of native ranches and the bloody exploitation of the Indians of his country by North American promoters.

**Iglesias, Miguel.** 1822–1901. Peruvian general and political leader. At the end of the WAR OF THE PACIFIC, 1879–1883, Iglesias was elected president of Peru under the influence of Chile, 1883–1886. Acceding to Chilean demands, he concluded the TREATY OF ANCÓN in 1883. After the Chilean troops of occupation were withdrawn in 1884, he lost power and was overthrown by a revolution led by CÁCERES, 1885.

**Iguala, Plan of.** A manifesto issued by the Mexican officer ITURBIDE in 1821 in the town of Iguala, situated in the state of Guerrero, 80 miles south of Mexico City. The plan led to Mexican independence and laid the groundwork for the future constitution, its principal points being equality of CREOLES and *gachupines* (Spaniards who settled in Mexico), continuation of Catholicism as the only acceptable religion, the establishment of an independent empire under the sovereignty of the Spanish king, FERDINAND VII, one of his brothers, or some other European prince, and the election of a congress to draw up a constitution. It was supported by GUERRERO and other patriots.

**Immigration.** The immigration of Spaniards into the American territories was encouraged from the beginning by land grants, tax exemptions, and other privileges. In the first decades of the 16th century a few foreigners were permitted to enter the colonies. Among the foreign immigrants Germans were particularly active in the Americas as traders and merchants. The policy of permitting non-Spaniards to immigrate into the Spanish New World colonies changed, however, in the late years of Charles V's reign and during that of PHILIP II because of the wars between Spain and almost all other nations. Sons and grandsons of Spanish Jews and Moors were also excluded from the colonies. In general, permits were given to people whom the government considered desirable. Yet, there were always some non-Spaniards who found their way to the Spanish colonies. Many Portuguese, for instance, especially during the period when Spain and Portugal were united under Spanish rule (1580–1640), arrived in Spanish America.

During the 19th century, huge waves of immigrants entered several Latin-American republics. Thousands of British, Swiss, and other Europeans arrived in Argentina in the 1850's to raise sheep and to found agricultural colonies. In the second half of the century there were also many Italian and Spanish immigrants finding their way into the Argentine republic. A number of immigrants who were refugees from German Nazism found a haven in the country in the years preceding World War II. Between 1810 and 1930 an estimated 3,500,000 immigrated into Argentina and settled there. An important French, Italian, and Spanish immigration took place in Uruguay in the 1830's and a majority of the population of Montevideo was of foreign origin at the time of the famous siege of this city by the BLANCOS (1843–1851). In Chile in the late 1840's there was an important immigration of 1,400 Germans who settled in the southern area around Valdivia and Osorno. In Brazil immigration developed after the passage of the QUEIROZ LAW of 1850, which eliminated the slave trade. In the last years of the 19th century and the first years of the 20th, about 3,000,000 Europeans arrived, mostly Italians, Portuguese, and Spaniards, whose work made up for that lost by the ABOLITION OF SLAVERY in 1888. In Peru many thousands of Chinese laborers were imported in the second half of the 19th century. They settled in the coastal valleys where their condition was as bad as that of slaves. Between 1857 and 1938 Argentina received about 4,170,000 immigrants; Brazil between 1820–1937 approximately 4,600,000; Cuba between 1903 and 1932 around 1,260,000; Uruguay between 1900–1937 close to 510,000. In Argentina the lot of the immigrant is not an easy one. If he settles on the land he usually has to be a tenant farmer or a farm hand. Rarely does he become even a small owner. This condition is common throughout Latin America and is one of the causes of the settling of so many immigrants in the large cities. Today Latin-American governments are setting even higher requirements for immigration. They want immigrants who can be easily absorbed into the native population and who have trades that will benefit the economy of the country. Farmers are especially wanted. The largest immigration to Latin America has been furnished by Italy, with more than 2,600,000 entering Argentina and more than 1,400,000 entering Brazil. Next come the Spaniards, with 2,000,000 going to Argentina, 500,000 to Brazil, and about 800,000 to Cuba. Thousands more went to Mexico after Franco's victory in the Spanish Civil War,

1936–1939. About 230,000 Frenchmen have immigrated into Argentina, and about 50,000 into Brazil. In 1939 there were more than 250,000 native-born Germans in Latin America and more than 1,300,000 descendants of Germans, most of them in Brazil, Argentina, Chile, and Paraguay.

Representatives of almost all the European and Asiatic ethnic groups can be found in small numbers in Latin America, and it is the view of some scientists that there will be a growth of a "cosmic race" made up of the fusion of all existing races.

**Incas.** One of the most civilized people in pre-Conquest America. Not much is known of their beginnings, but it is surmised that they originally came from the region around Lake Titicaca, then moved north into the Cuzco valley in southern Peru, probably in the 12th century A.D., and then expanded their domain. Before the coming of the Spaniards, they ruled over huge territories covering some 380,000 square miles, stretching from present-day Ecuador to a large part of Chile and northwestern Argentina, and east into the jungle of the Amazon basin. Politically the Inca state was organized along rigid lines, with the ruler or *Sapa Inca* having a quasi-divine status, since he claimed to be a descendant of the Sun, the deity worshiped by the Incas. Around the monarch were the members of the aristocracy, who enjoyed a great many privileges. Below were the members of the military class and the priesthood. The conquered peoples were kept in line by the well-organized armies of the Incas and by sweeping measures, such as population exchanges between interior provinces and newly-conquered districts. The life of the masses was well-regulated and bears striking similarity to modern state socialism. The activities of all persons were fixed by law and there were social security provisions for persons too old to work. Land was held communally, with each family being allotted a certain amount deemed necessary for its need. Violations of laws were severely punished. Communications were handled efficiently by a system of marvelous roads cut through the mountains, by swift runners, relay posts, and signalling devices. The Incas were famous for their building prowess. Their roads, aqueducts, and stone structures, all bear testimony to their extraordinary skills. Their irrigation projects were unique in their conception and scope. They were skilled weavers and potters. However, they had no system of writing. They did develop a system of numerical computation by means of knotted strands of rope called *quipus*. In some cases the *quipus* could even serve as records of historical events, although only to a limited extent. The capital of the Inca empire was at Cuzco, in the Andes mountains. Situated there were the Palace of the Inca, and the many temples where the supreme deity, the Sun, was worshiped. The Inca empire came to an end in 1532–33, when the Spaniards under Francisco PIZARRO conquered Peru and put the Inca ruler, ATAHUALPA, to death. Today there still are impressive remains of Inca roads, palaces, temples, and fortresses, especially at Cuzco.

**Inconfidência.** A Brazilian term meaning "movement of political unrest." It is applied usually to the colonial period, when there were a number of such revolutionary movements organized by the CREOLES against Portuguese authorities.

**Independence Movements.** Toward the end of the 18th century the CREOLES in the Spanish-American colonies were becoming more and more restive under Spanish colonial rule, which discriminated against them in the field of administration and imposed heavy taxes and economic restrictions upon them. At the same time the ideas of the French philosophers were beginning to find their way into the colonies. Moreover, the freedom achieved by the thirteen North American colonies made a deep impression on the educated classes in Latin America. The important concessions in the field of trade that Spain had made to the colonies in the latter half of the 18th century came too late to heal the widening rift between Creoles and the Spanish administration. In Brazil too there were indications that some Brazilians looked forward at least to the day when they would be independent from Portugal. A revolt led by the engineer and dentist Joaquim José da Silva Xavier, nicknamed TIRADENTES, was crushed in 1792. The first country in Latin America to achieve freedom was Haiti, whose independence from France was proclaimed in January 1804. In northern South America the Venezuelan patriot Francisco de MIRANDA tried to organize a revolt against Spain in 1806, but his attempt failed, for the population as a whole was not yet ready for revolution. After the Napoleonic invasion of Spain in 1808 and the loss by FERDINAND VII of the Spanish throne, Spanish rule was severely shaken in the Latin-American colonies. In 1810, the year when the Spanish Crown's fortunes were at an all-time low (Spain had been overrun by French troops), several important events took place in the colonies. In Venezuela, New Granada (Colombia), Chile, and Buenos Aires, the Creoles formed local juntas, ostensibly in the name of FERDINAND VII, and forced the Spanish authorities out of office. In Mexico the parish priest HIDALGO Y COSTILLA raised the banner of revolt, but his movement was soon crushed and he was executed in 1811. Meanwhile the central junta in Spain and later the Regency had tried to appease the colonies by giving them political equality with the people in Spain, but these concessions came too late, for what the colonies now really wanted was complete independence. Actually the War for Independence was just as much a civil war between revolutionists and loyalists, that is, elements remaining loyal to the Spanish Crown. It was mainly because of the strength of this pro-Spanish element that the war lasted as long as it did.

Venezuela proclaimed its independence in 1811 and in the same year a number of provinces in New Granada declared theirs. Under the leadership of the Venezuelan patriot and general Simón BOLÍVAR initial successes were scored by the patriot forces against the Spanish troops. However these successes were of short duration and by 1815 most of northern South America was again back under Spanish rule. Bolívar, who had been forced to flee to the West Indies, did not become discouraged, however, and in 1816 he was back in Venezuela to continue the struggle against Spain. Bolívar's ranks were swelled by the crack horsemen from the Venezuelan plains, the *llaneros*, who previously had fought with the Spanish troops, but had become disgruntled over the shabby treatment at the hands of the

Spaniards. Hundreds of foreign volunteers, among them many British, flocked to the colors of the "Liberator." By 1819 Bolívar felt sufficiently strong to march on New Granada. In a unique military move he crossed the Andes with his small army and fell upon the unsuspecting Spanish forces on the high plateau north of Bogotá. The Spanish troops were decisively defeated at the battle of BOYACÁ, August 1819, and the liberation of New Granada followed quickly. In June 1821, Bolívar crushed the Spaniards in Venezuela at the battle of CARABOBO, thus freeing, for all practical purposes, the country from Spanish rule. Meanwhile, to the south in the Río de la Plata, the United Provinces, including Buenos Aires, had proclaimed their independence from Spain in 1816 and had sent their able military leader, General José de SAN MARTÍN, to western Argentina to prepare for a march on Chile, where the independence movement had been crushed by the royalists. With a 5,000-man army San Martín made a daring crossing of the Andes in January 1817 and defeated the Spanish forces in Chile at the battles of CHACABUCO, 1817, and MAIPÚ, 1818. The Chilean patriot leader Bernardo O'HIGGINS was elected supreme director of liberated Chile. After the liberation, San Martín put his army on ships under the command of COCHRANE, a brilliant English officer discharged from the British navy, and moved on Peru, then still a Spanish stronghold. He landed in Peru in September 1820, and entered Lima in July 1821. Meanwhile, in 1820, a revolution had taken place in Spain, that had forced Ferdinand VII to grant some liberal reforms. The South-American patriots were heartened by the news, for this meant that the power of the Spanish Crown was weakening. San Martín could not effect single-handedly the liberation of Peru, for the pro-Spanish elements there were still too strong for his small army. He therefore waited for Bolívar, who meanwhile was coming down from the north, liberating the province of Quito with the help of his exceedingly capable lieutenant Antonio José de SUCRE. Bolívar and San Martín met in 1822 at Guayaquil, Ecuador, but apparently the two could not agree on future operations and policies. As a result, San Martín left the scene and returned to

Chile, leaving to Bolívar the task of liberating Peru. This the latter did, together with the brilliant Sucre. The Spanish forces were defeated at the decisive battles of JUNÍN, August 1824, and AYACUCHO, December 1824. Shortly afterward Sucre cleared the region known as Upper Peru (Bolivia) from Spanish forces, and the only Spanish army still holding out on the mainland of South America was the one at El Callao, the port of Lima. It too capitulated, in 1826. The island group of Chiloé, off Chile, was captured by Chilean forces in the same year. Spain had lost South America. In 1819 Bolívar had been elected president of the new republic of Great Colombia, including modern Venezuela, Colombia, and Ecuador, and by 1826 he was the much-acclaimed liberator of five South-American countries. However, his power was not to endure, for internal dissensions gnawed away at the foundations of Great Colombia and its different component provinces soon became independent republics. In 1830, instead of one republic there were three: Venezuela, New Granada, and Ecuador. The liberator himself, his health broken, died a discouraged man the same year. The other free republics of Bolivia, Peru, Chile, Uruguay, Paraguay, and the United Provinces of the Río de la Plata, began their turbulent careers together with the northern republics, facing problems of a political and economic character with which they are to a large extent still grappling today.

In Brazil the change from Portuguese rule to independence came rather peacefully, since the regent Dom Pedro, left behind by his father, the Portuguese king JOÃO VI, refused to return to Portugal when ordered to do so by the Portuguese parliament. He proclaimed Brazilian independence and was declared Emperor PEDRO I of Brazil, 1822. In the Caribbean, Spanish Santo Domingo revolted against Spain in 1821, only to be overrun by the Haitians. Cuba and Puerto Rico, both enjoying great prosperity because of sugar, and both having received many Spanish immigrants since the beginning of the 19th century, were not as eager for independence as were the other Spanish colonies, and both remained under Spanish rule until 1898. Central America broke with Spain in 1821. Fi-

nally, in Mexico, independence was achieved by treaty rather than by violence. After the abortive rebellions of HIDALGO, 1810–1811, and MORELOS Y PAVÓN, 1812–1815, the insurrection was almost crushed. But when in 1820 the liberal revolution took place in Spain, the Mexican conservatives, led by the Church, began to favor independence as a safeguard against possible liberal reforms forced upon them by the new Spanish regime. Their leader, Agustín de ITURBIDE, persuaded the few remaining revolutionists to join him and in 1821 he signed a treaty with the Spanish viceroy, providing for the withdrawal from Mexico of all Spanish forces and for the establishment of an independent Mexican monarchy under a Spanish Bourbon prince. The Spanish Crown refused to recognize the accord, but Mexican independence had been achieved, and in May 1822, Iturbide had himself proclaimed emperor of Mexico. In 1823, however, Iturbide was forced into exile and Mexico became a republic.

**Independent Citizens Party of Ecuador.** Political party formed in Ecuador before the presidential election of June 1948, opposing both the Liberal-Radical Party of Alberto ENRÍQUEZ GALLO and the Conservatives of Manuel Elicio Flor. Its candidate, PLAZA LASSO, former Ecuadorian ambassador to the United States, was victorious.

**Indians.** The most widely accepted theory today is that the American Indians are of Asiatic origin and at one time or another crossed the Bering strait onto the American continent. They then spread gradually over the entire Western Hemisphere until they occupied large areas from Alaska to Patagonia. In recent years, speculation as to the Polynesian origin of the Indians has been revived with some success. However, conclusive proof is lacking in this direction. At the time of the discovery, the more important groups of Indians were the AZTECS of Mexico, the MAYAS of Yucatán, whose civilization, however, was but a pale reflection of their glorious past, the savage CARIBS of the Antilles and Venezuela, the ARAWAKS of northeastern South America, the Brazilian TUPÍS, the GUARANÍS of what is today Paraguay, the CHIBCHAS of the Colombian plateau, the INCAS of Ecuador and Peru, and the ARAUCANIANS of Chile. The word "Indians" itself derives from COLUMBUS' error in mistaking the Caribbean aborigines for East Indians. Under the impact of the Conquest, the two great Indian empires of the Aztecs and the Incas crumbled. The Colombian Chibchas were equally subdued, as were the Indians inhabiting the coastal areas of Brazil and the Guaranís of the interior. The Indians of the Caribbean area were all but wiped out by harsh treatment at the hands of the conquering Spaniards and by disease. The only groups that successfully resisted Spanish conquest were the primitive plains Indians of the Río de la Plata area, those of what is today the southwestern United States, who were somewhat beyond the reach of Spain's main armed might, and the Araucanians of Chile, who, fiercely contesting every inch of ground, retreated into their mountains, never to be subdued by Spain. During the colonial period the fate of the Indians under Spanish and Portuguese rule was not a happy one. In spite of numerous attempts on the part of the Spanish Crown to protect them from the greed of the colonists, the natives suffered considerably. In the early days they were often reduced to open slavery. Indian slavery was abolished in the 16th century and Negro slaves were imported from Africa, but the Indians were not treated much better than chattels under the system of the *encomienda* and the *repartimiento*. Many of them perished because of the hard work in the mines of the West Indies, Mexico, and especially Peru, although probably not as many as the famous defender of the Indians, Father LAS CASAS, would have liked the world to believe. In some instances the missionary work of Christian friars proved beneficial to the natives, especially in Paraguay, where under the patriarchal regime of the JESUIT missions the Guaraní Indians were well-treated and lived in relative security. In the course of the 18th century the *encomienda* system went out of existence, but the position of the Indian hardly improved, for from the status of serf he moved to that of peon, forced to work forever on the *hacendado's* land because of his debts, which he could never pay off. In Brazil, Indian slavery was finally outlawed in the 18th century, but until Brazilian

independence the Indians were generally exploited by the CREOLES. The War of Independence in the Spanish-American colonies was as a whole a white man's war, although in many cases Indians were forcibly recruited for the Spanish and Revolutionary armies, and in some cases the uprising against Spain coincided with the rebellion of the Indian against his oppressors. This was the case in Mexico, where HIDALGO's revolt in 1810 was largely an Indian uprising. Independence did practically nothing for the Indian, who during the 19th century was little more than a peon or was left completely out of national life, living in areas outside of white civilization, looked down upon by white and MESTIZO alike. Occasionally an Indian would rise to prominence, as was the case of Benito JUÁREZ, the Mexican president who was a full-blooded ZAPOTEC Indian. Those lands that the Indians held communally before the Conquest and even during the colonial period were in many cases lost completely in the century following Latin-American independence. Sometimes the land was bought from them, sometimes it was simply stolen under one pretense or another. The most outrageous treatment of the Indians in this respect took place in Mexico under the administration of President DÍAZ, who permitted the powerful *hacendados* to appropriate as much Indian land as they wanted. PEONAGE was one of the features of his 30-year rule. The turn of the 20th century brought some changes, when the world became aware of the plight of the Indian. Atrocities committed by rubber gatherers in the Amazon basin and in Peru shocked many. Governments began to take measures to help their second class citizens. The Mexican revolution of 1910 was essentially a tremendous upsurge of the landless peon who wanted land and a place in the sun. In recent years Latin-American governments have made some strides in improving the situation. Brazil, where the great majority of Indians live outside the areas settled by the white man, has created a special commission with the aim of protecting the Indian. During the administration of Lázaro CÁRDENAS in Mexico, the INDIGENISTA movement was strong; the agrarian reforms were regarded as a return to the pre-Colombian system of land ownership, and attempts were made to revitalize Indian culture. In April 1940, the first inter-American Congress on Indian Life met at Pátzcuaro in Mexico and many recommendations were made regarding the economic status, political rights, health, arts, and education of the Indian. Today many problems still remain, and in spite of the fact that in four Latin-American countries the Indian element is the dominant one in terms of population, it still does not play an important part in the affairs of those countries, and economically it is still backward. In many cases the Indians themselves, having led a primitive life for centuries, are unwilling to adapt themselves to modern changes. Unsuccessful attempts have been made, for instance, to employ the wild Chaco Indians of Paraguay in lumbering and cotton raising. Many parts of Latin America still contain Indians who are completely out of contact with civilization; as is the case of most Brazilian Indians and of a great number of Mexican Indians. The countries in which the Indians form the majority of the population are Guatemala, Ecuador, Peru, and Bolivia. There are few Patagonian Indians left and the few remaining Araucanians in Chile are living on a reservation. In some countries the Indian element is negligible, as in the cases of Argentina, Chile, Uruguay and the Caribbean area.

**Indies, Council of the.** See CONSEJO DE INDIAS.

**Indigenismo.** Latin-American intellectual movement which considers that in the countries with a predominantly Indian population, the Indian constitutes an element apart from the European ruling group and urges the revival of Indian culture and the return of the Indian to a dominant position in national life. *Indigenismo,* sometimes incorrectly called *indianismo* found its most striking expression in Mexico, during and after the revolution of 1910–1917, especially during the administration of Lázaro CÁRDENAS, 1934–1940, when strong attempts were made to develop the country along lines conforming to its Indian heritage. *Aprismo* in Peru also stressed Indian heritage and even suggested changing the name Latin America to Indo-America.

**Inquilinos.** Spanish, meaning tenants or tenant farmers. The term is used particularly in Chile.

**Inquisition in Spanish America.** The Spanish Inquisition, founded in 1478, under the Catholic monarchs, FERDINAND and ISABEL, also operated in Spanish America in colonial times. Its purpose was to root out any religious heresy among the subjects of the king of Spain. However, its authority did not extend to the Indians, whose offenses against the faith were handled by the ordinary clergy. Its targets were converted Jews who continued the practices of Judaism, and Protestants, as well as lesser heresies and books containing ideas contrary to the rigid ideological standards set by the Catholic Church. Its control of thought, whether spoken or written, was complete, and its great powers, including the confiscation of property, caused it to be feared wherever it held sway. A decree issued in 1569 provided for the establishment of Inquisitorial tribunals at Mexico City and Lima. The Tribunal at Cartagena, New Granada, was set up in 1610. Actual burnings at the stake were comparatively few. It is estimated that during the whole colonial period in Mexico and Peru there were only a hundred persons executed in this manner. The institution ended with the achievement of independence by the colonies. In Brazil, although there were cases of heretics burned at the stake or imprisoned to be sent to Portugal for trial, no Inquisitorial tribunals were established.

**Institutional Revolutionary Party of Mexico.** Spanish, **Partido Revolucionario Institucional** or **P.R.I.** The dominant political party of Mexico, usually known as the "official party." Created in 1929 as the National Revolutionary Party (*Partido Nacional Revolucionario* or P.N.R.), the party has undergone several basic changes, each time changing its name to reflect the reorganization of the party structure. In the years immediately following the Revolution there was an absence of organized political life in Mexico; the government was controlled by the militant leaders of the Revolution. The assassination of President-elect Álvaro OBREGÓN in 1928 created a crisis that radically changed the political scene and brought about the birth of

175

the party. The retiring president Plutarco Elías CALLES, the single dominant political figure after the removal of Obregón, decided to perpetuate his control of the government and to circumvent the "no re-election" provision of the constitution by manipulating the machinery of political control through a one-party political system. The party was a coalition of local military and political chiefs under the leadership of Calles, who became the *jefe máximo*. From 1928 through 1934, three provisional presidents occupied the office of the president while Calles held the real power. During this period Calles continued to build up the strength of the party by attracting politically powerful elements to its ranks, and by undermining the strength of opposition or dissident groups. The powerful position attained by the party during the Calles period has not since been seriously challenged. In 1934 Lázaro CÁRDENAS became the candidate of the party and was elected to the presidency. Although Cárdenas had enjoyed the support of Calles during the presidential campaign, he had no intention of becoming another puppet president. Once in office Cárdenas successfully challenged Calles' position and sent the political boss into exile. The P.N.R. was reorganized by replacing the regional chieftain base of the party with nonregional units based on social and economic interests. The party was composed of military, labor, agrarian, and popular sectors, each represented in committees at national, state, and local levels. In accordance with its reorganization, the party took a new name in 1938 and became the Party of the Mexican Revolution (*Partido de la Revolución Mexicana*, or P.R.M.). In 1940 the P.R.M. candidate Manuel ÁVILA CAMACHO was elected to the presidency. The reorganized party was preserved with one exception: the military sector was dropped from the basic framework. Direct political action by the military was no longer considered desirable, but military persons could participate in political activities by affiliating themselves with civilian organizations grouped within the heterogeneous popular sector of the party. In January 1946, the P.R.M. changed its name to Institutional Revolutionary Party (*Partido Revolucionario Institucional*, or P.R.I.) thus emphasizing the

institutionalization of the reforms of the Revolution and the increasingly stable and conservative character of the party. The P.R.I. of the present day differs from its predecessors largely because of its broadened base and growing responsiveness to public opinion. These changes have come about through the affiliation of new and unlike organizations with the different sectors. Mexico today has essentially a one-party system, which is usually associated with authoritarian forms of government. Although the P.R.I. is the only effective political party in Mexico today and has become the "official party," it has not evolved into the one-party political system usually associated with tyranny and authoritarian forms of government. Paradoxically, the one-party system in Mexico has developed into a political system quite different from despotism. Under the P.R.I. the liberal and democratic ideals of the Mexican Revolution have increasingly become realities. Although the system is not without its shortcomings, it has become increasingly democratic since its inception and has led the way to wider participation in national decisions and the broadening of liberties in Mexico. The party has also evidenced the ability to bring to the presidency men who have political ability and are competent leaders of the nation.

**Integralistas.** Members of a Brazilian party (*Acção Integralista Brasileira*) founded by Plinio SALGADO similar to the German Nazi and the Italian Fascist parties. The *Integralist* Party advocated complete state control over all national activities. It was dissolved in 1937 by President Getulio VARGAS.

**Intendencias.** Administrative units into which the Spanish-American colonies were divided in the second half of the 18th century in order to increase the revenues of the Spanish Crown as well as to eliminate a number of abuses and to insure the welfare of the colonies. The system, introduced by CHARLES III (1759–88), was patterned after the French *intendancies*, which were set up under Henry IV and Louis XIII in the early 17th century. After local experiments with the system, the institution was introduced into the viceroyalty of Buenos Aires in 1782, into that of Peru in 1784, and into Chile and New Spain in

1786. By 1790 the plan had been put into operation throughout the Spanish colonies in the New World. There were twelve *intendencias* in New Spain, and eight in Peru and La Plata. Venezuela, Guatemala, and Cuba each formed a single *intendencia*. At the head of each *intendencia* there was a *gobernador intendente* invested with wide judicial, military, and financial powers.

**Inter-American Arbitration Act.** A treaty signed by the delegates of 20 American nations at the Pan-American Conference on Conciliation and Arbitration that met in Washington in 1928–1929. It made obligatory the settlement of disputes of a justiciable nature between American states by an international tribunal. Most of the American states subsequently ratified it, although with extensive reservations.

**Inter-American Commission on Territorial Administration.** An organ set up by an act signed by the delegates to the HAVANA CONFERENCE of the Ministers of Foreign Affairs of American States in July 1940. Its function was to take over the administration of any European possession in the Americas that was in danger of changing hands as a result of the war. The Commission was to be made up of one representative of each nation that would ratify the Act.

**Inter-American Conferences.** See PAN-AMERICAN CONFERENCES.

**Inter-American Defense Board.** An organization that was set up in consequence of the meeting of the ministers of foreign affairs of the American republics at Rio de Janeiro in January 1942. It was designed to co-ordinate the efforts of all the American countries in the war against the Axis powers. The body now acts as an advisory defense committee on problems of military co-operation for the ORGANIZATION OF AMERICAN STATES (OAS).

**Inter-American Financial and Economic Advisory Committee.** A body set up in 1940 for the purpose of relieving the economic plight of the Latin-American republics, who were almost completely cut off from European markets as a result of the European war. Efforts were made to increase trade between Latin America and the United States, and an important result of the efforts of the committee was the Inter-American Coffee Marketing Agreement signed on November 28, 1940. See COFFEE.

**Iquitos.** Town in northeastern Peru on the Amazon River. It is accessible to ocean liners coming 2,300 miles from the Atlantic. It is the commercial center for much of the upper Amazon territory. Population is about 58,000 (est. 1960). Founded in 1863, the town became very important during the rubber-boom period at the turn of the century but since then has lost much of its importance.

**Irala, Domingo Martínez de.** ca. 1509–1557. Spanish conquistador and colonial administrator. Irala accompanied Pedro de MENDOZA to the Río de la Plata region, 1535. After the departure and death of Mendoza, 1537, he served as governor of Paraguay, 1539–1542, and again from 1544 until his death in 1557. Paraguay at that time was an area that included all of present-day Paraguay, Argentina, Uruguay, most of Chile, and parts of Bolivia and Brazil. Irala took as wives the seven daughters of one of the principal Indian chiefs, thereby encouraging polygamy, and he established Indian slavery on a wide scale. CABEZA DE VACA came from Spain in 1542 and acted as governor for two years, but the colonists deposed him and re-elected Irala.

**Iron Industry.** There are large deposits of iron ore in a number of Latin-American countries, but unfortunately many rich beds are too distant from the means of transportation to make their development worthwhile. Brazil possesses the largest known iron ore reserves in the world. They are located in the states of Minas Gerais, Bahia, and Mato Grosso. The building of railroads into the Minas ore fields has permitted profitable exploitation. Today the Minas ore is shipped to the recently built steel mill of Volta Redonda, the largest in Latin America. At present Brazil produces about 5,787,000 metric tons of iron ore each year. About 2,205,000 tons of pig iron and ferralloys are produced annually in Minas Gerais as well as close to 2,970,000 tons of steel. Chile has large deposits of iron ore throughout the country. Its Huachipato steel plant near Concepción is the second largest in Latin America. In 1962 Chilean production of iron ore reached 6,673,000 metric tons, but iron and steel production was far below Brazilian figures. Iron ore is one of Chile's principal exports. Mexico possesses important ore fields, but because of the inaccessibility of many of them, development is carried out mostly in the states of Durango and Nuevo León. In Peru an estimated 500,000,000 tons of iron ore are located in the department of Ica. In Cuba there is an exceptionally rich deposit in the province of Oriente. These resources were formerly held in reserve by American companies who imported certain amounts from time to time.

**Isaacs, Jorge.** 1837–1895. Colombian novelist. b. Cali. Author of well-known novel, *María*, 1867 (translated 1890, 1918), *Poesías*, 1864, and others.

**Isabel I of Castile.** 1451–1504. Called **The Catholic.** Wife of FERDINAND V. She financed the expedition of COLUMBUS, and was opposed to his sending a cargo of Indians as slaves to Spain because she desired to protect the natives and to handle the new Spanish possessions in a Christian manner.

**Isabel, Princess of Brazil.** 1846–1921. Daughter of Emperor PEDRO II. Served as regent three times during her father's absence from Brazil, 1871–1872, 1876–1877, and 1886–1888. In 1888, while she was acting as regent, a bill freeing all slaves was proposed by the Crown and passed by a large majority of both chambers. Since there was no provision for compensation, the owners were deprived of hundreds of millions of dollars; the Brazilians called this measure the "Golden Law." The Count d' Eu, Isabel's French husband, was disliked by the Brazilian people and she was forced into exile when her father was overthrown in 1889.

**Italian-Latin American Relations.** It is mainly in the field of immigration that there has been contact between Italy and various Latin-American republics. Italian immigration has been especially heavy in Argentina, Brazil, and Uruguay. During the Fascist regime, Italy's propaganda made some inroads among the many persons of Italian origin, and Fascism scored some propaganda successes. In spite of this, Italian exports to Latin America in this period did not increase, but on the contrary, continued to decline. Today Italian trade with Latin America is far below that of other leading European nations, Italy absorbing usually not more than 3 per cent of Latin-American exports.

**Itata Affair.** An incident of the Chilean civil war in 1891. Chilean revolutionists, fighting the administration of President BALMACEDA FERNÁNDEZ, bought much-needed military supplies in the United States, which were loaded on the Chilean vessel, "Itata." The Chilean vessel, although detained by U.S. authorities who feared complications, escaped to Chile. When the "Itata" reached Chile, it was reluctantly surrendered by the revolutionists in accordance with international law and promises previously made to the U.S. government. It was conducted back to the United States by the U.S.S. "Charleston" where the vessel was tried by an American court for violation of U.S. neutrality laws. The courts eventually freed the vessel as improperly detained. The affair caused much bitterness among Chilean revolutionists and was one of the reasons for their hostility toward the United States after they succeeded in defeating Balmaceda and gained power. It was followed by the BALTIMORE AFFAIR.

**Iturbide, Agustín de.** 1783–1824. Emperor of Mexico. b. Valladolid, now Morelia. Fought on the Spanish side in the Mexican War of Independence. He was placed at the head of the army in 1820, but arrived at an understanding with the revolutionists, and in 1821 drew up the PLAN OF IGUALA, which was to give Mexico the status of an independent monarchy under a Bourbon prince. Iturbide won support of GUERRERO. Viceroy O'DONOJÚ accepted the provisions of Iguala. However, Spain did not, and Iturbide engineered a coup d'etat and had himself proclaimed Emperor Agustín I in 1822. A revolt by the republican party and the army forced him to abdicate and to exile himself to Europe in 1823. When he returned in 1824 to regain his throne he was seized, tried, and shot in July 1824.

**Ituzaingó, Battle of.** Battle fought between the armies of Argentina and Brazil on February 20, 1827, on the plains of Ituzaingó in the Argentine province of Corrientes. The Argentine forces of 7,000 men, under the command of Carlos ALVEAR, defeated the 9,000 Brazilians under Barbacena after a six-hour battle.

**Itzcoatl.** *ca.* 1360–1440. Chieftain of the AZTECS, reigning about 1427–1440. He made Tenochtitlán (now Mexico City) the most important center in the lake valley.

# J

**Jagunços.** Name applied to rogues of the Brazilian *sertões* (hinterland), and also to members of a Brazilian religious brotherhood.

**Japanese-Latin American Relations.** In the 17th century the port of Acapulco, Mexico, carried on a flourishing trade with the Far East by way of Manila. For a short while Japan took part in this trade, which declined because of opposition from the Spanish merchants in Seville and Japanese isolationist policies. Japan made a determined drive for Latin-American trade in the 1930's but achieved little. In 1935, Latin-American imports from Japan totaled 3.7 per cent, but declined subsequently. Japan's share in Latin America's exports has never reached 2 per cent. It was in Paraguay, in the 1930's, that Japan scored important trade successes. Through barter arrangements the Japanese were able to occupy first place for a while in that country's import trade, receiving Paraguayan raw materials in exchange for Japanese cotton. Between 1908 and 1934 about 180,000 Japanese immigrants entered Brazil, many of them settling in the Amazon Valley and in agricultural communities in the state of São Paulo. The tendency of Japanese immigrants to band together and to live outside Brazilian culture, and their unflinching loyalty to the Japanese empire, proved a subject of concern to Brazilian authorities, especially during World War II. Other important Japanese groups settled in the coastal regions of Peru and in northwestern Mexico. A long-range immigration agreement was signed by the Paraguayan and Japanese governments in 1959. The agreement permitted the settlement of 85,000 Japanese in Paraguay over a period of thirty years. A Japanese agency, the Japan Overseas Emigration Promotion Company has purchased about 233,000 acres of agricultural land in the department of Alto Paraná in eastern Paraguay for the settlement of 2,000 Japanese farmers.

**Jefe político.** Spanish, meaning political chief. A term used throughout Latin America referring to a local political boss.

**Jesuits.** Religious order founded in 1534 by the Spaniard Ignacio de Loyola. The Society of Jesus was organized along military lines, with a general at the top, and a strict discipline governing the members. In Latin America the Jesuits performed valuable services for the Spanish and Portuguese Crowns in establishing many missions in the far-flung American territories, and in converting the natives to Christianity and gathering them into settlements under Spanish and Portuguese domination. The order distinguished itself by its general efficiency, its educational institutions, and its great wealth. In the 17th century, Jesuits founded missions in present-day Arizona under Eusebio Kino and in Lower California under the leadership of Juan María Salvatierra. The most important missionary activity of the Jesuits in the New World took place in South America, in Brazil, and in territories later to become present-day Paraguay and Argentina. In 1608, they were authorized by a royal order issued by the Spanish king PHILIP III to Christianize the GUARANÍ Indians. The first Jesuit settlements, east of the upper Paraná River, were destroyed in 1629 by Brazilian slave hunters, and the inhabitants were forced to move south. New missions, or *reducciones*, were founded with the capital at Candelaria, on the Paraná River, the seat of the father superior. Each mission was governed by two Jesuit missionaries, one directing material affairs, the other charged with spiritual welfare. The villages had their own officials elected among the Indians, but all real power was in the hands of the Jesuits. The organization of the *reducciones* had a distinctly theocratic character with some socialistic features. The Indians' life and work was under constant supervision and all the products of their work were the property of the community. In spite of the lack of liberty the Indians had at least found protection from white settlers, who frequently made slaves of the natives living outside of the missions. Until the expulsion of the Jesuits in 1767, there was constant friction between the Jesuits in the missions and the white settlers of the territory, particularly with the citizens of Asunción. There were even bloody clashes between CREOLES and Indians trained and armed by the Jesuits. Other Jesuit missions in South America were founded in southern Chile among the ARAUCANIAN Indians, in Peru, Ecuador, Venezuela, and especially in Brazil. In the latter colony they gathered many Indians in villages, where, as elsewhere, they taught the natives better ways of cultivating the soil. When the settlement of São Paulo was attacked by a powerful force of savage natives in the 1560's, it was defended by Indians who had been converted by the Jesuits. The Jesuit Fathers NOBREGA and ANCHIETA distinguished themselves during the siege, and the heroism of Anchieta, who remained as a hostage among the Indians for five months, brought about a treaty with the hostile natives. In the 17th century Indian slavery was vigorously opposed by the superior of the order, Father Antônio VIEIRA (1608–1697), who in 1655 was granted by the Portuguese Crown full authority to regulate relations with the Brazilian Indians. Since the Jesuits protected the Indians from slave-hunting Portuguese, they incurred the hostility of the latter. In Brazil the Jesuit missions were generally closer to European settlements than in the Spanish colonies, and the natives of the missions were engaged in work

for the Creoles under Jesuit supervision or traded with their white neighbors. In 1759–1760 the Portuguese Crown, disturbed by the increasing power of the Jesuits and fearing that the latter were planning to do away with the power of the king, ordered their expulsion from Portugal and Brazil. In 1767 the Jesuits in the Spanish colonies were expelled by CHARLES III of Spain. There was no serious opposition to the expulsion, which was carried out with great speed. About 2,500 Jesuits were expelled from the Spanish empire, and about 600 from Brazil. Expulsion of the Jesuits was a severe blow not only to the missions (when they left, the Paraguayan missions disintegrated and the Indians went back to their former savage way of life), but also to education, because all Jesuit colleges were closed.

**Jews.** After the expulsion of the Jews from Spain in 1492, and Portugal in 1496, those who remained were those who had preferred conversion to expulsion. They were the New Christians or *conversos*. Whereas New Christians were excluded from Spanish territories in the early days of colonization, they were able to emigrate from Portugal to Brazil in considerable numbers in the 16th century. A Jewish nobleman, Fernão de NORONHA, was granted a concession to cut brazilwood for three years. A considerable Jewish colonization of Pernambuco and Bahia took place as a result. The Jews who did manage to enter the Spanish-American colonies suffered persecution as a result of the establishment of the INQUISITION in America in 1569. The actual number of Jews burned at the stake, however, was relatively small during the colonial period. Between 1580 and 1640 when Portugal and Spain were both under the Spanish Crown, many Portuguese of Jewish origin settled in the Spanish territories and engaged in trade. A number of them were burned at the stake in Lima in 1635, after the Inquisition arrested many merchants in that city on the charge that they were practicing Judaism.

In the 20th century there has been considerable Jewish immigration into Latin America. Many Russian and Polish Jews went to Argentina, Uruguay, and Brazil before World War I and the years following it. More Jews followed during the 1940's and in the first years of World War II. Several projects of Jewish settlements in agricultural communities have been tried with varying success, the most important being those in Argentina, promoted by Baron Hirsch at the end of the 19th century, and the Sosúa settlement in Santo Domingo, formed by German Jewish refugees from Nazi Germany in the 1930's, under the auspices of the Dominican Republic. Today Jews play an important role in the economic life of the Latin-American republics. They are particularly active in wholesale and retail trade and in the professions, the main centers of Jewish population being in the larger cities such as Buenos Aires, São Paulo, Rio de Janeiro, Santiago, Bogotá, and Mexico City. The largest Jewish group is located in Argentina, with Buenos Aires having a Jewish population of over 300,000. The policy of the various Latin-American governments toward their Jewish citizens is generally one of complete tolerance. However, Fascist propaganda in the 1930's and 1940's caused some growth of antisemitism, especially in Argentina and Mexico. In the field of immigration, Latin-American governments tend now to reject any increase in the influx of Jews.

**Jiménez, Mariano.** Mexican patriot who fought with HIDALGO against Spanish rule. He was shot at Chihuahua in October 1811.

**Jiménez de Quesada, Gonzalo.** 1495–1579. Spanish conquistador. b. Córdoba or Granada. Lawyer; came to America, 1535, serving as the chief magistrate of Santa Marta colony in New Granada (now Colombia) on the northern coast of South America. In April 1536 he set out at the head of an expedition to explore the interior; eight months of many hardships followed until he reached the country of the CHIBCHAS, whom he succeeded in defeating. Gold and emeralds were discovered there. He founded the city of Santa Fe de Bogotá in 1538, where he died in 1579.

**Jiménez Oreamuno, Ricardo.** 1859–1945. President of Costa Rica for three terms, 1910–1914, 1924–1928, and 1932–1936. He was an able statesman who succeeded in governing by law rather than force. He granted freedom of the press and did not persecute his enemies.

Under his administration Costa Rica boasted more school teachers than soldiers. He was pro-United States and sympathetic to the investment of American capital in his country.

**Jívaros.** Indians of the Ecuadorian *montaña*, or the semitropical zone on the eastern slope of the Andes. The Jívaros comprise a linguistically isolated group and are divided into four principal tribal divisions: Antipa, Aguaruna, Huambiza, and Achuale. They are chiefly known for their practice of cutting off the heads of their enemies and shrinking them. Repeated attempts to civilize and Christianize the Jívaros have had little lasting influence and they have remained generally unsubdued.

**João.** See JOHN.

**John (João) IV.** 1604–1656. King of Portugal. b. Villaviciosa. Son of the Duke of Braganza, Teodosio II. He was proclaimed king in Lisbon on December 1, 1640, as a result of an uprising against Spain, which at that time was in command of Portugal. John defeated the Spaniards and reorganized the administration of the country. During his reign Brazil was recovered from the Dutch.

**John (João) VI.** 1769–1826. King of Portugal. b. Lisbon. When his mother went mad in 1792, he became regent with the title of Prince of the Algarves. When he hesitated to ally himself with NAPOLEON I against England, French forces invaded Portugal and the regent, followed by his family and his court, went to Brazil, 1808. After his mother's death in 1816, he became João VI of the United Kingdom of Portugal, Brazil, and the Algarves. He fostered industry and commerce but created friction by giving most official positions to Portuguese and not to native Brazilians. He returned to Portugal in 1820, when Portugal expressed its displeasure at the king's continued absence from the mother country. He recognized the independence of Brazil in 1825.

**John Maurice of Nassau.** Full name, **Joan Mauritz Van Nassau-Siegen.** 1606–1679. Dutch colonial administrator. Sent by Holland to administer Dutch territories in Brazil, he arrived in Recife in January 1637, and by 1640 the Dutch occupied six provinces of Brazil. He reorganized the colonial government, enlarging educational and charitable institutions, removed restrictions, thereby increasing trade and commerce. Religious toleration was practiced and Jews were allowed to enter. He was a statesman of vision, interested in art and science; and the colony prospered under his wise administration. He met opposition from the Calvinist ministers and the directors of the DUTCH WEST INDIA COMPANY, was removed, and retired to Holland in 1644.

**Juan Fernández Islands.** Group of islands 400 miles west of Valparaíso, Chile, belonging to Chile. They consist of two main islands, a small islet, and scattered rocks. The two larger islands are Más a Tierra, 36 square miles, and Más Afuera, 33 square miles. Small Santa Clara Island is near Más a Tierra. They were discovered in 1565 by the Spaniard Juan Fernández. The Scotch sailor Alexander Selkirk spent the years 1704–1709 on Más a Tierra and his experiences inspired Daniel Defoe to write *Robinson Crusoe*.

**Juan y Santacilia, Jorge.** See ULLOA, ANTONIO DE.

**Juárez, Benito Pablo.** 1806–1872. President of Mexico. b. Guelatao, Oaxaca, of ZAPOTEC Indian parents. Lawyer, 1832–1846; served a term in the national congress during the war with the United States; governor of Oaxaca, 1847–1852; exiled by SANTA ANNA, 1853; joined ÁLVAREZ against Santa Anna, 1855; minister of justice under Álvarez; wrote the LEY JUÁREZ, a law which abolished special courts and reduced the power of the army and the Church; named head of the supreme court by COMONFORT, 1857; assumed executive power, with headquarters at Veracruz, 1858–1860, during the War of Reform; became constitutional president, 1861, but his term was interrupted by the French occupation of the country, 1862–1867, and the imposition of MAXIMILIAN as emperor, 1864–1867, despite the fact that Juárez refused to relinquish his position as president; leader of the independence movement against the French. After Maximilian was captured and shot, Juárez was again elected to the presidency, 1867; re-elected, 1871, for a fourth term. He was responsible for many important reforms. Forced to put down many revolts in the last years of his administration, he died in office, July 18, 1872. Often regarded as the greatest of Mexican leaders, he was the soul of the REFORMA.

**Junín, Battle of.** Battle fought on August 6, 1824, in the Peruvian department of the same name, between the liberation army of BOLÍVAR and the Spaniards. The entire battle was actually limited to a cavalry encounter in which the South-American cavalry, 900 strong, defeated 1,300 Spaniards after an initial setback. The 45-minute-long battle, in the course of which not one shot was fired, resulted in 250 Spanish deaths and in approximately 150 South-American casualties.

**Junta.** Spanish, meaning council, committee, board, or conference.

**Justicialismo.** See PERÓN, JUAN.

**Justo, Agustín Pedro.** 1876–1943. President of Argentina, 1932–1938; general and cabinet member under Marcelo ALVEAR; *anti-personalista*. Although a former radical, he was elected with the support of conservatives. A depression caused revolts that had to be suppressed, but gradually economic conditions improved and by 1935 the country was one of the few Latin-American nations that continued service on its foreign debts. He was succeeded by Roberto ORTIZ. Justo supported the democracies in their opposition to Germany and Japan, and opposed his government's attitude at the Rio de Janeiro Conference of 1942.

**Justo, Juan Bautista.** 1865–1928. Argentine physician and political leader. Founder of the Argentine Socialist Party and of the newspaper *La Vanguardia*, 1896; deputy for Buenos Aires, 1912–1924; senator, 1924–1928. He was the author of a number of works on historical questions and translated the first part of *Das Kapital* by Karl Marx into Spanish.

**Juzgado de Indias.** A branch of the CASA DE CONTRATACIÓN of Seville formed in 1545 in Cádiz at the demand of merchants, who resented the Seville monopoly over American trade and wanted some part of that trade for themselves. The *Juzgado* made it possible for ships to load and unload at Cádiz instead of undertaking the difficult ascent of the Guadalquivir to Seville. At the head of the *Juzgado* was a judge controlled by the *Casa*. In 1717, the *Juzgado* was transferred to Seville, and the *Casa* to Cádiz.

**Juzgado General de Indios.** A special court for Indians set up in Mexico in 1573. Indians were entitled to have Spaniards and CREOLES appear before the court and accusations against officials could be filed before it. The *Juzgado* mitigated, to a certain extent, abuses against Indians. A similar institution was set up in Peru in 1603.

# K

**Keith, Minor Cooper.** 1848–1929. American businessman who began to plant bananas in Costa Rica in 1872. He built a railroad from the east coast to San José, which shipped bananas; he later established banana plantations in Colombia and Panama, and in 1899 joined with other banana planters to create the famed UNITED FRUIT COMPANY.

**Kemmerer, Edwin Walter.** 1875–1945. U. S. economist. b. Scranton, Pennsylvania. Professor at Princeton University from 1912. He was asked by the Colombian government in 1923 to head a financial mission that would make an economic survey of the country. A new system of banking was introduced as a result and the currency was reformed. He was financial adviser to other Latin-American countries including Mexico, 1917, Guatemala, 1919, Chile, 1925, Ecuador, 1926–1927, Bolivia 1927, and Peru, 1931.

# L

**Labor.** Indian slave labor was used in the early days in the Spanish colonies as well as in Brazil, but Negro slaves, imported from Africa, at the instance of "humanitarians" who wanted to spare the Indians, soon supplanted the latter. In Brazil, however, Indian slavery continued until the middle of the 18th century, whereas in the Spanish colonies it was outlawed in 1542. Forced labor had existed in pre-Conquest America. In Mexico the *mayeques*, or serfs, were forced to perform work on public lands. In Peru, under the system of the *mita*, the Indians were required to accomplish a specific amount of work each year on roads, fields, palaces, temples, and mines. Under the *encomienda* system, which was introduced at an early date in the Antilles and was later such an important institution on the Spanish-American mainland, the Indians were often forced to work for the *encomenderos*, although the requiring of personal service was forbidden by the laws of 1542. After the abolition of Indian slavery and the prohibition—at least in theory—of personal service in the *encomiendas*, the Spaniards, in order to assure a continuous supply of labor, set up the *repartimiento* system, or forced labor with wage compensation. Under the *repartimiento* Indians were temporarily assigned to public works or to individuals.

Free labor in colonial Latin America was regulated by the craft guilds, patterned on the European guilds, and these to a large extent hampered the worker rather than helped him in advancing in his field. Free labor in the colonies in general was only a slight degree better off than slavery and forced labor, since most wages were very low and living condi-

tions poor. By the beginning of the 19th century forced labor had been legally abolished but, for all practical purposes, the Indians' lot was not much better than it had been under the colonial *encomienda* and *repartimiento* systems. Peonage, or debt slavery, became the rule for the Indians working on the large plantations, for they were unable to leave the *hacendado*'s property because of their inability to pay their debts.

With the progress of industrialization in the 20th century, an urban proletariat developed, and among the city workers, as well as among the miners, a labor movement arose. The growth of the movement, however, was slow, since there was much confusion in the objectives of the labor force. The movement generally developed along national lines and has been especially strong in Mexico. There the CROM (*Confederación Regional Obrera Mexicana*) of the 1920's gave way to the CTM (*Confederación de Trabajadores de México*) which, under the leadership of Vicente LOMBARDO TOLEDANO, was able to influence the government to enact much advanced labor legislation in the 1930's.

Elsewhere in Latin America, with the exception, perhaps, of Chile, Uruguay, and Costa Rica although there has been a labor movement, it has not been as successful. This is due largely to the strength of the conservatives of the countries, and the fear of the existing governments of too much power in the hands of labor. In countries like Brazil and Argentina, where in recent years VARGAS and PERÓN supported labor, the governments have nevertheless always maintained a strict control over the unions. An attempt was made in the 1930's to organize Latin-American labor into one confederation. This was brought about by Lombardo Toledano, who in 1938 organized the *Confederación de Trabajadores de la América Latina*. However, this organization was largely pro-Communist in leadership, and in order to combat this influence, an Inter-American Federation of Labor was set up in 1948. Much progress has been made by Latin-American labor in the past 30 years. Labor legislation includes such provisions as an eight-hour day, rest on Saturday in a few countries, including Argentina, paid vacations in some republics, collective bargaining in Venezuela between the employees of the foreign oil companies and their employers, dismissal wage, especially in Mexico, child labor laws, and workmen's compensation laws in almost all Latin-American countries. Mexico has the most advanced labor legislation in Latin America and, in certain respects, in the world. An attempt was made to enforce Mexican labor laws under the CÁRDENAS administration, 1934–1940, but since that time there has been a relaxation in the enforcement of the more advanced laws. At the first inter-American conference of labor ministers and labor union leaders, held in Bogotá, Colombia, May 6, 1963, all Latin-American countries were represented, with the exception of Cuba and Haiti. The U. S. government, with the co-operation of U. S. labor organizations, encouraged the participation of organized labor in Latin America in national economic and social development programs. U. S. labor leaders strongly urged the acceleration of social and economic progress through the channeling of ALLIANCE FOR PROGRESS aid into projects that would directly benefit Latin-American workers.

**Labor Parties.** Most non-Socialist and non-Communist Latin-American labor parties have been formed in relatively recent years, and they have usually been sponsored by political figures seeking the support of organized labor. A Mexican labor party was organized in 1920 in order to support the election of OBREGÓN to the presidency and the *Confederación de Trabajadores de México* (C.T.M.), a federation of labor unions formed in 1936, was incorporated into the labor sector of the REVOLUTIONARY MEXICAN PARTY (P.R.M.) when the party was reorganized by President Lázaro CÁRDENAS in 1938. In Brazil, Getulio VARGAS established a Brazilian labor party during the DUTRA administration and was victorious on its ticket in the 1950 elections. In Argentina the PERÓN regime provided the most thoroughly organized example of translating militant labor unionism into political power. Supporters of Perón formed two separate labor parties to secure his election in 1946, and labor was used effectively to create demonstrations and in other ways promote the goals of the regime. In Bolivia, the labor unions have been associated with politics through the NATIONAL REVOLUTIONARY MOVEMENT (M.N.R.), and labor elements have been tied to some extent to the *ibañistas* in Chile. See also SOCIALISM, COMMUNISM.

**Ladino.** Spanish, having different meanings in different areas. In some parts of Latin America the word means a sly, crafty, or cunning fellow, but in southern Mexico and Guatemala it means a MESTIZO. Elsewhere *ladino* refers to an Indian who speaks Spanish and has generally left his Indian customs, or any person who speaks a foreign language.

**La Fetra, Adelaide Whitfield.** Teacher from New York City who founded Santiago College, Chile, 1880, to enable women to have an elementary and secondary education. She had great influence on the life of the country.

**LAFTA.** See LATIN AMERICAN FREE TRADE ASSOCIATION.

**La Gasca.** See GASCA, PEDRO DE LA.

**La Mar.** See MAR, JOSÉ DE LA.

**Landa, Diego de.** d. 1579. Spanish bishop. Sent to convert the Mayas, he burned Mayan manuscripts in Yucatán. He is known for his classical description of Mayan society in his book *Relación de las cosas de Yucatán*, edited and published in Paris, 1864 (translated as Yucatán Before and After the Conquest, 1937).

**La Paz.** The capital of Bolivia and the highest capital in the world, situated on the western slopes of the Cordillera de La Paz in a canyon formed by the La Paz river. The altitude of the city is 11,910 feet above sea level. Population about 399,000 (1960). Since the city lies in a narrow canyon, many streets are graded and some are quite steep. The architecture of La Paz is generally modern. The roofs of the houses are made of red tile and corrugated iron, lending a distinctive air to the city. Outstanding buildings are the Cathedral, one of the largest in South America, the Presidential Palace, the Legislative Palace, the National Museum, and the stadium, which accommodates 50,000 persons. The city is linked by rail with Peru, Chile, Argentina, and Brazil, and by air with the rest of the country and neighboring nations. La Paz is the commercial and industrial center of Bolivia. There are textile mills and factories turning out shoes, paper, tiles, and soap. The city was founded in 1548 by Captain Alonso de Mendoza, who was then exploring the country to establish a city, at the request of Pedro de la GASCA, the president of the Lima *audiencia*. At first the town was given the name of Ciudad de Nuestra Señora de la Paz (The City of Our Lady of Peace), and in 1555 it was given, by the emperor CHARLES V, a coat of arms that is displayed to the present time. During colonial times it experienced many attacks by unconquered Indians and was besieged by them in 1781 and 1782. In 1809 a revolutionary group led by Pedro Domingo Murillo wrested control from the Spanish forces and issued the first declaration of independence from Spain in South America. However, it was able to remain in control but a short time. Throughout the War for Independence the city was the seat of revolutionary activity, and in 1825 it was finally liberated by the forces of General SUCRE. In 1827 it was renamed La Paz de Ayacucho, in commemoration of the great victory over the Spanish forces at Ayacucho in Peru (December 1824). During the 19th century, because it was easier to reach, La Paz grew faster than the capital, Sucre, and in 1898 it was made the *de facto* seat of the government.

**La Plata.** City. Capital of the province of Buenos Aires in Argentina. When in 1880 the city of Buenos Aires was federalized (made into a federal district) as the capital of the Argentine Republic, a new capital for the province was established about thirty miles downstream on the RÍO DE LA PLATA estuary.

**La Plata.** See RÍO DE LA PLATA.

**La Plata, United Provinces of.** Name given to the Argentine federation first formed by the constituent assembly meeting at Buenos Aires in 1813. The head of the federation was Gervasio A. Posadas, appointed "Supreme Director of the United Provinces." Serious difficulties arose immediately as the result of the antagonism between the UNITARIOS of Buenos Aires, who advocated a strong central government with the province and city of Buenos Aires holding first place, and the federalists of the provinces, who favored a federation of autonomous states. When the Congress of TUCUMÁN proclaimed the independence of the new nation in 1816, the provinces of Corrientes, Entre Ríos, Santa Fe, Córdoba, and Montevideo did not send any delegates. Subsequently civil war broke out between the provinces and Buenos Aires, and anarchy ruled over Argentina. It was not until 1826 that a constitution for the United Provinces was framed by a congress of representatives from all provinces meeting at Buenos Aires. The unitarios caused their views to prevail, and a centralized form of government was adopted, with Buenos Aires the capital of the United Provinces. Bernardino RIVADAVIA was elected first president and took office in the same year. The provinces, however, opposed the unitarian constitution and after the advent of ROSAS, 1829–1835, the name of the country was changed to Argentine Confederation, marking the end of unitarian power.

**Laredo Bru, Federico.** 1875–1946. President of Cuba. Soldier and political leader. He fought in the war of independence, 1898–1899, and led the revolt against ZAYAS Y ALFONSO in 1924. He was founder of the Union Nationalist party, and served as vice-president under José GÓMEZ. Serving as president of Cuba from 1936 to 1940, he was under the influence of BATISTA and the army to a considerable extent.

**Larreta, Enrique Rodríguez.** 1875–1961. Argentine writer and diplomat, author of *La* *gloria de don Ramiro*, considered one of the best historical novels ever written in Spanish.

**Las Casas, Bartolomé de.** See CASAS, BARTOLOMÉ DE LAS.

**Latifundismo.** The monopolistic system of concentrating large landholdings, *latifundia*, in the hands of a few. The system, in use in Spain before the discovery and conquest of the New World, developed into the characteristic form of land ownership in Latin America and has provided little incentive for a more effective use of the land.

**Latin-American Free Trade Association or LAFTA.** A group of Latin-American countries which have as their object the establishment of a free trade area to meet some of the economic problems in Latin-American trade. The association, which includes Mexico, Argentina, Brazil, Chile, Paraguay, Peru, and Uruguay, was established by a treaty signed at Montevideo on February 18, 1960. Colombia and Ecuador joined in 1961. The association, somewhat similar in plan to the European Free Trade Association, envisages the establishment of a common market by the elimination of all trade restrictions between the member countries within twelve years. LAFTA formally came into existence on June 2, 1961, when the treaty signed in 1960 came into force; on July 24, 1961, the first LAFTA conference was held in Montevideo to set up an administrative structure and to consider a preliminary list of goods on which the member countries were prepared to cut import tariffs. Rómulo de ALMEIDA of Brazil was elected to be the first executive secretary of its permanent organization. LAFTA began operations on January 2, 1962, when tariff reductions mutually accorded among member nations became effective. A second conference met in Mexico City in 1962 and was attended by all nine members. Resolutions were adopted to govern future tariff negotiations, to co-ordinate the economic policies of member countries, to provide standards for determining merchandise origin for tariff purposes, and tariff reductions were programmed. The 1962 conference also rejected Cuba's application for membership on the grounds that a Communist economy is not compatible with the market principles of free enterprise and free competition. Although the LAFTA countries traded very little with each other in the past, since 1961 limited steps have been taken toward reduction of duties and import tariffs, and trade between them has expanded. Mexican exports to other member countries rose 90 per cent in 1962, and in the first half of 1963, they doubled again. Trade between other LAFTA members, however, has expanded more slowly; intraregional trade in 1962 was increased about one-third over the preceding year. Tariff reductions have been made on more than 2,000 items, but these only covered about seven per cent of the total trade of the area in 1965.

**Latorre, Lorenzo.** Dictator of Uruguay. Colonel, leader of the *colorados*; ruler of Uruguay after Ellauri was overthrown by the army, 1875; assumed dictatorship, 1876, and ran country until March 13, 1880, when personal financial difficulties caused him to state it was impossible to govern Uruguay and he resigned. The most important achievement of his administration was a reform program effected in the educational system. He was forced to use harsh measures to remain in office, and in February 1879 was made the actual constitutional president. He reformed the army, modified the national expenditures, putting the country on surer economic footing, and changed the customs' service.

**Lautaro.** ca. 1535–1557. Famous ARAUCANIAN (Chilean Indian) chieftain known among the Spaniards as Alonso. For a few years he was the servant of the conquistador of Chile, Pedro de VALDIVIA, but in 1553 he escaped and joined fellow Indians who had risen against the Spaniards, and he quickly became the leader of the rebels. They routed the Spanish forces commanded by Valdivia on the banks of the Tucapel River, taking Valdivia prisoner and torturing him and the other Spanish prisoners to death. He followed up this victory with the capture of the city of Concepción in 1554, which later was abandoned by the Araucanians and then recaptured in 1555. After an unsuccessful advance on Santiago, Lautaro's troops were finally defeated by the successor of Valdivia, General Villagrán, at the Battle of Mataquito River, April 1557.

Lautaro, who perished in the battle, was a brilliant military leader and his feats are immortalized in the famous epic poem, *La Araucana*, by Alonso de ERCILLA Y ZÚÑIGA, published in three parts (1569, 1578, 1589).

**Lavalleja, Juan Antonio.** 1778–1853. Uruguayan military leader and patriot. b. Minas. Served under ARTIGAS; captured by Portuguese and taken to Rio de Janeiro. He went to Buenos Aires, where he remained until April 19, 1825, when he left for the Banda Oriental (Uruguay) at the head of 32 Uruguayan patriots (the "Immortal Thirty-Three"), his sole purpose being to liberate his country. They were joined by others, and after Brazilian forces had been defeated, the Banda Oriental was declared independent of Brazil, thereafter to be a part of the United Provinces of the Río de la Plata (Argentina), and Lavalleja was elected governor of the province. War between Argentina and Brazil followed the former's approval of the Uruguayan decision. After the establishment of the Republic of Uruguay, resulting from the treaty signed by Argentina and Brazil in 1828, Lavalleja was succeeded by Rondeau as governor, 1829. He was provisional president, 1830, and was succeeded in the same year by RIVERA, who was the country's first president. Leader of the BLANCOS in the civil war between *blancos* and *colorados,* 1832–1834, Lavalleja was defeated and sought refuge in Brazil. He was active in the civil war of 1836–1838 on the side of ORIBE, who, after being defeated by the *colorados,* was forced to resign and leave for Buenos Aires, 1838. Lavalleja was a member of the triumvirate that briefly ruled Uruguay in 1853.

**League of Nations.** All of the Latin-American republics with the exception of Mexico, Ecuador, and the Dominican Republic joined the League of Nations following the formation of that organization after World War I. Brazil was elected to the Council of the League. In 1931 Mexico joined the League, and three years later Ecuador and the Dominican Republic followed its example. However, as the League showed more and more its inability to cope with the serious international crises arising during the period between the two World Wars, most of the Latin-American countries withdrew from it. The League of Nations did perform some valuable services in Latin America during the LETICIA DISPUTE between Peru and Colombia, 1932–1933, when it contributed to the settlement of that problem, and during the CHACO WAR when it struggled to put an end to the war between Bolivia and Paraguay.

**Leclerc, Charles Victor.** 1772–1802. French general. b. Pontoise. Brother-in-law of NAPOLEON I. In charge of the expedition against Santo Domingo, he left France with veteran troops in December 1801, and in the space of three months had put down the rebellion. But after this victory, yellow fever struck his army and even the reinforcements sent from France suffered the same fate. TOUSSAINT L'OUVERTURE had been arrested and sent to France, and in general the actions of the French caused renewed rebellion which, with the aid of the British blockade, defeated the French. Leclerc withdrew to Tortuga Island where he died.

**Leguía, Augusto Bernardino.** 1863–1932. President of Peru. b. in the department of Lambayeque. Leguía received his early education in Chile. He served with Peruvian forces during the WAR OF THE PACIFIC, 1879–1883. He became a successful banker and insurance manager, 1886–1903; minister of finance, 1903–1908; president of Peru, 1908–1912; president of the Latin-American Chamber of Commerce, London, 1912–1919. Leguía returned to Peru, and aided by the army, overthrew Barreda, seized power, and became provisional president, 1919. A constitutional assembly made his presidency legal and he served until 1930, when he was overthrown by a military revolt. His administration was a mild dictatorship, but during his term as president, the TACNA-ARICA controversy was settled, road and irrigation systems were improved, and education was advanced. He lost his power with the coming of the world depression.

**Lemachez, Quirino.** See HENRÍQUEZ GONZÁLEZ, CAMILO.

**Lepe, Diego de.** *ca.* 1460–*ca.* 1515. Spanish explorer of the coast of Brazil on the upper side of the "Bulge" about four degrees south latitude; sailed northward; arrived back in Spain in June 1500.

**Lépero.** In Mexico, a term referring to a vagabond, one of the rabble, or a disorderly element.

**Lerdo de Tejada, Miguel.** *ca.* 1814–1861. Mexican statesman. Served as secretary of the treasury in the liberal administrations of COMONFORT and JUÁREZ, 1855–1859. He was judge of the Mexican supreme court, 1860–1861. Famed for his sponsorship of the LEY LERDO of 1856 that prohibited ownership of land by the Church or any corporation beyond its operating needs, he sponsored legislation that placed the Church and religious orders under government supervision and regulation. He was a noted liberal.

**Lerdo de Tejada, Sebastián.** 1825–1889. President of Mexico. b. Jalapa. Lawyer and political leader who served as judge of the supreme court, 1855–1857, and held cabinet posts, 1857–1867. He supported JUÁREZ during the French invasion. He was chief justice of the supreme court, 1867–1872, succeeded to the presidency upon the death of Juárez in July 1872, and was elected to that office for a four-year term in December of the same year. He had difficulty keeping harmony in his administration and was overthrown by Porfirio DÍAZ in November 1876. After several unsuccessful attempts at revolt, he went into exile and died in New York City.

**Lescot, Élie.** b. 1883. President of Haiti. b. Saint-Louis du Nord. Lawyer; minister to the United States, 1937–1941; president of Haiti, 1941–1946. He had a difficult administration, because when Haiti joined the United States in WORLD WAR II, the economic condition of the country was bad; prices rose, wages fell, and a lowering of the standard of living in Haiti meant starvation. This resulted in riots against the government, which was blamed for the many shortages, and Lescot was forced to resign in January 1946 and go into exile.

**Lesseps, Ferdinand Marie, Vicomte de.** 1805–1894. French diplomat and promoter of the Suez and Panama canals. b. Versailles. Minister of France at Madrid, 1848–1849.

He conceived the plan and owned part of the company that constructed the Suez Canal, 1859–1869. He was president of the French company that obtained a concession from Colombia in 1878 and worked on the construction of the Panama Canal from 1880–1888. He was the leading spirit of the enterprise; however, the company's resources, depleted by extravagance and gross mismanagement, scandalous handling of the funds, loss of employees from yellow fever and other diseases, made the completion of the job impossible, and the company was forced to abandon the project.

**Leticia Dispute.** The Leticia territory, located in the upper Amazon valley, was allotted to Colombia by virtue of a treaty between that country and Peru signed in 1922. A serious dispute arose in 1932 when a group of Peruvians took over the village of Leticia and ejected some Colombian officials. In spite of the fact that the Peruvian government refused to condone this action, armed clashes took place in the Leticia area at the beginning of 1933 between Peruvian forces and Colombian troops. Attempts at a peaceful settlement by the LEAGUE OF NATIONS and some American powers proved fruitless at first because of the uncompromising attitude of Peru's President SÁNCHEZ CERRO. After the assassination of Sánchez Cerro in April 1933, however, the new Peruvian president, General Oscar BENAVIDES accepted a plan of the League of Nations under which the Leticia corridor would be ruled by an international commission for a year. At the end of that term the area was handed back to Colombia.

**Ley Iglesias.** Law passed in Mexico in April 1857, during the liberal administration of COMONFORT, removing cemeteries from the control of the Church. It was part of LA REFORMA, along with the LEY JUÁREZ and the LEY LERDO.

**Ley Juárez.** Law formulated by the Mexican liberal leader Benito JUÁREZ and passed in November 1855. It limited the authority of the ecclesiastical and military tribunals, which had formerly had exclusive jurisdiction in cases involving clerics and army officers. The reaction to this loss of their *fueros* on the part of the clergy and especially of the army was so violent that partly because of it, the provisional president, General Juan ÁLVAREZ, was compelled to resign in December of the same year. The provisions of the law were included in the liberal constitution of 1857, and helped to cause the three-year civil war of 1858–1860.

**Ley Lerdo.** A law promulgated in Mexico on June 25, 1856, it was sponsored by Miguel LERDO DE TEJADA and restricted the right of civil or Church corporations to hold land beyond their operating needs; other land had to be sold. Part of the program of LA REFORMA, it led to the civil war of 1858–1860.

**Leyes de las Indias.** See RECOPILACIÓN DE LEYES DE LOS REYNOS DE LAS INDIAS.

**Liga Federal.** A league formed in 1816 by the Uruguayan patriot José ARTIGAS to counteract the growing power of Buenos Aires, and to cut the latter province off from the Argentine interior. It included the Banda Oriental (Uruguay) and the Argentine provinces of Córdoba, Corrientes, Entre Ríos, and Santa Fe. It was short-lived, however, for the Portuguese invaded the Banda Oriental in 1816 and were in control of the province by 1820, forcing Artigas to go into exile in Paraguay.

**Liga Litoral.** A league formed by the Argentine provinces of Buenos Aires, Santa Fe, and Entre Ríos in 1831. It established a form of Argentine federalist government that lasted until the adoption of the Constitution of 1853. See LIGA UNITARIA.

**Liga Unitaria.** A league formed by the Argentine provinces of Córdoba, Mendoza, San Luis, San Juan, Salta, Tucumán, Santiago del Estero, Catamarca, and Jujuy under the leadership of General José María PAZ. In an effort to consolidate *unitario* opposition to federalism, Paz assembled an army and won control of the interior provinces in 1829. His control of the interior was opposed by Estanislao LÓPEZ in the littoral provinces and Juan Manuel de ROSAS in Buenos Aires. In 1831 Rosas and López signed a federal pact uniting their forces in the LIGA LITORAL and in the same year captured the unitarian leader

Paz. By 1832 the *Liga Unitaria* was disrupted and resistance to federalism was quieted.

**Lima.** The capital of Peru, situated on the banks of the Rimac River, about 8 miles from its Pacific port of CALLAO. Population 1,262,107 (1960). The wide and fertile plain on which the city is located leads up to the foothills of the Andes at a distance of less than 50 miles. The city still has an Old-World aspect in spite of a growing number of modern constructions. It has the shape of a triangle and its streets are laid out at right angles. There are many plazas, palaces, and churches, which give Lima an air of historical distinction. Important buildings include the Cathedral, in which are to be found the remains of Francisco PIZARRO, the University of San Marcos (founded 1551), the Government Palace on Plaza de Armas, containing the residence of the president, the Congressional Palace, and the Torre Tagle Palace, housing the Ministry of Foreign Affairs.

The city is connected with the rest of the country by railroads and highways, and by air with other American nations. The Lima area is the leading manufacturing district of Peru and the headquarters of the country's mining and oil industries, as well as cotton and sugar enterprises. Lima was built by Francisco Pizarro in 1535 and was first named *La Ciudad de los Reyes* (The City of the Kings), probably because it was founded on January 6, 1535, the Day of the Kings. The name Lima itself derives from the Indian name of the Rimac River on whose banks the city stands. Until the end of Spanish power in South America, Lima was the capital of the viceroyalty of Peru. In its early days the city witnessed much bloodshed. In 1536 it was besieged over a long period of time by the INCAS; in 1541 Pizarro was assassinated there by the supporters of ALMAGRO; and until the middle of the 16th century the city was torn by constant civil strife. From then on, however, the city knew a long period of internal peace and expanded rapidly. It was subjected to a number of attacks from pirates during the 16th, 17th, and 18th centuries, and in 1746 it was wrecked by a violent earthquake. On July 28, 1821, independence was proclaimed there by José de SAN MARTÍN.

During the WAR OF THE PACIFIC (1879–1883) Chilean troops occupied the city from 1881 to 1883. In 1938 it was the site of the LIMA CONFERENCE (Eighth Pan-American Conference) which drew up the DECLARATION OF LIMA.

**Lima, Declaration of.** Act adopted by the LIMA CONFERENCE of December 1938, in which the American states manifested their solidarity and their firm resolve to defend American principles against foreign intervention. They agreed that in case of any threat to their peace, security, or territorial integrity, there should be a meeting of foreign ministers for consultation. This was a reaffirmation of decisions already made at the BUENOS AIRES CONFERENCE of 1936.

**Lima Conference.** The Eighth International Conference of American States that met in December 1938. A number of resolutions expressed the support by the delegates of the use of peaceful means in the field of international disputes, and their opposition to force as an instrument of policy, and to racial and religious persecution. The Conference adopted the DECLARATION OF LIMA expressing the solidarity of the American states against all foreign intervention or aggression, and the Declaration of American Principles summarizing inter-American international law.

**Lima e Silva, Luiz Alves de.** See CAXIAS, DUKE OF.

**Limantour, José Ives.** 1854–1935. Mexican financier. b. France. Son of French immigrant. Minister of finance under DÍAZ, 1893–1911, he was part of a group known as *científicos*, who served under Díaz and, although they approved the dictatorship, wanted an honest and scientifically efficient government with a greater degree of intellectual freedom. Limantour took the leadership of the *científicos* in 1895 on the death of RUBIO, and as minister of finance, he nationalized the railroads, abolished the *alcabalas*, and consolidated the internal and foreign debt at an interest rate of five per cent. He authorized a bank in each of the Mexican states and established a single gold standard which improved foreign trade. Internal improvements such as harbors, government

buildings, and communication lines were built, but all this apparent financial success benefited chiefly the upper classes and foreign business groups. A rival of Bernardo REYES to succeed Díaz, he negotiated with MADERO, but was forced to resign and follow Díaz into exile. He died in Paris.

**Linares, José María.** 1810–1861. President of Bolivia, 1857–1861. He favored the oligarchy of his country but attempted to institute reforms and improve the social and economic conditions. He was overthrown by ACHÁ in January 1861.

**Line of Demarcation.** See DEMARCATION, LINE OF.

**Linhares, José.** 1886–1957. Brazilian jurist. b. Baturite, Ceará. President of the Supreme Court of Brazil, he took over as acting president when VARGAS was removed from power in 1945. Linhares announced that the election would take place as planned on December 2, investigated the Brazilian bureaucracy, and appointed new men to replace those of the Vargas regime. He suspended mayors of all the cities for a period of two weeks on November 20 and announced the counting of ballots was to be supervised and honest. He then handed the government over to DUTRA who had won the election.

**Liniers, Santiago Antonio María de.** 1756–1810. b. Niort, France. French naval officer who served the Spanish. He commanded a force of CREOLES from Montevideo and defeated the British invaders of Buenos Aires, forcing General Beresford to surrender, 1806. Liniers, who had held only a minor post in the Spanish navy, was elected commander in chief by the *cabildo abierto*, and a force to defend the city was organized. He was made viceroy after defeating the British under General Whitelocke in July 1807 and was able to suppress an attempt made by ELÍO to overthrow him in 1808, but gave way to the new viceroy appointed by the central junta in Spain who arrived in July 1809. Liniers joined the revolt attempting to re-establish royal authority in May 1810, but was captured and shot, August 26, 1810.

**Lircay, Treaty of.** Treaty signed on May 1,

1814, on the banks of the Chilean river of the same name, between the Spanish general Gainza and the Chilean general O'HIGGINS, according to which the Chilean patriots agreed to recognize the sovereignty of the king of Spain and Gaínza agreed to evacuate the country. The treaty was not honored by either the Spanish viceroy or the Chileans.

**Lisbôa, Antônio Francisco,** called **O Aleijadinho.** 1730–1814. Considered the greatest rococo sculptor of Brazil; mulatto from Minas Gerais area; group of twelve statues of prophets at church of Congonhas do Campo (1800–1805), masterpiece of sculpture; *capela mor* (apsidal chapel) of São Francisco (1773–1794, Ouro Prêto), outstanding work of architecture.

**Literature.** Among the AZTECS and the INCAS poetry was cultivated and the philosophical sayings of Aztec and Inca rulers were preserved. The Incas composed tragedies dealing with epic themes and there was a religious drama in which masks were worn. On the whole, however, Indian literature never went beyond a primitive stage, mainly because of the lack of a well-developed system of writing. This was especially true in the case of the Incas, who did not even possess the pictographic writing of the MAYAS and Aztecs, and who had to rely totally on oral transmission. Spanish-American literature may be said to begin when Spanish chroniclers set down the history of the Spanish Conquest. The most interesting of these is Bernal DÍAZ DEL CASTILLO (1492–1584). A soldier in CORTÉS' army, he relates his experiences in a most vivid manner in the *Verdadera historia de la conquista de la Nueva España* (True History of the Conquest of New Spain), written about 1568, published in 1632. More than simply recounting the exploits of the conquistadors he gives an extremely valuable picture of Aztec civilization. Much interesting information on the traditions of the Incas is furnished by the Peruvian GARCILASO DE LA VEGA (*ca.* 1539–1616), son of a Spanish conquistador and of an Inca princess, in his *Comentarios reales* (Royal Commentaries), 1609, 1617. Epic poetry in early colonial times is represented by the Spanish nobleman Alonso de ERCILLA Y

ZÚÑIGA (1533–1594), who in *La Araucana* (1569–1589) recounts in unforgettable verse the courageous struggle put up by the ARAUCANIAN Indians of Chile against the advancing Spaniards. The Chilean poet Pedro de OÑA (1570–1643) composed another poem on the same subject entitled *Arauco domado* (Arauco Subdued), 1596, in which he praises the deeds of the Spaniards and expresses with great sensitivity his love for his native land. In the 17th century, Spanish-American poetry fell under the influence of Gongorism, the ornate and obscure style cultivated by the Spanish poet Luis de Góngora (1561–1627). Gongorism appears in the poetry of the Mexican Carlos de SIGÜENZA Y GÓNGORA (1645–1700) and of the erudite Peruvian Pedro de PERALTA BARNUEVO ROCHA Y BENAVIDES (1663–1743), author of the epic poem *Lima fundada* (The Founding of Lima), 1732. The influence of the great Spanish satirist Francisco de Quevedo (1580–1645) can be detected in the popular poetry of another Peruvian author, Juan del Valle y Caviedes (*ca.* 1653–1692), a drunkard, who directed his vitriolic satire mainly against doctors and whose vivid caricatures are still greatly admired today. But the two greatest literary figures of that period were Juan Ruiz de ALARCÓN Y MENDOZA (*ca.* 1581–1639) and Sor Juana Inés de la CRUZ (1651–1695), both Mexican. The former spent a great part of his life in Spain, where he created some of the best dramas ever written in the Spanish language. His talent for character study is at its best in *La verdad sospechosa* (Truth Made Suspect) and *Las paredes oyen* (The Walls Have Ears). Sor Juana Inés de la Cruz, the greatest poet of the colonial period, was a beautiful woman who after a brilliant sojourn at the viceregal court, where she was admired for her intelligence and beauty, withdrew to a convent at the age of 18. There she died at 44. In the convent she wrote secular and religious poetry, prose, and plays. It is her secular poetry that made her justly famous. Much of it deals with love, but she also composed ballads and satirical poems.

In colonial Brazil, literature first appeared in the form of letters and sermons by JESUITS, among whom José de ANCHIETA (*ca.* 1533–1597) is an outstanding example in this field in the 16th century, and Antônio VIEIRA in the 17th. Many works were written about Brazil itself. Among these is the *Tratado descriptivo do Brasil en 1587* by Gabriel Soares de Souza, and the *História do Brasil*, 1627, by Frei Vicente do Salvador, the latter being Brazil's first historian. Poetry was represented in the 17th century chiefly by Gregorio de Mattos Guerro (1633–1696), who became known as a satirist, and in the 18th century by José da Silva (1705–1739), who was burned at the stake by the Portuguese Inquisition in Lisbon; by José da GAMA (1740–1795), author of the anti-Jesuit poem *O Uruguay*, 1769; by José de Santa Rita DURÃO, author of the epic poem *O Caramurú*, 1781; and by Thomaz Antônio GONZAGA (1744–1807), who wrote the beautiful love poem *Marilia de Dirceu*, 1792.

The influence of the French philosophers of the 18th century and of the ideas of the French Revolution were strongly felt in Latin-American circles in the late 18th century and during the War for Independence. The outstanding writer of this period was the Mexican FERNÁNDEZ DE LIZARDI (1776–1827), advocate of Mexican independence and author of *El Periquillo Sarniento* (The Itching Parrot), 1816, the first Spanish-American novel. This is an extraordinarily vivid romance of roguery depicting Mexican society of the time, and one of the greatest of Mexican novels.

The Romantic movement in Spanish America, strongly under the influence of European, especially French Romanticism, and favored by such factors as exaggerated individualism, political passion, unsettled conditions, and the grandiose spectacle of tropical nature, is represented in the field of poetry by the Cuban José María de HEREDIA (1803–1839), author of the poem *Niágara*; the Argentine Esteban ECHEVERRÍA (1805–1851), who composed the romantic *Elvira o la novia de la Plata* (Elvira or the Bride of the Plata), 1832, and *El matadero* (The Slaughter House), a protest in prose against the tyranny of ROSAS; and in the field of prose mainly by the Argentine author and statesman Domingo Faustino SARMIENTO (1811–1888). The latter was forced to flee his native Argentina because of the reign of terror instituted there by the dictator Rosas. He sought refuge in Chile, where he became a journalist and a teacher. He was later president of Argentina (1868–1874). In Chile, Sarmiento carried on a famous controversy in 1842 with the Venezuelan scholar Andrés BELLO. The latter spent much of his life in Chile, where he acquired fame as an educator, and was the author of an outstanding Spanish grammar and of the *Silvas Americanas* (1827), in which he sings of the agriculture of the American tropic zones and of their plants. While Bello defended Classicism and Spanish culture, Sarmiento fought for Romanticism and French influence. Sarmiento won, and his triumph was symptomatic of what was happening everywhere in Latin America. In *Facundo o la civilización y la barbarie* (Facundo or Civilization and Barbarism), 1845, Sarmiento studies the life of one of Argentina's early *caudillos*, paints a picture of the Argentine countryside and its customs, and denounces the Rosas regime. The outstanding Spanish-American Romantic novels are *Amalia*, 1851–1855, by the Argentine José MÁRMOL, another vigorous protest against Rosas, and *María*, 1867, the story of an ill-fated love and one of the most widely-read novels in Spanish America, by the Colombian Jorge ISAACS (1837–1895). The 19th century also saw the development of the realistic novel, the greatest representative of which was the Chilean Alberto BLEST GANA (1830–1920), author of *Durante la Reconquista* (During the Reconquest), 1897, and *Los trasplantados* (The Transplanted), 1904, the latter a study of Chileans in Paris. Naturalism at the end of the century appeared in the works of the Mexican GAMBOA (1864–1939), who achieved fame with *Santa*, 1903. Other genres cultivated in the last century were: *costumbrismo*, or the description of everyday life and customs, by such authors as the Mexican Ignacio Manuel Altamirano (1834–1893), and the Peruvian Ricardo PALMA (1833–1919), who wrote the famous *Tradiciones peruanas* (Peruvian Traditions), 1872–1906; Argentine GAUCHO poetry, such as José HERNÁNDEZ' *Martín Fierro*, a truly epic poem about the outlawed gaucho; and the gaucho novel, such as *Soledad*, 1894, by the Uruguayan Eduardo ACEVEDO DÍAZ (1851–1924).

Toward the end of the 19th century a new movement called Modernism developed in Spanish-American literature. It was essentially a literary manifestation of the reaction against the realism and positivism of the 19th century, which was then setting in among Latin-American intellectuals, and reflected the trend toward a more spiritual and idealistic approach to life, the heightened interest in mankind in general and in the New World in particular, and the increasing awareness of the cultural unity of Spanish America. Modernism also reflected to a great extent the powerful influence that French culture and particularly French Parnassian and Symbolist poetry exercised on Spanish-American writers. Although the new trend manifested itself primarily in poetry, it also found its way into prose, mostly in essay form. Chief characteristics of the poetry of the representative Modernists are the emphasis on sound and color, a love for the exotic, a tendency to derive inspiration from French culture, the cultivation of art for art's sake, and an enriched vocabulary. The initiators of Modernism were the Cuban patriot and writer José MARTÍ (1853–1895), the Cuban Julián del Casal (1863–1898), the Mexican Manuel GUTIÉRREZ NÁJERA (1859–1895), and the Colombian José Asunción SILVA (1865–1896). The greatest of the Modernists was the Nicaraguan poet Rubén DARÍO (1867–1916), who is considered one of the greatest poets ever to have written in the Spanish language, and with whom Modernism came into its own. Darío spent much of his life in Buenos Aires, Paris, and Madrid, as a journalist and as a diplomat representing his country. Unfortunately he was a dipsomaniac and his dissipated life led to his premature death at the age of 49. Darío, besides achieving extraordinary perfection of form in his delicate verses full of color and music, was also an innovator and experimented with new metric schemes and with a new poetic vocabulary. He was a cosmopolite, at home in Europe as much as in America, but he did not lose sight of the tremendous importance of the Western Hemisphere in the world, and he wrote a number of poems on American themes. His work, which includes exquisite compositions in prose, is best appreciated in *Azul* (Azure),

1888, *Prosas profanas*, 1896, and *Cantos de vida y esperanza* (Songs of Life and Hope) 1905. Other modernists are the Mexican Amado NERVO (1870–1919), the Argentine Leopoldo LUGONES (1874–1939), the Peruvian José Santos CHOCANO (1875–1934), the Colombian Guillermo VALENCIA (1873–1943), and the great Uruguayan essayist José Enrique RODÓ (1872–1917), who in *Ariel*, 1900, contrasts Latin-American spirituality and North-American utilitarianism.

After the Modernist period, which ended around 1914, the Spanish-American contribution to literature has been chiefly in the field of the novel. The Spanish-American novel of the past 40 years has developed mainly along realistic lines, often expressing a radical point of view. At the same time, as the interest in the Indian and his problems have been awakened, an Indianist type of novel dealing with the suffering of the Indian at the hand of the white man, and with Indian folklore, has been cultivated, mainly in Bolivia, Peru, and Ecuador. Outstanding Indianist novelists are the Bolivian Alcides ARGÜEDAS (1879–1946) with *Raza de bronce* (Race of Bronze), 1919, the Ecuadorian Jorge ICAZA (1906–    ) with *Huasipungo*, 1934, the Mexican Gregorio López y Fuentes with *El Indio*, 1935, and especially the Peruvian Ciro ALEGRÍA (1909–    ) with *El mundo es ancho y ajeno* (Broad and Alien is the World), 1941. Other outstanding Spanish-American novelists of this century are the Mexican Mariano AZUELA (1873–1952), who in his masterpiece *Los de abajo* (The Underdogs), 1915–1916, deals with the Mexican Revolution; the Venezuelans Rufino BLANCO FOMBONA (1874–1944), with *El hombre de oro* (The Man of Gold), 1920, and Rómulo GALLEGOS (1884–    ), who in *Doña Bárbara*, 1929, has created an unforgettable female character of the Venezuelan *llanos;* the Colombian José Eustasio RIVERA (1889–1928), whose powerful *La vorágine* (The Vortex), 1924, describes the terrible plight of Colombian rubber gatherers in the upper Amazon jungle; the Chileans Joaquín Edwards Bello (1888–    ), with *El roto*, 1920, Pedro PRADO (1886–1952), with the symbolic novel *Alsino*, 1920, and Eduardo BARRIOS (1884–    ), a novelist who delves into emotional instability in *Hermano asno* (Brother Ass), 1922; the Uruguayan Carlos REYLES (1868–1938) with *El embrujo de Sevilla* (The Spell of Seville), 1935; and the Argentines Enrique Rodríguez LARRETA (1875–1961), author of the historical novel *La gloria de don Ramiro*, Benito LYNCH (1885–1951), author of gaucho novels, Ricardo GÜIRALDES (1886–1927), famous for his portrayal of the ideal gaucho in *Don Segundo Sombra*, 1926, and Manuel GÁLVEZ (1882–1962), whose *Nacha Regules*, 1919, depicts the sordid life of the Buenos Aires red-light district. Spanish-American drama since colonial times has had only two outstanding representatives, the Uruguayan Florencio SÁNCHEZ (1875–1910), author of *Barranca abajo* (Downhill) a somber drama of rural life, and *La gringa*, 1904, and the Mexican Rodolfo USIGLI (1905–     ), author of *Corona de sombra* (Crown of Shadows), which deals with Emperor MAXImilian of Mexico and his wife Carlota, *El niño y la niebla* (The Child and the Mist), and *El gesticulador*, 1944. Leading Spanish-American poets of today are the Chilean poetess Gabriela MISTRAL (1889–1957), winner of the Nobel Prize for literature in 1945, an intense humanitarian and a crusader against injustice, the Uruguayan Juana de IBARBOUROU (1895–     ), a poetess of love and nature, and especially the Chilean poet Pablo NERUDA (1904–     ), whose revolutionary convictions have frequently been expressed with great force in his verse.

The gallery of outstanding Spanish-American writers of this century would not be complete without the Mexican statesman and thinker José VASCONCELOS (1882–1959), author of *La raza cósmica* (The Cosmic Race) and *Indología*; the Mexican humanist, poet, and critic Alfonso REYES (1889–1959), author of *Visión de Anáhuac;* the Mexican poet Octavio Paz (1914–     ); the Guatemalan novelist and poet Miguel Ángel Asturias (1899–     ); the Venezuelan poetess Ida Gramcko (1925–     ); the Ecuadorian poet Jorge Andrade (1903–     ); the Uruguayan poetess Sarah Bollo; and the outstanding Argentine poet, short story writer and essayist Jorge Luis BORGES (1899–     ).

In Brazil the outstanding Romantic poets were Antônio Gonçalves Dias (1823–1864), a singer of the beauties of nature, and Antônio de Castro Alves (1847–1871), a staunch defender of republicanism. The greatest 19th-century poets were Olavo Braz Martins dos Guimaraes Bilac (1865–1918), who followed the style of the French Parnassians and achieved a rare perfection of form, and Joaquim Maria MACHADO DE ASSIS (1839–1908). The latter was also the most important novelist of the 19th century. In his most widely known work, *Quincas Borba*, he is at his best in blending his unusual capacity for psychological analysis with his somewhat melancholy sense of humor. The greatest realistic novel and perhaps the greatest work in Brazilian literature is the *Os sertões*, 1902, by Euclides da CUNHA (1866–1909), in which the author paints an unforgettable picture of life in the Brazilian *sertão*, or hinterland, at the time of the rebellion of Antônio CONSELHEIRO in 1896. Another great writer of the same period is GRAÇA ARANHA (1861–1931), the apostle of Brazilianism, author of *Canaan*, 1901, who with da Cunha exercised a decisive influence on the 20th-century Brazilian novel, which has developed along essentially nationalistic lines. The leading contemporary novelists are Erico VERÍSSIMO (1905–     ), José Lins do Rêgo (1901–     ), José Américo de Almeida (1887–     ), Jorge Amado (1912–     ), and Graciliano Ramos (1892–1953). The outstanding sociologist Gilberto FREYRE (1900–     ) is the author of *Casa grande e senzala*, 1933 (The Masters and the Slaves, 1946), a fine study of Brazilian life in the times when slavery was an established institution, and a work that has had an important influence on the present-day literature of Brazil.

**Llama.** One of the two domesticated members of the South American camel tribe derived from the wild GUANACO. The llama is found chiefly in southern Peru and Bolivia where it is used as a pack animal. When the Spanish conquistadors introduced horses and mules into South America the importance of the llama as a pack animal decreased somewhat, but to this day the llama is useful since it is thoroughly acclimated to the Andean climate, easy to keep, and can follow mountain paths that horses or mules would find difficult or impossible to negotiate. Llama is sometimes used to designate all the South-American *camelidae*. See ALPACA.

**Llaneros.** Spanish, meaning people of the LLANOS. The people of the vast plains, or *llanos*, of southwestern Venezuela and eastern Colombia. They are excellent horsemen and savage fighters; as lancers they provided invaluable services to both sides during the War of Independence. See BOVES and PÁEZ.

**Llanos.** Spanish, meaning plains. Name given to different regions of Latin America, principally to the great treeless plains of the Orinoco basin in southwestern Venezuela and eastern Colombia, particularly the lands around the Apure and Arauca rivers.

**Lleras Camargo, Alberto.** 1906– . Colombian president and statesman. Director-general of the PAN-AMERICAN UNION, 1947, and secretary general of the ORGANIZATION OF AMERICAN STATES, 1947–1954. He served as provisional president of Colombia when LÓPEZ resigned, July 1945–1946, and had served as ambassador to the United States. He resigned as secretary general of the O.A.S. in 1954 and was made rector of the University of the Andes in Bogotá, Colombia. He was elected president as the candidate of the Liberal Party and the National Front (*Frente Nacional*) in 1958 for a four-year term, and was succeeded in 1962 by Dr. Guillermo León Valencia.

**Localismo.** Spanish, meaning loyalty to one's particular region or locality. *Localismo* is characteristic of both Spaniards and Indians and an obstacle to political unity in many Latin-American countries.

**Lombardo Toledano, Vicente.** 1894– . Mexican labor leader. b. Teziutlán, Puebla. Son of a copper magnate who had lost all his wealth, he was secretary of and professor in the Mexican Popular University (a labor institution), 1917–1921, and professor of law and philosophy at the University of Mexico, 1918–1933. He was expelled from the University of Mexico for his radical views in 1933. He was secretary of the government of the Federal District, 1920, and governor of

the state of Puebla, 1923. A prolific writer and an excellent orator, he represented as an intellectual a new type of labor politics; organized a number of labor unions into a General Confederation of Workers and Peasants (C.G.O.C.), 1932, and was the guiding spirit in the creation of the Mexican Federation of Labor or C.T.M. (*Confederación de Trabajadores de México*), becoming secretary in 1936, and one of the foremost labor figures in the Western Hemisphere (1936–1946). He organized the C.T.A.L. (*Confederación de Trabajadores de América Latina*) together with Cuban, Chilean, Colombian, and other Latin-American trade unions that would work with him. Pro-Soviet since the 1930's, he proposed to substitute labor management for capitalist control throughout Mexican industry. His power declined after the C.T.M. repudiated his leadership, 1946. A challenge to his Communist-dominated C.T.A.L. was the formation of the new Inter-American Federation of Labor, with the A.F. of L. of the United States a member since 1948. He organized the leftist Popular Socialist Party (*Partido Popular Socialista* or P.P.S.), also known as the Popular Party (P.P.), 1947–1948, whose leadership was made up of past members of the official party, the P.R.I., who had broken with President ALEMÁN and the party.

**Lopes, Isidoro.** Brazilian general who led a revolution in the state of São Paulo on July 6, 1924, against President Bernardes, demanding lower taxes and reforms in the ballot and customs service, but it failed. On July 9, 1932, he again led a rebellion, this time against VARGAS, demanding the re-establishment of constitutionalism and a government willing to serve the needs of the people. This too failed, but it did make the government aware of the temper of the people.

**López, Carlos Antonio.** 1792–1862. President of Paraguay. b. Asunción. Educated in the secondary schools of Asunción, he became a professor of theology and philosophy, and later practiced law for a short time. He lived a secluded life outside of Asunción until the death of the dictator FRANCIA in 1840, and then shared a dual consulate with Mariano Roque Alonso (1841–1844). Chosen president of Paraguay, 1844, and re-elected by congress, 1854, and again in 1857, López did little to change the basic domestic politics of his predecessor and maintained a strong dictatorship that discouraged political opposition. The country was opened to foreigners and the complete isolation imposed by Francia ended. López re-organized the system of taxation and the courts; the first newspaper, a government organ called *El Paraguayo Independiente,* was published (1845); government monopolies controlled the most important products of the country including *yerba maté,* lumber, and hides; communications improved with a regular steamship service between Asunción and Buenos Aires and the building of a railway connecting the capital with Paraguarí. He demonstrated a particular astuteness in the field of foreign relations: Paraguayan independence was recognized by the United States and many European and Latin-American nations; trouble with Brazil was averted when treaties were signed on the question of mutual boundaries and the navigation of the Paraguay and Paraná rivers; and serious difficulties with the United States were skilfully handled (1859–1860). Less cruel to his enemies and with more respect for the constitution than other *caudillos,* López was nevertheless a dictator who granted little freedom of political thought and carefully arranged the succession of his son, Francisco Solano LÓPEZ.

**López, Estanislao.** 1786–1838. Argentine political leader. One of the chief federalist leaders who controlled the province of Santa Fe, 1818–1838; he was forced to serve as a lieutenant to ROSAS.

**López, Francisco Solano.** 1826–1870. President of Paraguay. Under the dictatorship of his father, Carlos Antonio LÓPEZ, he became his understudy, principal advisor, and confidant. Made brigadier general and commander in chief of Paraguayan army at the age of 18, he commanded an army sent to co-operate with anti-Rosas forces in Argentina in 1846 but participated in no battles. He was minister plenipotentiary in Europe, 1853–1854, where he met Elisa Alicia LYNCH, who became his mistress and remained with

him until his death. He was appointed minister of war, 1854, succeeded to the presidency with dictatorial powers, 1862, and ruled until his death. Brazilian intervention in Uruguayan internal affairs provoked López, 1864, into taking military action against Brazil, an act that led to the War of the Triple Alliance, or PARAGUAYAN WAR, against the combined armies of Argentina, Brazil, and Uruguay. After the first disastrous stages of the war López assumed command of the defense of the country. The brutal measures used by López in prosecuting the war and in continuing the war when his forces had been unquestionably defeated have contributed to an image of bestiality and extreme personal ambition. Although his enemies have exaggerated his worst traits, it is undoubtedly true that he evidenced little compassion for his countrymen. During the last years of the war he became suspicious of those around him. His brothers were executed and other officials were cruelly tortured and shot; in December 1868, after the battle of Lomas Valentinas, López was forced to flee to the north and to abandon his prepared defenses, but he continued to fight a guerrilla warfare until his death on March 1, 1870. Trapped in an encampment called Cerro Corá, the marshal-president refused to surrender and was killed by a Brazilian soldier; the war he had unleashed completely ruined Paraguay, costing more than half of its population and reducing the adult male population to 28,000.

**López, José Hilario.** ca. 1800–1869. President of New Granada (Colombia). General and political leader who served as president of New Granada, 1849–1853. A liberal, he instituted radical reforms including the expulsion of the JESUITS and the adoption of other anticlerical measures. He established civil marriage and abolished slavery in 1851 with compensation to the owners; political dissension was bitter.

**López, Narciso.** 1797–1851. Venezuelan who led filibustering expeditions into Cuba against the Spanish. b. Caracas. Began by fighting for the patriots in Venezuela and then went over to the royalists. He lived in Cuba and in 1848 organized a revolutionary group, but was defeated and fled to the United States,

1849. He organized a group of North Americans and went on other expeditions to Cuba to fight for independence. He was arrested and prosecuted in the United States, but he had public sentiment so much in his favor that a conviction could not be obtained against him, and he sailed again with another force. He was captured and executed in Havana.

**López, Vicente Fidel.** 1815–1903. Argentine historian and politician. Forced into exile in opposition to ROSAS, he wrote against him; in exile in Chile, 1840–1852. He supported URQUIZA when he returned to Argentina, from 1853 until 1861, when he was again forced to leave the country. He is best-known for his 10-volume work *Historia de la República Argentina,* 1883–1893.

**López Contreras, Eleazar.** b. 1883. President of Venezuela. In 1899 he took part in the revolutionary movement led by General Cipriano CASTRO and in the pacification campaign, 1900–1903. Promoted to the rank of colonel for his military services, between 1914 and 1920 he commanded a number of battalions and regiments; as "Director of War" from 1920 until 1925, he bought military supplies in Europe. He served as minister of war and marine, 1931–1935, and after the death of President Juan GÓMEZ in December 1935, he was elected president to serve until 1943. He asked to have the presidential term shortened to five years instead of the customary seven, and served until 1941. Under his administration Venezuela enjoyed a period of internal peace during which progress was made in the fields of public health, public works, and education. López Contreras refused re-election in 1941, an unprecedented gesture on the part of a Venezuelan president, and was succeeded by General Isaías MEDINA ANGARITA.

**López de Santa Anna, Antonio.** See SANTA ANNA, ANTONIO LÓPEZ DE.

**López Mateos, Adolfo.** 1910– . President of Mexico. b. Atizapán de Zaragoza. Attended the National University and received law degree, 1934; served as secretary to the governor of the state of Mexico, 1931; secretary to the head of the National Revolutionary Party (P.N.R.), precursor of P.R.I.; elected to a six-year term as a federal senator for the state of Mexico, 1946; chairman, Senate Foreign Relations Committee; chairman, Mexican delegation to the United Nations Economic and Social Council (UNESCO) meeting Geneva, Switzerland; managed campaign of the P.R.I. presidential candidate, Adolfo RUÍZ CORTINES, 1952; minister of labor and social welfare, 1952–1957; presidential candidate of P.R.I., 1957. Elected to the presidency, 1958, the first years of his administration were plagued by inflation and rising cost of living. The crisis in Cuba seriously divided Mexican public opinion and brought criticism of the government from both right and left. Faced with the problem of agrarian discontent, López Mateos accomplished more in the area of land reform and land distribution than any president since Lázaro CÁRDENAS. His attempts to diversify and expand foreign trade led to the development of new markets in the Far East and Mexico's participation in LAFTA. He scored a triumph in the settlement of the El Chamizal territorial dispute with the United States, 1963, when Mexico gained territory in the border zone between Ciudad Juárez and El Paso, Texas.

**López Pumarejo, Alfonso.** 1886–1959. President of Colombia. b. Honda. Educated in Colombia and the United States, López Pumarejo became a successful businessman, diplomat, and statesman. He served as minister to England, and was elected to the presidency as a candidate of the Liberal Party, 1934. He supported labor, proposed social legislation and a moderate "soak-the-rich" program that met great opposition in congress. He entered into a reciprocal trade agreement with the United States which assured the sale of Colombian coffee in the American market and American goods in Colombia. A more liberal constitution was passed in 1936. He was succeeded in 1938 by Eduardo SANTOS. He began his second term as president, 1942, receiving more opposition from congress than in his first administration, and there were many changes in his cabinet. War was declared on Germany, 1943; the coffee industry suffered and the country's economy was in difficulty. Scandal and revolts finally made López want to resign, which he was allowed to do in 1945. He was chief Colombian delegate to the United Nations General Assembly in 1945, 1948, and 1958, president of the United Nations Security Council, 1947, and ambassador to Great Britain, 1959.

**López Rayón, Ignacio.** See RAYÓN, IGNACIO LÓPEZ.

**Losada, Diego de.** *ca.* 1520–1569. Spanish colonizer. Founded Santiago de León de Caracas, the present capital of Venezuela, 1567.

**L'Ouverture, Toussaint.** See TOUSSAINT L'OUVERTURE.

**Lozada, Manuel.** Known as the **Tiger of Nayarit.** d. 1873. Mexican general of Indian origin. Took part in the internal struggles of the country after Mexico won back its independence, 1867. He led a revolt against the Republic and was given the name "Tiger of Nayarit" because of his cruelty and because his main theater of operations was the western territory of Nayarit. He was captured by federal troops and shot at Tepic.

**Lugones, Leopoldo.** 1874–1938. Argentine poet and writer. b. Río Seco. One of the foremost Modernist poets of Latin America, he wrote on a great variety of subjects, including love, country life, and the gauchos; author of *Las montañas del oro* (The Mountains of Gold), *Odas seculares* (Secular Odes), *Romances del Río Seco* (Ballads of the Río Seco).

**Luiz** or **Luis, Washington.** See SOUZA, WASHINGTON LUIZ PEREIRA DE.

**Lumber Industry.** Wood cutting was an important industry in the early days of Portuguese Brazil, when the Portuguese Crown derived considerable profit from Brazilian dye woods. In the 17th century British buccaneers initiated the logwood industry in the area of what is today British Honduras. With an area of more than 3,000,000 square miles in timber, the largest forest land area in the world, Latin America's sawn lumber today amounts

to only between 5 and 7 per cent of the world figure. The main reason for this low proportion is that most of the forest lands are made up of tropical rain forests that do not contain enough of the soft woods that are used in industry and construction. Hardwood is generally plentiful but in many cases transportation problems constitute a serious obstacle to the growth of the industry. In western South America, for example, the Andes make it almost impossible to transport lumber from the eastern forest lands to the Pacific coast. Brazil and Mexico are the homes of prosperous softwood industries, chiefly of pine, with the state of Paraná supplying most of Brazil's needs and exporting 200,000 to 300,000 tons annually. The Spanish cedar (*Cedrela brasiliensis*) is the wood in most demand in Latin America. It is used in construction and many other fields. Cabinet woods that have been popular in the world for centuries are still cut in the Caribbean area and in Brazil. Mahogany from Honduras, Mexico, and Cuba is still much needed in the United States. The forests of Paraguay and northern Argentina supply the extraordinarily hard quebracho wood which gives a highly-valued tanning extract for the leather industry.

**Luperón, Gregorio.** Leader of the so-called "Blues" in the Dominican Republic's internal strife in the years 1871–1882. A semiliterate Negro chieftain, he served as provisional president for a brief time in 1879 but was content to be the power behind the executive.

**Luque, Hernando de.** d. 1532. In 1524 he aided PIZARRO and ALMAGRO in obtaining funds to outfit an expedition of exploration into Peru. Luque had been a teacher in Darién and had lived as a priest on the Isthmus of Panama. He was made bishop of Túmbez, Peru, by the king of Spain with the approval of the pope, and was named "Protector of the Indians."

**Lynch, Benito.** 1885–1951. Argentine novelist, author of works dealing with Argentine country life; among his best-known novels are *Campos porteños, La evasión, El romance de un gaucho,* and *El inglés de los güesos* (The Englishman with the Bones).

**Lynch, Eliza Alice** or **Elisa Alicia.** 1835–

1886. Paramour of the Paraguayan dictator Francisco Solano LÓPEZ. b. Cork, Ireland. At the age of 15 she was married to Jean Louis Armand de Quatrefages, a surgeon in the French army, and lived with him until 1853 when they were separated. The marriage was considered void because certain legal formalities had not been executed; in the same year she met the young López in Paris, and when he returned to Paraguay the following year she accompanied him. She bore López five or six children during their years together. Although there is little basis for believing the tales of her leading Paraguayan women into battle during the PARAGUAYAN WAR, she often lived with López near the line of battle and accompanied him in his flight to the north of the country after his armies had been defeated. She was with him when he was killed in the last desperate resistance at Cerro Corá. After the war she wandered about Europe and then returned to Paraguay, only to be turned away. She went to the Holy Land, remaining there for three years. She was buried, forgotten, in a potter's field in Paris.

# M

**Machado de Assis, Joaquim Maria.** 1839–1908. Brazilian writer. b. Rio de Janeiro. Born in poverty, he was ugly and ill from epilepsy. He wrote for the press and had small government jobs but gained no success from his writing until his later years. He is best-remembered for his fine novels including *Memórias póstumas de Braz Cubas,* 1881, (translated as Epitaph of a Small Winner, 1953); *Quincas Borba,* (translated, 1954); and *Dom Casmurro,* (translated, 1953). See LITERATURE.

**Machado y Morales, Gerardo.** 1871–1939. President of Cuba. b. Santa Clara. General. Served in revolution against Spain, 1895–1898. As head of the Liberal Party, he served as president of Cuba from 1925 to 1933, acting as dictator. He suppressed freedom of speech, imprisoned or deported hundreds of people, and closed the national university. He had the constitution amended so that the presidential term was extended from four to six years and was re-elected in 1928 for a term ending in 1935. He suppressed a revolt in 1931, ordered a STATE OF SIEGE, and deprived the citizens of the right of appeal to the courts. He had a network of secret police. His enemies founded a party called ABC PARTY, plotted his overthrow, and a revolutionary movement followed. By withdrawal of army support from his regime and the activities of U.S. Ambassador Sumner WELLES, he was forced to resign and go into exile in the United States, August 1933.

**Mackenna, Benjamín Vicuña.** See VICUÑA MACKENNA, BENJAMÍN.

**Madero, Francisco Indalecio.** 1873–1913. President of Mexico. b. San Pedro, Coahuila. Son of a landowning family, he was educated in the United States and Europe. He had no military or administrative experience but was an honest liberal idealist. He opposed the re-election of DÍAZ in 1910 but failed to be elected and was imprisoned. Upon his release he went to San Antonio, Texas, where on October 7 he issued his Plan of SAN LUIS POTOSÍ, declaring himself provisional president, and with the help of ZAPATA, OROZCO, and VILLA, he forced Díaz to resign and go into exile. Elected president in October 1911, he served until 1913. He proposed a plan for effective suffrage and no re-election, but did not meet the popular demand for land and labor reforms, and it was left for Zapata to become the champion of the agrarians. Madero was confronted with one rebellion after another and put misplaced trust in Victoriano HUERTA, who plotted his downfall. After the "Tragic Ten Days" Huerta seized power and Madero was shot, supposedly attempting to escape when being transferred from prison to the train for Veracruz and exile.

**Magalhães, Botelho de.** See CONSTANT DE MAGALHÃES, BENJAMIN.

**Magellan, Ferdinand.** Portuguese, **Fernão de Magalhães.** *ca.* 1480–1521. Portuguese navigator in the service of Spain. With the approval of CHARLES V he sailed for the Spice Islands via a western route, leaving Spain on September 20, 1519, sighted South America near Pernambuco on November 29, and explored the La Plata estuary. Able to crush a mutiny, he sailed through the strait now known as the Strait of Magellan from October 21 to November 28, 1520, reached the Ladrone Islands in March 1521, and discovered the Philippines on March 16th. He was killed by natives on the island of Macatan on April 27, 1521. One of the vessels of his expedition completed the voyage in 1522, successfully circumnavigating the globe. Magellan noticed that the body of water on the other side of the continent, after passing through the strait was unusually calm, and he named it the Pacific Ocean.

**Magoon, Charles Edward.** 1861–1920. U. S. lawyer and administrator. Practiced law in Nebraska. He served as governor of the Canal Zone from 1905 to 1906 and provisional governor of Cuba from 1906 to 1909. Although accused of showing favoritism, a charge of which he was later cleared, there was bad feeling in Cuba at the time. He instituted a number of reforms including a new electoral law, April 1, 1908.

**Maine, U.S.S., Sinking of the.** On February 15, 1898, the battleship U.S.S. "Maine," which had been sent to protect American lives and properties endangered in the fighting in Cuba, sank in Havana harbor as a result of a mysterious explosion. More than 260 men lost their lives. The cause of the mishap has remained a mystery to this day, but popular opinion held Spain responsible and anti-Spanish feelings in the United States, already at a high pitch because of sympathy with the Cuban rebels, were fanned even more. Although Spain accepted almost all of the conditions of the American note calling for an armistice with the rebels, the United States, where war fever was constantly being whipped up by the "yellow press," declared war on Spain in April of the same year. "Remember the Maine" was the slogan of the war party.

**Maipú, Battle of.** Battle fought on April 5, 1818, on the plain of Maipú in the province of Santiago between the troops of the Argentine general SAN MARTÍN and the royalist forces under General Osorio. After six hours of fierce fighting the royalists were defeated, leaving 2,000 dead and San Martín taking more than 3,000 prisoners. General Osorio

escaped. San Martín's army suffered approximately 1,000 casualties. The battle brought independence to Chile.

**Malinche** or **Malintzin.** See MARINA.

**Mameluco Stock.** From Indian, *mamaruca*, meaning half-breed. In colonial Brazil, half-breeds of whites and Indians found mainly in the São Paulo region. Their cruelty toward the natives caused them to be compared to the Egyptian mamelukes, soldiers of the Egyptian rulers. Thus the Indian word *mamaruca* became *mameluco*.

**Managua.** The capital of Nicaragua and its largest city. Population 191,000 (1960). It is situated on the southern shore of Lake Managua at an altitude of 150 feet above sea level. The city has a number of modern buildings, including the National Palace, which blend with the old residential houses. It is the center of the country's trade, and a rail line links it with the port of Corinto on the Pacific. The PAN-AMERICAN HIGHWAY that passes through it, and the airlines provide communications with other parts of Nicaragua and with other countries. Managua became important in 1855, when it was made the capital of Nicaragua by agreement between the rivaling cities of León and Granada, which were trying to find a compromise for their differences. Before that date the city had been a relatively obscure community, but after being declared the capital, it grew rapidly. It was occupied by U. S. marines from 1912 to 1925 and from 1927 to 1932. In 1931 a large part of the city was destroyed by an earthquake, and in 1936 it was severely damaged by fire.

**Manco Capac.** Legendary first INCA. According to Inca myth Manco Capac and his sister were created by the sun god on the Isle of the Sun in Lake Titicaca (*ca.* 1100). Given a staff of gold they were instructed by the sun god to seek a place where the staff would disappear into the ground and on that spot to build their city. The pair journeyed north to a valley where the staff sank into the ground and there they started the city of Cuzco.

**Manco Capac II.** *ca.* 1500–1544. Emperor of Peru, brother of ATAHUALPA and HUÁSCAR.

Recognized by PIZARRO after the death of Atahualpa and Huáscar in 1533, he was crowned at Cuzco. At first he collaborated with the Spaniards, but in 1536 he raised an army and attacked them. He was defeated in 1537 and forced to flee to the mountains. He was assassinated by followers in 1544.

**Manso de Velasco, José Antonio.** b. 1688. Viceroy of Peru. b. Logroño, Spain. After extensive military service in Spain and Italy he went to Chile in 1737, where he served as lieutenant governor and captain general until 1744. He was noted as the founder of many Chilean cities, among them San Felipe, Copiapó, Melipilla, Rancagua, Curicó, San Fernando, Cauquenes and Los Ángeles. His successful career in Chile led to his appointment to the viceroyalty of Peru in 1744. He was succeeded by Manuel de AMAT Y JUNIENT in 1761. He was given the title of Conde de Superunda as a reward for his long service in Peru.

**Manufacturing Industries.** Handcraft had reached varying degrees of development in America at the time of the discovery. While the Caribbean Indians had remained on a rather primitive level of arts and crafts, the AZTECS, MAYAS, and INCAS had made great strides in gold and silver work, weaving, pottery, stone cutting, and carpentry. The Indians were proficient in wood and metal work, except in iron, which was not employed. Indian craft continued to be practiced in the colonial period, while European handcraft was introduced. In the early period the Spanish Crown encouraged colonial manufacturing, for it realized that Spain would be unable to provide the colonies with all the necessary manufactured products and because it was thought that exports from Spain would cause prices to rise. The textile industry developed at a very early period, and the silk industry flourished in New Spain until about 1580. Cotton and wool were in general use. Leather tanning and food processing were widespread throughout the colonies, as was shipbuilding. Manufacturing in the La Plata area was based mainly on the abundant herds of cattle roaming the plains. While in the later period the Spanish government from time to time attempted to limit colonial manufacturing, Spanish America always provided the greater part of its own population with most of its needs. In colonial Brazil, despite the general policy of the Portuguese Crown to discourage too much Brazilian manufacturing, some industries prospered. Shipbuilding flourished from the 16th century on, while gold and silver smithing developed in the 18th century. In 1785 Queen Maria of Portugal decreed that all manufacturing in Brazil be eliminated, so that agriculture and the sugar industry might be provided with more workers, and Portuguese exports to Brazil might find a larger market. The measure was highly unpopular in Brazil, and only increased the dissatisfaction with Portuguese administration. While the 19th century did not witness much progress in Latin-American manufacturing, the 20th century has seen great strides in this field. The depression of the 1930's during which imports declined sharply, the two world wars that forced Latin America to look to its own capacity for producing much-needed supplies, as well as growing nationalism, have been important factors in hastening the process. Foreign investments were welcomed at first and foreign concerns were treated with great tolerance. However, after the depression, Latin-American governments tended to clamp more and more controls on foreign capital and have expropriated large foreign-owned industries in many countries. The nationalization of foreign investments has usually been accomplished without adequate, prompt, or effective compensation and has done much to discourage further foreign investment in Latin America. In 1962 U. S. investors withdrew more money from Latin America than they invested, and in the following year, 1963, Argentina, Brazil, and Peru expropriated large U. S. investments in those countries. Measures for the protection of domestic industries, such as import quotas, were widely used to protect budding industries from foreign competition. In recent years, Brazil and Argentina, followed by Chile, Cuba, Mexico, Colombia, Peru, and Uruguay, have made the greatest strides in manufacturing. In other countries, like Paraguay and the Central-American republics where industrialization has still a long way to go, manufacturing consists chiefly in the production of essential consumer goods.

**Mar, José de la.** 1788–1839. Peruvian general. b. Guayaquil. Served with SAN MARTÍN, 1820–1821. From July 1827, he served as constitutional president of Peru, ousting SANTA CRUZ. In attempting to push the Colombian troops from his country, he was defeated by BOLÍVAR, and was overthrown by GAMARRA in 1829.

**Maracaibo.** The chief port and the second largest city of Venezuela, and the capital of the state of Zulia, situated on the west shore of the narrows between Lake Maracaibo and the Gulf of Venezuela. Population 460,000 (1960). The city is set in one of the richest oil areas in the world, and the crude oil produced there has been for the most part transshipped for refinement to the islands of Aruba and Curaçao by means of shallow-draft tankers, because a sand bar prevented ocean steamers from entering the harbor. Work on a canal through the bar was begun in 1953 and has been completed. Maracaibo also exports coffee, cacao, and sugar. The city was founded in 1529 by Ambrosio Alfinger. In 1667 Maracaibo and nearby Gibraltar were attacked by a Dutch pirate, and in 1669 it was captured by the British pirate Henry Morgan, who took much treasure with him when he left. A revolt against Spain broke out here in 1799, but was easily suppressed. The discovery of oil in 1914 made Maracaibo the important city that it is today.

**Maranhão Company of Brazil.** See CHARTERED COMPANIES IN LATIN AMERICA.

**Marcos, Fray.** See NIZA, MARCOS DE.

**Mariátegui, José Carlos.** 1895–1930. Peruvian Communist, editor, and writer. At first he was an associate of HAYA DE LA TORRE, but later turned to Communism when their relationship was severed. He was editor of a literary journal and review, *Amauta*, which was founded in 1925. A bedridden, but fiery figure who constantly wrote editorials and speeches, he was famous for his book of essays *Siete ensayos de interpretación de la realidad peruana*, 1928.

**Marina, Doña.** Also called **Malinche** and

**Malintzin.** Daughter of an AZTEC chieftain, she became interpreter and mistress of Spanish conquistador Hernán CORTÉS. Forsaking her own people, she rendered invaluable service to the Spanish cause. *Malinchismo* is a word of reproach for unpatriotic Mexicans in modern times.

**Mármol, José.** 1817–1871. Argentine writer. b. Buenos Aires. Romantic poet who gained fame for his writings against tyranny and the dictator ROSAS, who had banished him to Uruguay. His best-known works are the tragic historical novel *Amalia*, 1851, the poem *Hymn to the River Plate*, and his play *El cruzado* (The Crusader). See LITERATURE.

**Márquez, José Ignacio de.** 1793–1881. Colombian president. Lawyer, orator, and political leader, and member of the Civil Party, he was elected vice-president in charge of executive power, 1832, president in 1837, and served until 1841. He concluded an agreement with Venezuela and Ecuador for the apportionment of an old foreign debt of his country, in an effort to re-establish Colombia's credit by a partial payment of this debt. The last two years of his administration suffered from several revolts.

**Márquez, Leonardo.** Mexican general who fought on the side of the conservatives during the civil war of 1858–1860. His cruelty against enemy prisoners earned him the name of *Tigre de Tacubaya* (Tiger of Tacubaya).

**Marroquín, José Manuel.** 1827–1908. President of Colombia. Political leader and philologist. He served as vice-president under Sanclemente in 1898. He assumed the presidency when Sanclemente was removed by a *coup d'état* during a bloody civil war, serving as president from 1900 to 1904. A revolution in 1903 lost Panama. He is known also as an author of books on Castilian grammar and spelling.

**Martí, José.** 1853–1895. Cuban patriot and poet. b. Cuba. Wrote a political journal, *La Patria Libre*, 1869, in which he set forth the first expression of the necessity for Cuban independence. He was imprisoned and deported to Spain, where he studied at the Universities of Madrid and Saragossa, receiving degrees in philosophy and letters, and in law. He wrote his first pamphlet, *Political Imprisonment in Cuba*, 1871. From 1881 he lived in New York City where he worked as a journalist, but his main work was organizing a new revolution in Cuba. He founded the Cuban Revolutionary Party in 1892, organizing all Cuban exiles in the United States, and inspired the Cuban revolt of 1895. He commanded rebel troops after landing in Cuba, but was killed by the Spanish in the first weeks of fighting in May 1895. His two outstanding books of poetry are *Simple Verses*, 1891, and *Ismaelillo*, 1882, the latter containing many poetic innovations which helped to create a new school of modern poetry for Latin America.

**Martínez, Maximiliano Hernández.** b. 1882. President of El Salvador. General and political leader. Served as minister of war under Araujo. Vice-president in 1931, he was chosen by a military directorate to succeed Araujo to the presidency in December of that year, and confirmed by the congress in February 1932 and was president, 1931–1934. The United States, because he was ineligible under the treaty of 1923, did not grant recognition until 1934. Elected president in 1935, he managed to have himself periodically reelected until he was forced to resign his office in 1944. El Salvador was the only country other than Japan that recognized Manchukuo (May 1934); in February 1937, El Salvador signed a trade agreement of importance with the United States. Martínez, though considered a tyrant, supported social improvements in his country, including the division of land among the peasants; homes were built for workers, and an attempt was made to raise wages. The country resigned from the LEAGUE OF NATIONS in 1937. Martínez fell from power in 1944 as a result of a nation-wide strike that had paralyzed the country.

**Martínez, Tomás.** 1812–1873. President of Nicaragua from 1857 to 1867. A conservative, he fought against William WALKER and American filibusters in 1856–1857; constitution adopted on August 19, 1858. He was defeated in a war with Honduras and El Salvador, suppressed a revolution headed by Jerez in 1863, but in general his was a prosperous and efficient administration.

**Mascates.** Portuguese, meaning peddlers. The name given in the early 18th century by the inhabitants of the capital of Olinda in Pernambuco province (Brazil) to the Portuguese immigrants who had settled near the town, but closer to the harbor, at Recife. When, at the urging of the newcomers, the Crown decided in 1710 to make a separate town of Recife, fighting broke out between the Brazilians of Olinda and the *mascates*. The fighting lasted a year and did not come to an end until the forces on both sides were promised an amnesty by a new governor of the province.

**Masonic Orders.** There have been active Masonic groups, which generally have been anticlerical in nature, in Colombia, Ecuador, Mexico, and Brazil. Many leaders of the independence movement and of later governments, particularly in Mexico and Brazil, were Masons. The most active groups have been in Mexico. During the administration of President Guadalupe VICTORIA, 1824–1829, there were two politically active Masonic lodges, the Scottish rite Masons, called *escoceses*, organized in the first decade of the 19th century, and the York rite Masons, or *yorquinos*, established in 1825. The *escoceses* were mainly conservative and centralist in their political outlook, whereas the *yorquinos* were rather liberal and federal-minded. The latter were supported by the first U. S. envoy to Mexico, Joel POINSETT, and one of their members was President Guadalupe Victoria himself. The *escoceses* lost their political influence after the failure of the conservative revolts of 1827 and 1828. The influence of the *yorquinos* declined when the organization became split over the candidates to the succession of Guadalupe Victoria, one faction supporting Vicente GUERRERO, the grand master of the *yorquinos*, and the other throwing its support to Gómez Pedraza. Freemasonry was introduced into Brazil in 1807 and thereafter became a force for the propagation of liberal ideas during the last days of the colonial era. Anticlericalism was not a feature of Brazilian Freemasonry; in fact the organization gathered many ecclesiastics into its membership. Catholic members of the Brazilian lodges were faced with a dilemma in 1865, when Pope Pius IX placed a ban on Freemasonry. Among the distinguished membership of the Masonic lodges were numbered such eminent persons as the prime minister, Baron RIO BRANCO, and even the emperor, Dom PEDRO II. The peaceful relations that had heretofore existed between the Church and the Brazilian government were disrupted by the so-called *questão religiosa* precipitated by the papal encyclical. The conflict weakened the prestige of the monarchy and Freemasonry in Brazil.

**Matamoros, Mariano.** 1770–1814. Mexican priest and patriot. He served with MORELOS Y PAVÓN in revolt from 1811 to 1814, was captured at Puruarán on January 5, 1814 and executed at Valladolid on February 3. The town of Matamoros on the Río Grande is named in his memory.

**Maté.** Also **Paraguayan Tea.** A popular South American beverage, or infusion, prepared from the dried leaves of the *Ilex paraguariensis.* The small tree or shrub, usually called yerba, whose leaves produce this drink, belongs to the same genus as the holly and is found in a wild state in Paraguay and southern Brazil. Attempts to cultivate the plant in different areas have proved successful but Paraguay has continued to be the chief source of maté. The woods in which the plants grow are called *yerbales.* The origin of maté is obscure. There are many Indian legends linked to its use but there is no agreement concerning its origin. The indigenous population prepared the beverage long before the arrival of the Spanish conquerors, who quickly developed a taste for it. The tea is prepared in a calabash or gourd by adding boiling water to the roasted and pulverized leaves. The infusion is sucked by means of a *bombilla*, a metal tube that has a perforated bulb at its end to prevent particles of the leaves from being drawn into the mouth. Maté is a bitter drink that becomes more delicious as the taste becomes accustomed to it. During the summer heat it has become popular in Paraguay to prepare cold maté, a drink usually referred to by its GUARANÍ name, *tereré.* Yerba maté is an important product of Paraguay and is also grown in Argentina and Brazil.

**Mato Grosso.** The second largest state of Brazil, 484,486 square miles in size, bounded on the north by Amazonas and Pará, on the east by Goiás, Minas Gerais, São Paulo, and Paraná, on the south and southwest by Paraguay and Bolivia, and on the west and northwest by Bolivia and the Brazilian territory of Rondônia. Population 950,000 (1960). Much of the state is covered with forests, but the area east of Campo Grande is rich grazing land. The main cities are Corumbá, situated on the Paraguay River and on the recently completed railroad from São Paulo to Santa Cruz in Bolivia, and Cuiabá, the capital of the state, on a tributary of the Paraguay River. Both cities are connected by air with Rio de Janeiro and São Paulo. South of Corumbá there are great manganese deposits, but the relative inaccessibility of the town greatly reduces the possibility of profitable exploitation. Mato Grosso was first settled in 1718, when gold mines were discovered around Cuiabá by pioneers from São Paulo. It received its name Mato Grosso (Great Forest) in 1748, when it became a separate CAPITANIA. Its first capital was Villa Bella on the Guaporé River, but Cuiabá was declared the capital in 1820. In 1822 it was made a province of the Brazilian empire. It became a state in 1889. During the war with Paraguay (1864–1870) it suffered an invasion by Paraguayan troops.

**Mauá, Irineu Evangelista de Sousa, Baron of.** 1813–1889. Brazilian financier. b. Jaguerão, Rio Grande do Sul. Studied in Europe and decided to modernize his country. He organized the *Banco do Brasil*, 1851, established first Brazilian railroad, 1854, as well as steamboat-navigation of the Amazon river and a public gas-lighting system. He was deputy for Rio Grande do Sul and took an active part in the political activities of his time. He was the author of several books concerning the industrialization of Brazil.

**Mauritz, Jan.** Full name, **Joan Mauritz Van Nassau-Siegen.** See JOHN MAURICE OF NASSAU.

**Maximilian.** Full name, **Ferdinand Maxi-**

**milian Joseph.** 1832–1867. Brother of Emperor Francis Joseph of Austria. Likeable, well-educated prince, he served as archduke of Austria, and from 1864 to 1867 was emperor of Mexico. He served in command of the Austrian navy, 1854; married Princess Charlotte (Carlota) of Belgium, 1857. French intervention in Mexico was planned by Napoleon III to collect debts, suppress liberalism, and render Mexico a French puppet state. After the French had partially conquered Mexico, a group of Mexican conservative leaders offered the throne to Maximilian in July 1863. He accepted in 1864 and arrived in Mexico City on June 12, 1864. He alienated supporters in Mexico by refusing to restore the property that the Church had had to sell under the LEY LERDO. He attempted to establish a free press. Resistance by JUÁREZ forces continued throughout his reign, and in 1866 the United States, refusing to recognize Maximilian, requested the French troops to leave Mexico; Napoleon III broke his promise to Maximilian to continue support and withdrew the troops. Maximilian decided to stay after the French left, hoping for sufficient support from Mexican conservatives. Juárez renewed his attack in 1867, and Maximilian was forced to surrender. He was condemned by court-martial and was shot at Querétaro on June 19, 1867.

**Mayapán.** One of the ancient Mayan cities of the Yucatán peninsula in Mexico. For a long period before the end of the 12th century it formed part of a league, whose other two cities were CHICHÉN ITZÁ and UXMAL. The league established peace and prosperity, but this was followed by a period during which Mayapán, with the aid of NAHUA mercenaries, dominated the peninsula. Finally the ruling theocracy of Mayapán, the Cocoms, became so tyrannical that the two other cities rebelled. Early in the 15th century, as a result of these civil wars, that marked the decline of the Mayan civilization, Mayapán was destroyed.

**Mayas.** American Indians who developed a high civilization toward the beginning of the Christian era in Guatemala, northwestern Honduras, Mexico and especially in the Yucatán peninsula and state of Chiapas. The Mayas reached an astonishingly advanced level of cultural development, excelling in the building of massive stone temples and in sculpture. They evolved a hieroglyphic system of writing that can be only partly deciphered today, an amazingly accurate calendar, and were skilled in mathematical and astronomical calculation. During the Old Empire, which lasted to about the 8th or 9th century, the Mayas lived in large city-states and were probably ruled by priests. For unknown reasons the Old Empire came to an end, and the Mayan civilization shifted to northern Yucatán where it flourished in a New Empire that lasted from about 990 to 1200. During a long period of the New Empire the three cities of CHICHÉN ITZÁ, MAYAPÁN, and UXMAL, organized in a confederation, seem to have ruled the Mayas. This was followed by a period of domination by NAHUA immigrants from central Mexico, and then by bitter civil wars, which brought about a permanent decline of Mayan civilization. At the time of the Spanish Conquest, they still maintained, however, their skill in writing, the use of the calendar, and the making of pottery and textiles. Today impressive archaeological remains of the Mayan civilization are found in northern Yucatán, especially at Chichén Itzá, and in the tropical jungles of Guatemala and Honduras. A large proportion of the inhabitants of Yucatán, southern Mexico, and Guatemala today are of Mayan descent, and the Mayan language is still spoken. In the 1840's there was a rebellion of the Mayas against Mexican rule in Yucatán, which was finally suppressed at the end of the century. See COPÁN.

**Mayorazgo.** Spanish, meaning primogeniture, the institution aiming to preserve in a family certain property in favor of the eldest son. The term may also refer to the entailed estate thus passed from father to eldest son.

**Mazorca.** Spanish, meaning ear of corn. Name given to the political organization in the service of the Argentine dictator Juan Manuel de ROSAS. The name *mazorca* was adopted as a symbol of union. Rosas' enemies derided the organization by claiming that the name should be spelled *más horca* (more gallows). The group was originally organized as the *Sociedad Popular Restauradora*, devoted to the return of Rosas to the governorship of the province of Buenos Aires. No act proved too sanguinary or brutal for these agents of Rosas.

**McLane-Ocampo Treaty of 1859.** A treaty made with the JUÁREZ government during the Mexican civil war of 1858–1860. The United States, anxious to establish a trade route between the Atlantic coast and California, was given a perpetual right of transit across the Isthmus of Tehuantepec and was allowed to bring troops into Mexico to protect its property and enforce order. The United States was to pay to the Mexican government $2,000,000 and pay American citizens, who had claims against the Mexican government, another $2,000,000. The treaty was vehemently denounced in Mexico as a sacrifice of national sovereignty, and was rejected by the U. S. Senate as likely to cause U. S. intervention in Mexico on behalf of Juárez.

**Medina Angarita, Isaías.** 1897–1953. President of Venezuela. Came from the western Andean region; general; served as chief of staff, 1935; minister of war and the navy under LÓPEZ CONTRERAS from 1935 to 1940; president of Venezuela from 1941 to 1945. A well-intentioned, honest man, he wanted to institute a democracy, but it was a difficult task. He approved an income tax and insisted on freedom of speech and press. In a fight over free elections, he was overthrown by a revolt organized by the radical ACCIÓN DEMOCRÁTICA with the help of the military in October 1945, and Medina Angarita was forced into exile.

**Medina Zavala, José Toribio.** 1852–1930. Chilean historian and bibliographer. b. Santiago. Educated at the National Institute and the University of Chile. He received a degree as advocate, 1873, and practiced law for a short time. He saw military service during the War of the Pacific. Early in life he turned to history as a career, and is considered the outstanding bibliographer in the Western Hemisphere, being well-known for historical writings and many biographies of noted Chileans. He also published collections of documents related to the history of Chile.

**Meiggs, Henry.** 1811–1877. American railroad builder. b. Catskill, N.Y. After a bus-

iness failure in California in 1854, he went to South America. He acquired fame as a builder of railroads and laid lines across unbelievably difficult terrain, completing the road from Santiago, Chile, to Valparaíso in 1863, and the Mollendo-Arequipa line in Peru in 1871.

**Mejía, Tomás.** 1823–1867. Mexican soldier. Indian chieftain from the Sierra Gorda. He supported the conservatives during the civil war of 1858–1860, and French intervention. He was captured with MAXIMILIAN at Querétaro in 1867 by JUÁREZ forces and on June 19 was executed with Maximilian and MIRAMÓN.

**Meléndez Family.** Ruling family in El Salvador for fourteen years. Upon the assassination of President Araujo in 1913, the vice-president, Carlos Meléndez, succeeded to the presidency. In August of 1914, Meléndez' brother-in-law Alfonso Quiñonez assumed the reins of the government for a brief period but relinquished the position to Meléndez in February 1915, who was again elected president for a four-year term. Quiñonez took over the presidency again in 1918, until Jorge Meléndez, brother of Carlos, was elected and began serving his term in February 1919. Quiñonez was elected president in 1923 and served until 1927.

**Melgarejo, Mariano.** 1820–1871. President of Bolívia. b. Department of Cochabamba. General; after overthrowing ACHÁ and killing BELZÚ, he established himself as president and served from 1864 to 1871. He gave up Bolivia's claims to the nitrate areas in the Atacama Desert. A callous man without scruples, he cruelly suppressed his opposition and used public funds for his own purposes. When drunk, which was a frequent occurrence, he was capable of unbelievable atrocities. Overthrown by Morales in 1871, he is often regarded as the worst of all South-American *caudillos*.

**Mello, Custodio José de.** 1845–1902. Brazilian admiral who led a revolt of the entire fleet against the PEIXOTO government on September 6, 1893. He controlled the harbor of Rio de Janeiro for six months, but was forced to leave, largely through the forceful efforts of U. S. and European warships that prevented him from bombarding or blockading the port. The blockade collapsed on March 12, 1894, and he was forced to give himself up, April 16.

**Mello Franco, Afrânio de.** 1870–1943. Brazilian lawyer and statesman. b. Minas Gerais. Renowned jurist. Minister of communications and public works, 1918–1919; head of the Permanent Brazilian Delegation to the LEAGUE OF NATIONS; member of the Permanent Court of International Justice of The Hague (World Court), 1923–1929; minister of foreign affairs under VARGAS, 1930–1933; arbitrated the dispute between Peru and Colombia over the LETICIA area in the upper Amazon. He was author of many works dealing with jurisprudence and history.

**Mendes Maciel, Antônio Vicente.** See CONSELHEIRO, ANTÔNIO.

**Mendicta Montefur, Carlos.** 1873–1960. Cuban politician. b. San Antonio de las Vueltas. He took part in the revolution against Spain, 1895–1898 and led attacks against the administrations of MENOCAL and MACHADO Y MORALES. Arrested, 1931, he was forced to flee to New York City. In 1933, after Machado was deposed, he led the opposition to GRAU SAN MARTÍN and was made provisional president of Cuba, 1934–1935. He was recognized by the United States and granted credit to the amount of $10,000,000 for the purchase of food. He was forced to resign December 11, 1935.

**Mendoza, Antonio de.** 1490–1552. First viceroy of New Spain and viceroy of Peru. Appointed by the Crown as viceroy of New Spain (Mexico) in 1529, he served, 1535–1550, and proved to be one of the ablest administrators in Spanish colonial history. After his arrival CORTÉS' influence was reduced to practically nil. Mendoza was responsible for the first printing press in the New World, 1539. He sent the CORONADO Y VALDÉS expedition into New Mexico and Colorado. Appointed to Peru, his first act in 1551 was to prohibit the use of enforced labor. He died July 21, 1552, leaving the government of Peru in the hands of the *audiencia*.

**Mendoza, Pedro de.** *ca.* 1487–1537. Spanish colonizer appointed by CHARLES V, 1534, as governor and captain general of the Río de la Plata region, an area that began at the southern limits of the Peruvian conquests and extended southward for 200 leagues. He equipped, mainly at his own expense, an expedition that left Spain in August 1535 and succeeded in reaching the estuary of the Río de la Plata early in 1536. The first colony of Buenos Aires was founded as Nuestra Señora de Santa María del Buen Ayre, 1536. In addition to attempts at colonizing and exploring the region, Mendoza undertook to open communications with Peru, which was attempted by an expedition led by Juan de Ayolas. Because of bad health Mendoza decided to return to Spain and died at sea, June 1537.

**Menocal, Mario García.** 1866–1941. President of Cuba. Engineer and political leader. Educated in the United States and worked in the Nicaraguan canal company. He rose from the ranks to major general in the war for independence, 1895–1898. He was defeated by GÓMEZ in election of 1908; served as conservative president of Cuba, 1913–1921. Wealthy himself, he was honest in politics and his first administration was efficient and one of increasing prosperity; however, he was not very popular. In 1916, he suppressed a revolt of liberals that resulted in the landing of American troops, and he was re-elected. Cuba declared war on Germany in April 1917, its chief contribution to the Allied cause being an increased sugar production. General Crowder was sent by the president of the United States to Cuba to oversee the elections of 1921 and ZAYAS Y ALFONSO was elected. Menocal's second administration had been more extravagant and corrupt, and the country was left in financial difficulties. He was defeated by MACHADO Y MORALES for the presidency in 1924, attempted to run against BATISTA in 1939–1940, but was again defeated.

**Mera, Juan León.** 1832–1899. Ecuadorian poet and novelist. b. Ambato. Best known for the novel *Cumandá*, 1871. His poems deal mainly with Indians, and he used Indian songs as models. An excellent example of his work is the poetic romance *La Virgen del sol y las melodías indígenas* (The Virgin of the Sun), which takes place at the time of the Conquest.

**Mesta.** Short for *Real corporación de la Mesta.* Live stock breeders' guild, which was transferred to the colonies from Spain. It was established in Mexico in the first part of the 16th century and extended later to the other Spanish colonies in America. At first it included many small stock raisers, but in the course of time it became more and more an organization of the rich, those owning at least 1,000 head of cattle or 3,000 sheep.

**Mestizo.** From Spanish *mixto*, meaning mixed. Half-breed; the offspring of parents of different races. In Spanish America, mestizos are mainly the descendants of white fathers and Indian mothers.

**Methuen Treaty.** Commercial treaty between Great Britain and Portugal, signed in Lisbon in 1703 by the Portuguese government and the British ambassador, John Methuen, according to which woolen goods produced in Great Britain could enter Portugal subject to tariff of 23 per cent of their value. In exchange, Great Britain allowed Portuguese wines entering England to pay a tariff one-third less than that paid on French wines. As a consequence of the treaty Great Britain was able to control a large part of Portuguese trade, including especially that with Brazil.

**Mexican Federation of Labor.** See C.T.M.

**Mexican Revolutionary Party.** See INSTITUTIONAL REVOLUTIONARY PARTY OF MEXICO.

**Mexico.** The northernmost Latin-American republic, with an area of 760,375 square miles and a population of 43,675,000 (est. 1966), of which 60 per cent are mestizo, 30 per cent Indian, and 10 per cent white. The official language is Spanish although many Indian dialects are spoken. The monetary unit is the peso; 12.59 pesos equal the U.S. dollar. The majority of the people are Roman Catholic, but there is complete separation of church and state. Mexico is a federal republic composed of 29 states with two territories and one federal district. The president is elected for six years and cannot be re-elected. There is a bicameral congress with senators elected for six years and deputies for three. Suffrage is universal. Primary education is free and compulsory up to the age of 15. There are excel-lent institutions of higher learning, particularly in the capital, Mexico City. The country is in the shape of a horn and is bounded on the north and northeast by the United States, on the south by Guatemala and British Honduras, on the west by the Pacific Ocean, and on the east by the Gulf of Mexico, Gulf of Campeche, and the Caribbean Sea. The tip of the horn is formed by the peninsula of Yucatán, which extends northward into the Gulf of Mexico. The Sierra Madre Occidental mountain range runs north and south near the western coast, and on the eastern coast the Sierra Madre Oriental runs down almost as far as Veracruz. Between these two ranges lies the great Mexican central plateau with its temperate climate, its altitude varying from 5,000 to 8,000 feet. The southern part of the plateau is the most densely populated section of the country, where the soil is fertile and farming is facilitated by adequate rainfall. The lowlands along the coasts are hot and offer an abundance of tropical vegetation. The main cities and populations (1964) are Mexico City, the capital, 5,215,000 (includes environs and suburbia), Guadalajara, 830,-000. Monterrey, 615,009, Puebla, 290,000, and the ports of Veracruz (144,000) and Tampico (180,000).

The poverty of much of the soil, the nature of the terrain, and the lack of rainfall are major obstacles to agricultural development. Important crops are coffee (Mexico is the world's fifth largest producer), corn, rice, sugar, wheat, beans, cottonseed, copra, cotton, and tobacco. There is also considerable stock raising and fishing. Rich in minerals, Mexico is the world's largest producer of silver and is a leading producer of gold, copper, lead, and zinc. There are large oil deposits, and the petroleum industry has been gaining in importance (111,800,000 barrels in 1962). Manufacturing has developed in recent years, the principal products being textiles, beverages, vegetable oils, wheat flour, cotton yarn, copper, zinc, cement, iron, and steel. The United States purchases almost three-fourths of all Mexican exports. Railroad connections amount to 17,000 miles, and there are 18,000 miles of paved roads and an almost equal amount of surfaced roads.

Among the early inhabitants of Mexico

were the MAYAS, who established a flourishing civilization in the Yucatán peninsula. Much of southern Mexico was dominated by the TOL-TECS between the 8th and 12th centuries, until they were conquered by the CHICHIMEC tribes, one of which, the AZTECS, succeeded finally in dominating the area. They established a powerful empire that extended from the central valley down to Guatemala, and east to the Gulf of Mexico. Their capital, TENOCHTITLÁN, was built on the site of present-day Mexico City. The Yucatán peninsula was discovered in 1517 by Francisco Hernández de CÓRDOBA, and two years later, in 1519, Hernán CORTÉS landed near modern Veracruz at the head of a small expeditionary force. At the time of the landing the chief of the Aztecs was MOCTEZUMA. Although vastly inferior in numbers, Cortés and his army succeeded in crushing the Aztecs, mainly because of the help they received from other Indian tribes, enemies of the Aztecs. All southern Mexico was rapidly subjected to Spanish rule by Cortés and his lieutenants, while the Indians were converted to Christianity by missionaries accompanying the conquistadors. Mexico was made a viceroyalty of the Spanish Crown under the name of New Spain, the first viceroy being Antonio de MENDOZA (ruled, 1535–1550). Northern Mexico was gradually occupied during the latter decades of the century. During the colonial period, Mexico prospered in agriculture and in mining, and the silver from its mines provided the Spanish treasury with vast wealth. It was also a center of culture as the various religious orders of the Catholic Church fostered education. Patriotic societies, whose aim was the independence of Mexico, began to form toward the end of the 18th century, but the first open revolt did not occur until 1810, when the priest Miguel HIDALGO Y COSTILLA led a bloody uprising. After the defeat of this movement and the execution, 1811, of Hidalgo, another priest, José MORELOS Y PAVÓN, took charge of the revolutionary forces, but he in turn succumbed in 1815. Paradoxically, only in 1820, when a liberal revolution in Spain frightened Mexican conservatives, did Mexican independence become possible. The conservative General ITURBIDE, who had been commissioned by the viceroy to crush anti-

Spanish guerrillas, reached an agreement in 1821 with the revolutionary GUERRERO and declared the independence of Mexico. The following year he had himself proclaimed emperor. He was soon overthrown, 1823, by a movement led by General SANTA ANNA, and when he attempted to return to Mexico from exile, 1824, he was shot. Mexico then became a federal republic, its first president being Guadalupe VICTORIA, 1825. The next thirty years were marked by great internal instability, with the federal-minded liberals vying for power with the centralist-minded conservatives strongly backed by the Church, who feared that a liberal victory would mean the end of the many privileges it was still enjoying in the country. General Santa Anna was the dominating figure of that period, making and unmaking governments, allying himself first with one faction and then with another, and leading the country's military forces in the disastrous campaign against the Texans, 1836, which resulted in the independence of that state from Mexico, and in the war against the United States, 1846–1848, arising out of the American annexation of Texas in 1845, and ending in Mexico's defeat and the loss of huge territories in the north. Santa Anna took over the government once more in 1853, but was forced into exile in 1855 by Mexican liberals, who then had most of the country behind them.

The liberals took charge and, under the leadership of such men as President Ignacio COMONFORT (1855–1857), Miguel LERDO DE TEJADA, and the full-blooded ZAPOTEC Indian Benito JUÁREZ, launched a program of reform with the aim of establishing constitutional government, abolishing the independent powers of the clergy and the generals, and stimulating economic progress by putting into circulation the properties of the Church. Laws enacted to this effect, as well as the federalist constitution in 1857, aroused bitter opposition among the conservatives and the clergy, who in 1858 provoked a civil war that was to last for three years and is called the WAR OF THE REFORM (1858–1860). The leader of the liberal forces was then Benito Juárez, who had become president in December 1857, and who, in the middle of the war, issued new decrees against the clergy, involving the confiscation without compensation of all ecclesiastical property except the actual church buildings. Juárez was victorious and was re-elected in 1861 but did not enjoy his triumph for long. The Mexican treasury was empty and the country was in ruins. When the Mexican government suspended payments on foreign debts for two years, French, English, and Spanish forces occupied Veracruz, 1862. The British and the Spaniards soon withdrew, but the French Emperor NAPOLEON III decided to take advantage of the situation and establish a Mexican empire under French control. More French troops were sent to Mexico and soon overran most of the country, while President Juárez was forced to flee north. Napoleon installed the Austrian archduke MAXIMILIAN on the Mexican throne as emperor, 1864; Maximilian's empire was short-lived, however. At the end of the American Civil War the U.S. Government made France understand that it would not tolerate the presence of French troops on the soil of an American nation, and after the French troops were withdrawn from Mexico the liberals rapidly gained the upper hand and defeated Maximilian who was captured and shot, 1867. Juárez was re-elected, 1867, and under his administration the country experienced some economic progress. Juárez was elected again in 1871 but died the following year and was succeeded by Sebastián LERDO DE TEJADA, who was overthrown in 1876 by a movement led by Porfirio DÍAZ, a lieutenant of Juárez who had distinguished himself in the war against the French. Díaz ruled the country with an iron hand, 1876–1880, and 1884–1911, ruthlessly suppressing all opposition. He surrounded himself with *científico* politicians who placed the material progress of Mexico above all other considerations, and succeeded in stabilizing finances and in modernizing the country considerably, building up communications and developing mining and industry. Most of this was done with the help of foreign capital and the result was that the exploitation of the country's resources was mostly in foreign hands. Whereas the landed classes, the middle-class bureaucracy, the army, and the Church were deriving material benefit from the Díaz regime, the Indian peasant masses, who constituted the majority of the population, were generally badly treated. Their lands became the property of wealthy *hacendados* and they themselves were reduced to peonage.

Dissatisfaciton with the Díaz dictatorship gathered strength in the first decade of the 20th century, and in 1911, a revolutionary movement led by the idealistic Francisco MADERO, son of a wealthy northern landowning family, forced the dictator into exile. Madero, however, failed to make any substantial reforms, and was overthrown and assassinated, 1913, by the reactionary general Victoriano HUERTA. The Mexican Revolution then became a civil war in the course of which rival factions alternated in power. Huerta's dictatorship was overthrown in 1914 by forces led by CARRANZA, after which Carranza came into conflict with his former allies, Pancho VILLA and Emiliano ZAPATA, the latter being a fiery Indian leader from the state of Morelos, whose sole interest was to put the Indians in possession of land. By 1916, Carranza was firmly in power, and although a fairly radical constitution, authorizing agrarian reform, guaranteeing labor many important rights, nationalizing the country's subsoil, and drastically limiting the power of the Church, was adopted in 1917, he proceeded to govern as a dictator, disregarding the provisions of the new constitution. Carranza was ousted by Álvaro OBREGÓN, under whose administration, 1920–1924, the reforms promised by the constitution of 1917 were initiated, although at a slow rate. The U.S. Government, which had been drawn into the Mexican civil conflict on several occasions (Tampico incident, Veracruz occupation, 1914, Villa's incursions into U.S. territory) and which had refused to recognize Obregón, fearing for the economic interests of its nationals under a revolutionary regime, finally gave its recognition in 1923, after a compromise on outstanding differences (Mexican foreign debt, ownership of subsoil) had been reached. The term of Obregón's successor, Plutarco Elías CALLES, 1924–1928, was marked by the government's struggle against the Church and its supporters, which often took the form of bloody clashes, by a serious conflict with the United States over the oil question, and by the growth of the power of organized labor (see C.R.O.M.). Obregón was re-elected in 1928 but was assassinated the same year.

After a succession of presidents dominated by ex-President Calles, Lázaro CÁRDENAS was elected in 1934. He was determined to speed up the reforms which had been promised by the constitution of 1917 and which by that time had almost come to a halt, and to follow an independent course, free from the *callista* influence. He soon broke with Calles, who was sent off to the United States. The more striking features of Cárdenas' program included a greatly accelerated distribution of land to the Indian peasants, the granting to labor of an important share in the political, economic, and social life of the country, a rapid expansion in education, the expropriation of foreign oil holdings, 1938, and various governmental measures designed to revive native Indian culture. Cárdenas was succeeded by General ÁVILA CAMACHO, whose administration declared war on the Axis in 1942. Miguel ALEMÁN VALDÉS was elected president, 1946–1952, and was in turn succeeded by Adolfo RUIZ CORTINES. During and after the war, emphasis on reform gave way to stress on industrial growth and on development of the country's resources. Obstacles to overcome in the economic field included inflation and a shortage of dollars. Under Ruiz Cortines, a serious effort was made to eliminate graft and corruption in government and to place the economy on a stable basis. Rising inflation made it necessary in 1954 to devaluate the peso to the level of 12.50 to the U.S. dollar. Ruiz Cortines was succeeded, 1958, by Adolfo LÓPEZ MATEOS, the minister of labor during his administration. Political stability and economic progress was continued under the new administration and the distribution of land to Indian peasants was accelerated. By the latter part of 1962, the López Mateos administration had distributed almost 30,000,-000 acres of land, more than any other administration since Cárdenas. The president promised the breakup of the last of the great estates by the end of his term of office. U.S.-Mexican relations were troubled after 1960 by Mexican sympathy for Fidel CASTRO's reform movement in Cuba, but no important issues were precipitated by the Cuban crisis. In July 1963, the U.S. and Mexican governments announced a settlement to the 100-year-old border dispute over the El Chamizal territory located between El Paso, Texas and Ciudad Juárez. A shift in the course of the Rio Grande River, the international boundary between the two countries, about 100 years ago left Mexican territory on the U.S. side of the river. The 1963 agreement gave Mexico over 437 acres of the disputed land. Gustavo Díaz Ordaz was chosen president in 1964. Under Díaz Ordaz, Mexico has accelerated its industrialization program, offering a number of incentives to speed up action. In the summer of 1965 the country suffered heavily from torrential rains.

**Mexico City.** The capital and most important city of Mexico, it is also the oldest city in North America. It has a population of approximately 3,000,000 (1960), but the urban agglomeration figure is estimated at 5,215,000 (1964). Situated in the central valley of Mexico it enjoys a cool and dry climate due to its altitude, which is 7,800 feet above sea level. In the last 30 years the city has been expanding considerably, so that today it is a sprawling metropolis with an area of about 15 square miles. Because it is built essentially on the soft soil of a lake bed, a number of heavy buildings tend to sink into the ground as is especially the case of the Palacio de Bellas Artes, containing art galleries, various auditoriums, and the national theater. Not far from this building is the heart of the city, the famous square of the Zócalo on which stand the Cathedral and the National Palace. The modern business district to the west of the Zócalo contains the Avenida Madero, the Avenida Juárez, an avenue lined with shops, and the Alameda, a large park overlooked by a number of skyscrapers on Avenida Juárez. Further to the west is the beautiful Paseo de la Reforma, a tree-shaded avenue 200 feet wide lined with modern hotels. The castle of CHAPULTEPEC is situated at the southwest end of the Paseo de la Reforma, three miles from the heart of the city. Outside of Mexico City, important points of interest are the floating gardens of Xochimilco, the shrine of the Virgin of Guadalupe, and the famous pyramids of Teotihuacán. The capital is connected by rail with most of the cities of the country and with the United States, and it has air connections with the countries of the Western Hemisphere as well as with Europe. Industrial activities in the area of Mexico City include textile mills, repair shops for railroads, iron and steel foundries, auto assembly, tires, electrical appliances, and glass works.

The city was built in the 14th century by the AZTEC Indians on the islands dotting Lake Texcoco. It was given the name Tenochtitlán, and soon grew into a powerful metropolis, from which the Aztecs dominated a large part of Mexico. Its impressive ramparts, temples and houses, and the three causeways connecting it with the mainland, aroused the admiration of the Spaniards under Hernán CORTÉS, who entered it in 1519. Two years later, in 1521, after a bloody struggle, TENOCHTITLÁN was definitely conquered for Spain by Cortés, and since the city had been reduced to ruins, the Spaniards went to work at once to rebuild it. The lake was drained and a new city, Mexico City, was erected in a relatively short time. In the colonial period it was the seat of the Spanish administration in New Spain. By the middle of the 18th century there were about 90,000 inhabitants of Spanish origin in Mexico City, and toward the end of the century there were more than 100,000. Under the Viceroy REVILLAGIGEDO (1789–1794) the city was cleaned, pavements and a public lighting system were introduced, and new buildings were erected. In 1821 the city witnessed the entrance of Agustín de ITURBIDE, and the period of independence began. American troops occupied Mexico City briefly in 1847, and Emperor MAXIMILIAN made it his capital during his brief reign (1864–1867). During the Mexican revolution (1911–1917) the capital was the prize the different warring factions strove to gain. Throughout the upheaval, as the fortunes of the struggle changed, one group was forced to give way to another in the fight for control of the city. One memorable episode was the occupation of Mexico City by the forces of VILLA and ZAPATA toward the end of 1914. Under President CÁRDENAS (1934–1940) the city was developed as an industrial center and has become the largest industrial aggregate in the country. In July 1957 the city suffered a severe earthquake in which 56 persons were killed and more than 500 injured. Damage in the city was estimated at 200,000,000 pesos. Another earthquake occurred in May 1962 but was less severe.

**Mexico City, Inter-American Conference at.** Also known as the **Conference of Chapultepec.** Conference on Problems of War and Peace that met in Mexico City in February 1945. Among the important measures adopted by the conference was the Economic Charter of the Americas and the ACT OF CHAPULTEPEC. Argentina was not represented at the conference, for it had not joined in the war against the Axis powers, but the participating powers urged that country to support all measures adopted at the conference. The United States agreed to resume diplomatic relations with Argentina and support her admission to the UNITED NATIONS Conference at San Francisco if she declared war on the Axis.

**Milpa.** In Mexico, a plot of Indian maize land.

**Mina, Francisco Javier.** 1789–1817. Spanish soldier who fought with Mexican revolutionaries. b. Navarre. He fought against FERDINAND VII of Spain in 1814 as a young guerrilla fighter, and while in exile in England, Mina met Mexican liberals including Fray Servando de Teresa Mier who urged him to help them. He landed on the coast of Tamaulipas in April 1817, with a following of adventurers and revolutionaries, predominantly Anglo-Saxon. He went to Guanajuato but was received coldly by Mexican chieftains. He won several victories but was captured and shot in October 1817.

**Minas Gerais.** The fifth largest state of Brazil and the second-ranking in population and economic importance, situated inland west of the state of Espírito Santo and north of the state of Rio de Janeiro, with an area of 228,469 square miles and a population of approximately 9,550,000 (1960). Minas Gerais is important as a producer of agricultural products such as beans, maize, garlic, coffee, tea, and rice, and especially as a source of iron. It has the only two gold mines still being exploited in Brazil. Diamonds and manganese are also mined. Of great interest are the old colonial towns of the state such as Ouro Prêto, Diamantina, and Sabará, built during the gold and diamond rush at the end of the 17th century and the early 18th century. The capital of the state, Belo Horizonte, population approximately 583,000 (1960), is situated at an altitude of 2,500 feet amidst beautiful surroundings.

The importance of Minas Gerais dates from the discovery of gold in the area at the end of the 17th century and the discovery of diamonds in 1728. After the gold strikes there was a heavy influx of population. Considerable unrest resulted from the friction between the explorers from São Paulo, or *Paulistas*, whose explorations had led to the discovery of the gold and who considered the mines as their property, and the new immigrants, called *emboabas* by the *Paulistas*, among whom there were many Portuguese. Open warfare broke out between these two elements, and in the War of the EMBOABAS, 1709–1711, the *Paulistas* were defeated. In 1710 the captaincy general of São Paulo and Minas Gerais was established, and in 1720 Minas Gerais was detached from São Paulo and became a captaincy general in its own right. In 1789 it was the seat of the TIRA-DENTES CONSPIRACY directed against the Portuguese authorities, and in 1842 an unsuccessful republican revolution took place in the province. After the establishment of the republic in 1889, the state played an important part in the political life of the country, and a number of presidents in the first decades of the 20th century hailed from Minas Gerais.

**Mineiros.** The inhabitants of the state of MINAS GERAIS, Brazil.

**Mining Industry.** In pre-Conquest days the Indians seemed to have practiced placer mining, and the natives were in possession of fairly large quantities of gold and silver. The Spaniards were fascinated by the prospect of reaping huge riches from the gathering of precious metals in the Western Hemisphere, and mining began soon after the Conquest. It started first on the island of Hispaniola (Santo Domingo), 1492–1515, and was continued in Cuba and Puerto Rico, 1515–1530. Between 1501 and 1519 production in the West Indies amounted to 8,000,000 pesos, but after 1531 mining on the mainland by far surpassed that on the islands. Mining laws soon fixed the pattern of operation. Rewards were offered for discovering new lodes, and a number of privileges were granted to miners. The Crown, as the sole owner of the subsoil, granted the right to operate the mines and collected one-fifth of the produce. Mining played an important role in the economic development of the colonies as the production of precious metals stimulated the growth of population, trade, agriculture, and industry. Toward the middle of the 16th century the growth of mining was accelerated by the use of the *patio* process, by which quicksilver was employed in the extraction of silver from the ore. The role of quicksilver made the town of HUANCAVÉLICA in Peru an important mining center, for its soil was rich in mercury. In Mexico, mining hit its stride when the great silver mines of Zacatecas and Guanajuato were discovered in 1548 and 1558, respectively. In the first 80 years of exploitation the export of bullion from Mexico to Spain amounted to approximately 37,000,000 pesos. In Peru, the important period in mining opened in 1545 with the discovery of the Potosí silver mines, which soon became the best-known in the world. Their yield was highest from 1579 to 1635, when production at times went to 7,000,000 pesos a year. The main producer of gold during the colonial period was Colombia, where the gold produced until the end of the 16th century has been estimated to have reached approximately 4,000,000 ounces. Mining in the colonies was not, however, limited entirely to precious metals. Copper, tin, and bronze had been known to the Mexican and Peruvian Indians, and copper was mined after the Conquest in Chile, Cuba, Haiti, and Venezuela. Zinc and lead were also extracted, although in limited quantities. Mining continued to be important in the 17th and 18th centuries and continued to contribute to the economic prosperity of the colonies. In the 18th century the main share of the industry fell to Mexico, whose high years were 1796 to 1805, when the yield was about 25,500,000 pesos and 27,000,000 pesos respectively. Toward the end of the colonial period new techniques were introduced into mining science and a number of prominent European engineers went to the colonies to serve as advisers to the local mine operators. A school of mines was established in Mexico City and soon became one of the most important mining institutions in America. In Brazil the first gold mine was opened at the end of the 17th century in MINAS GERAIS, and Brazilian economy, then lagging, was stimulated as the rate of the population increase of the country was greatly stepped up. Soon after the discovery in Minas Gerais there were big strikes in MATO GROSSO in 1721, and Goiás in 1726. The economic development of Goiás was helped greatly by mining, and the territory became a captaincy in 1749. Another impetus to the economic growth of the country was derived from diamond production. Diamonds were discovered in Minas Gerais in 1728 and the quantity mined in the next 100 years was approximately 3,000,000 carats. In the 19th century, mining for a long time lagged behind other economic activities but was revived in the second half of the century, largely as the result of the stimulus of foreign capital, mostly British and American. In the first decades of the 20th century the industry again soared sufficiently to occupy a predominant place in the economy in several countries. In Mexico it was silver and copper; in Chile, nitrates and copper; in Peru, copper; and in Bolivia, tin. Today the leading producers of minerals in Latin America are Bolivia, Chile, Mexico, and Peru. Brazil, Colombia, and Ecuador are also mining countries but to a lesser extent. In Bolivia, tin mining is the country's important industry, but today it has to face increasing competition from Far-Eastern producers. Mexico is still the world's leading silver producer with a yield of about 41,250,000 troy ounces in 1962. Lead and zinc are also produced abundantly in that country. Chile produces the greater part of Latin America's copper, and ranks third in world production of the metal. There are rich iron deposits in Brazil (about 6,000,-000 metric tons of iron ore are mined yearly) and Cuba, and there are also large reserves of manganese in Brazil. Coal mining is actively carried out in Argentina, Brazil, Chile, Colombia, Mexico, Venezuela, and Peru. Transportation still presents great problems in Latin-American mining. In colonial days it was a relatively simple matter. After the smelting of ores had been carried out near the mines mules and sometimes LLAMAS were used to carry the bars of bullion to the coast. But today the use of pack animals even on a large scale could not possibly solve the problems presented by the transport of metals like copper, tin, and zinc, which do not have the value of gold and silver in proportion to weight and volume. The existing railroads and airlines have not been able to remedy the situation fully, and as a result, many rich areas are still inaccessible. The use of devices such as the steam shovel, suction dredges, power drills, the link belt, and the introduction of new smelting methods have increased the yield. In recent years there has been a growing government control over the industry, which often adversely affects the interests of foreign investors who have provided the greater part of the capital behind the industry. See COPPER and IRON INDUSTRY.

**Miramón. Miguel.** 1832–1867. Mexican general who served as provisional president, 1859–1860, succeeding ZULOAGA, with headquarters at Mexico City. He was recognized by European powers and Mexican conservatives but not by the United States. He headed the reactionary forces that fought against JUÁREZ, 1859–1860. Defeated on December 22, 1860, he was forced to flee into exile but returned to Mexico to support MAXIMILIAN, 1866–1867, and although a brilliant general, he was captured and executed with him.

**Miranda, Francisco de.** 1750–1816. Venezuelan revolutionist. b. Caracas. Most famous of the precursors of Spanish-American independence, he served as captain in the Spanish army, 1781–1782, against England in Florida and in the Bahamas during the American Revolution. He was accused of smuggling in 1782 and fled from Cuba; met Alexander Hamilton and Henry Knox in the United States and Europe and tried to persuade them to aid a revolution in the Spanish colonies; fought in French Revolutionary Army; unjustly accused of treason and imprisoned; went to England in 1798; secretly organized an expedition and sailed from New York in February 1806, for Venezuela; aided by Admiral COCHRANE in the West Indies; occupied the town of Coro, but was forced to withdraw; retired to England; returned to Venezuela in 1810 and became active in politics, serving in congress; worked with BOLÍVAR and achieved success when congress issued a declaration of independence on July 5, 1811. Forced to battle Spanish, on July 25, 1812, he agreed to lay down arms if the Spanish authorities would promise to spare the lives and property of Venezuelans. This agreement was violated and Bolívar, believing Miranda had betrayed him, handed him over to the royalists. He died in prison in Spain four years later.

**Missions.** Beginning with the Conquest and all throughout the colonial period many Christian missionaries, chiefly Jesuits, Dominicans, and Franciscans, went into outlying and unexplored territories in Latin America to convert the natives and to spread the influence of the Spanish and Portuguese Crowns. The primitive establishments of the early years gave place to well-planned towns built around the missions, called *reducciones*, and protected by Spanish armed forces. There Indians from the surrounding areas were gathered by the missionaries, who taught them agriculture and various trades; at times by the use of force and through persuasion, the missionaries made them stay there permanently. In the *reducciones* the Indians usually did not own any private property and each one worked for the whole settlement under the constant supervision of the missionaries. The most famous of these missions were the Paraguayan, which flourished in the 17th century, and those established in northern Mexico and California in the 17th and 18th centuries. The missions contributed greatly to the expansion of the power of the Spanish and Portuguese kings in the New World. They were also instrumental in bringing the Indian into close contact with European civilization and in protecting him from white slave hunters. See DOMINICANS, FRANCISCANS, and JESUITS.

**Mistral, Gabriela.** Real name, **Lucila Godoy de Alcayaga.** 1889–1957. Chilean poet. b. Vicuña. Schoolteacher; secretary of the Institute of Intellectual Co-operation of the LEAGUE OF NATIONS. She filled a number of consular posts in the service of her country

and won the Nobel prize for literature, 1945. Her poetry is filled with an intense sympathy for human suffering and indignation against injustice. Her most characteristic work, *Desolación*, 1922, won world-wide fame. She is also the author of *Ternura* (Tenderness), 1924, *Cinco canciones infantiles* (Five Children's Songs), *Lagar*, 1934, and *Tala*, 1938. See LITERATURE.

**Mita.** Name given to the system of forced labor to which Peruvian Indians had been liable under INCA rule, and which was continued under Spanish domination. The word is a short form of the Indian word *mitachanacuy*, which meant, to take turns by family. Through the *mita*, public works, and especially mines, were always assured of a steady supply of workmen. The distribution of the *mita* was determined by a system of lottery. The name was also applied to the tribute the Indians paid as substitute for their personal labor. The *mita* system prevailed throughout the colonial period and was not legally abolished until 1821.

**Mitla.** Official name, **San Pablo Villa de Mitla.** A town in the state of Oaxaca, Mexico. The town is famed for the important ruins of the ZAPOTEC civilization, which are the best-preserved in Mexico. Massive buildings include temples, subterranean tombs, and the impressive "Hall of Monoliths." Mitla is believed to have succeeded Monte Albán as the ancient Zapotec capital.

**Mitre, Bartolomé.** 1821–1906. Argentine president, statesman, soldier, historian, journalist. b. Buenos Aires. Worked as a journalist in Bolivia, Chile, and Peru as an exile during the ROSAS regime; fought in defense of Montevideo against Rosas and fought in civil wars in Bolivia. He returned to Argentina and supported URQUIZA against Rosas, taking command of the artillery in the Battle of Monte CASEROS, 1852. Elected deputy to the provincial legislature of Buenos Aires, he opposed Urquiza's federal plan of government; appointed minister of war for the province, 1853; commanded provincial forces against Urquiza in the Battle of CEPEDA, 1859; defeated; governor of Buenos Aires, 1860. He defeated Urquiza in the Battle of

PAVÓN, 1861, establishing the hegemony of Buenos Aires in the Argentine union. After a brief period as president *ad interim,* he became constitutional president, 1862–1868. During his administration Argentina made great progress. He reorganized the finances, improved communications, fostered public works and immigration, and increased the authority of the national government over the provinces. He served as commander in chief of the allied forces of Argentina, Brazil, and Uruguay in the PARAGUAYAN WAR, 1864–1868; conducted a diplomatic mission to Brazil, 1872–1873; candidate for president in 1874; upon his defeat he led an unsuccessful revolt; founded *La Nación* of Buenos Aires, which is still an important newspaper there. He was again candidate for president in 1891; author of *Historia de Belgrano y de la Independencia Argentina,* 1859–76, and *Historia de San Martín y de la Emancipación Sud-Americana,* 1887.

**Mixtecs.** Indian tribe inhabiting the western half of the Mexican state of Oaxaca. Together with the ZAPOTECS and other smaller groups they make up the Zapotecan linguistic family. They were conquered by the Spaniards under ALVARADO Y MESÍA in 1522.

**M.N.R.** or **National Revolutionary Movement of Bolivia** (*Movimiento Nacional Revolucionario*). Also called, the **National Socialist Party, National Revolutionary Party,** or **Movement of National Revolution.** A Bolivian political party organized by the followers of Lieutenant Colonel Germán BUSCH, an army officer responsible for the 1937 coup that overthrew the government of Colonel David TORO. Busch took over the government, 1937, and was elected to the presidency, 1938. When the new president died under mysterious circumstances, 1939, his followers organized the M.N.R. and adopted a radical program calling for the nationalization of the tin mines, the establishment of miners' unions, and the adoption of a pro-Axis policy in World War II. After suffering a decline in prestige and influence, it played an important part in the uprising of 1943, and many members of the M.N.R. were elected to congress in 1944. During the VILLARROEL administration, 1943–1946, it enjoyed official support and a number of M.N.R. members received posts in the government, among them the M.N.R. leader, Víctor PAZ ESTENSSORO, who became minister of finance. With the violent overthrow of the Villarroel dictatorship, 1946, the M.N.R. suffered a severe blow and many of its leaders were either killed or driven into exile. The party was not permitted to participate in the 1947 elections but did take part in the congressional elections of 1949. Unusual success at the polls encouraged party leaders again to attempt revolutionary methods to gain control of the government and led to a revolt verging on civil war, 1949. The election that was held in May 1951 gave the M.N.R. candidate, Paz Estenssoro, a sweeping victory. The election victory was annulled by the incumbent government but Paz Estenssoro succeeded in gaining control of the government by means of a popular revolt in April 1952. In May 1956, the party candidate, Hernán Siles Zuazo, was elected to succeed Paz Estenssoro, and in 1960 and 1964 Paz Estenssoro was re-elected. The party has been plagued by dissension within its ranks in recent years. In 1960 Walter Guevara Arze was chosen by a right-wing faction of the party, known as the Authentic M.N.R. (P.M.N.R.A.) and later as the Authentic Revolutionary Party (P.R.A.), as its candidate for the 1960 election. In 1961 further fragmentation of the party took place as several right- and left-wing splinter groups opposed M.N.R. policies. Conflict within the party caused the formation of two distinct groups in 1963, the leftists under Juan Lechín Oquendo and the orthodox members called the Paz Estenssoritos. In the 1964 elections the M.N.R. met strong opposition from the Popular Bolivian Alliance, a coalition of four major parties that included the Bolivian Socialist Falange (F.S.B.) and the Authentic Revolutionary Party (P.R.A.) but Paz Estenssoro was elected only to be overthrown later in the same year by General René Barrientos Ortuño, who held elections in 1966 and was elected president.

**Mocambo** or **mucambo.** In Brazil, a term referring to a fugitive-slave (*mocambeiro*) settlement (see QUILOMBO). Also, a hidden pasture for cattle or a hut in the woods.

**Moctezuma I.** Also, **Motecuhzoma** or **Montezuma.** *ca.* 1390–1464. AZTEC (Mexican) chief. Occupied the throne at the death of his brother Itzcoatl. His reign was characterized by many victorious wars that considerably aggrandized his territory. He governed with an iron hand, gave much power to the Aztec priests, instituted new religious ceremonies, and continuously offered human sacrifices to the gods. After the inundation of Tenochtitlán (Mexico City), Moctezuma ordered an enormous three-league-long wall built to protect the imperial city from further floods.

**Moctezuma II.** 1466–1520. AZTEC chief. b. Tenochtitlán (Mexico City). Occupied the throne in 1502; together with the kings of Texcoco and Tlacopán he attacked the republic of Tlaxcala, but was defeated on several occasions; fought against the MIXTECS and the ZAPOTECS, 1505, taking many prisoners who, in accordance with the prevailing custom, were sacrificed to the gods. He allowed the Spaniards under CORTÉS to enter Tenochtitlán on November 8, 1519, apparently because of a superstitious belief that they were agents of the god QUETZALCOATL; seized as a hostage by Cortés. In June 1520, when his people revolted against the Spaniards, he tried to calm them by haranguing them from the walls, but was severely wounded by stones thrown at him and died several days later, June 30, 1520. Moctezuma was extremely despotic, compelling the nobles of the Empire to walk barefoot in his presence and forcing them to leave their children as hostages whenever they left the court. He loved pomp and luxury and built many palaces for himself.

**Moderados.** Spanish, meaning moderates. Name given to the middle-of-the-road republicans who frequently dominated the Mexican political scene for some 30 years after the establishment of the republic in 1823. Composed mostly of the upper and professional classes of CREOLES, they favored constitutional government, and were opposed both to conservative demands for authoritarian rule under a monarchy, and to liberal demands for an attack on clerical wealth and power. With the outbreak of civil war between liberals and conservatives, 1858–1860, the *moderados*

ceased to play an effective role in Mexican politics.

**Molina Enríquez, Andrés.** Mexican author and anthropologist. Considered the intellectual father of agrarian reform and of Article 27 of the Constitution of 1917. He is the author of *Los Grandes Problemas Nacionales,* 1909, an attack on the agrarian policy of DÍAZ, which gained wide attention. He advocated restoration of the Indian system of communal landownership (EJIDO).

**Monagas, José Gregorio.** 1773–1858. President of Venezuela, 1851–1855. Put into office by his brother José Tadeo, he signed into law the ABOLITION OF SLAVERY, 1854.

**Monagas, José Tadeo.** 1784–1868. President of Venezuela. Liberal leader, general, and statesman. He fought with BOLÍVAR in the War for Independence, 1812–1821; rebelled against PÁEZ in 1831; defeated. He served as president of Venezuela, 1846–1851, 1855–1858. Virtually a dictator, he revised the country's constitution in 1857; was finally overthrown by a revolution in 1858 and sent into exile.

**Moncada, José María.** 1868–1945. President of Nicaragua, 1929–1932. Liberal; took leading role in the overthrow of ZELAYA in 1909; military general and principal leader of the revolutionary army, 1925–1928; elected president under supervision of United States, November 4, 1928, and agreed to have American officers supervise the congressional election of 1930.

**Monroe Doctrine.** A statement of U. S. policy made by President James Monroe in his message to Congress on December 2, 1823, although largely written by Secretary of State John Quincy Adams. The United States was alarmed by the threat of French intervention, supported by the powers of the so-called Holy Alliance (Austria, Prussia, and Russia), with the purpose either of restoring Spanish rule over the newly-liberated Spanish-American republics or of imposing monarchical government. In August British Foreign Secretary George Canning had suggested a joint Anglo-American declaration against such intervention, but the U. S. government preferred to act independently. The most important section of the Doctrine declared that: "With the Governments who have declared their independence and maintained it . . . we could not view any interposition for the purpose of oppressing them, or controlling in any other manner their destiny, by any European power in any other light than as the manifestation of an unfriendly disposition towards the United States." In another part of his message to Congress, with reference to Russian designs on the Oregon Territory, Monroe declared that "the American continents, by the free and independent condition which they have assumed, and maintain, are henceforth not to be considered subject to future colonization by any European powers." These positive principles were accompanied by two negative principles: the United States would not interfere with the existing colonies of European powers and would not participate in the wars of European powers in matters relating to themselves.

The Monroe Doctrine had little immediate influence on events, Latin America owing its security primarily to the diplomatic support of Great Britain. It was restated by President Polk in 1845, with reference to English and French diplomatic activities in Texas and British interest in Oregon and California, and was thenceforth regarded as a permanent principle of U.S. foreign policy. Its most important applications were in 1850, when British expansion in Central America was checked by the CLAYTON-BULWER TREATY; in 1867, when the French intervention in Mexico was terminated as a result of diplomatic pressure; and in 1895, when the United States insisted that a boundary dispute between British Guiana and Venezuela be settled by arbitration. In 1904, President Theodore ROOSEVELT announced what became known as the ROOSEVELT COROLLARY to the Monroe Doctrine, declaring that if a Latin-American republic failed to respect its obligations, the United States must prevent intervention by European powers by intervening herself. The Roosevelt Corollary was applied in the Dominican Republic, Haiti, and Nicaragua, but was strongly criticized throughout Latin America, causing the whole Monroe Doctrine

to be denounced as an expression of Yankee imperialism. The Corollary was repudiated in the CLARK MEMORANDUM written in 1928. At the Pan-American conferences in the 1930's the United States increasingly made it clear to the Latin-American nations that it did not consider the Monroe Doctrine to be an instrument that it might use to dominate its neighbors, but rather an instrument to be used by all the Pan-American nations for their mutual defense of the hemisphere. The ACT OF HAVANA (1940), in which the nations of Latin America and the United States jointly declared their intentions to prevent European possessions in the New World from falling into hostile hands, was an important step toward multilateralization of the Monroe Doctrine. The concept of a multilateral Monroe Doctrine was expanded in 1945 with the ACT OF CHAPULTEPEC and in 1947 with the Rio Pact, both of which have emphasized Pan-American solidarity and have created a hemispheric defense alliance. These developments were carried further by the establishment in 1948 of the ORGANIZATION OF AMERICAN STATES. The advent of a Communist regime in Cuba since 1959 has recently provoked statements concerning the Monroe Doctrine, but no use of force to implement the doctrine has been involved. Soviet Premier Khrushchev declared his intention to support Cuba and stated that the Soviet Union considered that the Monroe Doctrine had outlived its usefulness and was now defunct. President Eisenhower replied reaffirming the applicability of the doctrine to the situation in Cuba and warning the Soviets to keep out of the Western Hemisphere. President Kennedy did not invoke the doctrine in relation to the Cuban problem during his administration. Thus, the Monroe Doctrine has not been invoked in recent years but, goaded by Nazism and Communism, has been increasingly expanded into a multilateral doctrine belonging to all of the republics of the Western Hemisphere.

**Montalvo, Juan.** 1832–1889. Ecuadorian essayist and writer. b. Ambato. Renowned as a liberal thinker who wrote in opposition to GARCÍA MORENO from exile in Colombia, he was the author of many works reminiscent of

Cervantes; friend of, and had influence over Eloy ALFARO.

**Montaña.** Spanish, meaning mountain or a mountainous area. In Peru and Ecuador, the semi-tropical zone on the eastern slopes of the Andes. It corresponds to a similar zone in Bolivia known as the YUNGAS.

**Monte Albán.** Great ceremonial center of ZAPOTEC–MIXTEC civilization outside the city of Oaxaca in Mexico. It is an important archaeological site where ruins of pyramids and temples are found. Considerable gold and jewels were discovered there in 1932.

**Monte Caseros, Battle of.** See CASEROS, BATTLE OF.

**Montejo, Francisco de.** *ca.* 1484–1550. Spanish explorer. Attempted to conquer and govern Yucatán, 1527, having been commissioned an *adelantado* by CHARLES V, but there were constant revolts among the natives and the region was not finally subdued until after 1541. He was succeeded by his son and namesake.

**Montenegro, Roberto.** b. 1885. Mexican artist. b. Guadalajara. Best-known for his surrealist murals, he was the first director of the Museum of Mexican Popular Art, 1934.

**Montero Rodríguez, Juan Esteban.** b. 1879. Chilean lawyer, university professor, political leader, and president. b. Santiago. During the days of political unrest in July and August of 1931, Montero was twice minister of the interior, vice-president, and acting president; elected president in October 1931; served from November 1931 to June 1932. He co-operated closely with congress and governed according to the constitution, but economic conditions were so bad that he was obliged to resign when confronted by a coup d'etat.

**Montes, Ismael.** 1861–1933. President of Bolivia. Lawyer, soldier and statesman. President, 1904–1909; minister to England, 1911; again president, 1913–1917; minister to France, 1917; lived in France in exile from 1920. He returned to Bolivia to head the Liberal Party in 1928. His was an able and progressive administration during which

Bolivia enjoyed a period of peace and prosperity.

**Monteverde, Juan Domingo.** 1772–1823. Spanish naval officer who led a force into Trujillo and defeated the Venezuelan patriots in the War for Independence, 1812. Brutal in his massacre of the patriots he forced MIRANDA on July 25, 1812, to sign the Capitulation of San Mateo. On July 30 he entered Caracas, tricked Miranda by not living up to his agreement, and gave BOLÍVAR a passport to leave Venezuela.

**Montevideo.** The capital of Uruguay and of the department of the same name. Population approximately 1,200,000 (est. 1963), which is about one-third of the entire population of Uruguay. It was built on the north shore of the Río de la Plata on Horseshoe Bay. The 500-feet-high cone across the bay is the hill which presumably gave the city its name. There are two water accesses, an inner port and an outer one, separated by breakwaters, handling most of the country's foreign trade and enabling large ocean liners to dock there. The city, one of the cleanest and most attractive of South America, contains parks and museums, and while it has, itself, more than half a dozen fine beaches, it is the starting point for a number of beautiful resorts situated to the east on the Atlantic Ocean. Important buildings include the Cathedral, the huge Palacio Salvo, the Cabildo, and the Government Palace. The city is connected by rail and air as well as by ship with neighboring Latin-American republics. It is the industrial center of Uruguay, the main activities being meat packing, flour milling, clothing, and textile manufacturing. Montevideo was started in 1726 and officially founded in 1729 by Bruno Mauricio de Zabala. The city began to prosper in 1777, after the viceroyalty of La Plata was created in 1776, and when restrictions on trade between Montevideo and Spanish ports were removed. In 1807 the British occupied the city briefly and subsequently it found itself in the middle of fighting among its own citizens, Spaniards, Brazilians, and Argentines. It suffered an epic nine-year siege, 1843–1851, by Juan Manuel ROSAS, the Argentine dictator. It has considerably expanded in the 20th century and has been the site of a number of international conferences. In December 1939 the German battleship *Graf Spee* took refuge in its harbor after a pursuit by British warships, and was scuttled by its captain after Uruguayan authorities had ordered the ship to leave. U. S. President Eisenhower visited the city in March 1960, and although he was warmly received, his visit was marred by demonstrations of students who were sympathetic to Fidel CASTRO's reform program in Cuba and antagonistic toward the attitude of the U. S. government toward the Cuban government.

**Montevideo, Conference of.** The Seventh International Conference of American States, meeting in December 1933. It adopted an Antiwar Treaty of Nonaggression and Conciliation, providing for the peaceful settlement of all disputes between American states, and a Convention on the Right and Duties of States, declaring "that no State has the right to intervene in the internal or external affairs of another." In accepting this convention, the United States reserved its rights "by the law of nations as generally recognized." The United States accepted the Latin-American doctrine of nonintervention without any reservations at the CONFERENCE OF BUENOS AIRES in 1936.

**Montevideo Conference of 1941.** A meeting attended by Argentina, Bolivia, Brazil, Paraguay, and Uruguay in February 1941, at Montevideo, Uruguay. The aim of the conference was to promote closer economic cooperation between these states. The treaties signed provided among other things, for reciprocal preference for each other's products; for freer communications; for the promotion of tourist trade; for a regional parcel-post system; and for the setting up of a regional headquarters to put the treaties into effect.

**Montezuma.** See MOCTEZUMA.

**Montonera.** An undisciplined group of GAUCHO horsemen (or cavalry) who usually fought on the federalist side in the civil wars that marked the first years of independence in Argentina. Their leaders controlled most of Argentina outside the province of Buenos Aires.

**Montt Álvarez, Jorge.** 1845–1922. Chilean naval officer and president. b. Casablanca. Entered naval school, 1858; participated in the war with Spain, 1864–1866, and in the War of the Pacific, 1879–1883; named maritime governor at Valparaíso, 1887; commander of the navy in uprising against President BALMACEDA FERNÁNDEZ, 1891; became provisional president of Chile in April 1891 and elected to serve, 1891–1896. Although an honest administrator, he possessed few qualifications for the presidency. He reorganized the navy and the army of Chile; wanted to establish the gold standard and create a sound financial government policy but was hampered in his work by parliamentary opposition.

**Montt Montt, Pedro.** 1848–1910. President of Chile, son of Manuel MONTT TORRES. Defeated in the presidential campaign of 1901. Overwhelmingly elected in 1906 for a five-year term, his administration was primarily concerned with the building of railways and establishment of economic and financial operations, but he was prevented from developing an effective program because of the opposition of congress. He was supported for the presidency by the new National Union or National party, and by the Democratic Radicals. In 1910 Montt went to Europe for treatment of a serious illness and died in Bremen, Germany, before completing his term of office.

**Montt Torres, Manuel.** 1809–1880. President of Chile. b. Petorca. Educated on a scholarship in the National Institute; rector of the National Institute, 1835–1840; elected to the chamber of deputies, and chosen president of that body, 1840. During the administration of BULNES, 1841–1851, he served as minister of the interior on two occasions, and as minister of justice, worship, and public instruction. He saw to the abolition of the law of primogeniture; served as president of Chile for two five-year terms, 1851–1861. His administration was efficient and noted for progress in education, tax reform, and the construction of roads, railways, and telegraph service. Upon leaving the presidency in 1861, he became president of the supreme court; later elected senator; served as a counselor of state; sent on a diplomatic mission to Peru.

**Mora, José María Luis.** 1794–1850. Mexican thinker and political leader, one of the chiefs of the liberal party. Brilliant economist. Closely associated with GÓMEZ FARÍAS, Mora was the theoretician of Mexican liberalism and played an important role in the congress of 1833, which enacted a series of far-reaching reforms; in charge of education under Gómez Farías, 1833–1834; driven into exile by SANTA ANNA, 1834; went to England and visited Italy, 1838; appointed minister plenipotentiary in London by Gómez Farías, when the latter returned to power, 1847. Mora died in Paris. He was the author of *México y sus revoluciones*, 1836, *Catecismo político de la federación mexicana*. He had an important influence on Mexican political thought from 1855 to 1861.

**Mora Fernández, Juan.** b. 1784. First president of Costa Rica, serving from 1824 to 1833. b. San José. He established an efficient government, improved the economic and financial conditions of the country, and was succeeded by José Rafael de Gallegos, 1833–1835.

**Mora Porras, Juan Rafael.** 1814–1860. President of Costa Rica. After a period of seven years of political unheaval, Mora established a stable government, 1849–1859. He restored order, diminished the influence of the army, and fought the filibusters under WALKER in Nicaragua. Overthrown by a conspiracy, 1859, he was exiled, and then attempted an unsuccessful counterrevolution in which he was captured and shot.

**Moraes Barros, Prudente José de.** 1841–1902. President of Brazil. b. Itu (São Paulo). Studied law in São Paulo; member of legislature, 1866; from 1885 on, he openly manifested republican leanings in the national congress; governor of São Paulo, 1889; member of the Constitutional Congress, 1890; president of the senate, 1891–1894; elected President of the Republic in 1894, serving until 1898; he ended the civil war raging in the state of Rio Grande do Sul, 1895. He was considered the first "civilian president" of Brazil.

**Morazán, Francisco.** 1799–1842. President of the CENTRAL AMERICAN FEDERATION b. Honduras. Entered political life after Honduras gained its independence, 1821; helped to organize the new government; distinguished himself in the revolt led by Father DELGADO against ARCE, 1827–1830; elected president of the Central American Federation and served, 1830–1840, but failed to keep the country united and was forced to flee to Peru. He formed an army and invaded Costa Rica in the hope of reorganizing the Federation in 1842, but was captured, court-martialed, and executed on September 15, 1842.

**Morelos y Pavón, José María.** 1765–1815. Mexican priest and patriot. b. Valladolid (today Morelia) in the modern state of Michoacán. Worked as a laborer on an hacienda until the age of 25; studied at College of San Nicolás, Valladolid, under HIDALGO; was a priest at Carácuaro, Michoacán. He joined Hidalgo's uprising against Spain in 1810, was sent by Hidalgo to the south to organize revolution there, and took over leadership of the revolutionary forces after Hidalgo's death, 1811. A general of the first order, he waged such successful warfare on the royalists that within two years he controlled the whole of southern Mexico except the towns of Mexico, Puebla, and Veracruz. He called the congress of Chilpancingo, 1813, which proclaimed the independence of Mexico, and began to draft a constitution providing, among other things, for universal suffrage and a system of indirect elections, an executive department of three persons, and a supreme court. Morelos believed in racial equality, in the abolition of the FUEROS of the clergy and the army officers, and in breaking up of the great HACIENDAS into small holdings for the peasants. These ideas sketched by him at Chilpancingo, became the program of Mexican reformers for the following 100 years. After Chilpancingo the tide of war turned, and the revolutionary forces suffered defeat after defeat. Morelos was captured and executed on December 22, 1815.

**Moreno, Mariano.** 1778–1811. Lawyer, leading revolutionist of Buenos Aires. Secretary of military and political affairs in the revolutionary junta, 1810–1811, he sent expeditions to Paraguay and Upper Peru (Bolivia) to extend the authority of Buenos Aires to these regions, and ordered the execution of LINIERS and others for counterrevolutionary activities. He was founder and editor of the *Gaceta de Buenos Aires.* A convinced unitarian, he resigned from the junta in December 1810, when it decided to admit a number of provincial delegates. He died on a diplomatic mission to Europe.

**Morínigo, Higinio.** b. 1897. President of Paraguay. Army officer and political leader; served as minister of war from May to September, 1940, then was made provisional president when ESTIGARRIBIA was killed in an airplane crash; assumed absolute power in November 1940. Elected president for five-year term, 1943, he controlled the press and no word of criticism against the government was allowed. He ruled as a dictator and suppressed as many as 26 revolts during the first seven years of his administration. Despite suppression of political liberties, progress was made in education, health, sanitation, and in the economic condition of the country. Removed from office in June 1948, by a coup d'etat led by Colorado Party members, he was forced to flee the country.

**Morones, Luis N.** Mexican labor leader. Started as an electrical worker in the Federal District; member of *Casa del Obrero Mundial;* secretary general of the C.R.O.M. (*Confederación Regional Obrera Mexicana*), 1918, which was a craft-union organization somewhat like the A.F. of L. in the United States; leader of the C.R.O.M.'s *Grupo Acción* of 18 members who entered the field of politics in 1919 as a Mexican labor party; federal deputy, 30th and 31st legislatures; possessed great influence during administration of OBREGÓN, 1920–1924. When CALLES came to power, Morones was made minister of industry, commerce, and labor with the authority to enforce labor and industrial laws. Corrupt and open to graft, he was the worst type of labor leader but he kept labor satisfied with Calles, which was the reason for his appointment. Under the PORTES GIL administration the C.R.O.M. lost control of labor and became almost bankrupt, but Morones remained wealthy, although he lost his power. He was deported to the United States, 1936, but later returned to his homeland and to the leadership of the then ineffective C.R.O.M.

**Morrow, Dwight Whitney.** 1873–1931. Lawyer, banker, and diplomat of the United States. b. West Virginia. Partner in the banking firm of J. P. Morgan & Co., 1914–1927; U. S. ambassador to Mexico, 1927–1930; U. S. delegate to the London Conference, 1930; U. S. senator from New Jersey, 1930–1931. He succeeded in working out peacefully the oil and religious problems to the satisfaction of both Mexico and the United States, from 1927 to 1930.

**Mosquera, Tomás Cipriano de.** 1798–1878. President of Colombia. Served under BOLÍVAR; brigadier general at age of 30; president of New Granada, 1845–1849. An extreme conservative backed by the army and the Church during this administration, but later, when governor of the state of Cauca, he broke with the conservatives and went over to the liberals under General OBANDO. He headed the revolt of 1860–1861 and assumed power, 1861–1863. An assembly created the United States of Colombia and voted him dictatorial powers. He was elected president, 1863–1864, and again for 1866–1867. An ambitious and often unscrupulous leader, he was deposed in 1867 and banished from the country for a period of three years.

**Mosquito Coast** or **Miskito Coast.** Name given to a large section of the Caribbean coast of Nicaragua, because of the Mosquito or Miskito Indians who inhabit the area. The name is sometimes inaccurately used to designate the entire eastern seaboard of Nicaragua, and often given to the adjoining region of Mosquitia in Honduras. The area may be more accurately defined as the narrow strip, about 40 miles wide, extending from the Huahua or Wawa River south to the Rama River, a length of about 225 miles. Although discovered by COLUMBUS on his fourth voyage, 1502–1504, the Mosquito Indians did not come into contact with Europeans until the 17th century. As a result of the association with white and Negro peoples they are now a mixed race. They became subjects of a British protectorate in the 1830's. The activities of the British on the Mosquito Coast were regarded with disapproval by the United States. By the CLAYTON-BULWER TREATY of 1850, it was agreed that neither power could exercise dominion over any part of Central America, but Great Britain insisted that this proviso should not be interpreted retroactively. In 1860, however, after ten years of controversy, a treaty was signed with Nicaragua according to which Great Britain gave up its protectorate under the provision that the Mosquito Indians would be allowed to live in a reservation under their own government.

**Mountains.** Most of the mountains of Latin America are linked into one enormous chain, the *Cordillera*, which extends from northern Mexico to the Antarctic at Cape Horn. There are few gaps in the huge range, which includes the Sierra Madre of Mexico and the Andes of South America. The highest peaks (20,000 to 23,000 feet) are found in the Andes, where are found also some of the highest capitals in the world (La Paz, Bolivia, 11,910 feet; Quito, Ecuador, 9,400 feet; Bogotá, Colombia, 8,600 feet). The Cordillera constitutes an almost impassable barrier to east-west movement in many parts of the continent, but at the same time provides much-needed temperate zones in the tropical climates of Latin America. Much of the population of the tropical climates is concentrated on the high plateaus created by the mountain chain. There are numerous volcanoes in the mountain mass of the Cordillera, and earthquakes are an ever-present danger. The Cordillera is rich in minerals, and this factor has contributed a great deal to the prosperity of Latin America. Apart from the Cordillera, which in South America separates the Pacific coast countries from the lowlands to the east, the Brazilian plateau constitutes an important mountainous mass. Much lower than the Cordillera (average elevation 1,500 to 4,000 feet), it occupies an area of nearly 1,000,000 square miles and contains much of Brazil's population as well as much of the country's economic wealth. There is an additional mountainous area in the Guayanas and in southeastern Venezuela, much of it still un-explored. Finally, a great deal of the surface of Haiti, of the Dominican Republic, and of Cuba is mountainous, with some elevations in eastern Cuba rising to heights above 8,000 feet.

**Muñoz Marín, Luis.** 1898–      . Governor of Puerto Rico. b. San Juan. Son of the Puerto Rican patriot Luis Muñoz Rivera; spent much of his youth in New York and Washington; graduated from Georgetown University; secretary, Puerto Rican commissioner to the U.S. Congress, 1916–1918; member, Puerto Rican Socialist Party; member, Liberal Party, 1926; editor and publisher of *La Democracia;* urged complete independence for Puerto Rico; leader of Movement for Latin-American Unity; senator, 1932. Expelled from the Liberal Party, 1937, he organized the Popular Democratic Party (*Partido Popular Democrático* or P.P.D.), 1938. He disassociated himself from the independence movement believing that the island was not prepared for the economic responsibilities of independence or statehood; president of the senate, 1941–1948. Co-operating with the governor appointed by the U.S. government, he was responsible for the program to redistribute large landholdings, to improve the island's housing conditions, and to establish industrial and farm development corporations. He worked for economic improvement and self-government under U.S. tutelage. After World War II, he began "Operation Bootstrap," an accelerated program for economic growth and development. He was elected governor, 1948, when the U.S. Congress passed a law giving the islanders the right to elect their own chief executive, and was re-elected, 1952, 1956, 1960. Eminently successful in strengthening political democracy in Puerto Rico, establishing a program of economic growth for the island, and in giving the Puerto Rican people a sense of self-assurance and confidence they did not possess, he has worked patiently and successfully for gradually increasing autonomy and for the betterment of the Puerto-Rican people. He received the Presidential Medal of Freedom from President Lyndon Johnson of the United States, December 1963. He is the author of *Barrones,* 1917, co-author of *Madre Haraposa,*

1917, and contributed the section on Puerto Rico for *These United States*, 1925.

**Muñoz Rivera, Luis.** 1857–1916. Puerto Rican political leader and poet. b. Barranquitas. In the last years of Spanish rule, he demanded autonomy from Spain in editorials in the newspapers *El Pueblo* and *La Democracia*. He was a member of the autonomous government, 1898–1899. After the victory of the United States in the SPANISH-AMERICAN WAR, he went to the United States, and upon his return he became leader of the Federal Party.

**Murtinho Tariff.** A tariff put into effect by the Brazilian statesman Joaquim Murtinho in 1900 during the administration of President CAMPOS SALLES, 1898–1902. Murtinho believed that Brazilian coffee, which was then beginning its boom, would be damaged by a policy of excessive protectionism favoring Brazil's infant industry, since coffee growers would have to purchase European imports at high prices. Accordingly, his tariff was sufficiently high to be fair to industry, and to provide the federal government with adequate revenue and yet low enough to satisfy the coffee interests.

**Mutis, José Celestino.** 1732–1808. Spanish priest, physician, and naturalist. b. Cádiz. Went to New Granada (Colombia) where he served as physician to the Spanish viceroy in 1760. He collected many plants, making a special study of the various species of *cinchona*. A disciple of Linnaeus, he headed a botanical expedition for the study of plants, animals, and minerals in New Granada, sent out by the archbishop-viceroy Gondora. As a teacher in Bogotá he aroused a great deal of interest in science. He wrote the unfinished *Flora de Bogotá* that described thousands of specimens and had accurate, careful drawings of tropical plants, and received much attention among naturalists in Europe.

**Nabuco de Araujo, Joaquim.** 1849–1910. Brazilian liberal who fought for the ABOLITION OF SLAVERY; noted historian; statesman and diplomat; author of *O Abolicionismo,* a pamphlet against slavery, and *Um estadista do Imperio* (3 vols., 1897–1899), an important historical study. Largely responsible for the RIO BRANCO LAW of 1871, he was the first Brazilian diplomat with the rank of ambassador to represent his government in the United States, 1905–1910.

**Nacional Financiera** or **NF.** The foremost economic development agency of the Mexican government. NF was originally created in 1933 as a semi-private company to promote the sale of rural real estate. Its purpose was expanded in 1934 when it was given extensive control over enterprises in which the government had economic interest; it was also given the task of creating a Mexican stock market. Until 1941, however, NF operated mainly as an agricultural land credit agency. A new charter granted in the latter part of 1940 gave NF the right to regulate the securities market, provide funds for those sectors of the national economy where other credit sources were inadequate, promote capital investment in industry, and to act as trustee in the issuing of public securities. Interest rates on long-term credits were modest compared with those usually charged by Mexican individuals or lending agencies. The organization became an increasingly influential factor in the economic life of the country during the war years. In 1947 its mandate was again broadened, and it became the only agent authorized to negotiate foreign loans. Since

that time it has been eminently successful in obtaining needed credits from foreign sources to expand economic development in Mexico. In most NF operations the goal of making profits has been minimized, and it has adhered to its purpose of financing economic development with low-cost loans. In 1959 approximately 10 per cent of its funds was invested in public securities, while 90 per cent was invested in securities issued by private enterprises. Present plans include greater emphasis on agricultural improvements and on smaller industries requiring less capital investment.

**Nahuas.** Mexican Indians. The first of the Nahua-speaking tribes in Mexico, the TOLTECS, moved south into Mexican territory from a region along the Pacific coast far to the north. By the 9th and 10th century they had established a hegemony over a large part of south and central Mexico. Their capital, Tula, was established to the north of the Valley of Mexico, near the more ancient city of TEOTIHUACÁN. New Nahua invaders, the CHICHIMECS, came from the north after the Toltecs had entered a period of decline in the 12th century. These later Nahuas, seven tribes according to legend, settled around the lakes of the Valley of Mexico. Tribal wars brought about the rise of the AZTECS who had established their capital, TENOCHTITLÁN, on the islands of Lake Texcoco early in the 14th century. One hundred years later the Aztecs were the dominant Nahua tribe in the valley and had extended their control to the isthmus of Tehuantepec and to the east and west coasts of Mexico. The Nahua, or Nahuatl, language is the mother tongue of many Mexican Indians and is widely spoken in Mexico today.

**Napoleon I.** Full name, **Napoleon Bonaparte.** 1769–1821. Emperor of the French. When he took over Spain and appointed his brother Joseph king in 1808, he sent agents to the Spanish colonies. All attempts to force French influence in Latin America failed, and the French occupation of Spain led directly to Spanish-American independence movements that began in 1810. The Republic of Haiti gained its independence from France shortly before Napoleon became emperor, thereby becoming the first Latin-American country to free itself from European domination.

**Napoleon III of France.** Full name, **Charles Louis Napoleon Bonaparte.** 1808–1873. Son of Louis Bonaparte and nephew of NAPOLEON I. Proclaimed himself emperor, as Napoleon III, 1852; sent French army to Mexico, 1861, to enforce payment of debts due to French citizens, and to aid the clerical-conservative faction that had recently been defeated by the Mexican liberals headed by JUÁREZ; dreamed of establishing a French-Catholic empire in America, 1863–1867. After the French had occupied the chief Mexican cities, he sent Archduke MAXIMILIAN of Austria to Mexico and installed him as a puppet-emperor in 1864. Thwarted by the Mexican people under Juárez and the attitude of the United States, he was forced to recall the French army from Mexico, 1867. Shortly afterward Maximilian was captured and executed by the Mexican patriots.

**Nariño, Antonio.** 1765–1822. b. Bogotá. Colombian patriot who was arrested and exiled to Africa, 1795, for printing and distributing to Colombia, Venezuela, and Peru, copies of the French *Declaration of The Rights of Man and the Citizen*, printed in Spanish in New Granada (Colombia). He returned to New Granada, and when president of Cundinamarca, he undertook a campaign against the Spanish, but although at first successful, he was captured in May 1814, taken to Spain, and there freed. Upon his return he was made vice-president by BOLÍVAR, 1821. He

was regarded as the chief precursor of independence in Colombia because, although not a great military figure, his inspiration and influence on the group of Colombian intellectual leaders was profound.

**Narváez, Pánfilo de.** 1478–1529. Spanish explorer. b. Valladolid. Came to America in about 1498; aided in conquest of Cuba, 1511. Sent in April 1520 by VELÁSQUEZ, governor of Cuba, to Mexico to restrict the activities of CORTÉS, he was to follow him and make settlements in Mexico restricting his power. Instead, he was captured by Cortés near Veracruz and kept prisoner for two years. He was made governor of the region known as La Florida in 1526. In April 1528, he landed near the present Tampa Bay, and traveled through to the present Tallahassee, but was forced by hostile Indians to return. He was lost at sea in the Gulf of Mexico on the voyage back.

**Nascas.** Peruvian Indians who were settled in the Nasca valley south of Lima. They were polytheistic people who worshiped primarily the sun and the moon. The king, or chief, was the half-divine priest of his people. They created magnificent weaving and pottery products. The Nasca peoples fell under INCA influence about 1400 when after long and arduous campaigns they were reduced to submission.

**National Action Party of Mexico (Partido de Acción Nacional or P.A.N.).** Mexican political party organized in 1939 by a group of conservative business and professional men who were disturbed by what they believed to be the proletarian excesses of the CÁRDENAS administration. In 1940, having no presidential candidate of their own, they supported General Juan Andreu ALMAZÁN in opposition to ÁVILA CAMACHO, the government-sponsored candidate. The P.A.N. included Catholics (who were favorably impressed by Almazán's promises to exercise greater tolerance toward the Church), a number of former labor leaders, and some of the supporters of former president CALLES. Almazán campaigned vigorously but was no match for the government machine that succeeded in pushing through the election of Ávila Camacho. In 1946 P.A.N. merged its strength with the supporters of the main opposition candidate Ezequiel Padilla, but he was easily defeated by Miguel ALEMÁN, when they polled only about 8 to 10 per cent of the ballots cast. In 1952 the party attempted to broaden its base by adding to its ranks the leaderless peasant remnants of the SINARQUISMO movement. At the same time the party also included unions, both of workers and of white-collar employees. Those efforts produced few results at the polls and tended to split the party. In 1958 the party nominated Luis H. Álvarez, as its presidential candidate, with the same results. The party today, divided and lacking effective leadership, still maintains its position as the most significant of the minority parties.

**National Alliance of Peru.** A grouping of conservative parties in power in Peru in recent years. It includes the Revolutionary Union, the Republican Socialist Party, the Authentic Socialist Party, the Liberal Party, the National Party of Peru, and others.

**National Democratic Front of Peru.** The political coalition that supported the candidacy for the presidency of José Luis BUSTAMANTE in the 1945 elections. It included some conservatives (although the NATIONAL ALLIANCE boycotted Bustamante after his election), APRISTAS, who constituted the most important element, and even Communists. It succeeded in electing Bustamante.

**National Democratic Union of Brazil (União Democrática Nacional,** or **U.D.N.).** A political grouping formed to support the candidacy for the presidency of Eduardo Gomes in 1945. It came out in favor of lowering tariffs and of a more liberal economic policy. It derived its backing mainly from Brazilian liberals, intellectuals, and from Brazilian coffee interests who were interested in low tariffs. In the elections, the National Democratic Union received 90 seats in Congress, and for a few months collaborated with the Social Democratic Party of President DUTRA. In 1947 the Union refused to vote for the expulsion of Communist representatives from the Brazilian congress, but in 1948 it changed its stand, and its votes made the expulsion possible. In 1960 the U.D.N.

won the election with its popular candidate Jânio da Silva Quadros, but later lost considerable political prestige when the president resigned after only seven months in office.

**National Democrats of Argentina.** Name of the conservative party that controlled Argentine politics in the early part of the century and from 1930 to 1943. It supported Reynaldo Pastor in the election of 1951, but PERÓN, in an electoral campaign that was not free in the full democratic sense, was easily elected.

**National Proletarian Defense Committee of Mexico.** A committee set up in Mexico in 1935 at the suggestion of President CÁRDENAS for the purpose of organizing Mexican labor into a general confederation. Among the members of the committee was Vicente LOMBARDO TOLEDANO, who soon thereafter established the Mexican Federation of Labor, or C.T.M.

**National Revolutionary Movement of Bolivia.** See M.N.R.

**National Revolutionary Party of Mexico (Partido Nacional Revolucionario,** or **P.N.R.).** See INSTITUTIONAL REVOLUTIONARY PARTY OF MEXICO.

**National Union of Chile.** A right wing coalition that supported the candidacy of conservative Luis BARROS BORGOÑO in the Chilean presidential elections of 1920. Barros Borgoño lost to Arturo ALESSANDRI PALMA in a close election that was eventually decided by a special tribunal of honor.

**Navío de permiso.** Spanish, literally meaning permission ship. Privilege given to the British South Sea Company to send one ship a year to the fair of Porto Bello, Panama, during the colonial period. The right to send the ship, together with that of providing the Spanish colonies with slaves, had been granted by Spain to England after the War of the Spanish Succession, 1701–1713. By means of the *navío de permiso* the British were able to establish a profitable trade with Porto Bello, much of it clandestine, for the ship would be accompanied to the Panamanian port by supply vessels that would approach it at night and refill it with goods.

**Negroes.** Negro slaves were imported into the Spanish-American colonies from early in the 16th century, chiefly for work on plantations in tropical regions where the Indian population was rapidly dying off. Their importation was encouraged by some churchmen and royal officials who wished to protect the Indians. By 1600 there were in Spanish America approximately 40,000 Negro slaves, along with many persons of mixed white-and-Negro or Indian-and-Negro descent. By 1800 the Negro population had increased to more than 700,000, the majority being in the West Indies, while others lived mainly in the tropical coastal lowlands of Central America and northern South America. Except in the West Indies, slavery was not widely prevalent in the Spanish colonies. Many of the Negroes were legally free, although they suffered many social and economic disabilities. Slavery was more firmly established in Brazil, where large numbers of Negroes were imported through the entire colonial period, mainly for work on sugar plantations. By 1800 nearly 2,000,000 of the total Brazilian population of 3,250,000 consisted of Negroes and mulattoes, about 400,000 of them being free. Another section of Latin America in which the economy was largely based on slave labor was the French colony of Saint Domingue, now known as Haiti, which by 1790 had a Negro population of about 450,000. The Haitian Negroes secured their freedom by successfully rebelling against their French masters between 1791 and 1803. In the mainland Spanish countries, slavery was completely abolished, usually with little controversy, between 1821 and 1870, and it was ended in Cuba in 1885. In Brazil the problem caused more conflict, but a measure for gradual emancipation was adopted in 1871, and the Golden Law of 1888 made abolition immediate and complete. Today one Latin-American nation, Haiti, is predominantly of Negro origin, while persons wholly or partly of Negro descent form an appreciable part of the populations of Brazil, Cuba, Puerto Rico, and the Dominican Republic. Elsewhere Negroes no longer compose a clearly recognizable ethnic group, although there is a considerable Negro element in the populations of seaboard regions in Mexico, Central America, Colombia, and Venezuela. See ABOLITION OF SLAVERY.

**Neruda, Pablo.** Real name, **Neftalí Ricardo Reyes.** 1904– . Chilean poet. Occupied diplomatic positions and has taken an active part in Chilean politics, serving as consul in Calcutta, Rangoon, Madrid, Mexico, and senator of the Chilean Communist Party. His poetry, rich in symbols and metaphors, is often obscure and frequently shows traces of surrealism. His early work (until 1936) deals mostly with man's solitude in a hostile world, but many of his later poems bear the mark of his radical political views and express his sympathies for Republican Spain and the Soviet Union. Primarily, however, he expresses his faith in the common people. His works include the collections of poems *Crepusculario, Veinte poemas de amor y una canción desesperada* (Twenty Poems of Love and One Desperate Song), *Residencia en la tierra* (Residence on Earth), *España en el corazón* (Spain in the Heart), and others. Neruda is the poet who is most admired and most imitated by young Latin-American poets today. See LITERATURE.

**Nervo, Amado.** 1870–1919. Mexican poet of the Modernist school. Served as a diplomat in Spain and in Latin-American countries. The dominant notes in his poetic work are serenity, humility, and resignation before the trials of life. He was an introvert who constantly searched his soul and who, while emphasizing Christian virtues, often seemed closer to Oriental mysticism than to Western ideals. His works, published in 1920, include *Los jardines interiores* (The Inner Gardens), *Serenidad,* and *El estanque de los lotos* (The Lotus Pool). See LITERATURE.

**Netherlands Antilles.** Name given to the Dutch insular possessions in the West Indies. They are comprised of two groups of islands more than 500 miles apart. The southern group, off the Venezuelan coast of South America, contains Aruba, Bonaire, and Curaçao, and has a combined area of 377 square miles. In the northern group, part of the Leeward Islands, are Saba, St. Eustatius, and the southern part of St. Martin, having an area of 34 square miles. The population of both groups of islands totals about 198,000 (est. 1962). The southern group consists mainly of igneous rock and is generally flat, although Curaçao has hills in the north that rise to 1,230 feet. There is little change in temperature on the islands, the annual mean temperature being about 80 degrees. Because there is very little rainfall the vegetation is sparse and restricted to drought-resistant plants. The northern group of islands are volcanic rocks rising to an altitude of 2,821 feet on Saba, which has an area of only 5 square miles. The climate on the northern islands is not unlike that of the southern islands with the exception that they have more rainfall and lie in the hurricane zone. The Netherlands Antilles are an integral part of the kingdom of the Netherlands but have full internal autonomy. Executive authority is vested in a governor and a council of ministers who are responsible to a 22-member legislature elected by universal suffrage. Curaçao, the largest of the islands, has an area of 179 square miles and a population of 126,088 (est. 1962). The capital of both groups of islands is Willemstad, population about 50,000, located on Curaçao. Dutch is the official language, but natives also speak Spanish and a patois composed of European and African words called *Papiamento*. The principal economic activity of the islands is oil refining, which employs about one-third of the total labor force. The oil is brought from Venezuela, Colombia, and Trinidad, and is refined in the establishments of the islands. Curaçao and Aruba have large oil refineries. Other industries include tobacco processing, shipbuilding, and tourism. Most of the food for the islands has to be imported. Total imports were valued at 1,358,000,000 guilders in 1962; exports, 1,297,000,000 guilders. (A guilder is worth 53.02 cents.) The southern group of islands was discovered in 1499 by Alonso de OJEDA and settled by the Spanish in 1527. In 1634 the islands were wrested from the Spanish and have been ruled by the Netherlands ever since, except during the Napoleonic wars, when they were occupied by the British. The importance of these islands actually dates from 1916 and 1925 when oil refineries were built in Curaçao and Aruba, respectively. During World War II, at the request of the Dutch, U.S. troops were stationed in Curaçao to help defend it.

**New Galicia.** Name given during the colonial period to the region west and northwest of Michoacán, Mexico, conquered by Gonzalo Nuño de GUZMÁN in 1530–1531. The northern frontier was an ill-defined region that ultimately included the Californias and bordered on the Rio Grande. In 1548 an *audiencia* was established in Compostela but was later transferred to Guadalajara.

**New Granada.** Name given to present-day Colombia by JIMÉNEZ DE QUESADA in 1538 and used during the colonial period and in the first half of the 19th century. The region was made a captaincy general within the jurisdiction of the viceroy of Peru and in 1718 was raised to the rank of a viceroyalty. The viceregal office was abolished in 1724 and revived again in 1740 with authority over the region comprising present-day Colombia, Ecuador, and Venezuela. After the Battle of BOYACÁ in 1819, New Granada gained its independence, and BOLÍVAR was elected to the presidency when the Republic of Colombia was created by the CONGRESS OF ANGOSTURA in that same year. The new state was a union of the former Spanish possessions of Venezuela and New Granada. After the BATTLE OF PICHINCHA, 1822, secured the independence of Ecuador, that state also became a part of the Republic of Colombia. After Venezuela and Ecuador broke away from Colombia, 1830, the name New Granada (Estado de Nueva Granada) was again adopted. Under the Constitution of 1832, as modified in 1842 and 1843, the name was Republic of New Granada. In 1858 the country assumed the name of Granadine Confederation until it was again changed to the United States of Colombia in 1863. Finally, in 1886 the country was designated as the Republic of Colombia.

**New Laws of 1542.** Laws decreed by the Spanish Crown in 1542 with the aim of easing the lot of the Indians in the Spanish colonies in America. Partly under the influence of the famous defender of the Indians, Bartolomé de LAS CASAS, the government provided through the New Laws that all *encomiendas* (feudal estates) were to cease at the death of the holders and be returned to the Crown, and that no new ones would be granted; clerics and public officials who held *encomiendas* were to surrender them immediately; slavery was to be abolished; and the laws were to be published in the more important Indian languages. The New Laws aroused such violent opposition among the Spanish colonists that it proved impossible to enforce them, and the main provisions were repealed. Among these were the one stipulating that no new *encomiendas* were to be granted, and the one that provided for the return of *encomiendas* to the Crown at the death of the holders. Consequently the *encomienda* system continued in Spanish America until the 18th century.

**New Spain.** During the colonial period, the name given to the viceroyalty that made up the Spanish territories north of the Isthmus of Panama. The authority of the viceroy of New Spain extended north to the Californias and what is now the center of the United States, and eastward along the shores of the Gulf of Mexico to the peninsula of Florida. The Antilles and the Philippines, after their conquest had begun in 1565, also fell within the jurisdiction of the viceroy. The viceroyalty, established in 1535, was divided into a number of subordinate areas that included the captaincy general of Guatemala, the presidency of Guadalajara (NEW GALICIA), the Internal Provinces (*Provincias Internas*), created in 1776 and comprising the northern frontier, the captaincy general of Cuba, and the *audiencias* of Mexico, Santo Domingo, and Manila.

**New Vizcaya.** Name given during the colonial period to the immense Mexican areas that included the present-day states of Durango, Chihuahua, and Zacatecas, conquered by Francisco de IBARRA in 1554–1562. In size, Nueva Vizcaya comprised almost one-third of all Mexico.

**Nezahualcoyotl.** 1402–1470. NAHUA chieftain of Texcoco (Mexico). Famous for his victorious war against the Tepanecs, 1428, as a result of which he acquired enormous territories. He ruled over a large area of what is today Mexican territory in a triumvirate with the chieftains of TENOCHTITLÁN and Tlacopán.

He governed with wisdom, showing strong talent as an organizer, promulgating excellent penal and property laws. He was known to believe in one God, and was a gifted poet.

**Niagara Conference.** A meeting called by Argentina, Brazil, Chile, and the United States at Niagara Falls, Ontario, Canada, in May-June 1914, for the purpose of settling the Mexican civil war. The warring factions of Victoriano HUERTA and CARRANZA were represented at the conference by their respective delegates. It was proposed that Huerta resign the presidency and that a provisional government entrusted with the organization of the new elections be set up. While Huerta indicated his willingness to accept the compromise, Carranza demanded the unconditional surrender of his rival. Thus the efforts at mediation failed, and the Mexican civil war continued.

**Nicaragua.** The largest republic in Central America, between the Atlantic and Pacific Oceans, bounded on the north by Honduras and on the south by Costa Rica, having an area of 57,143 square miles; population, approximately 1,754,000 (est. 1966), of whom 68 per cent are MESTIZO, 17 per cent white, 10 per cent Negro, and 5 per cent Indian. Ninety per cent of the people of Nicaragua are concentrated near the west coast. The language is Spanish and the dominant religion Roman Catholic, although all faiths are tolerated. The monetary unit is the córdoba, worth about 7 cents. Nicaragua has a president who is elected for six years, a 42-member chamber of deputies to which the deputies are elected for six years, and a senate made up of 16 members who are elected for six years. Former presidents are automatically made members of the senate. Two mountain chains cross the country, and near the western coast there are two great lakes, Lake Nicaragua, approximately 92 miles long and 34 miles wide, and Lake Managua, about 32 miles long and 10 to 16 miles wide. The highlands have a healthy climate and are fertile, while the lowlands are tropical. The lowlands bordering the Caribbean, or MOSQUITO COAST, are inhabited by Indians, Negroes from the West Indies, and mixtures of both. The important rivers are the San Juan, the Bluefields

River, which is navigable for a distance of 65 miles, and the Río Grande. The main cities are MANAGUA, the capital, population 191,000 (1960) ; León, population 73,616 (est. 1960) ; Matagalpa, population 65,321 (est. 1960) ; and Jinatega, population 51,448 (est. 1960).

The country's chief agricultural products are cotton, cotton seed, corn, coffee, and sugar. Coffee is cultivated mainly south of Managua; production in 1960-1961 was about 26,000 metric tons and made up about 18 per cent of the country's total exports. Cotton production has been increased in recent years; 57,000 metric tons were produced in 1960–1961, an increase of 73 per cent over the previous year. Cotton made up about 36 per cent of the total exports and ranks first in Nicaraguan export trade. Sugar is produced in the west, around Chinandega; production in 1960–1961 totaled 67,000 metric tons. Bananas were once an important product of the country, but in the 1930's the *Sigatoka* sickness practically wiped out the plantations, which were located on the Atlantic coast. Today, however, bananas are still grown in great quantities in the east. In recent years, efforts have been made to plant bananas on the Pacific coast. Cattle raising and gold mining are important activities, with gold taking third place as an export product. Beef production increased more than 36 per cent in 1961–1962 over the previous year and totaled 15,000,000 pounds. Industries include sugar refining and the manufacture of textiles, shoes, hats, soap, cigarettes, and furniture. Transportation is still fairly backward, since there is only one railroad, the Pacific Railroad, linking the cities of Managua, Granada, León, Chinandega, and Corinto; there is steamship service on Lake Nicaragua. Roads are underdeveloped, the Pan American Highway from Costa Rica to Honduras through Managua being the only all-weather road. Nicaragua is served by its own national airline, Líneas Aéreas de Nicaragua, and by eleven foreign airlines. There are air connections with other countries from the Managua airport. In the field of foreign trade Nicaragua's main customer is the United States, which takes almost half of the country's exports. At the same time the United States provides more than 50 per cent of the coun-

try's imports. In recent years some improvements have been made in agriculture, industry, and communications, but today Nicaragua is still one of the most backward countries in Latin America, with the illiteracy rate exceeding 60 per cent.

The coast of Nicaragua was first discovered by COLUMBUS in 1502. In 1522, the western part of the country was explored by Gil González Dávila, and in 1524 the first Spanish city, Granada, was founded on the shore of Lake Nicaragua by the conquistador Francisco Hernández de CÓRDOBA, who also built the city of León on the north shore of Lake Managua. Nicaragua soon became part of the captaincy general of Guatemala and remained a province of the latter throughout the colonial period. In the 16th century fewer than 500 Spaniards settled in the country, but the natives, who outnumbered them by far, were torn by internal dissensions and thus offered no serious threat to the white settlers. From the beginning the Spaniards looked for gold, but they did not find any appreciable quantities of the precious metal. On the other hand they soon began to derive great wealth from commerce with Panama and the West Indies. In the latter part of the 16th century the inhabitants had to repel attacks by English privateers, and in the 17th century English settlements on the east coast posed an increasing threat to Spanish control over the area. In 1609 most of the city of León was destroyed by a volcanic eruption, and a new León was founded further to the west. Rivalry between the cities of León and Granada became intense with the passing of time, and was to mar the country's future history. In the 18th century there was rapid growth in agriculture in the lowlands, with sugar cane and cacao becoming the main products, and in cattle raising in the highlands. In 1786 England recognized Spanish control over the east coast, but it was not until the end of the 19th century that Nicaragua was able to establish complete sovereignty over the area when it took over Bluefields and ousted a native ruler who had been installed under British protection. In 1821, together with Honduras, Guatemala, El Salvador, and Costa Rica, Nicaragua proclaimed its independence from Spain, and in 1822 entered into the newly-formed Mexican Empire. After the fall of Mexico's Emperor ITURBIDE in the following year, however, Nicaragua became part of the CENTRAL AMERICAN FEDERATION, a group constantly troubled with internal conflicts, the antagonism between León and Granada contributing greatly to the unrest in Nicaragua. After the confederation was dissolved, 1838, Nicaragua became a republic under the leadership of the León liberals with León as its capital. The strife between the liberals of León and the conservatives of Granada continued to plague the country for years. The liberals engaged the services of the American adventurer William WALKER who entered the country with a handful of men and was soon able to gain control of the country and to have himself proclaimed president, 1856. However, he became involved in a conflict with Cornelius Vanderbilt, who after the California gold rush in 1849 had established a transport service across the country with river steamers and overland stagecoaches, and was operating the line with great profit to his company. When Walker tried to gain control over the trans-Isthmian Line, Vanderbilt supplied Walker's enemies with material aid and soon the combined forces of Nicaragua, Honduras, and Costa Rica forced the American to seek refuge on board a U.S. ship in 1857. Three years later, after he had tried another landing in Honduras, he was shot. The latter half of the 19th century was marked by constant conflict between liberals and conservatives, with the latter in power between 1863 and 1893, but there was considerable material progress. Agriculture developed further, especially the growing of coffee and bananas, and communications were improved.

In 1893 the liberals gained access to the presidency with José Santos ZELAYA, who governed the country for the next 16 years. Under his rule the Mosquito Coast was freed from British influence and an attempt was made to form a federation of Central American states with Zelaya as president, but the effort failed. In 1909 a revolution that had U.S. backing forced Zelaya to go into exile, and Adolfo DÍAZ became president, 1911. American marines were landed in the country, 1912, at the request of Díaz to help maintain order,

for the political situation had been steadily deteriorating. The marines were withdrawn, 1925, but returned when fresh disorders broke out, 1926. From then on until 1933, when the marines evacuated Nicaragua, there was sporadic guerrilla fighting between rebellious Nicaraguans and the marines, with Augusto SANDINO leading the Nicaraguan guerrillas. In 1937 the liberal leader General Anastasio SOMOZA became president. During his term a dictatorial form of government was developed to suppress opposition to the regime, and the economy of the country made little progress. In 1947 Somoza retired, but as minister of war he continued as the real power in the government. In 1948 a new constitution was adopted, and in 1950, when the incumbent president died, the congress of Nicaragua proclaimed Somoza president.

In 1948 Nicaragua became involved in a dispute with Costa Rica when Nicaragua accused Costa Rica, together with Cuba, Guatemala, and Venezuela, of plotting the overthrow of the governments of Nicaragua, the Dominican Republic, and Honduras. Nicaragua itself was accused by Costa Rica of sending supplies and men to the enemies of the Costa Rican government in that country. Upon the intervention of the ORGANIZATION OF AMERICAN STATES the conflict subsided. It broke out anew in January 1955, when Costa Rica was invaded from Nicaraguan soil by Costa Rican opponents of the FIGUERES government. The Organization of American States again intervened and set up a buffer zone between the two countries in order to prevent the anti-Figueres rebellion from turning into a full-fledged war between Nicaragua and Costa Rica.

President Somoza was assassinated, September 1956, and his son, Luis Somoza Debayle, was immediately chosen by the congress to finish his father's term. In February of the following year he was elected president for a six-year term. A long-standing dispute with Honduras over a common boundary brought a crisis, 1957, and intervention by the Organization of American States led to the controversy being referred to the International Court of Justice where a decision was handed down in 1960 in favor of Honduras. The Somoza regime was continually plagued by revolutionary activity aimed at the overthrow of the dictatorial dynasty. Political opponents of the new president invaded the country in June 1959, but the lack of popular support for the rebels and the fact that the National Guard remained faithful to Somoza brought about the failure of the insurrection. In reply to widespread criticism and charges of dynasticism Somoza promised a completely free election for 1963, one in which neither he nor any relation would be a candidate. The ensuing election resulted in the Somoza-backed candidate, René Schick Gutiérrez being chosen over his opposition. The retiring president entered the senate, a position automatically conferred on former chiefs of state. After Schick's sudden death in August 1966, Lorenzo Guerrero became president. Throughout recent years Nicaragua has co-operated in the ORGANIZATION OF CENTRAL AMERICAN STATES (ODECA) and the Central American Common Market, and, in spite of internal political difficulties, has had one of the best credit ratings in all Latin America. Economic activity has continued to expand in all areas and the country has had particular success in increasing agricultural production. See CENTRAL AMERICA.

**Niño, Pedro Alonso.** Known as **El Negro.** *ca.* 1468–1505. Spanish navigator who accompanied COLUMBUS on his third voyage in 1498 and participated in the first successful commercial voyage to America, 1499–1500. He returned to Spain with pearls and dye wood from the north coast of South America.

**Niza, Marcos de.** Known as **Fray Marcos.** d. 1558. FRANCISCAN missionary and explorer. b. Nice, Duchy of Savoy. Sent by Viceroy MENDOZA of New Spain to explore area known now as Arizona and western New Mexico, 1539. He saw Zuñi adobes from a distance and reported great wealth in that territory. He went with CORONADO Y VALDÉS on his expedition of 1540, reaching the upper Rio Grande valley. When the Spaniards found no wealth, his reputation was lost.

**Nóbrega, Manoel de.** 1517–1570. Portuguese JESUIT missionary in Brazil; accompanied Thomé de SOUZA to Brazil in 1549 with the first contingent of Jesuits to go to the New World. He founded the basis for Brazil's future religious and cultural life, and was considered a founding father of Brazil.

**Noronha, Fernão de.** Portuguese nobleman and wealthy merchant of Jewish descent, who in 1503 was granted for a period of three years a concession to develop the Brazilian wood industry. This concession initiated among Portuguese Jews, then suffering from persecution in Portugal, a movement to find a haven in Brazil, particularly in Pernambuco and Bahia. The name Fernão de Noronha is perpetuated in the islands off the eastern bulge of Brazil.

**No-Transfer Doctrine.** The doctrine setting forth that colonies in the Western Hemisphere cannot be transferred from one non-American power to another non-American power. It originated in an Act of the U.S. Congress of January 15, 1811. The threat of British occupation of the Floridas, then belonging to Spain, caused Congress to declare that it would regard such a step with "serious inquietude." Though antedating the MONROE DOCTRINE, the No-Transfer Doctrine has generally been regarded as a part of it and has been repeatedly reaffirmed by American presidents. It was accepted as a Pan-American doctrine by the Latin-American states at the HAVANA CONFERENCE OF 1940.

**Núñez, Rafael.** 1825–1894. President of Colombia, b. Cartagena. Educated in Cartagena and Bogotá; member of congress; held several government posts, 1853–1863; entered consular service and took up residence in Europe, 1863–1875; returned to Colombia and was an unsuccessful presidential candidate of the Liberal Party, 1875; member of the national senate and elected president of that body, 1878; president of the republic, 1880–1882; re-elected president, 1884–1886; suppressed the revolution of 1884–1885; supported the centralized and conservative constitution of 1886; again president on two occasions, June-December, 1887, and February-August, 1888; re-elected in 1892 but declined to serve because of ill health. Núñez's dramatic role as absolute dictator of Colombia began with his second term in office in 1884, and from that time until his death he maintained an undisputed control over the country. His earlier radical ideas and Liberal Party associations were abandoned and he became a strong advocate of conservative government. Power was concentrated in the central government, the chief executive was given dictatorial authority, the press was restricted, the former position of the Church was restored, and agreements were signed with the Vatican. Núñez's death left the Conservatives firmly in control of Colombia. A distinguished poet and writer, Núñez made notable contributions to Colombian literature.

**Núñez Vela, Blasco.** *ca.* 1490–1546. Spanish viceroy of Peru. Appointed in 1542, he landed at Túmbez with colonists on March 4, 1544, thereby initiating the first viceroyalty in South America. He was incompetent and his attempt to enforce the NEW LAWS was unpopular. He was imprisoned by Gonzalo PIZARRO, who forced the *audiencia* into naming him governor. He escaped and continued to fight in the northern part of Peru, and was killed in battle against Pizarro near Quito, 1546.

# O

**OAS.** See ORGANIZATION OF AMERICAN STATES.

**Oaxaca.** State in southern Mexico. Population 1,727,266 (1960). The state has an area of 36,365 square miles and is the fifth largest state in Mexico. It occupies the larger part of the isthmus of Tehuantepec and has a 329-mile coastline on the Pacific Ocean. The region is extensively mountainous and has broad fertile valleys lying in the *tierra templada* (temperate climate) zone; the lower regions are characteristically tropical. The Sierra Madre del Sur, or Sierra de Oaxaca, contains peaks reaching an altitude of over 11,000 feet, the highest being Zempoáltepetl with an altitude of 11,148 feet. Two railways cross the state—the Tehuantepec National, terminating at the Pacific port of Salina Cruz, and the Mexican National, running from south of the city of Oaxaca north to Puebla. Because of the mountainous terrain there are few good all-weather roads throughout the state. The PAN AMERICAN HIGHWAY crosses the state passing through the city of Oaxaca and following the Pacific coast through the isthmus of Tehuantepec into the state of Chiapas. The state is noted for the ZAPOTEC ruins at MONTE ALBÁN and MITLA, located near the capital of the state, Oaxaca.

**Oaxaca.** Officially, **Oaxaca de Juárez.** City in southern Mexico, capital of the OAXACA State. Population 68,545 (1960). A large percentage of the population is Indian, most of whom are MIXTECS and ZAPOTECS. The city lies in the broad picturesque valley of the Atoyac River, surrounded by mountains of the Sierra Madre del Sur, or Sierra de Oaxaca. The fine colonial architecture, the old convents and churches, and the fine Zapotec ruins of MONTE ALBÁN and nearby MITLA make the city a tourist attraction. It is the chief city of southern Mexico and is a trading, stock-raising, manufacturing, and mining center. Industries include flour milling, vegetable-oil extracting, tanning, cotton ginning, silversmithing, ceramics, and textile goods. The city is believed to have been founded about 1486 by soldiers of the AZTEC chieftain Ahuizotl. In 1521 it was taken by the Spaniards under Diego de Ordaz. It was successively given the names of Antequera and Segura de la Frontera. On April 25, 1535, Emperor CHARLES V granted it the title of *Ciudad*. In 1727 and in 1787 the city was severely damaged by earthquakes. In the 19th century the city played an important role in the political events of the times. During the 1810 independence movement, it remained loyal to Spain. The famous president Benito JUÁREZ was born in a nearby village and the city is the birthplace of the dictator Porfirio DÍAZ.

**Obando, José María.** 1797–1861. President of New Granada (Colombia). Led unsuccessful revolts in 1837 and 1839. Supported by the army and the *democráticos*, he was liberal president, 1853–1854, and called a constitutional convention that adopted a new federal type of government on May 20, 1853. It separated Church and State, granted freedom of worship, speech, and press, and universal suffrage. Obando was overthrown by a revolution, 1854, and was killed in a civil war, leading the liberals against the conservatives.

**Obrajes.** In colonial Spanish America, the name given to textile workshops. The first *obrajes*, turning out cotton and woolen products, were established in the first half of the 16th century and their number grew rapidly. The *obrajes* employed large numbers of Indian workers, frequently under a forced labor system. The Indians' lot was usually a miserable one.

**Obregón, Álvaro.** 1880–1928. Mexican statesman and soldier. b. near Álamos, Sonora. Employed as farmer and factory worker. He entered military service in 1912, in support of the MADERO government against the rebellion of OROZCO, and played a leading role in organizing resistance in Sonora against Victoriano HUERTA after the latter's seizure of power in February 1913. As commander of the army of the northwest, he won a series of battles against Huerta's forces, capturing Mexico City in August 1914. He supported CARRANZA in conflict with VILLA, becoming general of Carranza's army and defeating Villa at Celaya, April 1915, and other battles. He then returned to private life. He headed a successful revolt against Carranza, April 1920, and was elected president, serving 1920–1924. He began carrying out reforms promised in the Constitution of 1917, giving strong support to organized labor, especially to the C.R.O.M., initiating distribution of land to peasants, and launching program of building schools. He established better relations with the United States by settlement of oil and debt questions, and was granted recognition in 1923. After suppression of a revolt led by Adolfo de la Huerta, he was succeeded by CALLES in 1924. He was elected to the presidency for a second term in 1928 but was assassinated on July 17 by a religious fanatic.

**Ocampo, Melchor.** d. 1861. Mexican liberal statesman. Born into a wealthy landowning family; governor of Michoacán, 1846; forced into exile by SANTA ANNA to New Orleans. He served in JUÁREZ' cabinet and was responsible in part for the MCLANE-OCAMPO TREATY with the United States, December 1859. He wrote extensively against clerical power and privileges and became known as one of the leading exponents of the liberal program of LA REFORMA. He resigned from the government in 1861 and retired to his farm. In June, Leonardo MÁRQUEZ and his *guerrilleros* shot him.

**ODECA.** See ORGANIZATION OF CENTRAL AMERICAN STATES.

**O'Donojú, Juan.** 1755–1821. Viceroy of New Spain appointed by the Spanish liberal government in 1821. He arrived at Veracruz on July 30, 1821, and found ITURBIDE ruling the country. He signed an agreement with him known as the TREATY OF CÓRDOBA, August 24, 1821, which accepted Mexican independence along with the chief provisions of the PLAN OF IGUALA. He agreed to the withdrawal of Spanish troops, and served as one of five regents that governed Mexico until a regular constitutional government could take over. He died while regent of the country.

**Odría, Manuel.** President of Peru. General. A conservative, who served as provisional president of the country, 1948–1950, after a military revolution directed against the APRISTA movement, which had largely controlled the government during the administration of BUSTAMANTE. He was elected president, 1950, for a six-year term. His administration was characterized by liberal economic policies and rigid political control. He promoted education and the development of transportation and communication, and was succeeded, 1956, by former president Manuel PRADO Y UGARTECHE. See HAYA DE LA TORRE.

**Oficiales Reales de Hacienda** or **Oficiales Reales.** Royal officials in various territories of the Spanish colonies in America who were in charge of the collection and disposition of royal funds. In the reign of PHILIP II the *oficiales reales* were given judicial functions in relation to fiscal suits. The books of the treasurer and comptroller, along with all entries made, had to be countersigned by the *oficiales*; they witnessed all deposits of money or bullion, and their signatures were required on all public acts or communications. Monies were kept in a strong box, and each of the *oficiales reales* had a key to one of the three or four different locks on this box; in order for the box to be opened, they all had to be present. They often disagreed with the various governors, although they were outranked by them, and quarreled over expenditures. One of the NEW LAWS issued by CHARLES V in 1542–1543 directed the *oficiales reales* to issue a yearly report of receipts and expenditures to the COUNCIL OF THE INDIES.

**Ogé, Jacques Vicente.** *ca.* 1755–1791. Early mulatto leader of the Negro and mulatto revolt against racial discrimination and slavery in Saint Domingue (French portion of Hispaniola.) Educated in Europe where he was inspired by the radical ideas of the French Revolution, he returned to Saint Domingue where he agitated for equal rights for Negroes and mulattos and incited an insurrection, October 1790. The uprising was quickly suppressed by the French governor, the Comte de Peynier, who had Ogé and his followers cruelly put to death. Although Ogé accomplished little before his death, the insurrection he began became more widespread under new champions and eventually led to the independence movement that freed Haiti from French domination.

**O'Higgins, Ambrosio.** *ca.* 1720–1801. Irish soldier and colonial administrator in Spanish America. b. Ballinary, county of Sligo, Ireland. Went to Spain as a youth, and was employed by a firm of Irish merchants. A trading venture to Peru ended in disaster and resulted in his South American residence. After 1766 he became associated with the Spanish colonial administration; served in the Chilean cavalry as a captain, defeated the ARAUCANIAN Indians; founded the fort of San Carlos, 1770; built road from Santiago to Valparaíso; promoted to brigadier general, 1783; made intendant at Concepción, 1786; captain general of Chile, 1789–1796; was made a marquis after having rebuilt Osorno, 1792; viceroy of Peru, improving defenses and lines of communication, 1796–1801. He was the father of Bernardo O'HIGGINS Y RIQUELME.

**O'Higgins y Riquelme, Bernardo.** Called the **Liberator of Chile.** 1778–1842. Chilean dictator. b. Chillán. Illegitimate son of Ambrosio O'HIGGINS, he was not recognized by his father during early childhood; later accepted in his household and educated in

Lima, Peru, Spain, and England, where he met MIRANDA and other Spanish-American patriots; became the military leader of the Chilean patriots, 1810; commander of the army from 1813; served under CARRERA when defeated at Rancagua on October 2, 1814, and with him and 3,000 men escaped across the Andes to Mendoza; joined SAN MARTÍN and defeated the Spanish at CHACABUCO on February 12, 1817; leader of the radical wing of the patriot party; independence of Chile announced on February 12, 1818; declared dictator by San Martín. O'Higgins' was a relatively progressive administration, and he attempted to encourage education in Chile and instill a feeling of democracy in the then backward people. However he governed as a military dictator, only sharing authority with a senate of five members, and no congress was convened until 1822. High taxes were a cause of discontent, and in 1822, under the leadership of General Ramón FREIRE, the army revolted. In January 1823, a *cabildo abierto* in Santiago forced O'Higgins to resign and he retired to Peru.

**Oidor.** From Spanish *oír*, meaning to hear. In Spain and colonial Spanish America, the *oidor* was a magistrate of the *audiencia*, or High Tribunal. See AUDIENCIA.

**Oil.** See PETROLEUM INDUSTRY.

**Ojeda, Alonso de.** 1466–1516. Spanish explorer and colonial administrator. b. Cuenca, Castilla la Nueva, Spain. Joined COLUMBUS on his second voyage to America, 1493–1496, and took part in the conquest of Hispaniola (Santo Domingo), 1493–1495. He sailed from Spain with his own expedition accompanied by Juan de la Cosa and Amerigo VESPUCCI, explored the northern coast of South America, 1499–1500; gave Venezuela its name when an Indian village built on piles in the Gulf of Maracaibo reminded him of Venice; was appointed governor of the island of Coquivacao in the Gulf of Urabá, 1501; appointed by the Crown to govern the Colombian coast from Cape de la Vela to the Gulf of Urabá (Nueva Andalucía); unsuccessfully attempted to settle the coast of Cartagena, 1509; in 1510 founded a colony in the Gulf of Urabá (Gulf of Darién), the first founded on Colombian soil; returned to Hispaniola the same year.

**Olaya Herrera, Enrique.** 1881–1937. President of Colombia, 1930–1934; previously served as minister to the United States; liberal, elected president after many years of conservative administrations; at that time one of the few examples in Latin-American history of a change of government by peaceful election; problem of his administration was the necessity of instituting economic measures that would successfully combat the depression of the 1930's. The LETICIA DISPUTE with Peru in 1932 caused Olaya to appeal to the LEAGUE OF NATIONS for aid, and the dispute was settled amicably.

**Olid, Cristóbal de.** 1492–1524. Spanish soldier who served under CORTÉS in the conquest of Mexico, 1519–1521. In Michoacán, west of Mexico City, 1522–1524, he founded the town of Colima, and in 1524 he explored Honduras. He repudiated the leadership of Cortés and was executed by the latter's friends.

**Oliveira, Manoel Botelho de.** 1636–1711. Brazilian poet. Published a successful book of verses entitled *Música do Parnaso* in Lisbon, 1705, and *A Ilha da Maré*.

**Olmedo, José Joaquín.** 1782–1847. Ecuadorian poet and politician. b. Guayaquil. Best known for having written the *Canto a Bolívar* (Hymn to Bolívar) and *La victoria de Junín* (Victory of Junín), 1824. He wrote the charming *Silva a un amigo en el nacimiento de su primogénito* (To a Friend upon the Birth of his First Child).

**Oña, Pedro de.** 1570–*ca.* 1644. Chilean poet. b. Angol. Son of a Spanish army officer; educated at the University of San Marcos, Lima, Peru. He published his *El Arauco domado* (Arauco Tamed), 1596, dealing with the Spanish fight against the ARAUCANIANS. See LITERATURE.

**Orbigny, Alcide Dessalines.** 1802–1857. French naturalist; went on a scientific expedition to South America, 1826–1834, and wrote a series of works including *L'Homme Américain,* 1840.

**Orejones.** From Spanish *orejón,* meaning large ear. Former Indian tribe of Mexico inhabiting the territory of the present state of Coahuila. Also, a noble Indian caste of pre-Columbian Peru, inhabiting the town of Cuzco and constituting a sort of honor guard of the Incas. As a sign of distinction they pierced their ears and hung various objects from them, distending their lobes. Hence, the name given them by the Spaniards.

**Orellana, Francisco de.** *ca.* 1500–1549. Spanish soldier and explorer; served as lieutenant in Gonzalo PIZARRO's expedition from Quito eastward across the Andes, 1540–1541. To win fame for himself, he left Pizarro and continued the journey from Napo to the valley of the Amazon, exploring the course of the river from the Andes to the Atlantic Ocean, 1542, and returning to Spain by way of the West Indies. He returned to the Amazon basin in hope of establishing a colony, 1546, but the attempt failed.

**Orellana, José María.** 1872–1926. President of Guatemala, serving first as provisional president, 1921–1922, and then elected to the presidency, 1922–1926.

**Organization of American States.** Also, **O.A.S.** Although the Organization of American States actually dates back to 1890, when the Union of American Republics came into being, its juridical structure and its operations were defined by a charter signed by the American republics at the Ninth International Conference of American States at Bogotá, 1948. Ratification of the charter by the 14th state, which took place on December 13, 1951, gave legal validity to the treaty that had been in practical effect since its signing. The O.A.S. is a regional agency within the framework of the United Nations. Among its main goals are the settlement of disputes among member nations through peaceful means, and the furthering of the economic, social, and cultural development of the American republics. It functions essentially through the Inter-American Conference, the supreme body of the Organization, which meets every five years; the Meeting of Consultation of Foreign Ministers, called together at the request of any one of the republics in case of an international emergency; the Council of the O.A.S., its permanent executive body, which meets regularly at the PAN AMERICAN UNION in Washington, and which directs the work of the Pan American Union and the different inter-American agencies; and the Pan American Union, which is the General Secretariat of the O.A.S. The O.A.S. also acts through specialized Conferences, dealing with such matters as health, agriculture, Indian affairs, etc., and through specialized organizations. The first secretary general of the O.A.S. was a Colombian, Alberto LLERAS CAMARGO, who had been director general of the Pan American Union, 1947. Lleras Camargo resigned, 1954, and Carlos DÁVILA ESPINOZA of Chile was elected by the Council of the O.A.S. to finish the unexpired term (ending in 1958). When Dávila died, 1955, José A. Mora of Uruguay was elected, 1956, to complete his term and was re-elected secretary general, 1958, for a ten-year period. Some of the accomplishments of the O.A.S. have been the peaceful settlement of disputes between the Dominican Republic and neighboring countries, and the two successful mediations between Nicaragua and Costa Rica, the first in 1948, and the second in January 1955. In 1957 hostilities between Honduras and Nicaragua were brought to an end and the dispute over their common boundary was referred to the International Court of Justice. The execution of the Court's decision was successfully carried out by the Inter-American Peace Committee of the O.A.S., 1961. The subversive efforts of the Communist powers to gain a foothold in the Western Hemisphere have been effectively opposed by the O.A.S. in recent years. In 1962, at the Eighth Meeting of Consultation of Ministers of Foreign Affairs at Punta del Este, Uruguay, the ministers declared that the principles of Communism were incompatible with the principles of the Inter-American System and voted to exclude the present government of Cuba from participation in the O.A.S. A special security fact-finding committee empowered to investigate Communist subversion by the Cuban government throughout Latin America was approved, 1963. The committee recommended that cooperative security measures be taken to forestall Communist penetration. Since 1960 Cuba has repeatedly brought charges against the United States before the United Nations Security Council. This recourse to the Security Council rather than to the O.A.S. marks the first time that the Pan-American nations have not been able to solve their own problems through the medium of their own agency. Bolivia voluntarily withdrew in September 1962 from participation in all activities of the organization except the ALLIANCE FOR PROGRESS because of a dispute with Chile over the diversion of water from the Lauca River. A Haiti-Dominican Republic dispute, 1963, over diplomatic asylum was also brought to the attention of the O.A.S. Council. A committee was successful in conciliating the dispute and in preventing hostilities between the two countries. During the crisis in the Dominican Republic in 1965, the O.A.S. decided by a vote of 14 to 5 to establish an inter-American military force which would be sent to restore peace to the strife-torn Caribbean nation.

**Organization of Central American States.** Also known as **ODECA** from the initials of the Spanish name, **Organización de Estados Centroamericanos.** A regional organization composed of the Central-American states of Guatemala, El Salvador, Honduras, Nicaragua, and Costa Rica. The agency, created by the Charter of San Salvador in October 1951, represents the most recent attempt to achieve a unity that has been an ideal for many Central Americans since those countries gained their independence from Spain in 1821. A CENTRAL AMERICAN FEDERATION existed, 1823–1838, but because of internal dissensions was ineffective. Since then more than 25 official and formal attempts have been made to re-establish the union. The meeting of the foreign ministers of the five republics in San Salvador in 1951 was held with the purpose of discussing mutual problems and promoting closer economic, political, and cultural ties. The most significant result of the meeting was the creation of the Organization of Central American States, based on 18 articles that formed the Charter of San Salvador. The principal terms of the pact included the intention to conduct mutual consultations to promote peaceful relations, to maintain the concepts of juridical equality and nonintervention, and the common acceptance of the principles of the United Nations and the ORGANIZATION OF AMERICAN STATES. The main body of the new agency was to be composed of the foreign ministers of the five concerned governments, functioning by unanimous decisions, and was supposed to meet at least once each year. The charter was promptly ratified by all of the five republics. During the years immediately following the signing of the charter the organization did not function as planned and it was not until August 1955 that the first formal conference met in Antigua, Guatemala. Although Panama had declined a special invitation to join in the covenants, that nation was represented at the Antigua conference by observers. The participants in the conference chose José Guillermo Trabanino, foreign minister of El Salvador, as secretary general of ODECA for a four-year term. The five states agreed to contribute to an annual budget of $125,000.

Since its inception in 1951 the new agency has been confronted with political difficulties both within and between the member nations. Salvadorean charges that Guatemala was permitting and influencing Communist infiltration in Central America caused the Guatemalan government to withdraw from the organization in 1954 and it was not until 1955, after Carlos CASTILLO ARMAS had led a successful revolution against the left-wing government of ARBENZ GUZMÁN, that the Guatemalan government renewed its membership. In 1957 the boundary dispute between Honduras and Nicaragua was referred to ODECA but both nations refused its good offices; the issue was finally settled by the International Court of Justice. Other obstacles to the new regional agency have been an exaggerated sense of nationalism in the member states, a pride in national institutions, and a failure to appreciate representative government. The agency has met with more success in the field of economic co-operation. Proposals for economic integration have included such measures as tariff reduction or abolition, the integration of industries, a liberal policy with regard to intraregional travel, and the reduction or elimination of quota restrictions. In 1960, Guatemala, El Salvador, Honduras, and Nicaragua sent representatives to a conference on economic matters in Managua, Nicaragua. Several agreements were reached that promoted economic integration: A general treaty was negotiated that provided for the creation of a Central American Common Market, a convention for the equalization of external tariffs was signed, and the Central-American Development Bank was established. The entire economic program was put under the control of: an economic council, made up of the ministers of economy of the member countries; an executive council, composed of one delegate from each country; and a permanent secretariat headed by a secretary general. Costa Rica did not take part in the 1960 conference but later, in 1962, signed all of the agreements and became a full participant in economic integration. Despite pessimistic evaluations of the proposed strengthening of Central American ties, ODECA made considerable progress during its first decade of existence and in 1962 undertook to replace its original charter with a more comprehensive agreement. On December 14 of that year, the foreign ministers of the five countries signed a new charter that set up a supreme council composed of the heads of the member states, a conference of foreign ministers, an executive council, a legislative council comprising three legislators from each state, a court of Central-American justice, and a council of defense ministers. Although Panama has not joined ODECA, it has evidenced an increasing interest in the organization.

**Oribe, Manuel.** *ca.* 1796–1857. President of Uruguay. b. Montevideo. As a boy he served with the patriot army of Río de la Plata. One of the "thirty-three immortals" who helped liberate Uruguay from Brazilian rule after 1825, he served as minister of war under José Fructuoso RIVERA, 1833–1835. He was president of Uruguay, 1835–1838, friendly toward the *blancos* and ROSAS of Argentina. Overthrown by Rivera and forced to flee to Buenos Aires, he became leader of the *blancos*. With the help of Rosas, he returned to Uruguay and, at first, defeated the *colo-*

*rados* under Rivera, 1840–1842, but after nearly nine years of attempting to seize Montevideo, 1843–1852, Oribe and the Rosas forces were finally defeated, 1852, when the Argentine general URQUIZA revolted against Rosas and successfully invaded Uruguay.

**Orinoco River.** The principal river of Venezuela and one of the great waterways of South America. It rises in the Parima Mountains near the Brazilian border and winds in a semicircular course, flowing northwest to Colombia, then north along the Colombian border, then north-northeast through the center of Venezuela, and finally east to the wide delta on the Atlantic coast. The river, about 1,500 miles long, with its tributaries, drains an area of about 450,000 square miles. Its deep delta, which begins about 100 miles from the sea, near Barrancas, occupies about 150 miles of the coastline. Before entering the delta the river achieves its maximum width of 13 miles. The main city on the Orinoco is Ciudad Bolívar, about 262 miles from its mouth, which is also the farthest point on the river that can be reached by small ocean steamers. Between May and November, navigation is open to shallow-draught vessels between Ciudad Bolívar and San Fernando de Apure, about 300 miles to the west. The Orinoco was explored by the Spaniard Ordaz, 1531–1532, and subsequently many expeditions traveled on it, some with the purpose of finding the fabulous EL DORADO, and others for scientific reasons. Alexander von HUMBOLDT explored the upper reaches, discovering the linkage with the Amazon River system. The source of the Orinoco was not established until recent expeditions in 1931, 1943, and 1951.

**Orozco, José Clemente.** 1883–1949. Mexican painter. Associated with Diego RIVERA, SIQUEIROS, and others in the modern Mexican school of painting. Like Rivera and Siqueiros, he was radical in his political convictions.

**Ortega, Jesús González.** See Jesús GONZÁLEZ ORTEGA.

**Ortiz, Roberto Marcelino.** 1886–1942. President of Argentina. Served as minister of finance, 1935–1937; president, 1938–1942, but forced by illness into retirement, 1940. An *antipersonalista* radical who originally had the support of the conservatives, he went over to the radicals in 1940, severing relations with the conservative national democrats. He had the support of congress and attempted in his short time in office to restore an honest government to his country. He supported the United States at the Havana Conference held in 1940, in measures directed against Axis aggression. He was succeeded as president by Vice-President Ramón S. CASTILLO, who reverted to neutrality in foreign policy.

**Ortiz Rubio, Pascual.** 1877–1963. President of Mexico. Engineer; served as minister to Germany, 1923; ambassador to Brazil, 1926; president, 1930–1932, having been elected to succeed the provisional president PORTES GIL and to fill the unexpired term of OBREGÓN. He was forced to resign in September 1932, as a result of disputes with CALLES, and he retired to the United States.

**Ospina Pérez, Mariano.** b. 1891. President of Colombia, 1946–1950. Graduate engineer from Louisiana State University in the United States; rich man of good family; promised a liberal conservatism. Elected in 1946 as a result of split between two liberal candidates, he was the first successful conservative candidate in 20 years; attempted to institute reforms he had promised in his campaign but met with great opposition from congress; proposed a "cabinet of national unity" and divided the ministries equally between the liberals and conservatives, but made Laureano GÓMEZ, a reactionary, the foreign minister, the latter being forced to resign after the riots of 1948. In 1950, as a result of friction with congress, he offered to turn the government over to a bi-partisan commission to rule the country until 1954, but the proposal was rejected. Gómez was elected to succeed him in August 1950.

**Ospina Rodríguez, Mariano.** 1805–1875. President of New Granada (Colombia), 1857–1861. During his term the country was called the Granadine Confederation and a new constitution was promulgated on May 22, 1858, which established a federal form of government that granted the president a four-year term. It also granted each of the 35

245

provinces the right to elect its own governor and control its own local affairs but had difficulty in suppressing revolts in the provinces and asserting the authority authorized to the federal government. A clerical conservative, he permitted the Jesuits to regain power which brought about opposition to his regime.

**Ostend Manifesto.** In October 1854, the U. S. ministers to England, France, and Spain, James Buchanan, John Y. Mason, and Pierre Soulé, met in Ostend, Belgium, to exchange information and opinions regarding the acquisition of Cuba by the United States. They were directed to report their conclusions to Secretary of State William L. Marcy in Washington. The results of their conference, begun in Ostend but terminated in Aix-la-Chapelle, were enclosed in a dispatch that recommended that an effort should be made to purchase Cuba for not more than $120,000,-000, and that if such effort should fail—and if the island should prove dangerous to the United States—then the United States would be within its rights if it took possession of Cuba by force. Indiscretion on the part of the conferees caused the contents of the dispatch to become generally known, thereby creating the impression that a public statement had been issued by the trio. The document provoked much criticism in foreign capitals but was never officially recognized by either the Washington or Madrid governments.

**Ouvidor Geral.** A high judge in colonial Brazil. He was often ranked above the DONATÁRIOS, and was independent of the governor general.

**Ovando, Nicolás de.** 1460–1511. Spanish colonial administrator. Served as governor of Spanish possessions in the New World, 1502–1509, with headquarters at Santo Domingo on the island of Hispaniola. He started the first extensive importation of Negro slaves. An able and judicious man, he had the confidence of the Crown and succeeded in establishing many new towns and increasing agricultural production. He retired to Spain, where he died wealthy and with honors.

**Oviedo y Valdés, Gonzalo Fernández de.** 1478–1557. Spanish historian; official chronicler of the Indies. Author of *Historia general y natural de las Indias* published in 50 volumes. It is one of the first early histories of America and one of the best.

# P

**Pachacamac.** Supreme god of the INCA Indians. Although the sun, moon, and numerous gods were worshiped by the Incas, Pachacamac, meaning "creator of the world," was considered to be the supreme deity who had created all things. Pachacamac has been identified with the pre-Inca deity Viracocha. The name is also used to designate the Inca ruins and the nearby islands located just south of Lima, Peru.

**Pacific, War of the.** See WAR OF THE PACIFIC.

**Padilla, Ezequiel.** 1890–      . Mexican diplomat and political leader. Served under ZAPATA and VILLA in the Revolution; member of congress; foreign minister, 1940; eloquently advocated hemispheric unity against the Axis at the Rio de Janeiro Conference of 1942; considered over-friendly to the United States, seriously handicapping his candidacy for the presidency in 1946, forcing him to rely on the weak NATIONAL ACTION PARTY for support; defeated by ALEMÁN.

**Páez, Federico.** Provisional president of Ecuador selected by the army on September 26, 1935, called "Supreme Head of the State." Elected provisional president on August 10, 1937; involved in the boundary dispute with Peru; attempted to improve the economic conditions within his country by establishing co-operatives for farmers, and on February 4, 1937, the government fixed minimum wages for manual and agricultural laborers, and employees in private enterprises; attempts were made to increase the tourist trade. Revolts were unsuccessful, but the president unexpectedly resigned on October 22, and was succeeded by an administration of army officers.

**Páez, José Antonio.** 1790–1873. President of Venezuela. b. Orinoco Valley. Served as a soldier in the War for Independence, 1810–1823, and was responsible for dislodging the last royalist forces from Venezuelan soil, at Puerto Cabello, 1823; leader of the LLANEROS. A daring and popular leader of men, he won victories over the Spanish and was largely responsible for bringing Venezuela into the new republic of Great Columbia. He opposed the leadership of SANTANDER, revolted against BOLÍVAR in 1829, and was made the first president of the new republic of Venezuela, 1830. Páez' first term as constitutional president, 1831–1835, was relatively peaceful: freedom of the press was allowed; and the actions of the congress were independent. When VARGAS succeeded him and was unsuccessful, Páez was called out of retirement to serve again, 1839–1846. As leader of the conservatives, he led a revolt against President José Tadeo MONAGAS, 1847, was captured and imprisoned, from 1847 to 1850. He went into exile, but returned in 1858. He was made minister to the United States, 1860. He was again president with dictatorial powers, 1861. Forced to resign in 1863 he went into exile in the United States and died in New York. He has been called the "founder of the Venezuelan Nation."

**Paiva, Félix.** b. 1877. President of Paraguay. A revolutionist in his early years, he was vice-president of the republic under President Manuel Gondra, 1920–1921, and

247

was made provisional president after Gondra was overthrown, 1921. He became dean of the law school at the University of Asunción. He served as provisional president from August 15, 1937, until October 1938, when he was confirmed as president. He was successful in suppressing revolts led by Rafael Franco, and was succeeded by ESTIGARRIBIA on August 15, 1939.

**Palenque.** A center of ancient MAYAN civilization situated in the northern part of the Mexican State of Chiapas, 80 miles south of the Gulf of Mexico port of Carmen. The original name of the city having been lost, the modern name is taken from the nearby village of Santo Domingo de Palenque. On its site are found some of the oldest Mayan ruins. It may have been the capital of the old Mayan empire, which reached its zenith in the 6th century A.D. The site was totally abandoned in about the 12th century. Its impressive temples and pyramids with beautiful relief sculptures inside the buildings, set amidst the dense tropical forest, make it one of the most interesting sites of pre-CORTÉS civilization in Mexico. The ruins were discovered in 1750.

**Palma, Ricardo.** 1833–1919. Peruvian writer. b. Lima. Worked for the Peruvian National Library; strove for the expulsion of the JESUITS from Peru, 1886. Renowned as historical essayist, he was the author of *Los Anales de la Inquisición de Lima*, 1863, *Poesías*, 1887, and *Tradiciones peruanas*, a collection of Peruvian legends and folk tales. See LITERATURE.

**Pampa.** From Quechua Indian *pampa*, meaning plain. Name given to the immense South American plains, especially those of the RÍO DE LA PLATA region. The pampas of Argentina are characterized by their flat surface, fertile soil, the many lagoons that cover them, and the salt found in the soil. They cover an area of about 250,000 square miles, an area approximately the size of the state of Texas. In October the dry season begins, lasting from three to four months during which time there is practically no rain. The raising of livestock constitutes the main activity on the pampas, although in recent years there has

been a change, and now a great deal of the area is agricultural. The Indians who originally inhabited these regions were gradually forced back by the conquering Spaniards, but in the course of the 18th and at the beginning of the 19th century, they frequently raided Spanish settlements for cattle and horses, often precipitating bloody battles. Today the pampas are covered by a great number of *estancias*, whose cattle roam over the wide plains, and there are still a few GAUCHOS in their colorful costumes, riding swift horses and flinging their bolas. The area in general is treeless.

**P.A.N.** See NATIONAL ACTION PARTY OF MEXICO.

**Panama.** The fourth largest republic of Central America, bounded on the north by the Caribbean Sea, on the east by Colombia, on the south by the Pacific Ocean, and on the west by Costa Rica, with a maximum width of 110 miles and a length of 480 miles; the area embraces 28,753 square miles. The population is 1,308,000 (est. 1966), of whom approximately 65.5 per cent are mestizo, 13 per cent Negro, 11.1 per cent white, and 10 per cent Indian. The monetary unit is the balboa (linked to the dollar at 1 to 1). The official language is Spanish, and most of the people are Roman Catholic, although all other religions are tolerated. The chief cities are PANAMA CITY, the capital and important Pacific port, population approximately 285,000 (est. 1962); Colón, the principal port on the Caribbean, population 63,000 (est. 1962); and David, population 40,000 (est. 1962). The constitution of 1946 stipulates that the president, elected for a four-year term, may not succeed himself, and provides for a one-chamber congress consisting of 53 deputies who are also elected for four years. The country is mostly mountainous and covered with jungles; the climate is hot and humid. At its narrowest point Panama is crossed by the PANAMA CANAL which, together with a five mile strip of land on both sides of the canal, is under the jurisdiction of the United States in the form of a Canal Zone Government.

The canal is one of the pillars of Panama's economy, for the wages earned by Panamanians in the Canal Zone as well as the money spent by U.S. government employees constitute approximately 33 per cent of the country's income. Around 44 per cent of the population of Panama live in the central part of the country, in and around the cities of Colón and Panama, both of which are contiguous to the Canal Zone. Improvements in sanitation introduced by the United States in connection with the building and operation of the Panama Canal have been instrumental in raising the level of general health in the country. Aside from the wealth derived in connection with the operation of the canal, Panamanian economy depends mainly on agriculture, the chief product being bananas, followed by cacao and tobacco. In addition to agriculture, there are cattle raising and gold mining. The leading export is bananas, with the United States taking most of the supply. Education is compulsory and free between the age of 7 and 15, but more than 28 per cent of the population are illiterate.

The Isthmus of Panama was discovered in 1501 by the Spanish explorer Rodrigo de BASTIDAS, and in the following year it was explored by COLUMBUS, who founded Santa María de Belén, the first settlement on the American mainland. It was further explored in 1513 by BALBOA, who was the first occidental to set his eyes on the Pacific Ocean, originally named by him the Great South Sea. The city of Panama was founded in 1519 by the governor of Panama, Pedro ARIAS DE ÁVILA, and soon became the point of departure of the expeditions that conquered Peru and Chile. The port of Porto Bello, founded on the Caribbean side of the isthmus in 1597, was the most important port of the area for it was the site of the all-important fairs at which goods brought from Spain by the Spanish trade fleets were exchanged for products from Peru destined for Spain, including gold and silver. European goods were transported overland to Panama and from there were shipped to the South-American west coast. During the colonial period and until the 20th century the isthmus was an extremely unhealthy region, infested by deadly diseases, especially yellow fever, that claimed a heavy toll in lives among the merchants and travelers who ventured there. Attacks on Panama by English and French corsairs were a fre-

quent occurrence, the most serious of these being the sack of the city Panama by the English buccaneer Henry Morgan in 1671. In the 18th century Panama became a part of the viceroyalty of New Granada, and when it shook off the rule of Spain, 1821, it joined the Republic of Great Colombia, set up by BOLÍVAR, and remained a part of Colombia until 1903. Then the Panamanians revolted against Colombian rule after the Colombian congress rejected a treaty with the United States giving the latter the right to build a canal across the isthmus, retaining a zone six miles wide. A U.S. warship prevented Colombian troops from putting down the uprising, basing its action on the United States-New Granada (Colombia) treaty of 1846, which gave the United States the right to safeguard the neutrality of the isthmus and to maintain free transit in the area. Panamanian independence was recognized by the United States immediately after the revolt and the new republic signed a treaty with United States granting the latter the right to build a canal across the isthmus as well as a strip of land five miles wide on each side of the waterway in return for a payment of $10,000,000 and a further payment of $250,000 a year beginning nine years after the treaty began to operate. The canal was completed, 1914, after an epic struggle against natural obstacles and disease. After the dollar was devaluated in 1933, the annual sum paid the Panamanian government was $430,000, and by a new treaty signed between Panama and the United States, 1936, the latter yielded a number of rights acquired under the 1903 treaty, such as the right to intervene in Panama City and Colón for the purpose of preserving order.

The political history of the republic since 1903 has been stormy and there have been many internal upheavals. In WORLD WAR II the country collaborated with the United States, granting it bases. In recent years relations between Panama and the United States have been marred by questions concerning the Canal Zone. Anti-United States demonstrations have occurred as the result of Panamanian dissatisfaction with the division of canal income, and the question of sovereignty in the Canal Zone. In 1955 a new treaty was signed with the United States that increased the annual annuity from $430,000 to $1,930,-000, returned to Panama certain property no longer needed for the operation of the canal, and promised equality of opportunity for Panamanian citizens working in the Canal Zone. The election of Roberto F. Chiari in 1960 has brought still further demands from the Panamanian government. During 1960 President Eisenhower ordered the Panamanian flag to be flown in the Canal Zone and in the following year the last provisions of the 1955 treaty were carried into effect. Although a joint commission was set up in 1962 to resolve canal problems, its failure to satisfy Panama's claims led to its dissolution in 1963. On January 9, 1964, Panamanian demonstrators invaded the zone to protest a violation of the agreement to fly the Panamanian and U.S. flags together in the Canal Zone. During the violent rioting four American soldiers and twenty-one Panamanians were killed in an exchange of gunfire. President Chiari subsequently suspended relations with the United States and demanded a complete revision of the 1903 treaty. Despite efforts to resolve the crisis, the government of Panama formally broke relations with United States on January 17, 1964. Relations were later restored and in December President Johnson announced the United States' readiness to negotiate a new treaty for the canal. Under the administration of the new Panamanian president, Marco Aurelio Robles, negotiations with the United States concerning Canal Zone problems are continuing. See CENTRAL AMERICA, CENTRAL AMERICAN FEDERATION, and ORGANIZATION OF CENTRAL AMERICAN STATES.

**Panama, Declaration of.** At the Pan-American Conference on neutrality held in Panama, September 23–October 3, 1939, the American republics agreed to create a safety zone about the continent, exclusive of Canada, which was to present a united front against belligerents, and in this zone, varying from 250 miles to 1250 miles in width, no belligerent would be permitted to commit a hostile act. The area would be policed by the navies of the United States and the Latin-American countries. All governments concerned agreed to consult each other on matters pertaining to the European war. It was signed on October 3 and is known as the Declaration of Panama. The Declaration, however, became quickly ineffective, being violated in the fighting between the German pocket battleship "Graf Spee," and its British opponents. On December 13 the British drove the German ship into Montevideo harbor. On December 23, the American republics notified the governments of England, France, and Germany that vessels violating the Declaration of Panama would not be allowed to obtain supplies or go to American ports for repairs. In January 1940, both England and Germany refused to recognize the zone.

**Panama Canal.** This strategic waterway cuts across the Isthmus of Panama from the Caribbean ports of Colón and Cristóbal to the Pacific Ocean at Balboa in a northwest-southeast direction over a length of 40.27 miles. The distance between the channel entrances is 50.72 miles. Paradoxically, the Pacific entrance is 27.02 miles east of the Atlantic entrance. Ships passing through from either end are raised to an artificial lake in the center of the Canal Zone by locks 1,000 feet long, 110 feet wide, and 70 feet deep. Traffic moves in both directions, since all locks are double. It is operated by the PANAMA CANAL COMPANY, formed in 1951, which also administers business enterprises related to the canal, such as the Panama Railroad. The Panama Canal Zone, through which the canal cuts, is 10 miles wide and has an area of 553 square miles, including 191 square miles of fresh water. It is administered by the Canal Zone Government headed by a governor who is appointed by the President of the United States. Its population is 42,000 (1960). The idea of a canal linking the Caribbean Sea and the Pacific Ocean across the Central-American isthmus developed early in the 16th century, but no action was taken. It acquired renewed importance in the 19th century, especially after the war between Mexico and the United States, 1846–1848, when California was added to the United States and a canal would have facilitated travel to this new gold-rich territory. But aside from the building of a railroad across the isthmus by an American company, 1848–1855, as the result of an earlier treaty with Colombia, nothing constructive was done until a French company, under the leadership of Ferdinand de LESSEPS, who had built the Suez Canal, was granted a concession from Colombia, 1878, and began work on a canal, 1880. The project eventually ended in failure, 1889, because of disease and mismanagement. In 1902 the United States entered into negotiations with the Colombian government to obtain the Panama route. The HAY-HERRÁN TREATY with Colombia was signed in January 1903 but proved abortive because the Colombian senate refused to ratify the document in August of the same year. On November 3, 1903, a revolution broke out in Panama, where there was great disappointment over the failure of Colombia to accept the treaty. As a result of the revolution, which received United States support, Panama achieved independence and was recognized by the U.S. government on November 6, 1903. The new republic then signed the HAY-BUNAU-VARILLA TREATY, November 18, 1903, with the United States, providing for the construction of the canal by the United States and the creation of a 10-mile-wide Canal Zone under the perpetual control of the American government. The latter paid $10,-000,000 to Panama and promised to pay another $250,000 per year, a sum which was subsequently increased to $430,000 in 1933, and to $1,930,000 in 1955. Work on the canal was begun in 1904, and it was opened ten years later. The builders, including thousands of North Americans and many more West-Indian natives, had to overcome staggering difficulties in engineering and had to wage an unrelenting fight against yellow fever and malaria. The main credit for the success of the enterprise belongs to Colonel George W. GOETHALS, who was put at the head of the project in 1907, and to William Gorgas, surgeon general of the U.S. Army, whose efforts were chiefly responsible for eradicating yellow fever in the Canal Zone and for greatly diminishing the threat of malaria. The Panama Canal considerably facilitated communications between Europe and the Eastern United States on the one hand, and the countries along the Central-American and South-American west coasts on the other. It greatly stimulated trade between those parts of the world, and has been of vital military value to the United States.

**Panama Canal Company.** A corporation chartered by the government of the United States, organized in 1951 to take the place of the Panama Railroad Company. It operates the Panama Canal, the Panama Railroad, and such related businesses as stores and commissaries.

**Panama City.** The capital of Panama, situated on the Pacific side of the Panamanian isthmus close to the entrance of the PANAMA CANAL. Population is approximately 253,000 (1960). The city is a mixture of colonial and modern architecture. There are many modern buildings which alternate with very much older ones. Outstanding edifices are the President's Palace, the National Palace, the University, and the Cathedral. Panama City is linked by rail and by road with Colón, about 38 miles to the northwest, and David, close to the border of Costa Rica. It has air connections with South, Central, and North America. There are men's tropical clothing, soap, and nail factories, as well as furniture, beverage, and shoe plants. Panama City was established in 1672, after the old city of Panama, four miles away from the new city, had been captured and destroyed by the British pirate Henry Morgan in 1671. The old city had been one of Spain's proudest centers in the New World. It had been the receiving point for precious metals from Peru, and the point of departure of these treasures to Portobelo on the Caribbean. The new city was heavily fortified and was able to repel the numerous attacks launched against it in colonial times. In 1717 it became the provincial seat of the province of Panama in the viceroyalty of New Granada, and later it kept that title under the Republic of Colombia. In the 19th century it went through a period of feverish activity during the California gold rush. During the construction of the Panama Canal, 1904–1914, Panama City, although outside the jurisdiction of the United States, found itself within the area under the control of the United States and derived considerable prosperity from the project. A corridor linking the city with Panamanian territory was established in 1914.

**Panama Congress.** A congress held at Panama City in 1826 at the insistence of Simón BOLÍVAR, who wanted to establish an alliance among the newly-liberated Spanish colonies, and to discuss the possibilities of implementing the MONROE DOCTRINE with representatives from the United States, Brazil, and Great Britain. Only the delegates of Great Britain, Mexico, Central America, Colombia, and Peru attended the conference. A delegate from the United States died en route to the conference and the conference was concluded before a second appointee could make an appearance. The work of the congress ended in failure because treaties signed by the delegates of Spanish America, aiming at confederation and at united action on the part of these nations, were ratified only by Colombia. There was a second meeting scheduled at Tacubaya near Mexico City, but it never took place. The failure of the Panama Congress to achieve concrete results was a great disappointment for Bolívar.

**Panama Tolls Bill.** An act passed by the U.S. Congress in 1912 giving the president the authority to set the toll rate for all ships passing through the PANAMA CANAL. A clause in the act exempting coastwise vessels of the United States from all the tolls was protested by Great Britain as constituting a violation of the HAY-PAUNCEFOTE TREATY of 1901 which stated, "the canal shall be free and open to the vessels of commerce and of war of all nations . . . on terms of entire equality, so that there shall be no discrimination against any such nation or its citizens or subjects in respect to the conditions or charges of traffic or otherwise." The clause was revoked by the U.S. Congress in 1914, under the WILSON administration, but was included in a new Canal Act passed in 1921 by the U.S. Senate after the Republican victory in the election of 1921. However, the bill was not voted on in the U.S. House of Representatives and has remained in this state ever since.

**Pan-American Conferences.** The term "Pan-American conferences" is a generic term used to designate the various inter-American meetings in which the American republics have participated. The history of the Pan-American conferences may be divided into two periods, those held prior to 1889, and those held after that date. The earlier meetings were attended by representatives of some Latin-American states, but in none of these were all of the nations represented. The meetings, eight in number, were held to discuss matters of mutual concern; they largely dealt with political and juridical topics. In 1889 the Pan-American conferences assumed hemispheric proportions with the initiation of the International Conferences of American States. The term "Pan-American conferences" is frequently used to designate these latter conferences. Special or technical conferences and meetings of consultation of the ministers of foreign affairs have also been a feature of inter-American relations since 1889. The meeting of an inter-American conference was suggested in 1881 by U.S. Secretary of State James G. Blaine, primarily with a view toward promoting trade between the United States and Latin America. The first conference, officially called the First International Conference of American States, met in Washington in 1889. It agreed, among other things, to set up machinery for the arbitration of financial disputes and to establish the Commercial Bureau of American Republics, the name of which was afterward changed to the PAN AMERICAN UNION. Proposals for a lowering of inter-American tariff barriers produced no concrete results. The second conference met at Mexico City in 1902, and it was then decided that there would normally be such meetings every five years. The third conference convened at Rio de Janeiro in 1906, and the fourth at Buenos Aires in 1910. Delegates at the latter meeting signed resolutions covering copyrights and patents, and these decisions were implemented by most of the American states. The only real accomplishment of the fifth conference at Santiago, Chile, in 1923, was the adoption of the GONDRA TREATY, which established an inter-American commission of inquiry for the settlement of inter-American disputes. The sixth conference in Havana in 1928 was marked by Latin-American hostility toward the United States as a result of the latter's continued intervention in Haiti and Nicaragua. At the seventh conference at Montevideo in 1933 all the states, including the United States, accepted a convention prohibiting intervention by one state in the affairs of another; and the eighth conference held at Lima, Peru, in 1938 adopted a Declaration of American Principles summarizing the results of previous conferences. The ninth conference at Bogotá, Colombia, in 1948, although marred by a severe outbreak of rioting among opponents of the Colombian government, adopted the charter of the ORGANIZATION OF AMERICAN STATES, which transformed the Pan-American system into a regional agency within the framework of the United Nations. The tenth conference, held at Caracas, Venezuela, in 1954, was largely concerned with the problem of the Communist-dominated government of Guatemala.

Special inter-American conferences have been held from time to time in order to deal with specific or technical problems concerning all phases of inter-American activity deserving more detailed consideration. In 1936 a Conference for the Maintenance of Peace met at Buenos Aires and agreed upon immediate inter-American consultation in the event of any threat to the peace of the Hemisphere. The first meeting of ministers of foreign affairs, held at Panama City in 1939, adopted common neutrality policies. A second meeting, the HAVANA CONFERENCE OF 1940, gave Pan-American sanction to the no-transfer doctrine and declared that an attack on any American state from outside the Hemisphere should be regarded as an attack on all. A third meeting held at Rio de Janeiro in 1942 recommended that all American states break diplomatic relations with the Axis powers. The CHAPULTEPEC CONFERENCE OF 1945, held in preparation for the coming United Nations Conference at San Francisco, was largely concerned with the problem presented by Argentine neutrality, and also extended the Havana declaration to cover any act of aggression from within the Hemisphere. The obligation of all the American states to aid each other in the event of aggression was made binding in the form of a treaty at the RIO CONFERENCE OF 1947. In recent years the number of special meetings has increased

greatly. Among the more important conferences are the American Presidents Meeting at Panama City in 1956, the Buenos Aires Economic Conference of 1957, and the most significant of these specialized conferences, the Inter-American Economic and Social Conference in 1961 at Punta del Este, Uruguay, which established the ALLIANCE FOR PROGRESS.

**Pan American Highway.** A system of roads connecting the continental nations of the Western Hemisphere from the Texas-Mexico border to Buenos Aires in Argentina. The idea of a Pan American Highway was first proposed at the Fifth International Conference of American States held at Santiago, Chile, in 1923. In 1930 the U.S. government began assisting the Central-American countries in building the road, but it was not until 1936 that all the continental American republics signed and ratified a final agreement. The highway has been completed with the exception of a 362-mile gap, known as the "Darien bottleneck," which lies within Panama and Colombia. This final link, which will connect the American continents, is now under way. The highway, about 16,000 miles long, is not a single continuous route, but makes use of existing highways wherever possible and includes a number of branch highways that are considered to be a part of the system. The highway extends southward through Mexico and Central America and continues down the west coast of South America traversing every sort of terrain from desert to the high Andes. The road turns east in Chile and crosses the Andes through the Uspallata Pass into Argentina. From Buenos Aires on the east coast of South America, the highway turns north to Uruguay, Paraguay, and Brazil. The portion of the highway between Laredo, Texas, and Panama City is called the Inter-American Highway and is 3,142 miles long. This latter portion of the highway was opened for traffic in April 1963, even though a number of improvements were underway along the route.

**Pan American Union.** This central organ of the Pan-American movement, with headquarters in Washington, was set up by the first Pan-American conference in 1890, and until 1910, was called the Commercial Bureau of American Republics. Its governing board, made up of the ambassadors of the Latin-American republics, was presided over by the U.S. secretary of state until the Mexico City Conference of 1945 provided for the rotation of the chairmanship. At the same meeting it was decided, moreover, that the director general of the organization, who up to that time had always been a North American, would serve for ten years and that his successor would be of a different nationality. Under these new provisions the Colombian Alberto LLERAS CAMARGO was elected director general in 1947. After the ORGANIZATION OF AMERICAN STATES was established in 1948, the Pan American Union became the General Secretariat and principal administrative body of the O.A.S. and the governing board of the Pan American Union became the Council of the newly-created organization. The Pan American Union is also the central clearing house for public information on the O.A.S. and its activities. The functions of the Pan American Union are to arrange Pan-American conferences and promote cultural relations among the American republics. There are technical agencies, institutes, and all kinds of administrative units within or related to the Pan American Union. It also issues directives to three special organizations: the Inter-American Economic and Social Council, the Inter-American Council of Jurists, and the Inter-American Cultural Council. See ORGANIZATION OF AMERICAN STATES.

**Pando, José Manuel.** 1848–1917. President of Bolivia. b. La Paz. Colonel of the army and political leader of the liberals. Leader of the revolt of 1899 and president, 1899–1904. During his administration the boundary disputes with Brazil and Chile were settled.

**Paraguay.** A landlocked republic of South America bounded on the north by Bolivia and Brazil, on the east by Brazil and Argentina, on the south by Argentina, and on the west by Argentina and Bolivia, with an area of 157,047 square miles and a population of 2,030,000 (1965), most of whom are a mixture of white and Indian blood. The official language is Spanish, but Guaraní is also spoken by more than 90 per cent of the population. The monetary unit is the guaraní (1965 exchange rate, 126 to the U.S. dollar). Roman Catholicism is the official religion, but other religions are allowed. Under the constitution of 1940, the president is elected for five years by popular vote; a ten-man cabinet appointed by the president carries out the duties of the government; there is a one-chamber congress, whose members are elected by the people on the basis of one per 25,000 inhabitants; and an advisory body known as the council of state composed of the members of the cabinet, the archbishop, the rector of the University, the president of the central bank, and other leaders, all chosen directly or indirectly by the president. The chief cities are ASUNCIÓN, the capital, population 311,301 (1960, includes suburbia and environs), Encarnación, Concepción, and Villarrica. The country is divided into two main sections: that which lies between the two great rivers, the Paraguay and the Paraná, a region of highlands and rolling plains with 95 per cent of the population concentrated on the grasslands east of the Paraguay River, and the CHACO (95,338 square miles), an immense plain covered with scrub forest, marshes, lagoons, and unexplored tropical forests, situated north of the Pilcomayo River and west of the upper Paraguay River. The climate is subtropical, with moderate rainfall.

Paraguay is well-suited for cattle raising and agriculture; the country has about 45,-000,000 head of cattle. The main crops are cotton, manioc, corn, rice, and *yerba maté*; cotton production in 1963 was increased 70 per cent over 1962. Quebracho, a hard, heavy wood, present in great quantities in the forests of the Chaco, is an important product yielding the valuable quebracho tannin extract. The principal exports are meats, timber, tobacco, quebracho extracts, cotton, oilseeds, and hides; principal imports are textiles, foodstuffs, pharmaceutical products, vehicles, fuel and lubricants, machinery and motors, and iron and steel manufactures. Paraguay's chief trading partners are the United States, Argentina, and West Germany. Railroads and roads are still underdeveloped, and although there are 4,584 miles of roads, only 250 miles have paved surfaces. In spite of being an inland country, Paraguay is unique in that it has ready access to the open seas through the Paraguay and Paraná Rivers. Foreign vessels of sufficient size to sail the oceans of the world connect the capital city of Asunción with Europe, the United States, and many Latin-American ports. Smaller ships conduct an active trade between internal ports. The country has 1,865 miles of navigable waterways. Regular steamship service links Asunción with Buenos Aires and with Brazilian ports to the north. There are two domestic airlines operated by the government and seven foreign airlines that serve the country. According to the law, education is compulsory and free, but about 60 per cent of the people are illiterate. There are a number of higher institutions of learning, including the Universidad Nacional de Asunción.

The first European to explore present-day Paraguay was the Portuguese Aleixo García who was killed in 1525. Sebastián CABOT explored the area between 1527 and 1530, and established the settlement of Sancti Spíritu on the Paraná. Juan de Salazar de Espinosa, a member of the expedition of Pedro de MENDOZA, founded Asunción in 1537 and another member of the same expedition, Domingo Martínez de IRALA, became the most important figure in Paraguay for the following two decades. Although officially a part of the viceroyalty of Peru, it was given considerable freedom of development. Between 1608 and 1767, when they were expelled from the Spanish empire, the JESUITS made Paraguay the site of their famous Indian missions. In 1776 Paraguay became a part of the viceroyalty of La Plata. In 1811 the colony declared its independence from Spain and became a nominal republic under a junta. Dr. FRANCIA ruled from 1814 until his death in 1840 as absolute dictator of the country. He was followed by another dictator, Carlos Antonio LÓPEZ, who, in turn, was succeeded by his son Francisco Solano LÓPEZ in 1862. The latter plunged Paraguay into a disastrous war with Brazil, Argentina, and Uruguay, 1864–1870, as a result of which Paraguay lost more than half of its population. The CHACO WAR with Bolivia, 1932–1935, resulted in the acquisition of three-fourths of the disputed Chaco region, 1938, but the country was exhausted. During WORLD WAR II Paraguay co-operated with the United States. From 1940 to 1948 the country was ruled by the dictatorship of President Higínio MORÍNIGO. The last months of Morínigo's government were troubled by serious violence. In March 1947 a coalition of Liberals and FEBRERISTAS staged a revolt that developed into virtual civil war before it was ended by government forces. The elections of 1948 named Juan Natalicio González president but a coup upset his government early in 1949. Several provisional leaders headed the government before Dr. Federico Chaves brought the country relief from political anarchy. Another revolt brought a new president in 1954. General Alfredo Stroessner replaced Chaves in 1954 and has succeeded in controlling the country until the present time. He was re-elected in 1958 and again in February 1963, and his present term is not due to expire until 1968. The recent elections were boycotted by the Liberal and Febrerista parties but for the first time in thirty-five years an opposition candidate ran for the executive office. Ernesto Gavilán, candidate of the Renovación Party, polled less than one-tenth of the total vote but his party won twenty seats in the national legislature. In recent years there have been constant rumors of proposed invasions by Paraguayan exiles living in neighboring countries. A handful of rebels attempted to enter Paraguay in December 1959, but their insufficient numbers proved too feeble to oppose the strong dictatorship of Stroessner.

**Paraguayan War.** Also, **War of the Triple Alliance.** A conflict involving Paraguay on the one hand and Argentina, Brazil, and Uruguay on the other, 1864–1870. An undeclared war between Brazil and Paraguay broke out in November 1864 because of the Paraguayan government's refusal to accept Brazilian interference in the internal disensions of Uruguay. The decision of the Paraguayan dictator Francisco Solano LÓPEZ to send his armies across Argentine territory to attack Brazil, coupled with the victory of the Brazil-supported *colorados* in Uruguay, led Argentina, Brazil, and Uruguay to form an alliance and declare their intention to make war on Paraguay on May 1, 1865. The outbreak of the war has been attributed in the past to the personal ambitions of President López of Paraguay who became the ruler of his country after the death of his father, President Carlos Antonio LÓPEZ. His efforts to create a powerful army and make his country militarily superior to his neighbors, with whom Paraguay had a long history of tariff wars and territorial disputes, have led to that interpretation. Recent scholarship, however, has placed more emphasis on the political factors that led to the war and less on the individuals who took part in the conflict. In the initial phases of the war Paraguayan armies carried the war into Brazilian territory. López' forces attacked north into the Brazilian province of Mato Grosso and south across the Argentine province of Corrientes into Rio Grande do Sul in Brazil. Operating far from their sources of supply and against a numerically increasing enemy, the Paraguayans were eventually forced to retreat behind the river barriers that protected their homeland. In June 1865, Brazilian naval forces won a decisive victory at Riachuelo on the Paraná River below the city of Corrientes. That action severely crippled the Paraguayan navy and thereafter restricted its operations to a defense of the river approaches to Paraguay. By January 1866 the allied fleets had blockaded the rivers, but the assault on Paraguay proper was delayed until April of that year. Once on Paraguayan soil the allied forces, commanded by the Argentine president Bartolomé MITRE, suffered heavy losses at the hands of the stubbornly resisting Paraguayans. The allies were forced to fight in the swampy and muddy southwest corner of Paraguay for more than two years. During 1866 tremendous battles were fought that brought victory and terrible losses to both sides. After the overwhelming Paraguayan victory at Curupayty in September 1866, the allies did not mount an effective offensive for almost a year. In January 1868, Mitre was compelled to return to Buenos Aires and relinquished his command of the allied armies to the Brazilian Marquis of CAXIAS. In February, Brazilian ironclads forced a passage of the strategic river fortress HUMAITÁ and ascended the river to Asunción. The capital city was bombarded but no attempt was made to land troops. In July the famous fortress was abandoned by the Paraguayans and López moved his forces north to prepared defenses

near Villeta south of Asunción. In December of the same year Caxias attacked the new Paraguayan positions and all but annihilated the remains of López' army. The dictator was forced to flee north with a few of his followers. On January 1, 1869, Asunción fell to the allies, and in August a provisional government was set up under allied supervision. López continued to fight a guerrilla warfare until he was trapped and killed at Cerro Corá on March 1, 1870. The defeated country had suffered terribly from the war. Its population, numbering over 500,000 in 1865, was reduced to approximately 28,000 men and 200,000 women and children. In addition, about 55,000 square miles of territory claimed by Paraguay were lost as a result of the defeat. A Brazilian army occupied the country until 1876, and Paraguay was asked to pay heavy indemnities.

**Pardo, Manuel.** 1834–1878. President of Peru. b. Lima. Banker and political leader. Father of José PARDO Y BARREDA. Minister of finance and Peru's fiscal agent in London. Elected the first civilian president of Peru, 1872–1876, he attempted to solve the economic and financial problems of Peru, but it was almost impossible, particularly in the face of the world depression at the time. His administration was unfortunate in several ways: he established a national guard, diminishing the size and importance of the army, and as a result, when Peru was later called on to fight a war, it was unprepared; and he wanted to increase education for the people but was handicapped by financial difficulties that caused the banks in 1875 to suspend specie payments and the government to default on its foreign debt. In 1873 Pardo negotiated a treaty of alliance with Bolivia that ultimately led to war with Chile, 1879. In 1875, in an attempt to protect the GUANO industry of his country, he established a government monopoly of production. He was assassinated, 1878.

**Pardo y Barreda, José.** 1864–1947. President of Peru, 1904–1908. He opposed Chileanization of provinces of Tacna and Arica. He was president again, 1915–1919. A new constitution was inaugurated that granted religious liberty for the first time in the country's history. An able administrator, he attempted to improve the public school system.

His second administration was one of great prosperity for the country. He was friendly toward the United States and in 1917, after the United States declared war on Germany, he broke off diplomatic relations with that country.

**Paredes y Arrillaga, Mariano.** 1797–1849. Mexican general and political leader. Head of the conservative group that supported SANTA ANNA in 1841, he revolted against him in 1844; and again as leader of conservatism, he led a revolt against HERRERA in 1845. Having seized power as a spokesman of nationalism, he was president of Mexico from January to July 1846. When faced with the impossible task of a war with the United States, he was forced into exile in 1847.

**Party of the Mexican Revolution (PRM).** See INSTITUTIONAL REVOLUTIONARY PARTY OF MEXICO.

**Pastry War.** Name given to a minor conflict involving Mexico and France in 1838. Several foreign nations had claims against Mexico for losses suffered by their citizens during the disturbances in Mexico in the preceding years. As it became clear that the Mexican government would not meet the claims, a French fleet appeared off Veracruz demanding payment of reparations valued at 600,000 pesos. The episode was called by Mexicans the Pastry War because one of the claims was that of a French pastry cook, whose restaurant at Tacubaya, near Mexico City, had been wrecked by Mexican officers. The French bombarded the fortress of San Juan de Ulúa and the latter capitulated. Veracruz itself was briefly occupied. As a result of British mediation, France secured a guarantee of the 600,-000 pesos and the French fleet was withdrawn.

**Patiño, Simón Ituri.** *ca.* 1864–1947. Bolivian owner of tin mines and diplomat. b. Cochabamba. Mostly of Indian blood, with almost no education, he operated trains of LLAMAS and mules, and from a debtor obtained an interest in a tin mine. He worked the mine himself, and with the profits bought other mines, and in a few years was owner of the world's largest tin deposits. He served as minister plenipotentiary to Spain, 1922–1927, and to France, 1927–1940. It is said that he

financed the Bolivian war against Paraguay, 1932–1935, which was finally settled by a peace treaty in 1938. During World War II, he left Bolivia and never returned, living first in New York City, then in Europe. He owned Malayan mines and British tin smelters, and when he died he was one of the richest men in the world. Having built three palaces in Bolivia at a cost of $30,000,000, he never lived in two of them, and rarely visited the third. His family inherited his fortune.

**Patria boba.** Spanish, meaning foolish fatherland. The expression is used in Colombia to denote the first years of independence, 1810–1815, which were characterized by the ingenuousness of early patriot leaders.

**Patria chica.** Spanish, meaning little fatherland; region; province.

**Patrocinio, José de.** Brazilian Negro who fought for the ABOLITION OF SLAVERY in his country and helped form the Abolition Confederation in 1883.

**Patronato Real.** Privileges granted by the pope to the Spanish and Portuguese kings to appoint candidates to ecclesiastical benefices and in other ways making it possible for them to have control over the Church in Latin America.

**Pátzcuaro.** Town in the Mexican state of Michoacán, on the shores of Lake Pátzcuaro, one of the most beautiful lakes in Mexico. Near Pátzcuaro is the town of Tzintzuntzan, which in pre-CORTÉS Mexico was the capital of the Tarascan empire, and where ruins of that once-flourishing Indian civilization can be found today. See TARASCANS.

**Paulistas.** Inhabitants of the Brazilian federal state and city of São Paulo. They are historically famous for their pioneering initiative and aggressiveness which in the 17th century brought them together in expeditionary bands or *bandeiras*, having as their goal the exploration and settling of the interior, as well as the finding of gold and the bringing back of Indian slaves. See BANDEIRANTE.

**Pavón, Battle of.** Battle fought at Pavón, province of Santa Fe, Argentina, on September 17, 1861, between the forces of the Argentine Confederation commanded by Justo José de URQUIZA and a Buenos Aires army led by Bartolomé MITRE. Mitre's forces were victorious, and as a result of the victory a new national government was formed, the capital was transferred from Paraná, in the province of Entre Ríos, to Buenos Aires, and Mitre was made the provisional president of the Confederation.

**Paz, José María.** 1791–1854. Argentine general and statesman. Fought against the royalists in Upper Peru (Bolivia); fought in the war against Brazil, 1826–1827. Governor of the province of Córdoba, and one of the most liberal 19th-century leaders, he attempted to unify the unitary leagues of the interior provinces under Córdoban leadership. In a battle with the forces of Federalist Estanislao López, *caudillo* of Santa Fe, he was taken prisoner in May 1831, and escaped after eight years of imprisonment. He opposed ROSAS' dictatorship but because of discord among anti-Rosas leaders he retired to Montevideo, 1842. He directed the defense of Montevideo during the nine-year siege by the forces of Rosas and ORIBE, 1843–1851.

**Paz Estenssoro, Víctor.** 1907–    . President of Bolivia. Lawyer; deputy professor of economic history, La Paz University, 1939–1941. He was leader of the *Movimiento Nacional Revolucionario* (M.N.R.), whose aims were closely patterned after those of the German Nazis. Minister of the treasury in the VILLARROEL government, 1945, he escaped to Buenos Aires after the revolution of 1946 that overthrew Villarroel. Although in exile and lacking an organized political machine, he won the 1951 election with the support of a coalition of the M.N.R. and the *Partido Obrero Revolucionario*, a pro-Communist movement, but the government refused to recognize Paz Estenssoro's election, and a military junta assumed power, May 1951. His supporters overthrew the junta, 1952, and he took office. He launched a program of economic and social reform, nationalized Bolivia's three most important tin mining firms, October 1952, and subsequently took steps to distribute land among landless Indians. He had to suppress a number of revolts, 1953.

He maintained cordial relations with the United States and received substantial economic aid therefrom. He was the only president to complete his term of office since SAAVEDRA in 1925. Hernán Siles Zuazo, another M.N.R. candidate, was elected president, 1956–1960, and then Paz Estenssoro was re-elected to the presidency. Continuing economic difficulties provoked strikes and serious disturbances during his second administration, and supporters of Fidel CASTRO, supported by Communists and leftist elements, also attacked the government. The administration announced a ten-year development program, 1962, to strengthen the economy and raise Bolivian living standards. He was re-elected for a third term, May 1964, but was ousted in November 1964, by a military junta headed by General René Barrientos, who in turn was elected president in July 1966.

**Peçanha, Nilo.** 1857–1924. President of Brazil. Jurist and political leader from MINAS GERAIS who served as vice-president of Brazil, 1906–1909, and upon the death of PENNA became president, serving for the year 1909 to 1910. He served as foreign minister, 1917–1918.

**Pedrarias.** See ARIAS DE ÁVILA, PEDRO.

**Pedro I.** 1798–1834. King of Portugal and emperor of Brazil. b. Lisbon. Sent to Brazil at the time of NAPOLEON's invasion where he was joined by his family, and remained there as prince regent after his father, JOHN VI, returned to Portugal, 1821. When Brazil broke with Portugal, he was proclaimed Emperor Pedro I of the independent Brazilian Empire, December 1822. He granted a liberal constitution, 1824, and at the death of his father, abdicated his rights to the Portuguese Crown in favor of his daughter Maria. The unsuccessful war against Argentina, 1826–1827, his delay in putting into effect the Constitution of 1824, the increasing interest with which he viewed the affairs of Portugal, where the regent, his brother Miguel, had proclaimed himself king, and his open infidelity to his queen rendered him unpopular. After an uprising in the capital he abdicated the Brazilian Crown in favor of his son PEDRO II, April

1831. He left for Europe where, after a hard-fought campaign against Miguel, he entered Lisbon, sent his brother into exile, and made the Portuguese throne safe for his daughter Maria in September 1833. He died shortly afterward from the extertions of the campaign. He was responsible for the GRITO DO YPIRANGA of 1822.

**Pedro II.** 1825–1891. Second and last emperor of Brazil. b. Rio de Janeiro. Succeeded to the throne in 1831; declared of age, 1840, and crowned July 1841. He was immediately faced with federalist uprisings in different provinces; only toward 1850 was he able to govern a pacified country. He abolished slave trade, 1850, and was able to aggrandize Brazil's territory after the successful war against Paraguay, 1864–1870. He promulgated a law granting slaves gradual emancipation, 1871, introduced the metric system, fostered building of railroads, education, establishment of universal suffrage, etc. He was a liberal-minded monarch, was devoted to philosophy and science, and governed in accordance with the constitution and in co-operation with the elected legislature. He visited the United States, 1876, and Europe on three occasions. A revolution in November 1889 forced him to leave for Europe with his family. He died in Paris.

**Peixoto, Floriano.** 1842–1895. President of Brazil. General. One of the leaders who deposed the Brazilian emperor PEDRO II and established the republic, 1889. He became vice-president, 1891, under Manoel da FONSECA and when the latter was forced to resign, he became president, serving 1891–1894. His regime, corrupt and arbitrary, caused the people to fear the continuance of the military in power. There were revolts in many provinces, including one in Rio Grande do Sul, headed by the GAUCHO chieftain Saraïva. A navy revolt headed by Admiral MELLO started a bloody civil war. The insurgents were defeated by government forces at Camp-Osorio in June 1894, but the people, before the end of the fighting, had already elected a civilian, Prudente José de MORAES BARROS, a PAULISTA, to replace Peixoto.

**Pelucones.** Literally, bigwigs, derived from the Spanish word *peluca*, meaning wig. In Chile, the name given to the conservative political element in the contest for control of the government after independence had been achieved. The liberal opposition were termed *pipiolos*, or "greenhorns." Both parties were active for a long time in the political life of the country.

**Peña y Peña, Manuel de la.** 1789–1850. Provisional president of Mexico from September to November 1847, and from January to June 1848. Best known as a jurist, he served as a judge of the supreme court from 1824, and was its president. He was a cabinet officer in 1837 and 1845. During his last term as provisional president the TREATY OF GUADALUPE-HIDALGO was signed, which ended the war with the United States.

**Peninsulares.** Spanish, meaning people of the peninsula. Name given, during the Latin-American colonial period, to persons born in Spain.

**Penna, Affonso Augusto Moreira.** 1847–1909. President of Brazil. Political leader from the state of Minas Gerais; member of the commission that drafted the Brazilian Civil Code of 1888; patriotic supporter of the new republic, 1889; president of the Bank of Brazil, 1894–1898; senator, vice-president, 1902–1906; president, 1906–1909.

**Peonage.** After the elimination of the *encomienda* (fief) and *repartimiento* (forced labor) systems in the Spanish-American colonies in the 18th century, the Indians were theoretically free. However, most of them soon contracted debts with white landowners and were bound to work on the latters' properties until the debts were paid off. Often Indians would receive plots of land from white *hacendados* and would have to pay for the use of the plots by working a certain number of days a week on the land of the owners. Since the Indians could rarely pay off their debts, they were practically bound to the soil, and usually the debt was inherited by their children. This condition is called peonage or debt slavery. In the 19th century, peonage was especially prevalent in Bolivia, Peru, Ecuador, Guatemala, and Mexico, countries with large Indian populations. In Bolivia, Peru, and

Ecuador peonage is illegal, but it still exists in many districts. In Mexico, peonage flourished especially during the DÍAZ regime, but was declared illegal by the constitution of 1917 and has been largely eradicated through the agrarian reforms of the past 45 years.

**Peonías.** See CABALLERÍAS.

**Peralta Barnuevo Rocha y Benavides, Pedro de.** 1663–1743. Peruvian scientist, poet, and encyclopedist. Distinguished rector of the University of San Marcos at Lima, engineer, and astronomer. He wrote intense Baroque poetry, and was influenced by the Spanish poet Luis de Góngora (1561–1627). His published works, numbering more than 60, include such diverse subjects as astronomy, law, metallurgy, mathematics, civil engineering, history, navigation, poems in Spanish, Latin, French, and Italian, and drama. His best-known work is the epic poem *Lima fundada* (The Founding of Lima), 1732. See LITERATURE.

**Pereira de Souza, Washington Luiz.** See SOUZA, WASHINGTON LUIZ PEREIRA DE.

**Pérez Moscayano, José Joaquín.** 1800–1889. President of Chile. b. Santiago. After preliminary diplomatic service in the United States, Europe, and Argentina he became minister of the treasury, 1845, and four years later was appointed minister of the interior. He served as president, 1861–1871, and his administration was relatively calm and peaceful. The only exception was the year 1865–1866, when Chile, with Bolivia and Peru, fought against a Spanish bombardment of Valparaíso and a blockade of the coast, but the enemy withdrew. Mining developed, and there was general prosperity. After his presidency, he served as senator and counselor for several years.

**Pernambuco.** Indian words *pera nambuco*, meaning perforated rock. Federal state of the United States of Brazil, situated in the northeastern part of the country on the Atlantic Ocean, having an estimated population of 4,120,000 (1960). Its capital is RECIFE, also called Pernambuco, population approximately 798,000 (1960). The principal wealth of the state is derived from agriculture, especially sugar, cotton, and tobacco.

According to a legend, the coast of Pernambuco was discovered in 1484 by Martin Behaim of Nuremberg, Germany, traveling in the service of Portugal. It was also explored by COLUMBUS' friend, Vicente PINZÓN. The first to set foot on it was Pedro Álvares CABRAL on May 3, 1500, who took possession of it in the name of Portugal. In 1503 a colony was founded on the island of Itamaracá. In 1535 the region between Cape Agostinho and the São Francisco River was taken over as a captaincy by the captain general, Duarte Coelho Pereira, who was able to establish friendly relations with the Indians of the territory. Olinda, which for a long time was the capital of the captaincy, was founded in 1535. The region enjoyed prosperity during the 16th century, except for war with the Indians and the sack of Recife by the British in 1595. Olinda and Recife were captured by the Dutch in 1630, and from 1636 to 1644 the territory was governed by MAURITZ of Nassau, who treated the Portuguese settlers well and tried to insure the prosperity of the newly-acquired Dutch possession. The Dutch were finally dislodged by the Portuguese in 1654. For more than 60 years Pernambuco was the seat of the *quilombo*, or slave republic of Palmares, founded by escaped Negro slaves in 1630. Only at the end of the century were the whites able to destroy this movement. In 1710 the rivalry between the twin towns of Recife and Olinda broke out into open conflict, but peace was restored after a year of fighting. (See MASCATES.) Several republican uprisings took place in the province in the first half of the 19th century. After the failure of the first of these revolts in 1817, Pernambuco lost the *capitanias* of Alagoas, Paraíba, Rio Grande do Norte, and Ceará. In 1822 Pernambuco became a province of the Brazilian Empire. In 1824 Pernambuco republicans were joined by other provinces and proclaimed the Republic of the Equator, but this revolution was also suppressed. A third uprising, begun in 1848, failed when the revolutionaries failed in their efforts to take Recife by storm, 1849. In 1889 Pernambuco became a federal state of the Republic of Brazil.

**Perón, Juan Domingo.** 1895–     . President of Argentina. b. Los Lobos, Buenos Aires. Entered pro-German military academy, 1911; worked at general staff headquarters, 1930, took part in the military coup against President YRIGOYEN organized by General URIBURU, leading the troops into Buenos Aires; lieutenant colonel; military observer in Italy, 1938. He was in charge of training troops in Mendoza, where he organized the G.O.U. (Group of United Officers) with the aim of seizing power, in imitation of the German pattern in Europe, and establishing Argentina's predominance in South America. The G.O.U. supported seizure of power by army leaders, June 1943, and he was appointed vice-president, minister of war, secretary of labor and public welfare in the administration of General Edelmiro FARRELL, who took over from General Pedro RAMÍREZ, February 1944. He courted the favor of the workers by passing labor legislation and raising wages. His dictatorial methods caused the opposition to demand his imprisonment, and he was confined to the island of Martín García, October 1945, but the same month returned to Buenos Aires amidst the enthusiastic shouts of his lower-class supporters, the *descamisados* (the shirtless ones), who had been aroused to a frenzy in his favor by Eva Duarte, whom he married on October 26, 1945. He was elected president, 1946, and after his victory, began to push through his political, economic, and social program, which has been called *peronismo* or *justicialismo*, a system midway between capitalism and communism, analogous in many ways to Mussolini's fascism, but adapted to the historical tradition, temperament, and specific needs of Argentina. A five-year plan was set in motion to develop Argentine economy; a government corporation in control of imports and exports, the Trade Promotion Institute (IAPI) was organized; a National Economic Council was formed. The government established strict control over labor, the press, and the educational system; many professors opposed to Peronism lost their positions and the world-famous Buenos Aires newspaper, *La Prensa*, as well as other newspapers, such as the Socialist organ *La Vanguardia*, were closed. Perón launched a program of economic nationalization under which the banks,

railroads, and telephone and telegraph systems were taken over by the government. In other fields, mixed government and private organizations were created to foster economic growth, and British influence over the Argentine economy largely ended. Perón allowed political parties to exist (e.g., radicals and socialists) but opposition was strictly limited and operated under the control of the government. Perón consistently favored labor, enacted labor reforms and increased the workers' wages, and in return enjoyed continued support from the working people in his country. In foreign affairs, he encouraged Argentine agitation for the return of the Falkland Islands from Great Britain, and pushed Argentine claims to the Antarctic. He had the Argentine constitution amended, 1949, so that he could be re-elected, and in 1951, he managed to poll over 2,000,000 votes running against the Radical deputy, Ricardo Balbín, whose campaign was hampered by repressive measures established by the government to stifle opposition. Although decidedly anti-North American in the early days of his administration, partly because of the publication by the United States of the so-called *"Blue Book,"* 1946, showing that country's pro-Axis activity during the war, Perón later indicated his willingness to place relations with the United States on a basis of mutual respect and understanding and to foster better economic ties between the two countries, and in 1950 he obtained a loan of $125,000,000 from the United States. The death of Perón's wife, (María) Eva Duarte de PERÓN, 1952, proved to be a great loss to the dictator as she had been a valuable political asset and great favorite among his followers. An unsuccessful attempt on his life, 1953, when he was addressing a crowd of *peronistas* in Buenos Aires, was followed by severe rioting in the course of which *peronistas* wrecked a great deal of property belonging to both individuals and groups of the opposition. Perón lashed out against the Catholic Church, 1954–1955, accusing the latter of trying to undermine his regime, and a number of repressive measures were taken against ecclesiastics. The Argentine envoy to the Vatican was recalled for "consultation," and religious education in state-supported schools discontinued, April 1955; legislation aiming at the separation of Church and State was passed by the Peronist congress. A revolt, June 1955, although unsuccessful, severely shook the Perón dictatorship, and he was forced to make a number of conciliatory moves designed to pacify the growing opposition to his regime. By September, however, it seemed that he was once more firmly in control, after the Peronist-dominated Confederation of Labor, enthusiastically proclaiming its support for him, had refused to accept his resignation as president, and after the Argentine congress, acceding to his demand, had decreed a state of siege for the Buenos Aires area to prevent anti-Peronist demonstrations in the capital. However, a second, and more powerful revolt, involving the navy as well as important segments of the army, overthrew the Perón dictatorship, and he sought political asylum on a Paraguayan gunboat anchored in Buenos Aires harbor. He was given safe-conduct to Paraguay, September 24, 1955, by the revolutionary Argentine government. He went into exile in Spain. See ARGENTINA.

**Perón, María Eva Duarte de.** 1919–1952. Argentine political leader and wife of president Juan PERÓN. b. Los Toldos, Buenos Aires. Spent her early years in the town of Junín, then settled in Buenos Aires; actress. She was of invaluable service to Perón when she organized workers' march in Buenos Aires in 1945 demanding his freedom from detention on the island of Martín García. She married Perón on October 26, 1945, and after his election in 1946 she rose to power quickly and played an important part in accelerating Perón's social and economic program. She established control over a number of important departments of government and was highly influential with labor. She was in charge of the (María) Eva Duarte de Perón Foundation, which was established to promote public welfare and retain control of public sentiment; and she ceaselessly defended Perón's *justicialismo* program, and enjoyed great popularity with the common people. She toured Europe in 1947. She intended to run for the vice-presidency in 1951, but reconsidered. She died of cancer.

**Pershing, John Joseph.** 1860–1948. General of the U.S. Army. b. Laclede, Missouri. Graduated West Point, 1886; brigadier general, 1906; he commanded the expeditionary force that was sent into Mexico in 1916 to suppress the activities of Francisco (Pancho) VILLA, whom he failed to capture; major general, 1916; commander in chief, American Expeditionary Forces, World War I, 1917–1919; full general, 1917; chief of staff, 1921–1924; retired.

**Personalismo.** The practice of exalting the leadership of an individual over political ideologies, constitutional government, or political parties. In Latin America it is common for a political party to be founded on the personality of the leader rather than on political beliefs or issues. The leader's name is often used as a popularized name for the party or its followers, e.g., *villistas, peronistas,* or *ibañistas.*

**Peru.** The third largest republic in South America, and the fourth in all Latin America, with an area of 496,228 square miles (indefinite, as a portion of the frontier has not been delimited) and a population of 12,087,000 (1966), of which 53 per cent are white and mestizo, 46 per cent Indian, and 1 per cent others. Spanish is the official language, but Indian Quechua and Aymará are widely spoken. The monetary unit is the sol; 26.82 soles equal the U.S. dollar (1965). The Roman Catholic religion is the predominant faith, but there is general religious freedom. Under the amended constitution of 1933 the president is elected by direct suffrage for a six-year term as is the congress that consists of a chamber of deputies and a senate. The president is not eligible for re-election until the succeeding presidential period has passed. Voting is compulsory for males who are literate and are between the ages of 21 and 60 and voluntary for all citizens over 60. The chief cities and their approximate populations (1963) are Lima, the capital 1,730,000, Callao, the main port, 150,000, Arequipa, 150,000, and Cuzco, 70,000.

Peru is situated on the west coast of South America and is bounded on the north by Ecuador, on the northeast and east by Colombia and Brazil, on the southeast by Bolivia, and on the south by Chile. Its extreme width is 800 miles. The country may be divided into three main areas: a narrow coastal strip where most of the cities are situated; the great highland formed by the Andes Mountains which run north-south, where there are a number of peaks rising more than 19,000 feet above sea level; and the *montaña*, a tropical region in the Amazon Basin, to the east of the Andes. The great majority of the people are engaged in agriculture, the chief products being cotton (grown in the coastal area), sugar, corn, tobacco, wheat, and rice. The country is rich in minerals, which constitute about 60 per cent of its exports and include barite, bismuth, silver, tellurium, gold, iron, petroleum, vanadium, copper, lead, and zinc. Manufacturing industries are devoted principally to the production of goods for domestic consumption and include the production of food, tobacco, rubber, metals, paper, textiles, chemicals, leather goods, and cement. There are 2,262 miles of railroads and 18,600 miles of roads, and two of the rail lines are among the most striking engineering achievements in the world. The line extending from Callao and Lima to Oroya and Cerro de Pasco reaches an altitude of 15,000 feet in 80 miles, and that between Mollendo and Lake Titicaca climbs up to 12,000 feet. Peru still imports the majority of its manufactured goods as well as much food, the main sources for these imports being the United States, Great Britain, and West Germany. Much remains to be done in the field of education. More than 50 per cent of the people are illiterate, and there are too few schools outside the cities to educate the peasant masses. The cities have a number of good schools and universities, the most famous being the University of San Marcos in Lima, founded, 1551; opened, 1576.

In pre-Conquest times Peru was ruled by the INCAS, who had formed a vast empire including present-day Ecuador, Peru, Bolivia, and parts of Chile and Argentina. The flourishing civilization of these Indians was rivaled only by that of the Central-American MAYAS and the Mexican AZTECS. Many impressive ruins still standing today are witnesses of the achievements of this remarkable people. The Inca empire was crushed with

relative ease by Spanish conquistadors led by PIZARRO and ALMAGRO, 1532-1533, who conquered the huge territory in the name of the Spanish Crown. Lima, the present capital, was founded by Pizarro, 1535. Jealousy between Pizarro and Almagro soon resulted in a civil war among the Spaniards. This conflict, which cost both Pizarro and Almagro their lives, continued for a number of years and was followed by further unrest when the NEW LAWS, 1542, sought to protect the Indians from the greedy conquistadors. Disorders followed upon each other until the arrival of Viceroy Andrés HURTADO DE MENDOZA, 1556. The colony developed in peace, and with the discovery of silver in what is now Bolivia (then a part of Peru), it prospered.

During the colonial period Peru was one of the two leading Spanish viceroyalties of the New World. The Indians were generally exploited, apportioned to the Spanish settlers in *encomiendas* or fiefs and forced to work in the mines under the *mita* or forced labor system. There were a number of Indian revolts, the most important being the one led by TUPAC AMARU, 1780, which was ruthlessly suppressed. The movement for independence from Spain began in the first decade of the 19th century and continued into the second decade. But it was only in 1821, when General SAN MARTÍN entered Lima, that independence was proclaimed. San Martín served as "protector" of Peru until 1822, when he resigned. BOLÍVAR liberated those parts of Peru still under Spanish control and assumed dictatorial powers, 1824. He left the country in the hands of a council with SANTA CRUZ as president, 1826. The council was overthrown, 1827, and José de la MAR became president. In the 19th century the leadership of Peru changed hands many times with recurrent civil wars. After a war with Spain, 1864-1866, the country went through a period of great prosperity during the administration of José BALTA. The large income derived from GUANO exports permitted the government to launch a large-scale public works program, including the building of railroads, and also to further agricultural expansion. To deal with the labor shortage on the coastal plantations, many Chinese coolies were brought into the country.

Government by the military came to an end in 1872, when Manuel PARDO, the candidate of the Civilista Party, composed of rich planters and merchants as well as of liberal elements, was elected to the presidency. The disastrous WAR OF THE PACIFIC with Chile, 1879–1883, cost Peru the province of Tarapacá and also resulted in the occupation of Tacna and Arica by Chilean forces. Nicolás de PIÉROLA, president, 1895–1899, and his successors, gave the country more than a decade of peace, directing much of their efforts to the improvement of education. Peru was ruled by the dictatorship of Augusto LEGUÍA, 1908–1912, 1919–1930, who paid no attention to the liberal constitution of 1920. Leguía was overthrown, 1930, by a military uprising led by Luis SÁNCHEZ CERRO, who was forced to resign the following year because of poor economic conditions and military revolts. However, he was elected to the presidency the same year and served until 1933, when he was assassinated. During his administration Peru almost became involved in a war with Colombia over the LETICIA DISPUTE. His successor, General Oscar BENAVIDES, also ruled as a dictator until 1939, when the moderate Manuel PRADO Y UGARTECHE was elected. Peru broke diplomatic relations with the Axis in 1942, and the great demand for Peruvian copper as well as a large amount of financial aid from the United States resulted in prosperity for the country. In 1945 BUSTAMANTE Y RIVERO was elected president with the support of the left-wing political group, APRA, led by HAYA DE LA TORRE. The conservatives in congress and in the president's cabinet violently opposed the *apristas* who had three representatives in the cabinet and were determined to push through a number of social and economic reforms. The struggle between conservatives and *apristas* culminated in an uprising allegedly organized by the latter group in October 1948. The revolt was a failure, and Bustamante, although not connected with the movement, was ousted by the army. Severe measures were taken against APRA, and Haya de la Torre, its leader, was forced to seek refuge in the Colombian embassy at Lima and was only permitted to leave the country in 1954. General Manuel ODRÍA assumed power as provisional president

and served in that capacity until 1950 when he was elected for a six-year term, no other candidates being permitted to run in opposition. Odría's administration was characterized by liberal economic policies aimed at economic reconstruction and by rigid political control. The border dispute with Ecuador, ostensibly settled in 1942, flared up again in 1954. Despite efforts to reach an acceptable agreement no lasting settlement was achieved. Free elections were held in 1956 and former president Manuel Prado was elected to the presidency. The new president continued the conservative but enlightened policies characteristic of recent governments, but permitted far more freedom than his predecessors. The dispute with Ecuador continued to provoke trouble but neither country was willing to retreat from the position it had taken on the boundary question. In 1962 an avalanche of ice, boulders, and mud inundated an Andean community near Mt. Huascarán causing severe damage and killing more than 3,500 persons. The elections of June 1962 resulted in a confused situation that brought about a military coup and the establishment of a ruling junta. No candidate polled the necessary one-third of the votes cast and the selection of the president fell to the congress. Conservative military leaders, fearing the election of the liberal Haya de la Torre, seized the government and annulled the election. One year later a new national election was held and Fernando BELAÚNDE TERRY was chosen president. Though the new government pushed through a law aimed at the distribution of large estates to peasants, the country was harassed in 1965 by left-wing guerrilla activity which was finally brought under control by the armed forces.

**Peru-Bolivian Confederation.** A union of Bolivia and Peru effected in 1836 during the presidencies of José Orbegoso of Peru and Andrés SANTA CRUZ of Bolivia. Santa Cruz, whose army had invaded Peru to help Orbegoso put down a Peruvian army revolt in 1835, brought about the confederation after defeating the rebels. He divided Peru into two states: North Peru with President Orbegoso at its head, and South Peru, led by General Ramón Herrera. The two republics formed a confederation with Bolivia, of which General José Miguel de VELASCO was declared president, and Santa Cruz was proclaimed the "protector" of this new state, an office which was to be both lifelong and hereditary. The new regime was welcomed by the Peruvians, for Santa Cruz had displayed remarkable talents as an administrator in Bolivia. The confederation, however, was short-lived. In 1836 war broke out with Chile, whose relations with Peru had been steadily deteriorating because of financial questions, and because of the competition between the ports of Valparaíso and Callao. Chile also interpreted the confederation as a menace to its own position. In 1837 Argentina joined the conflict on the side of Chile, but the troops of the confederation defeated Argentine forces sent against Santa Cruz. Chile was not more successful at first, but in January 1839, a Chilean army, led by General Manuel BULNES PRIETO, routed the forces of Santa Cruz at YUNGAY and put an end to the confederation. Santa Cruz went into exile and José Miguel de Velasco remained as president of Bolivia, while GAMARRA took over the presidency in Peru.

**Pessôa, Epitácio da Silva.** 1865–1942. President of Brazil. Jurist and political leader from Paraíba. He was head of the Brazilian delegation to Versailles, and was elected president in 1919 to finish out the term of RODRÍGUES ALVES. Pessôa's administration did much to aid the drought-afflicted areas of the northeast by building dams and supplying means for storing water, and he served until 1922. He was a member of the World Court (Permanent Court of International Justice) at The Hague, 1924–1930.

**Pétion, Alexandre Sabes.** 1770–1818. Haitian general and political leader. b. Port-au-Prince. Well-educated mulatto who fought in the rebellion under TOUSSAINT L'OUVERTURE and RIGAUD, 1791–1797. He later supported Rigaud against L'Ouverture, and when L'Ouverture was victorious fled to France, 1800; returned with French, 1802, but soon turned against them. He served under DESSALINES, 1802–1806. After the assassination of Dessalines, when CHRISTOPHE proclaimed himself ruler of the island, Pétion established

the Republic of Haiti in the southern portions of the island to contest the authority of Christophe. He ruled moderately and well. He fought against Christophe, 1811–1818, and aided BOLÍVAR in 1816. He died in office.

**Petroleum Industry.** The leading petroleum producer in Latin America and the third in the world is Venezuela, where the first wells, lying close to Lake Maracaibo, started operating in 1917, and where a second oil-producing area in the eastern part of the country has been developed in recent years. Estimated production in 1963 amounted to 3,240,000 barrels daily. Most Venezuelan oil is refined on the Dutch West Indian islands of Aruba and Curaçao, off the Venezuelan coast. American and British interests almost exclusively control the industry. The second-ranking Latin-American petroleum source is Mexico, where production started at the turn of this century. In 1910 the country was producing 3,600,000 barrels and by 1921, 193,000,000 barrels, greater than today's production. In the early twenties the industry declined, partly because production in the Tampico field on the Gulf of Mexico decreased, and partly because foreign capital began to prefer Venezuela for investment purposes. The petroleum laws in Venezuela were more favorable to foreign investors than in Mexico, where all products of the subsoil had been declared the property of the nation by the constitution of 1917. In 1938 the Mexican government expropriated the petroleum holdings of 17 American and British concerns and today the industry is in the hands of the state-owned Pemex (*Petróleos Mexicanos*). Major Mexican oil fields are located in the states of Tamaulipas and Veracruz, along the coast of the Gulf of Mexico, and in the Tuxpan area, where the Poza Rica field now produces about half of Mexico's oil. In Colombia, the industry began to operate in 1919. Two long pipelines (262 miles and 335 miles long, respectively) link the Magdalena basin wells with the Caribbean coast. In 1963 Colombia registered the highest rate of production increase, 11 per cent, in all of Latin America. Recent oil discoveries, 1960, 1962, will augment Colombia's rising production figures. Most of Argentina's oil still comes from the province of Chubut, but new fields have begun production in other areas. A majority of the Argentinian petroleum industry is handled by the government-controlled concern *Yacimientos Petrolíferos Fiscales.* Production in 1963 was estimated at 263,000 barrels daily, a decline of 2.2 per cent from the preceding year. In Peru, where the first well in Latin America was opened in 1878, a 100-mile-long area extending along the northern coast contains the country's important oil deposits. In Bolivia oil is found in the southeastern lowlands and a large amount of the oil produced is exported to Argentina. With the completion of the Brazilian-financed railroad from Santa Cruz to Corumbá, Bolivian oil can now be exported to Brazil. In the latter country only the state of Bahia produces oil, and that in small quantities. In March 1955, oil was struck at Nova Olinda, in the Amazon basin, by the Brazilian government oil monopoly Petrobras (*Petróleo Brasileiro*). Efforts to locate more fields in the area are continuing.

**Philip II.** Also, **Felipe.** Known as **The Prudent.** 1527–1598. King of Spain, 1556–1598, and Portugal, 1580–1598. b. Valladolid. Succeeded his father, CHARLES I, as ruler of the Spanish and Portuguese areas of the New World, ruler of the Netherlands, and defender of the Roman Catholic religion. Determined to crush all opposition, his mighty Armada was defeated by the English, 1588. Interested in his possessions, he sent scientific expeditions to New Spain, but unfortunately not always good administrators were sent to the colonies, for those positions could be bought, due largely to the depleted treasury of the mother country. He took many shiploads of treasures, gold, silver, and whatever else he could get from the colonies as tribute. He was hard-working and conscientious, but a religious fanatic and of moderate ability. The decline of Spanish power began during his reign.

**Philip III.** 1578–1621. Son of PHILIP II. b. Madrid. King of Spain and Portugal, 1598–1621, inheriting all the Spanish and Portuguese possessions and problems. Spain at that time was a fading power and needed attention, but Philip was not interested and

turned over the affairs of his kingdom to the Duke of Lerma, who hastened the decline.

**Philip IV.** 1605–1665. King of Spain, 1621–1665, and Portugal, 1621–1640. b. Valladolid. Eldest son of PHILIP III. Left the administration to his favorite, Count Olivares, 1623–1643. Spain's commerce and industry continued to decline. When the Spanish Crown, for example, was bankrupt in 1633, Philip assigned out of royal revenues as much as 300,000 ducats a year for wine and oil to be used in the monasteries of New Spain and Peru. There was absolutely no sense of values, no attempt was made to work for a stable trade or economy, and the disastrous foreign wars that Spain fought against France, Germany, and Holland further ruined the country. Portugal regained her independence in 1640, and Holland was lost by the Treaty of Westphalia in 1648.

**Philip V.** 1683–1746. First monarch of the Bourbon dynasty in Spain. King 1700–1724, 1724–1746. Grandson of Louis XIV and son of Dauphin Louis and Marie Christine, daughter of Ferdinand Maria, Elector of Bavaria. b. Versailles. As Duke of Anjou he was educated in his youth by Fénelon. CHARLES II of Spain named him heir to the throne, and his accession to the throne marked the beginning of the War of the Spanish Succession, 1701–1714. He was recognized as king on the condition that a Bourbon would not occupy both the French and Spanish thrones at the same time. During his rule, he issued new reforms for New Spain: The mints were taken out of the hands of private contractors and were administered by the Crown; the new laws went into effect in New Spain, 1732–1733, but in Peru not until 1748. He tried to prevent the CREOLES from competing with Spain in trade and prohibited them, in 1729, from acting as agents of the exporting houses. Consequently, the creoles could only do business through Spanish merchants. He introduced French ideas into the Spanish courts. He abdicated in January 1724, in favor of son Luis, but the son died, and Philip returned to the throne, 1724–1746. He joined in the War of the Austrian Succession against Maria Theresa, 1741.

**Picado Michalski, Teodoro.** 1900–1960. President of Costa Rica, teacher, and lawyer. b. San José. Teacher of history, Liceo de Costa Rica, 1918–1923; practiced law, 1923–1930; minister of public education, 1932; deputy in the national congress, 1938; president of the republic, 1944–1948. Though he suppressed a revolution in 1945, his was a liberal, moderate administration. After the 1948 election, he was forced into exile.

**Pichincha, Battle of.** Battle fought on May 24, 1822, in the Ecuadorian province of the same name between the troops of the Venezuelan general SUCRE and the Spanish troops of General Aymerich. Sucre won and, as a result, was able to take Quito and to move on Peru.

**Piérola, Nicolás de.** 1839–1913. President of Peru. b. Camaná. General and political leader. Studied theology and law; married a granddaughter of Mexican emperor ITURBIDE. Exiled, 1866, he lived in Europe for three years, returning to Peru, 1869. He was minister of finance under BALTA and led revolts against Manuel PARDO, 1874–1875, and against Mariano Ignacio PRADO, 1879. He assumed the presidency, 1879, but was driven from office by Chileans during the WAR OF THE PACIFIC, 1879–1883, when they occupied Lima, 1881. He played a military role in War of the Pacific. After a period of travel in the United States and Europe, Piérola returned to Peru where he led another successful revolt, 1894, and again occupied the presidency, 1895–1899. His administration was characterized by strong and efficient leadership, increased stabilization in the currency, construction of public works, government control of the army. A civil marriage law was passed, 1897. He was an unsuccessful candidate for the presidency in 1903 and 1908.

**Pilar, Treaty of.** Compact signed in 1820 by the Argentine provinces of Buenos Aires, Santa Fe, and Entre Ríos, by virtue of which all three were to share in the government of Argentina.

**Pinedo, Federico.** Argentine finance minister, 1933–1938, who attempted to establish a stable economy in his country. He instituted an income tax law, 1934, created the National Grain Board, stimulated a free flow of international payments, and government control over the supply and demand levels in cattle and wheat, and encouraged industrial growth of the country. He wrote many works in the fields of government and economics.

**Pinto Díaz, Francisco Antonio.** 1785–1858. President of Chile. Descended from illustrious family of Santiago; became lawyer, 1806; member of revolutionary forces, 1810; minister to Buenos Aires; minister to England, 1813–1817; fought with SAN MARTÍN against royalist forces; appointed minister of interior and of foreign relations, 1824; served as intendant at Coquimbo; elected vice-president, 1827; succeeded FREIRE SERRANO as chief executive, 1827. He called a new congress that wrote a new constitution in 1828 giving more power to the central government. He attempted to institute other reforms, and when he was unsuccessful, he resigned, 1829. He became leader of the liberal political element, 1841.

**Pinto Garmendia, Aníbal.** 1825–1884. President of Chile, 1876–1881. b. Santiago. Held diplomatic posts in Europe; appointed intendant of the province of Concepción, 1862; served in the national chamber of deputies; elected senator, 1870. He entered the cabinet of President ERRÁZURIZ ZAÑARTU as minister of war and navy, 1871, and started the successful Chilean WAR OF THE PACIFIC with Bolivia and Peru in 1879. There were many economic problems during his administration, for the country was feeling the world depression of the 1870's.

**Pinzón, Martín Alonso.** ca. 1440–1493. Spanish navigator and explorer. b. Palos. With his brothers, Vicente and Francisco, he aided COLUMBUS in preparing the first expedition and commanded the "Pinta" on the voyage of 1492. Separated from the other ships after landfall at Guanahani, he joined Columbus at Haiti. On the return voyage, he was again separated from Columbus but managed to reach Palos on the same day, March 14, 1493. He died at La Rábida.

**Pinzón, Vicente Yáñez.** ca. 1460–1524. Spanish navigator. b. Palos. Aided COLUMBUS in gathering equipment for his expeditions.

Pinzón was in charge of the "Niña" on Columbus' voyage of discovery, 1492. In 1500, he reached the Brazilian coast, discovered the mouth of the Amazon River, and followed the shore north, going west for 2,000 miles and may have reached Costa Rica.

**Pipiolos.** Spanish, meaning novices or greenhorns. In Chile, the name given to the liberals in the contest for control of the government after independence had been achieved. The conservative opposition were called *pelucones,* or bigwigs. The two political parties continued to be active in Chilean politics for a long time.

**Pizarro, Francisco.** *ca.* 1470–1541. Spanish conqueror of Peru. b. Trujillo, Extremadura. First sailed to America, 1509. He settled in Panama, 1519, and joined ALMAGRO in his plan to explore the west coast of South America in 1522. The first expedition was a failure, 1524–1525, and after great hardships were endured during the second expedition, 1526, they explored the Gulf of Guayaquil. Pizarro returned to Spain for the purpose of getting permission from CHARLES V to conquer and govern new territories, 1528. He arrived in Panama with a large group in 1530, and the expedition got underway in 1531 and overcame the INCA chief ATAHUALPA in 1532. After a trial which was a travesty of justice, Atahualpa was executed, 1533. Pizarro reached Cuzco and captured it. He founded Lima, the new capital, in 1535. In a civil war with Almagro, 1537–1538, Almagro was defeated and executed, but Pizarro himself was killed by followers of Almagro.

**Pizarro, Gonzalo.** *ca.* 1506–1548. Spanish explorer, half-brother of Francisco, who went with him to Peru, 1531. He served as governor of Quito, 1539–1546. In October 1544, he occupied Lima and forced the *audiencia* to recognize him as governor. Power intoxicated him and he acted, although he made no such statement, as if he were "king of Peru"; this annoyed CHARLES V, who sent Don Pedro de la GASCA to take charge. The latter, a forceful and determined man, rallied an army, and in April 1548 when the armies met at Xaquizaguana, he was victorious. Capturing PIZARRO, Gasca had him executed for treason within a few days.

**Pizarro, Hernando.** *ca.* 1475–1567. Spanish explorer who joined his half-brother Francisco on the journey to Peru, 1531. He went back to Spain in 1534 with gold obtained from ransoming ATAHUALPA, returned to Peru, and was seized by ALMAGRO, 1537, but released. He defeated Almagro at head of his brother's army in 1538 and executed him. Sent to Spain as a spokesman for his brother, he was imprisoned by the authorities, 1540–1560, for having executed Almagro and for other reasons.

**Plata, La.** See RÍO DE LA PLATA.

**Platt Amendment.** Seven articles presented in the form of an amendment to the U.S. military appropriation bill for 1901–1902 by Senator Orville H. Platt of Connecticut, and adopted under pressure from the United States by the Cuban Constitutional Convention in June 1901. It prohibited Cuba from entering any treaties that might impair her independence and provided, among other things, that Cuba lease naval stations to the United States, and that the United States, whenever there existed a danger to life, property, and individual freedom was entitled to intervene in Cuba, and that this would also apply when Cuban independence was threatened. The last clause in particular aroused the dissatisfaction of Cuban patriots, but the Cubans had no choice but to adopt the amendment. Under the Platt Amendment, the United States intervened a number of times in Cuba's affairs. The amendment remained in force until 1934, when it was abrogated under the GOOD NEIGHBOR POLICY of the Franklin D. ROOSEVELT administration.

**Plaza Lasso, Galo.** 1906–    . President of Ecuador. b. Quito. Son of a president. Studied agriculture in the United States; became amateur bullfighter; wealthy rancher; minister of national defense, 1938; ambassador to the United States, 1944–1946; member of the Ecuadorian senate, 1946; elected president, serving 1948–1952 on the Independent Citizens Party ticket. He brought political stability to Ecuador, and tried to improve economic conditions by introducing modern farming methods. He pursued a consistently liberal policy aimed at political freedom and bettering the living conditions of the people. He visited the United States, 1951. He was succeeded by José María VELASCO IBARRA, 1952.

**P.N.R.** See INSTITUTIONAL REVOLUTIONARY PARTY OF MEXICO.

**Poinsett, Joel Roberts.** 1779–1851. American diplomat from South Carolina who served as U.S. commercial agent, and later as consul general, in Buenos Aires, Chile, and Peru, 1809–1816. He was the first U.S. minister to Mexico, 1825–1829. He opposed the conservatives, who were backed by his rival, the British minister, and supported President Guadalupe VICTORIA and advised him to use strong methods to curb the opposition. Poinsett was severely criticized for interfering in the internal politics of Mexico, and when the conservatives came to power, 1829, they demanded his recall. He served as U.S. secretary of war, 1837–1841. He was accused unjustly by the Mexicans of trying to foment civil war in order to facilitate seizure of Texas by the United States. He was often cited as an example of Yankee meddling and imperialism. The poinsettia, a tropical woody flowering plant, was named in his honor.

**Pombal, Marquis of.** Full name, **Sebastião José de Carvalho e Mello.** 1699–1782. Portuguese statesman. b. Soure, near Coimbra. Served as envoy to London and Vienna; minister of foreign affairs, 1750–1756; prime minister, 1756–1777. He instituted many reforms and developed the colonies. In a fight with the JESUITS, 1754–1759, he had them expelled from all Portuguese dominions, 1759. He is an excellent example of 18th-century benevolent despotism, influenced by liberalism and anticlericalism.

**Ponce de León, Juan.** Spanish discoverer of Florida. 1460–1521. b. León. He joined COLUMBUS on his second voyage, 1493, went to Puerto Rico, 1508, and became governor, 1510. He founded San Juan, 1511; set out with three ships in search of the Fountain of Youth, 1513, and discovered Florida on Easter Sunday of that year; visited Bahamas, 1513; second expedition to Florida in attempt to establish a settlement there, 1521, but was unsuccessful. Wounded by the natives, he died on return voyage to Cuba.

**Porras, Belisario.** 1856–1942. President of Panama. b. Las Tablas. Jurist. He was minister to the United States, 1910. The leader of the liberal party, he was elected to the presidency, 1912, and was acting president, 1918–1920. During his administration there was a short war with Costa Rica involving a boundary dispute. He was minister plenipotentiary to France and to Great Britain, 1925–1926, and to Italy, 1933; Porras was the unsuccessful presidential candidate of the Union Liberal Party, 1936.

**Portales Plazazuelos, Diego José Víctor.** 1793–1837. Chilean political leader and businessman. b. Santiago. He was the virtual dictator of the conservative government that came into power, 1830, after the civil war of 1829–1830, against the liberals. Wary of militarism, Portales dismissed from the army all officers who had participated in any revolt, ousted all liberals from public office, and took harsh measures against those who actively opposed him. He turned over the government to the newly-elected PRIETO, 1831, retired, but exercised considerable influence in government. He was appointed governor of Valparaíso, 1832, and was largely responsible for the conservative constitution of 1833, which remained in force until 1925. He was minister of war, 1835, and was killed by revolutionists, 1837. He was one of the ablest, most honest of all Latin-American conservative leaders.

**Port-au-Prince.** The capital and chief city and port of Haiti, situated on the southwest coast of the island of Hispaniola (Santo Domingo). Population 200,000 (1963). Built partly on hillsides, the city has a striking appearance because of its white buildings, among which the Cathedral, the National Palace, and the Palace of Justice stand out particularly. The city is well-kept and has many modern buildings including schools, hospitals, and stores. It is connected by road with the interior and by ship and air with the Dominican Republic and other American countries. The Port-au-Prince area produces chiefly sugar, rum, coffee, and bananas. Port-au-Prince was founded in 1749, and in 1770 it was declared the capital of French Saint Domingue (Haiti). In the same year a devastating earthquake wrecked the city, and since then it has been damaged many times by other earthquakes as well as by numerous fires and hurricanes.

**Porteños.** People who live in the port city of Buenos Aires, Argentina. The adjective *porteño* means pertaining to the city or port of Buenos Aires.

**Portes Gil, Emilio.** 1891– . Provisional president of Mexico. b. Ciudad Victoria, Tamaulipas. Lawyer, deputy to national congress, 1916–1920; governor of Tamaulipas, 1920–1924; minister of the interior under President CALLES, 1924–1928; appointed by congress as provisional president of Mexico after OBREGÓN was assassinated, serving from November 1928 to February 1930; minister to France, 1931–1932; minister of foreign affairs under CÁRDENAS, 1934–1936. The chief event of his term as provisional president was the consolidation of the powers of the ruling group by the organization of a new political party, the INSTITUTIONAL REVOLUTIONARY PARTY or P.N.R. The C.R.O.M. was smashed, Portes Gil giving his support to independent unions. A program of land distribution was carried out, and Portes Gil served as president of P.N.R. until 1936.

**Positivism.** A philosophical doctrine evolved by the French philosopher Auguste Comte (1798–1857), according to which philosophical investigation should concern itself only with natural phenomena. Positivism stressed the study of the exact sciences and the positivists put special emphasis on material development. In Latin America, positivism exercised a strong influence in the late 19th century. In Mexico the positivist credo was most consistently applied. Introduced into that country by the scientist and educator Gabino BARREDA, who had studied under Auguste Comte, positivism became the official doctrine of the Mexican school system in the 1870's. Under the DÍAZ regime its principles governed the actions of the *científicos*, who were striving to make Mexico a modern nation by increasing the output of mines and factories, and by extending the mileage of railroads and telegraph lines. While positivism brought material improvements to Mexico, the adoption of its doctrines of hierarchy and authority by the *científicos* greatly strengthened the dictatorship of Porfirio Díaz. In Brazil, positivism has maintained its influence to this day. In the 1880's it became popular in military circles, thanks to the teachings of Benjamin CONSTANT, a professor in the military school at Rio de Janeiro. Positivism promoted republicanism and thus played an important role in the overthrow of the Brazilian empire and the establishment of the republic, 1889. Today one of the manifestations of Brazilian positivism is the effort on the part of the government to improve the welfare of the MATO GROSSO Indians. The program was directed until recently by a well-known positivist, General Rondón. In Argentina the doctrine of positivism was merged with the social democratic doctrines of Esteban ECHEVERRÍA in the 1880's. The new scientific socialism was expressed in the writings of Juan B. JUSTO and José Ingenieros. During the PERÓN era the dictator attempted to identify his brand of national socialism with Argentine positivism.

**Potosí.** Department of the Republic of Bolivia bordering on Argentina to the south and Chile to the west. It has an area of 45,632 square miles and a population of about 535,000 (1950). During colonial times it was a province of the AUDIENCIA of Charcas. It is one of the world's richest regions in minerals, containing in abundance silver, gold, tin, copper, zinc, salt, and sulfur. Its capital, Potosí, population 53,528 (1960), situated at a height of 13,000 feet at the base of Mount Potosí, has ruins of the churches and palaces of the colonial period. The city was founded in 1546 by the Spaniards Villarroel, Centeno, and Cotamito. Within a short time the city's wealth became proverbial throughout the world and it remained a symbol of riches during the colonial period.

**Prado, Mariano Ignacio.** 1826–1901. President of Peru. b. Huanuco. General and political leader; fought in the revolution of 1854 under CASTILLA; overthrew President Pezet in opposition to his appeasement policy toward Spain, 1865; dictator of Peru, 1865–1867; declared war against Spain in 1866 in alliance with Chile, Bolivia, and Ecuador; defeated the Spanish fleet off Callao, 1866. Forced to flee the country, 1867, he returned and was elected president, 1876, serving until 1879, when his administration was overthrown by a revolt led by Nicolás de PIÉROLA. He retired and spent most of the rest of his life in Europe.

**Prado, Pedro.** 1886–1952. Chilean poet and novelist. He was the author of the philosophical novel *Alsino*, 1920, of the collections of poems *Camino de las horas* (March of the Hours), *Otoño en las dunas* (Autumn on the Dunes), and other works.

**Prado y Ugarteche, Manuel.** 1889– President of Peru. Trained as an engineer, he was a college professor and banker; president of the Central Reserve Bank of Peru, 1934–1939. Elected president of Peru, 1939–1945, by a 12-party coalition of rightist factions, he continued the policies of BENAVIDES. Despite a dispute with Ecuador over a boundary, his administration was generally peaceful, and he was re-elected to the presidency, 1956. He was deposed by a military coup at the end of his term, 1962, and replaced by a junta of conservative military officers. He was the candidate of the Unión Nacional Odrísta party in the abortive 1962 presidential election and, although he polled a significant number of votes, he was defeated by Fernando BELAÚNDE TERRY in the 1963 election.

**Prensa, La.** Argentine newspaper founded in 1869 by José C. Paz. One of the great newspapers of the world, it opposed policies of the PERÓN administration and was closed by the Argentine government in 1951. It was expropriated and turned over to the General Confederation of Labor, 1952, but after the fall of Perón in September 1955, *La Prensa* was restored to its owner, Gainza Paz.

**Presidio.** Spanish military installation, usually established in frontier regions, as in California. The Spanish word *presidio* has other meanings: garrison, penitentiary, fortress, imprisonment, or hard labor.

**P.R.I.** See INSTITUTIONAL REVOLUTIONARY PARTY OF MEXICO.

**Prieto, Guillermo.** 1818–1897. Mexican poet and liberal reformer. Aided JUÁREZ during the War of Reform, 1858–1860, and served briefly as minister of finance in his cabinet, where he introduced the innovation of double-entry bookkeeping. He was the author of *Musa callejera* (Street Muse), 1883, picturing the life among the Mexican poor, and *Romancero nacional*, 1885, a collection of ballads on patriotic subjects. He was a contributor to the *Diccionario universal de historia y geografía*, 1853–1856, and wrote his *Memorias* and numerous other works. Throughout his life he fought for liberal reform.

**Prieto Vial, Joaquín.** 1786–1854. President of Chile. b. Concepción. General and political leader; enlisted in the patriot ranks, and participated in the battles of CHACABUCO and MAIPÚ; served in various congresses, 1823–1828; head of the conservative revolt, 1829–1830; defeated FREIRE SERRANO, the liberal leader; president, 1831–1841, but his administration was under the strong influence of Diego PORTALES PLAZAZUELOS; a constitution was adopted in 1833; the revolt led by Freire was suppressed, 1836. The war against the Peru-Bolivian Confederation ended successfully, 1839. After his term he served as counselor of state, senator, intendant, and captain general of Valparaíso.

**Prío Socarrás Carlos.** 1903– . Cuban president. b. Bahía Honda. Member of constituent assembly, 1939; national senator, 1940–1948; member of GRAU SAN MARTÍN's cabinet; designated prime minister, 1945, and minister of labor, 1947; supported by Grau San Martín and the *auténticos*; elected president, 1948; deposed by a military *coup d'état* led by BATISTA on March 10, 1952.

**P.R.M.** Full name, **Mexican Revolutionary Party** (*Partido de la Revolución Mexicana*). Name adopted by the P.N.R. (*Partido Nacional Revolucionario*) in 1938. The change in name was accompanied by a change in structure, as control of professional politicians over the party was weakened by the admission of trade-union and peasant delegates. See INSTITUTIONAL REVOLUTIONARY PARTY OF MEXICO.

**Pronunciamiento.** Spanish, meaning military uprising, revolt. It is accompanied by a manifesto containing the charges issued against the existing authorities by those launching the revolt; also containing the promise that they, when in power, will institute new reforms.

**Protestantism in Latin America.** Protestantism has never been an important force in any Latin-American country. During the colonial period it was excluded by the Spanish and Portuguese governments, and in the Spanish colonies any persons suspected of Protestant beliefs were turned over to the INQUISITION. These were never numerous, and consisted chiefly of shipwrecked or captured British and Dutch sailors. After the establishment of independence, British and American Protestant churches carried on missionary activities but had relatively little success except in Brazil. The nationalism of Latin-American countries has been an obstacle to their efforts, and missionaries from the United States were often accused of being agents of "Yankee imperialism." Some Protestant immigrants from Britain, Germany, and other countries have settled in Latin America but have not generally taken any active part in politics. The number of Protestants in all Latin America is estimated at over 2,000,000.

**Provedor Mor.** In colonial Brazil, a high official who controlled the custom houses, collected taxes, supervised the subordinate *provedores*, and accounted for the royal income. The *provedor mor* had judicial power that pertained to his own functions, independent of the other courts.

**Puebla.** Official name, **Puebla de Zaragoza.** The fourth largest city of Mexico, capital of the state of Puebla, situated at an altitude of 7,150 feet, 84 miles southeast of Mexico City. Population 285,000 (est. 1960). Well-built, clean, and healthy, the town has more than 60 churches and an outstanding cathedral containing valuable paintings. Its architecture offers interesting examples of the Andalusian style. Among the many manufacturing establishments in the town are those producing textiles, glazed tiles, glass, and cigarettes.

Nearby there are extensive cotton mills. Other important products of Puebla are its well-known Talavera pottery, onyx wares, and palm leaf hats. Founded in 1531, Puebla was at first called Puebla de los Ángeles (City of the Angels) but was renamed for General Ignacio ZARAGOZA who won a decisive victory over the invading French forces in 1862. Its strategic location with respect to Mexico City gave it considerable military importance, and in the 19th century a number of battles were fought for its possession. It was taken by ITURBIDE in 1821 and by Winfield Scott in 1847, during the war between Mexico and the United States. In 1862 it repulsed the attacks of the French, but in the following year it surrendered to the French forces. In April 1867, it fell to Porfirio DÍAZ, victor over the troops of Emperor MAXIMILIAN.

**Puebla, Battle of (1862)** and **Siege of (1863).** An engagement between French and Mexican troops at the Mexican city of Puebla on May 5, 1862. The French army under General Laurencez, after having disembarked at Veracruz, undertook its march on Mexico City to put an end to the JUÁREZ administration and to pave the way for the establishment of a Mexican empire under French tutelage. At Puebla this army attacked a Mexican army of former *guerrilleros*, equipped with outmoded guns and led by amateur generals under the supreme command of Ignacio ZARAGOZA. The French army, however, took no precautions. At the order of Laurencez the soldiers flung themselves at the center of the Mexican fortifications, over a ditch and a brick wall, and up the steep slopes of the Cerro de Guadalupe. The French were repulsed with heavy losses (more than 1,000 casualties) and fled back to Orizaba and the coast. A year later, in 1863, another French army under General Forey renewed the attempt to take Puebla, putting the city under siege. The city, defended by 30,000 men under GONZÁLEZ ORTEGA, was attacked in March and was forced to surrender in May, after every animal in the town had been eaten, and every round of ammunition had been exhausted. The Mexican army was sent to Veracruz for shipment to France as prisoners, although a number of the officers, among them González Ortega and Porfirio DÍAZ, succeeded in escaping.

**Puerto Rico.** An island commonwealth associated with the United States, situated in the Caribbean Sea between the island of Hispaniola (Santo Domingo) and the Leeward Islands, with an area of 3,435 square miles and a population of 2,349,544 (est. 1965), making it one of the most densely settled territories in the world. The chief cities are San Juan, the capital and largest city, population 451,658 (1960), Ponce, 145,586 (1960), and Mayagüez, 83,850 (1960). The island enjoys complete local autonomy and the powers of administration are carried on by a governor and a congress, both elected by the islanders. A resident commissioner in Washington, D.C., has the right to a voice in the House of Representatives but has no vote. The island produces cane sugar and rum, along with tobacco, pineapples, and coffee.

Puerto Rico was discovered by COLUMBUS in 1493 and was conquered by PONCE DE LEÓN in 1508. San Juan was founded in 1521. In 1897 it was granted political and economic autonomy by Spain, and shortly afterward it became a possession of the United States as a result of the American victory in the Spanish-American War of 1898. Ruled by a U.S. military government until 1900, it was then placed under a civil administration. The Jones Act made the islanders citizens of the United States in 1917. An Act of Congress in 1947 stipulated that the governor of Puerto Rico would henceforth be elected by the popular vote of the Puerto Ricans, and in 1948 Luis MUÑOZ MARÍN was elected governor. In 1951 the Puerto Ricans voted for autonomy, and in July of the next year Muñoz Marín proclaimed the Constitution of the Commonwealth of Puerto Rico after it had been sanctioned by popular vote in the election of March 1952. The government of Muñoz Marín launched a program of industrialization under which 850 factories were to be established by 1960. By September 1959, 581 new factories had been established, creating 48,585 new jobs, and the net income from manufacturing was 50 per cent higher than the net income from agriculture. The expansion of the tourist industry has also been stimulated since 1956, as the result of encouragement of private investment in hotel building. The postwar years have been marked by a large-scale emigration of Puerto Ricans to the eastern United States, mainly to New York City. This migration to the U.S. mainland reached its height in 1953 when 69,124 Puerto Ricans emigrated to the United States. The number has been reduced to an annual figure of about 30,000 (1959) because of improved economic conditions on the island. Puerto Rican nationalists attracted world-wide attention in March 1954, when several members of the Nationalist Party fired a number of shots in the House of Representatives in Washington and wounded five congressmen. This act, carried out with the purpose of dramatizing the Nationalists' desire for independence, led to a roundup of Nationalists in Puerto Rico on the orders of Muñoz Marín, who was firmly opposed to the aims of the Nationalist Party. In the 1960 election Governor Muñoz Marín was re-elected for his fourth successive term in office, 1961–1965. He was succeeded by Roberto Sánchez Vilella.

**Pueyrredón, Juan Martín de.** 1777–1850. Argentine leader who aided SAN MARTÍN in the War for Independence. In 1816 a congress at Tucumán, representing the various provinces, elected him Supreme Director of the UNITED PROVINCES OF LA PLATA for a three-year term, and formally declared their independence. The congress adopted a constitution calling for a strong central government, 1819, and the leaders of the provinces protested. Pueyrredón refused a second term. He was one of the ablest statesmen of the independence period.

**Pulque.** A Mexican alcoholic beverage fermented from the juice of the Maguey plant.

**Puros.** Spanish, meaning pure ones. Name given to the more extreme Mexican liberals in the 30 years following the establishment of the republic in 1823. They championed social revolution, demanding the abolition of clerical and military FUEROS, the confiscation of clerical property, and the destruction of caste distinctions. They derived their strength mainly from the mestizo group and from the middle classes, who opposed the CREOLE landowning aristocracy. Outstanding *puros* were the economist José Luis MORA and Valentín GÓMEZ FARÍAS the leader of the liberal party for 25 years and acting president in 1846–1847. Their program was put into effect in the Reform Movement of 1855–1867.

# Q

**Quechua** or **Quichua.** Name given to the language spoken in the general area of the old INCA Empire, from Quito, Ecuador, to the provinces of Tucumán and Catamarca, Argentina. The language was called *runa-simi* (language of men) by the Indians themselves. The name Quechua, actually designating a small district of central Peru, was given to the language by the DOMINICAN friar Domingo de Santo Tomás in his grammar of the language of Peru. The origin of the Quechua language is unknown. It is still spoken today in many Peruvian localities. It is pleasing to the ear and has various dialects. Some Spanish words of Quechua origin that are used widely today are *pampa*, *puma*, and *guano*. The term is also applied to the Indians who speak the Quechua language.

**Queiroz Law.** Law drawn up in Brazil in 1850 and passed shortly afterward, prohibiting the slave trade. The passage of the law was prompted by British opposition to the trade, which manifested itself in the seizure of slave-carrying Brazilian ships even in Brazilian territorial waters.

**Queremistas.** From Portuguese *queremos*, meaning we want. Name given to Brazilians supporting VARGAS in 1945 for another term in office. Vargas himself was not a candidate, but the *queremistas* staged huge rallies during 1945, demanding that Vargas remain as president. An important leader of the *queremistas* was Vargas' brother. But Vargas was forced to resign in October by a bloodless coup of the military, and in December of the same year elections were held, resulting in the victory of DUTRA.

**Querétaro Literary Society.** In the year 1808 a society for the study of fine arts was founded in the city of Querétaro, 110 miles northwest of Mexico City. However, its members were more interested in Mexico's independence than in fine arts, and the society soon became a hotbed of revolutionaries. The members were able to win over to the cause of Mexican independence the CORREGIDOR of Querétaro, his wife, and a number of officers of the garrison.

**Quesada, Ernesto.** 1858–1934. Argentine jurist and author of *Goethe*, 1881, *San Martín*, 1900, *Spengler*, 1921, *The Social Evolution of the Argentine Republic*, 1911, and other works.

**Quetzalcoatl.** From *quetzalli*, a Mexican bird, and *cohuatl*, snake. Legendary TOLTEC deity and traditional half-god, half-hero of that Mexican tribe. Also worshiped by MAYAS in Yucatán under the name Kukulcán; also a divinity of the AZTECS. According to the most widespread popular version, Quetzalcoatl was of white skin, and had a long gray beard, and a red cross was painted on his dress. He preached universal peace and brotherhood, taught his people agriculture and architecture, and invented the calendar. After teaching his subjects the mysteries of religion, he left them telling them that he would return to them in the year *Ce Acatl*, one of the years of the Mexican calendar. He then proceeded to the east coast where he embarked on a raft made of serpents and floated eastward. Some scholars have thought that the legend may have some historical basis, and that this personage was an early Christian missionary who reached America in an unknown manner. Others have seen in the legend a story symbolic of the movements of the sun. In any event, the year 1519, when CORTÉS landed in Mexico, was by coincidence the year *Ce Acatl* in which Quetzalcoatl was to return, and when the Aztec emperor MOCTE-ZUMA first met Cortés, he treated him as if he were a representative of that legendary figure.

**Quiché Indians.** Central American Indians related to the MAYAS, inhabiting the western part of Guatemala. Their long history seems to go back to the 8th century. Government and religion were usually well developed in this culture, which also employed a system of pictorial writing. The city of Utatlán, near the Santa Cruz Quiché of today, was the capital. Their holy book, *Popol Vuh*, has come down to the present time in a manuscript composed in the 17th century by a Guatemalan Indian converted to Christianity. The Quichés were discovered by the Spanish conquistador Pedro de ALVARADO Y MESÍA in 1524. Today the Quiché language is spoken by the Indians of the departments of Quiché, Quezaltenango, Totonicapán, Retalhuleu, and Sacatepéquez in Guatemala. The modern Quichés live in villages in the highlands of Guatemala where, for the most part, they work on the large plantations and are held in a state of peonage.

**Quilombo.** In Brazil, in the days of slavery, a refuge for runaway slaves, usually situated in some inaccessible jungle or desert. In the 17th century the most famous of all *quilombos*, that of Palmares, was founded in the province of Pernambuco, 1630. It was inhabited by about 20,000 runaway slaves and maintained itself until 1697, when it was destroyed by the Portuguese. See MOCAMBO.

**Quiñones Molina, Alfonso.** b. 1873. President of El Salvador. Physician and political leader, he served as provisional president for a brief time in 1914 and 1915, and again in 1918 and 1919; vice-president from 1915 to 1923 and president from 1923 to 1927. See MELÉNDEZ FAMILY.

**Quintana, Manuel.** 1836–1906. President of

Argentina, 1904–1906. He served as minister of the interior under SÁENZ PEÑA and suppressed the Radical revolt of 1905. He was interested in the development of communications and had much to do with the first transandine railroad from Buenos Aires to Valparaíso. He died in office, March 11, 1906.

**Quintana Roo, Andrés.** 1787–1851. Mexican patriot. b. Mérida. Poet and scholar from Yucatán, he was a champion of the independence movement, and president of the Chilpancingo congress of 1813, which proclaimed Mexican independence. He was a senator, and a member of the supreme court. He published *El Federalista Mejicano*, and was the author of the poem *Al 16 de Septiembre de 1821*.

**Quinto** or **Quinto Real.** The royal fifth. In the Spanish-American colonies, the royalties derived by the Spanish Crown from the production of the mines, amounting to one-fifth of the yield. During the Middle Ages the royalties on bullion had been two-thirds of the total value, but to encourage the development of mineral resources in the New World the percentage was lowered. After 1500 it was reduced to a half, then a third, and in 1504 the *quinto real* was established for ten years but remained in effect until the 18th century. From time to time the royalties were reduced to an eighth, a tenth, or even a twelfth depending on local mining conditions and to encourage the development of new mines. In 1723 the *quinto* became a *diezmo* (a tenth) for all minerals with the notable exception of Peru where the silver royalty was not reduced until 1735.

**Quipus.** From QUECHUA *quipu*, meaning knot. Ropes of different colors tied in various knots, used by the INCAS to keep accounts. The *quipu* was usually formed by a thick woolen rope from 1 foot to 15 or 20 feet long, from which hung thinner ropes of different lengths and colors. They were used to record numbers and simple facts connected with numbers. A decimal system was apparently employed to facilitate the use of the *quipus*. For the forming and interpreting of the *quipus* there was a group of Indians known as the *quippu-camayoc* (accountants), educated in special schools.

**Quirino Lemachez.** See HENRÍQUEZ GON-
ZÁLEZ, CAMILO.

**Quiroga, Horacio.** 1878–1937. Uruguayan
short-story writer who spent many years in
the jungles of northern Argentina and turned
out stories often compared to Kipling's
*Jungle Book;* considered by many critics one
of the best short-story writers of Latin
America.

**Quiroga, Juan Facundo.** 1793–1835. Argentine CAUDILLO who ruled the western
provinces as a tyrant. He fought against
RIVADAVIA, and aided ROSAS, but was murdered in 1835 while on a mission for the
dictator in Córdoba. He was the subject of a
book by Domingo SARMIENTO, *Facundo, o la
civilización y la barbarie.*

**Quiroga, Vasco de.** 1470–1565. Bishop in
Michoacán, Mexico, who taught handicrafts
to the Indians, established schools and colleges, and became a legend as a kind and
helpful man.

**Quito.** The capital of Ecuador, situated 15
miles south of the equator. It is in a valley
surrounded by high peaks of the Andes, but
at an altitude of 9,400 feet. It has a temperate,
pleasant climate with few seasonal changes,
cool nights, and almost daily showers; mean
temperature 54.6 Fahrenheit. Population,
314,000 (est. 1960). Quito has retained
much of its Old-World appearance, with
narrow cobbled streets, over-hanging bal-
conies, and the ornate architecture of more
than 50 old churches. Important buildings
include the Government Palace, the Cathedral, the Central University (founded, 1787),
and the School of Fine Arts. Quito has air
connections with other American capitals,
and there is a rail line running down to the
Pacific port of Guayaquil. The city is situated
on the PAN AMERICAN HIGHWAY. An important
textile manufacturing center, Quito also turns
out chocolate, leather, and shoes. Once occupied by the Quitu Indians, in the 15th century
it became the northern capital of the INCA
empire under the Inca HUAYNA CAPAC (d.
1525), and was ruled over by the son of the
Inca, ATAHUALPA. In 1533 it was taken by the
conquistador Sebastián de BENALCÁZAR, who,
however, found Quito in ruins and built a
new city, San Francisco de Quito. In colonial
times Quito was known for its highly-developed art. In 1822 the city achieved independence from Spain after the Spanish forces
were defeated by SUCRE at the Battle of PICH-
INCHA in May of that year. In 1830 it became
the capital of the independent Republic of
Ecuador. It has been badly damaged by
earthquakes several times, notably in 1868.

**Quivira.** Mythical land that the Spaniards
believed was located in the present-day
United States, where there were supposed to
have been fish as large as horses and a great
king who ate from golden dishes and rested
under a tree hung with bells of gold. Searching for this country, CORONADO explored what
is now Kansas, 1541.

# R

**Radical Civic Union Party of Argentina.** Also, **Unión Cívica Radical, U.C.R.** A party formed in Argentina in 1891 by the Argentine liberal leader Leandro N. ALEM and called the *Unión Cívica Radical*. It grew out of the *Unión Cívica*, formed in the 1880's to do away with corruption in government but considered too moderate by Alem. The radical party advocated the adoption of political reforms and called for an end to political control by the conservatives. It revolted against the government in 1893, but the movement was put down by the army. Supported mainly by the growing middle class, the party vigorously advocated political democracy. Its growing strength induced President SÁENZ PEÑA in 1912 to adopt electoral reforms establishing universal male suffrage and the secret ballot. In 1916 the radical leader Hipólito YRIGOYEN, who had taken over as head of the party in 1896 after the suicide of Alem, was elected president, and the radicals came into power, but did not effect any significant reforms. They were satisfied with political democracy and were only mildly interested in improving economic and social conditions. They did, however, enact some labor legislation. After the election of Yrigoyen's successor, Marcelo de ALVEAR in 1922, there occurred a split in the party between those who followed Yrigoyen's leadership, known as *personalistas*, and those who favored the more independent course charted by Alvear, or *anti-personalistas*. In 1930, the *anti-personalistas* joined the army and conservative forces in overthrowing Yrigoyen, who had again been elected president in 1928. Alvear, however, soon rejoined the *personalistas*, who now constituted the

real radical party, still had wide popular support, and were opposed to the administration of the *anti-personalista* president Agustín JUSTO, inaugurated in 1932. In 1937 Alvear was the radical candidate for the presidency, but was defeated by the *anti-personalista* Roberto ORTIZ. Most of the radicals, however, threw their support to Ortiz when the latter split with the conservatives in 1940. In the same year the radicals lost power once more, when the conservative vice-president Ramón CASTILLO took over the reins of government from the ailing Ortiz. In the succeeding years their efforts were ineffective against the conservatives and the military groups that replaced the conservatives in 1943. Their candidate José Tamborini was defeated by Juan PERÓN in the election of 1946 and under Perón's regime, because of suppression, violence, and intimidation, they lost ground steadily. After the overthrow of Perón the party, split into two factions, lost the opportunity to strengthen constitutional democracy and to help re-establish effective civilian government in Argentina. The Intransigent Radical Civic Union (U.C.R.I.) led by Arturo Frondizi, and the People's Radical Civic Union (U.C.R.P.) aligned themselves with Ricardo Balbín. The 1958 presidential election gave an overwhelming majority to the U.C.R.I., and party-leader Frondizi became president for a six-year term, May 1958. After a revolt unseated Frondizi, 1962, the presidential election held in July 1963 gave the U.C.R.P. the largest share of the popular vote, and its candidate, Dr. Arturo U. Illia, became president, October 1, 1963. He was overthrown in June, 1966 by a military coup d'etat which virtually eliminated the influence of the party.

**Railroads.** A famous pioneer in railroad building in South America was William WHEELWRIGHT, who promoted the construction of the first railroad in South America, opened in Chile in 1852. He later built, with the aid of British capital, an Argentine line from Rosario to Córdoba. In 1880 there were 1,500 miles of railroads in Argentina, and after 1880 construction of railroads grew at a rapid pace. Today Argentina has about 27,000 miles of rail lines, the largest network in Latin America. In 1947–1948, the PERÓN administration purchased the British and French-owned railroads and the system thus became nationalized. The Argentine rail lines fan out from Buenos Aires to reach many parts of the country as well as all neighboring nations. Particularly impressive is the line from Buenos Aires to Santiago (originally envisioned by Wheelwright), which crosses the Andes Mountains and in the process climbs to heights of more than 10,000 feet. In Brazil, which has the second largest network in Latin America, about 24,000 miles, many of the important lines are owned by the federal government or the state governments. Particularly well-provided with railroads are the states of São Paulo and Minas Gerais. The Madeira-Mamoré line, built by American engineers around the rapids of the Madeira and Mamoré Rivers and opened in 1913, ranks as one of the most impressive lines in Latin America and in the world. Third in mileage is Mexico, with 17,000 miles. In Mexico railroad building made tremendous progress during the DÍAZ administration, 1876–1911. With the help of foreign capital, mileage spurted from a mere 429 miles in 1876 to 15,534 miles in 1911. There are lines connecting the American border with the central plateau, and the Atlantic Ocean with the Pacific Ocean, and most state capitals are linked by rail with Mexico City. In 1950 rail connections linked Baja California to the main body of Mexico, and at about the same time, another railway connected Yucatán with the mainland. Chile has about 6,000 miles and is connected with Peru, Bolivia, and Argentina. The Chilean system, 70 per cent of whose mileage is run by the government, serves all the most important cities except Arica in the far north, and Punta Arenas in the far south on the Strait of Magellan. In Uruguay (2,000 miles), where the lines fan out from Montevideo, the government bought in 1948 the British railroads controlling 90 per cent of the mileage. In Paraguay (750 miles), railroad building began during the administration of Carlos Antonio LÓPEZ (1844–1862). Under Eduardo SCHAERER (1912–1916), the line from Asunción to Encarnación on the Paraná was completed. In Bolivia (2,000 miles), after the line between Oruro and Antofagasta was opened in 1892, much construction was undertaken at the beginning of the 20th century with the help of money borrowed abroad. The line linking Lake Titicaca and La Paz was completed in 1903 and connected the Bolivian capital with the Peruvian port of Mollendo. In 1913 lines between La Paz and Arica, and La Paz and Oruro, were completed. In the 1920's a link was forged between the Bolivian and Argentine rail system. In 1954 another important line was completed, this time with Brazilian capital, the Santa Cruz-Corumbá stretch, connecting the Bolivian lowlands with Brazil. Considerable commercial progress resulted. This newest line is important for Bolivian economy insofar as it provides an outlet for the country's products, especially oil. In Ecuador the important line linking the port of Guayaquil with the capital, Quito, built by Americans, was completed during the administration of President Eloy ALFARO, 1907–1911. In Peru (2,300 miles) the majority of the lines are operated by British interests. Colombia has 2,200 miles of rail lines and Venezuela has 750 miles. Cuba, with 11,000 miles, is one of the best rail-served countries in Latin America. In Central America, the rail systems have not been developed to any extent except in Guatemala and El Salvador. Today relatively little railroad construction is being undertaken in Latin America. Most lines suffer from differences in the gauges, from deficits in operations, and from competition from cars, trucks, and the airlines. The tendency on the part of most Latin-American governments is to nationalize all rail lines, with the result that little foreign capital is being invested in Latin-American railroad building.

**Ramalho, João.** d. 1580. Portuguese lawyer who was shipwrecked off the coast of Brazil. He lived at Piratininga in the highlands, near modern São Paulo, where he formed a half-Portuguese, half-Indian colony. He met Martim souza in 1532 and helped him to found São Vicente, the first permanent settlement in Brazil.

**Ramírez, Ignacio.** 1818–1879. b. San Miguel el Grande, Guanajuato. Mexican liberal writer who was brilliant and eccentric. He took pride in his AZTEC ancestry and strongly opposed the Catholic Church. He was a liberal member of the convention of 1856 which worked for reform, and wrote the constitution that was completed in 1857. He served in JUÁREZ' cabinet but later turned against him and called him a dictator. He approved the PLAN OF TUXTEPEC and supported DÍAZ, 1876, believing that Díaz would establish a democracy and not the dictatorship that resulted.

**Ramírez, Pedro Pablo.** 1884–1962. Argentine president, after the military *coup d'état* that overthrew Ramón S. CASTILLO, from June 1943 until February 1944. A general, he served as minister of war under the Castillo regime. He was pro-Axis in sentiment, and kept the country neutral, but was finally forced to break relations with the Axis powers on January 26, 1944. He turned over the presidency to FARRELL.

**Ramos Arizpe, Miguel.** 1775–1843. Mexican patriot, priest, and economist. b. San Nicolás de la Capellanía. Educated in the College Seminary of Monterrey and the University of Guadalajara. Elected a deputy to the Cortes in Spain, he helped create the Spanish constitution of 1812, attempting to introduce some of his ideas into Mexico; secretly favored Mexican independence. He was imprisoned by FERDINAND VII; freed, 1820. He returned to Mexico, 1821, fought for economic liberation of the northern part of Mexico, abolition of colonial monopolies, internal free trade, and the establishment of a regional capital at Saltillo. He was a leader in the fight for a republic against ITURBIDE,

helped establish the republic, and was a leader of the new congress assembled to draft the constitution of 1824, which largely resembled that of the United States with the exception that there was to be no religious toleration and Catholicism was to be the state religion. Mexico was to be divided into 19 states and four territories, the states electing their own governors and legislatures. Ramos Arizpe was appointed minister of justice and ecclesiastical relations, 1824–1828, 1832–1833, deputy to the constituent congress of 1842, and dean of the Puebla Cathedral.

**Rayón, Ignacio López.** 1773–1832. Mexican fighter for independence. Became secretary of state in HIDALGO's revolutionary government at Guadalajara, 1810. After the capture of Hidalgo by the Spaniards, López Rayón, as head of the rebel army, led them from Saltillo into Michoacán, and established himself at Zitácuaro, fortified it, and set up a revolutionary government, 1811. He abandoned his stronghold to Spanish forces sent against him, but continued guerrilla warfare in Michoacán. He attended the congress of Chilpancingo, which met under the leadership of MORELOS Y PAVÓN and which declared Mexico's independence from Spain, 1813. After the capture of Morelos in 1815, he continued guerrilla activities for some time, but gave up the struggle in 1817 and submitted to Spanish authorities, who kept him a prisoner from 1817 to 1820.

**Real Cuerpo de Minería.** The association of mine owners in colonial Spanish America; established by royal decree in the viceroyalty of New Spain, 1777; *Ordenanzas de minería*, the ordinances that governed the miners' guild, were extended to Venezuela, Guatemala, New Granada, Peru, and Chile within a few years after their promulgation; provincial courts in New Spain, located in each mining district, had jurisdiction over cases affecting mine owners, and a central tribunal, composed of a director general, an administrator general, and three deputies general, established in Mexico City, became the executive organ for the entire mining industry and the board of directors of a mining bank that made loans to mine owners; the tribunal became a court of appeals (1793) in mining cases from the provincial courts; members of the *Cuerpo* enjoyed special privileges, including immunity from arrest for debt; a school of mines was established, 1792, by the *Cuerpo* to provide training in the theory and practice of mining and metallurgy soon after its inception; the Spanish engineer Fausto de ELHUYAR, associated with the guild, was the guiding spirit of the school which produced many leaders of the Mexican republic; the *Cuerpo* went out of existence in 1821.

**Recabarren, Luis.** d. 1924. Chilean political leader. Of humble origin, he worked as a printer. He was elected deputy for Taltal and Tocopilla on the Democratic Party ticket, 1906, but was expelled from congress upon his refusal to give oath in the name of God and the Scriptures. He settled in Iquique and founded the socialist newspaper *El Despertar de los Trabajadores* (The Awakening of the Workers), 1908. He formed the Socialist Labor Party, 1912, and in 1920 left it to found the Chilean Communist Party. He was elected deputy for Antofagasta on the Communist ticket, 1921. He founded the Santiago newspaper *La Justicia*, traveled to Russia, 1922, and returned disillusioned, 1923. He committed suicide, 1924.

**Recife.** Formerly, **Pernambuco.** The capital of the Brazilian state of PERNAMBUCO and the leading city in the north of the country as well as an important port of call for ocean liners. Recife has a population of 798,000 (est. 1960). It is composed of three parts, the port being situated on a peninsula, another portion on an island, and a third on the mainland. The three sections are linked by a number of bridges. The city has been modernized in recent years and there are broad avenues and tall buildings. Important products of the area include sugar, cotton, tobacco, and coffee. Manufactures include the production of textiles and the refining of sugar. The export through Recife of a number of such agricultural products as sugar, rum, and cotton renders it an important commercial center. The city was founded about 1548 and was the port for the town of Olinda. It was sacked by the British in 1595 and captured by the Dutch in 1630. From 1636 to 1644 it was ruled by the Dutch governor MAURITZ of Nassau and during this short period its name was Mauritzstad. The Portuguese reconquered it in 1654. Rivalry between the lower-class Portuguese inhabitants of Recife and the CREOLE sugar planters of nearby Olinda led to civil war between the two factions after Recife ceased to be a part of the township of Olinda and was elevated to the category of town in 1710. Recife was supported by the Portuguese authorities, and order was restored after a year of fighting. In 1817 Recife and the province of Pernambuco were the seat of an anti-Portuguese revolt that was crushed by government troops, most of its leaders being executed. In 1823 Recife was given the title of city. Another republican uprising, which was suppressed, occurred in 1824. During WORLD WAR II it was the site of an American air base.

**Recopilación de Leyes de los Reynos de las Indias.** Collection of laws and regulations relating to Spanish colonies in America, published in 1563 by Luis de Velasco, viceroy of New Spain. A more complete collection was brought out in Spain in 1596, another in 1628, and in 1681 the Spanish government published the definitive edition comprising nine volumes. An improved version of the latter, consisting of three volumes, was published in 1791, and another edition comprising twelve volumes was published in 1805 under the title *Novísima Recopilación de las Leyes de Indias*. This code covering all phases of colonial life is an impressive work on Spanish colonial legislation in the New World and an indispensable source of information concerning colonial Spanish America. It contained numerous humanitarian regulations protecting the Indians, but many were not effectively enforced.

**Reducciones.** Indian villages established in colonial Spanish America under the supervision of the Church or the royal authorities. The Indians were gathered into these settlements to be converted to Christianity and to furnish an easily available labor force. They were ruled either by missionaries or, in the case of civil *reducciones*, by their own native chiefs. The most famous *reducciones* under religious control were those established by the JESUITS in Paraguay in the 17th century.

281

By the second quarter of the 18th century there were 30 *reducciones* among the GUARANÍ Indians of Paraguay, with about 150,000 natives under their control. There were 10 such settlements among the equally fierce Chiquitos to the west and northwest, and the Jesuits also worked in what is now Uruguay and the western plains of Argentina. It is estimated that between 1610 and 1767, 700,-000 Indians were baptized in the Paraguayan missions. In Brazil, Indian villages set up under conditions similar to those governing the formation of the Spanish *reducciones* were called *aldeas*.

**Reed, Walter.** 1851–1902. U.S. Army surgeon and bacteriologist. b. Belroi, Virginia. With James Carroll, Aristides Agramonte, and Jesse Lazear, he was sent to Cuba to investigate the cause of yellow fever, 1900. He proved by controlled experiments that the disease was spread by a genus of mosquitoes, as Dr. Carlos FINLAY, a Cuban physician, had already suggested. The carriers were destroyed and the disease controlled. Walter Reed Hospital, Washington, D.C., is named in his honor.

**Reforma, La.** The name given to the Mexican political and social revolution that occurred between 1855 and 1867. The protagonists of the Reform, most of whom belonged to the middle class and were largely of MESTIZO descent, proposed to establish a constitutional government, to abolish the independent powers of the clergy and the generals, and to stimulate economic progress by putting into circulation the properties of the Church. They assumed power in 1855 by the Revolution of AYUTLA, which overthrew the conservative dictatorship of SANTA ANNA. Under the administration of Ignacio COMONFORT, 1855–1858, the LEY JUÁREZ of 1855 abolished the clerical and military *fueros*, the LEY LERDO prohibiting the Church from owning land was passed in 1856, and the federalist constitution of 1857 was adopted. The conservatives violently opposed the reforms, and the antagonism between the liberals and conservatives resulted in the three-year civil war called the War of the Reform, 1858–1860. The conservatives under ZULOAGA, after forcing Comonfort into exile, gained control of

Mexico City, while the president recognized by the liberal party, Benito JUÁREZ, entrenched himself in Veracruz. During the war, Juárez promulgated even more drastic anticlerical legislation. By the LAWS OF LA REFORMA of July 1859, all ecclesiastical properties except the actual church buildings were to be confiscated without compensation. All monasteries were to be suppressed immediately, cemeteries were to become national property, and marriage was to be a civil contract. After a long struggle the liberals were victorious and the War of the Reform came to an end in 1860. Juárez, however, did not stay in power long. In 1863 French intervention forced him to flee to northern Mexico and for the next four years the liberals fought against French domination of the country, and against the Emperor MAXIMILIAN, who had been installed on the throne of Mexico by NAPOLEON III of France. The departure of the French and the liberal victory in 1867 permitted Juárez, who was re-elected to the presidency, to continue his reform program until his death in 1872.

**Reforma, Laws of La.** Mexican laws promulgated by the liberal government of Benito JUÁREZ in July 1859, during the three-year civil war, 1858–1860. They provided for: the confiscation without compensation of all ecclesiastical property except the actual church buildings, the immediate cessation of operation of all monasteries and the suppression of all nunneries at such time as their occupants had died, the nationalizing of all cemeteries, civil marriages, and the division of Church estates into small farms and the sale of the same. These provisions were subsequently incorporated into the Mexican constitution.

**Regidor.** In Spain and Spanish America, a member of the *cabildo*, or town council, entrusted with the government of a town. There were 8 to 12 *regidores* in the town councils of the main cities and 4 to 6 in the others. Only inhabitants of the town could be *regidores*, and they were nominated by royal officials. Positions could be bought from late in the 16th century, but in the 17th century they became largely hereditary. Although the *cabildos* had little actual power, it was one outlet through which the CREOLES could express their wishes.

**Reinões.** Portuguese, meaning people of the kingdom. During the Brazilian colonial period, *reinões* was used to designate persons born in Portugal.

**Remón Cantera, José Antonio.** 1908–1955. President of Panama. b. Panama City. Educated in the Mexican military academy; joined Panamanian national police force, 1931; made national chief of police, 1949; brought about the resignation of President Chanis, 1949. He overthrew the administration of President Arnulfo Arias, 1951, and was elected president, 1952. He stabilized the country's finances, outlawed the Communist party, and took measures designed to render Panama's economy less dependent on the Panama Canal. He was assassinated in January 1955.

**Rengifo Cárdenas, Manuel.** 1793–1845. Chilean statesman, businessman, and diplomat. b. Santiago. Business associate of Diego PORTALES, he was appointed minister of finance, 1830–1835. He attempted to stabilize the economy of the country and develop Valparaíso as the most important port of Chile and the Pacific coast. He encouraged the investment of foreign capital in the country, and served again in 1842 as minister of finance under BULNES PRIETO. He established a bureau of statistics in 1843, set up laws of weights and measures, and regulated tariffs.

**Repartimiento.** Spanish, meaning distribution. In the Spanish-American colonies, the term meant distribution of Indians for forced labor. The *repartimiento* was used when the economic upkeep of the New-World territories required it. Indian labor was drafted to insure the cultivation of land, the operation of mines, and the carrying out of public works. The laws dealing with this system stipulated that Indians were to be paid and protected against abuses, but often these laws were not enforced and the Indians suffered, especially in the gold and silver mines of Peru, which exacted a heavy toll of Indian lives. In Peru the *repartimiento* system was often called the *mita* and in Mexico the *cuatequil*. The word was often used interchangeably with *en-comienda*, which theoretically meant only the right to collect tribute from the Indians but in practice often included the exaction of labor. *Repartimiento* also came to be known in colonial days as the forced sale of goods to the Indians by the *corregidores*.

**Residencia.** In colonial Spanish America, the judicial review of an official's conduct made at the end of his term of office. The first instance of use of a *residencia* occurred in 1501 when Nicolás de OVANDO, appointed governor of the Indies, conducted a *residencia* of Francisco de BOBADILLA who had been his predecessor. When a *residencia* was to take place, an announcement was made, and all people, including Indians, could come forward and give evidence or testimony. The judge, appointed by the viceroy or president, prepared his report and submitted it to the COUNCIL OF THE INDIES or, in some instances, to the local AUDIENCIA. Appeals could be made to the Council if a man felt he had been misjudged. These appeals were usually heard by the district *audiencia*. The *residencia* was intended primarily to insure better government but also to maintain a hold over agents of the government by the Crown. The punishments for an unfavorable report included heavy fines, imprisonment, confiscation of property, or all three.

**Restrepo, Carlos E.** 1867–1937. President of Colombia, 1910–1914. A conservative, he was the candidate of the *unión republicana*, a coalition party opposed to Rafael REYES. Later he was minister of the interior, 1930–1934, and ambassador to the Vatican, 1934.

**Restrepo, José Manuel.** 1782–1863. Colombian statesman and historian. b. Envigado. Fought for independence with BOLÍVAR, and held many important government posts; author of an important 10-volume work, *Historia de la revolución de la República de Colombia*, 1827.

**Revillagigedo** or **Revilla Gigedo, Francisco de Güemes y Horcasitas, Count of.** 1682–1766. Viceroy of Mexico. b. Oviedo, Spain. Became viceroy in 1746, reorganizing the finances of the Mexican viceroyalty and bettering the economic condition of the country. His son Juan Vicente (1740–

1799), second count of Revillagigedo, was appointed viceroy in 1789, and his was perhaps the best viceregal administration Mexico ever had. He reorganized administration, fostered agriculture and industry, education and communications, and created weekly mail deliveries in the provinces. He had Mexico City partly rebuilt and organized a census that revealed that the viceroyalty had 4,483,569 inhabitants in 1793.

**Revillagigedo** or **Revilla Gigedo Islands.** An uninhabited archipelago belonging to Mexico and forming part of the state of Colima. These islands, located in the Pacific Ocean, 475 miles west of Manzanillo, on the west coast of Mexico, have an area of 320 square miles and consist of three main islands, Socorro, San Benedicto, and Clarión. There are several smaller islets, among them Roca Partida and Roca de la Pasión. Socorro Island, 24 miles long and 9 miles wide, is the largest of the group and rises to a height of 3,700 feet. A new volcano appeared on San Benedicto Island in September 1952; within six weeks it had attained a height of over 1,000 feet.

**Revolutionary Mexican Party** (*Partido Revolucionario Mexicano*). Also, **PRM.** Name given to the dominant political party in Mexico, formerly known as the NATIONAL REVOLUTIONARY PARTY (PNR) and later as the Party of the Mexican Revolution (PRM), after it had been reorganized in 1938 during the administration of Lázaro CÁRDENAS in order to give greater representation to labor and peasant organizations. The name was later changed to INSTITUTIONAL REVOLUTIONARY PARTY (PRI).

**Reyes, Alfonso.** 1889–1959. Mexican writer, poet, and diplomat. b. Monterrey. He held a number of diplomatic posts, including those of ambassador to Brazil, 1930–1936, and to Argentina, 1936–1937. He was president of the Colegio de México, 1938, professor of philosophy and letters at the National University of Mexico, 1941, and at the Colegio Nacional, 1944. Reyes did outstanding work in history and literary criticism, and is one of the most important essayists in the Spanish-speaking world. His many works include

*Cuestiones estéticas,* Paris, 1911; *Visión de Anáhuac, 1519,* 1917, second edition, Madrid, 1923; and *Cuestiones gongorinas,* 1927. See LITERATURE.

**Reyes, Bernardo.** 1850–1913. Mexican general and political leader. Most efficient of DÍAZ' governors, he ruled Nuevo León and held the military command of the northeast, 1885–1900. Under his administration, the first workmen's compensation law in Mexico was put into effect. A mestizo, he was opposed by the CREOLE oligarchy but hoped to become Díaz' successor. He was made secretary of war by Díaz, 1900, quarreled with minister of finance LIMANTOUR, and was sent back to Nuevo León, 1903. He was sent to Europe by Díaz in 1910, and upon his return he rebelled against MADERO, but was captured. He headed a revolt again in 1913 in Mexico City but was killed immediately.

**Reyes, Rafael.** 1850–1918. President of Colombia. Explorer, scientist, soldier, writer, and conservative political leader. With his brothers he explored the tributaries of the Amazon in the southeastern part of Colombia. He was commander in chief, Colombian army, and in Washington, D.C., as his country's representative at a discussion on Panama, 1903. On August 7, 1904, he assumed dictatorial powers. He modified the constitution, quarreled with congress, and censored the press, but instituted many important economic reforms. In 1909 when his suggested treaty with the United States recognizing the independence of Panama was rejected, he resigned.

**Reyles, Carlos.** 1868–1938. One of Uruguay's most important novelists. b. Montevideo. A naturalist in his early days, he later wrote on the GAUCHO theme. He is especially known for *El embrujo de Sevilla* (The Spell of Seville), 1922, his masterpiece.

**Riesco Errázuriz, Germán.** 1854–1916. President of Chile. b. Rancagua. Served in a minor position in the ministry of justice for five years. He was appointed relator, and later prosecutor, in the court of appeals, and made prosecutor in the supreme court. He was a senator in the national congress, 1899. A liberal member of the Alliance Party, he was president of Chile, 1901–1906.

**Rigaud, André.** 1761–1811. Haitian mulatto general. He opposed TOUSSAINT L'OUVERTURE but was defeated. He went to France, and returned to Haiti with LECLERC, 1802. During the rebellion he was captured with Toussaint L'Ouverture, and sent to imprisonment in France, but managed to escape to Haiti, 1810. He set up an independent state, controlling the southern peninsula, but died soon after.

**Rio Branco, José Maria da Silva Paranhos, Baron of.** 1845–1912. Brazilian diplomat and statesman. b. Rio de Janeiro. Son of Viscount of RIO BRANCO, he represented Brazil at the International Congress at St. Petersburg, Russia, 1884, directed the negotiations with France and Argentina on border disputes, and obtained favorable decisions for his country. He was appointed foreign minister, 1902, and settled the ACRE TERRITORY controversy with Bolivia, and the boundary questions between Brazil, Peru, and Uruguay. He was one of Brazil's outstanding jurists.

**Rio Branco, José Maria da Silva Paranhos, Viscount of.** 1819–1880. Brazilian statesman. b. Bahia state. Governor of the province of Rio de Janeiro, 1864; minister plenipotentiary to the RÍO DE LA PLATA area during the war with Paraguay, 1864–1870. He won approval of RIO BRANCO LAW providing for gradual abolition of slavery, 1871, and fostered development of Brazilian agriculture and communications. He was premier from 1871 to 1873.

**Rio Branco Law.** A law passed in Brazil in 1871 through the leadership of Viscount RIO BRANCO and NABUCO DE ARAUJO. It provided for the freedom of all children born of slaves, although their owners might use the labor of such children until they reached the age of 21. The law was an important step in the full emancipation of Brazilian slaves, which was finally decreed in 1888.

**Rio Conference of 1947.** A conference at which the American states signed the Inter-American Treaty of Reciprocal Assistance or Rio Pact, September 2, 1947. It stipulates that in case of aggression against an Ameri-

can state—whether from outside or within the Western Hemisphere—all other American states will come to the aid of that state. The determination that an act of aggression has taken place requires a two-thirds vote of the contracting parties. No member is required to furnish armed forces without its consent. The treaty went into effect in December 1948.

**Rio Conference of 1954.** Official name, **Inter-American Conference of Ministers of Finance or Economy.** An economic conference of the 21 American republics meeting at Petropolis near Rio de Janeiro in November 1954, for the purpose of examining the fundamental problems of the economy of the Western Hemisphere. U.S. delegates included George M. Humphrey, secretary of the treasury and head of the United States delegation, Henry F. Holland, assistant secretary of state for inter-American affairs, Senator Alexander Wiley, chairman of the Senate Foreign Relations Committee, Samuel C. Waugh, assistant secretary of state for economic affairs, and Andrew Overby, assistant secretary of commerce. A total of 49 resolutions met with approval. Most of them asked for a thorough study of the main economic problems of the Western Hemisphere, including transportation, price fluctuations of coffee, the formation of an inter-American stabilization fund, attracting foreign capital, and technical co-operation.

**Rio de Janeiro.** The second largest city of Brazil, the third largest city in South America. Population 3,307,163 (1963). The city, situated on the Atlantic Ocean, is among the most beautiful in the world. Its matchless 15-mile harbor, the unusual shapes of the mountains surrounding it, and the splendid coloring of the sea and the hillsides make an unforgettable impression on the visitor. It is rapidly becoming an ultramodern metropolis, with its many skyscrapers, boulevards, and parks. Among its avenues the most beautiful is the recently built Avenida Presidente Vargas, a 10-lane thoroughfare, cutting through the city from east to west and lined with skyscrapers. Lining the magnificent 5-mile shore drive along the sea are the well-known suburbs of Copacabana, Ipanema, and Botafogo. The famous Pão de Açúcar

(Sugar Loaf Mountain), 1,230 feet, and Corcovado (The Hunchback), 2,300 feet, tower above the city. The most important buildings include the Catete Palace, which houses the federal government, Guanabara Palace, residence of the president of the republic, the Federal Senate, the Chamber of Deputies, the Municipal Hall, the Municipal Theater, the National Library, the largest in South America, and the church of Our Lady of Gloria. The building housing the ministry of health and education is an ultramodern edifice. The peak of Pão de Açúcar, situated in the southern area, can be reached by cable car, and that of Corcovado by a cog-wheeled railway. The city is connected with other Brazilian centers by two rail lines, and with other countries in the Western Hemisphere and Europe by air and steamship service. The important economic activities are the production of textiles, clothing, glass, electrical and household appliances, chemicals, motors, trucks, and rubber tires. Rio is also a major import-export center, having splendid harbor facilities that enable large vessels to berth near the heart of the city. Although the site of Rio de Janeiro (River of January) was discovered in January 1502, it was settled only in 1555, and then by the French under VILLE-GAGNON, who founded a colony on an island in the harbor. The Portuguese were able to establish a settlement only in 1566, calling it São Sebastião do Rio de Janeiro. A year later they consolidated their grip on the bay by expelling the French. The town grew rapidly and in 1572 it was made the capital of the southern half of the colony. In 1576, however, the city of Bahia supplanted Rio de Janeiro as colonial capital. In 1711 the city was sacked by the French, but subsequently it kept expanding. In 1763 it was made the capital of the Brazilian colony, and in 1808 it became the seat of the Portuguese royal court. In 1822 it was proclaimed capital of the Brazilian Empire, and in 1834 it was administratively detached from Rio de Janeiro province and became part of a neutral *municipio*, which in 1891 was renamed a federal district. Until the beginning of the 20th century Rio de Janeiro was plagued by frequent yellow fever epidemics, but during the administration of RODRIGUES ALVES (1902–

1906) this scourge was eradicated from the capital under the direction of the great Brazilian physician Oswaldo CRUZ. The city was the scene of the 1906 Pan American Congress, and in 1942 the Third Inter-American Conference of Foreign Ministers met there. Rio de Janeiro ceased to be the capital of the Brazilian nation when, on April 21, 1960, the new federal capital, BRASÍLIA, was inaugurated.

**Río de la Plata.** The 180-mile-long estuary between Uruguay and the Argentine province of Buenos Aires. The Río de la Plata is the estuary of the continent's second largest, but most important, river system which includes the Uruguay, Paraguay, and Paraná Rivers. It is widest, 130 miles, where it enters the Atlantic, measures 65 miles across at Montevideo on its northern shore, and 35 miles at Buenos Aires on its southwestern shore. Although the Río de la Plata carries a tremendous volume of water that it drains from a basin of over 1,500,000 square miles, it is generally shallow, ranging from 8 to 18 feet deep over most of its length and reaching its greatest depth of 65 feet near the open sea. The presence of shoals requires frequent dredging to permit ships to ascend it to Buenos Aires and to the entrance to the Paraná and Uruguay Rivers. It combines the characteristics of a river estuary and an ocean gulf, being a fresh-water body in its narrower northwestern portion and increasing in salinity beyond a line joining Punta Piedras (Argentina) and Montevideo. The first Europeans probably arrived in the region in 1502 in the voyage of Amerigo VESPUCCI. The search for a passage through the continent to the Orient brought the Spaniard Juan DÍAZ DE SOLÍS in 1516 and the estuary subsequently was given the name of Río de Solís. In 1526 Sebastián CABOT sailed upon it and then ascended the Paraná and Paraguay Rivers. Because of the silver that Cabot bought from the Indians in that area, and of reports of the existence in the same region of a "Great White King" who was in possession of much silver, the river was later renamed Río de la Plata (Silver River).

**Rio Grande do Sul.** The southernmost state of Brazil, bordering on Uruguay to the south and Argentina to the west, with an area of 110,150 square miles and a population of about 5,448,823 (1960). The state capital, Pôrto Alegre, with a population of 382,000, is a growing industrial city and the leading commercial center south of São Paulo. Along the Atlantic coast are lagoons, of which the largest is the Lagôa dos Patos, 150 miles long and 30 miles wide. At the entrance of this lagoon stands the important port and distribution center of Rio Grande, 1,000 miles south of Rio de Janeiro. Rio Grande do Sul is one of the leading agricultural states in Brazil, and its cattle industry, especially in the southern grasslands, is also one of the most important in the country. In colonial times the area was a constant source of quarrels between Portugal and Spain. In 1763 the territory was formally given to Portugal, but the Spaniards stayed on. The limits of Portuguese and Spanish possessions were definitively traced in 1800. During the early period of the Brazilian empire a serious revolt aiming at the independence of the province broke out in Rio Grande do Sul, but the insurgents finally surrendered to the central authorities after an amnesty had been promised, 1835–1845. Many Germans settled in Rio Grande do Sul in the 19th century, and today German is still spoken by a considerable number of people in certain districts of the state. In 1923 an uprising was put down by the government, and in 1930 a country-wide revolt, in which the state played an important part, made the governor of Rio Grande do Sul, Getúlio VARGAS, provisional president of the republic.

**Ríos Morales, Juan Antonio.** 1888–1946. President of Chile. Lawyer and statesman. b. Cañete. Of humble parents, he worked his way through the University of Concepción and became a successful and well-to-do man. A member of the moderate wing of the Radical Party, he opposed the Communists. He was a senator, minister of the interior, and also minister of justice, 1932. He was an unsuccessful candidate for the presidency in the convention of 1938. A friend of the democracies, he was elected, 1942, and kept the country neutral until 1943, when WELLES accused Chile of being too lenient to Axis

agents. Ríos Morales denied the charges, broke relations with the Axis powers, and the United States sent economic and industrial aid in an attempt to alleviate the country's problems. Ríos Morales set price ceilings, but the black market flourished; disagreements within the party caused difficulties, and at the convention, his candidate was defeated. He took a leave of absence in January 1946 as the result of ill health and died five months later.

**Rivadavia, Bernardino.** 1780–1845. Argentine diplomat and statesman. He fought in the War for Independence, 1811–1814, served as minister of war, 1811–1812, at Buenos Aires, and served as Argentina's envoy in London, Paris, and Madrid, 1814–1820. He was minister of state of Buenos Aires, 1820–1823, instituting a number of reforms. He founded a university and improved primary education. He was president of the Argentine Confederation for the year 1826–1827, during which a treaty was made with Brazil, recognizing the Banda Oriental (Uruguay) as Brazilian territory. This action, taken in the midst of the war with Brazil, was very unpopular, and Rivadavia repudiated the treaty and wanted to continue the war, but resigned July 1827. He spent most of his remaining years in exile in Spain.

**Rivera, Diego.** 1886–1957. The most prolific, controversial, and widely-known of Mexican painters. b. Guanajuato. A leader of the group of artists appearing early in the 1920's who devoted themselves to expressing and propagandizing the ideals of the Mexican revolution. Primarily a muralist, most of his pictures deal with Mexican history, glorifying the Indian heritage and modern radicalism, and castigating Spanish colonialism, Catholicism, and modern capitalism. Outstanding examples of his work are to be found in the National Palace, the Secretariat of Education in Mexico City, the National Agricultural School in Chapingo, and the Palace of Cortés in Cuernavaca.

**Rivera, José Eustasio.** 1889–1928. Colombian writer, author of the powerful novel *La vorágine* (The Vortex), 1924, in which he gives an account of the plight of rubber workers in the South American jungle. See LITERATURE.

**Rivera, José Fructuoso.** 1790–1854. First president of Uruguay. b. Paysandú. Descendent of GAUCHOS. General and statesman, he fought for Uruguayan independence under ARTIGAS, submitted to Brazilian occupation of Uruguay, 1820, but later joined the liberation movement of 1825, which led to war between Argentina and Brazil and resulted in Uruguayan independence, 1828. He led the revolution of 1830 and became the first president of the country, 1830–1834. He led a *colorado* revolt, 1836–1838, that overthrew ORIBE. He was president again, 1839, and led the *colorados* for a number of years in the great civil war, 1840–1851, against the *blancos* under Oribe who were supported by ROSAS and the Buenos Aires forces. He was forced into exile to Brazil by his own supporters, 1846. He was chosen as one of the three to administer the provisional government of Uruguay, 1853, but died the following year.

**Roca, Julio Argentino.** 1843–1914. President of Argentina, 1880–1886, 1898–1904. General; participated in war against Paraguay. Minister of war under AVELLANEDA, he led troops into the southern PAMPA, 1878–1879, defeating the hitherto unconquered Indians and opening up a great area of fertile land for stockraising and agriculture. During his first administration, he strengthened the central government, built railroads, encouraged immigration and foreign trade, and the country's prosperity increased. He was appointed minister of the interior under Pellegrini, 1890–1892. During his second administration the boundary dispute with Chile was settled.

**Rocafuerte, Vicente.** 1783–1847. President of Ecuador, 1835–1839. b. Guayaquil. Wealthy CREOLE who spent most of his early life in Europe and was educated there. He served as American deputy in the Spanish Cortes and represented Mexico in England. He was leader of the liberals in Guayaquil, opposed Juan FLORES, and then surprisingly became the latter's choice for the presidency. Rocafuerte was not a good administrator, ruled arbitrarily, and his anticlerical legislation

caused a split in opinion which divided the country. Flores returned to office in 1839 and became a dictator. Rocafuerte and other liberals staged an unsuccessful revolt, and he was forced into exile. He wrote many political essays and articles.

**Roca-Runciman Agreement.** Accord signed in 1933 between the vice-president of Argentina, Julio Roca, and Lord Runciman of Great Britain. By its terms, Argentine meat was to receive a privileged position on the British market, and in return Argentina would increase the import of British manufactured goods.

**Rodó, José Enrique.** 1872–1917. Uruguayan author. b. Montevideo. Considered the outstanding and most influential modernist of Uruguay. A liberal, he was twice member of congress. He won fame for his criticism and philosophical essays, his main thesis being that although the material and practical are essential to life, spiritual and cultural values are vastly more important. Outstanding among his works are *Ariel*, 1900, which was very influential for its criticism of the materialism of the United States, and widely read as the leading expression of "Yankee-phobia"; *Motivos de Proteo*, 1909, which stressed the development of the individual and human spirit, following the creative evolution ideas of Henri Bergson; and *El mirador de Próspero*, 1913. See LITERATURE.

**Rodrigues Alves, Francisco de Paula.** 1848–1919. President of Brazil. President of São Paulo, 1900–1902, 1912–1916. He was president of Brazil, 1902–1906, and again elected president, 1918, but was unable to serve as the result of ill health. He succeeded in instituting a program of municipal improvements that made Rio de Janeiro a magnificent city and approved a campaign against yellow fever that rid the capital of the disease.

**Rodríguez, Abelardo K.** 1889–1967. Provisional president of Mexico. b. San José de Guaymas. General and wealthy banker. He served as provisional president of Mexico, 1932–1934, after ORTIZ RUBIO resigned. He was generally regarded as a puppet of CALLES, and his administration was moderately conservative and peaceful, although there was some conflict with the Church.

**Rodríguez, Manuel.** 1786–1818. Chilean patriot. Graduate of the University of San Felipe; lawyer; secretary to José CARRERA. He fought as a leader of the guerrillas who paved the way for Bernardo O'HIGGINS in the fight for independence. Because of jealousy, and the fact that he had once worked for Carrera, he was arrested, 1818, and shot by members of the police guard.

**Rodríguez de Cabrillo, Juan.** See CA-BRILLO, JUAN RODRÍGUEZ DE.

**Rojas Uturguren, José Antonio.** 1732–1817. Chilean patriot. b. Santiago. Aided the men who fought for independence from Spain, propagandized for "The Rights of Man" and other revolutionary ideas, Rojas played an important part in the revolution of 1810. After the restoration of Spanish rule in 1814, he was deported to the island of Juan Fernández. He was later given permission to move to Santiago, where he died.

**Romaña, Eduardo López de.** President of Peru, 1899–1903. He was a civil engineer and political leader whose administration was a relatively quiet one.

**Romero, José Rubén.** 1890–1952. b. Cotija. Mexican novelist and diplomat. Ambassador to Brazil, 1937–1939, and Cuba, 1939–1943; author of *Mi caballo, mi perro y mi rifle* (My Horse, My Dog, and My Rifle), *La vida inútil de Pito Pérez* (The Useless Life of Pito Pérez, 1967), and other works. See LITERA-TURE.

**Romero Rubio, Manuel.** d. 1895. Mexican political leader. b. Mexico, D. F. Liberal supporter of JUÁREZ. He became rich and more conservative, and served as Sebastián LERDO DE TEJADA's political manager but was forced into exile, 1876. After 1884 he became an important part of DÍAZ' political machine, serving as secretary of the interior, managing congress, and controlling the police. He married his daughter to Díaz. He was the leader of the *científicos*.

**Roosevelt, Franklin Delano.** 1882–1945. Thirty-second president of the United States.

Intensely interested in the solidarity of the Western Hemisphere and the promotion of Pan-American relations. Famous for his GOOD NEIGHBOR POLICY, Roosevelt was more admired and better liked in Latin America than any other United States president.

**Roosevelt, Theodore.** 1858–1919. Twenty-sixth president of the United States. With Leonard WOOD he organized a volunteer cavalry regiment known as the Rough Riders, and first as lieutenant colonel and then as colonel, served in Cuba in the SPANISH-AMER-ICAN WAR, 1898. When president, he recognized the Republic of Panama after its revolt and declaration of independence from Colombia, November 3, 1903, and promoted the building of the PANAMA CANAL. In 1905, he negotiated a treaty with the Dominican Republic that set up machinery for the United States to administer the customs of that country in order to pay off foreign debts. This made it clear that the United States would interfere in Latin America in order to guarantee the good relations of Latin-American nations with other countries and to prevent intervention by European powers. When on an expedition of exploration to South America in 1914, he discovered a tributary of the Madeira River. He was disliked in Latin America for his BIG STICK imperialism. See ROOSEVELT COROLLARY.

**Roosevelt Corollary.** An extension of the MONROE DOCTRINE, expounded by President Theodore ROOSEVELT in December 1904. Roosevelt interpreted the Monroe Doctrine as imposing upon the United States the duty to intervene in the affairs of Latin-American nations in order to forestall the intervention of European powers. Said Roosevelt: "Chronic wrongdoing may in America, as elsewhere, ultimately require intervention by some civilized nations, and in the Western Hemisphere, the adherence to the Monroe Doctrine may force the United States, however reluctantly, in flagrant cases of such wrongdoing or impotence, to the exercise of an international police power." This doctrine led to American intervention in the Caribbean area and aroused much ill feeling in Latin America toward the United States. It was repudiated by the United States in the CLARK

MEMORANDUM, written in 1928 and published in 1930.

**Rosas, Juan Manuel de.** 1793–1877. Dictator of Argentina. b. Buenos Aires. Head of the Federalist Party from 1828, he was a landowner, who had his own GAUCHO army, and was governor of Buenos Aires, 1829–1831, 1835–1852. He joined other Argentine provinces in a form of union and ruled over them all as a dictator, although he was, technically, only the governor of Buenos Aires. He claimed to be for the people but only to retain power; favored the Church and big landowners; aided ORIBE in war against the *colorados* of Uruguay, 1840–1851, hoping to take over that country. During his administration he was constantly at war, first with SANTA CRUZ, ruler of Bolivia and Peru, then with Uruguay, France, and Great Britain. He was defeated by URQUIZA on February 3, 1852, in the Battle of CASEROS, and was forced to flee to England where he lived in exile, 1852–1877. His regime was one of the cruelest dictatorships in Latin-American history. However it was important in maintaining the unity of Argentina and stimulating a feeling of nationalism.

**Roto.** Spanish, meaning broken, ragged. The name *roto* in Chile refers to a member of the lowest class.

**Rubber Industry.** The *Hevea brasiliensis* tree, source of crude rubber, and native to the Amazon valley, catapulted that area into the first rank of world rubber production in the first decade of the 20th century. Brazil was the world's leading exporter, but Bolivia, Colombia, Ecuador, Peru, and Venezuela also contributed important amounts of wild rubber to the world market. By 1912 exports of rubber from the Amazon basin amounted to 45,000 tons. Very soon, however, the Amazonian boom collapsed when competition from southeastern Asian plantations displaced South-American rubber from its dominant position. In spite of the combined factors of energetic measures taken by the Brazilian government to restore the country's product to its former prominence, the setting up of Ford plantations on the lower Tapajós River, and the work of the Rubber Development Corporation in World War II, production in the Amazon has not come up to expectations. The best rubber today is grown in the Acre Territory in western Brazil, and in northern Bolivia. Brazilian rubber production for 1962 amounted to approximately 37,000 metric tons. Synthetic rubber production is an ever-growing threat to the industry.

**Ruiz de Apodaca, Juan.** 1767–1835. Viceroy of Mexico, 1816–1821. Arriving in Mexico toward the end of the anti-Spanish uprising, Apodaca offered amnesty to all who were willing to submit, and this measure, combined with military successes won by the royalists, ended the revolution for all practical purposes. After King FERDINAND VII of Spain was forced to recognize the Spanish constitution of 1812, as a result of a revolution in Spain in 1820, Apodaca proclaimed the constitution in Mexico, and in the ensuing elections the creoles were victorious. At the beginning of 1821, the viceroy was confronted by a new independence movement organized by Agustín de ITURBIDE, to whom Apodaca had entrusted a command over military forces to be used against the rebel chieftain GUERRERO and by the summer of that year the movement had become irresistible, and Apodaca was recalled to Spain.

**Ruiz Cortines, Adolfo.** b. 1891. President of Mexico, 1952–1958. b. Veracruz. Had elementary schooling; enlisted in revolutionary armies and rose to rank of major; government clerk after the war. He became a close friend of Miguel ALEMÁN VALDÉS, and in 1937 the latter appointed him his administrative assistant. With the support of Alemán, he rose to the governorship of Veracruz, 1944, and became minister of the interior, 1948, during Alemán's term as president. Elected president, 1952, he launched a strong drive against graft and corruption in government, gave Mexican women full citizenship rights, including the vote. He pushed industrial expansion of Mexico, continuing the work of previous administrations, devalued the Mexican peso to encourage investments and increase exports, developed a Mexican hydraulic program that increased power sources, established flood control, and improved and irrigated more than 2,700,000 acres of farm land. A friend of the United States, his administration, 1952–1958, was dedicated to implementing policies initiated by his predecessors and, although few innovations were made, the complicated machinery of government ran more smoothly and there was a noticeable improvement in the morality of public service in Mexico. He was succeeded by Adolfo LÓPEZ MATEOS, 1958.

**Rurales.** Mexican rural policemen of the DÍAZ regime. They wore broad felt hats, gray uniforms with red ties and silver buttons, and silver-embossed saddles adorned their horses. They frequently applied the *ley fuga* (law of escape), which gave them the right to shoot their prisoners who attempted to escape. There were more than 10,000 cases of *ley fuga* during the Díaz regime. They suppressed banditry and rendered Mexico safe for travelers, but often exercised tyrannical powers over the underprivileged.

**Russell, John H.** Brigadier General of the U.S. Marine Corps. Appointed high commissioner of Haiti in 1922, acting as diplomatic representative of the United States. Under his administration the economic and financial condition of the country was greatly improved. The Public Works Service, under the direction of U.S. Navy doctors, organized hospitals and clinics; agriculture was stimulated and new methods of farming introduced. By 1930, when Sténio VINCENT became president, Russell's work was ended and the military occupation terminated, 1931.

**Russian-Latin American Relations.** Before WORLD WAR II Russia had diplomatic relations with but few of the Latin-American nations. During World War II the Soviet Union made strenuous efforts to win the sympathies of Latin Americans and, in a number of cases, succeeded. Chile was an important example. As a result of the U.S.S.R.'s friendly relations with Chile, the Chilean Communist Party gained much ground during the war. Throughout Latin America Communist Parties capitalized on the normalization of relations with the Soviet Union and spread their propaganda, especially through the medium of newspapers. They were also active in the labor unions, winning their greatest strength in Brazil, Chile, and Cuba. The Soviet Union's uncompromising attitude toward the West after the war lost her many friends in Latin America. Brazil was first to break relations with the U.S.S.R., 1947, closely followed by Chile. After Stalin's death, 1953, the U.S.S.R. tried to impress Latin America with her "new look" policies and endeavored to regain the ground lost after World War II. Soviet bloc trade with the Latin-American area has increased in recent years, but by 1958 it accounted for only 2 per cent of the total trade. In the latter years of the 1950's and to the present time the attempts of the Soviet Union to cultivate better relations with Latin America have enjoyed limited success. The revolution in Cuba has afforded the Soviets the opportunity to capitalize on Latin-American distrust of the United States and to promote better relations. The Sino-Soviet ideological quarrel has brought about a split among Latin-American Communists, but most of these have continued to support the Soviet argument and the disagreement has not seriously affected Soviet relations with Latin America. See COMMUNISM IN LATIN AMERICA.

# S

**Sá, Mem de.** *ca.* 1500–1572. Portuguese statesman. Third governor of Brazil, who drove the French out of Fort Coligny and founded Rio de Janeiro, 1566–1567. He was governor of Brazil, 1557–1572, and during his administration cities were founded, schools were established, Indian labor was supplemented by the importation of Negro slaves from Africa, and tobacco and sugar were added to the meager list of crops of the country.

**Saavedra, Cornelio.** 1760–1828. Leader of the War for Independence in Argentina, and president of the junta, 1810–1811. An Argentine soldier, he defended Montevideo against the British, 1806, and led a legion of *patricios* in fight for independence of 1810. He became president of the junta of Buenos Aires, was opposed by MORENO, and attacked for being too moderate. Forced to take refuge in Chile, he was absolved by the congress of Buenos Aires in 1818 that appointed him chief of staff of the army.

**Saavedra, Juan Bautista.** 1870–1939. President of Bolivia. Well-known jurist; leader of the Republican, or Liberal party. He was president, 1921–1925, and succeeded in obtaining loans from banking interests in the United States for the purposes of building railroads and developing the oil and tin industries. He was able to suppress a political revolution in the province of Santa Cruz where a secession movement was in operation, July 1924.

**Saavedra Lamas, Carlos.** 1878–1959. Argentine lawyer and statesman. b. Buenos Aires. Conservative lawyer; responsible for the Saavedra Lamas Law of 1912 which practically excluded all foreign sugar from Argentina and thereby provided a national subsidy for the Tucumán producers. He served as foreign minister under Agustín JUSTO, 1932–1938, and presided over the conference in Buenos Aires, 1935, which ended the CHACO WAR. Unfriendly to the United States, he worked for the consolidation of South-American states under Argentina's guidance and urged neighboring nations, who were having constant disputes, to try to settle their problems with as little help as possible from inter-American or international sources. He served as president, however, of the Assembly of the LEAGUE OF NATIONS, 1936, and was awarded the Nobel Peace Prize, 1936.

**Sacasa, Juan Bautista.** 1874–1946. President of Nicaragua. b. León. Educated at Instituto de León and Columbia University. Liberal leader, served as vice-president under Solórzano, 1925, but was forced to flee the country when CHAMORRO VARGAS seized power. The United States refused to recognize Chamorro and the presidency was given to DÍAZ. Sacasa was minister plenipotentiary to the United States, 1929–1931, and elected president, 1933. In February 1933, he made peace with SANDINO, who had been in revolt against the government. When Sandino was assassinated, Sacasa attempted to punish the guilty, and as a result was forced to resign, June 1936, and went into exile in the United States.

**Sáenz Peña, Luis.** 1823–1907. President of Argentina. As a result of the formation of a coalition known as the *Acuerdo,* although opposed by the radicals, Sáenz Peña was elected president, 1892, but had a difficult administration because of a severe economic depression in the country, resulting in discontent. He succeeded in suppressing a radical revolt, 1893. He called a special session of congress to discuss the problem of the threatening war with Chile and the financial crisis within the country. In January 1895, he was forced to turn the government over to vice-president URIBURU.

**Sáenz Peña, Roque.** 1851–1914. President of Argentina. Served as a volunteer in the Peruvian army during the war against Chile, 1879–1883, and as a public official both in domestic posts and as an envoy to foreign countries. A conservative member of the Nationalist Party, he succeeded Figueroa Alcorta as president of Argentina, 1910. An idealist interested in introducing democratic reforms into his country, he succeeded in pushing through congress his Reform Bill of 1912; this legislation established for the first time the secret ballot and provided for universal male suffrage; proportional representation was granted to minority groups; voting was compulsory, and punishment by fine was imposed for unexcused absence from the polls. Sáenz Peña also promoted conservation of natural resources. He died in office in August 1914.

**Salamanca, Daniel.** 1863–1935. President of Bolivia. He was elected president by a republican-liberal coalition in 1931, broke off diplomatic relations with Paraguay, 1931, and declared war on Paraguay, 1933. The CHACO WAR was the result of disputes over the ownership of the Gran Chaco, where oil was being discovered. The war was disastrous, costing many lives, and the financial burden was enormous. Salamanca was overthrown in 1934.

**Salas Corvalán, Manuel de.** 1755–1841. Chilean educator. b. Santiago. Set up the Academia de San Luis at Santiago at the end of the 18th century, with courses in arithmetic, geometry, and mining engineering. He was a leading member of the Santiago trade tribunal, the *consulado*. He was the author of *Memorial on the State of Chile,* 1796 (published, 1843), based on Spanish reforms and the ideas set forth by Adam Smith (Scottish political economist and author of *Wealth of Nations,* 1776) on economic liberty and political economy. He worked with Manuel BELGRANO of Argentina and fought for reform in Chilean agriculture, commerce, mining, and education. He was interested in free trade and stressed its importance to an exporting nation like Chile.

**Salaverry, Felipe Santiago.** 1806–1836. Peruvian general. A daring young *caudillo* who led a revolt against GAMARRA, 1834, he set himself up as chief of Peru, 1835–1836. He was defeated in battle by SANTA CRUZ of Bolivia and executed, although he had surrendered on the trust that his life would be spared.

**Salvador.** Formerly, **Bahia** or **São Salvador da Bahia de Todos os Santos.** The capital of the Brazilian state of BAHIA and the oldest and fourth largest city in Brazil. The population in 1960 was 591,000. Salvador is one of the most important ports and airports of Brazil. Divided into two parts, linked by cable-car service, the city has attractive squares and gardens as well as many impressive public and business buildings, hotels, and private residences. It occupies a leading position in the tobacco and cacao trade, and is an important sugar refining center, also producing cotton and jute. It is linked by rail and by air with Rio de Janeiro to the south and with Recife to the north. Salvador was founded by Thomé de SOUZA in 1549, after an earlier settlement (1534) had been destroyed by Indians, and soon became the most important town in the colony. It was the capital of Brazil until 1763. The sugar industry of the state of Bahia declined after the ABOLITION OF SLAVERY in 1888, and the city lost much of its economic importance. It regained its prominence in the economy of the country, however, when it became a leader in the fields of cacao and tobacco.

**Sam, Villbrun Guillaume.** d. 1915. President of Haiti, 1910–1915. He led a revolution in January 1910 and seized the presidency. He executed 167 of his political enemies, provoking a revolt that caused the United States to intervene, landing troops to restore order, on

July 28, 1915, the day when Sam himself was murdered.

**Samaná Bay.** A bay 30 miles long and 10 miles wide, situated on the northeast coast of the Dominican Republic. It has an excellent harbor, which can be used by the largest ships. In 1869, under the administration of President Ulysses S. Grant, two treaties were signed between the United States and the Dominican Republic, one providing for the annexation of the Dominican Republic to the United States, and the other for a 99-year lease of Samaná Bay. The U.S. Senate, however, refused to ratify these treaties, 1870, and further efforts of the Grant administration to change the opinion of the lawmakers did not meet with any success.

**Sánchez, Florencio.** 1875–1910. Uruguayan playwright. Perhaps the foremost Latin-American dramatist; author of *M'hijo el doctor*(My Son the Doctor), 1903, *La gringa*, 1904, *Barranca abajo* (Down the Hill), 1905, a somber drama of rural life, and others. See LITERATURE.

**Sánchez Cerro, Luis M.** 1889–1933. President of Peru. b. Piura. Became colonel; military commander at Arequipa. On August 22, 1930, he led a revolt against LEGUÍA, who was forced to resign, and Sánchez Cerro became provisional president, serving for six months, when he was forced by the troops to resign, due to the discontent and opposition of the people. He was elected president in the voting of October 1931 and became constitutional president. Sánchez Cerro played an important part in the LETICIA DISPUTE and refused to allow the LEAGUE OF NATIONS to bring about a settlement. He was assassinated on April 30, 1933.

**Sánchez Errázuriz, Eulogio.** 1903–    . b. Santiago. Organizer of the *Milicia Republicana* (Republican Militia) in Chile, 1932, composed of armed and well-disciplined volunteers whose purpose was to prevent uprisings against the government. A national group with 50,000 members, it was unpopular with liberal elements of the country. Its dissolution was brought about in 1935 because constitutional government and legal order had been sufficiently strengthened, and because the *Milicia* itself was becoming a menace to the public peace. Sánchez sought to unite the organization under the new name of *Acción nacional* to oppose the administration of President ALESSANDRI PALMA, 1936.

**Sandino, Augusto César.** 1893–1934. Nicaraguan guerrilla leader. He supported a liberal revolt in 1926, seized American property, refused to lay down arms as long as U.S. forces were in Nicaragua, and waged guerrilla warfare against the U.S. Marines in an attempt to cause them to withdraw, 1927–1932. When U.S. forces were withdrawn, 1933, he was forced by both liberals and conservatives to come to terms with the government. He was assassinated in Managua, and is regarded by many as the patriotic champion of Nicaraguan independence from U.S. domination.

**San Domingo Improvement Company.** An American company set up under the statutes of the state of New Jersey. By virtue of an agreement in 1892 with the administration of President Ulises HEUREAUX of the Dominican Republic, at the time in dire financial straits, it took over the collection of Dominican customs, the proceeds being distributed to the Dominican government and its creditors. Aside from its customs-collecting activities, the company issued loans and engaged in the building of railroads. When, in 1901, the administration of President JIMÉNEZ, who assumed control after the assassination of Heureaux, 1899, barred the company from the collection of customs, it appealed to the U.S. Government. Negotiations began and in 1903 the company agreed that it would relinquish its interests in the Dominican Republic in exchange for $4,500,-000 to be paid monthly out of the revenue from certain ports. It was further agreed that a financial agent, named by the United States, would take charge of a number of customhouses if the Dominican government did not fulfill its obligations. As it turned out, the government did not make any payment on the American debt and the Puerto Plata customhouse was taken over by a financial agent appointed by the U.S. government, October 1904.

**Sanfuentes Andonáegui, Juan Luis.** 1858–

1930. President of Chile, 1915–1920. He kept his country neutral during WORLD WAR I, improved the financial situation of the country, and instituted military and administrative reforms.

**San Jacinto, Battle of.** The last important battle of the War for Texan Independence. On April 21, 1836, 783 Texans under General HOUSTON crushed about 1,500 Mexicans under SANTA ANNA. The Texans with a shout of "Remember the Alamo" stormed the breastworks thrown up by Santa Anna and within 20 minutes destroyed organized resistance. The battle then turned into a slaughter with 600 Mexicans being killed and the rest taken prisoner. Santa Anna himself was made a prisoner and negotiated armistice terms to end the war.

**San José.** The capital of Costa Rica, situated at an altitude of 3,800 feet above sea level, about 100 miles west of the Atlantic port of Limón and 50 miles east of the Pacific port of Puntarenas, with a population of about 157,679 (1963). It is one of the most beautiful cities in Central America, with many parks, and many of its buildings still preserving an Old-World look. Because of frequent earthquakes its houses have been built low and generally do not exceed a height of two stories. Outstanding buildings include the National Palace, the Muncipal Palace (finished in 1937), the National Library, the U.S. Embassy (considered the finest building in the city), and the Cathedral. San José is the center of the Costa Rican coffee trade and is linked by rail with the Atlantic and Pacific. Its airport assures flight connections with other countries.

San José was founded in 1738. In the second half of the 18th century it became of increasing importance because of tobacco grown in the area. In 1815 the construction of the University of Santo Tomás was begun. The inhabitants of San José espoused the cause of freedom soon after the beginning of the independence movement in Spanish America, and gave their wholehearted support to the establishment of Central-American independence in 1821. Two years later, in 1823, San José became the capital of Costa Rica, after the town of Cartago, until then the capital, had been almost destroyed by an eruption of the volcano Irazú. In 1948 San José was the scene of severe fighting during the antigovernmental revolt led by José FIGUERES FERRER.

**San Luis Potosí, Plan of.** A proclamation issued by Francisco MADERO at San Antonio, Texas, in October 1910. It declared the recent Mexican elections null and void and called for a general insurrection against the dictatorship of Porfirio DÍAZ. It also demanded effective suffrage and no re-election, the restoration of the constitution of 1857, and the return to the Indian villages of the land illegally taken from them. A year later the revolution had triumphed and Madero was elected president.

**San Marcos, University of.** Official name, **Universidad Nacional Mayor de San Marcos de Lima.** One of the oldest universities in the New World, in Lima, Peru, established by royal order in 1551 and opened in 1571–1576. By the end of the 18th century it had 15 professorial chairs. Today it is an important center of learning in Latin America, having approximately 13,500 students and an academic staff numbering about 1,300.

**San Martín, José de.** 1778–1850. South American patriot, general, and statesman. b. Yapeyú, now in Argentina, on the Uruguay River. Taken to Spain by his family, 1785, he served in the Spanish army, 1791–1811; arrived in Buenos Aires from Europe, 1812, and offered his help in the fight for independence; defeated the Spaniards in 1813 and succeeded BELGRANO as commander in chief, 1814. In Cuyo province, Argentina, he organized an army and crossed the Andes in January 1817, one of the greatest exploits in military history, since only by careful preparation and skill in deceiving his enemies could such a task be accomplished. With General Bernardo O'HIGGINS, he defeated the Spanish at CHACABUCO, Chile, 1817, and captured Santiago; at MAIPÚ he won a decisive battle, 1818, enabling him to establish the independence of Chile; developed a Chilean fleet, with the aid of Lord COCHRANE, and left for Peru, 1820. Winning over the Peruvians, he entered Lima, July 1821, and as the Spanish withdrew, established the independence of

Peru, and assumed dictatorial powers as "Protector of Peru." Refusing to oppose BOLÍVAR, and more anxious to aid Peru than to gain glory for himself, a gesture unparalleled in history, he resigned in September 1822. San Martín was largely responsible for the success of Bolívar in later victories over the Spanish. He sailed for Europe, 1824, and when upon his return to Buenos Aires five years later he was met with coldness, without disembarking he returned to Europe where he died in obscurity at Boulogne, France, 1850. His remains were moved to the cathedral at Buenos Aires in 1880. He was farsighted, honest, able, and one of the greatest figures in Latin-American history.

**San Martín, Juan Zorrilla de.** See ZORRILLA DE SAN MARTÍN, JUAN.

**San Mateo, Treaty of.** A capitulation signed by the Venezuelan patriot revolutionary Francisco de MIRANDA and the Spanish commander Juan Domingo MONTEVERDE on July 25, 1812, providing for the re-establishment of Spanish rule in Venezuela in return for immunity for Venezuelan patriots. The Spanish violated the treaty after the revolutionaries had capitulated, and the patriots thought that Miranda had betrayed their cause. Miranda was taken into custody by his friends, including BOLÍVAR, and handed over to the Spaniards.

**San Nicolás, Pact of.** A compact signed on May 31, 1852, at San Nicolás de los Arroyos in the province of Buenos Aires, Argentina, by the governors of the Argentine provinces. It renewed the federal pact of 1831 and called for a constitutional convention. At the same time General URQUIZA, the recent victor over ROSAS, was given executive, civil, and military powers, until the constitutional convention could meet.

**San Salvador.** The capital of El Salvador, situated at an altitude of 2,200 feet above the sea, and a distance of 23 miles from the Pacific port of La Libertad. Population about 453,293 (est. 1963). Laid out in the shape of a cross, the city is essentially a modern capital with fine parks and private houses. Outstanding buildings are the National Palace, the National Theater, and the Cathedral. Near the city is a beautiful stadium built for the Caribbean Olympic games in 1935. San Salvador is connected by road with the port of La Libertad and with Guatemala City, and by rail with Guatemala City and Puerto Barrios, as well as with the Pacific port of Acajutla. It is connected by air with neighboring countries. The city is in a coffee-growing district, and other crops include rice, sugar, and tobacco. Among the products produced in the capital are silk goods, cigars, beer, soap, and shoes. San Salvador was founded about 1528 by Jorge de Alvarado, brother of Pedro de ALVARADO Y MESÍA, the conquistador of Guatemala. It was not built at the present site, however, but at some distance from today's city. San Salvador has suffered many earthquakes. In the 19th century it was wrecked twice, and in 1917 it again underwent extensive damage.

**Santa Anna, Antonio López de.** ca. 1795–1876. Mexican dictator, general, and revolutionist. b. Jalapa. Served as a soldier in the Spanish army. Leader of revolt against ITURBIDE in 1822, he supported GUERRERO, 1829, but later turned against him in favor of Anastasio BUSTAMANTE, then revolted against Bustamante, and served as president, 1833–1835. In an attempt to crush the Texan revolution of independence, he captured the ALAMO, 1836, but was defeated by Sam HOUSTON at SAN JACINTO and captured on April 21, 1836. He was in control of the government, 1841–1844, until finally overthrown and exiled. He was called back and was made provisional president when he commanded the army against the United States, 1846–1847, but he was defeated at the battles of BUENA VISTA and CERRO GORDO, and driven by General Scott from Mexico City. He was exiled again in 1848, but once more recalled and made dictator, 1853–1855. Following the revolution of AYUTLA, he went into exile, 1855, and lived in Colombia, Venezuela, and the United States, 1855–1874. He returned to Mexico City in 1874, where he died poor and neglected. Although unscrupulous and with little actual administrative ability, he had dominated Mexican politics for 25 years. He changed his ideas and politics to suit the opportunities of the times, but generally was on the side of the conservative elements and the Church.

**Santa Cruz, Andrés de.** 1792–1865. Dictator of Bolivia. Born a mestizo on the shore of LAKE TITICACA, he claimed descent on his mother's side from the royal INCAS, and had a large following among the Indians in both Peru and Bolivia. He fought with the Spanish during the Peruvian war for independence but joined SAN MARTÍN's army, 1821. He served under BOLÍVAR and governed Peru as the Liberator's lieutenant at the head of a council, 1826–1827. He was president of Bolivia, 1829–1839, and instituted a number of reforms; planned a union of Peru and Bolivia and became head of the PERU-BOLIVIAN CONFEDERATION, 1836–1839. At the BATTLE OF YUNGAY, 1839, he was defeated by General Manuel BULNES of Chile. Overthrown, he lived in exile in Europe.

**Santa María González, Domingo.** 1825–1889. President of Chile. b. Santiago. Educated in National Institute and University of Chile; professor and minor official in ministry of justice and public instruction. He supported the re-election of BULNES and was appointed intendant of Colchagua. He was exiled during the administration of Manuel MONTT TORRES. He was minister of finance, diplomat, minister of court of appeals, appointed to the supreme court under PÉREZ, and held three cabinet posts, including that of war and marine, during the WAR OF THE PACIFIC. He served as president of Chile, 1881–1886. He brought the war with Peru and Bolivia to a successful conclusion, 1883, and put down uprisings of the ARAUCANIAN Indians. He had a problem with the Church which refused to support the liberal government, causing Santa María González' administration to pass laws of restriction, including enforced civil marriage, removal of public cemeteries from the control of the Church, and the granting of freedom of worship.

**Santana, Pedro.** 1801–1864. President of the Dominican Republic, 1844–1848, 1853–1856, 1858–1861. A general, he was the leader of the revolution that separated Santo Domingo from Haiti, 1844. He was made first president under the new constitution. His administration was marked by invasions from Haiti, which he threw back, and by internal unrest. He invited Spain to re-annex the Dominican Republic, for he felt that his country needed the help of a foreign power to protect itself from Haitian attacks. When Spain re-annexed the Dominican Republic, 1861, he was made governor and captain general, and also became senator of Spain and Marquis de Las Carreras. He was dissatisfied with Spanish rule, and resigned, 1862.

**Santander, Francisco de Paula.** 1792–1840. Colombian patriot and statesman. b. Rosario de Cúcuta. A general, he served in the revolutionary war, and led a division in the battle of BOYACÁ, 1819. He was vice-president of GRAN COLOMBIA under BOLÍVAR, 1821–1828, and acted as president of the country in Bolívar's absence, 1821–1826, 1827–1828. He was a good administrator, but after a dispute with Bolívar, went into exile, 1828–1832. He returned and was elected president of the Republic of New Granada (Colombia), serving until 1837. He settled boundary and financial disputes with Venezuela and Ecuador, and also did much to expand the educational system of the country.

**Santiago.** The capital of Chile and the fourth largest city in South America. Population about 1,914,539 (1963). Santiago is situated in Chile's central valley, 116 miles by rail southeast of Valparaíso, 1,700 feet above sea level, and is crossed by the Mapocho River. It has one of the most beautiful settings in Latin America. The snow-capped Andes are visible for the greater part of the year, and the Cerro San Cristóbal, in the northeast, towers over the city. Santiago has developed into a modern metropolis, with noisy traffic and many skyscrapers as well as numerous ultramodern apartment houses. The most important avenue is the 325-feet-wide Avenida Bernardo O'HIGGINS, which runs through the city for a length of two miles and is lined with beautiful homes. Important buildings include the Congressional Palace, the Palacio de la Moneda (the residence of the president), the Cathedral, the Palace of Fine Arts, and the central building of the University of Chile. The city is connected by rail with all parts of the country, with Argentina and with

Bolivia, and by air with other Latin-American countries, as well as with North America and Europe. Santiago is the manufacturing center of Chile, the leading products being textiles, iron and steel goods, cosmetics, paper, and furniture. The city was founded in 1541 by Pedro de VALDIVIA, accompanied by 150 Spanish soldiers after a long trek south from Peru. For a long time the settlement faced the attacks of the Indians, who almost succeeded in wiping it out six months after its establishment. It became the capital of the republic of Chile in 1818 after the victory of SAN MARTÍN and patriot forces over the Spaniards at the battle of MAIPÚ (April 5).

**Santo Domingo.** Former name, **Ciudad Trujillo.** The capital of the Dominican Republic, situated on the west bank of the Río Ozama and on the southern coast of the country, with a population of approximately 367,000 (est. 1960). Its climate is warm (mean temperature 77 degrees F.). Today it is a modern city with wide avenues and fine parks. The most important thoroughfare is Avenida Mella, running southwest from the bridge over the Río Ozama. On the south side of Parque Colón is the famous Cathedral of Santa María, built in 1514–1540, containing the reputed tomb of Christopher COLUMBUS. The other points of interest are the Alcázar de Colón, the castle of Columbus' son Diego, the University City, which contains the University of Santo Domingo (founded, 1538), one of the three oldest universities in the New World, and the Presidential Palace. The city is the main port of the Dominican Republic and its harbor can accommodate the largest ocean liners. It is connected by good highways with the rest of the country and by air with important cities in North and South America. The main economic activity of the area is the exporting of sugar cane and the making of rum. Other exports include coffee, cacao, and hides. There are sugar mills, distilleries, textile and clothing plants. The town of Nueva Isabela was founded before Santo Domingo in 1496 on the east bank of the Río Ozama by the brother of Columbus, Bartolomé. In 1502 the city was wrecked by a hurricane and was moved to the west side. It was then given the name of Santo Domingo

de Guzmán, the first permanent settlement in the New World. The city was the center of Spanish power in the Americas before the conquests on the mainland were consolidated. Subsequently the city lost its importance in the Spanish colonial empire. In 1844 it witnessed the revolution that freed it from Haitian rule. Between 1916 and 1924 U.S. marines were stationed in the area. On September 3, 1930, a devastating hurricane almost completely destroyed the city. It was reconstructed and in 1936 was renamed after the dictator of the Dominican Republic, Rafael Leonidas TRUJILLO MOLINA. The city again became known as Santo Domingo after the overthrow of the dictatorship in 1961. After the revolution of 1965, which overthrew the regime of Donald Reid Cabral, it was the scene of bloody fighting between conservative and liberal forces.

**Santos.** Brazil's coffee port and the most important coffee port in the world, about 200 miles southwest of Rio de Janeiro and 45 miles southeast of São Paulo. The population is 295,000 (1960). Standing on the coastal island of São Vicente off the mainland, it has been considerably modernized in recent years and has become an important resort because of its fine beaches and the beautiful views in its suburbs. Its docks can accommodate a large number of steamers. Santos is linked with São Paulo by a double track railroad, which ascends the precipitous coastal escarpment (2,600 feet) by means of cables, and by a modern four-lane highway. It is connected with Rio de Janeiro by steamer. The city was settled in 1543–1546, after the first Portuguese post had been established on the São Paulo coast in 1532. In 1591 the settlement was captured by English privateers. Santos replaced São Vicente as the chief seaport after São Paulo became the capital of the captaincy in 1681. The development of coffee cultivation in the interior of São Paulo in the 19th century, and the completion of the railroad across the coastal escarpment in 1867, contributed greatly to the prosperity and growth of the city.

**Santos, Eduardo.** b. 1888. President of Colombia. b. Bogotá. LL.D. from the National University of Bogotá; studied in Paris. He joined his brother in the publication of Bogotá's liberal daily, *El Tiempo*. He was a member of the house of representatives and its president, a senator and president of the senate. As president of Colombia, 1938–1942, he co-operated with the United States during WORLD WAR II, breaking diplomatic relations with the Axis after Pearl Harbor. His administration was characterized by the improvement of agriculture, industrial development, and the extension of education. A pact with the Vatican, 1942, ended clerical control of education and stipulated that bishops must be citizens of Colombia and approved by the Colombian government.

**Santos-Dumont, Alberto.** 1873–1932. Brazilian pioneer aeronaut. b. São Paulo. Built a cylindrical balloon with a gasoline engine, that he flew in France, 1898. In 1901 his airship won a prize for making the first flight from St. Cloud, around the Eiffel Tower, and back. He built the first airship station at Neuilly to house his dirigibles, 1903. In an airplane similar to a box kite, he flew 715 feet, 1906. He built a monoplane that weighed only 260 pounds, 1909. A large airport in Rio de Janeiro is named in his honor.

**São Paulo.** Federal state of the Republic of Brazil, bounded on the north by MINAS GERAIS, on the east by Minas Gerais, Rio de Janeiro, and the Atlantic, on the south by the Atlantic and Paraná, and on the west by Paraná and MATO GROSSO. The state has an area of 95,800 square miles and a population of 12,930,000 (est. 1960). Due to its average altitude of 2,600 feet above sea level, its climate is not tropical but temperate. From the point of view of economic development São Paulo is the leading state in Brazil. It is the richest as well as the most industrialized state. Coffee is its main agricultural product and its big export, but cotton, sugar cane, and tobacco are also important. Today São Paulo grows nearly 50 per cent of Brazil's coffee and 50 per cent of its cotton. Its capital, São Paulo, founded in 1554, is the fastest growing city in the Western Hemisphere. The São Paulo region was colonized by Martim Affonso de SOUZA in 1532. The area, known as the captaincy of São Vicente, was rapidly settled by Portuguese and people of other nationalities

who, intermarrying with the Indians, formed a race of halfbreeds called *mamelucos*. The latter were generally an unruly lot, and in the 17th century they organized adventurous groups or *bandeiras* with the aim of finding gold and capturing Indians for slavery. Their slave-raiding expeditions brought them into frequent conflict with the JESUIT missionaries, who were doing their best to protect the Indians from the greedy PAULISTAS. Some of the *paulista* explorers discovered gold in Minas Gerais in 1695, in Mato Grosso in 1719, and in Goiáz in 1725, and thus caused a considerable shift of population from the coast to the interior. In 1710 the captaincy of São Vicente became the captaincy general of São Paulo and Minas Gerais, the latter being established as a separate jurisdiction in 1720. The captaincy of São Paulo remained under the sovereignty of Rio de Janeiro until 1765, when it became a captaincy general. Its great wealth dates from the last decades of the 19th century, when the coffee boom and the settling of huge numbers of European immigrants assured its prosperity. It took a leading position in the political life of the country and in the first four decades of the Brazilian republic a number of presidents were *paulistas*.

**São Paulo.** The capital city of the Brazilian state of SÃO PAULO, the fastest-growing city in the Western Hemisphere and one of the fastest-growing in the world. It is the largest city in Brazil and the second largest in South America, with a population of about 3,850,000 in 1963 (in 1920, it had only 580,000). Situated at an altitude of approximately 3,000 feet, it is about 45 miles northwest of the port of Santos and 220 miles southwest of Rio de Janeiro. The climate is excellent. The city has been recently modernized by the construction of a large number of broad thoroughfares, of which the most notable is the Anhangabahú, which runs through the center of the city. There are many modern buildings including such skyscrapers as the São Paulo State Bank and the Martinelli Building. Other important edifices are the huge Companhia Brasileira de Investimentos Building, the impressive Municipal Market, the new Municipal Library, and the beautiful Municipal Stadium, the most modern in South America.

São Paulo is the industrial and commercial heart of Brazil and the center of the all-important coffee and cotton trade of São Paulo state. Important industries include textiles, automobiles, truck assembling, tires, paper, chemicals, cement, iron, construction materials, clothes, and food processing.

An important factor behind São Paulo's phenomenal growth is the availability of a great amount of water power. Two huge reservoirs drawing their supply from the many streams formed on the São Paulo plateau, as well as from the heavy rainfall, keep a number of hydroelectric plants humming and give power to both São Paulo and Santos. In November 1954, a 200,000-kilowatt steam power plant was opened at Piratininga, outside São Paulo. The city is linked by rail with Rio de Janeiro, Santos, and the interior, as well as with the south and Uruguay; by road with Santos, Rio, and other centers; and by air with all areas of Brazil and with other countries, including European and North-American nations. The city was founded by missionaries in 1554. In 1681 the seat of the captaincy was transferred to São Paulo from São Vicente, and in 1711 it was granted the title of "city" by John V of Portugal. In 1822 the independence of Brazil was proclaimed from the banks of the Ypiranga. In 1889 it became the capital of the state. In 1954 it celebrated its fourth centennial with a number of expositions, fairs, and festivals.

**Sarmiento, Domingo Faustino.** Popularly called the **Schoolmaster President.** 1811–1888. Argentine educator, journalist, author, and president of the republic. b. San Juan de la Frontera. Imprisoned for opposition to dictator ROSAS, he escaped to Chile, 1839, and returned, 1841, to join the resistance to Rosas but his efforts were ineffective. He became involved in Chilean politics, established the first normal school in Chile, and traveled to Europe, Africa, and the United States to study educational methods. He helped to defeat Rosas in the Battle of MONTE CASEROS, 1852, opposed President URQUIZA of the Argentine Confederation, and retired to Chile until 1856. He taught school and was in charge of public education in Buenos Aires when the province was an independent state.

He was governor of San Juan, 1862–1864, appointed minister to Chile and Peru, 1864, and to the United States, 1865–1868. He was influenced by Horace Mann's ideas when in the United States. As president of Argentina, 1868–1874, he successfully concluded the war against Paraguay. With the aid of AVELLANEDA he reorganized the school system of the country by extending the primary system and introducing the teacher-training normal school. He served as a senator during the administration of Avellaneda, became director of the provincial schools of Buenos Aires, and editor of *El Nacional,* 1878. He was minister of the interior, 1879, and made national superintendent of schools, 1881. He died at Asunción, Paraguay. He was the author of the famous Latin-American classic *Facundo o la civilización y la barbarie,* 1845, the story of the *caudillo* of La Rioja, Juan Facundo QUIROGA, *Viajes,* 1849, *Recuerdos de provincias,* 1850, *Vida de Lincoln,* 1866, *Las escuelas: base de la prosperidad y de la república en los Estados Unidos,* 1866, and many other works. A statue of Sarmiento by Rodin is at Buenos Aires. See LITERATURE.

**Schaerer, Eduardo.** President of Paraguay, 1912–1916, being the first president of that country in 20 years to complete his term of office. He served as minister of the interior under Navero, 1912. The notable achievements of his administration include the extension of the railroad system to Encarnación on the Paraná, construction of wharves at Concepción, Encarnación, and Pilar, installation of a tramway system in Asunción, and expansion of the public education system. Normal schools were established at Villarica, Encarnación, and Barrero. A program for the expropriation of land for national and foreign agricultural colonies was begun, and important economic legislation was passed, including a homestead act and the establishment of an agricultural bank for farmers in need of relief.

**Sedeño, Antonio de.** d. 1540. Spanish conquistador. Setting out from Puerto Rico, he conquered the island of Trinidad, 1530, but was forced to give up the island because of strong Indian resistance, 1532.

**Senado da Câmara.** City council in colonial Brazil, the equivalent of the *cabildo* in the Spanish-American colonies. Composition of the *senado da câmara* was limited to the chief *fazendeiros* (planters), merchants, and professional people of the town, while many poor whites, Negroes, mulattoes, Indians, Jews, and women were excluded. Some members held office on a hereditary basis, and others were elected. The *câmara*'s powers dealt with local taxes, customs duties, public works, etc. A legal agent represented the *câmara* in Lisbon and defended its interests at the Portuguese court. Although the institution dated from the beginning of Brazilian colonization, its greatest development took place in the 18th century, for it was then that city life in Brazil received its greatest impetus. The *câmara* often defied the governor's authority and acted on its own initiative, as in the case of the expulsion of the JESUITS from São Paulo and Maranhão by the local city councils. It was around the *câmara* that Brazilian nationalism developed.

**Senzala.** On the Brazilian plantation the *senzala* was the slave hut.

**Sertão.** Plural, **sertões.** In Brazil an isolated, little-known place, distant from the centers of population and from agriculturally developed areas. Usually the term is used to refer to the hinterland of northeastern Brazil, an area that is semiarid, covered with sparse, spiny vegetation, and very sparsely populated —it is the *sertão par excellence*. *Sertão bruto* refers to such a place that is entirely uninhabited.

**Sesmaria.** In colonial Brazil, a land grant.

**Seven Cities of Cíbola.** Legendary cities that were supposed to contain great wealth and were believed by the early Spanish conquerors to be located somewhere north of New Spain. Álvar Núñez CABEZA DE VACA brought stories of the famous cities to Mexico after his trek through those regions and inspired the exploring expeditions of Fray Marcos de NIZA and Francisco Vázquez de CORONADO Y VALDÉS.

**Sierra, Justo.** 1848–1912. Mexican educator, writer, and historian. b. Campeche. A liberal reformer, he taught at the National Prepara-

tory School; served as minister of education in the DÍAZ cabinet, established schools, and re-established the Autonomous University, 1910; author of *México, su evolución social* (3 vols., 1900–1902), *Juárez, su obra, su tiempo* (1905–1906), and other works.

**Siete Leyes.** Spanish, meaning seven laws. Name given to the Mexican constitution of 1836, a distinctively conservative and centralist instrument of government.

**Sigüenza y Góngora, Carlos de.** 1645–1700. Outstanding scholar, scientist, poet, historian, philosopher, and critic of the colonial period. He was interested in mathematics, and taught at the University of Mexico. He wrote *Libro astronómico*, an important contribution to the study of astronomy; author of *La primavera indiana*, dealing with the Virgin of GUADALUPE, and many other religious and historical poems. See LITERATURE.

**Siles, Hernando.** 1881–1942. President of Bolivia, 1926–1930. A jurist, the leader of the Nationalist Party, he was elected, 1926. Economic problems caused a crisis that forced him to resign in May 1930, and he fled to Brazil when revolts broke out in June of that year.

**Silva, José Asunción.** 1865–1896. Colombian poet. He had an unhappy life: he lost his family's fortune; his sister died; his best verses were lost in a shipwreck; and he committed suicide. He was a pessimist and a romantic at heart, as well as a forerunner of the Modernist movement by virtue of the musical, impressionistic style of his poetry. Perhaps the most famous of his poems is the beautiful *Nocturno*, an elegy on the death of his sister. See LITERATURE.

**Silva Xavier, Joaquim José da.** See TIRADENTES CONSPIRACY.

**Sinarquismo.** A Mexican fascistic movement founded in either 1936 or 1937. The word means "with order" and hence is the opposite of anarchism. The *Sinarquistas* claimed that Mexico had achieved its greatest prosperity under Spanish rule, and proposed to set up an authoritarian government based on Catholic principles, like that of the viceroys. The movement was a protest against various excesses and shortcomings of the revolution and against anticlerical legislation. Sinarquismo was hostile to Communism, to all forms of liberalism, and to the United States, and sympathetic to Franco and to the Axis. Having its headquarters at León, Guanajuato, the movement won wide support from peasants who had failed to benefit from the agrarian reforms of the revolution, and by 1941 it claimed 1,000,000 members. In 1944, the movement split into two factions, one group shunning politics while the other formed the Popular Force Party. Since that time further disputes among the Sinarquista leaders, the increasing national prosperity, and the opposition of the government (which resorted to ridicule rather than to repression), have resulted in a considerable decrease in its strength. In 1952, the *Partido de Acción Nacional* (PAN) attempted to broaden its base by bringing the peasant remnants of the Sinarquistas into its files. In recent years the Sinarquistas—still politically active chiefly in demanding more powers for the Catholic Church—no longer constitute any serious threat to democracy.

**Siqueiros, David Alfaro.** 1898–    . Mexican painter. b. Chihuahua. Took an active part in the Mexican revolution and became an officer in the revolutionary army. He was the leader of the Syndicate of Technical Workers, Artists, and Sculptors, 1922; advocated a national popular art; traveled to Moscow, New York, and Havana, and was an officer on the side of the loyalists during the Spanish Civil War, 1936–1939. He painted world-famous murals and frescoes that express violent opposition to existing social conditions, and is known for new techniques in mural painting. His major works are in the National Preparatory School and the National Institute of Fine Arts in Mexico City. Many paintings are in museums in the United States. His imprisonment, 1962–1963, for political beliefs aroused protest from artists in the United States. See also RIVERA.

**Smuggling.** The severe restrictions imposed by Spain, and to a lesser extent by Portugal, on colonial trade gave rise to much smuggling by Latin Americans throughout the colonial period. At the same time foreign nations, aware of the huge profits to be reaped from trade with the Latin-American colonies, were heavily engaged in illegal traffic with Spain and Portugal's New-World possessions. The activities of the smugglers were facilitated by the willingness of CREOLES to engage in illegal trade, and by the connivance of many royal officials. Contraband started early in the 16th century when English and French ships traded in the Caribbean and along the coast of Brazil, and brought back the famous wood of Brazil. Throughout the 16th century French and English traders carried manufactured goods and slaves to the Latin-American colonies and exchanged them for such colonial products as sugar, cotton, tobacco, cacao, hides, and brazilwood, as well as gold and silver. In the early 17th century the Dutch traded heavily with the Spanish Main, and the Dutch capture of Curaçao in 1634 gave them a valuable center for contraband in the Caribbean. They established control over the trade in cacao and tobacco from the northern coast of South America, and the Spanish government was forced to take the drastic step of forbidding the growing of tobacco in Venezuela to check the illegal trade with the Dutch. British conquest of Jamaica, 1655, gave them an important base for smuggling in the Caribbean, and the French annexation of the western end of Hispaniola in 1664, as well as their control of Tortuga Island, permitted France to take an ever-growing part in contraband activities. Some of the most effective smuggling was carried out by the Portuguese. The goods they brought to the RÍO DE LA PLATA were transported across South America to Upper Peru and, once there, entered competition with goods imported over the legal route from the Isthmus of Panama to Lima. In the 18th century the town of Colonia on the Río de la Plata across from Buenos Aires was the main center for Portuguese smuggling and, for the same reason, the object of frequent Spanish military expeditions from Buenos Aires. Toward the end of the 18th century U.S. ships entered this field of illicit traffic, and competed actively with the French and the British for Latin-American trade.

**Socialism.** A form of socialism was found

in the organization of the INCA empire in pre-Conquest South America. There was no private ownership of land among the Incas, and all able-bodied men were forced to work for the state, whether in agriculture or in manufacturing. A somewhat similar system prevailed in the missions set up by the JESUITS in Paraguay in the 17th century. Compulsory work by all the Indians in the missions, male and female, for the benefit of the community was enforced by the Jesuits, and there was no ownership of private property. Toward the end of the 19th century Marxian socialist ideas began to make their way into Latin America. In Argentina, where there had been a forerunner in the person of the poet and intellectual radical Esteban ECHEVERRÍA, who had propagandized utopian socialism in the 1840's, a Socialist Party was formed in 1896 and in time it became the most important socialist group in Latin America. Although weakened by serious splits between 1917 and 1919, when one group broke away to form the Communist Party, and in 1927, when another group set up the Independent Socialist Party, the Argentine socialists steadily increased their strength in the first three decades of the 20th century. They were especially strong in Buenos Aires and other large cities. They exerted relatively little influence among the working class, their main support coming from the intellectuals, but they were to a large extent responsible for the enactment of some labor legislation and the creation in 1929 of the Argentine trade-union organization, the *Confederación General de Trabajadores*. They published the important newspaper *La Vanguardia* and constantly preached reform. Under the PERÓN regime they suffered a damaging split in their ranks in 1953, when their left wing went over to Perón, and their influence has been generally negligible. Some forms of socialism have been adopted by the government of Uruguay acting along lines somewhat similar to the pattern followed in Scandinavian countries. Public utilities, as well as a very high proportion of the rail network, are operated by the government. Banking and insurance are chiefly in government hands, and a national refrigeration plant maintains a monopoly on domestic meat. In Brazil, where Marxist ideas were introduced mainly by German and Italian immigrants, a Socialist Party was formed in 1916. Socialism never was influential in Brazil, however, in spite of some gains in the cities, chiefly São Paulo. In Chile, Marxist ideas were received with special favor among the nitrate workers of the north in the first two decades of the 20th century. The socialist leader Luis RECABARREN founded the Socialist Labor Party in 1912 but later went over to communism and organized the Communist Party of Chile with members of the Socialist Labor Party. The bulk of Chilean labor, however, was at that time unaffected by Marxism and gave its support to Arturo ALESSANDRI PALMA, who won the presidency in 1920 on a platform of social reform. A full-fledged socialist experiment was tried in 1932 by the HUNDRED DAYS GOVERNMENT of Carlos DÁVILA ESPINOZA and Marmaduque Grove, but quarrels between them, plus an army uprising shortly thereafter, prevented the carrying out of the far-reaching reforms that had been promised. The APRISTA movement in Peru, which reached its zenith after WORLD WAR II, borrowed some of its ideas from Marxian socialism but aimed at the bettering of the conditions of the Indo-American peoples through means corresponding to their specific needs. In Colombia a small Socialist Party appeared in the 1920's and in 1929 received many votes in the Bogotá municipal election; otherwise, it did not have much influence on political developments in the country. In Mexico, socialist ideas were introduced during the DÍAZ period, spreading underground among workers and intellectuals, and having some influence on the program of the revolution as expressed in the constitution of 1917. The agrarian and labor reforms that have been put into effect since 1920 have been chiefly attempts to deal with Mexico's own peculiar problem along non-Marxian lines but have continued to show some socialist tendencies, especially during the administration of CÁRDENAS, 1934–1940, as exemplified in experimental and co-operative farming and in the nationalization of the oil industry and some other state enterprises.

**Solís, Juan Díaz de.** See DÍAZ DE SOLÍS, JUAN.

**Somoza, Anastasio.** 1896–1956. Dictator of Nicaragua. b. San Marcos. Educated at the Instituto Nacional de Oriente and at Pierce Business School in Philadelphia. He was minister of war and marine during the administration of SACASA and was elected president, 1936, serving from 1937 to 1947. By a new constitution in 1939 his term of office was extended to eight years, and he became commander of the national guard to insure his keeping control of the country. He allowed Leonardo Argüello to become president as the candidate of the government party, the *Partido Liberal Nacionalista,* and when no longer satisfied, he had him declared incapacitated and sent into exile. He permitted his uncle, Román y Reyes, to serve as president, but he died and Somoza became provisional president, May 1950. Again elected president, 1951, his administration was marked by progress in agriculture, cattle raising, and mineral production. He extended the public-school system, built hospitals and hydroelectric plants, improved the country's roadways, and maintained close relations with the United States. He was shot by an assassin on September 21, 1956, at León and died eight days later. His successor in office was his eldest son, Luis Anastasio Somoza Debayle, who served as provisional president after his father's death, and who was elected for a six-year term in 1957. A second son, Anastasio Somoza Debayle, became president on May 1, 1967.

**Sosúa.** A settlement of Central-European Jewish refugees established in 1940 at Sosúa in the northern section of the Dominican Republic, under the auspices of General TRUJILLO, who donated an estate of 26,000 acres to the project. In 1941 he gave another 50,000 acres. About 500 refugees, German Jews for the most part, settled at Sosúa during 1940. The colony received technical aid from a number of philanthropic organizations in the United States, which helped to solve problems of sanitation, electrification, etc. The project has not been a notable success, and the number of colonists has decreased since establishment of the settlement. By March 1953, only 181 refugees were still living at Sosúa.

**Soto, Hernando de.** 1499–1542. Early Spanish explorer. b. Jerez de los Caballeros, Extremadura, Spain. Accompanied ARIAS DE ÁVILA on his second expedition to Darién, 1519; explored the coast of Guatemala and Yucatán, 1528; and was in Peru as lieutenant of PIZARRO. He returned to Spain and was granted the approval of CHARLES V for an expedition of exploration to Florida, 1537, where he landed May 1539. He explored the area of the southern United States, north and west of Florida, fighting off hostile Indians. In 1542 he turned back, discouraged at not finding gold and treasure; he died of fever, and was buried in the Mississippi River.

**Soublette, Carlos.** 1790–1870. President of Venezuela. Fought under BOLÍVAR during the War for Independence; appointed governor of the territory of Venezuela, 1822; appointed to a diplomatic mission to Spain to conclude a treaty of peace and commerce, 1835; served as secretary of war, 1836–1839. A conservative, he was president of Venezuela, 1843–1846. He was forced into exile, 1848–1858.

**Soulouque, Faustin Élie.** 1785–1867. Emperor of Haiti. A Negro general, he was put into power by a group expecting to control him and was made president of Haiti, 1847. He proclaimed himself Emperor Faustin I, 1849, and ruled as a dictator. He was deposed, by Geffrard, 1858, and lived in exile from January 1859 until his death. His cruelty terrorized the elite of the island.

**Souza, Martim Affonso de.** *ca.* 1500–1564. Portuguese colonial administrator. Sent with settlers, cattle, and seed to colonize the Portuguese possessions in the New World, 1530, he spent two years exploring the coast from the Amazon to present-day Rio Grande do Sul and in 1532, with the aid of RAMALHO, founded the first permanent European colony in Brazil at São Vicente, and was made captain general, where he introduced sugar cane. He returned to Portugal, 1533, and was appointed governor of Portuguese India.

**Souza, Thomé de.** *ca.* 1510–*ca.* 1564. First captain general of Brazil. In April 1549 he reached Brazil with six ships of colonists and the first JESUITS to arrive in America. He founded the settlement of BAHIA, and served as leader of the colony until 1553.

**Souza, Washington Luiz Pereira de.** 1869–1957. President of Brazil. b. Macaé, Rio de Janeiro. *Paulista* who gave more than 30 years to public service in various administrative positions; able organizer and executive, governor of São Paulo, 1920–1924; senator, 1924–1926, and president, 1926. Economic problems made it difficult to institute many of the reforms and improvements he had hoped to inaugurate, but he succeeded in building roads, and suppressed revolts in 1927. In 1930 the world depression caused severe economic problems for Brazil. In October 1930 VARGAS resorted to arms; Souza was forced to resign; Vargas became provisional president. Souza went into exile in Europe and did not return to Brazil until 1947.

**Spanish-American War.** The conflict involving Spain and the United States in 1898. For years the United States had looked with sympathy on the Cuban fight for independence from Spain (the latest uprising had begun in 1895) and had manifested its hostility toward the Spanish policy of repression in Cuba. At the same time, the United States was concerned over the investments of about $50,000,000 by American citizens in Cuba, and American public opinion, already emotionally prepared for imperialistic adventures and war, was constantly aroused against Spain by the propaganda of the more sensational newspapers. The immediate cause of the war was the mysterious blowing up of the American battleship "MAINE" in the harbor of Havana on February 15, 1898. Although the origin of the explosion was never ascertained, the United States blamed Spain, and the American government sent a strong note to the Spanish government demanding that an armistice be conceded to the Cuban insurgents. Spain then softened her policy in Cuba and attempted to have the dispute arbitrated by the pope. On April 9, 1898, she gave in to the American terms, but the United States had gone too far on the road to war to stop. War against Spain was declared on April 25, 1898. It was to be a conflict of short duration,

for the Spanish navy was no match for the better-equipped ships and better-trained crews of the American navy. In Far Eastern waters a Spanish fleet was annihilated by Admiral Dewey's naval squadron in Manila Bay on May 1, and the Spanish ships under Admiral Cervera were destroyed off Santiago, Cuba, in July. On land, Spanish ground forces in Cuba were overwhelmed by an American expeditionary force, but not without having offered fierce resistance in the Santiago area in July. After these defeats, Spain realized the futility of continuing the war, and peace was signed in Paris on December 10, 1898. By the terms of the treaty, Spain recognized the independence of Cuba and ceded Puerto Rico to the United States, thus losing her last possessions in the New World. She also relinquished to the United States the island of Guam, in the Pacific, and the Philippine Islands, the latter for the sum of $20,000,000. The war underscored the decline of Spain as a world power. The country had come to the lowest point on the downhill road she had been following ever since she had reached her zenith at the end of the 16th century. On the other hand, the United States, as the result of its victory, emerged as a great power, dominant in the Caribbean, and destined to play an increasingly important role in world affairs.

**Spooner Act.** An act passed by the U.S. Congress in 1902, authorizing the president to acquire the concession held by the French New Panama Canal Company for $40,000,000, provided that the Republic of Colombia would yield a strip of land across the Isthmus of Panama "within a reasonable time" and upon reasonable terms. In the event Colombia refused, Congress authorized the president of the United States to enter into negotiations with Nicaragua for the construction of a canal. As a result of the act, the president purchased the French concession and the United States negotiated the HAY-HERRÁN TREATY with Colombia.

**State of Siege.** Spanish, *Estado de Sitio.* Under certain conditions of emergency, Latin-American presidents have the authority to suspend the guarantees contained in the constitutions of their countries, and to act as absolute dictators. Such powers have been granted in various forms by the constitutions of Argentina, Brazil, Bolivia, Chile, Haiti, Panama, and Paraguay, and they have all used the term "state of siege." Other Latin-American countries have used such terms as "suspension of guarantees," "state of national emergency," "extraordinary powers," and "measures of security" to define the power to suspend constitutional guarantees. In the past this power was used frequently, ostensibly to meet a grave danger or crisis caused by foreign wars or domestic disturbances, thus providing a legal pretext for the maintenance of dictatorial regimes. In recent years, however, the power to declare a state of siege has been used with more discretion and in some countries, as Mexico and Chile, this action has become the exception in the past few decades rather than the rule.

**Strangford Treaty.** An accord signed in 1810 between the Portuguese Crown, then residing in Brazil, and Great Britain, represented by Lord Strangford, British minister at the Portuguese Court. The treaty provided for the export of Brazilian agricultural products to Great Britain and the import of British manufactured goods, British warships were permitted to use Brazilian ports to replenish their supplies, English Protestants were given the right to worship freely in Brazil, and British nationals in Brazil were to be tried only by magistrates appointed by the British government. According to the agreement no other nations were to be permitted to enjoy the commercial privileges granted to Great Britain. Although the treaty was a severe blow to the new Brazilian manufacturing industries, it contributed strongly to the economic development of the country.

**Sucre, Antonio José de.** 1795–1830. Liberator and president of Bolivia; general. b. Cumaná, Venezuela. Served as chief lieutenant to BOLÍVAR in Quito against Spain, 1821. He won the Battle of PICHINCHA, 1822. He was again with Bolívar in Peru, and at the Battle of JUNÍN, 1824, and won the final great battle of the war at AYACUCHO, 1824. When the assembly was convened in Upper Peru he declared the new state independent of Spain and gave it the name of República Bolívar. Although Bolívar was named first president, Sucre became the first elected constitutional president, 1826–1828, establishing an orderly administration and a sound fiscal system. Because of opposition evidenced by the native Bolivians, he resigned and was assassinated in Colombia, June 4, 1830. He was one of the ablest generals and most patriotic statesmen in Latin-American history.

**Sugar Industry.** Sugar cane was planted on the island of Hispaniola (Santo Domingo) as early as 1493, and before long huge profits were derived from this fast-growing industry. In 1520 there were more than 28 mills on Hispaniola, most of them powered by water. Sugar cane also became the main agricultural product of the islands of Puerto Rico and Jamaica, and was introduced into Mexico soon after the Spanish conquest of that country. Due to difficulties of transportation from the lowlands of the coast to the central plateau, Mexican sugar cane was grown on the highlands, and by 1800 about 160,000 tons of sugar were being consumed within New Spain. In Brazil the industry developed rapidly in the 16th and 17th centuries, and from about 1550 to 1650 Brazil occupied first place in world sugar exportation. Full exploitation required a large supply of manpower, and this need contributed enormously to the growth of Negro slavery. In Brazil especially, the industry was the economic reason for the great need for slaves. In Cuba sugar growing acquired particular importance during the 18th century, and by 1825 approximately 440,-000 cases were produced annually on the average. Contributing to the rapid progress of Cuban sugar growing were improvements in production methods. Mules took the place of the slower oxen in the mills, more water-power plants were built, and steam engines were introduced. While there were 473 sugar factories *(ingenios)* in Cuba in 1775, there were 780 in 1817. Other important producers in the colonial period were Venezuela (from the end of the 18th century), Peru, and Ecuador. Production in Latin America continued to grow in the 19th century, but in the 20th, the industry has experienced setbacks, partly because of overproduction, and partly because of the increasing competition from beet sugar in Europe and the United States, resulting in high import tariffs in the beet sugar producing countries. In Cuba overproduction in the 1920's resulted in a collapse during the depression of the 1930's, when the country was unable to sell its surplus on the world market. The serious economic crisis that followed was remedied somewhat by the Sugar Stabilization Act of 1934, under which Cuba was allowed to sell almost 2,000,000 short tons of sugar to the United States, while import duties were lowered sufficiently to assure a profitable price for the product. At the same time the Cuban government took measures to regulate the grinding of sugar cane. Cuban production was about 6,577,000 short tons in 1958–1959 but then decreased in 1962–1963 to 4,100,000 short tons. However by 1965 the sugar harvest (amounting to 6,200,000 short tons) returned to pre-CASTRO levels. In Brazil similar steps have been taken to control production; the 1962–1963 output was about 3,544,000 short tons of refined sugar, approximately 9 per cent less than the previous year. In Argentina 858,000 short tons were produced in 1962–1963, and the output is controlled to insure that it will not exceed the demands of the domestic market. In South America another leading sugar producer is Peru; in the Caribbean area, beside Cuba, the Dominican Republic and Mexico are the most important growers.

# T

**Tacna-Arica Question.** Often called, **Question of the Pacific.** A long dispute between Peru and Chile over the territories of Tacna and Arica. After Peru, allied with Bolivia, had lost the WAR OF THE PACIFIC against Chile, 1879–1883, it signed the Treaty of ANCÓN with Chile. By the terms of the accord, Chile received the Peruvian province of Tarapacá, while the provinces of Tacna and Arica were to be held by Chile for ten years. At the end of this period a plebiscite was to determine final possession of the territories. The two countries could not agree on the conditions under which the plebiscite should be held, and relations between them remained bad. The United States attempted to mediate the dispute, 1922–1926, but the effort produced no immediate result. However it led to direct negotiations between Chile and Peru, and in 1929 an agreement was reached. Peru received Tacna, was granted an indemnity of $6,000,-000 and certain other concessions, while Chile retained Arica.

**Tacubaya, Conference of.** A meeting agreed upon by the members of the PANAMA CONGRESS of 1826 before adjourning. The conference which was to have taken place at Tacubaya, near Mexico City, was never held.

**Taft Agreement.** Compromise between the United States and Panama arrived at in the fall of 1904 by U.S. Secretary of War William Howard Taft, then visiting the Isthmus, and Panamanian authorities, concerning trade in the Canal Zone. The agreement limited imports into the Canal Zone to goods earmarked for the United States and its employees, or for sale to ships passing through the canal. Furthermore the general public was not allowed to buy or sell at the stores established by the American authorities. The Taft agreement was abrogated by the United States on June 1, 1924, but the United States continued to bar the general public from trading at the commissaries and in general to exclude private business from the Canal Zone.

**Tajes, Máximo.** 1852–1912. President of Uruguay. b. Montevideo. General of the army and minister of war; elected president of Uruguay, 1886–1890. He was able, through a particularly successful policy, to get the cooperation of the dissatisfied elements in the country, diminish the political influence of the army, and maintain peace in the country.

**Talambo Affair.** The immediate cause of the war between Peru and Spain, 1864–1866. After a group of Basque immigrants had been the object of a vicious attack at the hands of Peruvian laborers on the HACIENDA of Talambo, the Spanish government sent a royal commissioner to Lima to demand satisfaction, but the Peruvian government, resenting the title of the envoy, refused to have anything to do with him. As a result a Spanish fleet occupied the CHINCHA ISLANDS belonging to Peru, and war began.

**Tamarón y Romeral, Pedro.** Bishop of Durango, Mexico, one of the largest dioceses in colonial America. He traveled through Mexico and into part of what is now the United States, 1759. His book *Demostración del Vastísimo Obispado de la Nueva Vizcaya,* written 1764–1765, tells of the results of his surveys.

**Tamayo, Rufino.** 1899– . Mexican painter who has gained an international reputation for his colorful, highly individual modern paintings; excellent examples of his work can be seen at the Museum of Modern Art in New York City, as well as in Mexico, Brazil, and other capitals. He spends much of his time in the United States.

**Tamborini, José P.** 1886–1955. Argentine physician and leader of the RADICAL CIVIC UNION PARTY. b. Buenos Aires. Served as minister of the interior under Marcelo ALVEAR, 1925–1928, and had an honest reputation as senator. The candidate of the *Unión Democrática*, a coalition of the Radical Party, socialists, communists, and other minor groups that opposed PERÓN, he ran for the presidency, 1946. He was not as dynamic or as young a man as Perón, who was backed by the Church because he supported compulsory religious education in the schools at the time, while Tamborini was for separation of Church and State. Many votes were cast for Perón after the U.S. State Department's publication of the BLUE BOOK, a denunciation of Perón's pro-Axis activities during WORLD WAR II, which Argentines resented as an attempt to intervene in their internal affairs. Perón's supporters set fire to Tamborini's campaign train, destroyed the offices of newspapers supporting him, tore down posters, etc., and he was not elected.

**Tampico Incident.** See VERACRUZ INCIDENT.

**Tarascans.** Indians inhabiting the state of Michoacán, Mexico. In pre-Conquest times they were led by chieftains who lived beside Lake PÁTZCUARO. In the period of the AZTEC empire they fought fierce battles against the Aztecs and managed to preserve their independence. When they learned that the Aztecs had been conquered by the white men, they decided to offer their allegiance to the invaders and sent gifts to CORTÉS. The latter sent Cristóbal de OLID to Michoacán, and Olid, disregarding the instructions of Cortés, ordered the Tarascan idols smashed and plundered the tribe. The Tarascans were treated with kindness by friars who came in the wake of the conquistadors and who performed baptisms and built convents. But in the 1530's a new scourge fell upon them in the person of Gonzalo Nuño de GUZMÁN, former president of the AUDIENCIA of New Spain. Guzmán seized several thousand Tarascans to act as porters and ordered the chieftain burned because he was unable to furnish all the gold the Spaniards asked of him. Guzmán later established himself in Jalisco, where he built towns. In modern times the Tarascans benefited greatly from the reform policy of the CÁRDENAS administration, 1934–1940. Cárdenas, himself a former governor of Michoacán with Tarascan blood in his veins, saw to it that the Tarascans derived the maximum benefit from the government's policy of distributing land to the Indians, established schools, and revived Indian culture. Today the Tarascans form one of the most prosperous Indian groups in Mexico. They are famous for the products of their native crafts, and their colorful communities around Lake Pátzcuaro attract a considerable number of tourists every year.

**Taxation.** See FINANCIAL ADMINISTRATION IN THE SPANISH-AMERICAN COLONIES.

**Tecpantlaca.** Special class of AZTEC workers who cultivated the fields and stored the produce of the *tecpan* (lands of the local chief). They were generally exempted from almost all other tribute.

**Tegucigalpa.** The capital of Honduras, situated at an altitude of 3,000 feet, approximately 62 miles from the Pacific port of San Lorenzo. Population about 125,000 (1963). The city is connected by road with San Lorenzo, and by air with the rest of the country and with other nations. Gold and silver mining are the main activities in the surrounding area. It was founded about 1579, when important discoveries of mineral deposits were made in the region. Due to the wealth of its soil it acquired great importance, especially in the 18th century. During the 19th and 20th centuries Tegucigalpa was involved in the civil and foreign wars that were besetting the Central-American republics, and in 1907 it was occupied by the troops of Nicaragua.

**Tejada Sorzano, José Luis.** 1881–1938. President of Bolivia, 1934–1936. Served as vice-president under SALAMANCA. As president, he succeeded in signing a truce with Paraguay, June 12, 1935, concluding the war in the CHACO. He authorized a workmen's compensation law but it did not prevent a general strike, May 15, 1936, and Tejada Sorzano was ousted by a *coup d'état* led by the army.

**Tenochtitlán, Conquest of.** Tenochtitlán was the magnificent capital built by the AZTECS over a period of nearly 200 years, from which they had conquered an empire comprising almost the whole of southern and south-central Mexico. This great city became, in modern times, Mexico City. Hernán CORTÉS was determined to capture the Aztec capital, after having had to retire from that point on June 30, 1520. In the spring of 1521 his army, aided by thousands of Indian allies, who were enemies of the Aztecs, advanced on Tenochtitlán along two of the causeways across the lake then surrounding the city. Supporting the army was a fleet of 13 brigantines that had been disassembled, transported overland, then reassembled, and a great number of Indian canoes. After an initial setback in which he was wounded and almost lost his life, Cortés was able to lay siege to the city. Offering fanatic resistance, the Aztecs held the Spaniards at bay for a long time but finally capitulated when their chieftain, CUAUHTÉMOC, was made prisoner when he tried to escape in a canoe. When the Spaniards entered the city in August 1521, it was in ruins and almost all of the Aztecs were dead.

**Teotihuacán.** An important center of TOLTEC civilization, situated in the valley of Mexico to the northeast of modern Mexico City. It reached its zenith of splendor in the 9th or 10th century and was abandoned at some period before the 13th century, when the Toltec empire dissolved. At Teotihuacán the Toltecs built magnificent pyramids and temples as well as dwellings for priests. Today visitors can still admire the two great pyramids of the sun and the moon; and the impressive remains of the temple of the feathered serpent, QUETZALCOATL, the chief deity of the Toltecs, which are decorated with feathered serpents and obsidian butterflies.

**Terra, Gabriel.** 1873–1942. President of Uruguay. b. Montevideo. Elected president, 1930, by one of the parties split from the *colorados*, he took office March 1931, in the midst of world economic depression, and was granted extraordinary powers to meet the emergency. He attempted to increase employment and improve business conditions, dissolved congress and council, and in 1933 assumed dictatorial powers. A new constitution was drafted, calling for a strong executive, restricting the powers of congress, and establishing compulsory voting for women as well as men. It was put into effect on April 19, 1934. In the same year Terra was re-elected president, which had also been provided for in the constitution. He was able to suppress revolts, and although there was much opposition to his government, he did put through some beneficial legislation, which included low-priced houses for people of low income, laws for protection of labor, old-age pensions, subsidies on meat exports, development of the nation's industries, and in 1937 a refinery for petroleum was completed. He decided that since his program had been put into effect he would not seek re-election, and stepped down in March 1938.

**Terreros, Pedro.** Mexican mine owner. Reopened the Biscaina Vein, San Luis Potosí, 1762, and by 1774 drew a profit of more than 5,000,000 pesos, equivalent to more than $10,-000,000. He was granted the title of Conde de Regla.

**Texas.** The territory of Texas was colonized by the Spaniards shortly after the middle of the 17th century, most of the settlers establishing themselves in the western part of the area. In the second decade of the 18th century *presidios* and missions were set up in eastern Texas, and in about 1731 a number of settlers from the Canary Islands arrived. There was recurrent friction with the French along the Louisiana-Texas frontier, but after 1763, when Louisiana was ceded by France to Spain, interest in eastern Texas was largely lost and many of the settlements were abandoned. Spain granted several Americans the right to people the Texas territory with colonists. After Mexico obtained its independence, the new settlers were unmolested provided they paid a nominal price for their land and assumed all the responsibilities of Mexican citizenship. The offer of cheap land where cotton would flourish attracted thousands of American settlers, most of them from the southern states. Within ten years Texas had a white population of from 20,000 to 30,000, in addition to a number of Negro slaves imported to work in the cotton fields. Soon Mexican authorities began to regret their decision to let Americans settle in Texas. There was constant friction between the settlers and Mexican officials, and in view of the well-known American interest in the territory, it was feared that the Texans would serve as an advance guard of American expansion, and would eventually join the United States. In 1829 President GUERRERO, in order to discourage American ·immigration, issued a decree for the ABOLITION OF SLAVERY, but in Texas the decree could not be enforced. The following year it was decreed that no more colonists should be admitted from the United States and that customs duties should be collected along the Louisiana frontier. At the same time, Texas was joined to the Mexican state of Coahuila to form one state. The Texans resented these measures, and there were a number of riots. Austin went to Mexico to persuade Vice-president GÓMEZ FARÍAS, then in charge of the government, to allow the Texans to govern themselves as a separate state. His efforts failed, and he was put in a Mexican prison where he remained for 18 months. In 1835 the Texans rebelled openly against Mexican rule, and in December of that year a Mexican army was defeated at San Antonio.

On March 2, 1836, a Texan convention proclaimed the independence of Texas, naming David Burnet provisional president. The Texans suffered a setback when the ALAMO was taken by a Mexican army under SANTA ANNA in March 1836, but they won a smashing victory over Santa Anna at SAN JACINTO in April of the same year. The Mexican commander himself was captured and signed a treaty with the Texans recognizing their independence. The Mexican government, however, refused to recognize Texas. Under Mirabeau Bonaparte Lamar, president of Texas from

1838 to 1841, relations between Mexico and the infant republic were exceedingly bad. Texans raided Santa Fe and Mexicans raided San Antonio. A Texas army, which invaded Tamaulipas, was forced to surrender, escaped into the mountains, and was recaptured, after which every tenth man was shot and the remainder imprisoned. In March 1845, Texas was annexed by the United States and this brought relations between the United States and Mexico to the breaking point, for the Mexican government had previously declared that annexation of Texas by the United States would be considered an act of war. Fighting broke out when American troops, under Zachary Taylor, who had entered the no man's land between the Nueces and the Río Grande, claimed but never occupied by Texas, and established themselves on the Río Grande. They clashed with Mexican troops in April 1846. In May the U.S. Congress declared war on Mexico.

**Texcocans.** See ACOLHUAS.

**Texcoco.** A city built in ANÁHUAC, the central valley of Mexico, by the ACOLHUA Indians, who were one of the NAHUA tribes that took possession of Anáhuac after the fall of the TOLTECS. The Acolhuas were first to assert their supremacy over the other peoples of the valley, and the chieftains of Texcoco became the overlords of Anáhuac. They carefully preserved whatever had survived of the learning of the Toltecs. The Acolhuas were subsequently overshadowed by the rise of the Tepanec city of Atzcapotzalco. Early in the 15th century Texcoco was compelled to pay tribute, and its lawful chieftain, NEZAHUALCOYOTL, was driven into exile. After the destruction of Atzcapotzalco in 1431, Nezahualcoyotl regained his throne and from then on reigned as chieftain of Texcoco for 40 years. During the first half of the 15th century Texcoco entered into a confederacy with two more cities, Tacuba and Tenochtitlán, the latter the home of the AZTECS, who rapidly asserted themselves as the dominant partners and who became the true rulers of Anáhuac. Texcoco was also the name of the lake on whose islands the Aztecs built their city, Tenochtitlán, in the 14th century.

**Tiahuanaco.** Town in Bolivia in the department of La Paz, 38 miles from La Paz, near Lake TITICACA. It is famous for the ruins of Indian monuments located in its neighborhood. These ruins, among the oldest of all those found in South America, are an admirable testimony to the architectural accomplishments of a pre-Incan civilization.

**Tiempista Party of Paraguay.** Name given to Paraguayan liberals active in 1944 who campaigned for civil liberties and against the dictatorship of Higinio MORÍNIGO. They took their name from the newspaper, *El Tiempo*, which printed their views. When the dictator felt that the activities of the *tiempistas* might become dangerous to his regime, he took drastic steps against them and many were jailed.

**Tiradentes Conspiracy.** Plot against the Portuguese government organized in 1788 in the MINAS GERAIS region by the Brazilian patriot Joaquim José da Silva Xavier, a man who had at times occupied himself as a businessman, minor army officer, amateur physician, and dentist—the latter occupation earning him the nickname Tiradentes, meaning, tooth-puller. He was captured in 1789 and executed in 1792. Tiradentes is considered the precursor of Brazilian independence.

**Tithe.** In colonial Spanish America, a tax of ten per cent levied for ecclesiastical purposes on all fruits of the earth, livestock, and dairy products. A papal bull issued on November 16, 1501, granted the Spanish Crown the right to exact tithes for ecclesiastical purposes with the proviso that the Spanish sovereigns take full responsibility for founding and maintaining churches and for converting the natives. The collection of tithes was, therefore, handled by the government, but the greater part of the proceeds came into the hands of the Church, the Crown receiving only one-ninth of the amount collected. Indians were generally exempt from most of the tax, since the amount required for the maintenance of the local church was deducted from the tribute paid to the king or to the *encomendero*.

**Titicaca, Lake.** The largest lake in South America, situated at an altitude of 12,500 feet, located partly in Peru and partly in Bolivia. The lake is 110 miles long, 35 miles wide, and has an area of 3,200 square miles. It is divided into two sections, Lake Chucuito and Lake Uinamarca, by the Strait of Tiquina. The lake contains many islands, two of which, Titicaca (Sun) and Coati (Moon), are famous for the Incan and pre-Incan ruins that have been found there. According to Indian legend, the Incan civilization originated on these islands.

**Tlaxcalans.** One of the NAHUA tribes that took possession of the central valley of Mexico after the fall of the TOLTECS. The Tlaxcalans moved eastward and settled in what is now the state of Tlaxcala. They fought bitter battles with the AZTECS and managed to preserve their independence. During the Spanish conquest, they first fought CORTÉS but then became his loyal allies against the Aztecs. The Tlaxcalans helped Cortés fight the Aztecs at TENOCHTITLÁN, and when the Spaniards were forced to abandon the city with great losses and returned to Tlaxcala, they received them, attended to their wounds, and gave them food. In 1521, under the direction of a Spanish shipwright, they built the ships that gave Cortés command of Lake TEXCOCO and aided considerably in the siege of Tenochtitlán. After the conquest of Tenochtitlán, the Tlaxcalans contributed troops for further conquests in Mexico.

**Tobacco Industry.** Tobacco is indigenous to the American continent and was grown by the Indians in pre-Conquest times. During the colonial period it became an exceedingly important crop, especially in the Caribbean area. From an early date, Venezuelan tobacco was greatly prized in Europe. Other leading centers were Cuba and Mexico (especially the Guadalajara area), and tobacco was also important in Peru and Chile. After the middle of the 18th century the Spanish Crown established a monopoly over the industry, granting special permits for planting the crop and prohibiting the growing of the plant except in areas specifically earmarked for it. The monopoly (*estanco real de tabaco*) was set up in Peru in 1752, in Chile in 1753, and in New Spain (Mexico) in 1764. In the latter colony only the Orizaba, Córdoba, and Veracruz areas were allowed to grow tobacco. The Crown's revenue from the monopoly in New Spain was enormous. The same restrictions prevailed in Venezuela where, after 1777, only the districts that had been granted permission by the monopoly could grow tobacco. Since there were only few such privileged areas, Venezuelans were forced to import contraband tobacco from Brazil to satisfy their needs. In Cuba production spurted toward the end of the 18th century and between 1789 and 1794 about 250,000 *arrobas* (weight of 1 *arroba*, 25 pounds ) were produced annually. By 1822–1825 production reached 300,000 to 400,000 *arrobas* annually on the average. In Brazil the tobacco crop became important toward the middle of the 17th century, when it was able to reach world markets as the result of Dutch smuggling. Its importance increased in the 18th century, when the leading center was Bahia. As in the Spanish colonies, the Portuguese Crown established a tobacco monopoly and derived a large revenue from it. Today tobacco is still an important crop in most Latin-American countries, especially in Cuba, Mexico, Brazil, and Paraguay.

**Tobar Doctrine.** The view of the Ecuadorian diplomat Carlos R. Tobar (1856–1920), who declared in 1907 that "the American Republics . . . ought to intervene in an indirect way in the internal dissensions of the Republics of the Continent. Such intervention might consist at least in the nonrecognition of *de facto* governments sprung from revolutions against the constitution." The Tobar Doctrine was incorporated into the Central-American peace treaties of 1907 and 1923, each of which was negotiated in Washington under the leadership of the United States. It was repudiated in 1934, when all the signatories of the treaties granted recognition to the Maximiliano MARTÍNEZ regime in El Salvador, which had seized power by *coup d'état* three years earlier.

**Toledo y Figueroa, Francisco Álvarez de.** *ca.* 1515–1584. Viceroy of Peru, 1569–1581. He attempted to bring law and order to the territory, and as chief founder of the Spanish colonial system in Peru, he established a code of laws that was used throughout the colonial period. Included in it were not only the rules for handling Indians, but rules on mining, finance, irrigation, municipal operations, etc. This code was written after Toledo had conscientiously made a tour of the territory that is now Peru and Bolivia and investigated the conditions prevailing throughout. The laws and customs of the natives were taken into consideration, but unfortunately his record of just treatment of the Indian is spoiled by the execution of the Incan leader, Tupac Amaru. He permitted the INQUISITION to be introduced into Peru, and endowed the University of San Marcos, 1576.

**Tolsa, Manuel.** 1755–1816. Spanish sculptor, active in Mexico toward the end of the 18th century. He introduced the classical style in art and founded a school of sculpture in Mexico City. Considered one of the best sculptors of his day, he is most famous for his equestrian statue of CHARLES IV in Mexico City.

**Toltecs.** An Indian tribe that dominated much of southern Mexico between the 8th and 12th centuries. Apparently belonging to the NAHUA group, these people seem to have migrated from the Pacific Northwest early in the Christian era, and to have settled in and around the Valley of Mexico, also known as ANÁHUAC. They probably built the pyramids and temples of TEOTIHUACÁN and the pyramid of Cholula. Although culturally inferior to the MAYAS, they made some technological advances, including the use of metals. The Toltec hegemony ended sometime before the 13th century, apparently because of internal dissensions, after which the area they had controlled was occupied by another group of invading Nahua tribes, among them the AZTECS. But much of the Toltec religion and culture was transmitted to the Aztecs, especially the legend of QUETZALCOATL.

**Tordesillas, Treaty of.** A treaty signed June 7, 1494, at Tordesillas, in the Spanish province of Valladolid, stipulating that the line drawn by Pope ALEXANDER VI in 1493 (Line of Demarcation) was to be changed to 370 leagues west of the Cape Verde Islands. While most of America was thus granted to Spain, the eastern part of Brazil fell on the

Portuguese side of the line and led to the eventual possession of this territory by Portugal.

**Toro, David.** 1898–    . b. Sucre. President of Bolivia. Assumed dictatorial powers as a result of a *coup d'état* by a joint civil and military junta against TEJADA SORZANO, May 17, 1936. He established a virtual government monopoly over the petroleum industry, confiscating the Standard Oil properties in March 1937. He also made attempts to control mining and banking as well, but his policies were opposed and his fellow army officers drove him from power on July 14, 1937.

**Torre, Carlos de la.** b. 1858. Cuban naturalist, teacher, and statesman. b. Mantanzas. A founder of the School of Arts and Crafts, Havana, he was professor of natural history and physiology at the Puerto Rico Institute, 1883, taught comparative anatomy and zoography at Havana University, 1884, held various public offices, and helped organize the public school system. He taught again at Havana University and was at one time its president. He took a part in the overthrow of the MACHADO Y MORALES government, 1933, and was president of the Council of State, 1934. He was the author of several books.

**Torre, Lisandro de la.** 1868–1939. Political leader in Argentina. b. Rosario. Lawyer, populist leader of the agrarian bloc, and head of the *Partido Demócrata Progresista*, a party formed by splitting away from YRIGOYEN and the Radical Party. Considered one of the outstanding parliamentary figures in the history of Argentina, he struggled against JUSTO's policies but was unable to defeat the economic measures passed by the voting power of the *concordancia* in the senate. He took his own life.

**Torre, Miguel de la.** d. 1838. Spanish general who defended the town of Angostura, Venezuela, against the Venezuelan patriots in 1817, and later commanded the forces defeated by BOLÍVAR and PÁEZ at the Battle of CARABOBO, 1821. He was appointed civil and military governor of Puerto Rico, 1823, and proclaimed the Spanish Constitution of 1837 in Puerto Rico. He received the title of Count of Torrepando.

**Torres, Camilo.** 1766–1816. Colombian patriot and leader in the fight for independence. b. Popayán. Important CREOLE member of the consultative assembly of the Viceroyalty of New Granada, he defended the cause of the *Quiteños* and the CREOLES, and his celebrated *Memorial of Grievances and Rights*, Nov. 29, 1809, became the cornerstone of Colombian independence and is considered an outstanding contribution by a creole thinker. He was secretary of foreign relations of the junta, set up in 1810. As a federalist, he opposed NARIÑO, and as president of the newly-formed congress, he denounced the dictatorial tactics of Nariño. In 1813 he encouraged BOLÍVAR, and was made head of the government of New Granada when the Spaniards were already victorious, 1815. Forced to resign in the spring of 1816, he was captured by the Spaniards and executed.

**Torres Bodet, Jaime.** 1902–    . Mexican scholar and statesman. b. Mexico City. Professor of French literature at the University of Mexico, 1924–1928. He was appointed chief of the diplomatic department of the foreign affairs ministry, 1936. He was undersecretary for foreign affairs, 1940–1943; minister of education, 1943–1946; minister of foreign affairs, 1946–1948; director general of UNESCO, 1948–1952.

**Tosta, Vicente.** d. 1930. Provisional president of Honduras, May 3, 1924. He successfully suppressed an attempt at further revolution by Gregorio Ferrara, August through October of the same year. Under a new constitution he was replaced by Miguel Paz Barahona as president, 1925. During the 1928 presidential election campaign Tosta evidenced his disagreement with the leadership of the Liberal Party by bolting and forming the Independent Party with himself as candidate but later withdrew in favor of a coalition candidate, Dr. Mejía Colindres.

**Totonacs.** A tribe of Indians inhabiting the shores of the Gulf of Mexico in what is now the state of Veracruz. They were subdued by the AZTECS in the 15th century and were forced to pay tribute to their conquerors. When the Spaniards under CORTÉS set foot on the Mexican shore in 1519, the Totonacs greeted them as friends and asked their help against the Aztecs. The Spaniards entered the Totonac city of Cempoala and converted the Indians to Christianity, tearing down the idols and cleansing the temples of blood from the victims of the human sacrifice ritual. A number of Totonac nobles and porters accompanied Cortés on his first expedition to the Aztec capital of TENOCHTITLÁN (Mexico City).

**Toussaint L'Ouverture** or **Louverture, Pierre** (or **François**) **Dominique.** Original surname, Breda. *ca.* 1743–1803. Haitian general and liberator. b. Saint Domingue (the French portion of Hispaniola). His surname Breda was changed to L'Ouverture in token of his bravery in causing a gap to be made in the enemy lines. Born of African slave parents, he worked as a coachman and taught himself to read and write. He joined the insurrection forces of OGÉ that sought freedom for the slaves, 1790, and when Spanish and English forces invaded Saint Domingue, 1793, L'Ouverture joined them in their war against the French. He later transferred his allegiance to the French army when the French government ratified an act declaring freedom for the slaves and helped to drive out the invaders. When the entire island came under French control (Treaty of Basle), 1795, he became the virtual ruler of the island, defeated dissident mulatto elements under RIGAUD in the southern portions of the island, and proclaimed a constitution and the independence of the country, assuming the title of governor general, 1801. He was captured as the result of an act of treachery by the French general, LECLERC, 1802, and sent to France where he died in the prison of Joux the following year. He was an outstanding man of courage and ability and was eulogized in poems written by Wordsworth, Lamartine, and Whittier.

**Tresguerras, Francisco Eduardo.** 1745–1833. Mexican architect and sculptor. He worked in his native town of Celaya and also in Guanajuato. He built a number of churches, including his masterpiece, the church of Our Lady of Carmen at Celaya, completed in 1807. He is the last figure of importance in Mexican art until the 20th century.

**Troncoso de la Concha, Manuel de Jesús.** 1878–1959. President of the Dominican Republic. b. Santo Domingo. Judge of supreme court, 1908; secretary of justice and education, 1911; secretary of public works, 1912; national attorney general, 1914; adviser to the World Court, 1914; secretary of the interior and war, 1923; special minister to the United States, 1937; vice-president of the Dominican Republic, 1938; president of the republic, 1940–1942; president of the senate, 1943; acting president early in 1940, when President Peynado was incapacitated. Upon the death, March 8, 1940, of Peynado, he became constitutional president. Difficulties with the United States over the control of the Dominican customs were settled, and the United States withdrew its commissioner of customs and relinquished control of customs collections.

**Trujillo Molina, Rafael Leonidas.** 1891–1961. President of the Dominican Republic. Self-made man, he was a mulatto of humble origin who started as an errand boy, worked as a cattle hand, became a colonel in the national guard in six years, and rose rapidly politically. He used the army through a revolutionary coup to put himself in power, 1930, and had the constitution amended to suit his needs. In complete control of the country, he was re-elected four times, even though he allowed relatives and friends to become president on several occasions. He was generalissimo of the armed forces, renamed the capital Ciudad Trujillo, 1936, was founder and supreme chief of the *Partido Dominicano*, and owned the newspaper *La Nación* and controlled the Dominican press. He suppressed uprisings of all types by bloody methods, the worst being the massacre of 7,000 Haitians when they drifted into Dominican territory to work cutting sugar cane, 1937. He also controlled the sugar, match, and other monopolies of the country. The system of terror used by the dictator to silence opposition and to perpetuate his control of the country gradually generated hostility in the outside world toward the Dominican government. Following his attempt to bring about the assassination of President BETANCOURT of Venezuela, 1960, the majority of American republics severed relations with the Trujillo government. Trujillo was himself assassinated, May 30, 1961.

**Tucumán, Congress of.** The congress that on July 9, 1816, proclaimed Argentine independence from Spain. It named Juan Martín de PUEYRREDÓN the Supreme Director of the new nation, then known as the UNITED PROVINCES OF LA PLATA. The delegates to the congress disagreed as to the future form of government to be given the United Provinces. Monarchy under a French, Spanish, Portuguese and even an INCA candidate was discussed at length, and the deliberations continued into the year 1817, when the congress moved to Buenos Aires. There it promulgated a constitution in 1819, establishing a centralized form of government, but the opposition of the provinces to the Buenos Aires unitarians forced the dissolution of the congress in the following year.

**Tupac Amaru II.** Real name, **José Gabriel Condorcanqui, Marquis of Oropesa.** 1740–1781. Indian chieftain and revolutionist of Peru. Descendant of the Incan Tupac Amaru, who was beheaded by the Spaniards, 1579. He led a great Indian uprising against the Spanish authorities, 1780, which was at first highly successful, spreading over large areas in Peru. He abolished tributes and *mitas*, but was finally defeated and captured, and was put to death by the Spaniards. The revolt continued under other leaders and was finally suppressed, 1783.

**Tupí-Guaraní.** The second most important South-American linguistic group, deriving its name from the two most important tribes of this stock, the Tupís and the GUARANÍS. At the time of the Portuguese occupation of Brazil the Tupís inhabited the Brazilian coastal region from the mouth of the Amazon River to what is now the state of Rio Grande do Sul, while the Guaranís occupied an area of the southern Atlantic coast and extended westward to the Paraná and Paraguay rivers, and southward to the Río de la Plata estuary.

The Tupís were a primitive race practicing cannibalism and usually at war among themselves. Many of them became the slaves of the Portuguese, and but few survived the harsh treatment and diseases. The language of the Tupís was made the *língua geral* (common language) of Brazil by the missionaries, and is still used today in the Amazon Basin. The Guaranís, although also given to cannibalism, engaged in agriculture, fishing and hunting. They grew corn, manioc and tobacco, and lived in lightly-built communal houses. They were skilled in working with stone, in weaving, and in pottery. In the 17th century they were gathered by the JESUITS in the famous Paraguay missions, but upon the expulsion of the Jesuits, 1767, many scattered into the interior. In modern Paraguay there are comparatively few pure Guaraní Indians; the mass of the people are a mixture of Spanish and Guaraní. The Guaraní language is still spoken in Paraguay and is as important as the Spanish language.

**Turbay, Gabriel.** 1901–    . Colombian diplomat and political leader. b. Bucaramanga. Served as minister plenipotentiary to Italy and Belgium; national senator and president of the senate; minister of government; minister of foreign affairs; leader of the Liberal Party; ambassador to the United States, 1939. He was defeated for the presidency by OSPINA PÉREZ, 1946.

**Tuxtepec, Plan of.** A revolutionary plan proclaimed by Porfirio DÍAZ, 1876, in which he demanded the resignation of the Mexican president, LERDO DE TEJADA (who was seeking a second term), the application of effective suffrage, and a constitutional prohibition against re-election of presidents. Díaz did not meet with immediate success. He was defeated and forced to seek refuge in the United States. But he returned to Mexico and in November 1876, he defeated Lerdo de Tejada's forces. On May 5, 1877, Díaz took office as constitutional president of Mexico to rule as a dictator from 1877 to 1880 and from 1884 to 1911. The demands for effective suffrage and no re-election were revived by MADERO in 1910.

# U

**Ubico, Jorge.** 1878–1946. President of Guatemala. b. Guatemala City. Leader of sanitary campaigns against yellow fever, 1918, 1920; chief of general staff, 1920; military commandant of Guatemala City and minister of war, 1921; president of Guatemala, 1931–1944. He had a constitutional amendment passed, 1937, that permitted him to stay in office another six years, and a constituent assembly voted, 1941, to permit him to stay in office until 1949. He was overthrown by a revolt, July 1944.

**U.C.R.** See RADICAL CIVIC UNION PARTY OF ARGENTINA.

**U.D.N.** See NATIONAL DEMOCRATIC UNION OF BRAZIL.

**Ulate Blanco, Otilio.** 1895–  . President of Costa Rica. b. Alajuela. Began career as a journalist and publisher. He has been director of *La Prensa Libre*, and *La Tribuna* since 1921, and publisher of *Diario de Costa Rica* since 1936. He was deputy to the national congress, 1930–1938; elected president in 1948, and took office in 1949, after a constituent assembly had confirmed his election; resigned, September 1952, but in October of the same year he returned to the presidency once more and remained in office until 1953.

**Ulloa, Antonio de.** 1716–1795. Spanish colonial and naval official, scientist, and writer. b. Seville. Educated in the *Guardias Marinas*, Cádiz. First visited America, 1730–1732, and was then commissioned by the king, together with another naval officer, Jorge Juan y Santacilia (1712–1773), to accompany a French scientific expedition to South America

and to report on the scientific data accumulated and on the condition of Peru and Ecuador, 1735–1744. He published, with Jorge Juan, an account of his experiences entitled *Relación histórica del viaje a la América meridional*, (5 vols., 1748, translated into English as A Voyage to South America). Again with Jorge Juan, he published another important work, *Noticias secretas de América*, written 1749 and published 1826, which told of the abuses of colonial rulers and the conditions existing in the viceroyalty of Peru. He was governor of Huancavélica, Peru, 1758–1764. Governor of Louisiana, 1766–1768, he was ousted by a revolt of the CREOLES. He was promoted to rear admiral. He published *Noticias Americanas*, 1772, a comprehensive account of Spanish South America and the southeastern part of North America. He was vice-admiral and chief of naval operations at the time of his death.

**Ultramar, Conselho do.** See CONSELHO DO ULTRAMAR.

**Unitarios.** Name given in Argentina in the early decades of the 19th century to those advocating a strong central government, and opposing federalism, or the autonomy of provinces within a confederation. The *unitarios* were bitter enemies of the Argentine dictator Juan Manuel de ROSAS and had their strongest supporters among the upper-class inhabitants of Buenos Aires.

**United Fruit Company.** A concern formed in 1899 by the North American Minor C. KEITH and others, designed to grow BANANAS in tropical America and to export the fruit.

It soon operated in most of the Central-American republics and northern South America, carving huge plantations out of the jungle, building railroads from the interior to the ports in order to facilitate the export of bananas, operating fleets of ships to transport them, and soon becoming an important element in the economic life of the countries in which it had been established. A number of times it became involved in the politics of the Central-American republics, and in some cases it undoubtedly exercised undue influence in that field. At the beginning of its career it was accused of monopolizing the banana industry and of using harsh methods in order to rid itself of competitors. Recently the United Fruit Company became involved in a dispute with the government of former President ARBENZ GUZMÁN in Guatemala. The Guatemalan government began to confiscate lands held by the company in order to turn them over to landless Guatemalan peasants. This policy would probably have been continued if the CASTILLO ARMAS revolution of June 1954, had not overthrown the Arbenz regime. Today the most important United Fruit Company banana plantations are in Honduras, Costa Rica, Guatemala, and Panama. The company also has plantations in Colombia, Ecuador, the Dominican Republic, and Jamaica. Other commodities produced by United Fruit include sugar, from Jamaica, cacao from Costa Rica, Panama, and Ecuador, and African palm oil from Costa Rica, Honduras, Guatemala, Nicaragua, and Colombia. The company acts as agent for the U.S. government in the growing and processing of abacá (Manila hemp) in Guatemala, and formerly did so in Costa Rica, Honduras, and Panama. It also has plantings of rubber, quinine, essential oils, and a variety of tropical hard and soft woods. Before the advent of CASTRO in Cuba the company had developed extensive holdings in sugar cane plantations and in cattle raising in that country, but since 1959 the company has been stripped of its Cuban properties. United Fruit has been a favorite target for ardent nationalists who have accused it of influencing local governments to its advantage, of having an adverse effect on the local economy, and of exploiting the workers. In earlier years these charges were no doubt based on just grounds, but in recent years the company has adopted the policy that whatever is best for the countries in which it operates is best for the company. United Fruit plantations are worked mainly by natives who receive good wages and enjoy a number of benefits, such as good medical care in modern hospitals maintained by the company. Today it is recognized as one of the most intelligently operated of all the U.S. companies abroad.

**United Nations.** The Latin-American republics participated in the setting up of the United Nations Organization at San Francisco in 1945 and have, since then, all been represented in it. During the drafting of the charter the Latin-American states were instrumental in clarifying the relationship of regional systems, such as the Pan-American movement, to the new international system then being formed. Until 1955 the 20 republics wielded considerable influence in decision-making as they made up one-third or more of the General Assembly's voting strength, but with the continuing growth in membership of the United Nations, their influence has lessened. Latin-American statesmen have held many responsible positions in the UN: the Security Council customarily includes two Latin-American states, the Economic and Social Council has four, the Trusteeship Council has two, and the International Court of Justice has four. Every four years a Latin American usually serves as president of the General Assembly. With regard to the maintenance of international peace and security, the Latin-American nations have a consistent record of supporting Western-sponsored proposals. In 1950 Colombia provided a contingent of troops as well as a naval unit to the UN command in its Korean operation, and both Brazilian and Colombian troops were included in the UN force sent to the Middle East during the Suez crisis. Latin-American states have generally favored the extension of self-government and independence and have taken a position opposed to colonialism on most questions involving dependencies and nonself-governing peoples. They have worked for and evidenced a strong interest in programs concerned with economic development

—their own underdeveloped regions have no doubt made them cognizant of those problems. They have usually voted as a group on important issues of world politics. The UN has not intervened in any Latin-American disputes, for these come under the jurisdiction of the ORGANIZATION OF AMERICAN STATES. In 1954 the ARBENZ GUZMÁN government of Guatemala tried to bring the matter of the revolt against it before the United Nations, but the latter referred the matter to the Organization of American States.

**United Provinces of Central America.** See CENTRAL AMERICAN FEDERATION.

**United Provinces of La Plata.** See LA PLATA, UNITED PROVINCES OF.

**United States Bases.** See BASES, NAVAL AND AIR.

**United States-Latin American Relations.** From the beginning of the Spanish-American struggle for independence there was great sympathy in the United States for the cause of the Spanish colonies. As early as 1783, the Venezuelan patriot Francisco de MIRANDA discussed plans for revolution in Spanish America with important North-American personalities. In 1811 a resolution, approved by the U.S. Congress, declared that the United States looked favorably upon the establishment of independent nations in Spanish America. An official American agent, Joel Roberts POINSETT, went to South America and spent the years between 1810 and 1814 in Buenos Aires and Chile. Moreover, during the Spanish-American War for Independence, a number of American citizens fought in the revolutionary armies. The independence of Colombia and Mexico was recognized by the United States in 1822; that of Chile and Argentina in 1823; Brazil and Central America in 1824; and Peru in 1826.

The MONROE DOCTRINE in 1823 indicated, among other things, that the United States would oppose any attempts of European powers friendly to Spain to help the latter to regain her lost provinces in the Americas. In the 1820's there was constant rivalry in Latin America between the United States and Great Britain, but in most instances

England was victorious. Competition was especially sharp in Mexico, where the first American ambassador, Joel R. Poinsett, did not succeed in dispelling growing Mexican fears of North-American land hunger, fears that were constantly kindled by the British. The Texas problem increased friction between the United States and Mexico, and the secession of Texas from Mexico in 1836 led to annexation of the territory by the United States and to war between the two countries, 1846–1848, a war that resulted in the cession of huge territories by defeated Mexico. In the same decade rivalry between the United States and Great Britain became more accentuated in Central America. Both countries vied for Central-American trade and at the same time tried to gain control over the routes leading across the Central-American isthmus. While Great Britain extended its holdings in the Belize area (British Honduras) and increased its influence on the east coast of Honduras and Nicaragua, the United States in 1846 secured from New Granada (Colombia) the right of transit across the Isthmus of Panama by any means. Anglo-American rivalry was more or less settled in 1850 by the CLAYTON-BULWER TREATY, which guaranteed the neutrality of any canal that might be constructed across the Central-American isthmus.

In the Caribbean the United States became interested about the middle of the 19th century in acquiring Cuba and tried to purchase the island from Spain, but Spain refused to sell it. During the Mexican War of the Reform, 1858–1860, the subsequent French intervention, and the MAXIMILIAN interlude, U.S. sympathy was with the liberals led by Benito JUÁREZ, but the United States could take no effective action against foreign intervention in Mexico because of its own Civil War. Upon the termination of this conflict, however, the American government made it clear to French Emperor NAPOLEON III that it would not tolerate the presence of French troops on the territory of an American state, considering it an infringement of the Monroe Doctrine. At the same time the United States began to mass troops on the Rio Grande and provided the armies of Juárez with war supplies. The French were forced to withdraw

319

from Mexico early in 1867, and shortly afterward Juárez gained final victory.

American interest in Latin America became particularly strong in the late 19th century. American investments began to flow into Latin America especially in Mexico, Central America, and the Caribbean, at an ever increasing pace, and the United States became strongly interested in securing Latin-American markets for its products. It was mainly with the aim of fostering inter-American trade that the American government called the first Pan-American conference at Washington, D.C., in 1889. For the United States, Pan-Americanism at this early stage meant closer trade relations with Latin America, and the next three PAN-AMERICAN CONFERENCES were concerned mainly with trade. In South America, the United States played the role of arbitrator in such disputes as the WAR OF THE PACIFIC, 1880, the dispute between Venezuela and Great Britain, 1895, and the Chile-Argentina controversy of 1898.

Increasingly confident in its own power, the United States was determined to play a dominant role in the Caribbean and in Central America, all the more so since American investments in that area had become quite heavy. Victory in the SPANISH-AMERICAN WAR of 1898 permitted the United States to play a decisive role in the Caribbean. By virtue of the authority conferred upon it by the PLATT AMENDMENT, the American government intervened in the affairs of Cuba a number of times in the first two decades of the 20th century. At the beginning of the century, the United States supported the Panama independence movement in 1903 and secured from the infant republic of Panama the right to build the PANAMA CANAL, a monumental project completed in 1914. The ROOSEVELT COROLLARY, enunciated in 1904 by President Theodore ROOSEVELT, declared it to be the right and duty of the United States to intervene in the affairs of Latin-American countries who were reluctant to pay their bills, if this intervention prevented the interference of European powers bent on the forcible collection of debts and protecting the interests of their nationals. This doctrine, motivated to a large extent by U.S. fear that a European power might take advantage of the inability

of one or several of the Caribbean nations to pay their debts to European creditors, in order to extort territorial concessions, led to constant intervention in the Caribbean and Central-American area. Roosevelt's highhanded manner of intervening in the Caribbean republics was typical of his BIG STICK diplomacy and created considerable bitterness toward the United States. The administration of President William H. Taft, 1909–1913, was characterized by a preoccupation with U.S. investments abroad and a desire to increase U.S. exports. Taft's secretary of state, Philander C. Knox, an advocate of a spirited foreign commercial policy, forcefully implemented the policy that was branded DOLLAR DIPLOMACY. President Woodrow WILSON, 1913–1921, was emphatically opposed to his predecessor's policies in Latin America and particularly hostile to "Dollar Diplomacy." At the beginning of his first term in office he sincerely tried to place United States-Latin American relations on a basis of friendship and mutual understanding. It was not long, however, before Wilson, due partly to the force of circumstances, became involved in an even sterner intervention policy than that of his predecessors. In the Mexican civil war that pitted the dictator HUERTA against the constitutionalists CARRANZA and VILLA, Wilson was friendly to the aims of the latter faction, but unfortunately he did not wait for a constitutionalist victory and picked a quarrel with the Huerta government, 1914, after an incident involving American sailors at TAMPICO on the Gulf of Mexico. The dispute led to American seizure of the port of VERACRUZ, an operation in the course of which many Mexicans were killed. A year later the United States intervened in Haiti, and American forces remained in occupation in that country until 1934.

In the Dominican Republic, American intervention had begun in 1905 with the establishment of a customs collectorship under U.S. control, and from 1916 until 1924 the country was occupied by American marines. In Central America, Wilson's policy of withholding recognition from any government having come into power by force, involved the United States, in 1917, in a dispute with the Costa Rican dictator Federico Tinoco, and this same policy, nine years later, indirectly caused American intervention in Nicaragua. The United States had intervened in Nicaragua with armed force as early as 1913, and from then until 1925, U.S. marines had been stationed there. A second intervention occurred in 1926, and marines remained in the country until 1933. The nonrecognition policy was also applied to President OBREGÓN of Mexico, who had been elected in 1920 after a revolt had toppled the Carranza administration. Obregón was finally recognized in 1923, after a number of disputes involving the two countries, including a controversy over oil property owned by American citizens in Mexico, had been settled. During World War I, trade between the United States and Latin-American countries increased greatly, since it was difficult for Latin Americans to purchase goods in Europe, and in spite of opposition to the U.S. policy in Latin America, a number of countries joined the United States in the war against Germany. Trade between the United States and Latin America continued to grow after the war, and the same can be said of American investments, which by 1928 amounted to more than $5,500,000,000 in all of Latin America. In the 1920's, under Republican administrations, the United States tried to establish more friendly relations, terminating interventions in Cuba and the Dominican Republic, and settling disputes with Mexico by negotiation. Under the Franklin D. ROOSEVELT Democratic administration, intervention was definitely abandoned and a new approach, the GOOD NEIGHBOR POLICY, was inaugurated.

The change in the American attitude was in evidence at the Seventh Pan-American Conference at Montevideo, Uruguay, December 1933, when the United States signed a convention declaring that "no state has the right to intervene in the external or internal affairs of another." Although the United States had taken part in Pan-American conferences since 1889, effective inter-American co-operation began only at the Montevideo Conference. This policy was continued in the following years and was evidenced at subsequent Pan-American meetings. Pan-Americanism was now more than a mere word. By 1939, when WORLD WAR II broke out, the United States and most Latin-American nations were in full agreement on hemispheric solidarity and on the defense of the American continent against foreign aggression. Political and economic co-operation between Latin America and the United States reached its highest point during World War II. Most Latin-American countries declared war on the Axis powers or broke diplomatic relations with them soon after Pearl Harbor. They gave the United States valuable aid in the form of vital raw materials and naval and air bases on their territories. Two countries, Brazil and Mexico, even sent armed forces to the fighting fronts. Argentina alone remained nonco-operative almost to the end, refusing to abandon neutrality until January 1944, when the war was almost over. The United States, on the other hand, extended important financial aid to Latin-American nations through the EXPORT-IMPORT BANK and provided other types of economic assistance to its southern neighbors. Economic and cultural relations were given great impetus with the creation of the Office of the Co-ordinator of Commercial and Cultural Relations in 1940, later given the title of Office of Inter-American Affairs. Co-operation with Latin America continued after the war. It was implemented by the Inter-American Treaty of Reciprocal Assistance signed at the RIO CONFERENCE OF 1947, the BOGOTÁ CONFERENCE OF 1948, and the adoption of the charter of the ORGANIZATION OF AMERICAN STATES at this meeting, the CARACAS CONFERENCE of 1954, and the economic parley at Rio de Janeiro in the same year.

In more recent years events have occurred that have caused both the United States and the Latin-American nations to make an agonizing reappraisal of their relations with one another. The false sense of serenity concerning those relations that prevailed in most of the United States was shattered when the latent distrust and antagonism in Latin America toward the United States was manifested in clear and unmistakable terms. In 1958 when Vice-President Richard M. Nixon was booed, shoved, stoned, and spat upon in his nightmarish good-will tour of South America, President Eisenhower dispatched a contingent of marines and paratroopers to

U.S. bases in the Caribbean to insure the vice-president's safety. In 1959 the Cuban revolution that overthrew the BATISTA regime and created what became the first Communist state in the Western Hemisphere accented the tragic failure of U.S. policies in Latin America. To offset the mounting bitterness in Latin America toward U.S. intervention and economic exploitation, whether real or imagined, officials in Washington laid plans to bring about a better rapport with the nations to the south. The bad feeling generated by hostile attacks on the United States served to accelerate the pace of inter-American economic and social co-operation. U.S. officials responded to Brazilian President Kubitschek's 1958 proposal of an economic development program on a grand scale (called "Operation Pan America") by establishing the Inter-American Development Bank, which provided an additional source of capital to promote economic growth in Latin America. Economic aid was further expanded by the Act of Bogotá in 1960, and in 1961 the ALLIANCE FOR PROGRESS, a truly comprehensive long-range economic and social development program, was begun. Despite sporadic outbursts against the United States, such as the Panama riots, January 1964, and the almost constant agitation by communists and Cuban sympathizers, and despite recent U.S. intervention in the Dominican Republic (1965), the determined efforts of the United States and the Latin-American nations to promote better relations have made real, if limited, progress. The Alliance for Progress has not succeeded in transforming the Latin-American scene in its first years of operation, but once out of the organizational stage the program gives real promise of accomplishing what it set out to do. If relations between the United States and its southern neighbors have suffered a decline and at the present time are less than desirable, there is hope in the knowledge that the elements of common interest are far greater than the elements of opposed interests and that the current decline is not likely to be long-lasting or permanent.

**Universities.** Higher education played an important role in Spanish colonial life, since its main function was to turn out royal officials and churchmen who would render important service to king and Church. A number of universities were established by the Crown, and others by the Church, but control by the Church over all of them was undisputed. Students came mainly from the upper classes, and the faculties were made up mostly of JESUITS, DOMINICANS, and FRANCISCANS. University education, patterned on the system in force at the Spanish university of Salamanca, consisted chiefly in the teaching of theology, with some courses on civil law, mathematics, medicine, and Indian languages. Instruction was conducted in Latin. Up to the middle of the 18th century the general level of university education was low, because of the neglect of the sciences and languages in favor of theology, attributable to the all-pervading control of the Church, which usually stifled any attempts at independent thinking. In the second half of the 18th century new ideas imported from Europe began to infiltrate the universities, and the traditional Aristotelian metaphysics governing all academic thought until then began to give way to Cartesianism. Cartesian thought, however, was compatible with Catholic orthodoxy, and to the end of the colonial period the Church prevented the teaching of anything that might undermine Catholic dogma. Brazil never had a university during its colonial period, and Brazilians received their higher education at the University of Coimbra in Portugal.

The earliest universities to be established in Spanish America were: that of Santo Domingo, founded by a papal bull in 1538; the University of Mexico, established by Emperor CHARLES V in 1551 and opened in 1553; and San Marcos in Lima, Peru, founded in 1551 but opened in 1571–1576. Other early institutions included the University of Bogotá, Colombia, and of Córdoba, Argentina. In modern times Latin-American universities have seen a consistent widening in the range of their curricula. While law and medicine are still dominant, such subjects as engineering, dentistry, pharmacy, and agriculture have taken on an ever-increasing importance. The outstanding institutions in Latin America today include the University of Mexico, whose old buildings in the capital have recently been completely replaced by modern structures in the outskirts of the city; the University of Brazil (formerly Rio de Janeiro); the Universities of Buenos Aires, La Plata, and Córdoba in Argentina; the University of Montevideo in Uruguay; the University of San Marcos at Lima, Peru; the National University of Colombia at Bogotá; the National University of Chile at Santiago; the University of Havana in Cuba; and the University of Santo Domingo in the Dominican Republic. Latin-American students are usually intensely interested in the politics of their countries, and there have been many cases of their having taken part in antigovernment demonstrations, even resorting to open violence to underscore their hostility. At times Latin-American universities have been centers of open resistance to the governments of their countries. One example is the University of Havana, whose students took a strong part in political activities against the MACHADO administration, 1925–1933. Their hostility to Machado resulted in violent clashes with the police, in the course of which many students lost their lives.

**Urbina, José María.** 1808–1891. President of Ecuador. b. Ambato. Seized power after overthrowing Noboa, 1851. He considered himself a liberal and had taken part in the March revolution of 1845. He forced the JESUITS out and adopted a mild anticlerical policy; chief accomplishments were the abolition of Negro slavery, 1854, and the outlawing of the tributes the Indians had been compelled to pay. However, there were not many slaves and the Indians' lot did not improve. He was succeeded by Robles, but he was still in control and retained power. Peru attacked Ecuador and revolts forced Robles and Urbina to flee. Urbina was in exile in Peru, 1856–1876, but returned to become commander of the army of Ecuador, 1876–1878.

**Uriburu, José Evaristo.** 1831–1914. Argentine president and diplomat. b. Salta. He was mediator in the dispute between Chile and Bolivia at the conclusion of the WAR OF THE PACIFIC, 1879–1883, and envoy to Chile at the time the Chilean President BALMACEDA took

refuge in the Argentine legation at Santiago, 1891. Elected vice-president, 1892, he became president upon the resignation of SÁENZ PEÑA, 1895. During his administration, 1895–1898, Uriburu consolidated peaceful relations with Chile; reorganized the armed forces, and built the military port at Bahía Blanca. He was senator of Buenos Aires, 1901–1910, and served as interim president in 1903.

**Uriburu, José Evaristo.** b. 1880. Argentine financier, diplomat, and historian. b. Peru. He was director of the *Banco de la Nación Argentina* (Bank of the Nation), 1919; ambassador to Great Britain, 1927–1931; vice-president of the Central Bank, 1935–1940. He was the author of *Historia del general Arenales, Memorias de Dámaso de Uriburu,* and other historical writings.

**Uriburu, José Félix.** 1868–1932. Argentine general who led the movement that overthrew Hipólito YRIGOYEN, 1930; provisional president, 1930–1932; established a dictatorship and took harsh measures against opposition. He handed over power to Agustín JUSTO after the latter was elected, 1932. Uriburu died in Paris.

**Urquiza, Justo José de.** 1800–1870. Argentine president. Governor of province of Entre Ríos, 1842–1854, he protested against the ROSAS trade policy which hurt other provinces, declared the province of Entre Ríos no longer in the control of Rosas under the Federal Pact of 1831, and led his army into Uruguay. Others joined him and Rosas was defeated at Monte CASEROS, February 1852. Urquiza became the new ruler of Argentina on May 31, 1852, gaining control of all military forces, and a constitution was adopted on May 1, 1853. He was inaugurated president of the Argentine Confederation, March 5, 1854, with the capital at Paraná, but Buenos Aires remained independent. He dissolved the legislature and installed a regime under his own control, signed treaties with Great Britain, France, and the United States, which opened the Paraná and Uruguay rivers to international commerce, and remained president until 1860. He commanded the federal army after 1860, and was again governor of Entre Ríos. He was defeated at the Battle of PAVÓN by Buenos Aires forces under MITRE in 1861. Urquiza was assassinated.

**Urrutia Lleó, Manuel.** 1901– . Provisional president of Cuba. b. Yaguajay. Educated at University of Havana, he received his law degree in 1923 and was appointed municipal judge, 1928. He opposed the dictatorship of MACHADO Y MORALES. Restored to the judiciary during the first BATISTA regime, and appointed judge of the urgency court, 1949, he resisted the illegal usurpation of power by Batista, 1952. His defense of members of Fidel CASTRO's revolutionary army, 1957, made him a national symbol of opposition to the Batista government, and he went into voluntary exile in the United States, 1957–1958. He was made provisional president by Castro, January 2, 1959, but when charged with treasonous actions by Castro, Urrutia resigned his position, July 1959.

**Ursúa, Pedro de.** *ca.* 1510–1561. Spanish governor of Bogotá, believed to have been killed by Lope de AGUIRRE while exploring the Amazon River.

**Uruguay.** The smallest republic in South America, it is bounded on the north and east by Brazil, on the south by the Atlantic Ocean and the Río de la Plata estuary, and on the west by Argentina. With an area of 72,172 square miles, it has a population of about 2,845,000 (est. 1965), most of whom are of European origin. The language is Spanish, and the monetary unit is the peso, valued in 1966 at 70 pesos to the U.S. dollar; it has fluctuated wildly in recent years. The dominant religion is Roman Catholic, but there is complete religious freedom. Uruguay was ruled by a national council of government, composed of nine men elected for four years. The chairman of the council was nominally the president of the republic. The post of chairman rotated each year among four of the six-member delegation of the leading party; the second ranking party received the other three seats on the council. In late 1966 Uruguay voted to return to a four-year presidency. There is a bicameral general assembly consisting of a chamber of deputies and a senate. There is universal suffrage. The chief cities and their populations (est. 1963)

are Montevideo, the capital, 1,200,000, Paysandú, 86,944, and Salto, 92,595. Most of Uruguay is flat or slightly rolling, with many rivers crisscrossing the land. The most important river is the Uruguay, which forms the western border of the country. The basic economic activities of the country are sheep and cattle raising. The small percentage of land that is used for the raising of crops produces wheat, corn, and flax. The most important industry is meat processing, 2,000,000 head of cattle and sheep being slaughtered yearly. The main export is wool, followed by meats and hides. Uruguay imports machinery, vehicles, gasoline, sugar, and textiles. The greater part of the exports go to Great Britain, the United States, the Netherlands, and West Germany, and the country's main suppliers are the United States, Great Britain, West Germany, and the Soviet Union. The British-owned railroads, which controlled 90 per cent of the mileage until 1948, were purchased by the government in that year. There are now more than 1,800 miles of railroads. All education is free, and primary education is compulsory. About 12,000 students attend the University of Montevideo. About 15 per cent of the population is illiterate.

It is probable that the area of the RÍO DE LA PLATA was first discovered by Amerigo VESPUCCI, 1501–1502, but it was not explored until the Spaniard Juan DÍAZ DE SOLÍS went there in 1516. The territory became known as the Banda Oriental, or eastern bank of the Uruguay River, and to this day the Uruguayans like to call themselves *Orientales.* The Portuguese founded the settlement of Colonia in 1680 and carried on considerable smuggling in the Plata area. The settlement of Montevideo was begun in 1726 by a number of families from Buenos Aires, from Spain, and from the Canary Islands. In the 18th century Portugal and Spain constantly fought for the territory, with Spain succeeding in placing it under her control in 1778. Starting in 1811 Uruguay fought for independence, led by the cattleman José ARTIGAS, who was forced to battle the Spaniards, the forces of Buenos Aires, and the Portuguese from Brazil. The territory was occupied by the Portuguese in 1816, and Artigas, who had maintained the struggle for independence, was decisively defeated by them in 1820. The following year Uruguay was incorporated into Brazil. In April 1825, when the 33 patriots, the "Immortal Thirty-three," crossed the Río de la Plata from Buenos Aires under the leadership of LAVALLEJA, the *Orientales* rose against the Brazilians and proclaimed their union with Argentina. War then followed, with Argentina and the *Orientales* on one side and Brazil on the other. Largely with the help of British mediation, a treaty was signed in 1828 between Brazil and Buenos Aires, which created the new, independent República Oriental del Uruguay, a buffer state with a population of 70,000. A republican form of government was established in 1830, and from that time until the beginning of the 20th century the history of the country was essentially a struggle for power between the conservative *blancos* and the liberal *colorados*. The important episodes in the 19th century and early 20th century were the siege of Montevideo by the troops of the Argentine dictator ROSAS, under the command of the *blanco* ORIBE, 1843–1851; the War of the Triple Alliance (Argentina, Brazil, and Uruguay) against Paraguay, 1864–1870, coming on the heels of a civil war between *blancos* and *colorados*; and the administrations of José BATLLE Y ORDÓÑEZ, 1903–1907, 1911–1915, who put an end to political unrest and introduced far-reaching political and social reforms. A new constitution, adopted in 1917 and in force from 1919 to 1933, provided that the executive powers of government would be shared by a president elected by direct popular vote and a national council of administration consisting of nine members elected for six years, with elections to be decided under the system of proportional representation. In 1933 the *colorado* president Gabriel TERRA dissolved the congress and ruled by decree. The new constitution of 1934 did away with the national council, giving its powers back to the president. Terra ruled as a virtual dictator until 1938, when Alfredo BALDOMIR succeeded him.

Uruguay broke diplomatic relations with the Axis powers in 1942 and declared war on Germany and Japan in February 1945. Since WORLD WAR II Uruguay has had to face such economic problems as inflation, public debt, and the lack of adequate world markets to absorb its large wool and meat production. An important event in the postwar history of Uruguay was the constitutional reform of 1951 which restored the national council. The elections of 1958 gave a majority of the vote to the *blancos*, or Nationalists as they are now called, who had not won an election for 93 years. Internal dissensions among the *colorados*, inefficient operation of the government, and economic depression brought about the 1958 upset. The change of parties, after almost a century of one-party rule, was peacefully accomplished and gave proof of the effectiveness of Uruguayan democracy. In April and May of 1959 the country experienced disastrous floods, which were followed in 1960 by serious drought. The economic distress was somewhat alleviated through international aid. The *blancos* won the national elections again in 1962 and retained control of the national council of government despite the fact that the party was torn by internal strife. In the elections of November 1966, won by the *colorados*, Uruguayans voted to replace their Swiss-style rotating presidential system with a one-man chief executive. On March 1, 1967, a retired air force general, Oscar Daniel Gestido, became the first full-term president of the country in 15 years. Relations with the United States have been marred in recent years by Uruguayan sympathy for Fidel CASTRO's efforts at reform in Cuba, and by Communist propaganda directed at United States imperialism in Latin America. Vice-president Richard Nixon, President Eisenhower, and U.S. Ambassador Adlai E. Stevenson visited Uruguay, 1958–1961, and although they were received warmly, their visits were marred by demonstrations that revealed a hostile attitude on the part of certain political elements. On August 5–18, 1961, the economic and financial ministers of the American republics met at Punta del Este in southeastern Uruguay to seek an agreement on the ALLIANCE FOR PROGRESS program proposed by U.S. President John F. Kennedy. Today Uruguay is in many respects the most advanced country in Latin America; its constitution provides for old-age pensions, workmen's compensation, free medical care for the underprivileged, an eight-hour day and a 48-hour week, cheap housing for laborers, state care for mothers, a minimum wage, and the right of labor to strike and to bargain collectively.

**Usigli, Rodolfo.** 1905– . Mexican playwright. b. Mexico City. One of the outstanding dramatists of Latin America, he is the author of *Corona de sombra* (Crown of Shadows), a play dealing with Emperor MAXIMILIAN of Mexico and his wife Carlota, *El gesticulador*, and others. See LITERATURE.

**Uxmal.** Important center of MAYAN civilization on the Yucatán peninsula of Mexico, which for a long period before the end of the 12th century formed a league together with the other two centers, MAYAPÁN and CHICHÉN ITZÁ. The league brought peace and prosperity to the peninsula, but this was followed by a period during which Mayapán, aided by NAHUA mercenaries, dominated Yucatán. Finally, the rulers of Mayapán became so tyrannical that Uxmal joined Chichén Itzá in a revolt against Mayapán. After the latter's destruction at the beginning of the 15th century Uxmal and Chichén Itzá fought against each other. These civil wars brought about a permanent decline of Mayan civilization.

**Vaca de Castro, Cristóbal.** *ca.* 1492–1558. Spanish administrator in Peru. Sent by CHARLES V as VISITADOR (inspector general) to investigate the affairs of Peru, where the PIZARRO and ALMAGRO factions were fighting. He was shipwrecked but managed to reach shore and continued the journey overland. He was supported by the Pizarro faction, defeated the rebellious younger Almagro in the Battle of Chupas, 1542, and had him executed. He was replaced by the first viceroy of Peru, NÚÑEZ VELA, 1544, who suspected Vaca de Castro of siding with Gonzalo Pizarro. Vaca de Castro was sent back to Spain and imprisoned. After many years, he was cleared of the charges.

**Valdivia, Pedro de.** *ca.* 1500–1553. Spanish conquistador and governor of Chile. b. La Serena, Extremadura, Spain. Fought in Flanders and at Pavia in Spanish military service; took part in the conquest of Venezuela, 1535. He joined PIZARRO in Peru, 1537, and was given permission by him to undertake an expedition to attempt to conquer and settle Chile, 1539. He left Cuzco, 1540, with a small force of Spaniards, about 1,000 Indians, and sufficient supplies to establish a settlement. When he reached the irrigated valley where Copiapó now stands, he took possession of the land. He founded the city that he called Santiago de la Nueva Extremadura, 1541, now Santiago. He returned to Peru to help Pedro de la GASCA suppress a rebellion led by Gonzalo Pizarro, 1547. He founded the city of Concepción, 1550. Faced with an uprising by ARAUCANIANS, he was captured in a battle with LAUTARO and tortured to death.

**Valencia, Guillermo.** 1873–1943. Colombian writer and political leader. Modernist poet, he was the author of the volumes of poems, *Ritos* (Rites), 1898, *Sus mejores poemas,* 1919, and *Catuy,* 1928. The leader of the conservative party, he was a brilliant orator, and a candidate for the presidency in 1918 and 1930.

**Valparaíso.** The second largest city of Chile and the leading port on the South-American west coast, situated on the Pacific Ocean 75 miles northwest of Santiago. Population approximately 274,000 (1960). The city stands on a number of hills, connected with the port by funicular railroads. It has an essentially modern appearance, because it had to be rebuilt following the severe earthquakes of 1906 and 1907. Important buildings include the Chilean Naval Academy, the Intendencia, nerve center of the provincial government, and the fine Universidad Técnica Federico Santa María, one of the most important schools of engineering in South America. A number of manufacturing establishments produce textiles, refined sugar, leather, chemicals, pharmaceuticals, and cosmetics, and there are several important foundries. Valparaíso is connected by rail with Santiago and by the trans-Andean railroad with Buenos Aires, Argentina. Air and steamship lines provide connections with other countries. In 1536 the Indian fishing village of Quintil was discovered by the Spanish conquistador Juan de Saavedra and was renamed by him Valparaíso (Vale of Paradise). It lacked importance in colonial times because it was too distant from the important centers of Spanish power in the New World. In 1578 it was seized by Sir Francis Drake and was sacked by Richard Hawkins in 1595. It was again sacked in 1600 by a Dutch pirate. In 1866 during the war in which Chile was involved on the side of Peru in a short conflict against Spain, the port was shelled by Spanish naval forces. During the civil war of 1891 the Chileans wrecked a large part of the city. Valparaíso has suffered a number of violent earthquakes, particularly disastrous being those of 1730, 1839, 1873, 1906, 1907, and 1939.

**Vaquero.** Spanish, meaning "cowboy"; the Portuguese equivalent is **vaqueiro.**

**Varas de la Barra, Antonio.** 1817–1886. Chilean educator, financier, and political leader. b. Cauquenes. Self-made man; first head of the Mortgage Bank of Chile. He was the leading minister in MONTT TORRES' cabinet, 1851–1859. Influential in Chilean land and banking interests, he was a conservative with a long record of government service, but strong opposition to Varas led to revolt, and he was forced to renounce his candidacy for the presidency. He was replaced by Montt with José PÉREZ MOSCAYANO. Varas de la Barra was a member of the chamber of deputies, 1862, and was famous for brilliant oratory.

**Vargas, Getúlio Dornelles.** 1883–1954. President of Brazil. b. São Borja. Rose to prominence in politics as finance minister to President W. Pereira de SOUZA, 1926. He was president of RIO GRANDE DO SUL, 1928–1930, and led the successful so-called GAUCHO revolution, charging fraud when congress selected Prestes as victor in the election of 1930. Vargas was made provisional president, 1930–1934, and developed a strong central government, taking powers away from the states. There were many outbreaks of violence and uprisings against his early regime, including the PAULISTA outbreak, 1932, but he was able to suppress them all, and a new constitution was put into effect in 1934. He also established the University of São Paulo in that

year. Although trade unions were allowed to organize, a police force kept strikes under control. He held tight reins on industry, kept strong government control, and the elections set for 1938 never took place. Vargas abolished the 1934 constitution, November 1937, and decreed a new one that inaugurated his famous New State or *Estado Novo*. He served as head of a "constitutional" dictatorship, and dismissed all state governors. He declared war on Germany and Italy, August 1942, conferred with President Franklin D. ROOSEVELT at Natal, January 1943, and military aid and supplies were sent to Brazil for its aid in WORLD WAR II. He resigned as president after a coup on October 30, 1945, but was re-elected October 1950. Accused of intrigue with PERÓN, he faced strong opposition that culminated in the army's demanding his resignation, and he committed suicide, August 24, 1954. He was the author of a political history of Brazil, *A nova política do Brasil,* published in nine volumes, 1938.

**Vasconcellos, Bernardo Pereira de.** 1795–1850. Brazilian statesman. b. Vila Rica (now Ouro Preto). Studied law at Coimbra, Portugal. Elected deputy for the province of MINAS GERAIS, he was known for his liberal views and criticism of the administration of Emperor PEDRO I. He was the chief author of the ATO ADICIONAL OF 1834, which granted more self-government to Brazilian provinces. He opposed regent FEIJÓ, 1835–1837, was minister of justice under regent ARAUJO LIMA, 1837, and became gradually more conservative. He was a senator after 1838.

**Vasconcelos, José.** 1882–1959. Mexican writer and political leader. b. Oaxaca. Studied law in Mexico City. A member of the anti-re-electionist club established by MADERO; supported Madero, 1910–1913; joined CARRANZA's forces in 1913, but broke with him; in exile in the United States, 1915–1920; rector of the National University, 1920; minister of education, 1920–1924; reorganized schools and universities; founded new schools and libraries and carried out the huge task of raising the general cultural level of the country. Rural schools were built, an active campaign for literacy among the Indians was conducted, and government patronage was given to artists like RIVERA. He broke with CALLES, 1924, was an unsuccessful candidate for the presidency, 1929, and was again in exile in 1929 but returned as head of the National Library. He was one of the outstanding intellectual figures of Latin America, and the author of many works, including *El movimiento contemporáneo de México*, 1916, and *La raza cósmica*, 1925, which takes the position that America as a whole is contributing a completely new culture to the world. In *Indología*, 1927, he advocates the joining of the New World Indian and European cultures for a bright common future, and in *Quetzalcoatl* he discovers a spiritual kinship between the AZTEC myth and basic Christian ideals. His autobiography, *Ulises criollo*, 1935, (Mexican Ulysses, 1963) is one of the leading works of Mexican literature. See LITERATURE.

**Vásquez, Horacio.** 1860–1936. President of the Dominican Republic. b. Ciudad Moca. Provisional president after the assassination of President HEUREAUX, 1899, he was elected vice-president, 1902, led a revolt that overthrew President Jiménez, 1902, and about that time organized the National Party, which he dominated until 1930. The government was overthrown, 1903, and he fought unsuccessfully to regain control of the country. He remained in retirement during the military administration of the United States, 1916–1924. He was elected president, 1924, and the U.S. marines were withdrawn from the country. He had the constitution revised so that he could succeed himself as president. He was determined to continue in power, but a revolt led by Rafael TRUJILLO forced him from office, February 1930.

**Veintemilla, José Ignacio de.** 1830–1909. Dictator of Ecuador. b. Cuenca. General who led liberal military revolt against President Borrero, he convened the constituent assembly and was provisional president, 1876–1878. He was elected president, 1878, and he abolished the concordat with the Church, 1878. He was overthrown by revolt and civil war, 1883, and exiled.

**Velasco, José Miguel de.** 1795–1859. President of Bolivia. b. Santa Cruz de la Sierra. Served as provisional president, 1829, and

following the defeat of SANTA CRUZ, 1839, he was declared president of the republic in June 1839. A popular but not very capable president, he had constant trouble with revolts led by military opposition, and was overthrown, 1841, by followers of the exiled Santa Cruz. He served again as provisional president after the resignation of José BALLIVÁN, 1848, and was president of the republic from August to December of 1848.

**Velasco Ibarra, José María.** b. 1893. President of Ecuador. Distinguished lawyer; conservative president who took office with a coalition cabinet, 1934; confronted with depreciated currency and need for modifying the so-called KEMMERER Laws for economic reform. When his economic program failed to win support of congress, he offered to resign, but his resignation was refused. He dissolved congress and tried dictatorial power, but when faced with a threatened military *coup d'état*, he resigned, August 20, 1935. After the overthrow of the ARROYO DEL RÍO government, 1944, he was placed in power by a revolutionary junta that included Communists and socialists, and a new liberal constitution was adopted, 1945. After experiencing difficulties in his administration, he suspended the new constitution and re-established that of 1906, but was ousted by the army, 1947. Again elected president, 1952, his administration was characterized by ardent nationalism expressed in an anti-U.S. attitude and the revival of the chronic boundary dispute with Peru. Re-elected to the presidency, 1960, he was overthrown by an air force coup, November 1961.

**Velázquez, Diego de.** ca. 1460–ca. 1524. Spanish soldier and first governor of Cuba. b. Cuéllar, Spain. Sailed on second voyage with COLUMBUS to Hispaniola; sent on an expedition to conquer Cuba, 1511; by 1514 he had completed the occupation of the island; governor of Cuba, 1514–1521; assisted in his administration by NARVÁEZ; sent out expeditions under Francisco CÓRDOBA, 1517, under GRIJALVA, 1518, and was determined to send CORTÉS on an expedition to Mexico, 1518, but changed his mind and countermanded his orders only to have them ignored. He sent Narváez to compel Cortés to return, but

Narváez was defeated. Even though Cortés was Velázquez' brother-in-law, there was jealousy between them. He was replaced as governor of Cuba, 1521, but returned to office, 1523.

**Vélez Sársfield, Dalmacio.** 1800–1875. Argentine jurist and political leader. b. Córdoba. Deputy and senator for the province of Buenos Aires, he was minister of finance and of the interior of the province of Buenos Aires, 1856–1857, 1859. He was one of a prominent group of men who were in stróng opposition to ROSAS and URQUIZA and is famous as the author of Argentina's civil code.

**Venezuela.** The northernmost republic of South America, bounded on the north by the Caribbean Sea, on the west and southwest by Colombia, on the south by Brazil, and on the east by British Guiana, with an area of 342,143 square miles and a population of 9,228,000 (est. 1966), of which 70 per cent are mestizo, 20 per cent white, 8 per cent Negroes, and 2 per cent Indian. The language is Spanish, the monetary unit is the bolívar (4.50 to the U.S. dollar), and while most of the people are Roman Catholics, religious freedom is guaranteed. It is a federal republic composed of 20 states, two territories, and a federal district. The constitution of 1961 provides for a president elected for five years by direct universal suffrage, a senate, and a chamber of deputies. Voting is compulsory for all citizens 18 years of age and over. Primary and secondary education are compulsory, and although all education is free, illiteracy still runs to about 50 per cent. The chief cities and their populations (est. 1963) are Caracas, the capital, 1,372,435 (including environs and suburbs), Maracaibo, the great oil center, 456,000, Barquisimeto, 204,000, and Valencia, 165,000. Venezuela may be divided into four areas: the tropical and unhealthy lowlands of the coast; the mountainous area in the west, the north, and northeast; the Orinoco basin, consisting of the grass-covered LLANOS or plains, well-suited for cattle raising, and of huge forest lands, deriving its name from the 1,700-mile-long Orinoco River, which, with its tributaries, drains about four-fifths of Venezuela; and the southern highlands, large portions of which are still unexplored.

The two principal occupations are agriculture and stock raising, the main crops being coffee and cacao, as well as sugar, tobacco, cotton, and corn. Manufacturing is relatively underdeveloped. Minerals include gold and iron ore, the mining of the latter having been begun relatively recently by American companies. However petroleum is the mainstay of Venezuelan economy and the factor that explains the unprecedented boom through which the country is passing today. Most of the country's oil is located on the northwest shore of Lake Maracaibo, where it is drilled and then shipped to the United States via oil refineries on the islands of Curaçao and Aruba. Venezuela claims to be the third petroleum producer in the world (average daily production in 1963 was 3,240,000 barrels). Oil exports, constituting 92 per cent of the country's exports, keep the treasury replete and give it a favorable trade balance. The principal imports are machinery, chemicals, manufactured goods, and foodstuffs, the United States being the main supplier. Aside from oil the chief exports are iron ore, coffee, and cacao. Railroad mileage is small (about 700 miles) but there are more than 13,000 miles of roads, including the 790-mile-long Trans-Andean highway that runs west of Caracas and crosses the Andes at more than 14,000 feet, continuing on to Cúcuta in Colombia.

The eastern coast of present-day Venezuela was discovered by COLUMBUS in 1498, and in 1499 an expedition led by the Spaniard Alonso de OJEDA discovered an Indian village built on wooden poles on Lake Maracaibo. The village was given the name of Venecia, because it reminded the Spaniards of Venice, and subsequently it was called Venezuela or Little Venice. This was the name later given to the whole territory that makes up the country today. The first Spanish settlement was established in 1507 on the island of Cubagua off the coast. It became a center of pearl fisheries, but in about 1535 the oyster beds began to be depleted. In 1528 the German banking house of the WELSERS obtained from the Spanish Crown the right to exploit a large portion of the Venezuelan coast. The project resulted in failure because of the cruel methods used by the German leaders to subjugate the Indians, and the concession was withdrawn, 1546–1556. The only important contribution made by the German settlers was that they explored hundreds of miles of previously unknown territory. Overcoming fierce resistance by the Indians, Spanish colonists expanded the Spanish holdings in the area and founded a number of towns, including Caracas, 1567. In the 17th century the colony was the target of many attacks by English, French, and Dutch pirates, and Caracas itself was sacked twice.

From 1728 until 1781 the Guipúzcoa Company of Caracas held the monopoly of Venezuelan trade, establishing trading posts in Caracas, La Guaira, Puerto Cabello, and other towns, and introducing cotton and indigo into the area. At the end of the 18th century the most important Venezuelan exports were indigo, cotton, cacao, coffee, tobacco, and hides. In 1777 the province of Venezuela was made a captaincy general. Forerunners of the Venezuelan independence movement were the Negro uprising of 1795 in Coro, the plot of La Guaira in 1797, aiming at the establishment of a republic, and the landing of the Venezuelan patriot Francisco de MIRANDA in the country to raise the banner of revolt in 1806, which proved unsuccessful. Venezuelan patriots proclaimed the independence of their country in 1811 and Miranda was named general in chief of the revolutionary army. Simón BOLÍVAR, who served under Miranda in the war against the Spaniards, took over the command of the Venezuelan forces after turning Miranda over to the Spaniards, following a misunderstanding, 1812. Years of fighting followed, and in 1821 Bolívar's victory at CARABOBO insured the freedom of the country from Spain. In 1829 Venezuela broke away from the Republic of Great Colombia established by Bolívar and declared itself an independent republic. The first president was José Antonio PÁEZ, 1831–1835, whose administration was peaceful and prosperous. For the next 37 years, however, the history of Venezuela was characterized by internal instability and civil strife. From 1870 to 1888 the country was

ruled by the dictatorship of the liberal GUZMÁN BLANCO, one of the chief features of his administration being his struggle against the Church. Another dictatorship was that of Cipriano CASTRO, 1899–1908, who involved Venezuela in a dispute with Great Britain, Germany, and Italy over compensation to foreign property holders for damages suffered in the course of Venezuelan revolutions. After the coast was blockaded in 1902 by warships of these nations, the United States offered to mediate, and Castro was forced to accept the decisions handed down by arbitration commissions. He was succeeded by his vice-president, Juan Vicente GÓMEZ, who ruled the country for the next 27 years. Gómez fostered oil production and built good highways but did little to raise the general standard of living of the people and ruthlessly suppressed all opposition. Under LÓPEZ CONTRERAS, 1936–1941, there was general prosperity, but the new president did not hesitate to resort to dictatorial methods when left-wing opponents won the congressional elections of 1937, accusing a number of elected congressmen of being Communists, and having them arrested.

During WORLD WAR II Venezuela co-operated with the United States and her oil was of considerable value to the Allied war effort. Diplomatic relations were broken off with the Axis in December 1941. A military uprising in October 1945 set up a provisional government under the leadership of Rómulo BETANCOURT, the head of the left-wing *Acción Democrática* A liberal constitution was adopted in 1947 and in the same year the famous Venezuelan novelist Rómulo GALLEGOS was elected president with the support of the same party. In the fall of 1948, however, Gallegos was overthrown by an army coup headed by Colonel Carlos Delgado Chalbaud. After the latter's assassination in 1950, a military junta took charge, promising general elections. Elections for a constituent assembly were held in 1952 and Colonel Marcos Pérez Jiménez was named provisional president by the army in December of that year. The constituent assembly subsequently confirmed his election even though he had been clearly defeated in the election. From 1953 to 1958 Pérez Jiménez imposed a strict dictatorship on the country. The wealth of the country brought about increasing prosperity as well as the enrichment of the dictator and his associates. In January 1958 Pérez Jiménez was ousted by a military coup and replaced by a junta headed by Admiral Wolfgang Larrazábal. Elections held in December 1958 chose Rómulo BETANCOURT, candidate of *Acción Democrática*, president for a five-year term. Under President Betancourt the government inaugurated a program to develop the communications network, modernize agriculture, and implement industrial expansion. The new administration was plagued from the beginning, however, by political unrest and economic difficulties. The petroleum industry suffered a decline and mineral production in general decreased. Despite the creation of new jobs by industrial expansion, unemployment was a major economic concern. Political extremists, particularly the Armed Forces for National Liberation (FALN), employed terrorist methods to bring about the fall of the Betancourt government before the expiration of the president's term. On December 1, 1963, elections were held and Dr. Raul Leoni, candidate of *Acción Democrática* and the choice of the retiring president, was chosen. Efforts of the FALN to disrupt the election failed completely. President Leoni began his term as president in February 1964. After a period of political stability, an upsurge of terrorist activity in late 1966 led the government to order the army to carry out an occupation of the 18,000-student National University, suspected of being a base of operations of terrorist groups. This action abrogated the institution's traditional right to autonomy in all police matters within its gates.

**Veracruz.** The chief port of entry of Mexico, on the Gulf of Mexico, 200 miles east of Mexico City. It has a population of 144,232 (1963). The city is provided with an excellent harbor. The architecture is a blending of colonial and modern styles, and the most interesting building is the old fort of San Juan de Ulúa, built in 1565, situated on an island one mile from the mainland. Veracruz is connected by rail and road with Mexico City. Around the city, agricultural products,

such as cotton and sugar, are grown, and the oil industry is becoming increasingly important. There are textile mills, and soap, beer, and cigar manufacturing establishments. When Hernán CORTÉS landed in April 1519, he called the Indian village that he found there La Villa Rica de Vera Cruz (The Rich Town of the True Cross). It was at Veracruz that Cortés first met the envoys of the AZTEC emperor MOCTEZUMA, and it was from there that Cortés started his march on the Aztec capital. During the colonial period the city was the object of frequent attacks by foreign pirates, and in the 19th century its fortress of San Juan de Ulúa was bombarded by a French fleet in 1838. It was the headquarters of JUÁREZ and the liberals during the civil war of 1858–1860 and was occupied by French, English, and Spanish troops in the early 1860's. The last French troops to leave Mexico embarked from there in March 1867. In 1911 the Mexican dictator Porfirio DÍAZ left Mexico through Veracruz on his way to Europe and exile. In April 1914, during the Mexican civil war, American marines were landed at Veracruz and occupied the port for several months.

**Veracruz Incident.** The American occupation of the Mexican seaport in 1914 during the civil war between HUERTA and the Constitutionalists. It had its origin in the "Dolphin" incident, taking place on April 9, 1914, at Tampico, Mexico, when the crew of the U.S.S. "Dolphin" was arrested by Mexican authorities and held for an hour and a half after landing. When Victoriano Huerta, the president of Mexico, refused a salute of 21 guns to the American flag demanded by the American commander as a form of apology, President WILSON of the United States sent an American fleet into the Gulf of Mexico. On April 21, hearing that the German merchantship "Ypiranga" was on its way to Veracruz with munitions for Huerta, Wilson ordered the seizure of the seaport. Veracruz was occupied by American forces, but only after hard fighting, in the course of which Mexican troops lost about 200 men. As a result of the incident, even Venustiano CARRANZA, one of the opponents of Huerta in the civil war raging in Mexico, denounced the American action, and Huerta was able to pose as the champion of Mexican independence. By preventing Huerta from obtaining war supplies, however, the American action contributed to the victory of the Constitutionalists, which occurred in August. Veracruz was evacuated by American forces in November 1914. See TAMPICO INCIDENT.

**Verissimo, Erico.** 1905–    . Brazilian novelist. The main subject of his writings is life in the southern state of Rio Grande do Sul, especially in its capital, Pôrto Alegre. His works include *O resto é siléncio*, 1943, (The Rest is Silence, 1946), *Olhai os lírios do campo*, 1938, (Consider the Lilies of the Field, 1947), *Caminhos cruzados* (Crossroads, 1943), and others. See LITERATURE.

**Vespucci, Amerigo.** 1451–1512. Italian navigator. b. Florence. Famous because his name was used by Waldseemüller, the German geographer, in 1507, calling the New World "America." Vespucci made voyages to the west, 1497–1503, and claimed to have been a member of the OJEDA expedition that first reached the mainland, but his claims have not been substantiated.

**Viceroy.** Spanish, **Virrey.** The Spanish king's direct representative in the Spanish-American colonies and the highest authority in the colonial government. The viceroy was selected by the king and the COUNCIL OF THE INDIES and was usually a member of a high-born Spanish family, and, in theory at least, held his post from three to five years, although in practice there was little uniformity in the length of his term in office. There were at first two viceroys, one in New Spain and one in Peru. Viceroys of La Plata and New Granada were added in the 18th century. Among the many duties of the viceroy were enforcing the laws, insuring the collection of the Crown's revenues, and seeing that the Indians were converted to the Christian faith. He appointed most minor officials and had the power to grant ENCOMIENDAS. In his capacity as captain general of the territory under his control, he commanded the military forces in the viceroyalty. His salary was high, and he lived in great luxury, but although his power and prestige were great, he was closely watched by the king and the Council of the Indies. He was not permitted to engage in commercial activities, and at the end of his term in office he had to submit to the RESIDENCIA, an inquiry into his acts. Moreover, he was limited in his power by the AUDIENCIA, which at Mexico and Lima functioned as his advisory council and as a court of appeal where people considering themselves injured by his acts could present their grievances. The first viceroy appointed to the Spanish colonies in the New World was Antonio de MENDOZA, viceroy of New Spain, 1535–1550; the first viceroy of Peru was NÚÑEZ VELA, 1544–1546. In Brazil, during the first century and a half of colonization, the governor general was the equivalent of the viceroy in the Spanish colonies, but in the second half of the 17th century a viceroy replaced the governor general.

**Victoria, Guadalupe.** Real name, **Juan Manuel Félix Fernández.** 1789–1843. Mexican president, leader in fight for independence. b. Durango. When a student, he joined the revolution under HIDALGO, 1810. After its failure, he refused to give up the cause and fled to the mountains above Veracruz. All of his followers had deserted him, and the Spaniards attempted to starve him out, but he lived for two and one-half years alone in the forests, and changed his name to Guadalupe Victoria to show his devotion to his cause. He was not satisfied with the independence won under ITURBIDE and adhered to the PLAN OF IGUALA, 1821. He joined SANTA ANNA in the revolt against Iturbide, 1823, and was president of Mexico, 1824–1829. He was not a strong president, but his administration was more peaceful than those to follow. He had been a liberal at the outset of his administration but turned more to the conservatives toward the end, and finally turned over the presidency to GUERRERO. He was the only president, for many years to come, who served the full four years of his term.

**Vicuña.** The smallest of the four representatives of the South-American camel tribe. The vicuña, like its relative the guanaco, is wild, although efforts to domesticate the animal have met with fair success. It inhabits the bleak and elevated regions of the Andes from

Ecuador to Bolivia and ranges over those parts in small herds. The wool of the vicuña is greatly valued for weaving, being used in its natural orange-brown color by the natives. See ALPACA, GUANACO, and LLAMA.

**Vicuña Mackenna, Benjamín.** 1831–1886. Chilean historian, revolutionist, journalist, politician, and diplomat. b. Santiago. Forced to live in exile, 1851–1856, he was a successful journalist, 1856–1858, but was again forced into exile, 1858–1863. He was special envoy to the United States, 1865, and Europe, 1870; during ERRÁZURIZ ZAÑARTU's term, 1871–1874, served as intendant in Santiago, and was responsible for the modernization and beautification of the city. A candidate for the presidency, 1876, he was defeated. Although Vicuña Mackenna wrote more than one hundred volumes, they are characterized by carelessness and a lack of seriousness. His principal works include *El ostracismo de los Carreras*, 1857, *El ostracismo del general D. Bernardo O'Higgins*, 1860, and *Historia crítica y social de Santiago*, 1868.

**Vieira, Antônio.** 1608–1697. Portuguese JESUIT missionary in Brazil. b. Lisbon. Educated in Bahia, Brazil; became Jesuit, 1625; ordained, 1635; gained fame as an orator at the time of the Dutch war with Brazil, 1638–1640; became adviser of King JOHN IV. A liberal and ahead of his times, he advocated freedom for and good treatment of the Indians, opposed the INQUISITION, and believed in civil rights for Jews. He was sent on various missions to various courts of Europe, and then to Maranhão, Brazil to direct missions and take care of Indians. He was finally driven from Brazil by slave owners and traders, who wanted ill-treated, uneducated Indians. In Lisbon he was forbidden to preach against the Inquisition, and went to Rome, 1669, staying there six years and gaining fame as the papal preacher of Clement X; he became a friend of Queen Christina of Sweden. He returned to Brazil to care for the Indians, 1681. His prose writings rank high in Portuguese literature and 15 volumes of sermons were published, 1679–1748; he is the author of *Esperanças de Portugal*, 1863–1864, and other works.

**Viera, Feliciano.** b. 1872. President of Uruguay, 1915–1919. A COLORADO, he followed in the footsteps of BATLLE Y ORDÓÑEZ and introduced such innovations as an eight-hour working day, a national inheritance tax, government control of telephone and telegraph lines, workmen-compensation laws, old-age pensions, better education, a national bank, and government control of one-third of the nation's railroads. He instituted the secret ballot, put into effect, 1917; and the constitution of that year included provisions that limited the powers of the president, and the separation of Church and State. His foreign policy favored the United States, and he broke diplomatic relations with Germany during WORLD WAR I.

**Vieytes, Hipólito.** 1762–1815. Argentine publisher. b. Buenos Aires. Edited and published the *Semanario de Agricultura, Industria y Comercio*, the first issue of which appeared September 1, 1802. The *Semanario* was for merchants, lawyers, and businessmen, and the subject matter was concerned chiefly with society and economy. The articles were generally on improved methods of farming, applied chemistry, and the trades, but the invasion by the British, 1806, caused suspension of the publication. With BELGRANO, he edited *Correo de Comercio*, which began publication in 1810, the articles being mainly on the subject of revolution, along with accusations against the Spanish government.

**Villa, (Francisco) Pancho.** Real name, **Doroteo Arango.** 1877–1923. Mexican revolutionary leader. As a boy he escaped from PEONAGE on an HACIENDA in Durango, and became a bandit chieftain, taking part in the MADERO revolution, 1910. After Madero's murder, 1913, Villa fought the HUERTA dictatorship and against CARRANZA, 1914–1915; captured Mexico City in December 1914. In revenge against the munitions embargo placed against him by the United States, which was supporting Carranza, he crossed the American border into New Mexico, killing several people in the town of Columbus. Troops under PERSHING were sent to pursue him into Mexico, 1916, and he continued guerrilla warfare in Chihuahua. After the victory of

OBREGÓN over Carranza in 1920, Villa was bribed into submission by the gift of an hacienda in Durango, but he was assassinated in the summer of 1923 by, it is believed, government men who feared that he might oppose the succession by CALLES to the presidency.

**Villa-Lobos, Heitor.** 1884–1959. Brazilian composer. b. Rio de Janeiro. Considered the foremost Latin-American composer, he was incredibly prolific. Influenced by Brazilian folk music, he is noted for five operas, six symphonies, *chôros* (serenades), piano solos, songs, symphonic poems, cello concerti, etc. His best known works are *Bachianas Brasileiras* No. 5 (in two parts), 1930, *Aria*, 1938, *Dansa*, 1945, and *São Sabastião*, an *a capella* mass. He organized an orchestra in Rio de Janeiro, 1933, and was the director of Brazil's department of music education, 1932–1959.

**Villarroel, Gualberto.** 1908–1946. Bolivian soldier and military leader. Head of the government that came into power, December 1943, as a result of a coup against the Peñaranda government. Most of the American republics, including the United States, withheld recognition, for Villarroel was supported by the pro-Axis National Revolutionary Movement, the M.N.R., and because the overthrow of the Peñaranda government had been prepared in Buenos Aires with the complicity of German agents. Recognition was granted, June 1944, after Villarroel had taken steps to weaken the M.N.R. position in the government and had ordered the expulsion from Bolivia of a number of Germans and Japanese. At the end of the year the M.N.R. regained its influence in the government, however, and from then on Villarroel's regime was a dictatorship characterized by ruthless suppression of all opposition; a revolt, July 1946, overthrew the regime, and Villarroel was murdered by a mob in La Paz.

**Villazón, Eleodoro.** 1849–1939. President of Bolivia, 1909–1913. b. Cochabamba. Minister of finance in CAMPERO administration, 1880; foreign minister, 1900; settled many problems concerning boundaries with Paraguay, Brazil, Peru, and Chile; elected president, 1909; reorganized finances, introduced reforms in education, and fostered public works; minister plenipotentiary to Argentina, 1924.

**Villegagnon, Nicolas Durand de.** 1510–1571. Leader of French colony in Brazil. Naval officer who, with the support of Henry II and Admiral Coligny, established a French colony in the area of the unoccupied bay of Rio de Janeiro, hoping to establish a settlement for refugee Huguenots, but Villegagnon quarreled with his Protestant followers; the two ministers sent by Calvin to the colony were sent back by Villegagnon. The colony maintained itself for several years, having established friendly relations with the Indians with whom the settlers traded. The colonists were finally attacked and defeated by the Portuguese under Mem de SÁ, 1560.

**Vincent, Sténio Joseph.** 1874–1959. President of Haiti, 1930–1941. b. Port-au-Prince. Lawyer and statesman. Founded the newspapers *L'Effort*, 1902, and *Haiti-Journal*, 1930; anti-United States in attitude. On October 1, 1931, Haiti took over control of its own affairs from the United States with the exception of the office of financial adviser and general receiver, and the control of the national guard. An agreement was finally reached whereby the U.S. marines would be withdrawn by October 1, 1934; Vincent went to Washington to confer with President Franklin D. ROOSEVELT, April 1934, and as a result all the marines were withdrawn by August 15, 1934. Haiti signed a reciprocal trade agreement with the United States, 1935, and a new constitution was ratified, June 1935, which extended the term and powers of the president. Vincent signed contracts with French and U.S. construction companies to build highways, irrigation and drainage systems, water supply and port improvements, schools, rural electrification, and public buildings, and he arranged for a census to be taken. In 1937 Haitian peasants looking for work in Santo Domingo were driven back by Dominican soldiers and thousands were killed. Through the intervention of several other American republics, Vincent received $750,000 in damages. In December 1939, he again went to Washington to get credit from the EXPORT-IMPORT BANK in order to build additional irrigation and drainage works. A constitutional amendment of 1939 provided that the national assembly should elect the president, and in 1941 it elected LESCOT, who pledged to carry out Vincent's policies.

**Virginius Affair.** An episode in the first (and unsuccessful) Cuban war for independence, 1868–1878. In October 1873, Spanish authorities seized the blockade-running ship "Virginius," a vessel that was owned by Cuban insurrectionists and had been notoriously running arms and supplies into Cuba for several years. She was captured while sailing under papers obtained by fraud, while illegally flying the American flag, and carrying munitions and a party of revolutionists. The ship was taken to Santiago, Cuba, where, after hasty and secret trials, fifty-three members of the crew were executed. Among the victims were a number of American and English citizens. Had it not been for the intervention of a British warship, many more members of the crew would have been shot. The "Virginius" affair and other incidents of the same type, which resulted in the death of Americans, aroused public opinion in the United States against Spain and led to demands that the American government intervene to put an end to the war. The dubious character of the "Virginius" had a sobering effect on U.S. officials and led to moderate demands on the Spanish government. Eventually an amicable settlement was reached with Spain, which included a payment of $80,000 to the families of the executed Americans and called for the release of the surviving members of the crew of the "Virginius."

**Visitador.** In Spanish colonial America, an official, or inspector general, appointed by the king, charged with investigating the administration of the viceroy and of other officials during their term of office. At the end of this inquiry or *visita*, the *visitador* sent a report to the king on the competence and honesty of the official. An unfavorable report could lead to the removal of the person in question. The most famous of the *visitadores* was José de GÁLVEZ, who spent the years 1765–1771 in New Spain.

**Walker, William.** 1824–1860. American adventurer. b. Nashville, Tennessee. Admitted to the bar, New Orleans. Interested in a scheme to colonize part of Mexico, with a small force he invaded Lower California, 1853, proclaimed Lower California and the Mexican state of Sonora an independent republic, and declared himself president; finally defeated and forced out of Mexico; led group of 58 adventurers called "filibusters" in a revolutionary battle in Nicaragua, 1855; attacked Granada, captured it, and became master of Nicaragua. He secured the appointment of Patricio Rivas as provisional president but retained the real power of commander in chief of the army for himself. The new government was formally recognized by the United States, 1856. When he seized property belonging to the Vanderbilt interests, he was ousted by a coalition of Central-American powers that were backed by the strong pressure and financial position of Vanderbilt. Walker was finally forced to flee, 1857. He attempted another landing in Central America but was arrested by the U.S. Navy and returned to the United States. He returned to Central America, 1860, and tried to instigate a revolt in Honduras, but was captured by British naval authorities, surrendered to the Honduran government, and was executed. He was known by his admirers as the "grey-eyed man of destiny."

**War of the Pacific.** A conflict between Peru and Bolivia on the one side and Chile on the other, 1879–1883. Chilean companies exploiting nitrate deposits on the southern Peruvian coast and in the Bolivian Pacific province of Atacama became involved in frequent disputes with the Peruvian and Bolivian governments. Moreover, there was a standing disagreement between Bolivia and Chile over possession of the Antofagasta area. A treaty signed by both countries in 1873 recognized Bolivian control north of the 24th parallel but the taxes paid by the Chilean concerns were not to be increased by the Bolivian government within the next 25 years. In 1875 the holdings of the Chilean nitrate companies were expropriated by the Peruvian government, and three years later Bolivia, which had signed a secret alliance with Peru in 1873, confiscated the property of the nitrate-producing Anglo-Chilean company, basing this action on the refusal of the company to pay a new tax on the shipping of nitrates from the Atacama territory. Chile reacted by taking possession of Antofagasta in February 1879. When Chile's request to Peru to revoke its alliance with Bolivia was rejected, the Chilean government declared war on Peru in April 1879. Chile's superiority on the sea and its better-trained land forces soon decided the war in its favor. Peru's navy was beaten at Iquique in May 1879, and the allied armies suffered a severe defeat at Tacna in May 1880. After this defeat Bolivia ceased to be a factor in the war, and the Chilean navy, now undisputed mistress of the sea, shelled Peruvian coastal towns and clamped a blockade on the port of Callao. U.S. efforts to promote peace between the belligerents failed when Peru and Bolivia refused to cede their nitrate-producing provinces to Chile. There was more fighting, and at the beginning of 1881 Lima was occupied by the Chilean army. Peace between Chile and Peru was signed in 1883. The TREATY OF ANCÓN signed on October 20, 1883, ratified by both governments on May 8, 1884, left Chile in possession of the province of Tarapacá and gave Chile the right to occupy the provinces of Tacna and Arica for a period of ten years, after which their fate was to be decided by a plebiscite. Bitterness between the two countries made the holding of the plebiscite impossible, but in 1929 an agreement was reached which turned Tacna over to Peru and Arica to Chile. A truce was arranged with Bolivia in 1884, but a peace treaty between Chile and Bolivia was not signed until 1904. The treaty provided, among other things, that the Chilean government would build a railroad between Arica and La Paz.

**War of the Triple Alliance.** See PARAGUA-YAN WAR.

**Washington Conference of 1889.** The first Pan-American conference, which convened under the auspices of the United States and was attended by delegates of all the Spanish-American republics, except the Dominican Republic. It established the Commercial Bureau of American Republics, later called the PAN-AMERICAN UNION, and adopted a resolution for settling financial disputes by compulsory arbitration. Other problems such as communications between the American nations, uniform customs, uniform weights and measures, sanitation, and extradition were also discussed. Actually, the only concrete result of the Washington Conference was the establishment of the Pan-American Union. See PAN-AMERICAN CONFERENCES.

**Washington Treaties of 1907 and 1923.** A series of conventions, adopted by all Central-American republics except Panama on two occasions in Washington, D.C., aiming at the establishment of peace and stability in Central America. At the first meeting in 1907, the Washington Conference set up a Central-American Court of Justice, comprising five judges, one per republic, whose function it was to hand down decisions on Central-American controversies, and the Central-American states pledged themselves to avoid giving support to revolutions in that area.

Other treaties designed to foster co-operation were adopted. At the second, in 1923, the Central-American Court of Justice was replaced by a new court, the Central-American Tribunal of Arbitration, made up of a number of judges from Central America and other countries. It was essentially a board from which arbitrators could be chosen by the Central-American nations involved in controversy. Another important convention adopted provided for nonrecognition of governments having come into power by means of revolution. The Central-American states also promised not to give shelter to revolutionists plotting to overthrow governments in adjoining countries. It was further agreed upon to set up international commissions that would look into future disputes.

**Washington Treaties of 1929.** In 1929 the Washington Conference on Conciliation and Arbitration drafted two multilateral treaties, one providing for the conciliation of disputes likely to lead to war, and the other making obligatory the arbitration of all disputes of a justiciable nature by an international tribunal. These treaties were subsequently ratified by the United States and most of the Latin-American states, though with a number of reservations.

**Waterways, Inland.** In colonial times inland waterways were used especially in Brazil and the RÍO DE LA PLATA basin. In the 18th century there was an active inland trade carried on between Belém (Pará) and MATO GROSSO over the AMAZON-Madeira-Guaporé system, or over the Xingu or Tapajós rivers. In the Río de la Plata area there was much traffic over the Río de la Plata, Paraná, and Uruguay system, and many river boats were constructed in Buenos Aires. Today the leading inland-waterway network is the Río de la Plata system. There is traffic between Buenos Aires and Corumbá, in Brazil, on the Paraná-Paraguay for a distance of 1,800 miles, and movement between Rosario, Santa Fe, and the Argentine capital is heavy. The 950-mile-long Uruguay River, which forms the eastern arm of the Río de la Plata system, is navigable up to Salto, and there is regular service between Buenos Aires and Montevideo on the north side of the Río de la Plata estuary.

The 900-mile-long Magdalena River in Colombia ranks second after the Río de la Plata system as an inland waterway. Stern-wheel vessels with flat bottoms can ply up and down the river between the Caribbean port of BARRANQUILLA and La Dorada, at a distance of approximately 560 miles from Barranquilla. Between La Dorada and Bogotá there is a regular rail service and there is also a highway for motor traffic. From time to time sand bars and shallows hamper traffic along the river, and navigation then has to await the rise of the water. Although the 3,900-mile-long Amazon River can carry ocean steamers to Iquitos, in Peru, over a distance of more than 2,000 miles, traffic is relatively small. A number of ships moving along the Amazon and its tributaries carry on local transportation and trade. Along the tributaries of the Amazon, navigation is often hampered by rapids, and different types of craft are used, some of them particularly well-adapted to certain rivers. Portages have to be used where rapids or waterfalls make navigation impossible. Today there is some movement on the 1,500-mile-long Orinoco River in Venezuela, chiefly up to Ciudad Bolívar, about 370 miles from its mouth. Inland navigation in Mexico and Central America is of negligible importance.

**Water Witch Incident.** In 1853 the U.S. government undertook a scientific survey of the rivers of the Río de la Plata system and assigned the U.S.S. "Water Witch," under the command of Lieutenant Thomas Jefferson Page, to accomplish that mission. After initial success in accomplishing his assignment, Lieutenant Page became involved in a dispute between the management of an American company operating in Paraguay and President Carlos Antonio LÓPEZ of Paraguay. The controversy resulted in the departure of the Americans in 1854, and in Paraguayan waterways being closed to foreign warships. Early in 1855 while exploring the Paraná River, an international waterway, the "Water Witch" was fired upon while near the Paraguayan Fort Itapirú. The helmsman of the vessel was killed and several other American sailors injured. The "Water Witch" returned the fire, killing and injuring several

Paraguayan soldiers. The incident was finally settled in 1859 when the U.S. government sent a naval force to Paraguay to force the settlement of several disputes and claims that were disturbing relations between the two countries. The López government made an apology for the attack on the vessel and agreed to pay an indemnity of $10,000 to the family of the helmsman of the "Water Witch."

**Welles, Sumner.** 1892–1961. American diplomat. b. New York City. Graduated, Harvard University. He was secretary to the American Embassy in Buenos Aires, 1917–1919; first assistant, then chief of the division of Latin-American Affairs in the Department of State, 1920–1922; served in the Dominican Republic, 1922, 1929, and in Honduras, 1924. He was largely responsible for the details of the GOOD NEIGHBOR policy. He served during the Franklin D. ROOSEVELT administration as ambassador to Cuba, 1933, assistant secretary of state, 1933–1937, undersecretary of state, 1937–1943, and served as U.S. delegate to the conference of 21 American republics held at Rio de Janeiro, January 1942. He resigned his position in the State Department, 1943, in policy disagreements with Secretary of State Cordell HULL. After World War II he devoted his time to writing on foreign affairs, and was author of *Naboth's Vineyard*, 1928, *The Time for Decision*, 1944, *We Need Not Fail*, 1948, *Seven Decisions that Shaped History*, 1951.

**Welsers.** A German banking firm in the city of Augsburg that received from the Spanish King, CHARLES I (who was also Holy Roman Emperor with the title Charles V), a concession to establish a colony in Venezuela, 1528. The colony did not prosper and shortly after the middle of the 16th century the grant was revoked. See VENEZUELA.

**West Indies.** See ANTILLES, THE.

**Wheat.** The Spaniards introduced wheat into America, and during colonial times it became an important crop in most of the Spanish colonies, especially in Chile, the Río de la Plata area, the north coast of South America, and Mexico. Today the leading wheat-growing nation in Latin America is Argentina, ranking second after Canada in world export, and growing about 60 to 70 per cent of all Latin-American wheat. Production fluctuates between 125,000,000 and 250,000,000 bushels a year. Another important wheat grower is Chile, whose production in 1962–1963 was 12,200,000 metric *quintals* (the Chilean *quintal* is equal to 101.43 pounds), a sufficient amount to waive the usual need for wheat imports.

**Wheelwright, William.** 1798–1873. Railroad builder. b. Newbury, Massachusetts. Shipwrecked off Buenos Aires, 1822; U.S. consul, Guayaquil, Ecuador, 1824–1829. He inaugurated a steamship line along the west coast of South America between the ports of Callao and Valparaíso, Chile, 1840, which developed commerce and travel between that country and the United States and Europe. He built the first railroad in South America, that ran from the mining town of Copiapó to the port of Caldera, a distance of 51 miles, 1849–1852, and built the first telegraph line in South America in Chile, 1850. With British capital he built a railroad from Rosario to Córdoba, Argentina. He started the construction of the important railroad from Valparaíso to Santiago, and introduced into the towns electric telegraphs, gas-lighting, and water-supply systems. He is most famous for the trans-Andean railroad linking Argentina on the Atlantic and Chile on the Pacific, planned during his lifetime, but not completed until 1910. A statue in Valparaíso honors his many contributions to that city.

**Williman, Claudio.** 1862–1934. President of Uruguay. b. Montevideo. Doctor of law and social sciences, 1887; rector of the University of Montevideo, 1902; served as COLORADO president of Uruguay, 1907–1911. He followed the reform program of BATLLE Y ORDÓÑEZ, and instituted an important reorganization of the government. Capital punishment was abolished, university education was given added impetus with the building of the University of Montevideo and the Military and Naval School, and many rural schools were also built. The harbor at Montevideo was improved, a divorce law passed, and a treaty signed with Brazil providing for a condominium of the two countries over the Merimi Lagoon and the Yaguarón River. A treaty with Argentina, recognizing the *status quo* in the Río de la Plata question was signed. When he turned over the government in 1911 to Batlle, there was a sizable surplus in the national treasury, and he was chairman of the board of directors of the National Bank, 1915.

**Wilson, Henry Lane.** 1857–1932. American lawyer and diplomat. b. Crawfordsville, Indiana. Practiced law at Spokane, Washington. U.S. minister to Chile, 1897–1904; minister to Belgium, 1905–1909; ambassador to Mexico, 1909–1913. Author of *Diplomatic Episodes in Mexico, Belgium, and Chile*, 1927. Concerned chiefly with the protection of U.S. business interests, he was hostile to the MADERO government in Mexico, regarding it as incapable of maintaining order; he supported the *coup d'état* of HUERTA, February 1913, and urged prompt recognition of the new regime. His refusal to intercede with Huerta to prevent the murder of Madero has been almost universally condemned. Wilson resigned as ambassador, October 1913.

**Wilson, Woodrow.** 1856–1924. 28th president of the United States serving from 1913 to 1921. President of Princeton University. When he came into office he was opposed to the BIG STICK POLICY of the preceding administrations and sought to establish truly friendly relations with the Latin-American republics, based on peace and constitutional methods. His idealism, however, soon proved no match for the force of circumstances. After having lifted the arms embargo in favor of the Mexican constitutionalists during the Mexican revolution in early 1914, he became involved in a dispute with the HUERTA regime over the TAMPICO INCIDENT and ordered American forces to seize Veracruz. In 1916 he ordered General PERSHING to lead an expedition into Mexico to capture (Francisco) Pancho VILLA. In the Caribbean area the political instability in Haiti and the Dominican Republic led his administration to intervene openly in the affairs of those countries, 1915–1916, and in Central America his refusal to extend American recognition to any government seizing power by revolutionary methods resulted in the dispute with the Tinoco regime in Costa Rica in 1917.

**Wilson Plan.** A plan designed by Woodrow WILSON and the U.S. government to stabilize political conditions in the Dominican Republic was presented, August 1914, to the rival Dominican factions that were keeping the country in a state of anarchy. It called for an end to disorder, for the selection of a provisional president, and for the holding of free and fair elections under American supervision. It threatened that the United States would name a provisional president itself and install him in the event the Dominican factions failed to select one. The plan was accepted and Ramón Báez was chosen as provisional president, although further disorders led to occupation by American forces in 1916.

**Wood, Leonard.** 1860–1927. American army officer and colonial administrator. b. Winchester, New Hampshire. Co-operated with Theodore ROOSEVELT in organizing the "Rough Riders" and served as colonel in battle of Las Guásimas, Cuba, 1898. He was appointed military governor of Santiago, where he established order, and was then appointed military governor of all Cuba and served from December 1899 to May 1902. He did much to promote education and public health. In July 1900 Wood called a constitutional convention to meet in Havana in November, and a democratic form of government was agreed upon with the election of a president and a vice-president for four years, a two-house congress, and the separation of Church and State; a constitution was signed, February 2, 1901. Wood was governor of Moro province in the Philippines, 1903–1908, chief of staff of the U.S. Army, 1910–1914, and served as governor general of the Philippines, 1921–1927.

**Wool.** In pre-Conquest time LLAMA wool was worked by the Andean Indians. During the coonial period sheep wool was woven especially in New Spain (Mexico), at Texcoco, and later at Guadalajara and Saltillo; in Ecuador, at Riobamba, La Tacunga, and Ambato; and in Chile. In Peru, the wool obtained from the llama, VICUÑA, and GUANACO was important. Today the production of wool is the main industry of Uruguay (average annual production about 95,000 short tons, greasy)

and is an important activity in other Latin-American sheep-raising countries, such as Argentina, Brazil, Peru, Chile, Bolivia, and Mexico.

**Wooster, Charles Whiting.** 1780–1848. American naval officer and commander in chief of the Chilean navy. Served during the War of 1812 in command of the privateer "Saratoga" and captured two British vessels; served in the merchant marine until José Miguel de CARRERA and Manuel de Aguirre interested him in the Chilean struggle for independence. He was commissioned a captain in the Chilean navy by Bernardo O'HIG-GINS, and was in command of the "Columbus," which he bought and outfitted himself. When he arrived in Valparaíso from New York on April 25, 1818, the "Columbus," given to the Chilean government, was renamed "Araucano." In October 1818, in command of the man-of-war "Lautaro," he succeeded in bottling up the "María Isabel," a Spanish warship, and boarded her. He played an important part in operations that were responsible for breaking the royalist blockade of Valparaíso, enabling the patriots to gain control of the sea on the west coast of South America. Because of differences with Lord COCHRANE, who took command, Wooster retired, January 1819. He re-entered service as chief of the Chilean naval forces, March 1822. On November 27, 1825, he attacked the last stronghold of the Spanish in Chile at the island of Chiloé. He was made a rear admiral, 1829, left Chile, 1835, and died in poverty in San Francisco, 1848.

**World War I.** At the beginning of World War I, Latin America suffered heavily from a sharp drop in trade with Europe. Soon, however, exports to Europe rose again and Latin America benefited from the demand for its products in the warring European nations. At the same time there was a great increase in imports from the United States, for European goods were becoming increasingly scarce. After the United States declared war on Germany in 1917, Brazil, Cuba, Haiti, and all Central-American republics except El Salvador followed the example. The Dominican Republic, Ecuador, Peru, Bolivia, and Uruguay broke diplomatic relations, and Argentina, Chile, Colombia, Paraguay, Venezuela, El Salvador, and Mexico remained neutral. The contribution of the Latin-American nations in the war on the side of the Allies was mainly in the form of raw materials supplied to the latter, although Brazil also sent a naval force to help the Allies in the Atlantic.

**World War II.** At the outbreak of World War II, in September 1939, the Latin-American republics joined the United States in the DECLARATION OF PANAMA, which asked the warring powers to respect the waters around the American continents and requested that they commit no warlike acts in these areas. A naval battle between the German pocket battleship "Graf Spee" and several British cruisers, fought off the Uruguayan coast in December 1939, led to the German ship's seeking refuge in Montevideo harbor and then to the scuttling of the vessel by its crew when the Uruguayan government ordered it to leave its waters. At Havana, in 1940, the American republics declared that they would not permit any European possessions in the New World to fall into the hands of a rival European nation and that they would consider an aggression against any American state as an attack against all of them. The closing of European markets to Latin-American goods threatened the economic stability of the Latin-American countries, but by various means, especially loans, the United States effectively helped the Latin-American republics. At the same time efforts were made to stimulate trade between the United States and its southern neighbors. U.S.-Latin American co-operation was further evidenced when a number of Latin-American nations granted the United States air and naval bases on their territory, and many German and Italian-controlled airlines in South America were either discontinued by the respective South-American governments or taken over by them. After the United States entered the war, a conference at Rio de Janeiro in January 1942 voted a recommendation that all American states break diplomatic relations with the Axis powers. All states quickly complied, many of them also declaring war, except Chile, which delayed until January 1943, and Argentina, which waited until March 1945. During the war, co-operation between the United States and Latin America reached an all-time high level. The United States extended considerable financial aid to Latin-American nations and the latter supplied the allies with many vital raw materials. They took effective measures to curb Axis espionage and sabotage, co-operated with Allied forces on the sea, and two of them, Brazil and Mexico, sent forces to the fighting fronts, Brazilian troops going to the Italian front, and a Mexican air squadron taking part in the war in the Pacific. Argentina tried to maintain its neutrality to the last, and its reluctance to co-operate with the rest of the American nations in the war against the Axis led to severe criticism of its policy in other American nations, especially in the United States, and most of the American countries withheld recognition from the FARRELL government after its seizure of power in the revolution of 1944. Its decision in March 1945 to declare war on the enemy stemmed from a desire to be admitted to the UNITED NATIONS, and was due also to the CHAPULTEPEC CONFERENCE.

# Y

**Yanacona.** A class of perpetual servants in the pre-Conquest Incan realm. After the coming of the Spaniards the *yanacona* were joined by countless others and formed an itinerant proletariat that furnished a source of labor for the conquerors. In modern Peru, *yanacona* means a tenant farmer holding land in return for labor.

**Ydígoras Fuentes, Miguel.** b. 1895. President of Guatemala. Educated at the Military Academy of Guatemala and the National University; military attaché to Washington and Paris; governor of four departments; minister to United Kingdom, 1945–1950; presidential candidate, 1950; minister and later ambassador to Colombia, 1955–1958; president, 1958–1963. His administration was characterized by political unrest; fears that extremists and Communist-oriented politicians were being given too much freedom in the forthcoming elections were claimed as the reason for the coup led by defense minister Enrique Peralta Azurdia, which toppled the government in March 1963. General Ydígoras sought refuge in Nicaragua. See GUATEMALA.

**Yegros y Ledesma, Fulgencio.** d. 1821. Paraguayan patriot and political leader. President of first junta to rule Paraguay, 1811–1813. He shared the chief magistracy with FRANCIA when a consulate was adopted, 1813–1814. He was involved in a plot against Francia, and when the conspiracy was discovered, was executed at the latter's order.

**Yellow Fever.** This acute, infectious disease, transmitted by a mosquito, has in the past ravaged many sections of Latin America, especially tropical and semitropical regions, and today it is still a menace in a number of areas. In colonial times many epidemics of the dread disease carried off untold numbers of people and as late as 1871 an epidemic in Buenos Aires is said to have killed 24,000 persons in the space of two months. It was not until the turn of the 20th century that yellow fever was successfully attacked and eliminated in a number of Latin-American countries. It was eradicated in Havana by William C. Gorgas of the U.S. army, during his work as chief sanitary officer, 1898–1902, and in the Panama Canal Zone also by Gorgas in his capacity as chief sanitary officer of the Panama Canal Commission, 1904–1913. In Brazil a campaign against yellow fever in Rio de Janeiro was undertaken during the presidency of Francisco de Paula RODRIGUES ALVES, 1902–1906. The physician Oswaldo CRUZ, in charge of the program, succeeded in rendering Rio de Janeiro safe from yellow fever. In Haiti, American occupation authorities conducted a vigorous campaign against that scourge as well as other diseases through the Public Health Service in the 1920's. In other parts of tropical America the International Health Division of the Rockefeller Foundation, in co-operation with several Latin-American countries, carried out an exceedingly effective anti-yellow fever program. Today the disease is kept under control by the joint efforts of the World Health Organization, which in Latin America works through the Pan-American Sanitary Bureau, and specialized agencies of the ORGANIZATION

343

OF AMERICAN STATES. See Carlos FINLAY and Walter REED.

**Yerba Maté.** See MATÉ.

**Yorkinos** or **Yorquinos.** Spanish, meaning men of York. Members of the Masonic lodge adhering to the York rite, which was organized in Mexico in 1825 with the aid of the U.S. minister Joel POINSETT. The *yorkinos* were liberals and federalists, and the keen rivals of the conservative, centralist ESCOCESES, the Masons of the Scottish rite. In 1828 there was a split in the ranks of the *yorkinos* on the problem of who would succeed President Guadalupe VICTORIA. Vicente GUERRERO was finally chosen as the *yorkino* candidate to oppose Gómez Pedraza, who refused allegiance to either faction of the Masonic lodge. The internecine quarrel weakened the lodge and it soon lost its influence on the political life of the country.

**Yrigoyen, Hipólito.** 1850–1933. President of Argentina. b. Buenos Aires. Basque ancestry; active in the revolution of 1890; had been active in politics for 40 years when he finally became president, serving 1916–1922 and 1928–1930; leader of the radicals. A successful cattle raiser, he gave his salary, first as a teacher in state schools and later as president, to charity. He rode to his inauguration in a street car and lived modestly. He was interested in introducing democratic methods into government but did not make much progress except in pushing through better labor legislation. He kept Argentina neutral during World War I and Argentina profited by selling her products at high prices on the world market. He was re-elected in 1928 by his followers, known as the *personalistas*, but he found it difficult to delegate authority. This resulted in a great lack of efficiency in his administration. World depression became a problem in 1930, and Yrigoyen was taken prisoner by General José Félix URIBURU and confined for more than a year. He was re-arrested by JUSTO, 1933, but released after two months, a seriously ill man. The people demonstrated upon learning of his death, for they had had great affection for this remarkable man.

**Yucatán.** Peninsula separating the Caribbean Sea from the Gulf of Mexico. The peninsula at present comprises two Mexican states, Campeche and Yucatán, and one Mexican territory, Quintana Roo, as well as British Honduras, and the northern portion of Petén, Guatemala. It is mainly a vast plain, partly covered by immense forests, and at times arid and sandy. The climate is tropical, with very little rainfall. The Indians have conserved their old Mayan language and customs, once part of the famous Mayan civilization. The origin of the MAYAS is still shrouded in mystery. It is thought today that shortly before the first millennium A.D. the Maya-Quiché race had come to the region, organized it, and left the imprints of its culture through its many and skilfully built monuments. The most famous ruins are those at CHICHÉN ITZÁ and UXMAL. The wars of the 14th and 15th centuries marked the decline of Mayan civilization, and when the Spaniards discovered Yucatán there were relatively small states, each one governed by a CACIQUE.

Several Spanish expeditions explored the coastal region, among them that of Hernán CORTÉS in 1519. The Conquest, begun in earnest in 1527, was later consolidated with the founding of the cities of Campeche, 1541, and Mérida, 1542. An insurrection in 1546 was suppressed after a long struggle. Except for frequent attacks by pirates, the colonial history of Yucatán was not marked by any outstanding events, and the territory developed but slowly due to the absence of mineral and agricultural wealth. After the establishment of Mexican independence, Yucatán showed great reluctance to accept the central authority of Mexico, and in 1839 a revolution broke out at Tizimín, followed in 1840 by the proclamation by Colonel Anastasio Torrens of Yucatán's independence from Mexico as long as federalism was not restored in the republic. After a period of struggle, the Yucatán government asked to be readmitted into the Mexican Republic, 1848, as a defense against a general uprising by the Mayan Indians, which by then was in full swing. This Indian war continued until the beginning of the 20th century, when the rebels finally withdrew into the forbidding regions of the Quintana Roo territory. The latter area was created by a law of November 1902, thus completing the division of the Yucatán peninsula, begun in 1858 with the separation of Campeche from Yucatán. The chief occupations of the Yucatán peninsula are the growing of henequen and chicle.

**Yungas.** The temperate zone on the eastern side of the Bolivian Andes.

**Yungay, Battle of.** Battle fought on January 20, 1839, near the town of Yungay in the Peruvian department of Ancash, between the troops of the president of the PERU-BOLIVIAN CONFEDERATION, SANTA CRUZ, and the Chilean and Peruvian supporters of a separate Peru and Bolivia, led by Manuel BULNES PRIETO of Chile. The battle ended in victory for the forces of Bulnes and marked the end of the confederation.

# Z

**Zaldúa, Francisco Javier.** 1811–1882. President of Colombia. b. Bogotá. President of the Río Negro Convention, 1863; rector of the University of Bogotá; minister in the Trujillo administration, 1879; governor of the province of Socorro; elected president, 1882. He died several months after taking office, but together with Ezequiel Rojas, he codified the laws of the country. Zaldúa was one of the outstanding jurists of Colombia.

**Zambos.** In Spanish America, people of part African Negro and part Indian blood. During the colonial period they suffered the same discriminations as other people of mixed blood. They could not hold public office, and in the 18th century they were barred from education and could not, therefore, enter any profession.

**Zapata, Emiliano.** 1880–1919. Mexican Indian agrarian revolutionist. b. state of Morelos. Leader of the revolutionary movement that championed the Plan of Ayala, 1911, demanding the return of the land to the Indians. He fought MADERO when he failed to carry out his promise of restoring land, illegally taken from Indians, to its rightful owners. With VILLA he captured Mexico City toward the end of 1914. He fought against CARRANZA and was the leader of peasant rebels who controlled most of southern Mexico during the revolution. Led into a trap and assassinated by Carranzist officers, he became the hero of legends and songs of the Mexican Indian.

**Zapotecs.** Indians inhabiting the southeastern portion of the Mexican state of Oaxaca, forming part of the Zapotecan linguistic family, which also includes the MIXTECS and other tribes. They fought against the AZTEC warriors of MOCTEZUMA, and together with the Mixtecs were able to preserve their independence from the Aztec empire. The Zapotec civilization was highly advanced and has left us the impressive ruins of MONTE ALBÁN and MITLA. The Zapotec Indians to this day speak their ancient language, although in a changed form. The famous president of Mexico, Benito JUÁREZ, was of pure Zapotec blood.

**Zaragoza, Ignacio.** 1829–1862. Mexican general and liberal leader. Minister of war under JUÁREZ. He was in command of the Mexican army defending Puebla against the French, and in a battle fought on May 5, 1862, he flung back the attacking army, which had to withdraw to the Atlantic coast after suffering heavy losses. The city of Puebla was renamed Puebla de Zaragoza in honor of his victory over the French.

**Zavala, Lorenzo de.** 1788–1836. Mexican historian and political leader. b. Mérida, Yucatán. Deputy for Yucatán to the Spanish Cortes, 1820. He was a member of the federalist party, and was governor of the state of Mexico, and took an active part in the revolt of the ACORDADA, 1828. He was minister of finance in the GUERRERO government, 1829, traveled in the United States and Europe, and was minister plenipotentiary to France, 1833. He fled from Mexico during the SANTA ANNA dictatorship, 1834, settling in Texas where he supported Texan independence, and was deputy for Harrisburg, losing his Mexican citizenship upon accepting the post. He was a delegate to congress in Washington, D.C., when Texan independence was proclaimed, and was the first vice-president of Texas, 1836. He was the author of *Ensayo histórico de las revoluciones de la Nueva España*, 1831–1832, and *Viaje a los Estados Unidos*. He was regarded in Mexico as a traitor because of his support of Texans.

**Zayas y Alfonso, Alfredo.** 1861–1934. President of Cuba. Fought for Cuban independence, and with José GÓMEZ was responsible for the revolution against ESTRADA PALMA, 1906. He served as vice-president in the Gómez regime, 1909–1913, and was elected president, 1921–1925. Although he opposed the interference of the United States in Cuban affairs, he was forced by financial conditions to accept aid. Criticized for graft and corruption in his administration, he did not win renomination, 1924, and supported MACHADO. He was director of *La Habana Literaria*. A poet, historian, and linguist, he was the author of *Lexicografía antillana*, 1914.

**Zelaya, José Santos.** 1853–1919. President of Nicaragua. b. Managua. Chief of the Liberal Party, he became president as a result of revolution, and served, 1893–1909, as a virtual dictator. He introduced civil marriage and secular instructors in schools, and fostered commerce, industry, agriculture and the building of railroads. He refused to send delegates to the San José conference aiming at insuring peace in Central America, 1906, invaded Honduras, and overthrew the government there. He attempted to start a revolution in El Salvador, with the ultimate goal of forming a Union of Central America under his leadership. When Guatemala prepared to help El Salvador, Mexico and the United States offered to mediate. The Washington Conference of 1907 was held and all five Central-American nations signed important agreements. Zelaya ignored these agreements, and as a result the United States supported a revolution against him, and he was forced to resign, 1909.

**Zenteno del Pozo y Silva, José Ignacio.** 1786–1847. Chilean patriot and political leader. b. Santiago. Secretary of SAN MARTÍN;

minister of finance and of war under Bernardo O'HIGGINS, 1817–1821. His problems included repair of the destruction of the port of Valparaíso, caused by an earthquake, raising money for the Peruvian campaign, and attempting to break the Spanish colonial tax systems. He requisitioned property, readjusted customs duties, applied new tariffs, and took over the tobacco monopoly for the government. He was also important as one of the signers of the declaration of independence of the Republic of Chile and creator of the Chilean flag. He was governor of Valparaíso, 1821–1826, represented the departments of Santiago and La Victoria in the national congress, and was vice-president of the chamber of deputies. He was the founder and first editor of *El Mercurio*, Valparaíso.

**Zipa.** Name given to the chief of a number of CHIBCHA tribes in pre-Conquest Colombia.

**Zorrilla de San Martín, Juan.** 1855–1931. Uruguayan poet. His first well-known work was the patriotic *La Leyenda Patria*, 1879, but he is best known for his poetic legend, *Tabaré*, 1886. Educated at the University of Chile, he founded the Catholic newspaper, *El Bien Público*, in Montevideo. He served in diplomatic appointments to the Vatican, France, and Spain.

**Zuloaga, Félix.** 1814–1876. Mexican soldier and political leader. He supported the liberal COMONFORT, 1855–1858, but in 1857 urged him to become dictator, led the movement of conservatives to end liberal reforms, and seized Mexico City. He forced Comonfort to accept his Plan of TACUBAYA and was declared president, January 1858, when Comonfort went into exile. The Laws of Reform were repealed and he was the leader of the Conservative Party in the civil war against the liberals under JUÁREZ. He was in power until December of that year, when he was ousted by MIRAMÓN as conservative leader.

**Zumárraga, Juan de.** 1468–1548. Spanish Franciscan prelate and chief founder of the Church in Mexico. Appointed first bishop of Mexico City, 1528, he championed the rights of the Indians, opposed President Nuño de GUZMÁN and the AUDIENCIA, and excommunicated them, 1529. He was instrumental in the founding of Santa Cruz de Tlaltelolco, a college for education of the Indians. He was appointed Inquisitor of New Spain, 1535, aided in founding the first printing press in the New World, 1535–1538, and wrote several works published by the press. He established missions throughout Mexico and Central America and co-operated with Viceroy Antonio de MENDOZA. He was accused, probably falsely, of having burnt Indian manuscripts. He was made archbishop, 1547.